A CULTURAL HISTORY OF
LATIN AMERICA

D0147845

The following titles drawn from
The Cambridge History of Latin America edited by Leslie Bethell
are available in hardcover and paperback:

Colonial Spanish America

Colonial Brazil

The Independence of Latin America

Spanish America after Independence, *c.* 1820–*c.* 1870

Brazil: Empire and the Republic, 1822–1930

Latin America: Economy and Society, 1870–1930

Mexico since Independence

Central America since Independence

Cuba: A Short History

Chile since Independence

Argentina since Independence

Ideas and Ideologies in Twentieth Century Latin America

Latin America: Politics and Society since 1930

Latin America: Economy and Society since 1930

A Cultural History of Latin America

A CULTURAL

HISTORY OF

LATIN AMERICA

*Literature, Music and the Visual Arts
in the 19th and 20th Centuries*

edited by

LESLIE BETHELL

*Emeritus Professor of Latin American History
University of London
and
Professorial Fellow
St. Antony's College, Oxford*

CAMBRIDGE
UNIVERSITY PRESS

CAMBRIDGE UNIVERSITY PRESS
Cambridge, New York, Melbourne, Madrid, Cape Town, Singapore, São Paulo

Cambridge University Press
The Edinburgh Building, Cambridge CB2 2RU, UK

Published in the United States of America by Cambridge University Press, New York

www.cambridge.org
Information on this title: www.cambridge.org/9780521623278

© Cambridge University Press 1998

First published 1998
Reprinted 1999

A catalogue record for this publication is available from the British Library

ISBN-13 978-0-521-62327-8 hardback
ISBN-10 0-521-62327-8 hardback

ISBN-13 978-0-521-62626-2 paperback
ISBN-10 0-521-62626-9 paperback

Transferred to digital printing 2005

CONTENTS

PREFACE

The Cambridge History of Latin America (CHLA), edited by Leslie Bethell, is an international, collaborative, multi-volume history of Latin America during the five centuries from the first contacts between Europeans and the native peoples of the Americas in the late 15th and early 16th centuries to the present day.

A Cultural History of Latin America brings together, in Part One, chapters from CHLA volume III *Latin America: from Independence to c. 1870* (1985) and CHLA IV *Latin America: c. 1870 to 1930* (1986) and, in Part Two, chapters from CHLA X *Latin America since 1930: Ideas, Culture and Society* (1995) to provide in a single volume a history of literature, music and the visual arts in Latin America in the 19th and 20th centuries. This, it is hoped, will be useful for both teachers and students of Latin American history and culture.

There is a small degree of overlap between the second of the two chapters in Part One, a general survey of Latin American literature, music and the visual arts, which ends in 1930, an economic and political rather than a cultural watershed, and the separate chapters on narrative, poetry, music, architecture, and art in Part Two, all of which begin appropriately *c.* 1920.

A companion CHLA 'student edition' *Ideas and Ideologies in Twentieth Century Latin America* (1996) includes an essay by Richard M. Morse, 'The multiverse of Latin American identity, *c.* 1920–*c.* 1970', of particular interest to readers of this *Cultural History of Latin America.*

The bibliographical essays which accompanied these ten chapters in CHLA volumes III, IV and X, and which have been omitted here for reasons of space, can be found, revised and updated, in the supplementary volume to the *Cambridge History of Latin America*, CHLA volume XI *Bibliographical Essays* (1995).

Part One

1

LITERATURE, MUSIC AND THE
VISUAL ARTS, *c.* 1820–1870

It is difficult to make sense of the cultural history of Latin America in the nineteenth century without an understanding of the age of revolutionary struggle and independence with which it begins. This would be true even if the Latin American experience at the time had not itself been so firmly inserted within the context of international events following the revolutions of 1776 and 1789, the incipient industrial revolution in Europe and the spread of liberalism following the century of enlightenment. The historical transition from European colony to independent republic (or, in the case of Brazil, from colony to independent empire), corresponds broadly to the beginning of a transition from neo-classicism, which itself had only recently replaced the baroque, to romanticism in the arts. Triumphant romanticism is the characteristic mode of the new era, particularly in literature – though the continuing influence of neo-classicism in the other arts, especially painting and architecture, is much more persistent than is generally appreciated. Hugo's equation of liberalism in politics with romanticism in literature applies more forcefully, though even more contradictorily, in Latin America than in Europe, where much of the romantic impulse was in reality an aristocratic nostalgia for the pre-scientific, pre-industrial world. This brings the historian, at the outset, up against an enduring problem in using labels for the arts in Latin American cultural history. Terms such as neo-classicism and romanticism are often inaccurate approximations even in Europe where they originated, yet critics frequently assume that they designate entire historical periods of artistic development, rather than denote the formal and conceptual contradictions of historical processes as these are reproduced in art. In Latin America these same labels can at times appear to become completely disembodied, losing all direct concrete relation to historical determinants, giving rise to a persistent perception among

3

Americanist artists of a conflict in which America's 'natural' and spontaneous realities are repeatedly constrained and oppressed by Europe's coldly rational 'cultural' forms.

Spain was the nation which had given Europe the picaresque novel and Don Quijote, but was also the colonial power whose Holy Inquisition had prohibited the writing and diffusion of prose fiction in its American territories and, especially, of all works about the native Americans, the Indians. It was therefore both appropriate and profoundly ironic that the first outstanding literary work of the independence period in Spanish America should have been a picaresque novel, *El periquillo sarniento* (1816), by the Mexican José Joaquín Fernández de Lizardi (1776–1827), a satirical survey of opportunism and corruption which looked for the first time at the structure and values of contemporary Mexican society, using the themes and expression of popular culture in a clear emancipatory gesture characteristic of the novel's generic function at that time. Lizardi, self-styled *El Pensador Mexicano* (the title of his first newspaper, 1812), was a journalist, politician, bureaucrat and man of letters, and the close relationship between journalism and literature forged by his generation continues in the continent to this day. In addition to his newspaper articles, he published innumerable satirical pamphlets and broadsheets demanding freedom of expression and claiming for the still adolescent press the role of orientating public opinion and taste: 'Public opinion and the freedom of the press are the muzzle and leash for restraining tyrants, criminals and fools.'[1] Ironically enough, Lizardi appears to have wrapped his ideas in fictional guise not out of an artistic vocation but in order to avoid censorship and imprisonment or worse, but his characteristically heterogeneous works give us our most complete picture of those turbulent and ambiguous times. It is tempting to link him with the Argentine Bartolomé Hidalgo (1788–1823), whose *cielitos* and gaucho dialogues on contemporary politics during the revolutionary period convey vividly the language and mentality of the age. Lizardi's educated wit and Hidalgo's popular humour were, however, the exception. The staple fare of the neo-classic period was a diet of heroic hymns, patriotic odes, elegies, madrigals, epigrams, fables, and comedies and tragedies framed by the poetics of Horace, Boileau and

---

[1] From his last newspaper, the *Correo Semanario de México* (1826), quoted by Carlos Monsiváis, *A ustedes les consta. Antología de la crónica en México* (Mexico, 1980), 19. All translations in the text are the author's.

Luzán. Divorced from the emotions and conventions which created and conditioned such works, it is difficult for the modern reader to identify with them; yet most of the literary expression of the revolutionary period is clothed in such forms. Among writers neo-classicism gradually came to be associated with the more conservative versions of Enlightenment doctrine and with the authoritarian outcome of the French Revolution, in view of its association with the contemporary cultural policies of the Portuguese and Spanish empires. Little wonder, then, that writers were searching for something new. What they found was a European romantic movement at first sight tailor-made for them, whose combination of political passion and private sentimentality would make a particularly lasting impact on Latin American literature and art generally precisely because it corresponded to the early decades in the history of the new republics. Germán Arciniegas has gone so far as to assert: 'The republics that were born romantically in the New World constitute the greatest achievement, the masterwork of the Romantic spirit.'[2] And another modern critic, Luis Alberto Sánchez, individualized the idea by declaring that Simón Bolívar himself was an intrinsically romantic spirit who became the focal point of Spanish American artistic expression: 'How long might it have taken for our romanticism to emerge without the stimulus of a man and a writer like Bolívar? And to what extent would Bolívar have been able to realise himself without the literary and romantic aura which surrounded him?'[3]

The pre-independence and independence period in Spanish America was an age of travellers, intellectuals, journalists, poets and revolutionaries. Many men were all these things by turns or at one and the same time, and they embodied the Americanist concept by living, learning, working and fighting in other men's countries, like Byron, who called his yacht *Bolívar* and longed to go to America, and Garibaldi, who did go, and who wore an American poncho as a mark of rebellion to the end of his days. The interwoven lives of men like the Mexican Father Servando Teresa de Mier (1765–1827), the Venezuelans, Francisco de Miranda (1750–1816), Simón Rodríguez (1771–1854), Bolívar (1783–1830) and Andrés Bello (1781–1865), or the Guatemalan, Antonio José de Irisarri (1786–1868), are as remarkable in their peripatetic majesty as anything the Enlightenment or revolutionary periods in Europe have to show. The Ecuadorean José Joaquín Olmedo (1780–1847) expressed the Bolivarian dream in

[2] Germán Arciniegas, *El continente de siete colores* (Buenos Aires, 1965), 391.
[3] Luis Alberto Sánchez, *Historia comparada de las literaturas americanas* (Buenos Aires, 1974), II, 230.

verse: 'Unite, oh peoples,/ to be free and never more defeated,/ and may the great chain of the Andes make fast/ this union, this potent bond.' The dream dissolved, as is known ('we have ploughed the sea'), but its memory echoes still both in contemporary politics and literature. In those early days, before even the provisional boundaries of the new republics had been finally determined, many writers anticipating the new order – which would be *criollo* and bourgeois in intention, if not yet in reality – would have approved the 1822 declaration by José Cecilio del Valle (1780–1834), a Honduran who was also an ardent Central-Americanist: 'From this day forth America shall be my exclusive occupation. America by day, whilst I write; America by night, whilst I think. The proper object of study for every American is America.' After the revolutionary period the Americanist theme lived on, but circumscribed and directed now by nationalism, as men and republics came down, albeit reluctantly, to earth.

In the meantime, however, a number of writers were already seeking a new expression to communicate their new perspective on American reality. A writer like Lizardi, for example, although undoubtedly more innovatory than most, still really belonged to the Enlightenment and appeared to see his immediate task, not unreasonably, as that of helping his countrymen to catch up by filling in the gaps in their knowledge and correcting the errors of the past and present rather than constructing the new republican culture that was on the horizon. Had everyone attended to the foundations as he did, more castles – or, rather, government palaces – might have been built on the ground instead of in the air. The theatre was vigorous for a time in many regions, with a predominance of dramas in which morality and patriotism fused almost to the point of synonymity, but none of the plays of that period are ever performed today. Only lyric poetry managed to effect tolerable adaptations to the changing circumstances, so that a small number of poems by Olmedo, Bello or the young Cuban, José María Heredia (1803–39), are as close to the hearts of educated Latin Americans today as are a few well-known paintings of Bolívar, Sucre and San Martín and the scenes of their triumphs in battle. These, however, are no more than isolated landmarks in a vast and mainly uninhabited landscape.

The most characteristic poet of the era is José Joaquín Olmedo, whose lasting fame was secured by his celebratory *La victoria de Junín. Canto a Bolívar* (1825). It is one of the very few serious works which deals with the independence struggles as such. Olmedo was quite unable to find a

suitable form for his romantic subject, but perhaps this is appropriate. At
any rate, the famous cannon thunder of the opening verses is memorable,
though it provides the first of many examples of Latin American literary
works which have no lived experience of the reality they are attempting
to communicate. In that opening salvo we have Olmedo, who was not
present at the battle, purporting to recreate it by 'firing away', as Bolívar
himself felt obliged to point out, 'where not a shot was heard'. Sarmiento
would later write romantic – and enduringly influential – evocations of
the Argentine pampa without ever having seen it, and his twentieth-
century apostle, Rómulo Gallegos, would emulate him by writing *Doña
Bárbara* (1929) having spent a total of five days on the Venezuelan llanos
where his apparently authoritative novel was to be set. In this respect,
however, the classic predecessor of them all was Chateaubriand, who set
Atala (1801) on the banks of the Mississippi, although – or perhaps
because – he had never travelled that far. No wonder some critics say, not
altogether fancifully, to judge by the writings of artists and intellectuals,
that America has been more dreamed about than lived.

　　Neither Olmedo nor his more important contemporary, the Venezuelan Andrés Bello, introduced any innovations in versification or style
and their poetry remained essentially neo-classical: measured, harmonious, exemplary and impersonal. What had changed were the themes or,
more precisely, the attitude towards them. Those new themes were
American nature, virginal again as the Spaniards had conceived it at the
time of the conquest (for now it belonged to new masters); the Indian,
viewed for the moment not as a barbarian or forced labourer, but as a
noble savage ripe for redemption; and political and cultural liberation
inaugurating a new social order. Bello would have been one of Latin
America's great men had he never written a word of poetry (in this regard
he is similar to José Bonifácio de Andrada e Silva in Brazil), but he did.
His *Alocución a la poesía* (1823) correctly assumed the eventual triumph of
the revolutionary forces and effectively inaugurated nineteenth-century
literary independence in Spanish America. It was later used by the
Argentine writer, Juan María Gutiérrez, as the introductory work in his
América poética (Valparaíso, 1846), the first important anthology of Latin
American poetry. The *Alocución* was in some respects closer to Virgil or
to Horace than to Victor Hugo, but it clearly perceived the great themes
of the American future, calling on poetry to 'direct its flight/ to the
grandiose scenarios of Columbus' realm/ where the earth is clothed still
in its most primitive garb'. Nevertheless, Bello's own rather ponderous

verse (more eloquent than poetic, in Pedro Henríquez Ureña's phrase) was itself an indication that this world of nature, mother of poetry, would remain largely unexplored during the nineteenth century, a 'poetry without poets', to plagiarize Luis Alberto Sánchez's verdict on the state of the Latin American novel a century later. What Bello was effectively demanding, of course, was what would later be called *nativismo* or *criollismo*, both forms of literary Americanism which would indeed gradually emerge from the later romantic movement. In his second major poem, *La agricultura de la zona tórrida* (1826), the descriptions of the American landscape and its vegetation recall the Guatemalan priest Rafael Landívar's earlier evocation (*Rusticatio Mexicana*, 1781) or the Brazilian José Basílio da Gama's *O Uraguai* (1769), and anticipate the equally admirable *Memoria sobre el cultivo del maíz en Antioquia* (1868) by the Colombian Gregorio Gutiérrez González (1826–72) towards the end of the romantic era. For a long time, however, despite Bello's passionate plea, and despite innumerable beautiful anthology pieces now largely forgotten by criticism, Latin America's natural regional landscapes would be merely 'backcloths', 'settings', not truly inhabited by the characters of literature. There was to be little internalization of landscape, except in Brazil, where both social and literary conditions were different and where Portuguese traditions obtained. At the same time it must be said that much dismissive criticism of nineteenth-century Spanish American poetry and prose as descriptive or one-dimensional is itself unthinking and superficial. Peninsular Spanish literature had little or no tradition of natural observation, and the European travellers to the New World at this time were only more successful in evoking its landscapes and inhabitants because their works implicitly communicated the necessarily limited view of the outsider. Latin Americans themselves were secretly searching not for reality but for emblematic images – the Indian, the gaucho, the Andes, the tropical forests – in literature and painting, just as they had to search for them as themes for their national anthems, flags or shields.

Bello and Olmedo were both mature men approaching middle age when they wrote their famous poems and were too set in the Enlightenment mould to discard their neo-classical formation. They were both fortunate, however, to witness what Olmedo called the triumph of the Andean condor over the Spanish eagle in the southern continent. Other revolutionaries did not live to see that day. One of the most revered is the young Peruvian Mariano Melgar (1791–1815), a rebel executed by the

Spaniards. After a classical education, he wrote love poems which are still recited in Peru, including impassioned Inca-style *yaravíes* which made him, according to Henríquez Ureña, 'the first poet to give voice in a consistent fashion to Indian feeling in Spanish poetry'.[4] In his famous 'Ode to Liberty', he saw the intellectual and the people united in the romantic new world to come: 'Cruel despotism,/ horrid centuries, darkest night,/ be gone. Know ye, Indians who weep,/ despised sages, the world entire,/ that evil is no more, and we have taken/ the first step towards our longed for goal . . ./ And those who called my land/ an "obscure country",/ seeing it so fertile in wonders/ now say, "Truly, this is indeed a new world".' Melgar did not live to see that world, but his youthful and passionate poetry make him a genuine precursor of it.

Different but also tragic was the poet of frustrated independence, the Cuban José María Heredia, the most authentically lyrical poet of the period and the first great poet of absence and exile (see especially 'Vuelta al sur' and 'Himno del desterrado', both from 1825). Critics disagree about his literary definition, but many view him as a precursor and some as even the initiator of Latin American romanticism. His precociousness, political failure and tragic destiny have encouraged such a view, which, despite his clearly neo-classical point of departure, is persuasive. *En el teocalli de Cholula* (1820), which he wrote at the age of 17, and *Niágara* (1824), inspired partly by Chateaubriand, have become literary symbols of Latin America's natural majesty as also of historical imminence. When it became clear that Cuba was not to share in the exhilaration of a triumphant independence struggle, Heredia, moving to the United States, Venezuela and Mexico, gradually gave himself up to despair. In 'La tempestad' (1822), he was already lamenting, 'At last we part, fatal world:/ the hurricane and I now stand alone'; and, in 'Desengaños' (1829), he at once reproves his passive compatriots and acknowledges his own surrender to despair and domesticity ('the novel of my fateful life,/ ends in the arms of my dear wife'). He was not to know that those who did see political liberation would themselves be lamenting its dissipation in many of the new republics until well after mid-century.

Brazil's evolution was less turbulent, but more productive. As the only Portuguese colony in the New World, Brazil arrived earlier at a distinctively national conception of its literary identity, in a movement which, coinciding with the high-point of neo-classical *arcadismo* or pastoral literature, spread from Minas Gerais to Rio de Janeiro and then

---

[4] Pedro Henríquez Ureña, *Las corrientes literarias en la América hispánica* (Mexico, 1949), 112.

to Pernambuco from about 1770 to 1820. Brazil, moreover, had been the theatre of one of the earliest responses to advanced European and North American thought in the shape of the Inconfidência Mineira (1788–9). By far the greatest writer of the period, however, was José Bonifácio de Andrada e Silva (1763–1838), tireless promoter of Brazil's literary independence and patriarch of its relatively peaceful political independence in 1822. He was an Enlightenment figure who distinguished himself in scholarship and scientific research, whilst occupying a number of important administrative posts in Portugal and Brazil. His literary career followed a path from Virgilian classicism to an almost Byronic romanticism, though possibly his most representative works are his patriotic verses. A man with some of the qualities of both a Miranda and a Bello, he was perhaps the most widely read and productive man of letters of the era in Latin America.

The period from the 1820s to the 1870s saw a violent and often incoherent struggle to restructure the Latin American societies. The interests of the rural sector, its regional caciques and oligarchs predominated, but the project of the era was clearly urban and bourgeois. Liberalism was espoused, slavery abolished everywhere but Brazil and Cuba, education was revolutionized and culture gradually refurbished on national lines. All the arts except literature languished or declined at first in most regions, because they required a level of wealth, investment and stability lacking in Spanish America generally – the Brazilian case was very different – until the 1870s or later. Relatively few important buildings were erected and few paintings or musical compositions were officially commissioned before mid-century, other than the traditional religious works for churches. The academies founded in some large cities in the last years of the colonial period remained immersed in the most unimaginative versions of classical doctrine and style. The political functions of art were not immediately perceived, except in Brazil, where continuity of monarchical and aristocratic perspective allowed the reconstruction of Rio de Janeiro to be undertaken, mainly in French neoclassical style. Literature, however, retained all its traditional social functions and acquired new ones. Most of the best-known writers of the nineteenth century would be men of action. Yet when these patriots and revolutionaries found time to look around them, they found themselves in a vast, barbarous continent which was less welcoming than Bello, for example, had remembered when he dreamed about it through the mists of his London exile. It was an empty, overwhelmingly rural and agricultural continent, whose only significant industry was mining. In 1850 the total population was only 30 million scattered among twenty countries. Most cities remained in appearance much as they had in colonial times; apart from Rio de Janeiro, which had almost 200,000 inhabitants, only Mexico City, Havana and Salvador (Bahia) had populations of more than 100,000.

Since the project of the era was to build new republics with new cultures, it is appropriate to begin with architecture. The end of the eighteenth century had seen the triumph of neo-classical architecture throughout the western world. It was to be particularly welcome in Latin America in the early nineteenth century because of its misleading identification with the French Revolution (its identification with Napoleon's empire received less emphasis, at least from liberals), whilst the baroque became identified with Spain and Portugal, perhaps unreasonably since the discord between structure and ornamentation which characterizes its Latin American versions may itself be interpreted as a sign of rebellion. The baroque style, at any rate, had unified Latin American art. As the continent became more accessible – perhaps vulnerable would be a better word – to contemporary European influences other than those of Spain and Portugal, neo-classicism in architecture and painting, and later romanticism in other fields, gave art a secular function, and reinforced this unity.

In a few Spanish American cities, particularly those like Buenos Aires which had little distinguished colonial architecture, the independence struggle gave an impetus to architectural innovation which would symbolize the rejection of Spanish colonialism. Many buildings in Buenos Aires were constructed according to non-Hispanic principles, and French, Italian and British architects were frequently employed. Nevertheless, it is essential to recognize that this process was already under way at the end of the colonial period. Neo-classicism's cooler, more rational lines were already visible in, for example, the Palacio de Minería in Mexico City built by the Spaniard Manuel Tolsá (1757–1816), also known as the sculptor of the equestrian statue of Carlos IV on the Paseo de la Reforma, in the churches and great houses constructed in the Bajío region of Mexico by Tolsá's pupil, Francisco Eduardo Tresguerras (1759–1833), in the dome and towers designed for the metropolitan cathedral in Mexico City by Damián Ortiz de Castro (1750–1793) and in Santiago's Moneda Palace built in the last years of the eighteenth century by the Italian architect, Joaquín Toesca (1745–99). At the same time, it is equally important to acknowledge that the continuing existence of colonial architecture, dominant in strictly quantitative terms, and the place it has held in conservative minds, meant that Spanish American architecture after independence, taken as a whole, remained unavoidably provincial (as it did until the 1930s). Unlike Brazil, most of the new republics were too impoverished to undertake a great process of reconstruction in the so-called anarchic period between the 1820s and the 1860s. Nevertheless, what innovation did take place was in general accord with neo-classical taste, symbolizing the adoption by the new rising elites of European rationalism and positivism, and pointing the way in the process to the specific economic and political future of Latin American societies as perceived at the time. Nothing shows more clearly than architecture what the nineteenth-century project was all about, for nothing materializes more dramatically the selection of the Enlightenment and France as the Latin American cultural and ideological model, frequently translated, it has to be said, into the Versailles of Louis XIV and the Paris of Napoleon. If any reconstruction of colonial culture is inevitably the view from the monastery or the fortress, the edifice containing Latin America's nineteenth-century culture would remain, in effect, despite the apparent predominance, first of romanticism and then of modernism, a neo-classical academy, and the impact of this on Latin American art would be enduring. (In Mexico the Academia de San Carlos, founded in 1785, survived to serve as one of the pillars of institutionalized artistic activity there until well into the twentieth century.) If the baroque spoke of an identity, however contradictory, between church and state, neo-classicism symbolized bourgeois liberties and civil society, the growth of secular education and a general process of integration into the wider European world order. For this reason European educationalists like Lancaster and Thompson were invited to Caracas and Buenos Aires by Bolívar and Rivadavia as early as the 1820s, at the same time as droves of French and Italian architects arrived to build new neo-classical edifices alongside colonial structures, much as the Spaniards had once built on top of pre-Columbian monuments. As early as 1816 during the residence of Dom João in Rio de Janeiro, a French Commission on Fine Art led by Joachim Lebreton (1760–1819) arrived to advise on future construction and, in effect, to lay down a blueprint for artistic policy for the rest of the century. Auguste-Henri-Victor Grandjean de Montigny (1776–1850) was the principal architect; he designed the Academy of Fine Arts in Rio and many other buildings. Later Louis Léger Vauthier built the theatres of Santa Isabel in Recife, Belem de Pará and São Luís de Maranhão. Italian architects and other artists remained influential in most Spanish American republics until the 1870s, when French models finally triumphed, but as early as 1823 it was a French architect, Prosper Catelin (1764–1842), who completed the façade of the cathedral in Buenos Aires in neo-classical style seventy years after it had been started; and another Frenchman, François Brunet de Baines (1799–1855), founded the first school of architecture in Chile, though it was a Chilean, the famous writer and thinker Benjamín Vicuña Mackenna (1831–1886), who later redesigned the city centre and earned the name 'the Chilean Haussmann'.

The transition from the American baroque's peculiar combination of the sacred and the paganistic – concealing many tensions and contradictions even as it flaunted them – to neo-classical rationalism and positivism was also a transition to an architecture which was actually severely hierarchical in its symbolism, and this permitted – indeed, it imposed – an increasingly tyrannical academicism in Latin American art which would in the long run become reactionary and archaic, and was not finally to be shaken until the First World War a century later. It is partly for this reason that artists in many fields have been led to believe that the baroque – shaped by instinct and intuition – is the true vehicle and expression for the Latin American *mestizo* character, and that colonial art is therefore closer to Latin American reality. This is highly problematical, needless to say, but it seems evident that baroque ornamentation gives more scope for hybridization and syncretism than any version of the classical.

The French Artistic Mission in Rio dismissed the work of the incomparable Brazilian architect and sculptor, Aleijadinho (1738?–1814), as a 'curious gothic antique'. His true worth would go unrecognized for more than a century, and the values of foreign experts determined the course of Brazilian architecture and the plastic arts for most of the nineteenth century, illustrating another general problem for the art historian. The vertebral division in Latin American art from the early nineteenth century until the present day is between Americanist–nativist and European–cosmopolitan currents, a distinction which has frequently caused more difficulties than it has resolved. In the last century, however, there was another side to this problem. Within Latin American art itself, unlike the situation during the colonial period, there opened up a particularly wide – indeed, a virtually unbridgeable – gap between academic art (*arte culto*) and popular art (*arte popular o semiculto*). The latter, of course, was not perceived as having any history, for it was only in the 1840s that some Europeans, under the spell of romanticism, began to conceive of the concept of folklore. Latin Americans would take a long time to assimilate such lessons and spent most of the nineteenth century attempting to suppress or conceal their own uncultivated and implicitly shameful folk art and music, until the moment when strong regionalist movements finally emerged and socialism made its first tentative appearance on the Latin American stage. If we look at the case of painting, for example, in Mexico it was later artists like Diego Rivera who recognized the full worth of popular engravers like Posada or Gahona, just as it was Frida Kahlo who rehabilitated the popular tradition of *pulquería* wall painting; in Peru, likewise, it was artists, not critics, who most lovingly recalled the contribution of 'El mulato Gil' (José Gil de Castro, 1785–1841) to Peruvian and Chilean post-independence culture and the contribution of the great popular artist, Pancho Fierro (1803–79), later in the century. Latin American art criticism was overwhelmingly provincial and subjective, concentrating almost exclusively on historical, biographical and generally 'literary' aspects, with very little aesthetic insight in evidence. Almost all art criticism appeared in newspapers and most of the critics were poets and writers, so that purely plastic criteria were effectively ignored. The great writer, thinker and future president of Argentina, Domingo Faustino Sarmiento (1811–88), was one of the first art critics in the continent and almost certainly the earliest in Argentina, whilst Vicuña Mackenna takes precedence in Chile. The first exhibitions in Buenos Aires were held in 1817 and 1829, but for the next half century such events were few and far between in most other cities.

Despite the predominance of neo-classicism in architecture and, at first, through the influence of the academies, in the plastic arts, the quest for a national art and literature was, as we have seen (remembering Bello and, later, Sarmiento), a grand continental theme from the moment of independence; but the ideal was a very long time in the achieving. For most of the nineteenth century Latin American painting was almost exclusively descriptive. Brazilian painting, for example, which had been particularly backward during the colonial period (unlike music, sculpture and architecture), set out to take a more determinedly nationalist course after independence in 1822, but nationalism as channelled through French and Italian tutors not infrequently produced a merely insipid version of a supposed 'universalist', in fact thoroughly Europeanized, art. Academic painting encouraged the depiction of historical personages and events in the style of David and Ingres. The imperial government invited teachers to Brazil from Paris and Rome and sponsored young artists to travel and study in Europe. The most important of the artistic immigrants was Nicolas Antoine Taunay (1755– 1830), who came with the French Artistic Mission and painted many portraits and landscapes, including *O morro de Santo Antônio em 1816*. As well as his famous scenes of slave life, Jean-Baptiste Debret (1768–1848) painted portraits of João VI, the *Sagração de D. Pedro I*, and the *Desembarque de D. Leopoldina, primeira Imperatriz do Brasil*. Brazilian painting proper only really began in the 1840s, when Jean Léon Pallière Grandjean de Ferreira, who was a grandson of Grandjean de Montigny, returned to Brazil after spending most of his early life in France and galvanized the artistic world with the latest European techniques. Manuel de Araújo Pôrto Alegre (1806–79), barão de Santo Angelo, equally well known as a poet, was a notable disciple of Debret, best known for his *Coroação de D. Pedro II*. But this was court painting at its least audacious, and in the works of even the most accomplished later artists like Vítor Meireles (1832–1903), Pedro Américo (1843–1905), José Ferraz de Almeida Júnior (1850–99) and Rodolfo Amoêdo (1857– 1941), the dead hand of European academicism reaches well into the Brazilian republican period after 1889.

In other countries also the most significant phenomenon of the first half-century after independence was the arrival of a succession of artists from Europe, intrigued by the colourful types, scenes, customs and landscapes of the newly liberated continent. Artists like Vidal, Fisquet, Nebel, Verazzi, Menzoni and, above all, the German Johann-Moritz Rugendas (1802–58) and the Frenchman Raymond-Auguste Quinsac de Monvoisin (1790–1870), went to work, teach and write, and exerted an influence out of all proportion to their real status in their own countries or in the history of art. Frequently they sent their works back for reproduction or for sale to collectors of the picturesque. In Chile, for example, artists like the English naval officer, Charles Wood (1793– 1856), who painted marine views around Valparaíso, Rugendas, who lived there from 1834 to 1845 after visiting Brazil and Mexico and was a friend of Andrés Bello, Monvoisin, who was also there in the 1840s, and E. Charton de Treville (1818–78), between them provided most of the scenes which thereafter illustrated Chilean histories of the period. Not until the 1870s did significant native-born artists appear. In Mexico the most influential painters of the period were the conventional Catalan Pelegrín Clavé (1810–80), brought to Mexico by Santa Anna in 1846 to reorganize the Academy, and the Italian Eugenio Landesio (1810–77), known for romantic landscapes such as *Chimalistac, Valle de México*, and *Vista de la Arquería de Matlala*, exhibited in 1857, and also tutor to Mexico's most important nineteenth-century artist, José María Velasco (1840–1912). Such travelling foreign artists were in many cases the first to record Latin American life in the early republican period, and it took some time in a number of countries before national artists – for example, Ramón Torres Méndez (1809–85) in Colombia, Martín Tovar y Tovar (1828–1902) in Venezuela – were able to adopt the genres and styles which these frequently more romantically inclined Europeans had laid down.

The only way in which most artists, other than popular painters, could conceive of their search for a national art was through *costumbrist* painting. In Argentina the first important national painter was Carlos Morel (1813–94), who painted portraits of Rosas and his mother but was best known for his scenes of gauchos, Indians and local customs in the late 1830s and early 1840s, with titles like *La carreta, Payada en una pulpería, La familia del gaucho*, or *Cacique pampa y su mujer*. These works, many of which first appeared in his 1844 album *Usos y costumbres del Río de la Plata*, have been reproduced on innumerable occasions. In such pictures, and those of other Argentine painters like Carlos Pellegrini (1800–75), we see a varied, colourful, social and natural world constrained in painting which is ultimately one-dimensional. These were artists viewing their own reality – though of course the underlying point here is that it was not yet truly their own reality – partly through European eyes. Yet they were generally well in advance of the men of letters, largely because they moved in much wider social circles than the salon life to which writers of the period were often confined. Indeed, as in peninsular Spain and other parts of Europe, many *costumbrista* poets and writers who reproduced the picturesque and the picaresque learned their skills of observation primarily from their contemporaries among the painters. A case in point was the leading Argentine romantic, Esteban Echeverría (1805–51), who was in the same art class as Carlos Morel when they were both students, and may well have been inspired to write his brutal novella *El matadero* (1838) partly as a result of a picture by the English painter, Emeric Essex Vidal.

Portraiture had developed only slowly during the eighteenth century, but expanded rapidly during the first sixty years of the nineteenth century. Neo-classicism encouraged an austere, voluminous style of portrait painting, as exemplified in the works of travellers like Rugendas. Indeed, most artists made a living painting portraits of the rising bourgeoisie, although of course the trade declined abruptly after about 1860 with the spread of the daguerrotype, at which point many painters like Morel and Prilidiano Pueyrredón (1823–70) in Argentina also became photographers. Pueyrredón, son of the famous general, was, unlike most painters, a member of the social elite and spent much time in Europe, where he was influenced both by David and Delacroix. He produced a vast output of more than two hundred paintings, of which more than half were portraits in oils. The most famous was his portrait of Manuelita Rosas dressed in Federal red (1850), but he also painted outstanding portraits of his father (1848), his friend, Don Miguel J. de Azcuénaga (1864), both also from life, as well as pictures of Rivadavia and Garibaldi. Typical of men of the age, Pueyrredón was in fact a trained engineer and architect who was responsible for many of the public buildings erected in and around Buenos Aires between 1854 and 1864 after his return from a second sojourn in Europe. He also produced such well-known landscapes as *Un alto en el camino* (1861) and *San Isidro* (1867), and numerous scenes of native customs.

Only with the gradual triumph of romanticism in the plastic arts and literature, however, were painters like Pueyrredón in Argentina, Almeida Júnior in Brazil, Velasco in Mexico and Juan Manuel Blanes (1830–1901) in Uruguay able to begin the move out of academic, descriptive or merely *costumbrist* painting in the direction of a more specifically individualistic and to that extent – at this stage – national style. In the second half of the century, when romanticism had been more profoundly absorbed and had itself in turn given way to Courbet's naturalism, a few painters, often influenced by the findings of archaeological expeditions (those of J. L. Stephens and E. G. Squier, for example), made the first faltering attempts to gain inspiration from a historically grounded but formally romantic return to aboriginal roots. Francisco Laso (1823–69) of Peru, for example, seems to foreshadow *indigenismo* in his attempt to travel this road by uniting individual and national identity in pictures like *El habitante de la cordillera* (1855).

In music the national concept was barely reflected at all until well after mid-century, at a time when conservatories and other formative institutions had developed or were being newly founded. Before that it was largely left to the chapel-masters of the great cathedrals, such as José Maurício Nunes Garcia (1767–1830) and Francisco Manuel da Silva (1795–1865) in Brazil, or José Antonio Picasarri (1769–1843) in Argentina, to lay the foundations of national musical life, often forming schools of music, philharmonic societies and ensembles, and thereby ensuring that patriotic or nativist currents did not take art music too far from its religious base in the continent. In Mexico the musical scene was dominated in the post-independence period by José Mariano Elízaga (1786–1842), known in that most patriarchal century as the 'father of Mexican music'. San Martín is said to have had a fine singing voice and to have intoned Parera's *Marcha patriótica* to the massed crowds in Santiago de Chile in 1818, whilst in later years Juan Bautista Alberdi wrote numerous salon pieces for piano. In Brazil Pedro I himself wrote the Brazilian Hymn of Independence, as well as an opera whose overture was performed in Paris in 1832. By that time the minuet and mazurka, polka and waltz had arrived in Latin America, rapidly became acclimatized and then gave birth to local versions and variations.

But if every educated man and woman had an interest in music, its public performance and development were securely in the hands of foreigners after the chapel-masters had had their day. In Chile, exceptionally, German influences were strong; but there as elsewhere, Italian opera had been popular since the early eighteenth century and continued to dominate the scene, initially through Rossini and Bellini. When new theatres were opened it was usually with opera in mind, since the performance of symphonic and chamber works only really became feasible, even in the larger republics, in the last quarter of the century. Opera apart, the main musical fare consisted of piano and song recitals, and light musical theatre, particularly the Spanish *género chico* of *zarzuelas* and *sainetes*, usually performed by Spanish touring troupes.

Argentina and Brazil are the most interesting countries in terms of music during this period. In Argentina as elsewhere, patriotic music in particular flourished alongside the more vernacular *cielitos*. At the same time European salon music grew rapidly in social acceptance after 1830, in somewhat ironic counterpoint to the rural music of the gaucho *payadores* and their pampa *gatos*, *vidalitas* and *tristes*. Yet despite the aura of barbarous spontaneity which appears to have surrounded such folk music at the time, its European heritage is obvious, and the gauchos, for all their alleged savagery as denounced in contemporary literature, were not remotely as beyond the pale as the Indians and negroes who predominated in other nations. In this sense it is not surprising that the River Plate region, even before the waves of European immigration in the last quarter of the century, should have largely followed European trends in developing its musical culture. Buenos Aires, moreover, was always an especially welcoming host to Italian operas, which appeared regularly from the 1820s – Rossini's *Barber of Seville* was premiered in 1825 – until by 1850 some two dozen operas were being mounted regularly in Buenos Aires each year. More than a dozen theatres opened in the city during the nineteenth century, including, in 1857, the Teatro Colón, which would in time make Buenos Aires a world opera capital.

In Brazil, where the development of culture moved through successive organic rather than revolutionary transformations, Italian opera was even more effectively acclimatized. The transfer of the Portuguese court to Rio de Janeiro in 1808 and the establishment of an independent empire in 1822, whilst initially stifling such creativity as had been apparent in the late eighteenth century, provided for a more stable and continuous evolution over the ensuing decades than was possible elsewhere. The mulatto priest, José Maurício Nunes Garcia, although primarily an outstanding composer of sacred music, including an admired Requiem Mass (1816), is credited with having written, in 1809, Brazil's first opera, *Le du gemelle*. In the 1840s his pupil Francisco Manuel da Silva reformed the orchestra of the Imperial Chapel and galvanized musical activity in the capital; he established the national conservatory in 1847. In 1856 Manuel de Araújo Pôrto Alegre, the celebrated poet and painter, provided the Portuguese text to music by Joaquim Giannini, an Italian professor at the conservatory, to produce *Véspera dos Guararapes*; and in 1860 Elias Alvares Lôbo went further, himself composing the music for an opera *A noite de São João*, staged at the new Opera Lírica Nacional, with a libretto based on narrative poems by the most important novelist of the era, José Martiniano de Alencar (1829–1877). The following year saw a still more significant event, the performance of *A noite do castelo*, the first work by Antônio Carlos Gomes (1836–96), destined to be nineteenth-century Latin America's most successful composer, above all with *Il Guarany* (1870), based on Alencar's already famous novel *O Guarani* (1857). It remains the only Latin American opera in the international repertory to this day.

Only negligible attention has been paid to the history of the theatre in nineteenth-century Latin America, and the casual observer might conclude that there were few if any theatres, playwrights or plays. This is far from being the truth, although it is true that theatres were mainly confined to national or provincial capitals and that the standard of artistic achievement appears to have been generally low. Moreover, as we have seen, most theatres were opened with opera or light musical comedy in mind. Nevertheless, the theatre was a central focus of literary activity at a time when literature was still far from acquiring the essentially private character it has assumed today, occupying the same place in the construction of the imagination as the cinema and television now. Thus, when the young Sarmiento arrived in Santiago de Chile for the first time in 1841, he conceived it as a 'theatre' full of unknown personages in which he was called upon to act.

Taking Mexico City as an example, there were already two theatres in operation in the 1820s, one of which served to finance the hospital while the other was built on the site of a cockpit and continued to be associated with this activity in the popular mind. A play entitled *México libre* was produced at the Coliseo Nuevo in 1821, the year of Iturbide's triumph, in which Mars, Mercury and Liberty together defeated Despotism, Fanaticism and Ignorance on Mexican soil, while in the succeeding years of the decade dramas with titles like *El liberal entre cadenas* and *El despotismo abatido* were performed. Most of the leading impresarios and actors were Spaniards, a tradition only temporarily interrupted by their expulsion after 1827. Manuel Eduardo de Gorostiza (1789–1851), a doughty liberal campaigner and outstanding dramatist – *Contigo pan y cebolla* (1823) is his best known work – was one of the unfortunate exiles of the period. Censorship was still prevalent, despite independence, though most of its motivation remained religious and moralistic rather than political. By 1830 in Mexico City, as in Buenos Aires and Rio de Janeiro, the opera had become the favourite pastime of the upper classes. The city was also visited by French ballet troupes, foreign conjurers and balloonists, exotic performing animals and, in due course, other diversions such as Daguerre's diorama in 1843 and wrestling in 1849. Almost all such events took place in or directly outside the theatres. The age of the impresario had dawned, and show business was just around the corner. By the end of the 1830s European romantic drama had arrived, above all in the shape of Hugo's plays, and as early as 1840 Mexican imitations such as *El torneo* by Fernando Calderón (1809–45), or *Muñoz, visitador de México* by another young romantic, Ignacio Rodríguez Galván (1816–

42), were appearing, while the *costumbrist* works of the Spaniard Manuel Bretón de los Herreros were soon filling theatres in Mexico as they would elsewhere in Spain and Latin America for over half a century.

Needless to say, during the nineteenth century and particularly the romantic period up to the 1880s, the theatre was not only an artistic phenomenon but an important focus of social activity, and theatre criticism often seemed as much concerned with the behaviour of the audience and the state of the auditorium as with the drama and its performance. Most of the plays and authors have long since been forgotten, but in its day the romantic theatre, both historical and *costumbrist*, was a closer reflection of contemporary reality than either the novel or poetry. In 1845, for example, the recognition of the independence of Texas by the United States inspired a Mexican drama entitled *Cómo se venga un texano*. At the same time the continuing influence of Spain in theatrical and musical tradition must not be overlooked. In the 1850s the *zarzuela* was revived in the Peninsula and transferred to Spanish America, proving particularly popular in Mexico. José Zorrilla, whose *Don Juan Tenorio* was staged in Mexico in 1844, only six months after the first performance in Spain, spent much time in the Mexican capital. Many other foreign touring companies and star performers visited Latin American countries with increasing regularity throughout the nineteenth century, sometimes at great personal risk, and a number of them died of diseases such as cholera and yellow fever.

In the 1850s four more theatres opened in Mexico City and the Teatro Nacional in 1858 saw the first performance of an opera by a Mexican composer – this was in fact the only Mexican thing about it – *Catalina de Guisa* by Cenobio Paniagua (1821–82). Soon afterwards a comic opera treating national customs, *Un paseo a Santa Anita*, was launched and became an overnight sensation, the forerunner to the *revistas* so important in later Mexican popular theatrical history. After Júarez's triumph in 1861 theatre censorship was removed and specifically Mexican works were positively encouraged. The two leading dramatists of the period were Juan A. Mateos (1831–1913) and Vicente Riva Palacio (1831–96), Júarez's close collaborator, who was also an excellent short-story writer. Riva was the author of the famous satirical song. *Adiós, mamá Carlota*, which heralded the expulsion of the French in 1867, an event also celebrated by Felipe Suárez's romantic drama *El triunfo de la libertad*, about a Mexican guerrilla fighter who arrives in the nick of time to save the honour of La Patria, his Mexican sweetheart. The following year *La*

Patria became the title of another play, by the poet Joaquín Villalobos, whose central character was an Indian maiden of that name aided jointly by Father Hidalgo and Minerva to defeat the French invaders.

Only Peru could approach Mexico's abundance of theatrical activity during this period, with two particularly outstanding playwrights, the conservative Felipe Pardo (1806–68), author of *Los frutos de la educación* (1829), and Manuel Ascensio Segura (1805–71), author of the celebrated *El sargento Canuto* (1839) and *Ña Catita* (1856). They represented two integral aspects of Lima society and both in their different ways foreshadowed Ricardo Palma's sharp but cynical observation (see below). Brazilian theatre had few really outstanding names in the nineteenth century, although in Brazil as elsewhere most well-known poets and novelists also wrote for the stage, including opera. One romantic playwright who deserves to be remembered is the founder of Brazilian comedy, Luís Carlos Martins Pena (1815–48), although the poet Gonçalves de Magalhães is, historically speaking, the true originator of Brazilian theatre. Martins Pena's comedies of manners – *Ojuiz de paz da roça* (1833, staged 1838) is the best example – though light and superficial, were also accomplished and entertaining. Unlike the theatre of the Spanish American republics, they were the product of a relatively stable society, where veiled criticism was not considered dangerous, and were based on a vigorous representation of all the social classes of Rio. Pena was very successful at giving the public exactly what it appeared to want. As Samuel Putnam rather cruelly puts it, 'His countrymen saw themselves and their daily lives in all their mediocrity mirrored in his creations, had a chance to laugh at their own reflections, and went away satisfied.'[5]

There can be little doubt, however, that despite its social importance, the theatre in Mexico, Peru, Brazil, or the rest of Latin America, was the least distinguished of the literary genres. Let us then turn to those other forms of literary expression, and in particular to the impact of the romantic movement in the continent. It is logical to remain with Brazil, since that country undoubtedly saw the most complete and 'European' version of the movement, although perhaps lacking some of the more dramatic features precisely because Brazil's relations with the outside world were generally less turbulent than those of most Spanish American nations. Independence was achieved with few heroics in 1822 (even the monarchy survived), which meant that the transition from neo-classi-

5 Samuel Putnam, *Marvelous journey: a survey of four centuries of Brazilian writing* (New York, 1948), 161.

cism to romanticism was less abrupt and much less contradictory than in Spanish America. As a result, Brazil's classicalist tendency has been more persistent over time, harmonizing more fluently in this period with a romanticism which itself was on the whole more sentimental and less agonized, with little to show in terms of revolutionary impulse. The various parts of fragmented Spanish America have been forced to speak to one another, in however sporadic and spasmodic a fashion, and this has produced an Americanist dimension more profound and enduring in that part of the continent than in Brazil, which has on the whole pointed largely in the direction of Europe, with few deviations. By contrast Brazil, itself of continental proportions, experienced a far more complex regionalist dialectic than most Spanish American nations.

The first flowering of romanticism in Brazil was in poetry, beginning in 1836, when Domingos José Gonçalves de Magalhães (1811–82), a member of the *Niterói* group resident in Paris, published there his *Suspiros poéticos e saudades*, while another, Manuel de Araújo Pôrto Alegre, who was also a painter, as we have seen, published *A voz da Natureza*. Gonçalves de Magalhães did not give himself over to the new virile romanticism of Hugo as much as to the sentimentality of the Chateaubriand who had written *Atala* and *Le Génie du christianisme*. An aristocrat abroad, his talents were largely imitative and much of his rhetoric remained arcadian rather than romantic, but his contemporaries felt that here in intention was a new poetry with its combination of religiosity and langorous scepticism, of exultation and melancholy.

Probably the greatest Brazilian romantic poet was Antônio Gonçalves Dias (1823–64), who produced four collections of poetry between 1846 and 1857 (the first prefaced with lines from Goethe and Chateaubriand), a drama *Leonor de Mendonça* (1847), and one of the earliest Indianist poems of Latin America, *Os timbiras* (1848) (the latter prompting Gonçalves de Magalhães to produce his own influential *Confederação dos tamoios* in 1856). For many Brazilian critics this composer of opulent, pantheistic hymns to the tropics, at once nostalgic and assertive, patriotic, Americanist and Indianist, combining fluency and formal elegance, is the greatest of all Brazilian poets. Certainly he is the leading poet of Brazilian nationality, notably for his repeatedly quoted 'Canção do exílio', written in Coimbra: 'My land has palm trees,/ wherein sings the sabiá bird;/ he sings a sweeter note by far than ever here is heard./ Our sky has more stars,/ our bushes have more flowers,/ our forests have more life in them,/ more loves that life of ours.' Gonçalves Dias died in a shipwreck within sight of land, retrospectively underlining the characteristic *saudade* of his great poems. His important 'O canto do guerreiro' is similar to Longfellow's *Song of Hiawatha*; other works even recall Hernández's later *Martín Fierro*. He is characteristic of Brazilian romanticism, but his greatness bursts its limitations to become, as so many critics have said, the first truly Brazilian voice.

After Gonçalves Dias, romantic *indianismo* and *paisagismo* gained momentum. The aristocratic background of many Brazilian poets permitted a more patriarchal, Hugoesque style than most Spanish Americans were able to adopt, within a generally nationalistic perspective. The Indian stood in reality for a defeated and largely eliminated culture, and was therefore quite safe to adopt as the basis of a nationalist myth. He is far more in evidence in Brazilian literature before 1870 than the negro, on whom the economy still largely rested. Landscape was another romantic concern, but genuine interest in the rural world and the real conditions of its inhabitants was glaringly absent. Instead a certain mysticism and fatalism, which many critics have chosen to see as a projection of some Brazilian national character, was much in evidence, a sense that God and nature had determined man's destiny within the vast cosmic expanse of Brazil. One of the most representative romantic poets was Francisco Adolfo de Varnaghen (1816–78), author of *Epicos brazileiros* (1843), editor of the famous anthology *Florilégio da poesia brasileira* (1850), and an important promoter of national historiography; another was the errant Luís Nicolau Fagundes Varela (1841–75).

However, a succeeding generation of romantic poets (it is customary for critics to speak of four such generations) were entirely lacking in any sense of religiosity. They formed the Satanic school, a 'lost generation', according to Samuel Putnam, writers of a 'homicidal literature', in Afrânio Peixoto's words,[6] sufferers long before anyone in Spanish America from the *mal de siècle* or *taedium vitae* of decadent romanticism, much given to alcohol and other artificial paradises, for whom both nationalism and Americanism were empty concepts. The nearest equivalent in the Spanish-speaking countries would probably be the Mexican, Manuel Acuña (1849–73), who committed suicide aged 24 when the more normal tradition among young romantic poets in his country was to die for political causes. Most of these young Brazilian poets also died before their time. The most characteristic of them was the child prodigy of Brazilian romanticism, Manuel Antônio Alvares de Azevedo (1831–

[6] Afrânio Peixoto, *Noções de história da literatura brasileira* (Rio de Janeiro, 1931), 161.

52), who was like Byron or Baudelaire at their most morbid. Called the 'poet of doubt', he proposed his own epitaph: 'He was a poet, he had dreams, he loved.' These writers were more individualistic and aesthetically oriented than their more complacent, patriarchal forerunners, though much of their work was in reality, as critics have pointed out citing one of Azevedo's best known works, a long dark 'night in a tavern'. Nonetheless, another of them, Casimiro José Marques de Abreu (1839–60), became one of the most lastingly popular of Brazilian poets as the author of verses for lovesick adolescents.

Quite a different phenomenon was another short-lived romantic poet, Antônio de Castro Alves (1847–71), Brazil's greatest social poet of the era and, for some, a finer poet even than Gonçalves Dias. He was known as a *condoreiro* or condor poet, of lofty wingspan and high ambitions, unmistakably Hugoesque in range but innately Brazilian in sentimental orientation. His first impact on public consciousness was in 1867 with his drama *Gonzaga ou a revolução de Minas*, based on the life of the great mineiro poet of the late eighteenth century, Tomás Antônio Gonzaga. Castro Alves's poetry was public and private by turns, declamatory and intimate, Hugoesque or Byronic. A mulatto from Bahia, he filled his work with compassion and tropical sensuality. Erico Veríssimo has justly said of him that while other romantic poets were picking at their own sores, Castro Alves attended to the wounds of his suffering compatriots, not least the black slaves, and the indignant 'O navio negreiro' remains his single best-known poem. *Espumas flutuantes* (1871) was the only collection in book form to appear during his lifetime.

Castro Alves reminds us that the nineteenth century was the century of *Uncle Tom's Cabin*. It was also the century of *The Last of the Mohicans*. In Brazilian fiction the Indianist motif was represented most comprehensively and lastingly by the country's greatest romantic novelist, José Martiniano de Alencar. There had, however, been two memorable novels before Alencar's first triumph in the late 1850s. One was the famous *A moreninha* (1844) by Joaquim Manuel de Macedo (1820–82), a naive and touching novel still much read and loved by Brazilian women today, and the first truly popular work of Brazilian literature. The other, entirely different at first sight, was *Memórias de um sargento de milícias* (1853), by Manuel Antônio de Almeida (1831–61). At first reading the work appears to have been produced decades before its time, possessed of a startling objective realism; critics have noted, however, that its underlying impulse, though well-disguised, was romantic; it looked back fondly through a *costumbrist* prism to the good old days of João VI's residence in Brazil at the beginning of the century. Another more visibly romantic novelist was Antônio Gonçalves Teixeira e Sousa (1812–61), a mulatto best known for *A Independência do Brasil* (1847), but also the author of novels of a kind then being written all over the rest of Latin America, after the style of Alexandre Dumas and Eugène Sue, with titles like *Fatalidades de dois jovens* (1856), or *Maria ou a menina robada* (1859). They were immediate precursors of Alencar's works, typical of the romantic movement in their obsessive emphasis on young lost lovers (with an exotic tinge always available through an emphasis on their racial differences), in the treatment of wild sylvan settings, and with a gothic frisson evoked by themes of incest, cannibalism or headhunting. A novelist influenced, like Alencar himself, by the more serious Walter Scott was João Manuel Pereira da Silva (1817–98). Like most other major Brazilian writers of the time, he was able to reside in Europe, notably Paris, for long periods, and there he wrote *Jerónimo Corte Real* (1839), set in the sixteenth century, and his *História da fundação do Império brasileiro* (1864–68).

José de Alencar, an aristocratic politician from a Pernambucan family, who also wrote a number of plays and much poetry, including the Indianist *Os filhos de Tupan* (1867), was, however, the unrivalled master of Brazilian romantic fiction. He set out, almost like a Balzac, to cover the entire range of Brazilian historical periods and themes. No novelist of the era from Spanish America can match his achievement in terms of breadth, narrative fluency and grasp of detail. Curiously, though, as in the case of Gonçalves Dias, it is for his Indianism that he is remembered today. Like Fenimore Cooper, with whom he is sometimes unconvincingly compared, he owed a large debt to Walter Scott, and as much to Chateaubriand, though he was more skilful than the latter in terms of detail and general management of action, and not inferior in his symphonic mastery of prose which is sonorous and rhythmical. Sentimental, platitudinous, but unmistakably accomplished, his works are probably the highpoint of nineteenth-century Indianism in Latin America and of the romantic novel as a whole, reminiscent of Hugo, Lamartine and Chateaubriand, with his powerful use of emotion, lyrical landscapes and high moral tone. In addition, he frequently used Brazilian popular idiom and regional themes. The best-known novels include *O Guarani* (1857), *Iracema* (1865), about a beautiful Indian girl who falls tragically in love with a Portuguese soldier, *O gaúcho* (1870), *Ubirajara* (1875), *O sertanejo* (1875), and the posthumous *Lembra-te-de-mim* (1887). *O sertanejo* went further than his previous works in detailing popular customs, but these remained divorced from their true social and economic content. His characters were spiritual rather than social beings, and a novelist from a later era, José Lins do Rego, commented unkindly but rather appropriately that Alencar 'moved them about as if they were trees'.[7]

Just as Brazil's historical experience during the first three quarters of the nineteenth century was different from that of the Spanish American republics, so her romantic movement developed differently, both more complete and less dramatic than the movements in the sister states, where political and social upheaval produced a literature with more imperfections in which the passionate, affirmative and committed current in romanticism was stressed. Furthermore, there can be little doubt that the melancholy and misty religiosity of Brazilian romanticism derived from the aristocratic background of many of the poets involved, nor that its muted pessimism was shaped unconsciously by the fear that the social order which gave them their stable way of life, based as it was on slavery, was slowly but surely drawing to its end.

The romantic phenomenon, viewed as a movement, appeared earlier and more vigorously in Argentina than elsewhere. Indeed, such was the importance of Argentine literature up to the 1870s that, perceived through the standard histories, Spanish American literature as a whole can often seem to be almost reducible to the history of literature in that one republic, with even Mexico and Peru in subordinate roles. Echeverría, Mármol, Varela, López, Mitre, Sarmiento, Alberdi, Gutiérrez, gauchesque poetry: there appears to be an unbroken dialogue, a continuity, even in its conflictiveness, typical of western European literatures. Only Brazil's less convulsive but even more organic development can compare in this regard. Indeed, it is arguable that Argentine and River Plate literature (with close ties to Chilean literature up to 1850) is one history, and that of all the other Spanish American republics another during this period. This is particularly striking because of course what was now Argentina had been a distant outpost, a zone of strictly secondary importance during most of the colonial period. Now, however, Argentina, with less of the heritage of Spanish colonialism and with its political and literary elites most strongly influenced by England and France, became almost inevitably the home of nineteenth-century Spanish American literature until the time of *modernismo*, which in Argentina

[7] Quoted by Putnam, *Marvelous journey*, 148.

came curiously late perhaps precisely because that nation had its own authentic literary-social trajectory to develop.

It was in Argentina where a number of enduring themes in Latin American cultural history emerged most emphatically. Thus, in Argentina, from the very start, the opposition between a civilized Europe and a barbarous America was established, with Buenos Aires perceived as a far-flung outpost of civilization marooned in a savage, empty continent. The theme is well expressed in an 1843 poem by L. Domínguez, 'El ombú', which laments the unmarked grave of 'one of those brave men/ worthy of glory and fame/ who, because they were born out here/ left no memory of their name'. Such concepts are essential to an understanding of the Argentine literary mentality to this day. The perceived emptiness encouraged the development of two further themes, both of them conducive to a romantic cast of mind – solitude and distance – and both appear even in the titles of some of Latin America's great works of literature. They are themes which have emerged wherever white Europeans have settled vast areas with sparse aboriginal populations (Australia comes particularly to mind). Rómulo Gallegos, in all the novels he wrote about the previous century, above all *Canaima* (1935), evoked that 'unfinished world' of Genesis, a world not only uncompleted by God but by man: uncharted, unsettled, undeveloped, unknown. The entire continent awaited exploration by the emotions and the senses – the project of romanticism – and by scientific empiricism – the project of positivism – though not ideally, perhaps, in that order. Unfortunately intellectuals tended to act as though each of the new nations really was as empty as it seemed, a cultural vacuum, a ghostly blank sheet of paper bequeathed not by Spain or Portugal but by the French Enlightenment, on which they could write whatever future they saw fit. The *conquistadores* had dreamed of El Dorado; nineteenth-century intellectuals dreamed of utopias. They were bitterly disappointed in those early decades and nowhere more so than in Argentina, where the expectations were highest. The dilemmas were acutely perceived by the brilliant young thinker and writer Juan Bautista Alberdi (1810–84), at that time a journalist who modelled himself on the Spanish writer Mariano José de Larra. In 1838 Alberdi wrote:

The revolution has taken us abruptly out of the arms of the middle ages and has placed us quite unprepared alongside the nineteenth century. These two civilizations have married in our country, but they live ill-wed, as one might expect. The young century, sparkling with elegance and youthful energy, cannot but smile ironically all the while at its silly, decrepit and ridiculous wife. Such heterogeneous arrangements are to be found in every situation, in every misadventure of our society.[8]

The leader of the rebel intellectual generation in post-independence Argentina, founder of the Generación Joven and the Asociación de Mayo in 1837 and 1838, and author of the seminal *Dogma socialista* (1837), was Esteban Echeverría, who wrote the first self-consciously romantic poems in the Spanish language. He had spent the period 1826–30 in Paris, during the years of Vigny's *Cinq mars* (1826), and Hugo's *Cromwell* (1827) and *Hernani* (1830), and then almost literally imported the movement back into Argentina with his other baggage. In Europe he had read Schiller, Goethe and, above all, Byron, realizing that the new movement was, in Pedro Henríquez Ureña's words, 'a spiritual revolution which paved the way for each national or regional group to find its own expression, the complete revelation of its own soul, in contrast to the cold, ultra-rational universality of classicism'.[9] Although Echeverría had little instinct for poetry, his temperament undoubtedly predisposed him to the new movement, as a fragment from his reflections, 'On my thirtieth birthday . . .' (1835), will reveal: 'Between the ages of eighteen and twenty-six my passions and emotions became gigantic, and their impetuosity, bursting all limits, shattered into fragments against the impossible. An insatiable thirst for knowledge, ambition, glory, colossal visions of the future . . . all these things I have felt'. In 1894 the critic García Mérou commented that the defining characteristics of Echeverría's works, typical of his generation, were 'the protests and complaints of those who aspire to a higher destiny, but fail to attain it'.[10]

On his return to Buenos Aires he found a nation wracked by the struggle between unitarians and federalists. Rosas, already governor of Buenos Aires province, was soon to become dictator. By that time Echeverría had published his poems *Elvira o la novia del Plata* (1832) and *Los consuelos* (1834), and was preparing his best-known poetic work, the narrative *La cautiva* (1837), about a passionate heroine who braves the dangers of the savage pampa in an effort to save her lover from bloodthirsty Indians. His real talent, however, as the remarkable and now classic novella *El Matadero* (1838) shows, was for vigour and clarity in prose writing, although in his own day he was celebrated particularly

---

[8] 'Del uso de lo cómico en Sud América', *El Iniciador* (Buenos Aires), no. 7 (15 July 1838), quoted in Juan Carlos Ghiano, *'El matadero' de Echeverría y el costumbrismo* (Buenos Aires, 1968), 69.
[9] Henríquez Ureña, *Las corrientes literarias*, 121.   [10] Ghiano, *'El matadero'*, 11

for his rather wooden and ultimately cerebral romantic poetry. This is characteristic of the entire era: until the end of the century Argentine critics remained convinced that national achievement in poetry was far superior to the quality of prose writing, whereas quite the opposite was actually the case. When the liberal revolution of 1839 failed, Echeverría's band were forced to flee, mostly to Montevideo. He devoted himself to his writings, a broken man – impotent rage, as we have seen, character-izes the literary work of most of the *proscritos* at this time – and died a year before Rosas was finally defeated at Caseros. His impact on his contemporaries was immense, and is visible in the early works of Juan María Gutiérrez (1809–78), whose *Los amores del payador* appeared in 1833, and equally in *Santos Vega* (1838) by Bartolomé Mitre (1821–1906), one of the great men of the century in Argentina.

In the year of Echeverría's death, one of his young disciples, José Mármol (1817–71), completed his long novel *Amalia*, parts of which had been appearing since 1844. It was the outstanding fictional work of the era, though other interesting novels were also being written: Mitre's *Soledad* (1847), *Esther* (1850) by Miguel Cané (1812–63), *La novia del hereje o la Inquisición de Lima* (1840) by Vicente Fidel López (1815–1903), and Gutiérrez's *El capitán de Patricios* (1843), most of them composed in exile and only published much later. They were mainly pale copies of Walter Scott, and Argentina's own lack of historical tradition made it difficult for writers far from home to produce convincing works of fiction based on such a model. The period also saw the emergence of Argentina's first important female novelist, Juana Manuela Gorriti (1818–92), who married the Bolivian politician Manuel Isidoro Belzú and produced a number of early romantic Indianist works such as *La quena* (Lima, 1843). Mármol's *Amalia*, however, was more interesting than any of its contemporary rivals. It is Latin America's first novel about dictatorship. Its one-word title, a woman's name, is characteristic of the era, with its hyperbolic individualism and the identity it presupposes between indi-vidual, nation and history. Unlike most romantic novels after Scott, *Amalia* deals with the immediate past, although, as Mármol explained in the prologue, it was written as if distant in time to make its point of view immediately accessible to future generations. It dramatizes the heroic struggle of two young men against Rosas's regime embodied in the Mazorca. The beautiful Amalia, a young widow, is the beloved of one and cousin of the other: all are children of heroes of the wars of independence. When first we see Amalia in her scrupulously tasteful home, furnished entirely in European style, she is reading Lamartine's *Méditations*, whilst outside is Rosas's world of asphyxiating terror. Unfortunately, only the villains come alive – Rosas's depiction is unforgettable – whereas the heroes are aristocratic supermen whose idealized behaviour and eventual fate, despite some exciting episodes, leave the modern reader cold. As a document of the times, however, even in its ideological bias, *Amalia* is invaluable. By chapter five, Mármol has diagnosed his fellow countrymen as: 'ignorant by education, vengeful by race, excitable by climate . . . a wild horse rampaging from Patagonia to Bolivia, kicking out at civilization and justice whenever they try to put a brake on its natural instincts'. The image is suggestive, similar to Echeverría's view of Rosas's bloodthirsty supporters in *El matadero* and an anticipation of Sarmiento's portrayal of the gaucho in *Facundo*. Yet Mármol's own narrative clearly demonstrates that his fellow intellectuals were largely ignorant of the true condition of the Argentine Republic, which Rosas understood only too well. The caudillo's popularity with the lower orders was intolerable to the representatives of liberal civilization – whom he enraged still further by dubbing them 'filthy, savage unitarians' – and history incubated a long dialectic which would see the whole phenomenon repeated and magnified with the rise and fall of Perón.

Mármol had been imprisoned whilst still a student for distributing propaganda against Rosas, and it was in prison that he wrote his first poems, although most of his work was produced in exile. After being forced to escape from Montevideo also in 1844, Mármol began his Byronic *Cantos del peregrino*, often considered, despite its unevenness and imperfections, one of the outstanding works of romantic poetry in Spanish. The poet reflected as he sailed the stormy seas: 'Glory longs for bards, poetry for glories,/ Why is there no harmony, voice and heart all gone?/ Europe sends forth no more lyres nor victories,/ Songs died with Byron, glories with Napoleon'. Mármol's annual poetic maledictions against Rosas, written each 25th of May from exile, have become anthology pieces and count among the most violent diatribes ever written in the language ('Savage of the pampa vomited by Hell . . ./ Ah, Rosas, we cannot celebrate May/ without sending you our dread, eternal curse'). Unlike Echeverría, Mármol lived on to respectability in more peaceable days, renounced writing and became, like so many famous Argentine writers after him, director of the National Library.

Clearly, one of the principal reasons for the intensity of literary activity among nineteenth-century Argentines was the intensity of the nation's political life, and in particular the bitterness of a whole generation of intellectuals who felt cheated by the Rosas dictatorship of their right to rule. Argentina was therefore an early and leading producer of writers from exile, writer politicians and political writers, a seemingly permanent Latin American phenomenon ever since. Most of the great authors of the century, accordingly, were also great journalists. In 1852 Mitre, in *Los Debates*, quoted Lamartine's famous dictum:

Each age has its own dominant, characteristic passion: a source of life, if well understood, a source of death when unrecognized. The great passion of our time is a passion for the future, a passion for social perfectibility. The instrument of this passion for bringing about a moral world is the press, the prime civilizing instrument of our epoch.

Mitre, of course, would later found *La Nación* (1870). Many of the writers who had opposed Rosas would gain power after his demise, above all Mitre himself (president, 1862–8) and Domingo Faustino Sarmiento (president, 1868–74). Sarmiento's ideological adversary, Alberdi, the 'citizen of solitude', as Rojas Paz called him in a celebrated biography, never attained real power but his *Bases* were nevertheless instrumental in the elaboration of the 1853 Constitution.

As we have seen, the exiled Argentine rebels took refuge mainly in Montevideo, until Rosas besieged it, and then in Santiago de Chile. It was there, in a much more stable, prosaic and conservative environment – already characteristically a home of realism rather than romanticism – that the famous polemics of 1842 took place, between Andrés Bello and Sarmiento, over the appropriate form of a Latin American linguistic identity, and between Sarmiento's friend Vicente Fidel López and Bello's disciple José Joaquín Vallejo, 'Jotabeche' (1809–58), over romanticism in literary creation. The debates soon became generalized and moved on to overtly political ground, when Sarmiento began to equate grammar with conservatism of every stripe. José Victorino Lastarria (1817–88), a leading Chilean intellectual for the next forty years, was one of the prime movers of the debate, declaring that literature should be 'the authentic expression of our nationality'. It was at this time also that Francisco Bilbao (1823–65), author of the explosive *Sociabilidad chilena* (1844), and Vicuña Mackenna were making their mark in the Santiago intellectual milieu, where most young men were still under the distant spell of Fígaro, the great Spanish poet and journalist Mariano José de Larra. Bello, who had perhaps not expected such buffetings in the Chilean capital, retired wounded from the fray and set about preparing his famous *Gramática* (1847). Once the tutor of Bolívar, although less of an influence than the passionate Simón Rodríguez, he had lived in London from 1810 to 1829, editing epoch-making magazines and composing his famous poems, and had then moved to Chile, where he had become the first rector of the university and perhaps the most widely and consistently enlightened writer in Spanish in the nineteenth century: his contributions to law, literature, criticism and philosophy were all outstanding, and he was the dominant influence in the cultural reorganization of the Chilean republic. Such Latin American patriarchal sobriety as he and Olmedo represented, was as much British as Hispanic. Bello even managed to domesticate Hugo when he translated him later in life.

Sarmiento is at first sight Bello's polar opposite, except in his breadth of achievement. He remains one of a handful of undeniably great literary figures of nineteenth-century Latin America, despite the fact that he almost never wrote works of a purely literary character. He was not interested in following 'models', for 'inspiration' was one of the wellsprings of his existence; at the same time, like Echeverría, he was more comfortable writing about political and philosophical concerns, however passionately expressed, than imaginative literature, and he wrote exclusively in prose. So important is he that the dates of his birth (1811) and death (1888) are frequently used as the boundaries of the Spanish American romantic movement as a whole, especially since the year of his death coincides with the publication of Rubén Darío's *Azul*, the inaugural work of *modernismo*. *Facundo: civilización y barbarie* (1845), produced in exile in Chile, although primarily a work of sociology or 'essay in human geography', is one of only a handful of nineteenth-century works that can still be read for pleasure today. In it a personality imbued with the romantic spirit of self-affirmation is able to identify itself with the present and future of a national territory and, paradoxically, to sound more like the dictator and gauchos he is almost literally loving to hate, and less like that idealized cerebral world of European culture which, the more he exalts it, the more ethereal and unreal it sounds and the more abstract and unsatisfying his text becomes. Most astonishing of all is Sarmiento's certainty: he really seems to *know* that the future belongs to him (Rosas's downfall is accurately predicted in the text), and is palpably talking about a material world over which he intends to take power. At the same time, there is nothing aristocratic about him: he uses the concept of civilization as a club with which to beat his enemies, not as a fan to waft away the unpleasant smell of the masses. His works have none of the abstract distance with which writers like Martínez Estrada, Mallea or Murena would gaze on that same territory a hundred years later. Sarmiento was a dreamer, but also an intensely practical man. He was profoundly interested in the natural sciences (transformation and cultivation of the land) and in education (transformation and cultivation of the people). He founded the first teacher training school in Latin America in Santiago in 1842, and that capital's first serious newspaper, *El Progreso*, in the same year. When Bello argued for a renovated classical mode of language at this time, Sarmiento retorted that 'a correct purist style can only be the fruit of a completely developed civilization', and himself wrote vigorously and spontaneously, like the self-taught romantic he was. He gives the characteristic note to Spanish American – as opposed to Brazilian or European – romanticism: the epic of challenge, construction, achievement. Indeed his texts, vigorous as they are, are only a pale reflection of his continuously active, tempestuous life. There were many tragic figures in the period after Spanish American independence, as we have seen: Heredia, Melgar, Echeverría, Acuña. And there were plenty of sentimentalists, for example, the Colombian Jorge Isaacs, who was really more like a Brazilian of the era. But Sarmiento is the true man of his century. Byron, then, becomes less relevant after the 1840s, except to Brazil's Satanic Generation; even Chateaubriand becomes secondary, though still enormously important – especially in Brazil – and the inspiration of a number of seminal works. The fundamental figures are Victor Hugo in poetry and drama, and Walter Scott in narrative fiction.

If Sarmiento was a man of the future, at a time when other romantic writers had set out to portray the landscapes of the continent in poetry, or to depict the types and customs of its inhabitants, part of the contradictory romantic impulse was to the past. Walter Scott and Washington Irving had initiated the tradition of the historical romance, which Dumas and Sue had continued and, by vulgarizing it, made one of the most enduring forms of popular literature. Its true significance is sometimes misunderstood, however. When the romantics exhume the past it is not always from a merely conservative impulse of nostalgia; it can also be to provide their own post-mortem on it, in which case they are rewriting history according to the bourgeois view of the world. Similarly when they divine the soul of the people in myth and folklore, it is to take possession of that excessively fluid and combustible mass by representing it. In the prologue to his romantic novel *Soledad* (1847), Mitre remarked:

South America is the poorest part of the world in the matter of original novelists. This is why we should like the novel to put down deep roots in America's virgin soil. Our people are ignorant of their history, their barely formed customs have not been studied philosophically. . . . The novel will popularize our history, taking hold of the events of the conquest and colonial period, and our memories of the wars of independence.

Fifteen years earlier Heredia had written a prescient *Ensayo sobre la novela* (1832) on the relation between history and fiction, in which he drew an essential distinction between the historical novel and the sentimental novel.

Thus the development in nineteenth-century Spanish America of two sub-categories of the historical romance, the *leyenda* and the *tradición*, may not always correspond to the more conservative wing of romanticism, as was normally the case in the European context. The lapse of the Spanish realist tradition after the sixteenth and seventeenth centuries and the absence of either a satisfactory historical tradition or of a national store of myths, legends and popular traditions, left the Latin American writer in each new republic in a position where there was no choice but to improvise. If his instincts were concrete, he would turn to the *cuadro de costumbres*; if mystical and sentimental, to the *leyenda*, usually a narrative in prose or poetry about the mysterious past, some local religious miracle or strange natural phenomenon. Eventually the tendency would find its classic expression in the *tradición*, a genre invented by the Peruvian Ricardo Palma. Although the Latin American historical novel proper derives mainly from Scott, Dumas and Sue, the *cuadros de costumbres*, *leyendas* and *tradiciones*, all embryonic forerunners of the short story, were modelled primarily on the works of Spanish writers like the Duke of Rivas, Larra and Zorrilla (the 1843 anthology *Los españoles pintados por sí mismos* was the highpoint of the movement), and only in the more accomplished cases on the critical realism inherent in the French *roman de moeurs*. Although these Spanish writers were aristocratic by birth or inclination, the genres they developed underwent important modifications when transplanted to American soil. At the same time, it is true that each work must be examined on its own specific terms: some were modern in spirit, but archaic in subject matter; others appeared to be exploring contemporary customs, but from a reactionary standpoint. The search for national authenticity often degenerated into mere picturesqueness or local colour and moral superficiality. Where contemporary realist fiction (Balzac and his imitators), which came late both to Spain and Latin America, would attempt to typologize and individualize at one and the same time, *costumbrist* writers would tend to typify and stereotype, and although they frequently reproduced the dialect and idiom of popular culture, their intention was often to satirize and caricature whilst avoiding true social comment and overlooking misery and oppression.

It is not surprising that the *leyendas* and *tradiciones* are to be found primarily in the more traditional 'colonial' regions of the former Spanish empire. Two of the pioneers, for example, are Guatemalan: José Batres Montúfar (1809–44), known as 'Don Pepe', creator of the influential *Tradiciones de Guatemala*, whose best-known book is the very entertaining *El relox*, reminiscent of Byron's lighter work; and Antonio José de Irisarri, best known for his semi-autobiographical *El cristiano errante* (1845–7), who had shown himself a master of satire and slander in similar short pieces. Other Guatemalans worthy of mention are Juan Diéguez Olavarri (1813–66) and José Milla y Vidaurre ('Salomé Jil', 1822–82), author of *Don Bonifacio* (1862), a narrative in verse, *La hija del Adelantado* (1866), and the famous *Historia de un Pepe* (1882), in which the tenacious influence of Scott, Dumas and Sue was visibly giving way – at last – to other more realist models at the close of the romantic era.

Mexico produced many accomplished exponents of the romantic historical novel, but none of them achieved either true greatness or genuine continental significance. Manuel Payno (1810–94) was one of the first, with the novel *El fistol del diablo* (1845), and also one of the longest-lived, spanning the entire romantic period and beyond. The poet Juan Díaz Covarrubias (1837–59) wrote the characteristically entitled *Gil Gómez, el insurgente o la hija del médico* (1858), in the year before he was executed by the forces of reaction. Vicente Riva Palacio composed a series of lurid novels about the Inquisition, with titles like *Calvario y tambor* (1868) or *Monja y casada, virgen y mártir* (1868). Since Riva was such a close collaborator of Juárez, his works were nationalist, anti-Spanish and anti-clerical in orientation, with definite symptoms of a nascent desire to recuperate the indigenous past. In Mexico the dialectic between civilization and barbarism was from the beginning viewed in terms far more complex and ambiguous than in the Río de la Plata. The Indian question was never couched in such simplistic and dramatic terms as in Argentina, and the redemptionist current was visible rather earlier than in Brazil. Ignacio Ramírez, 'El Nigromante' (1818–79), while not a novelist, was a seminal literary figure of the era; but the greatest influence of all on Mexican literary life in the Reform period and after was Ignacio Altamirano (1834–93), himself an Indian like Juárez, author of the romantic *costumbrist* novel *Clemencia* (1869), the nostalgic and much loved *La Navidad en las montañas* (1871), and the adventure novel, *El Zarco* (written 1888, published 1901), a tale of banditry set in the early 1860s. The theme had already been broached in *Astucia* (1866) by Luis G. Inclán (1816–75), and was treated again in Payno's lastingly popular *Los bandidos de Río Frío* (1891). As in Spain, the bandit is a favourite figure in Mexican fiction, not only because, like the pirate, he was exalted by the romantics, but because he corresponded to a significant social reality. Altamirano, however, was more important as a cultural promoter than as a novelist. He it was who initiated the famous *Veladas Literarias* late in 1867, inviting all the leading writers and critics of the time; and who in 1869 founded the magazine *El Renacimiento*, which began the conscious search for a national culture and a nationalist literature. Mexico had 'still not heard the Cry of Dolores', in her literature, proclaimed Altamirano, and his call for national renovation was to echo down the following decades and into the 1920s, although Altamirano himself was really one of the last of the romantics rather than the transition to something genuinely new.

Cuban romantic fiction was passionate, as one might expect of novelists convulsed by the conflicting pressures of Spanish colonialism at its most ruthless and the national struggle for liberation. Gertrudis Gómez de Avellaneda (1814–73), who spent most of her turbulent life in Spain, wrote *Sab* (1841), a courageous if sentimentalized abolitionist novel, one of the first American anti-slavery works since Lizardi's *El periquillo sarniento*, which contains a memorable condemnation of the system. Anselmo Suárez Romero (1818–78) began his novel *Francisco* in 1832, but it was published, posthumously, only in 1880. It told the story of two slaves in love who commit suicide when that love cannot be realized, a plot typical of the romantic era and repeated with numerous variations both in Cuba and elsewhere. Similar in its orientation (and in its publishing history) was Cuba's best-known nineteenth-century novel, *Cecilia Valdés o la Loma del Angel*, by Cirilo Villaverde (1812–94), begun in 1839, finally completed only in 1879 and eventually published in 1882. In nineteenth-century Cuba writers could never be confident that their works could or would be safely published.

The greatest writer of prose fiction in nineteenth-century Spanish

America, though a late arrival – confirming the thesis that it was only around 1870 that the romantic movement there found its definitive focus – was the Peruvian Ricardo Palma (1833–1919), creator of the *Tradiciones peruanas*, which he began to produce in embryonic form in the 1850s but only published regularly between 1870 and 1915. He is a nineteenth-century classic, at once characteristic and unique, whose masters are really Cervantes and Quevedo and whose irony allows him both to preserve and to undermine colonial tradition. Faintly anti-aristocratic and anti-clerical, attacking injustice with humour and satire rather than denunciation, Palma's stories are consistently entertaining, communicating the love of their author for his native city, warts and all, with a subtle mix of everyday language, Spanish proverbial sayings and Peruvian vernacular dialogue. Manuel González Prada called them a 'bitter-sweet falsification of history', whilst Eugenio María de Hostos protested that so much erudition should go to waste on mere diversions in which the critique of colonialism was almost invisible. Nonetheless, Palma's works clearly imply a shift from the early *costumbristas*, who at bottom were in reality providing a critical parody of the new classes emerging after independence. The *leyenda*, predecessor to the *tradición*, had been an unmistakably romantic form, treated in verse by Zorrilla and in prose by Bécquer within peninsular tradition. Palma's *tradición* was in effect a combination of the *leyenda* and the *cuadro de costumbres*, radically updated in the direction of the short story, which in Brazil appeared through Machado de Assis as early as the 1860s but in Spanish America did not properly emerge until well into the *modernista* period. His works helped to recover, albeit in a distorted mirror, a lost colonial past, laid the bases of a national literature, and, indeed, became a precursor both of Borges's incomparable 'fictions' and of the so-called magical realist current in twentieth-century Latin American narrative. He evidently hoped that his fictionalized historical fragments would actually *become* Peruvian 'traditions', connecting national history and folklore through the genre of literary romance. In the introduction to his early *tradición*, 'Un virrey y un arzobispo', first published in 1860, he had written:

In America traditions have hardly any life. America still has the freshness of the recent discovery and the value of a fabulous but as yet barely exploited treasure. . . . It is up to our young people to ensure that traditions are not lost altogether. This is why we ourselves pay such close attention to tradition, and to attract the interest of the people, we think it appropriate to clothe each historical narrative in the garb of romance.

Palma's first series of definitive *Tradiciones peruanas* appeared in 1872. He later became an important member of the literary establishment and long-time director of the National Library from 1884 to 1912.

What the *leyendistas* had been attempting to solve with their newly developed genre, and what Palma did partially resolve, was the problem of finding an American form for American subject matter. As the Peruvian was composing his small literary jewels, the Colombian Jorge Isaacs (1837–95) managed to find a persuasive mould for the romantic novel, just before it finally became entirely archaic. The result was *María* (1867), the most successful of all Spanish American romantic works. It is a novel in the line of Rousseau's *La Nouvelle Héloïse*, Bernardin de Saint Pierre's *Paul et Virginie*, Lamartine's *Graciela*, or Constant's *Adolphe*. The most direct influence on Isaacs, however, was Chateaubriand: the characters of the novel themselves spend much time reading *Atala* and *Le Génie du christianisme*, fittingly enough, for in later Spanish American fiction many a heroine can be found, bathed in tears, reading *María*, which remains a powerful force today in popular fiction, drama and cinema. A close Brazilian equivalent is Alfredo d'Escragnolle Taunay's enduringly popular *sertão* romance *Inocência* (1872). With Chateaubriand in mind, Efraín, the narrator of *María*, says of his beloved that 'she was as beautiful as the poet's creation and I loved her with the love that he imagined'. In reality the novel was largely compensatory. Isaacs had mismanaged the family estate El Paraíso (which has the same name in the novel) after the death of his father during Colombia's plague of civil wars, and wrote most of it in a tent high in the tropical forests at a camp called La Víbora, earning a living as an inspector of roads. The work combines the nostalgic adolescent purity of one branch of romanticism with the willed desire for innocence of the liberal sector within a landed, slave-owning aristocracy. The result is a tropical pastoral symphony, gentle, tragic, tearful: objectively false but emotionally true. What was new was that Isaacs had based his novel not on other works of literature, as one might imagine, but on largely autobiographical experiences and on a real setting, the beautiful Cauca valley, whilst ruthlessly suppressing all but the most indirect social dimension to the work. (Isaacs, a converted Jew and embattled landowner, a liberal and a conservative by turns, was heavily involved in civil and military campaigns, but there is no trace of such things in the novel.) As the Colombian critic, Mejía Duque, has said, 'for thousands of readers *María* goes on living with the warmth common to the sweetest dreams and the most tenacious myths'.[11]

It was at this time that *Indianismo*, that version of historically inclined romanticism which exalted the Indian of the pre-conquest era whilst ignoring his contemporary descendants (the movement which defended them would begin later and be called *Indigenismo*), reached its zenith in Spanish America, as it had somewhat earlier in Brazil with Alencar. It may seem paradoxical that Spanish Americans were only able to achieve in the 1870s what French novelists had done in the wake of the Enlightenment, but that is how long it took them to distance themselves sufficiently from their own reality to achieve aesthetic perspective – and then only to see their American compatriots as distantly in time as the Europeans had in space almost a century before. It is a still more striking fact, as we have seen, that until the very last years of the century the Indian was given a heroic role only in countries like Brazil, where he was not the major social 'problem', or like the Dominican Republic, where he had long before been exterminated. Lins do Rego would later comment caustically that 'Alencar, by way of fleeing Brazil, sought out the jungle; by way of escaping from the Brazilian, he discovered the Indian'. Certainly the Indian who appears in nineteenth-century Latin American literature is invariably the childlike noble savage of the fifteenth and sixteenth centuries, used as a symbol of liberation after nineteenth-century independence, and not the downtrodden and malnourished figure who has worked on virtually feudal estates up and down the continent to this day. As Henríquez Ureña said, the living Indian was not considered poetical.

In 1879 the Ecuadorean Juan León Mera (1832–94) published his celebrated exoticist novel *Cumandá*, subtitled 'a drama among savages', which was full of sexual titillation including the almost obligatory danger of incest between unwitting relatives, and set among the head-hunting Jivaro Indians of the Amazon jungle. Like *María*, this was a late-flowering, voluptuous bloom, a highpoint of American Indianism. In the Dominican Republic, meanwhile, the conservative José Joaquín Pérez had produced a series of narrative poems, *Fantasías indígenas* (1877), exalting the Indians of the early colonial period, whilst between 1879 and 1882 Manuel J. Galván (1834–1910) published his long novel *Enriquillo*, set in the same period, and now recognized as one of the great historical

---

[11] Jaime Mejía Duque, 'Jorge Isaacs: el hombre y su novela', in Mirta Yáñez (ed.), *La novela romántica latinoamericana* (Havana, 1978), 373–442 (p.442).

works of the last century for its grasp of detail and its progressive critical perspective. In 1888 the Uruguayan Juan Zorrilla de San Martín (1855–1931), published *Tabaré*, the most famous verse narrative of the nineteenth century, about the son of a Spanish woman and an Indian chief. Zorrilla, both Catholic and romantic, mourned the passing of the Indian race through his tragic romance, but without conviction; his verse, however, already showed traces of the symbolist current which distinguished Darío's *Azul*, published that same year. Zorrilla later became the 'national poet of Uruguay' and was commissioned to write his *La epopeya de Artigas* in 1910 for the independence centenary.

Romanticism, as we have seen, launched first an Americanist, and then a Nationalist project, but succeeded on the whole only in producing a narrowly provincial, descriptive literature which rarely advanced beyond Spanish *costumbrismo*. Very late in the day, writers like Alencar, Isaacs and Mera brought the movement to its highest artistic point, but at the cost of carefully excluding all traces of social or historical realism. It was in the 1870s, and more particularly in the 1880s, that romanticism began to bifurcate into a realist narrative strand arising out of the *cuadro de costumbres* and historical novel, and a more rigorously specialized poetic strand in which the emotional exuberance of romantic poetry and the carefully chiselled artifice of the *tradición* combined to produce a more precise, musical and artistic modernist movement. Before this moment, the outstanding works, like Echeverría's *El matadero* or Sarmiento's *Facundo*, had been strange, anarchic creations, frequently a product of unforeseen hybridizations and fusions. One of the greatest of all such works was the gauchesque poem, *Martín Fierro* (1872) – with its sequel, the *Vuelta de Martín Fierro* (1879) – by the Argentine writer José Hernández (1834–86). Although it is customary to categorize gauchesque poetry separately, it is clear that this River Plate phenomenon is a nativist current among others, and part of the romantic impulse to commune with the spirit of the folk. It emerged very early – with the first manifestations of romanticism itself, during the emancipation period – and not in the latter part of the nineteenth century with *Indigenismo* and other such movements. This can be explained by the precociousness of Argentine and Uruguayan romanticism, which from the start saw the rural songs and music of the gauchos as adaptable to art literature, in the same way that the *romances viejos* had been imitated by urban poets at court in sixteenth-century Spain. Gauchesque poetry, accordingly, was written not by gauchos but by educated city dwellers.

Its origins, however, lay back in the eighteenth century, in oral tradition, and it was Bartolomé Hidalgo who, at the time of independence, captured it for written literature and history, reminding Argentinians and Uruguayans of the gaucho contribution to the defeat of the Spaniards and giving permanent impetus to the *criollista* tendency. After all, the existence of the gaucho, however much Sarmiento and his contemporaries may have considered him a barbarian, made it all the more easy to render the Indian invisible to literature, before he was finally exterminated at the end of the period under review.

It was Hilario Acasubi (1807–75) who most decisively perceived the potential in the gaucho theme for producing a national literature based on rural life, with rustic speech and popular songs. His best known works are *Paulino Lucero*, begun in 1838 and full of anti-Rosas sentiment (not at all characteristic of the real gauchos), and *Santos Vega* (1850, published 1872). Even more urban in its perspective was *Fausto* (1866), by Estanislao del Campo (1834–80), a city man who, on returning to Argentina from exile, saw in the rural gaucho a somewhat comic symbol of Argentine nationhood. The work recreates an ingenuous gaucho's impression of Gounod's *Faust*, which had recently been performed in the celebrated Teatro Colón, then in its first decade of operation. Del Campo's poem is sophisticated, entertaining and very characteristic of Argentine literary tradition.

Unlike most important Argentine writers of the nineteenth century, Hernández himself had been a *rosista* until Rosas fell in the poet's eighteenth year. He had also led the life of a gaucho, and in 1882 he published a knowledgeable *Instrucción al estanciero*. He was for much of the time at odds with post-Rosas Argentina, not least during the presidency of Sarmiento. His poem, *Martín Fierro*, is a popular epic with an individual voice, one of the greatest achievements of romantic poetry in Spanish. Like *Don Quixote*, it manages to evoke the landscapes in which it is set without actually needing to describe them. Hernández is so closely attuned to gaucho culture that the reader is persuaded by the picturesque dialect he invents for his narrative, even though, as Borges has remarked, no gaucho ever spoke as Martín Fierro does. The poem provides an implicit critique of the direction being taken by Argentine society and, indeed, of the Europeanized writers who were setting the pace. Hernández, instead, evokes the solitude and extension of the pampas, the everyday heroism of its inhabitants, and the simple Hispanic romanticism of the horse, the road and the horizon, all framed by a song sung to guitar, which would have so many literary miles to travel in both South and North America over the century to come. It is the single most important work of Argentine literature, viewed from the nationalist perspective. Leopoldo Lugones in 1913 called it the 'Argentine national epic'. At the same time, its elegiac quality is clearly evident, for the freedom of the prairies had been increasingly circumscribed by the advance of civilization and private property since independence. More-over, it was the gaucho, and the rural population in general, who were to suffer most directly from the wave of immigration which, when the poem was composed, was only just beginning. Hernández' definitive expression of a gaucho nationalist mythology retrospectively re-empha-sized the importance of Sarmiento's *Facundo*, as well as of other gauchesque poets since Hidalgo, and prepared the ground for Gutiérrez's *Juan Moreira* (1879) and Güiraldes's *Don Segundo Sombra* (1926).

From the 1860s, then, the age of realism had slowly begun to dawn in Latin America. Even Hernández' sober and stoical gaucho demonstrated that. Men still looked back with envy or nostalgia to the heroic days of the independence era, but for the most part were beginning to feel that such heroics were not for them. If romanticism, on the whole, seemed to have been a partially negative reaction to the rationalism of the Enlight-enment, realism demonstrated anew the Enlightenment's decisive con-tribution to the shaping of the western mind, and the growth of industrialization and urbanization in Europe had reinforced the trend. The result in Latin America was a fairly unproblematical development out of the historical and *costumbrist* modes of romanticism into realism or, more frequently, its variant, naturalism. One might even say that these schools were the more cosmopolitan, more specifically urban counter-part to a *costumbrism* that had been – and, in the many areas where it continued to flourish, still remained – unvaryingly provincial, leading to a further distinction to be made when we reach the twentieth century, between a regionalism which is the attempt by city-based novelists to rehabilitate life in the interior from within a progressive perspective on artistic nationalism, and a *criollismo* which embodies the conservative impulse to keep both society and literature very much as they are for as long as possible.

Looking back, the independence and post-independence periods set the national rather than continental patterns for Latin American culture. It

was not only a time of passionate upheaval followed by national introspection – imposed partly by willed choice and more by immovable
circumstance – but also one when the integration of the independent
republics into the rapidly evolving international economic system had
still barely begun. Although the period 1780 to 1830 had seen many Latin
American intellectuals travel to Europe (and the United States), few
other than Brazilian aristocrats were able in the decades after 1830 to gain
first-hand experience of the continent whose philosophical ideas and
artistic modes they nonetheless continued, inevitably, to adopt and
imitate. This is perhaps the true explanation for the aridity and alleged
'inauthenticity' of much Latin American artistic expression between the
1820s and the 1870s (with the partial exception of Brazil): not so much
that the European forms did not fit Latin American reality, as is usually
said, though this certainly remains an important theoretical consideration; more that the Latin American writers and artists themselves were
not fully able to inhabit those forms; and if through lack of lived
experience, they could not master foreign forms, they were hardly likely
to be able to apply them to their own autochthonous reality with any
conviction. This dual character of their inauthenticity derived from a
two-fold failure of assimilation. The more 'authentic' a Latin American
artist actually was – that is, the less he was affected by Europe – the more
inauthentic his works were likely to seem, with occasional exceptions
like José Hernández. The decisive sea-change would come only after
modernismo (*parnasianismo* – *simbolismo* in Brazil) from the 1880s to the
1910s, because for the most part that movement merely reversed the
process: with the improvement in communications (which itself derived
from the closer integration of Latin America into the international
economic system) writers became more proficient with the tools of
literature – language and ideas – by sharing the experiences of the
Europeans they were bent on imitating, but were for the most part too
alienated from their own reality, either because they actually lived in
Europe or were, sometimes literally, dying to go there, to apply the new
tools to native materials. The latter process got fully under way only in
the 1920s. Having said this, it is important not to repeat the
commonplaces of most criticism of Latin American art by dismissing
implicitly or explicitly all that does not conform to 'European' taste in
literary and artistic expertise and production, particularly since so many
of the shortcomings perceived in that art derive precisely from the effort
to mimic those distant models. Moreover, European art itself would

look very different if its story were told without reference to the concepts of 'masterpieces' or 'works of genius'. Latin America's historical reality has always produced Latin America's proper cultural expression: if so much of that art, particularly in the nineteenth century, now seems to have deformed or disguised Latin American realities, then that in itself is a Latin American reality for which artists alone cannot be held responsible. If critics or historians are 'disappointed' by what they find in the art and literature of Latin America of this period, it behoves them to explain what they were expecting to find, and on what assumptions. Even more than in other contexts, it is their task and their duty to grasp the movement and direction of Latin America's cultural history, which has always been, for every artist, at once a search for personal, national and continental self-expression which will lead the way from a colonial past to some freer, better future. Nowhere are the hopes and disillusionments of that quest better exemplified than in the early national period.

2

LITERATURE, MUSIC AND THE
VISUAL ARTS, 1870–1930

INTRODUCTION

By the time the great romantic writer Domingo Faustino Sarmiento (1811–88) became president of Argentina in 1868 irresistible changes were sweeping over Latin America which were reflected in each of the arts, though above all in literature. Most works produced at that time still seem romantic to modern eyes, but perceptible differences were emerging, how much or how soon depending largely on the city or region in which they originated. Some of the changes arose from purely internal factors, but the period around 1870 also saw the beginning of the intensification of the international division of labour and the more complete integration of the Latin American economies, including many regions of the interior, into the world economic system. The population of Latin America doubled during the second half of the nineteenth century, and the process of urbanization quickened: by 1900 Buenos Aires had one million inhabitants, Rio de Janeiro three-quarters of a million, Mexico City more than half a million, and a number of other cities, including São Paulo – which in 1850 had only 15,000 – were over a quarter of a million in size. By 1930 in some of the fastest growing cities 30 to 50 per cent of the population were European immigrants, mostly Italian and Spanish, or children of European immigrants. If the period 1830–70 had been mainly one of introspection and internal frustration, particularly in Spanish America, the period from 1870–1914 saw the continent looking outwards again, though an extra dimension of disillusionment, for peoples already sobered by decades of internal strife,

47

was added when Latin American nations began to wage large-scale wars on one another, as in the Paraguayan War (1864–70) and the War of the Pacific (1879–83). Most men began to see things more clearly in this new age of bourgeois 'realism', though others among them – those, ironically, who would call themselves 'modernists' – soon decided that they would rather not see anything at all, and tried to retreat into fantasy and evasion.

The relation of Latin American culture to European models has always involved the complexity of response to be found in any colonial or neo-colonial relationship with the metropolitan centres. A review of the relation during the period 1870–1930 reveals the most varied hybridizations and disjunctures, fusions and fissures, and the most elementary questions of form and content become problematical in such a context. These overlap in any case with such enduring themes in the history of aesthetic philosophy as the relation of mind to emotion, which in the nineteenth-century practice of artistic expression was juxtaposed as the antagonism, firstly of neo-classicism, then of realism, to romanticism. On the whole Latin American artists have tended to opt for passion, spontaneity and intuition, which explains the continuing influence of nineteenth-century romanticism and the special importance of surrealism in the twentieth century. Moreover, in Latin American art as a whole the search for knowledge and self-knowledge – whether undertaken by the mind, the emotions or the senses – characteristic of all Western art since the Renaissance, when European explorers 'discovered' Latin America, has been combined in that region since the early nineteenth century, as in other ex-colonial territories, with the quest for national and continental identity and self-expression.

This chapter will trace the path taken by Latin American writers and artists, architects and musicians, through the labyrinth of Latin American culture from the 1870s to the 1930s. It will treat not just literature but all the arts, and will compare and contrast the cultural experience of both Spanish America and Brazil. This requires a carefully planned approach and implies a complex architectural structure built on solid foundations and then tracked cinematographically from one part of the edifice to another until the picture is complete. In the arts the period 1870–1930, probably the most decisive in the continent's history, falls conveniently into two phases, 1870 to 1900 and 1900 to 1930, though the period 1900–14 is as much a transition as a part of the second era, due to Latin America's neo-colonial destiny as a late developer in the field of cultural activity. At the same time the arts themselves may be conceived, during both these phases, as advancing simultaneously on two fronts – whose paths unite only in the most outstanding cases in the early part of the period, but with increasing frequency after 1920 – namely, those of nativism and cosmopolitanism broadly understood. The generalized divorce in European art after romanticism, between 'realism' and what may loosely be termed 'impressionism', or between objective and subjective approaches to experience, seen most vividly in Latin America in the literary divide between *naturalismo* and *modernismo* from the 1870s to 1914, was prolonged in the continent after the First World War in the contrast between *regionalismo* and *vanguardismo* (or *modernismo*, confusingly, in Brazil). The greatest artists, on the whole, are those who manage to resolve, or rise above, the dilemmas posed by such radical alternatives.

Our broad strategy, then, is to treat the arts as ultimately indivisible, examining each of the major art forms in turn and within them outlining notable trends and illustrating these by reference to leading artists and their works; and to treat Latin America as a cultural unity (however contradictory at any given moment), whilst nonetheless giving full and proper regard to national and regional variations. Since positivism was the unifying ideology of the age,[1] we begin with its most direct reflection in artistic expression, the realist–naturalist narrative, accompanied by a brief survey of Latin American theatre in this same era. There follows an exploration of the contrasting cosmopolitan movements – especially fertile in poetry – known as *modernismo* in Spanish America and *parnasianismo-simbolismo* in Brazil. Music and painting, usually ignored in histories of this kind, are then briefly reviewed, bringing to an end the first phase of the period and the first half of the chapter. Once the scene has been set for the early 1900s, architecture is treated both retrospectively and prospectively, looking back at the nineteenth-century experience and revealing how, with the rise of the great cities and mass culture, Latin American architecture suddenly zoomed up to date and came to symbolize the continent's coming of age at the height of modernity. The chapter then doubles back upon itself by immediately picking up the story in painting and music and following the trends up to the end of the 1920s, thereby setting the stage for the completion of developments in

---

[1] See Charles A. Hale, 'Political and social ideas in Latin America, 1870–1930', *Cambridge History of Latin America* vol. IV (1986), reprinted as 'Political ideas and ideologies in Latin America, 1870–1930' in Leslie Bethell (ed.), *Ideas and ideologies in twentieth century Latin America* (Cambridge, 1996).

narrative and poetry, so dependent during this period on the discoveries in music, the plastic arts and architecture. The story of the 1920s is viewed primarily in terms of the continuation of realist forms through regionalism, together with the rise of a new revolutionary aesthetic advanced by young avant-garde groups from the new generation born with the century

THE LATE NINETEENTH CENTURY

The novel

So strong was the influence of positivism in the last decades of the nineteenth century that literature was either against it, as in the case of modernism, or went over to it wholesale, as in the case of naturalism. Whilst romanticism would remain a permanent feature of the Latin American self-image, because of its identification with independence, its ingredients would now be variously adapted, condensed or re-interpreted; and although both naturalism in fiction and the theatre, and modernism in poetry, would each retain certain continuities with the preceding movement, their divergences from it are more striking. In Europe the realism of Balzac and Stendhal preceded the naturalism of Zola and Maupassant; but Latin America had produced no Balzacs between 1830 and 1860, since the conditions which had produced him were entirely absent. Most Latin American novelists of realist persuasion thereafter relapsed into an anachronistic romantic version on the model of Scott, or degenerated into the less subtle naturalist mode. Realism, after all, is a historical product of the European bourgeoisie after the formation of nation states. It requires sociological complexity, psychological subtlety and a sure grasp of historical process; whereas all the vulgar naturalist has to do is swear by science, concentrate on the sordid and the shocking, and ensure that his characters are determined by the iron laws of heredity and environment. What could have been more suitable as a form for containing the contradictions of a historical moment in which the mainly white elites chose to blame the cultural backwardness of their respective nations on the supposed biological inferiority of the races with whom they were unfortunate enough to share their nationality? Contrary to first appearances, however, naturalism was in many respects an optimistic movement. Its desire to shock, which in the hands of superficial or conservative writers was merely a romantic throwback to the melodramatic or the gothic, was meant to galvanize, not dismay; and its interest in the sordid was really a desire to undermine the residual ideology of precisely those remaining romantics who still believed in some immanent realm of spirituality, or the catholics who continued to imagine that truth was metaphysical. For the naturalist, man lived in an entirely material world, and was an animal: when that was understood, progress was possible.

Given the relatively fluent assimilation of influences from Europe in the nineteenth century, and the close relation between Brazilian and French literature throughout the period, it is not surprising that naturalism flourished more vigorously in Brazil than elsewhere. And it was the north-east particularly which produced the outstanding naturalist writers between 1870 and 1920, just as it would produce the regionalist movement in the 1920s. Part of this regional–naturalist impulse stemmed from the harsh realities of slavery and its abolition and the transition from *engenho* to *usina*. This was hardly an equivalent process to the conflicts between capital and labour which had helped to focus naturalism in Europe, but it was certainly more perceptibly dramatic than most contemporary labour conflicts in Spanish America, and it also involved the racial question. The Negro had been virtually invisible in romantic fiction: only one novel, *A escrava Isaura* (1875), by Bernardo Joaquim da Silva Guimarães (1825–84), stood up at all for the blacks in the way that Castro Alves (1847–71) had in poetry. A transitional figure, Guimarães was one of the first to treat seriously the folklore of the interior, in this case Minas Gerais, and he dealt also with banditry, the *sertão* and contemporary social themes (as, for example, in *O seminarista*, (1872)). Unfortunately, although bohemian and scandalous in real life, his literary style was colourless.

The true precursor of the naturalist school was the north-eastern polemicist Franklin da Silveira Távora (1842–88), author of an early historical novel, *Os índios do Jaguaribe* (1861), followed by more sociologically informed works such as *Um casamento no arrabalde* (1869), *O cabeleira* (1876) and *O matuto* (1878). The first systematic employer of history and folklore – as against mere romance and local colour – in Brazilian fiction, Távora is so concerned with his documentary materials emphasizing the relation between character and environment, that his personages are frequently overwhelmed and denied the gift of life. A liberal humanitarian and militant republican, he is especially remembered for his vitriolic attacks upon José de Alencar's patrician detachment from reality. As a northerner, he resented Alencar's efforts to move the centre of literary gravity to the south at a time when coffee was beginning to alter the hegemonic pattern of the national economy. Like Argentine defenders of the *pampas* and later advocates of the Venezuelan *llanos* or the Peruvian *sierras* in symbolic fiction, Távora, the authentic precursor of the 1926 regionalist movement, believed that the soul of Brazil lay in the north-east, whilst the south was the port of entry for alien cosmopolitan influences.

The first unmistakably naturalist novelist, and the first Brazilian to live by pen alone, was Aluísio de Azevedo (1857–1913), who had read both Zola and Eça de Queirós. His literary stance is more conscious and uncompromising than that of any Spanish American novelist of the age. His first novel, *Uma lágrima de mulher* (1880), was still lingeringly romantic, but Azevedo developed astonishingly quickly – suggesting that programmatic naturalism is the inverse of an exalted but disappointed romanticism – and *O mulato* (1881) created a sensation, although a mild one as things turned out compared with the scandal provoked by *O homem* (1887), a case study of female sexual hysteria. Other important works were *Casa de pensão* (1884) and *O cortiço* (1890), an urban naturalistic classic. The very titles of these works reveal a more theoretical, almost sociological dimension to the movement in Brazil. Azevedo's books caused bitter controversy, provoking the same uproar in church and landowning circles as Clorinda Matto de Turner (see below) would elicit in conservative Peru at the end of the 1880s. Despite this, or because of it, Azevedo enjoyed great popular success.

Azevedo was by no means alone. Some critics assert that *O coronel sangrado* (1877) by Herculano Marcos Inglês de Sousa (1853–1918) is the first true naturalist novel in Brazil. Better known today is *O missionário* in which a priest falls in love with an Indian girl in the Amazon wilderness, a favourite naturalist motif. Most Zolaesque of all was Júlio César Ribeiro (1845–1890), a writer involved in all the great issues of his time, who achieved great success with *A carne* (1888), although to the modern reader only the scenes of sex and sadism seem convincingly achieved. Similar was Adolfo Ferreira Caminha (1867–97), as famous for his scandalous relationship with a married woman as for his novels, *A normalista* (1893), about small-town prejudice, and *Bom crioulo* (1895), about homosexuality in the navy, both denounced as immoral by the authorities. The response was another, equally scabrous work, *Tentação* (1896).

The cultivation of style seemed inappropriate to those naturalists attempting to change the way polite Brazilian society liked to view itself; yet in France the confluence of naturalist prose and parnassian poetry in Flaubert, Gautier and Maupassant had initiated a line which would eventually lead to Proust, Joyce, Virginia Woolf and the *nouveau roman*. Brazil produced two novelists closer to that model than to Zola. The first, Raul d'Avila Pompéia (1863–95), author of *Uma tragédia no Amazonas* (1880), is best known for *O Ateneu* (1888), a satirical recreation of his adolescent boarding-school experiences. Sometimes compared to Dickens, both for his subject matter and a certain eccentricity of perspective, he is normally considered a symbolist, for the glowing stylishness of writing which hovers between realism and impressionism whilst showing rare psychological insight. The other writer is for some the greatest of all Latin American novelists, Joaquim Maria Machado de Assis (1839–1908), the 'myopic, epileptic quadroon', who came to be considered the 'quintessential Brazilian'.[2] Born in poverty, later a typesetter and proofreader, then a journalist and critic, it was he who founded the Brazilian Academy in 1897. Devoted to his country yet intensely critical, he longed for full social acceptance and bitterly resented his treatment as a mulatto. His novels share with Pompéia's a command of the inner life: framed by social structures, but more psychological than sociological in emphasis. Aesthetically a parnassian, philosophically a determinist, Machado gave an oblique but accurate portrait of Brazil under the Second Empire. The first great novel, after his early poetic phase, was *Memórias póstumas de Brás Cubas* (1881), which begins with the death of its protagonist (recalling Sterne) and concludes: 'I had no progeny, I transmitted to no one the legacy of our misery.' Two other masterpieces of parody are *Quincas Borba* (1891) and *Dom Casmurro* (1899), both marked by precision, a finely balanced irony, sceptical humour and pervasive melancholy. The style is subtle, ingenious, sardonic, profoundly self-conscious; but also socially acute, even worldly-wise, recreating a world view circumscribed by all the determinants known to learned men at the time; also aware, finally, that

[2] See M. Seymour-Smith, *Guide to modern world literature* (4 vols., London, 1975), III, 152.

the imagination itself and its creations have their own relative autonomy, making this the first genuinely self-referential fiction in Latin America (though there were incipient signs in Lizardi's *El periquillo sarniento* at the beginning of the century) and anticipating twentieth-century developments. Machado also wrote poetry, drama, criticism and much journalism, contriving always to distance the immediate and the dramatic through the formal perfection of art. He was *sui generis*, a writer like Swift, Sterne, Kafka or Borges. Samuel Putnam declared in 1948 that no United States novelist – even Henry James – could compare with Machado, whilst William Grossman called him 'the most completely disenchanted writer in Occidental literature'.[3]

No republic in Spanish America can match the richness of Brazilian naturalism, but there too it soon predominated. A typical precursor was the Uruguayan Eduardo Acevedo Díaz (1851–1921), whose historical novels were radically different in focus from anything produced by romanticism. The best known Uruguayan naturalist, influenced by Azevedo, was the prolific Javier de Viana (1868–1926), noted for brutal short stories of life in the rural sector, like *Campo* (1896), or melodramatic novels after the manner of the polemical Spaniard Blasco Ibáñez (1867–1928), like *Gaucha* (1899). Carlos Reyles (1868–1938) wrote *Beba* (1894) and *El terruño* (1916), before turning to the more impressionist *El embrujo de Sevilla* (1922) and his masterpiece *El gaucho Florido* (1932). A wealthy landowner, Reyles combined imperious authoritarianism with a curiously sensitive aestheticism, revealing how close modernism and naturalism really were, as two sides of the same coin.

Nowhere in Latin America is the dialectic between city and country more complex, dramatic and continuous in this period than in Argentina, where the important 1880 generation of 'gentleman writers' carried Sarmiento's message forward after two decades in which the spectre of barbarism, in the shape of Indians, gauchos and general social anarchy, appeared to have been banished. The vivid documentary classic, *Una excursión a los indios ranqueles* (1870), by Lucio Mansilla (1831–1913), gives a remarkably humane soldier's view of the frontier between European civilization and the nomadic Indians a decade before Roca's notorious expedition, whilst Eduardo Gutiérrez (1851–89) produced in *Juan Moreira* (1879) a novel about the legendary gaucho bandit which, although rudimentary in technique, provided the first sign that the gaucho, after the age of Martín Fierro, was on his way to the cities. These works preceded those of the 1880 generation proper, men of leisure with time to enjoy the benefits worked for by others like Sarmiento who, as he remarked without bitterness near the end of his life, had struggled 'so that everyone might take part in life's banquet, which I could but do on the sly'.[4] The result was a naturalism without militancy, as revealed in *La gran aldea* (1884) by Lucio V. López (1848–94), which surveys the transformation of Buenos Aires in the first tide of immigration. As in *Juvenilia* (1884) by Miguel Cané (1851–1905), childhood reminiscences which can be read in revealing conjunction with Sarmiento's *Recuerdos de provincia*, we can sense the growing awareness of a newly cosmopolitan elite, in the era of the Grand Tour, bent on mythologizing its own past formation and securing its claim to the present and the future. Having defined themselves in opposition to the Indian and the gaucho, they would now define themselves in opposition to the waves of immigrants flooding into their republic. The Argentine version, then, would be a somewhat selective brand of naturalism.

Some immigrants were acceptable. Eduardo Wilde (1844–1913), son of an English aristocrat, typified the newly mobile Buenos Aires elite, and Paul Groussac (1848–1929), the half-French author of *Fruto vedado* (1884), semi-autobiographical reminiscences, became director of the National Library from 1885–1929. Even the fiction of the more tempestuous Eugenio Cambaceres (1843–88), arguably Spanish America's first genuine naturalist, contained numerous autobiographical elements, albeit less fondly and self-indulgently recalled. Cambaceres's works are written with the furious bitterness of the recent convert from romanticism: *Música sentimental* (1884), on the relationship between Buenos Aires and Paris; *Sin rumbo* (1885), on the relation between Buenos Aires and the provinces, with the most shocking scenes of sex and violence seen in Argentine literature up to that time; and *En la sangre* (1887), a thesis novel on heredity, environment and the dangers of immigration. Later works about changing Buenos Aires were *La Bolsa* (1891) by 'Julián Martel' (José Miró, 1867–96), dramatizing the rampant materialism of the era, and the stories of 'Fray Mocho' (José S. Alvárez, 1858–1903), a journalist on Mitre's *La Nación* whose books, like *Memorias de un vigilante* (1897), revealed a shabbier, more violent city than that of the literary gentlemen, and anticipated the tango era.

---

[4] See P. Henríquez Ureña, *Las corrientes literarias en la América hispánica* (Mexico, D.F., 1949), 140.

Chile's Alberto Blest Gana (1830–1920), persistently underestimated, is perhaps the nearest any nineteenth-century Latin American comes to emulating a Balzac or Galdós. His novels combine facets of the romantic historical novel, comedy of manners and naturalist slice of life, fused by a dominant realist intention. The best is *Martín Rivas* (1862), set in the Santiago he knew, though his most popular work was *Durante la reconquista* (1897), about the independence era. Similar in style though even less well known was the Bolivian Nataniel Aguirre (1843–88), whose *Juan de la Rosa* (1885) also recreated the independence struggles. Its genuinely popular Americanist standpoint makes it one of the most readable novels of the liberal era.

After Peru's shattering defeat in the War of the Pacific, two militant women novelists emerged, Mercedes Cabello de Carbonera (1845–1909), whose virulent assaults on corruption and social decay in *El conspirador* (1892), *Blanca Sol* (1889) and *Las consecuencias* (1889), provoked a counter-attack by the literary acolytes of the Lima oligarchy which eventually drove her into the municipal asylum; and Clorinda Matto de Turner (1854–1909), generally considered the first Latin American novelist to have produced a true indigenist novel, *Aves sin nido* (1889). Dedicated to González Prada (see below), the work caused scandal and led to excommunication and voluntary exile. She had followed Ricardo Palma, the creator of *Tradiciones peruanas*, with a series of *Tradiciones cuzqueñas* (1884–6), and her novel was tinged with romantic melodramatic hues, though genuinely anticlerical and anti-oligarchical. She directed a newspaper, *El Perú Ilustrado* (1892–5), a tribunal for social criticism, and produced another naturalist novel, *Herencia* (1893), on immigration and heredity. Interestingly, one of the first Bolivian indigenists was also a woman, Lindaura Anzoátegui de Campero (1846–98), indicating an intuitive empathy between different oppressed social groups. When so many naturalist novels were set in brothels, it is refreshing to find women looking elsewhere with critical insight and purpose.

The outstanding Colombian novelist of the era was Tomás Carrasquilla (1858–1940), an early *criollista* – not merely a costumbrist, since his grasp of folklore, social types and dialogue was always profoundly contextualized. His particular variant of naturalism, from *Frutos de mi tierra* (1896) to *La marquesa de Yolombó* (1926), anticipated the regionalist mode of the 1920s which he lived to see. With greater mastery of technique to match his observation and linguistic virtuosity, he would have become one of the major realists. By contrast José María Vargas Vila (1860–1933) cunningly used stock naturalist themes with a voluptuous late romantic, almost modernist style, to produce works of decadent allure and great popular appeal, including generous doses of anarchism and anti-imperialism, to produce a heady brew with titles like *Aura o las violetas* (1886) and *Flor de fango* (1895), works which allowed him, exceptionally, to live off their amoral earnings.

In Mexico nineteenth-century fiction had been curiously retarded, with a continuity of rather episodic, costumbrist narratives, provincial rather than regionalist. The effect of the war with the United States and the French invasion was to prolong romantic style and subject matter until well after the era of Ignacio Altamirano. José López Portillo (1850–1923), with *La parcela* (1898), anticipated the fiction produced during the revolutionary period, turning to the rural sector in search of a nationalist literature. Other novelists of the time were Rafael Delgado (1853–1914), best known for *La calandria* (1891), and Emilio Rabasa (1856–1930), who, in *La bola* (1887), pointed the way to a genuinely modern critical realist perspective. Federico Gamboa (1864–1939) was Zola's most direct disciple in Spanish America: the protagonists of *Del natural* (1888) and *Suprema ley* (1896) were syphilis and alcohol (modernist works of the period were more likely to feature tuberculosis and opium), with humans mere incidentals acting according to thesis and therefore to type, exemplifying the subordination of character to theme which defines Latin American fiction to this day. *Metamórfosis* (1899) was about a nun who, abducted from the convent, gives herself up to lust; and *Santa* (1903), a name as well known now in Mexico as Zola's *Nana*, was another laboratory demonstration concerning the tragic life of a country girl who, seduced by a soldier, becomes a Mexico City prostitute.

The theatre

The theatre was stagnating in most Latin American countries in the last decades of the century. During the post-independence period, although the quality of writing and performance had not been high, a dramatized sense of history itself had given impetus to the form. Thereafter most writers, responding to public demand, would become known first for their novels or poetry and only then feel secure in turning to the stage. Few of these works of secondary enthusiasm have survived; yet playwrights who were not already novelists found it difficult to get plays performed, since theatre owners preferred to play safe. Thus foreign plays, operas, actors and singers predominated. Sarah Bernhardt and the great soprano Adelina Patti, for example, made well publicised visits to cities like Rio de Janeiro, Buenos Aires and Mexico City.

At the same time, other entertainments developed to compete with the theatre. In the 1870s the *can-can* reached Latin America, to the disgust of many and delight of more, and could be guaranteed to fill theatres when more sober fare was flagging. French comic opera was introduced during the same decade, and Bizet's *Carmen*, 'the Spanish cigarette girl who speaks French and dances Cuban', became the rage. Not to be outdone by Gallic invaders, the Spanish *género chico*, in particular the *zarzuela*, likewise grew more popular at the expense of local theatrical activity; it was at the same time more easily Americanized, particularly in Mexico, where by the end of the century titles like *Viva México* were becoming common. The first truly Mexican *zarzuela*, *Una fiesta en Santa Anita* (1886) by Juan de Dios Peza (1852–1910) and Luis Alcaraz, caused a popular sensation. In the great capitals the *café dansant* and the nocturnal restaurant, frequented by dandies, bohemians and intellectuals, and deplored by the *gente decente*, became fashionable. By the early 1880s most people of moderate income had queued to hear the first phonographs in local theatres. In the 1890s American *vaudeville* reached Latin America, and in the same decade the first cinematographs arrived and developed with astonishing rapidity, auguring badly for the theatre's potential growth in countries where a national tradition had never really been established.

Thus, in most Latin American countries drama, which had never scaled the aesthetic heights, entered upon relative popular decline. Naturalist theatre, however, slowly gained momentum. In Mexico Ibsen's *Ghosts* arrived only in 1896, and went unappreciated, but already in 1894 the stolid Federico Gamboa had tried to emulate his achievement. It was Gamboa who in 1905 produced *La venganza de la gleba*, the first mexican drama to condemn the feudal system of land tenure, though characterized more by 'Victorian' sentimentality than by any revolutionary impulse. So dire was the general situation in Mexico that in 1906 Justo Sierra, education minister at the time, launched a drama competition to save the nation from the stranglehold of the music-hall. Sixty plays were entered; all have been forgotten. The situation was similar in most of the other major Spanish American republics, and in Brazil.

All this makes the astonishing theatrical renaissance of the River Plate region at the very high-point of *modernismo* all the more remarkable. This can be explained not only by the rapid growth of Buenos Aires and Montevideo, but also by the particular nature of the transition between country and city and the need for a unifying national mythology at a time of great internal change and heavy immigration. An Uruguayan impresario, José Podestá (1857–1937), began to combine performances in his circus in Buenos Aires with pantomimes and dramas using gaucho themes and trick riding, not unlike William Cody's Wild West circus in the United States. Podestá's first show in 1884 was based on Gutiérrez' *Juan Moreira*, mimed at first and then, in 1886, recited. His family formed travelling companies which toured Argentina and Uruguay, finally moving in 1901 from the suburbs to Buenos Aires, when gaucho themes began to be supplanted by other dramas which attracted a broadly based audience. More ambitious writers now emerged to fill the gap between this popular native theatre inspired by rural themes and the classical European theatre performed by foreign companies in the elegant zones of the city. In 1902 Martiniano Leguizamón (1858–1935), with *Calandria*, and Martín Coronado (1850–1919), with the Ibsenesque *La piedra del escándalo*, achieved overnight acclaim. An important stimulus to serious theatre was the critic Juan Pablo Echagüe (1877–1950), whose erudite commentaries were collected in *Puntos de vista* (1905) and *Teatro argentino* (1917). But the key figure of the era was the Uruguayan Florencio Sánchez (1875–1910), who produced a score of dramas, *sainetes* and comedies during a brief career, showing most clearly how quickly Argentine theatre moved from the melodramatic, mythologized deeds of gaucho outlaws to the real conflicts of ownership and exploitation in the rural sector at the time. His best known works, informed by anarchist and socialist thought, and his intimate acquaintance with suburban down-at-heel Buenos Aires and the outlying rural districts, were *M'hijo el dotor* (1903), *La gringa* (1904), the sombre masterpiece *Barranca abajo* (1905), and *Los muertos* (1905), a naturalist thesis drama written in two days about alcoholism, which, with tuberculosis and poverty, was what sent the great playwright to an early grave.

Poetry

In both Spanish America and Brazil during the late nineteenth century, we see one of those moments where form and content move into sharp contradiction, with prose, under the influence of Positivism, moving firmly in the direction of naturalism and poetry moving in the direction of *modernismo*, broadly speaking an amalgam of the European literary movements then in vogue and corresponding thereby to the moment of impressionism. In Brazil poets merely emulated the French movements – parnassianism (Leconte de Lisle, Gautier) and symbolism (Mallarmé, Verlaine) – and used the same names. It would be difficult to demonstrate a significant process of Brazilianization. Yet it was only in Brazil, as we have seen, that a Pompéia or Machado could unite the formal exquisiteness of parnassian poetry with the social relevance of naturalist fiction to produce the narrative masterpieces of the era. No Spanish American novelist came close to this achievement, in view of the more radical separation of poetry (including 'poetic' short prose) and narrative.

It is sometimes tempting to conclude that the Brazilians were right: Parnassianism possibly would have been the best name for that movement which swept the entire continent from 1870 to almost 1920, and Modernism would have been better reserved – as in Brazil – for the avant-garde currents after the First World War. (This would also have been less confusing to European and North American critics.) At first sight, indeed, there seems nothing in the least 'modern' in those rather ethereal would-be aristocrats, literary poseurs who sang of swans and princesses and seemed to long for ancient regimes. Yet the cries of 'Art for Art's sake' (Darío always wrote the word Art with a capital letter) were really more desperate than defiant, for most of these young poets were journalists and stood in quite a different relation to the literary mode of production than might be guessed from their published poems. Moreover, on closer examination *modernismo* was less apolitical than some critical mythologies suggest. In contrast to the romantic period, politics was expelled from the poetry itself. But most of the *modernista* poets maintained close relationships with leading *pensadores*; many were anarchists or socialists; almost all were nationalists and anti-imperialists.

The 'modernism' or modernity claimed was to be understood above all as a *modernisation of poetry*. This is more significant than the uninitiated might suppose, since the pompous sterility and oratorical arthritis of

Spanish poetry a century ago is difficult now to recapture. Latin American poetry was not truly modern by the end of modernism, but was fully ready to become so. The range of formal and thematic innovations of the movement was extraordinary. The subject matter of poetry, though extremely limited in tone and mood, ranged far and wide in time and space. Latin American themes, considered essential throughout the romantic period, now lay neglected by most poets. Latin America, after all, was not modern, and viewed from Parnassus or Olympus was hardly a suitable subject for aesthetic exploration. The poets would only return to it when they themselves had become modernised.

Much critical time and space has been occupied in debating when Spanish American modernism began – no one disputes that it was Rubén Darío who made it visible with the publication of *Azul* in 1888 – and who were its pathfinders and pioneers. One poet universally considered a 'precursor', even though he outlived Darío, was Manuel González Prada (1848–1918). His earliest works showed a precision and artistry quite foreign to poetry in Spanish at that time, Bécquer excepted, with an astonishing variety of experimental forms and metres. Like his contemporary Martí, González Prada saw literature generally as a high civic calling, but considered poetry pure and autonomous. Such a stance, which would seem astonishing today in a man of his orientation, only underlines the reversion at that time to the classical distinction imposed between poetry and prose. González Prada never troubled to diffuse his poetry, however, and had only limited influence outside Peru.

Another important 'precursor' of *modernismo* was the Cuban José Martí (1853–95). As a poet, he stands as one of the greatest of all time in Spanish, for his remarkable combination of simplicity, ingenuity and vigour, appearing classical even when his verse was in reality intricate and innovative. In prose, he was, along with Juan Montalvo (Ecuador, 1832–89)[5] – best remembered for his famous boast, 'My pen has killed him', when the dictator García Moreno was assassinated in 1875 – one of the great stylists of the period. As the supreme journalist of the era, Martí had the ability to coin phrases which have become part of Spanish American culture. Exiled at sixteen, after a year in prison, Martí devoted

---

[5] Juan Montalvo's best-known articles were collected in *El Cosmopolita* (1866) and *El Regenerador* (1872). *Capítulos que se le olvidaron a Cervantes* followed in 1873. In 1883 he began to publish his *Siete Tratados,* and in 1886, exiled in Panama, he published the famous *Las Catilinarias* followed by four series of essays under the title *El Espectador* (Paris, 1886–9).

his entire adult life to the Cuban revolutionary cause; when unable to return to Cuba, he contributed to the literary and civic culture of every country he visited (notably Mexico and Guatemala), and spent fourteen years in the United States. In this respect his career was similar to his Puerto Rican contemporary, Eugenio María de Hostos (1839–1903), who also devoted his life to the struggle against Spanish colonialism and who, like Darío, travelled the entire Latin American region, campaigning, writing and teaching wherever he went. Martí wrote the first modernist novel, *Amistad funesta* (1885), and his children's stories, *La edad de oro* (1889), have become classics of the genre. Much of his poetry, such as *Versos libres* (c. 1883) and *Flores del destierro*, was published posthumously. Collections which appeared during his lifetime were *Ismaelillo* (1882), delightful miniature masterpieces inspired by his absent baby son; and *Versos sencillos* (1891), as diaphanous and direct as the poet's own existence. He was killed in 1895 leading a military expedition against the Spaniards in Cuba. His example as man of action and man of letters, poet and patriot, is one whose impact on Latin American history could scarcely be exaggerated.

Because Martí and González Prada were greater as men than other modernists, critics have been tempted to see them, in their courage, their heroic individualism and political constancy, as romantic writers; but it is a distortion of the movement to seek to remove from it all whose life or work contained political content, or to assume that those who died young (Silva, Casal – see below) or gloriously (Martí) were really late romantics. On the contrary, what gave the movement its unifying force and differentiated it from contemporary Brazilian developments was precisely the fact that *modernismo* was not only a Spanish American version of parnassian–symbolist formal refinement, but a retarded assimilation of the full philosophical weight of romanticism, whose impact (due to the emphasis on political and historical currents) had been incomplete in Spanish America, together with an incorporation of the second, decadent phase of European romanticism: the 'romantic agony'. The genius of Darío, to whom we shall shortly be turning, is that only in his poetry and his person did all three phases – an accumulation of the entire European poetic experience of the nineteenth century – reach true harmony. Thus *modernismo* was not a school but a broad historical movement which influenced all important poets in the region after 1888; and which can be divided into two periods, before and after Darío's *Prosas profanas* in 1896, at which point a shift takes place from the north of the continent, where it first gained momentum, to the south. Many poets may have seemed, or may actually have been, tormented romantic personalities, or even men of action (Díaz Mirón, Gómez Carrillo, Chocano – see below), but their means of expression had changed irremediably.

Martí and González Prada, then, were part of the modernist tide, but both swept beyond its more limited, merely ornamental positions. One who was a *modernista* pure and simple, before Darío, was Manuel Gutiérrez Nájera (1859–95), founder of the celebrated *Revista Azul* (1894–6) in Mexico City. Curiously, he was from a humble background, but became the most aristocratic of the new writers (his pseudonym was 'El duque Job'); moreover, almost uniquely, he never left his native city, but acted and wrote, with extraordinary intuition, as if he were the best travelled and most experienced of writers. His early models were romantic (Musset, Bécquer), but already refined by his own sense of style; as each new poet – Leconte de Lisle, Verlaine, Baudelaire, Poe – became fashionable, Gutiérrez Nájera absorbed them and dosed them into his own frivolous, sophisticated but remarkably accomplished and musical poetry and newspaper pieces. One of his poems, the charming 'La duquesa Job', is a modernist classic. This writer of innately likeable poetry was as delicate as his verse, and died at the age of thirty-six. As though to demonstrate how different modernist poets can be, his Mexican contemporary, Salvador Díaz Mirón (1853–1928), has been called 'un montonero de las letras'.[6] Twice imprisoned for shooting enemies dead in gun battles, exiled by Porfirio Díaz, his life was of a turbulence only equalled by Martí and Chocano (see below). His famous verse, 'Some feathers cross the swamp/ and bear no stain: such is my plumage', shows not only his provocative temperament, but his insistence – for the phrase also has a literary connotation – that the new poetry need not avoid all serious or substantive content to be 'pure' and beautiful. Only González Prada equalled his determination both to innovate and to avoid all frivolity, and careful readers can trace the path by which American romanticism – Díaz Mirón's first heroes were Byron and Hugo – becomes transformed from an oratorical, essentially external impulse into a more contained, because more carefully internalized, perspective; from his first collection of *Poesías* (1886) to *Lascas* (1901).

More like Gutiérrez Nájera was the Cuban Julián del Casal (1863–93).

---

[6] L. A. Sánchez, *Historia comparada de las literaturas americanas* (4 vols., Buenos Aires, 1976), III, 191.

Dogged by ill-health, personal misfortune and the island's tragedy, his profoundly anguished version of *mal-de-siècle* decadence nourished a longing to escape to Europe ('Mine is the city's impure love/ and to this sun forever up above/ I much prefer the gaslight's flickering glow'). Neurotic, pessimistic, melancholy, he was influenced by Gautier, Baudelaire and his half-French compatriot, José María de Heredia (1842–95), a leading parnassian whose *Les Trophées* appeared in the year of Casal's death. Similar, but even more authentically tragic, was the life and death of the Colombian José Asunción Silva (1865–96), whose biography is worthy of a Keats or Shelley half a century before him. Like his friend Jorge Isaacs and Casal, Silva suffered the collapse of his family's fortune; his sister Elvira, for whom he felt an obsessive love, died aged twenty-one (Isaacs wrote a famous elegy); he lost most of his writings in a shipwreck; suffered, perhaps more than any of his contemporaries, the despair of romanticism's collision with positivism and materialism; and finally shot himself. Profoundly influenced by Poe, Bécquer and Baudelaire, his *Nocturno* ('Una noche,/ una noche toda llena de murmullos . . .') is among the most famous of Spanish American poems, and his novel, *De sobremesa*, is one of the most characteristic prose works produced by the *fin-de-siècle* mentality. Silva was tortured by the narrow provincial environment of Bogotá, and typifies the sense of marginality and alienation behind much modernist poetry. Positivism denied the artist's right to a central position, denied even that art was important; saw it, rather, like everything else, in instrumental terms, as entertainment, ornamental, decorative, diversionary; whereupon most poets, themselves dimly hankering after a pre-capitalist system of patronage, confirmed the perceptions of the positivists by retreating into a poetry that seemed largely intranscendent, evasive and – at first sight – irrelevant to Latin America's real needs.

The man who moulded the entire modernist movement – and gave it its name – was Rubén Darío (1867–1916), the child prodigy from a small town in Nicaragua who became the most influential poet in the Spanish language since Góngora. Critics now commonly deny his poetry's aesthetic quality, but nothing can shake his place in history, for as Pedro Henríquez Ureña correctly stated, 'Faced with any poem written in Spanish, one can state precisely whether it was written before or after Darío.'[7] He escaped for a long time from the tragic sense of life which

---

[7] Henríquez Ureña, *Corrientes literarias*, 173.

carried Casal and Silva to early graves, but he too, in the end, succumbed to the same anguish ('Not knowing where we are going/ nor whence we have come . . .') and the same undermining of his own health. Darío's exemplary trajectory ('Strong with Hugo and ambiguous with Verlaine'), viewed entire, confirms that beneath the opulent surface modernism was indeed a simultaneous assimilation of the still unabsorbed aspects of European romanticism ('Who that is, is not a romantic?') and of parnassianism–symbolism, all within Latin America's invariable tendency to the baroque. It brought poetry in Spanish to formal perfection for the first time since Quevedo and Góngora at precisely the moment when all conventions of metre and verse, like all other artistic conventions, were about to be exploded: that is, just in time, for there was no inevitability about this. Yet Darío's gesture was still more expansive. It was also a celebration, an assimilation of the whole European tradition going back to the Renaissance, which Spain had largely denied or rejected, including romanticism itself, which Spain had been unable fully to absorb and which Spanish America had partly denied. Modernism is to be understood, then, not as 'French poetry written in Spanish', as some have averred, but as a profound rejection of the still living Spanish medieval tradition, a liberation both symbolic in general terms and concrete in the special cases of Puerto Rico and Cuba. At the same time, since Latin American romanticism had, for obvious reasons, largely excluded the classical, biblical and medieval motifs so characteristic of European romanticism, *modernismo* now incorporated these whilst purging them of any possible Hispanic content: that is, Spain now became one more cosmopolitan option among others, a normalization of cultural relations that said much for the sophistication of that poetic generation. In throwing off once and for all the Spanish cultural heritage – indeed, in reversing the process by beginning to influence the mother country – they paved the way for the full literary modernization of the continent, visible immediately in the 1920s with the emergence of poets like Huidobro, Vallejo and Neruda, and narrators like Asturias, Carpentier and Borges. North American poetry also now exerted some influence through two seminal figures: Poe and Whitman. As for France, it lured Latin Americans not only for the obvious positive reasons – the Enlightenment, the Revolution, the continuous ability to produce artistic schools with precise philosophies and practices – but also for equally obvious negative ones: it was Latin, but not Spanish or Portuguese; and it was modern, but not Anglo-Saxon.

Darío was not only the greatest *modernista* poet in terms of fluency, flexibility and musicality, he not only synthesized the movement as a whole within his eclectic, morally opaque but aesthetically diaphanous poetry; he was also the most travelled of the leading poets and indeed, most strikingly, he travelled throughout Latin America. It was in Chile that he published *Abrojos* (1887) and *Azul* (1888), and in Argentina, *Los raros* and *Prosas profanas* (1896); but everywhere he enthused poets young and old, inspiring clubs and associations, and writing innumerable articles for newspapers in each country he visited. In Europe he spent long periods of residence both in Paris, home of the new, and Spain, home of the old, where *Cantos de vida y esperanza* was published in 1905. Exoticist, taking in all the romantic places which, in that newly mobile age, he had seen or dreamed of seeing; nostalgic for past ages of which aristocratically inclined Americans wished to consider themselves heirs, particularly Greece and Rome; cosmopolitan in his desire, shared by the entire generation of elite groups of the region, to transform Latin America into a 'universal' culture, centred on Paris but inspired by Versailles (itself, as heir to classical antiquity, the inspiration for the new monumental city centres of Buenos Aires and Porfirian Mexico); frivolously aesthetic, finally, with a New World hedonism and an innocent eroticism in the midst of the knowing *belle époque*, Darío encapsulates the movement and unifies it. Poets after the Great War would find in socialism a new substitute for religion; Darío claimed to live for art, but art failed to comfort him in his middle years, and sexual distraction merely underlined the transience of life. The poetry of his last years ceased to be merely pictorial or musical composition, however exquisite and compelling, and searched anew for meaning; in the words of Anderson Imbert, 'he poeticized, with incomparable elegance, the joy of living and the terror of dying.'[8] But he was never capable of very precise thinking, confining himself in the vaguest – symbolist, impressionistic – terms to what Sánchez calls his 'movement of enthusiasm towards freedom and beauty'. His contribution to the cosmopolitan element within modern Spanish American culture is as great as Martí's contribution to its specifically Americanist side: Martí universalized all things American; Darío Americanized all things universal. Between them they effectively systematize the movement and the era. Only Darío could unify it, however, partly because of his virtuosity, partly because of

---

[8] E. Anderson Imbert, *Historia de la literatura hispanoamericana* (2 vols., Mexico, D.F., 3rd edn., 1966), I, 407.

his very eclecticism, his refusal to accept any ideological centre except that of Art itself.

As we have noted, the impetus for modernism came from the north of Latin America – Mexico, Central America, the Caribbean and Colombia. In Argentina it came late and would perhaps not have become as important or taken the form it did had Darío not stayed there after 1890 and exerted his powerful influence through Mitre's *La Nación*. Two names above all stand out: Julio Herrera y Reissig (Uruguay, 1875–1910), another short-lived poet, elitist and escapist, the most baroque and Gongorist, but, for a minority of critics, the most innately talented of all; and Leopoldo Lugones (1874–1938), one of the most influential writers in all Argentine literature, whose prose poems *Las montañas de oro* (1897) really initiated Argentine modernism. His prestige was secured in 1905 by *Los crepúsculos del jardín* and the prose epic, *La guerra gaucha*. *El payador*, his study of gaucho troubadours, appeared in 1916. Its nostalgic romantic perspective revealed his increasingly nationalist position, and in 1924, having begun as an anarchist and atheist, then become a socialist, he identified himself with fascism and catholicism. Embittered at his ensuing rejection by the younger generation, he eventually committed suicide. He has since been recognized as a fundamental figure both in Argentine literature and in modernist poetry generally, symbolizing, as Luis Alberto Sánchez has said, 'the almost arrogant will to triumph characteristic of the Argentines of his generation'.[9]

Similar to Lugones in many respects was the Peruvian poet José Santos Chocano (1875–1934), the great hothead of Spanish American poetry, who at his height was conceded the title 'poet of America', which Rodó (see below) had felt should be denied to Darío. Frequently imprisoned, married three times but never divorced, enemy and friend of dictators, briefly secretary to Pancho Villa, sentenced to death in 1920 in Guatemala, he became a fascist in 1925, murdered the young Peruvian intellectual Edwin Elmore, and was himself murdered by a schizophrenic on a tram in Santiago de Chile. He was perhaps the least modernist of the poets of his era. Dante, Byron, Hugo and Whitman were his models, the American landscape and its inhabitants, both human and animal, his themes, from *Alma América* (1906) and ¡*Fiat Lux*! (1908). He initiated a movement called *mundonovismo* ('I am the singer of America,

---

[9] Sánchez, *Literaturas americanas*, III, 191.

autochthonous and wild . . .'), and was the first major poet to treat positively the themes of *indigenismo* and *mestizaje*. Yet his literary persona was egocentric and grandiloquent, his poetry essentially demagogic, Hispanic and oratorical (his public declamations were celebrated throughout the region). His achievement was to carry some of the great uncompleted themes of romanticism forward to the 1920s, where they fused with the new regional, telluric and criollist movements.

Other important modernists were Darío's lifelong friend, Francisco Gavidia (El Salvador, 1863–1950), Aquileo J. Echevarría (Costa Rica, 1866–1909), Darío Herrera (Panama, 1870–1914), Ricardo Miró (Panama, 1883–1940), Fabio Fiallo (Santo Domingo, 1866–1942), Luis Llorens Torres (Puerto Rico, 1878–1944), the Mexicans Manuel José Othón (1858–1906), Francisco A. de Icaza (1863–1925), Luis G. Urbina (1869–1934), Efrén Rebolledo Hidalgo (1877–1929) and José Juan Tablada (1871–1945), the Venezuelans Rufino Blanco Fombona (1874–1944), well known also as a novelist and historian, and his sworn enemy, Andrés Mata (1870–1931); the Colombian Guillermo Valencia (1873–1943), author of *Ritos* (1899), a wealthy poet who was perhaps the most 'classical' of the modernists; José María Eguren (Peru, 1874–1942), whose very personal vision carried him beyond the movement's typical banalities; Ricardo Jaimes Freyre (1868–1933), a Bolivian who spent many years in Argentina, politically radical yet author of *Castalia bárbara* (1899), suffused by strange nordic myths; and his compatriot Franz Tamayo (1879–1956).

The movement was waning before Darío died in 1916. In 1911 Enrique González Martínez (1871–1952) travelled from the provinces to Mexico City with his poems, *Los senderos ocultos*, including one which began: 'Wring the swan's neck, his plumage deceives/ though he lends his white note to the fountain's blue,/ he parades his pale beauty, but has no clue/ to the voice of the earth, or the spirit it breathes'. Since the swan was one of Darío's most characteristic images, it was clear that the Mexican was proposing an end to modernism. It is, however, arguable that the Darío of *Cantos de vida y esperanza* had already initiated precisely the kind of shift from formal complexity to bare simplicity demanded by González Martínez. Such a shift, needless to say, would not have succeeded without the sureness of touch and technique which modernism had already effected. Just as Lugones, after *Lunario sentimental* (1909), had changed the direction of Argentine poetry (anticipating Arrieta, Carriego, Fernández Moreno, Banchs, Capdevila, Méndez, the early

Borges), so González Martínez, conservative by nature, prepared the way for a line of Mexican poets – López Velarde, Pellicer, Torres Bodet, Villaurrutia – who would undertake the poeticization of everyday life. Much of the force behind the new direction came from a regionalist impulse, and thus anticipated developments in fiction after 1918. Amado Nervo (Mexico, 1870–1919), the most popular modernist of all after Darío – especially, thanks to his trite mysticism, with middle class women readers – though one who has worn least well, took the path towards greater simplicity. His success was itself a sign that modernism's ability to stimulate individualized responses in its audience or changes in poetic form was effectively extinguished. The title of his best-known collection, *La amada inmóvil* (posth., 1920), is eloquent in this regard.

The increasingly complex division of labour and pressures of big-city life, the expansion of travel and the new social and geographical mobility, the growth of newspapers and shortage of space within them, all conspired to encourage writing that was brief and to the point, fresh and immediate in its impact. The bourgeoisies in power had created the great Latin American newspapers in the late nineteenth century, such as *La Nación* in Buenos Aires, *La Epoca* in Santiago (its owner, MacClure, was Darío's *Rey burgués*) or *La Opinión Nacional* in Caracas, satisfying the demand of their newly rich readers for news of the elegant social and cultural milieux of Europe during the *belle époque*. All these circumstances taken together encouraged specific developments in modernist literary production: brief lyric poetry (and very little narrative verse), including the *hai-kai*; prose poems; short stories, sometimes less than a column in length (Ricardo Palma in Peru was the precursor of this art form, though the great age of the Latin American short story did not begin until the 1920s); and, most characteristic of all, the *crónica*.

The *crónica* was a curious mixture of genres: word poem, art reportage, interview converted into narrative, imaginative or literary essay, life of a writer, review of a book, exhibition, musical performance or literary evening, autobiographical note, disguised brief narrative or travel tale, and so on. Darío was one of the innovators, but the acknowledged master of this *pot-pourri*, halfway between literature and journalism, the eternity of Art and the fugacity of Life, was the Guatemalan Enrique Gómez Carrillo (1873–1927), who saw a vision of the future when, as a young man, having served the wife of the French ambassador to Guatemala in the lingerie store where he worked, he embarked on a brief passionate affair with her. The rest of his life was a succession of such *frissons*, all grist to his literary mill, until he married Spain's most popular singer and film star of the day, Raquel Meller, and, it was rumoured, had a passionate affair with Mata Hari before betraying her to the French authorities. A brilliant manipulator of newspaper owners and politicians (he represented Estrada Cabrera's dictatorship in Europe for many years), Gómez Carrillo spent all his adult life in Paris, wrote never a word about Guatemala, but travelled the length and breadth of the old world in search of 'sensations' for his readers: 'What I seek in a travel book is not the soul of the countries which interest me. I look for something more frivolous, more subtle, more picturesque, more poetic and more positive: sensations . . . Nature is sensitive and changeable like a woman . . . The pleasure of travel is in the journey itself . . .'[10] Nothing shows more clearly than the *crónica,* as practised by Gómez Carrillo, how much modernism was in reality a tacit celebration of the insertion of Latin America, the historically invisible continent, into the international economic and cultural networks, by those who nonetheless adopted the world-weary pose of the spiritual aristocrat in an age of merchants. It was a genre virtually unknown before the 1870s and effectively dead by 1930. No modernist was more eagerly read than Gómez Carrillo, purveyor of mildly intoxicating, titillating but stylish literary gossip, and none more quickly forgotten.

Yet perhaps we should pause a while with Gómez Carrillo in the Paris of the *belle époque,* cultural capital of Latin America and mecca for those with social or aesthetic aspirations. Many wealthy families spent their winters there, or moved the whole household for years at a time. Paris, after all, was the home of Art, and if one could 'conquer' her one could return to one's native land with the laurel – nay, the certificate – of success. Numerous short-lived reviews were published there by figures like Ventura García Calderón (Peru, 1887–1959), Gonzalo Zaldumbide (Ecuador, 1884–1962), Hugo Barbagelata (Uruguay, b. 1887) the ubiquitous Venezuelan Alberto Zérega Fombona, Isidro Fabela (Mexico, 1882–1964), and Alberto Ghiraldo (Argentina, 1874–1947), author of the essay *Yanquilandia barbara.* Like Gómez Carrillo, many of these writers came to seem more important than they really were because Paris gave them prestige and material access to its publicity outlets. Most of them thought of Paris and Europe as autumnal, but were less keenly

---

[10] *La psicología del viaje* (1919), quoted by M. Henríquez Ureña, *Breve historia del modernismo* (Mexico, D.F., 1954), 395–6.

aware that they too were autumnal: they had prepared Latin American culture for modernity, but were not themselves modern. After the First World War, the dilettantes from the ruling class had to make way for a new generation of artists from the petty bourgeoisie, although it was the former who continued to provide the social connections and to finance the magazines.

As usual, what had happened swiftly and violently, convulsively and unevenly, in Spanish American modernism, happened more organically – more closely following European models – in Brazil. After the gradual dissipation of romanticism, literary activity there continued to be organized under the same labels as in France, so that Parnassianism and Symbolism, names which have little resonance in Spanish American literature, are the generic terms applied to developments in the last thirty years of the nineteenth century and the first twenty years of the twentieth. Most critics are agreed that naturalism and parnassianism were at bottom different expressions of the same scientific spirit of anti-romantic revolt. The phenomenon was visible as early as the late 1860s in poetry such as Machado's *Crisálidas* and *Falenas*. He and Luís Guimarães (1845–98) were precursors of a new spirit – methodical, correct, restrained. The polemic which heralded the style began in 1878 in the *Diário do Rio de Janeiro*, and was later known as 'The Battle of Parnassus'. The highpoint was Machado's famous article, 'The new generation', in the *Revista Brasileira* in 1879. At this time no one yet spoke of parnassianism, however – the term was not adopted until 1886 – but of such positivist values as realism, social relevance and the scientific spirit. Although such themes may surprise the modern reader – certainly the reader familiar with Spanish American poetry of Darío's era – the movement was opposed to the unrestrained individualism and subjectivism of the romantics, which is why Machado's own prose works may plausibly be included within a so-called parnassian–realist ambit.

Erico Veríssimo said that parnassian verses 'have the cool and reposeful beauty of the Greek temple',[11] as befits the spiritual counterparts of Leconte de Lisle, Gautier, Proudhon and Heredia. Early exponents were Raimundo Correia (1859–1911), philosophical and pessimistic ('All is pain . . .'), and Alberto de Oliveira (1859–1937), a brilliant, dispassionate technician, encoder of intricate literary riddles,

---

[11] E. Veríssimo, *Brazilian literature: an outline* (New York, 1945), 76.

once called the prince of Brazilian poets. Both, however, indulged in poetic licence, forsook grammatical exactitude and resorted to Gallicisms. This was viewed with disfavour from the lofty heights of Parnassus – for poetry in Brazil had not escaped from the academicism constricting all the arts at the time – which opposed all looseness of metre, vagueness and sentimentality. The movement really reached maturity with Olavo Bilac (1865–1918) whose *Poesias* appeared in 1888, the year of Darío's *Azul*. Popular, sensual and fluent, Bilac was also a literary craftsman able to turn his two great loves – the Brazilian landscape and Brazilian women – into finely chiselled images ('Turn, perfect, uplift and polish/ your phrase; and at the last/ set the rhyme on each golden verse/ like a ruby'). Bilac remains the most readable of the parnassians, because in him alone the ideal was combined with the real. In the end, though, the movement was reduced to art for art's sake and effectively died of the cold.

Parnassianism had no sooner been identified and named than symbolism arrived to replace it. In one sense, it was a resurgence of romanticism, in its vagueness and sensuousness, its suggestiveness and musicality, and languid decadence. Perhaps best understood as the literary equivalent of impressionism, its purpose, according to Ronald de Carvalho, was 'to evoke intuitively, through the spontaneous rhythm of words, what the older poetic schools had sought to suggest through an exact representation of things'.[12] Erico Veríssimo declared that 'it had few followers in my country, where colour shades and mists are rare . . . We have few cases of introversion in our literature'.[13] But this was an overstatement. For example, one of its adherents, João da Cruz e Sousa (1861–98), whose *Broquéis* (1893) signals its advent, must be counted among the great poets of Brazil. Known as the 'Black Swan' of Brazilian symbolism, he was born into slavery of two Negro parents, and his life was marked by conflict, resentment and despair. His poetry is by turns bitter, sceptical and melancholy, with a decadent satanic note that many have considered Baudelairian. At the same time he was a vigorous abolitionist jornalist, though he never found the sort of appointment for which his talents fitted him and spent much of his life as a railway clerk, before dying of tuberculosis. His best known books are *Tropos e fantasias* (1885), *Broquéis*, *Faróis* (1900), and *Ultimos sonetos* (1905), all marked, like his brilliant prose poems, by a sonorous musicality. Other important

[12] R. de Carvalho, *Pequena história da literatura brasileira* (Rio de Janeiro, 7th edn, 1944), 348.
[13] E. Veríssimo, *op. cit.*, 81–2.

symbolists were the mystical Alphonsus de Guimaraens (1870–1921), from Minas Gerais, the main theme of whose wilfully archaic poetry is chaste, virginal love; and Augusto dos Anjos (1884–1914), whose work is imbued with his readings in science and philosophy, a despairing view of the human spirit wracked in a mechanistic, deterministic universe. His best-known poems have titles like 'Hymn to pain' or 'The obsession with blood', communicating a naturalistic horror at existence, an almost cosmic pessimism.

Music

Literature was undoubtedly the dominant mode of cultural expression in nineteenth-century Latin America, circumscribing the form and inter-pretation of all the other arts. This merely reinforced the academicism which characterized the century, all the more inevitably in a continent of young nations which had rejected the Iberian heritage with its irrational baroque artistic forms and set themselves the project of constituting new political and cultural systems as a means of integrating Latin America within the wider European order of which they felt destined to be part. Nowhere was literature's influence more evident than in music, which by 1870 was developing rapidly, with numerous theatres and conservatories in most major capitals.

Melesio Morales (1838–1908) guided musical endeavour in Mexico after the national conservatory was instituted in 1866. Of his eight operas, one, *Ildegonda*, was premiered in Italy – the ultimate accolade – in 1868, and he composed a celebrated programme piece, *La locomotiva*, for the opening of the Mexico City–Puebla railway in 1869. When Cenobio Paniagua (1822–82) had staged his pioneering opera *Catalina de Guisa* (composed 1845) at the National Theatre in 1858, some critics sourly noted that its only Mexican feature was its composer; in 1871 Aniceto Ortega (1823–75) produced a one-act opera, *Guatimotzín*, on the last days of the Aztecs, with Cuauhtémoc as tenor and Cortés as bass, starring the renowned Mexican soprano Angela Peralta (1845–83). The Cuban Laureano Fuentes Matons (1825–98) composed the equally indianist *La hija de Jefté* (1875), and Gaspar Villate (1851–91), one of the great propagators of the *danza habanera*, had three operas performed in Europe between 1871 and 1888. The first opera in Venezuela was *Virginia* (1873) by José Angel Montero (1839–81); in Colombia, *Ester* (1874), by José María Ponce de León (1846–82). The romantic titles tell all. The first

'Peruvian' opera, *Atahualpa*, was composed by the Italian Carlo Enrique Pasta (1855–98) and performed in Lima in 1877. Francisco A. Hargreaves' *La gatta bianca*, premiered in Italy in 1875, is generally considered the first Argentine opera. It was in Brazil, however, that the most significant developments took place, culminating in the work of Antônio Carlos Gomes, who, already under the spell of Verdi, lived in Italy from 1864. *Il Guarany*, based on Alencar's novel, triumphed at La Scala in 1870 and was staged in Rio to celebrate the emperor's birthday. Here was an American theme, the noble savage, treated in the most sumptuously lyrical manner in the home of opera. It remains in the international repertory to this day. In 1880 Gomes was persuaded to write on the more dangerous contemporary theme of slavery, but the librettist transformed Negroes magically into Indians when the opera, *Lo schiavo* (which includes the well-known 'Dance of the Tamoios'), appeared in 1889. Gomes has been rejected by nationalist critics, but there are undoubtedly some national and even popular elements embedded in his works.

The style and conventions of European opera were extremely resistant to change. Latin American composers could do little other than join the current, with mere gestures in the direction of national expression. Although increasingly vigorous attempts were made between 1850 and 1880 to master the form and produce Latin American versions, physical and cultural limitations tended to concentrate effort elsewhere. The romantic era was the heyday of the piano virtuoso, the solo song, and the symphonic poem, each ideally suited to Latin American conditions, and musicians like the Venezuelan pianist, composer and singer Teresa Carreño (1853–1917), the Cuban violinist José White (1836–1918) and the Mexican soprano Angela Peralta, achieved international recognition. Thus the era of musical nationalism, the second phase of romantic influence, began timidly in the 1870s, gathered pace by the end of the century and reached its peak in the 1920s. It incorporated both a regional, or nativist, and a national dimension in its essentially emotional expressiveness, multiplying the variety of rhythmic, melodic and harmonic phraseology available (though few Latin Americans saw its more radical possibilities at first) and preparing the way for the musical avant-garde of the 1920s.

Gottschalk's triumphant tour of Latin America in 1869 had made national themes and styles more acceptable, as long as they remained at a superficial level of picturesqueness and local colour. Composers increasingly adopted the European example of Glinka or Borodin,

Albéniz or Granados, Smetana or Dvorak, by incorporating popular national songs and dances, incidentally producing such Americanized European forms as the 'tropical waltz' or 'Paraguayan polka'. Not until the 1920s would Latin American composers definitively master the art of recreating national style from within, at precisely the moment when the international avant-garde was rejecting even the most sophisticated musical nationalism. In Brazil *A sertaneja* (1869) by Brasílio Itiberê da Cunha (1846–1913) was one early localist expression, but it was the famous piano piece *Tango brasileiro* (1890) by Alexandre Levy (1864–92) that first gave the nativist current positive panache. His *Suite brésilienne* (1890) later became part of Brazil's popular repertory, particularly its last movement, 'Samba', inspired not by personal experience but by a description in Ribeiro's novel *A carne* two years before. Hargreaves (1849–1900) was the first Argentine composer to draw regularly on folk music, beginning with the piano polka *El pampero*, also stylizing typical rural forms (*cielito, gato, estilo, décima*) in his *Aires nacionales* (1880). The Colombian José María Ponce de León, who had studied under Gounod in Paris, composed early nativist works such as *La hermosa sabana* and *Sinfonía sobre temas colombianos* (1881), with romantic adaptations of folk dances like the *bambuco, pasillo* and *torbellino*.

In Cuba, with perhaps the richest musical heritage in Latin America, Nicolás Ruiz Espadero (1832–90) produced a work for piano, *Canto del guajiro*, subtitled 'Typical Cuban scene', which illustrates perfectly how romantic rhetoric could smother rhythmic spontaneity. More convincing precursors of 1920s Afro-Cubanism were Manuel Saumell (1817–70), the 'father of the *contradanza*', and Ignacio Cervantes (1847–1905), 'Cuba's Glinka', who studied at the Paris Conservatoire and whose exquisite *Danzas cubanas* (1871–95) were Cuba's most important contribution to nineteenth-century art music. Signposts along Mexico's route to national expression were *Jarabe nacional* (1860) by Tomás León (1826–93) and *Ecos de México* (1880) by Julio Ituarte (1845–1905). The leading piano composer was the Otomí Indian, Juventino Rosas (1864–94), a member of Angela Peralta's touring company and author of the French-style waltz series, *Sobre las olas*, so popular that it was frequently attributed to Strauss. The piano virtuoso Ricardo Castro (1864–1907) achieved the ultimate ambition when *Légende de Rudel* (1906) was performed and applauded in Europe. The price was an essentially mimetic art, even though Castro was also producing arrangements of regional dances like the *jarabe* and the *danza mexicana*.

The father of musical nationalism in Brazil was Alberto Nepomuceno

(1864–1920), who was taught by Grieg how to compose music which was at once national and universal. In 1887 he composed *Dança de negros*, and in 1897 *Série brasileira*, the first orchestral suite based on Brazilian vernacular themes, using a wide range of forms and rhythms, and still popular today. Argentina's central figure was the prolific Alberto Williams (1862–1952), who studied at the Paris Conservatoire in 1882 under César Franck, eventually composing more than a hundred substantial works, including nine symphonies. In 1889 he toured Buenos Aires province to 'saturate myself in the music of my homeland', thereafter writing 'not mere transcriptions, but artistic music with native atmosphere, colour and essence'.[14] The first result was the elegiac *El rancho abandonado* (1890); but when *Aires de la pampa* appeared in 1893 Williams had evolved to writing his own *milongas, gatos, cielitos* and *sambas*. Although he strikes the modern ear as both incorrigibly academic and profusely sentimental, like his contemporary, Arturo Berutti (1862–1938), composer of the *Sinfonía argentina* (1890) and the operas *Pampa* (1897) and *Yupanki* (1899), Williams made an outstanding contribution to regional and national musical integration, especially during the decisive period 1890–1910. Modern critics, however, favour the less ambitious *criollista* Julián Aguirre (1868–1924), a friend of Albéniz, whose piano adaptations, *Huella* and *Gato,* remain in the international repertoire. Another prolific composer was the director of the Colombian national conservatory from 1910 to 1935, Guillermo Uribe Holguín (1880–1971), whose three hundred *Trozos en el sentimiento popular* for piano, based on folk dances, form an enduring legacy.

The most prominent figure in Mexico during this period was Manuel Ponce (1882–1948), universally known as the composer of the irresistible middlebrow hit, *Estrellita* (1914). After working in Paris and Berlin, he carefully studied and re-elaborated Mexico's *corridos, sones, jarabes* and *huapangos*. The results are often compared unfavourably with the later works of Chávez: critics consider Ponce 'folkloric', confined to quoting Indian or *mestizo* materials rather than using them as structural principles. Nevertheless, his works continue to be played world-wide as no other Mexican composer's are, and his mainly anonymous role as creator of many of Segovia's guitar pieces has recently come to light. Like

[14] See G. Béhague, *Music in Latin America: an introduction* (Englewood Cliffs, N.J., 1979), 108–10. Béhague's work is indispensable, and has been drawn upon extensively in the preparation of this section.

Nepomuceno, Uribe Holguín and Williams, Ponce provided the essential bridge for nativism to cross from romanticism to the avant-garde.

Painting

Even more than music, nineteenth-century painting was in the grip of academicism and social convention. Open-air painting was unknown in Latin America well into the century, and impressionism arrived after its end, more than two decades later than its literary equivalent, *modernismo*, and almost half a century after its European model. Although the delay was understandable, the failure to assimilate impressionism was particularly unfortunate, since European painting in the last third of the century was in the vanguard of changes in artistic perception. Given the specificity of the plastic arts, there was no repertory of popular styles to quote from as in music; and if in the first phase of nineteenth-century painting the depiction of native themes was learned from European travellers in search of the picturesque, in the second, after 1870, Latin American visitors to Europe invariably returned to their homelands with the latest version of academic painting, blind to the new visions of Monet, Renoir, Manet, Pisarro or Cézanne, men who really had put the stifling influence of academic neo-classicism behind them. When impressionism did arrive, early in the new century, the results were timid and its very lateness permitted its conversion, despite general public hostility, into a new academicism. As with music, it was not until the 1920s that Latin American painters finally – and all the more suddenly – joined the international avant-garde.

In Brazil continuity of monarchy and empire encouraged a wilfully grandiose style, midway between the classical and the romantic, based on the French school of battle painting, whilst landscape, as Fernando de Azevedo has written, was generally 'no more than a background of hills, a corner of woods or a curve in the river, as accessories to a bit of sacred, classical or national history'.[15] The two great exponents and most popular painters of the era were Vítor Meireles (1832–1903) and his friend Pedro Américo (1843–1905). Both had spent significant periods in Paris in the 1850s and 1860s. Meireles's *Primeira missa no Brasil* (1861) was the first Brazilian painting exhibited at the Paris Salon, whilst his two best-known works were the *Batalha dos Guararapes* (1869) and *Batalha*

15 F. de Azevedo, *Brazilian culture* (New York, 1950), 294.

naval do Riachuelo (1872). Two of his disciples, both born in Portugal, produced typical late-romantic works: Augusto Rodrigues Duarte (1848–88), with *Exéquias de Atalá*, following Chateaubriand, and José Maria de Madeiros (1849–1926), with *Iracema*, inspired by Alencar's novel. Pedro Américo's Italian-style nude, *A carioca* (1864), was one of his first successful canvases, but he is most remembered for the *Batalha do Avaí* (1877), exhibited in Florence in the presence of the Brazilian emperor himself, and the massive *Independência ou morte!* (1886). Rodolfo Amoêdo (1857–1941) also studied in Paris, where he did his best work, moving from biblical canvases and romantic works like the nude *Marabá* (1883), or the celebrated *O último tamoio* (1883), to the Manet-like *Más notícias* (1888) in the age of naturalism. José Ferraz de Almeida Júnior (1850–99), by contrast, was the first genuinely nationalist Brazilian painter in both form and subject matter, and for many the greatest Brazilian painter of the century. He had travelled to Paris at the height of the impressionist controversy, but his depictions of rural São Paulo, like *O derrubador brasileiro*, *Caboclo no descanso*, *Caipiras negaceando* and *Picando fumo*, were neither documentary nor merely picturesque, revealing rather 'a mind unequivocally Brazilian, unconsciously barbarous and fertile – a necessary consequence of a young land, which no foreign artist could translate'.[16] After these painters a decline set in. Typical of the ensuing transitional period was a decadent romantic current, often masquerading as a timid impressionism or Art Nouveau, exemplified in the work of Antônio Parreiras (1864–1937), a painter of historical canvases like *A conquista do Amazonas* or of 'Parisian' nudes lascivious in intent but uninspiring in effect, like his late *Flor do mal* (1922). Eliseu Visconti (b. 1864), superficial in conceptualization but perhaps most accomplished of all in purely pictorial terms, experimented successively with all the modes of the era, from academicism (*Maternidade*) to the almost pre-Raphaelite *Dança das Oréadas* (1900), and thence to *modernismo*.

In the River Plate republics, as in Brazil, a radical gulf opened between the objective and subjective approaches to painting (naturalism and impressionism), which would characterize all the arts henceforth. The Uruguayan Juan Manuel Blanes (1830–1901) effectively combined both approaches, albeit within an ultimately costumbrist perspective, successfully applying the formal lessons of European masters to American

16 *Ibid.*, 296.

subjects. His gauchesque and rural paintings, like *La cautiva* or *Las boleadoras*, historical paintings like the *Juramento de los 33 Orientales*, battle scenes like the *Batalla de Sarandí* or the famous humanitarian canvas *El ultimo paraguayo*, and social works like *Dos caminos* and *Fiebre amarilla* (1870), made him a key influence in the River Plate region, a symphonist of light who ranks with Prilidiano Pueyrredón, Almeida Júnior or José María Velasco (see below) as one of the unequivocally great Latin American artists of the nineteenth century. Patronage and taste, however, were in the hands of a small minority, whose predominantly academic orientation could be tyrannical. In 1887 the painter Eduardo Sívori (1847–1918), who had previously concentrated mainly on traditional subjects like *Tormenta en la pampa* or *A la querencia*, presented a canvas, *El despertar de la sirvienta*, which was deemed too 'pornographic' for exhibition in Buenos Aires, despite a successful Paris showing, partly because it was an uncompromising naturalistic nude in the manner of Courbet, but also – no doubt – because of the unmistakably critical social thesis it conveyed. Even more challenging canvases, in an Argentina where urban problems were rapidly replacing gaucho themes, were *La sopa de los pobres* (1883) by Reinaldo Giudici (1853–1921), *Sin pan y sin trabajo* (1894) by the socialist painter Ernesto de la Cárcova (1866–1927), and *La hora del reposo* (1903) by Pío Collivadino (1869–1945), all of which treated urban labour themes with incipient social realism. And even these painters of naturalist works, whether bourgeois or socialist in intention, found public acceptance more easily than those who took the impressionist route. The naturalists were at least narrative painters, and this the critics – invariably literary in orientation – could understand. Martín A. Malharro (1865–1911) renounced romanticism after a visit to Europe and produced works like *En plena naturaleza* or *Las parvas*, saturated with colour and its vibrations. Although his whole purpose, ironically, was to make people begin to *see*, his first exhibition in 1902 was savagely ridiculed and he died a virtual outcast; whereas Fernando Fader (1882–1935), effectively a naturalist like his German mentor Von Zugel, by merely enlivening his painting with an attenuated impressionist veneer, gained immediate critical acceptance in 1905 and became a lasting influence through the Grupo Nexus, such that his brand of 'impressionism' was almost the status quo by 1914. Critics interpreted as impressionist what was in fact, in Fader's essentially *criollista* recreations of the landscapes of rural Córdoba – like *Aclarando en la higuera*, *En el*

potrero or *Tarde de otoño* – a characteristically metaphysical interpretation
of Argentina's solitude and silence.

By far the greatest Mexican painter of the late nineteenth century was
José María Velasco (1840–1912), who ran the gamut from romanticism
through realism to the edge of impressionism, which he first viewed only
in 1889. His best-known series of works were eight canvases on the
theme of *El Valle de México* (1894–1905), including the magnificent
Valle de México visto desde el cerro de Guadalupe (1894) and the
famous railway painting *El Citlaltépetl* (1897). Velasco effected a
synthesis of emotion, aesthetic impulse and visual mastery to achieve,
like Almeida Júnior and Blanes, an almost impossible individuality in
that century of servile academic mimeticism disguised as lofty universality. Their historical achievement is that of Nepomuceno, Williams
and Ponce in music, pioneers in an inevitably arid landscape.

THE EARLY TWENTIETH CENTURY

The period after the turn of the century was one of great ideological,
cultural and artistic confusion in Latin America. Economic and social
changes moved faster than thinkers and artists could follow. In Spanish
America José Enrique Rodó (1871–1917) inaugurated the century with
his epoch-making essay *Ariel* (1900), at the zenith of *modernismo*, two
years after the defeat of Spain in Cuba, and at the very moment when the
United States had begun its irresistible rise, first to hemispheric and then
to world supremacy. Despite his claims to social relevance (his classic
essay had concluded that the innately elitist Darío was 'not the poet of
America'), Rodó is really to the essay what Darío is to poetry: elegant,
superficially assured and, ultimately, aestheticist. His assault on the
cultural barbarism of the North American Caliban typifies Latin
American thought at the time, in its incorrigible voluntarism and
idealism. After the First World War, the Mexican and Russian
revolutions, and the 1918 Córdoba student revolt, such spiritual anti-
imperialism would be supplanted by a keener perception of social and
economic struggle, and art would take on a class character. Although
Ariel is routinely considered the start of a twentieth-century debate, it is
better understood as a last despairing attempt, in the face of modernity,
to recuperate the neo-classical project of the emancipation era, now
buried in an incoherent jumble of contradictory philosophies and styles.
Nevertheless, Rodó's serene prose, with the clarity of line of a Greek

temple, did lay the foundation for the debate to follow and re-established the dignity of art after its devaluation by Positivist philosophy.

Architecture

If architecture best exemplifies the rather abstract and ultimately academic direction of nineteenth-century culture, it can equally dramatize the confusing scene at the beginning of the twentieth century. Although colonial styles were largely discontinued, the absence of experienced architects, craftsmen and material resources meant that the neo-classical architecture which predominated before 1870 was generally mediocre, despite the grandiose dreams of statesmen. Even in Brazil, where conditions were most favourable, the lack of coherent planning meant that 'the best buildings were still the oldest',[17] and cities took on their rather shapeless contemporary appearance. Buenos Aires grew more consistently than most on neo-classical lines, and in the two decades before the war underwent a building boom which produced its present image as the most nineteenth-century great city in Latin America. Most others remained largely colonial in layout, though the Haussmann pattern was imposed where feasible (the Paseo de la Reforma in Mexico, the Alameda in Santiago, Rio Branco and Beira Mar avenues in Rio). The national oligarchies erected imposing buildings and monuments in the last years of the century to give that sense of balance, measure and stability which Positivism required, symbolizing generalized prosperity and an officially ordained culture.

And so the *belle époque* dawned, an age of great government edifices, legislative palaces, grand theatres, huge private residences, at the very moment when neo-classicism finally faltered in the face of a chaotic romantic revivalism involving neo-colonial and neo-indigenist elements, Art Nouveau and other early harbingers of 'Modernism'. All planning disappeared and architects began an indiscriminate imitation of new foreign styles and historical models. The only major exception was Havana, which added a relatively coherent neo-classicism on Spanish lines to the basic colonial pattern, virtually excluding French or Anglo-Saxon inputs. Elsewhere a forest of diverse transplanted forms grew up in city centres, vitiating the effect of remaining colonial buildings, but accurately reflecting the eclecticism of Latin American culture generally

[17] *Ibid.*, 309.

at this time. Among the more distinguished constructions, the Teatro Colón in Buenos Aires was planned by Víctor Meano and built in 1908 by Julio Dormal (1846–1924) and the Palacio San Martín by Alejandro Christopherson (1846–1946), whilst the notoriously multi-styled Palacio de Bellas Artes (1903–34) was begun in Mexico City by Adamo Boari. The Brazilian critic Monteiro Lobato called the triumph of flamboyant bad taste the 'architectural carnival'.

Modern architecture reached Latin America in the 1920s through functionalism which, if nothing else, wiped the architectural slate clean; but it was yet another artificial imposition, a product of northern developed societies imported into tropical and mainly agricultural republics. The dominance of the international monopolist bourgeoisie was communicated to Latin Americans in the very industrialization of the construction materials, steel and concrete, in a new capitalist style which was simple, flexible and rapid. Unlike Europe and North America, where the movement also corresponded to the growth of middle-class suburbs, it was required in Latin America to solve the housing problems of the emergent working masses, whilst the middle classes themselves not infrequently returned to colonial styles, albeit 'functionalized', which many architects thought better adapted to Latin American climates and societies.[18]

The Mexican movement began with José Villagrán García (b. 1901), who had graduated, like so many of his muralist contemporaries, from the Academia San Carlos. Seizing upon the most dehumanized of Le Corbusier's theories ('a house is a machine for living in'), he advocated a technologically advanced, socially oriented architecture. As architect to the Public Health Department, he built the Institute of Hygiene and Sanatorium of Huipulco (1925) and the Sanitary Farm at Tacuba (1926), later becoming director of the new National School of Architecture in 1932. Juan O'Gorman (1905–83), a protégé, was also a painter and sculptor, ideally qualified to effect the integration of visual and spatial arts sought by the ideologues of the soon-to-be institutionalized revolution, who argued that such integration characterized both pre-Columbian and baroque techniques. Yet O'Gorman's militant functionalism (from which he recanted only much later, eventually participating in the construction of the integrationist University City) asserted that aesthetics were irrelevant: architecture should be strictly utilitarian, a

---

[18] See R. Vargas Salguero and R. López Rangel, 'La crisis actual de la arquitectura latinoamericana', in R. Segre (ed.), *América Latina en su arquitectura* (Mexico–Paris, 1975), 186–203.

mere branch of engineering, with maximum return from minimum expenditure. He built the first functionalist schools and private houses, including one for Diego Rivera, organizing the School of Construction after 1932.

In reality the expansion of capitalism in Mexico required that great public works be executed as rapidly as possible, but with a subtle mass manipulation involving mystical exaltation of the Indian peasant and urban proletarian. Most architects, painters, sculptors and musicians of the 1920s avant-garde, however lucid and well-intentioned, had been completely absorbed by the state by 1930. The Argentine case was quite different. There the French fine art tradition was at its strongest, and the vogue of the *hotel particulier* as urban mansion was the ideal of wealthy Argentines. The conservative bureaucracy did little to encourage the emergence of a modern architecture: during the first phase of the modern movement in the 1920s and 1930s, pioneers such as León Durge, Alberto Prebisch and Antonio and Carlos Vilar received little of the state support enjoyed by their contemporaries in Mexico and Brazil, and private commissions remained the rule until Perón's day.

In Brazil, as in Mexico, functionalism swept aside traditionalist debris and cleared the ground for new concepts. After the 1922 Semana de Arte Moderna, Gregori Warchavchik (1896–1972) launched his *Manifesto da Arquitetura Funcional* (1925), clearly influenced by Le Corbusier (who visited Brazil in 1929, and again, most decisively, in 1936: his example eventually led to the construction of Brasília). In Brazil, however, the modern movement took on grandiose overtones from the start, perhaps because there was no need, as in Mexico, to conceal the potential role of private capital as partner to the state. Brazil's new architecture was presented as an overtly multi-class movement, combining nationalism and populism with Le Corbusier's elegant European aesthetics and fantasies. The results were frequently dazzling, especially in the 1930s, and Brazil, where almost any dream could apparently come true, leaped to the forefront of contemporary architecture in its first decade in the international fray. Lúcio Costa (b. 1902), director of the National School of Fine Art, worked closely with Warchavchik, influencing the generation of the great Oscar Niemeyer (b. 1907).

Countries like Venezuela or Colombia, which in the nineteenth century had been too anarchic or too impoverished for major public works, hurtled straight from colonial to modern architecture with little difficulty, since the new movement of Gropius, Le Corbusier and Mies

Van der Rohe represented such a complete break with the past. In the late 1920s, as trans-national oil companies began to exploit new finds, Carlos Raúl Villanueva (1900–78) returned to Venezuela from Paris to a post at the ministry of public works. Over twenty years, through a brilliant combination of traditional and modern methods in construction and design, he expanded his range and eventually built the new Central University, bringing himself and Venezuelan architecture world renown.

Painting

The 1920s, then, was the decade when Latin American architecture, painting and music finally began to come into parallel focus with international developments, and a few leading exponents in each field attained international reputations. Yet the situation in the plastic arts at the turn of the century had been particularly unsatisfactory, as we have seen. Latin American versions of impressionism were timid and tentative, resulting in an unscientific, merely instinctual movement disconnected from its social and economic base. Nevertheless, although long since outmoded in Europe, impressionism had determined all the new ways of seeing reality and understanding art, giving artists licence to experiment and paving the way for the avant-garde explosion after 1910 and its crystallization in the 1920s, when Latin America itself made the first great landfall in its voyage of self-discovery.

In Mexico the celebrated 'Dr Atl' (Gerardo Murillo, 1875–1964) linked the great engraver José Guadalupe Posada (1851–1913), a key figure in the dialectic between popular and national culture, to the generation of world-famous muralists whom Murillo himself taught at the Academia San Carlos. Dr Atl really belonged to the previous era – his favourite subject was Mexico's topography, typified in his *La mañana en el Valle* – but his dramatic approach to techniques and applications of colour had lasting impact. Atl was a militant in all things, anarchist and socialist by turns, and after founding the Artistic Centre in 1910, encouraged young artists like Orozco and Siqueiros to paint murals on its walls. Although developments were interrupted by the Revolution (whose most important visual chronicler was Francisco Goitia, with paintings like *El ahorcado*, 1916), minister of education Vasconcelos gave renewed momentum to the movement after 1921, unleashing a vast programme of cultural renovation – with the explicit purpose of reconciling fine art with popular arts and crafts – launched by the 1921 exhibition for which Atl wrote the guide.

The best-known painter of the movement was Diego Rivera (1886–1957). During his crucial years in Europe (1907–21), he absorbed a succession of influences (Picasso, Gris, Modigliani, in Paris; Zuloaga and Sorolla, in Madrid) finally moulded into definitive synthesis by the Revolution itself. After eighty Cubist canvases like *El despertador* (1914), or *Paisaje de Piquey* (1918), had built him a solid reputation, a visit to Siena in 1920 helped forge a controversial synthesis of Renaissance fresco techniques (long admired by his early tutor, Atl), pre-Columbian integrated art, the styles and images of Mexican contemporary popular culture (mediated principally through Posada), and Soviet-style social realism. He concluded that avant-garde postures and socialist commitment were incompatible, renounced the easel and became a muralist. After studying his country in depth, he painted the results on the walls of the Ministry of Education (1923–8), the Chapingo Agricultural School (1923–7, see especially *La tierra liberada*), and the National Palace (1930–5). Rivera's trajectory is a paradigm, comparable with Pablo Neruda's journey to his later *Canto general*: documentary (*La molendera*, 1926), illustrative, replete with stock images, propaganda, folklorism (*Retrato de niña*, 1928) and hyperbole, but undeniably grandiose. The sometimes despised muralism of Rivera and Siqueiros foreshadowed Picasso's *Guernica* and much other political painting this century, not to mention North American action painting (following the uproar, both political and aesthetic, provoked by Rivera's visit to the U.S. in the 1930s) and pop art generally. No debate on the possibilities of a Third World art can ignore them.

David Alfaro Siqueiros (1896–1974) studied with Atl and Orozco at the Academy, followed by five years as a young revolutionary soldier which moulded his world view definitively. Like Rivera and Frida Kahlo, he became a communist. In Barcelona in 1921 he issued his famous Manifesto to the Plastic Artists of America, calling for 'a public art, a monumental and heroic art, a human art . . . pre-Columbian in inspiration and workerist in orientation'. In 1922 he was a founder member of the union of artists and technicians, whose purpose, declared their equally famous manifesto, was 'to liquidate the decadence of modern art . . . socialize artistic expression, and destroy bourgeois individualism'. The union's principal organ was the now legendary magazine, *El Machete*. Siqueiros never ceased to be involved in controversy (the plot to assassinate Trotsky, for example), though he did return to easel painting and achieved wide popularity with the Mexican public, beginning with pictures like *Madre campesina* (1929), *La niña muerta* (1931) and *Zapata* (1931).

Most critics now consider José Clemente Orozco (1883–1949) the greatest of the big three Mexican muralists, perhaps because he was least circumscribed by political considerations. The 1922–3 murals at the National Preparatory School, a composite masterpiece, show none of Rivera's penchant for rhetoric or decoration, whilst the vibrant coloration of pictures like *La trinchera* (1922–3), *Soldaderas* (1922–7) and *Zapatistas* (1931), or stark expressionism of *Prometeo* (1930) and *Cristo destruye la cruz* (1934) is well known, perfect in their fusion of concept and plasticity within a broadly political conception which is more Americanist than narrowly Mexican. From his earliest works, which exude loathing for Porfirian Mexico, Orozco communicates a longing for the identity, however tortured, of artistic form and spiritual content in a world of materialist determination.

Rufino Tamayo (1899–1991) was the first great artist to emerge from the shadow of the muralists. Deeply rooted in the indigenism that underpinned the muralist movement, he too underwent an early political phase, but later insisted that art is primarily plastic and poetic and can have 'no political or ideological manifestations'. Influenced by Picasso and Braque in the 1920s, he was always able to instil a sense of some personal mythology into his use of such models, as witness his *Retrato fotográfico* (1928) or *La niña bonita* (1932). Despite rejecting documentary realism and narrowly referential art, he has searched for forms which can communicate his specifically Mexican experience whilst engaging simultaneously with universal currents. Even before this, the Guatemalan Carlos Mérida (b. 1891) became perhaps the first to move entirely beyond mere folklore in Latin American nativist art. Influenced by Picasso's blue period during an early visit to Paris (1910–14), Mérida returned home to search for some Americanist synthesis of folklore, archaeology and modern plastic concepts. *Imágenes de Guatemala* (1914–27) conveys his evolution from stylized figuration to semi-abstraction, whilst remaining faithful throughout to the undulating spirit of his Mayan inspiration. Although in Mexico from 1919, he abandoned all romantic, picturesque or anecdotal approaches before the muralist movement had even begun, and began to treat native motifs with the same autonomy that Braque and Picasso had applied to their neo-primitivist work. (Among indigenist writers, his fellow Guatemalan, Miguel Angel Asturias, was influenced by this ultimately more fertile approach in his *Leyendas de Guatemala* of 1930, whilst others would travel Rivera's documentary road.) In 1927 Mérida returned to Paris to work on surrealist and musical analogies, moving now from quasi-geometrical indigenous stylizations, like *Perfiles* (1928), to almost complete abstraction by the time of *Máscaras* (1932). His achievement is comparable to that of Tamayo or Torres García (see below) in painting, Chávez or Villa-Lobos in music, Vallejo or Neruda in poetry.

In the Caribbean area modern Cuban art was taken out of provincialism and plunged into the Parisian cross-currents of the 1920s by Amelia Peláez (1897–1968), whilst retaining, for example in paintings like *Mujer* (1928) or her numerous *Naturalezas muertas* composed of blue tropical fruits, a distinctive *criollo* identity. Cuba's best-known painter abroad was Wifredo Lam (1902–82), whose celebrated *La jungla* came later (1943), but typified his fetishistic tropical exuberance, out of Matisse by way of Picasso, a close personal friend. Haitian art only really entered the modern period after 1930, but was influenced by the Afro-Caribbean movements initiated earlier in Cuba and Puerto Rico. Further south, one of the great painters of tropical America was the eccentric Venezuelan recluse, Armando Reverón (1889–1954), virtually ignored until after his death, who became deranged and withdrew to Macuto with his wife, his mistress and the rag dolls filled with sawdust which he used as models. His first outstanding works were *Las mujeres en la cueva* (1919), *Los cocoteros* (1920), *Figura bajo un uvero* (1920) and *Juanita junto a la tripoide* (1921). He painted numerous outstanding nudes and unforgettably vibrant coastal landscapes. After returning to Venezuela in 1921 following a tour of Europe, he became increasingly preoccupied with light – passing through blue, sepia and white periods – until it became an almost literally blinding obsession. Examples of his most characteristic mode are *Fiesta en Caraballeda* (1924), *El árbol* (1926) and *Macuto en oro* (1931). Although consumed by the local, he was in no sense a provincial or costumbrist artist.

In the Andean region nativism swept all before it, although it proved a pale reflection of the Mexican example. Peruvian art in general was bitterly divided between the reactionary Hispanicizing current represented in literature by Palma and Riva Agüero, and the new indigenism advocated by González Prada, Valcárcel, Mariátegui and Haya de la Torre (see below). Mariátegui, whose review *Amauta* was in the political if not the artistic vanguard, declared that futurism, dadaism, cubism and the rest were 'mere pirouettes of the decadent bourgeoisie', quite alien to Peru and its contemporary needs. Unfortunately, Peruvian painting after Pancho Fierro (1803–79) had been grimly academic and derivative, and there was no tradition of simple painterly proficiency on which to build. The new movement was led by José Sabogal (1888–1956) from Cajabamba, initially a painter of undistinguished landscapes lying somewhere between the academic and picturesque. A European visit in 1919 introduced him to Zuloaga, the Spanish master who combined local colour with technical virtuosity; then in Mexico in 1922, he was dazzled by the muralist synthesis of nativism and nationalism, and returned to Peru a militant indigenist and doctrinaire aesthetic nationalist. Although his own painting was a rather crude grafting of Mexican social realism on to Spanish *costumbrismo* (and thereby reminiscent of the 1930s fiction produced by his compatriot Ciro Alegría), Sabogal led the indigenist movement for the next thirty years and there is no denying his lasting impact on the national perception of native arts and crafts. His doctrine can be summed up in his phrase, 'Art is the translation of man and nature'. Unfortunately the translator frequently remains outside the world he is trying to convey. Not until Fernando de Szyszlo (b. 1925) would Peruvian art find a means of representing the pre-Columbian world without mere figuration or socio-economic reflectionism. In Ecuador and Bolivia, meanwhile, movements like Peruvian indigenism have sprung up only since the 1930s. Today the cry is for an 'Indian' – rather than indianist or indigenist – art.

In the southern cone such nativist movements as have existed tend to be labelled *criollista*, and it can fairly be said that even vernacular culture tends to become Europeanized. The Uruguayan lawyer Pedro Figari (1861–1938), a genuinely American artist and undisputed classic, only took up painting seriously after the age of sixty. He moved first to Buenos Aires (1921), then to Paris (1925–34), passing determinedly through the modern kaleidoscope to find the style *he* needed, which crystallized in a uniquely personal post-impressionist mode reminiscent of Bonnard. With his historical canvases like the *Grito de Asencio* or *Asesinato de Quiroga*, and his familiar *criollista* titles like *El gato*, *La doma*, *Potros en la pampa*, *Candombé*, *El Circo*, *No te vayas mi viejo*, *Recordando al finado*, and *Don Segundo Sombra*, Figari's River Plate landscapes, historical recreations and domestic scenes, filtered through his subjective vision and artistically recast, made him Uruguay's best loved painter.

The most influential is Joaquín Torres García (1874–1949), who returned with his family to their native Catalonia in 1891, where he was influenced successively by Gaudí, Toulouse-Lautrec and Picasso. He gradually evolved into an idiosyncratic theorist of Latin American art who, after gravitating to abstract thinkers like Mondrian and Kandinsky in Paris, sought in his own artistic trajectory, through cubism, fauvism and neo-plasticism, to fuse figuration and abstraction, coming at last to equate classicism, humanism and universalism through a unique personal synthesis. The cubist *Album de Nueva York* (1920), the fauvist *Marina de Villefranche* (1924), and the typically personal *Constructivismo* (1929), give some sense of the stages of this journey towards a geometrical aesthetics. He is best known for works like the latter, with their rectangular divisions of the canvas based on his own mystical humanist philosophy, 'Constructive Universalism' (later summarized in *Metafísica de la prehistoria indoamericana*, 1939, and *Universalismo constructivo*, 1944). Few American artists have matched either his force of vision or theoretical complexity.

Argentine artistic circles in the 1920s were still overwhelmingly influenced by Paris at a time when the French capital, though still a great home of culture, was no longer the home of modernity itself. In Argentine painting, misdirected by Fader's pseudo-impressionism, what could be termed post-impressionist art emerged *after* cubism, causing confusion well into the 1930s. Emilio Pettoruti (1892–1971) had been an early futurist in Italy, but thereafter followed the cubist path of Braque and Picasso, with paintings like *La mesa del estudiante* (1917), *El filósofo* (1918), *Pensierosa* (1920), *Carolita* (1925), or *El quinteto* (1927). He was arguably the first Latin American artist to assimilate European avant-garde models through a personal artistic vision, sense of structure and mastery of colour; but when he returned in 1924 to Buenos Aires, where Figari was all the rage, he was shunned by academicians and social realists alike as 'superficial' and 'decorative'. Yet he was a master of formal rigour, contemptuous of all improvisation in his brilliant reconstructions of planes, and effectively introduced the constructivist method of geometrical abstraction into Latin America, with paintings whose forms construct light rather than reflect it, as exemplified in his controversial classic, *El improvisador* (1937). Pettoruti's only supporters were the young men of the avant-garde Martín Fierro movement. In that seminal year 1924, their review of the same name was launched, the influential society Amigos del Arte was formed, Pettoruti's first exhibition was held, and Alejandro Xul Solar (1887–1963) returned to Argentina. Solar was typical of the era, a wilfully mysterious world traveller obsessed with spiritualism, mythology and astrology, inventor of personal labyrinths, a Jungian, cubist and surrealist by turns, and a bohemian who hated to sell his paintings. Some assert that he was the first Argentine artist to dispense altogether, in his geometrical yet dynamic works, with Renaissance concepts of space. The 'floating' quality of his paintings, typified in *Figura y serpiente* or *Juzgue* (1923), is most reminiscent of Klee.

The young intellectuals of the always effervescent Buenos Aires art milieu were divided at the time between the notorious Florida and Boedo factions. Florida artists, based in the most elegant zones, were cosmopolitan and experimental, and communicated directly with the European avant-garde, despite the deceptively nationalist name of their magazine, *Martín Fierro*: writers like Oliverio Girondo, Eduardo González Lanuza, Ernesto Palacio, Bernardo Canal Feijóo, Jorge Luis Borges, Leopoldo Marechal, and artists like Pettoruti, Solar, Figari, Gómez Cornet and Raquel Forner. Boedo's style was social realist, international only in its political commitment, with occasional infusions of expressionism to give militancy and dynamism: writers like Leónidas Barletta, Elías Castelnuovo, Alvaro Yunque, Abel Rodríguez, the brothers Enrique and Raúl Tuñón, and artists – especially engravers – like José Arato, Adolfo Bellocq, Guillermo Facio Hebécquer and Abraham Vigo. The division into opposing groups underlined and perpetuated a divorce between political and artistic vanguards which has been particularly bitter and intractable in Argentina. Antonio Berni (1905–81) was one painter who managed to communicate a socialist ideology through avant-garde techniques, using his experience in Paris in the mid-twenties to develop a 'new realism' tinged both with surrealist and expressionist elements, as in *Desocupados* (1934), *Manifestación* (1934) or *Chacareros* (1935). Berni claimed that no Latin American artist of conscience could choose any subject other than the suffering of colonized peoples: avant-garde formalists were led 'like stupid children' through an 'imaginary, abstract and ornamental world', outside of history, without notion of concrete time and space. However, when the flamboyant Mexican Siqueiros arrived in Buenos Aires in 1933, he and Berni disagreed. Although Berni went in for large canvases, he argued that mural painting was inappropriate in a bourgeois-dominated nation like Argentina, and felt justified when the only walls Siqueiros could find were at a newspaper director's country estate. Although Juan del Prete (b. 1897) introduced fully abstract art in 1926, Argentina only finally developed its own distinctively original movements, in painting as in music, and within a generally cosmopolitan conception of Modernism, in the 1940s, at which point it became the unchallenged leader of the Latin American avant-garde.

Brazil, always similar to other Latin American nations in broad outline but always different in detailed focus, discovered its artistic identity in the 1920s – confirmed historically by the architectural explosion of the 1930s – a complex and colourful tapestry of regionalism, nationalism and cosmopolitanism all under the banner of *modernismo*, launched officially by the 1922 Semana de Arte Moderna in São Paulo. Leading figures were the expressionist painter Lasar Segall (1891–1957), a Lithuanian emigré who worked social themes like *Navio de emigrantes*, *Guerra*, or *Mãe negra* (1930); Anita Malfatti (1896–1964), who, after studying in Paris and meeting Marcel Duchamp in New York, scandalized São Paulo art circles in 1917 with the first avant-garde exhibition in Latin America; and Tarsila do Amaral (1886–1973), whose Paris studio was an avant-garde crossroads in the 1920s. Her neo-primitivist paintings, like *O mamoeiro* (1925) or *Antropofagia* (1928) led Oswald de Andrade to posit first the 'Pau-Brasil' style, then in 1927 the 'Antropofagia' movement, Brazil's version of indigenism based, with typical humour and self-confidence, on a theory of aesthetic cannibalism. By the 1930s Amaral herself had turned to social realism, with paintings like *Morro da favela* or *2a classe* (1933).

The German expressionist mode popularized by Segall was developed by the 'revolutionary romantic' Flávio de Rezende Carvalho (1899–1973), also an outstanding sculptor, celebrated for his semi-abstract portraits, bold and vivid coloration and dynamic composition, combining in a bizarre lyrical representationalism. The outstanding avant-garde painter of the generation, however, was Emiliano Di Cavalcanti (1897–1976), who adapted Picasso's neo-classical phase from the olympian to the tropical, as in his 1927 study of a seated nude. Like Toulouse-Lautrec, he concentrated on women – black, in this case – graceful even in oppression, from a lucid social perspective. His remarkable versatility – including brilliantly mobile lithographs and etchings – created an astonishing variety of Brazilian scenes, human and natural, combining vivid colours, flowing forms and great emotional empathy. Yet even he was overshadowed by Cândido Portinari (1903–62), who is to painting what Villa-Lobos is to music, the great vehicle of artistic nationalism during the late 1920s and the 1930s, simplifying and developing the lessons of Mexican muralism after assimilating cubism, expressionism and surrealism, the examples of Braque, Picasso and Rivera. Among his most familiar paintings are *Cabeça de índio, Futebol* (1931–2), *Trabalhador rural* (1934), and *Café* (1935). The only Latin American painter outside Mexico to create a vast national pictorial epic, he eventually painted a set of murals, 'The Epic of Brazil', for Costa and Niemeyer's Ministry of Education building, with a fluent mixture of lyricism, realism and traditionalism. Some critics consider him too 'sociological'; others, the 'most modern of the ancients'; most agree, however, that his grandiose record of Brazilian history and landscape is one of Brazil's most important cultural landmarks.

Sculpture

Modern sculpture was slow to develop in Latin America, perhaps surprisingly in view of the vigorous religious and popular traditions. Most nineteenth-century sculptors were routinely occupied on commissioned busts and small neo-classical statues. One of the few large-scale monuments not imported was Noreña's bronze statue of Cuauhtémoc for Mexico City in 1889. The statue of Sarmiento unveiled in Buenos Aires in 1910, year of the International Exposition, was by Rodin, who, with Bourdelle, was an overwhelming influence on Latin American sculpture during that transitional era. As Argentine prosperity gave scope for increasingly ambitious monumentalism, Rogelio Yrurtia (1879–1950) produced his striking statue of Dorrego and the monument to Rivadavia, and Alfredo Bigatti (1898–1964) and José Fioravanti (1896–1982) subsequently carried out numerous commemorative commissions, including the homage to the national flag in Rosario. Uruguay had a similarly influential monumental sculptor in Bernabé Michelena (b. 1888). In the 1920s Latin American sculpture finally began to make strides similar to, though less dramatic than, those in painting. In Argentina Antonio Sibellino (b. 1891) with his *Composición de formas* (1926), produced what is by general consent the first abstract sculpture by a Latin American; other innovators were the cubist Pablo Curatella Manes (1891–1962) and Sesostris Vitullo (1899–1953). Chile's immensely rich modern developments fall outside our period. Brazilian sculpture had been no more than conventionally respectable in the nineteenth century; but the Italian immigrant Vítor Brecheret (1894–1955), an influential participant in the Modern Art Week, was probably the greatest sculptor since Aleijadinho. Generally, though, it was only after the 1920s indigenist movements, although largely figurative, had indicated the historical potential of the pre-Columbian heritage, that the genre really developed. A key precursor was Ignacio Asúnsolo (1890–1965), a Mexican who effected fusions between European examples like Rodin and Amerindian models. Ten of his monuments stand in Mexico City, devoted mainly to poets and politicians. Even countries with little in the way of pre-Columbian relics took up the theme, sometimes opting for solutions like those of Mérida or Torres García in painting. Eventually sculpture came fully into its own everywhere with the new vogue, essentially Mexican in origin, for integrated architecture, painting and sculpture.

Music

Latin American music between 1900 and 1930 shows clearly how rapidly the arts were moving into mutual focus. In 1906 the Italian composer Chiafarelli remarked that Brazil was still hardly more than 'a musical province of Italy', and even in 1916 Saint-Saëns unambiguously dubbed Buenos Aires 'Conservatoriopolis'; yet the slavishly mimetic or aridly academic traces they detected were clues to the past, not signs to the future. Although romanticism survived, particularly in regional music and urban popular song, it had lost its vitality; but those same popular forms, in their raw state, were becoming increasingly assertive and beginning – thanks, ironically enough, to Bizet – to reach a world audience. Songs like the *habanera*, *Tú* (1894), by the Cuban Eduardo Sánchez de Fuentes (1874–1944), and Ponce's *Estrellita*, swept through Latin America, whilst *habaneras*, *contradanzas* and *tangos* successively reverberated around Europe between 1890 and the 1920s. In art music meanwhile the trend was a refinement of romanticism through the French impressionism of Debussy and Ravel, perhaps the final phase in the organic evolution of European music since the Renaissance.

Carlos Chávez (1899–1978), most probably with Villa-Lobos the greatest name in twentieth-century Latin American music, belonged to that generation which came to prominence after the First World War, when so many artistic problems suddenly became soluble at last. Chávez, indeed, is an exemplary figure in the process of internalizing a chosen past, fusing it with the nationalist demands of the present whilst incorporating international developments. To say that he sought an 'Aztec Renaissance' is to simplify his intentions, which were not to recreate pre-Columbian musical patterns or techniques as such, but to connote them and thus disinter 'one of the deepest layers of the Mexican soul', as he declared in 1928. His modal or pentatonic melodies signified an indigenist commitment but did not reconstruct Indian reality past or present: rather, the process used made the past finally communicate with the present and thus compelled its assimilation. Despite adolescent piano arrangements of revolutionary songs like *Adelita* and *La cucaracha*, Chávez was always wary of popular music, placing his main emphasis on classical Indian forms, and two-thirds of his compositions contained no intrinsically Mexican content. His use of folk or popular materials involved extensive distillation and synthesis, far more than was the case with Copland, Vaughan Williams, Falla or even Villa-Lobos. The most characteristic pieces combine modernist and primitivist elements in a manner reminiscent of the early Stravinsky, as in the youthful ballet *El fuego nuevo* (1921). Later Chávez demanded the incorporation of autochthonous musical instruments, studiously avoided all romantic chords and dispensed with harmony, employing devices such as repetition, parallelism, frequent changes of tempo and rhythm, syncopation, and both pentatonic and diatonic modal melodies. In 1925 he produced another ballet, *Los cuatro soles*, followed by *Seven Pieces for Piano* (1926–30). In 1932 the anti-imperialist ballet *Caballos de vapor (H.P.)* was produced in Philadelphia by Stokowski, with sets by Rivera. This was Chávez's most militant phase, during which he instituted workers' concerts and composed populist works such as *Llamadas: sinfonía proletaria* (1934). Like other indigenists, he saw thematic links between pre-Columbian cultural motifs, contemporary indigenous culture and the march of socialism. In 1935 the *Sinfonía india* was performed, the work with which he is associated internationally.

Just as the 1920s saw the first great formative phase in the development of national art galleries, so it was the era of the symphony orchestra. The contribution of the Mexican national symphony orchestra under Chávez to Mexican musical life was unsurpassed; innumerable nationalist works were premiered in the late 1920s and early 1930s. Chávez's assistant throughout the period was Silvestre Revueltas (1899–1949), an outstanding composer in his own right. Where Chávez was austere, even magisterial, Revueltas was exuberantly populist and drew mainly on contemporary folk and popular music, as well as writing film scores. His first full orchestral piece was *Cuauhnáhuac* (1930), the best-loved perhaps the government-commissioned film piece *Janitzio* (1933). Later came a homage to Lorca and in 1938 *Sensemayá*, a vibrant evocation of Nicolás Guillén's Cuban poetry.

Not everyone in Mexico was engaged in nationalist exploration. Julián Carrillo (1875–1965), although of Indian extraction, was closely associated with the Díaz regime and spent many years in Europe. In 1920 he was appointed director of the national symphony orchestra for the second time, and took part in Vasconcelos's contradictory campaign of Indianist nationalism and – Carrillo's own preference – neo-classical revivalism. Thereafter, with his academic and romantic-impressionist phases behind him, Carrillo launched his celebrated theory of micro-tones, called 'Sonido 13' (symbolizing, according to Slonimsky, 'the field of sounds smaller than the twelve semitones of the tempered scale'),[19] on which he had been working since 1895, together with a new system of notation for which he became internationally recognized, although the theory was never widely applied. His first exposition of the system was with his own *Preludio a Colón* in 1922.

Such was the vitality of popular music in Cuba and so deadening the Spanish academic heritage, that it was difficult for serious composers to find a stylistic foothold in the recently liberated island before the 1920s. It was the Grupo Minorista of poets, artists and musicians who from 1923 provided the intellectual basis for renovating Cuban musical culture. *Afrocubanismo*, inspired in part by the great folklorist and ethnomusicologist Fernando Ortiz (1881–1969), who was particularly influential as a university teacher in Havana between 1909–18, found its most striking exponent in the mulatto composer Amadeo Roldán (1900–39), composer of the pathbreaking *Obertura sobre temas cubanos* (1925), *Tres pequeños poemas* (1926), and *La rebambaramba* (1928), from a story by Alejo Carpentier, who was not only to become a world-famous novelist but also, like Mário de Andrade in Brazil, a leading authority on national music. Another Carpentier story led to Roldán's second ballet, *El milagro de Anaquillé* (1929), and in 1930 he wrote *Motivos de son*, based on Guillén's poems, perfecting his intricate fusion of native folk elements, including syncopation, with sophisticated cosmopolitan orchestration and a mixture of native and European instruments. The work of Alejandro García Caturla (1906–40) was equally striking. Dazzled in Paris by

[19] See N. Slonimsky, *Music of Latin America* (New York, 1945), 229.

Stravinsky, Satie and Milhaud, he maintained his identification with black culture, adapting the *conga, son, comparsa* and *rumba*; and his *Tres danzas cubanas* (1928) and the suite *Bembé* (1929) reveal sure mastery of both traditions. Like Roldán, he collaborated extensively with Carpentier, for example on *Dos poemas afrocubanos* (1929), or the ritualistic symphonic poem *Yamba-O* (1928–31), and adapted various poems by Nicolás Guillén. Although his basic model was the *son*'s essentially pentatonic melody, he wrote an orchestral piece entitled *La rumba* in 1933.

On the whole Peruvian erudite culture has failed to achieve the artistic miscegenations of other parts of the continent. This is evidently due to a deep-seated reluctance to integrate indigenous culture, but is ironic in view of the extraordinary quality of its pre-Columbian arts and crafts, or its contemporary folk music. Teodoro Valcárcel (1902–42) composed the indigenist pieces *Sacsahuamán* (1928) and *Suite incaica*, but could not get his works satisfactorily orchestrated in his native land, whilst the Bolivian José María Velasco (1900–70) wrote a ballet *Amerindia* to glorify 'the new Indian of tomorrow' in the early 1930s, but had to wait until 1938 to see it performed in Berlin courtesy of the German ministry of propaganda.

Nativism has been the exception in Chile, but Carlos Isamitt (1887–1974) and Pedro Humberto Allende (1885–1959) pioneered research among the Mapuches. Allende also quoted mainstream *mestizo* folk music in the symphonic suite *Escenas campesinas chilenas* (1914), the tone poem *La voz de las calles* (1920) and the *Tonadas de carácter popular chileno* (1922). Carlos Lavín (1883–1962), another indigenist, composed *Mitos araucanos* and *Lamentaciones huilliches* (1928) for contralto and orchestra, and *Suite andina* (1929) for piano. Quite different in orientation was Domingo Santa Cruz (1899–1987), who composed the neo-classical *Cuatro poemas de Gabriela Mistral* in 1928.

In Argentina and Uruguay the picture was particularly complex after 1918. The nationalist rural-gauchesque tradition remained vigorous beyond 1940, complemented by emerging Andean and *porteño* currents. Italian immigrants were especially influential, and the opening of the Colón in 1908 both confirmed Buenos Aires as a world centre for Italian opera and stimulated a spate of nativist operas in the tradition of Williams and Aguirre (see above). Felipe Boero (1884–1958) wrote numerous operas, such as *El matrero* (1929), clothing folk legends in Italian garb, like Juan Bautista Massa (1885–1938), whose full-blown operatic style culminated in the symphonic poem *La muerte del Inca* (1932). Another Italianizer of Argentine folklore was Constantino Gaito (1878–1945), with *Flor de nieve* (1922), *Ollantay* (1926), and a symphonic poem *El ombú* (1925) evoking that symbol of Argentine solitude.

A more authentic regionalist was Carlos López Buchardo (1881–1948), whose symphonic poem *Escenas argentinas* (1922) was one of the most admired *criollista* works of the period. Floro M. Ugarte (1884–1975) composed *De mi tierra* (1923), a tone poem based on Estanislao del Campo's gauchesque poetry, and Honorio Sicardi (b. 1897) wrote *Tres poemas sobre Martín Fierro*. The most effective *criollista*, however, was Luis Gianneo (1897–1968), a member of the influential Grupo Renovación, who composed *Pampeanas* (1924), *Coplas* (1929), based on popular poetry, and the indigenist symphonic poems *Turay-Turay* (1928) and *El tarco en flor* (1930). Uruguay's most influential nationalist work was *Campo* (1909), by Eduardo Fabini (1882–1950), first performed only in 1922. It was to Uruguay that Francisco Curt Lange (b. 1903) emigrated in 1923, later to become one of the continent's foremost musicologists.

In the River Plate countries, however, there was always a certain suspicion of regionalism, and its exponents themselves not infrequently later renounced their youthful enthusiasms, as Borges did the poetry of his 'fervent youth'. Juan Carlos Paz (1901–72) of the Grupo Renovación was resolutely and irascibly opposed to all nationalist music as one more version of programme composition, like 'literary' references, which he also despised. Paz at first adopted a neo-classical style, but later advocated Schoenberg's serial techniques and the work of other avant-garde composers like Weber, Varèse and Berg. Significantly, it was at precisely the moment, in the late 1920s, when nationalism began to falter and cosmopolitanism again became a virtue, that Argentine music, like its painting, began to come into its own.

The Brazilian panorama was dominated by the giant figure of Heitor Villa-Lobos (1887–1959), 'the Rabelais of Latin American music', incomparably the most popular serious composer to have emerged from the continent. He composed over a thousand works for all media and in all genres, fusing the musical traditions of Portuguese, Negro and Indian into one vast synthesis, embracing every Brazilian region and social stratum past and present. No wonder he boasted: 'I am folklore; my melodies are just as authentic as those which originate in the souls of the people'. Once a popular musician himself, he spent eight years travelling the country, learning its music through intuition whilst repeatedly rejecting academic training. His early works were *Suite dos cânticos sertanejos* (1910), already based on folk sources, *Amazonas* (1917), *Lenda do caboclo* (1920), and *Nonetto* ('A quick impression of all Brazil', 1923). He met Milhaud in Rio in 1916 and was a major participant in the São Paulo Modern Art Week in 1922. In Paris from 1923, his 'primitiveness', exaggerated with the born impresario's instinct for playing to his audience, ensured success. The French composer Florent Schmitt called him 'three-quarters god, with blazing eyes and crocodile teeth'.[20] Villa-Lobos instinctively accommodated – indeed, he anticipated – the vogue for combining formal innovation with primitive content. Far from falling for his own image, he underwent a period of intense creativity. *Rudepoema*, completed in Paris and dedicated to Rubinstein, is one of the most complex piano pieces of the century, yet he was simultaneously composing children's songs and his most important nationalist works, the 16 *Choros*, ranging from relatively abstract pieces to completely programmatic and even onomatopoeic evocations of the Brazilian landscape. The nine *Bachianas brasileiras* (1930–35) adapted baroque counterpoint to Brazilian popular music, including a structural exploration of the *modinha*. In the 1930s, perhaps appropiately, the gargantuan Villa-Lobos became involved in Getúlio Vargas's gigantic education programme, organizing immense musical rallies of up to 40,000 people.

It was difficult to live in Villa-Lobos's shadow, but Oscar Lorenzo Fernández (1897–1948) wrote a *Canção sertaneja* (1924), an Amerindian tone poem *Imbapara* (1929) and an opera *Malazarte* (1933) to a libretto based on Graça Aranha's drama about the Brazilian folk hero. Fernández collaborated frequently with Mário de Andrade, whose seminal *Ensaio sôbre a música brasileira* appeared in 1928. It was Andrade who, with Luciano Gallet (1893–1931), pioneered the study of Brazilian folk music. Gallet's *Canções populares brasileiras* appeared in 1924 and the piano piece *Nhô Chico* in 1927. Other associates of Andrade's worthy of mention were Camargo Guarnieri (1907–93) and Francisco Mignone (1897–1986).

The novel

The first decade of the twentieth century saw the broad cultural movement of which literary modernism and naturalism were at once

---

[20] Béhague, *Music in Latin America*, 186.

opposing and complementary faces, visibly drained of vitality, at a historical moment when the widespread stability of the later nineteenth century was threatened by diverse factors, not least the gathering impact of immigration and the rise of workers' movements. Once the pace of modernization began to accelerate and true modernity appeared on the horizon, Spanish American *modernismo* was doomed, and would become superseded with astonishing rapidity by the post-war avant-garde; as concepts of class struggle overtook the biological and racial perspectives of social Darwinism, naturalism was bound to re-develop, creating new versions of the 'realist' impulse such as regionalism (including *criollismo*, usually conservative in impulse, and *indigenismo* and *afroamericanismo*, both usually progressive) and the social-realist novel.

Spain's defeat in 1898 had put an end not only to the century but to an old world, though Latin Americans were uncomfortably aware that they were the creatures of that world, and that it had been overcome by other, more technologically and economically advanced Americans; new ideas from Europe, notably Bakunin and Marx, arrived to challenge the old and were diffused by a new generation of thinkers and politicians. Positivism, still advocating orderly progress, after several generations in which revolutionary thought had barely existed in the continent, gave way to more explicitly political ideologies, as early socialist parties formed, followed in the 1920s by communist parties. All the more surprising, then, in retrospect, that Rodó's *Ariel* should so have influenced two generations of artists and politicians (like Batlle in Uruguay and Yrigoyen in Argentina) with its message of truth, beauty and spirituality based on Guyau, Carlyle, Emerson and Renan, but then the new generation, particularly the students, were looking almost desperately for some message of hope at the bleak dawn of the new century. Although the magisterial gravity of Rodó's Graeco-Roman prose seems more than eighty years away from us now, it inspired those who themselves were wishing to become educators, not of children but of the workers and peasants.

The First World War was a watershed. Literary developments evolving gradually to 1914 seemed suddenly complete by 1920. Poetry in particular underwent a revolution in form and function, shifting from ear to eye and breaking free of metre, rhyme and rhetoric to become either hermetically avant-garde or wilfully commonplace and prosaic. Prose, always weighed down by history itself, was slower to react, but the naturalist novel rapidly became more historical, political and economic, less biological and sociological; or, as in Reyles (see above) or Güiraldes (see below), inched towards the poetic pattern by fusing with the modernist novel. Before 1910 realist novelists, within a world view almost exclusively liberal in contexture, had been able to take up vague abstract commitments to 'civilization', 'progress' or 'justice'; after 1918 such political innocence was lost and writers who were apolitical or wished to conceal their allegiances would have to evade or confuse the issue. Before 1900 the progressive writer was against Spain, then the United States; after 1918 he had to oppose the landowners as well, and possibly even capitalism. The Mexican Revolution, the Russian Revolution, the First World War and the University Reform Movement at Córdoba together launched a complex tidal wave, some of whose impact was immediate, some short and some long-term, but whose effect remains today. In 1900 Latin American intellectuals were still assimilating Darwin, Spencer, Nietzsche and Bakunin; now Marx, Lenin, Trotsky, Freud, Bergson and Einstein arrived in rapid succession, not to mention diversionary eccentrics like Spengler and Keyserling, accelerating the development of realist narrative away from biological determinism to a more overtly political perspective based on a newly emerging class consciousness and the alliance between intellectuals and workers advocated by González Prada (for example, in his speech 'El intelectual y los obreros', 1905).

An early symptom of the change was the Chilean Baldomero Lillo (1867–1923), whose story collections *Sub terra* (1904) and *Sub sole* (1907) have usually been dismissed as late naturalist or regionalist, when he was one of the very first to view the proletariat as workers rather than members of the 'lower reaches' of society. Lillo himself was from a poor southern family, and spent many years as an employee in a mining *pulpería*. *Sub terra*'s mining stories include two, 'La compuerta número 12' and 'El chiflón del diablo', which, in their stark unsentimental realism and apparently spontaneous structural logic, represent early masterpieces of the genre. Lillo's concentration on the worker's own experience of industrial labour signals the transition from mechanistic naturalism to a new version of realism grounded in economics and politics, giving rise to the great age of the Latin American social novel between the wars.

In Bolivia, Alcides Arguedas (1879–1946), despite the pessimistic *Pueblo enfermo* (1909), was the first to point Latin American indigenist fiction in a more sociological direction. *Wata Wara* (1904) is a story of Indian lovers brutally mistreated by a *gamonal*, which, instead of the usual sentimental romanticism or brutal naturalism, examines the real social condition of the Indians and even ends with them exacting just revenge. Virtually ignored, Arguedas re-elaborated the book during a period of fifteen years, giving it a more panoramic perspective and an epic dimension which make its definitive version, *Raza de bronce* (1919), the precursors of all the great indigenist works of the next two decades, and inaugurating the theme of 'beggars on golden stools' in the implicit contrast between the soaring, grandiose landscapes of the Andes and the sordid and unjust condition to which its inhabitants have been reduced.

The third great precursor was the Uruguayan Horacio Quiroga (1878–1937), whose life was marked by repeated tragedy. Poe, Maupassant, Chekhov and Kipling were his principal models, and his stories contain a gallery of horrors almost without parallel in Latin American fiction. His first poems, *Los arrecifes de coral* (1901), were dedicated to the Argentine modernist Lugones, who included Quiroga in an expedition to the forests of Misiones. There the Uruguayan writer was destined to spend most of the rest of his life, far from urban civilization, producing numerous outstanding collections of stories: *Cuentos de amor, de locura y de muerte* (1917), *Cuentos de la selva* (1918), *El salvaje* (1920), *Anaconda* (1921), *El desierto* (1924) and *Los desterrados* (1926). Quiroga is the nearest Latin America comes to a Conrad. His stories deal with ordinary, uneducated men struggling against the two equally barbarous worlds of wild nature and human society, and usually end in horrifying defeat. Critics have not found it easy to categorize Quiroga: some, thinking of Poe, have called him 'gothic'; others, anticipating Arlt, have preferred 'expressionist'. Their difficulty is that while Quiroga undoubtedly synthesizes a number of currents within early twentieth-century fiction, his own bleak, almost hallucinatory vision is entirely unique. He is also, however, the first, and one of the very greatest, of the new wave of regionalist writers who, in the social realist era, became the first generation of Latin American novelists – in the 1920s – to come to international attention.

The historical phenomenon which attracted the world's gaze to the continent was the Mexican Revolution (1910–20). In Mexico itself, where the narrative tradition since Lizardi at the beginning of the nineteenth century had been consistently worthy and vigorous but somewhat undistinguished, the Revolution stimulated that well-known regional sub-genre, the 'novel of the Mexican Revolution'. The label has perpetuated a misconception that Mariano Azuela (1873–1952) and Martin Luis Guzmán (1887–1976), for example, were revolutionary novelists. Azuela was, in fact, profoundly sceptical about the Revolution and Guzmán took an almost conservative perspective. The crucial point was that both had lived through the conflict: like Lillo, who knew everything about the mines, like Arguedas, brought up on a semi-feudal estate, or Quiroga, who had lived and suffered in the jungle. It would be misleading to suggest that these literary chroniclers of the Revolution really did manage to reproduce the lives of their characters across the abyss of class, race and lived experience, but this was undoubtedly the era – the only one so far – when middle-class novelists in every country began to reach out and touch the lives of their hitherto alien and still largely illiterate compatriots to speak on their behalf. After 1945 the social-realist current would again return to minority status as novelists undertook the appraisal of their own class which European fiction had completed by the First World War, but which only Machado de Assis had been able to bring to a fine art in Latin America.

Mariano Azuela almost literally leaped at the historical opportunity afforded by the Revolution. A supporter of Madero, whose ideology he shared, Azuela's first important work was *Andrés Pérez, maderista* (1911), which communicates his disenchantment with the early months, when his own political ambitions were frustrated. His lasting claim on literary history, however, was *Los de abajo* (1915), written partly in the heat of battle – Azuela was a doctor in Villa's army – and partly in its disillusioned aftermath. Effectively Spanish America's first modern novel, the speed, exhilaration and confusion of its revolutionary content created a nervous, tersely impressionistic style and a structure which appears to accelerate the reader, along with the characters, to his disillusionment and their doom. In its freshness and vivacity, pioneering approach to popular dialogue and national humour, and frank depiction of the gulf between those who labour by hand and by brain, the novel provides an unforgettable, almost cinematographic view of the revolutionary era.

Los de abajo was virtually unread until 1924, and the other so-called novels of the Revolution appeared between 1926, when Guzmán's *El águila y la serpiente* appeared, and 1939 – coinciding more closely, therefore, with the golden age of Mexican cinema which followed the Revolution than with the contemporaneous muralist movement. Guzmán's famous novel is really a documentary dramatizing the novelist's own experiences. He too had been a *maderista* and could not subsequently identify with the positions of Villa (who nevertheless became a lifelong obsession), Carranza, Obregón or Calles. Ideologically sceptical, almost classical in its choice of expression, no artistic work of the era has more lastingly influenced the Revolution's perception by later generations. Guzmán's interest is in 'los de arriba'; the peasant revolutionaries are seen only in the mass, as if across a vast social abyss. Yet we obtain a crystal-clear (one would not wish to say 'true') impression of Guzmán's experiences, artfully composed yet apparently as natural as breathing; and an illuminating if unconscious insight into the relation between the middle-class novelist and his peasant or proletarian characters. His next novel, *La sombra del caudillo* (1929), was a bitter critique of the Calles regime, and, though rarely quoted, one of the continent's most important literary explorations of the authoritarian impulse. A third novelist, Gregorio López y Fuentes (1897–1967), although less talented than Azuela and Guzmán, was an important link between the novel of the Revolution and other genres, with *Campamento* (1931), a brief narrative which develops techniques for conveying mass psychology typical of the era; *Tierra* (1932), on the agrarian struggle launched by Zapata; and *El indio* (1935), condemning the treatment of Indian communities both during and after the conflict.

In general, then, the Revolution produced fiction which, for the first time since Mármol's *Amalia* (1851), saw history not as something in the distant past, like the colonial or independence periods, but as both a reality and a concept which could at once mobilize and fix the perception of social, political and economic events. Henceforth this historical awareness would sharply distinguish social realism from the more complacent *criollista* mode within the general movement of realism. The trend is illustrated by Latin America's most famous jungle novel, *La vorágine* (1924) by the Colombian José Eustasio Rivera (1888–1928), whose reputation is deservedly growing. It concerns a Bogotá poet who elopes with his mistress to the Amazon, and is sucked into a whirlpool of social, economic and natural disaster. The protagonist is a theatrical, anachronistic and essentially romantic personality whose first-person narration reproduces his own temperament. This has induced most critics to conclude that the novel is an unrestrained piece of tropical hyperbole, when in fact it subtly undermines the narrator's moral status and gradually transforms itself into a semi-documentary work exposing the exploitation of the Amazon rubber gatherers during the process of primitive accumulation. Rivera was another writer recasting his own experiences, having worked as a boundary commissioner in the Amazon. His newspaper reports on conditions for workers trapped by the *enganche* system in the almost inaccessible forests, combined with the impact of the novel, helped to change government labour policies.

The last line of *La vorágine*, 'the jungle devoured them', has been used ironically by critics to indicate that this fiction remained inherently deterministic, its characters dwarfed and ultimately obliterated by the vast natural landscapes of these novels. Such criticisms have their justification, but ignore the context in which writers were working. Latin American fiction had not yet explored, still less inhabited those vast open spaces, because they had not yet been fully developed in reality. It was hardly surprising that the continent remained largely a 'novel without novelists', in Luis Alberto Sánchez' phrase.[21] Again, critics have condemned both the collective characterization of this fiction and the apparent passivity of its characters; but here too the uneven nature of Latin American development meant that workers' movements appeared on the scene before Latin American fiction had experienced the 'classical' moment of European bourgeois realism, whilst, on the other side, such was the state of development of the early workers' movements in the 1920s that any triumphalist interpretation of their consciousness and achievements would have involved serious distortion.

One country where nature really had been largely domesticated and where the epic phase was past, was Argentina, whose greatest regional novel of the 1920s was *Don Segundo Sombra* (1926) by Ricardo Güiraldes (1886–1927), a wealthy landowner with an *estancia* in Buenos Aires province and apartments in Paris. His gauchesque masterpiece, published long after the golden age of the gauchos had passed into legend, creates a myth to inspire young Argentines to grow up straight and true. Like Jack Schaeffer's *Shane* (1954), the novel employs the device of viewing the cowboy hero through the eyes of a young person, its

---

[21] It is the title of his influential book, *América, novela sin novelistas* (Santiago de Chile, 1933). Sánchez's perplexities took on a still more metaphysical turn in 1945 when he produced a work entitled *¿Existe América Latina?*.

nostalgic force underlined by the dramatic contrast between its exquisite symbolist-impressionist form and the often brutal, always harsh subject matter. Few novels are more dishonest, however: purporting to exalt the cowboy of the pampas but written by a landowner (whose own father, moreover, employed the man on whom the fictional hero is based); mourning the gaucho's loss of freedom when it was families like the author's who fenced off the open ranges and turned the nomadic gauchos from knights of the prairies into hired hands; providing a disingenuous apology for *machista* values – interpreted inevitably as a continuingly valid code of honour – which ruled not only the pampas but the patriarchal world of the Argentine ruling class; in short, regretfully evoking a world uncomplicated by immigration, proletarian mass movements and industrialization, when landowner and gaucho supposedly shared the same individualist, stoical and epic philosophy of life, and the same love of the land. As Don Segundo rode into a tearful sunset, he eclipsed most other works of the pampas, but there are many more: Lugones's *La guerra gaucha* (1905) and *El payador* (1916); *Los gauchos judíos* (1910), by the Russian immigrant Alberto Gerchunoff (1883–1950); a number of books by Manuel Gálvez (1882–1962), polemical author of the well-known novel *La maestra normal* (1914); *El inglés de los güesos* (1924) and *El romance de un gaucho* (1933), by Benito Lynch (1885–1951); Reyles's *El gaucho Florido* (1932), and *El paisano Aguilar* (1934) by his compatriot Enrique Amorim (1900–60). The essential interpretive work for reading such fictional constructs in the light of River Plate history is the brilliant essay *Radiografía de la pampa* (1933) by the Argentine *pensador* Ezequiel Martínez Estrada (1895–1964).

More deluded than hypocritical was the writer generally considered to be, if not the greatest, then the most important Spanish American regionalist: the Venezuelan Rómulo Gallegos (1883–1969), author of the famous *Doña Bárbara* (1929) and many other novels. Bolívar's fatherland had endured the most unhappy of nineteenth-century experiences of *caudillismo*, prolonged into the contemporary period by the dictatorship of Juan Vicente Gómez (1908–35), apparently justifying Gallegos in resurrecting Sarmiento's opposition between civilization and barbarism in *Facundo*. No writer shows more clearly the achievements and limitations of the period. His identification of the essential themes was matchless in its time, and only Vargas Llosa among later novelists has shown his Conradian breadth of ambition. Unfortunately his ideas and arguments are as interesting outside the novels as within, and few of his characters are blessed with life. Like Rodó, Gallegos, a great educator, repeatedly offered cultural solutions for economic problems, showing no more insight into the psychology of his characters than into national politics. (Like Sarmiento he later became president, but was swiftly deposed.) Simplistic distinctions between civilization and barbarism are unhelpful in the face of capitalism and imperialism, and the delusion reached a climax in *Doña Bárbara* when Gallegos somehow persuaded himself and a generation of readers that his protagonist, the idealistically named Santos Luzardo, is a representative of civilization because he replaces an anarchic, inefficient semi-feudal agriculture with a more organized but equally paternalistic system. Nevertheless, he first gave literary form to myths which others would later elaborate, and no writer more lucidly and ambitiously set out to explore and colonize the natural landscapes of the continent through fiction, thereby undertaking the essential task, as Alejo Carpentier described it, of pointing his finger and naming things, like Adam. Without him the fiction of the 1920s could not have appeared so visibly the foundation of all that has happened since.

Nowhere was the confluence of realism and regionalism more decisively established in the late 1920s than in Ecuador, where the Grupo de Guayaquil in 1931 published a joint collection of stories, *Los que se van.* Those involved were Demetrio Aguilera Malta (1909–81), Joaquín Gallegos Lara (1911–47) and Enrique Gil Gilbert (1912–75), the last two communists, joined by Alfredo Pareja Diezcanseco (b. 1908) and José de la Cuadra (1904–41), one of the great Spanish American short-story writers and author of the novel *Los Sangurimas* (1933). Aguilera Malta, however, became the best known, with *Don Goyo* (1933) and *Canal Zone* (1935). This committed, neo-realist, unusually cohesive group were perhaps the nearest literary parallel to the Mexican muralist movement. Ecuador's best known writer of the century was Jorge Icaza (1906–78), from Quito, whose brutal indigenist novel *Huasipungo* (1934) is the culmination of the social-realist current, appearing, appropriately enough, at the moment when Zdhanov was imposing the official Soviet doctrine of socialist realism in the USSR. It traces the chain of exploitation from Chicago to the Ecuadorean sierras. No novel has been more vituperated – for its crude language and technique, its depiction of Indians reduced by priests and landowners to subhuman status – but no novel has so obstinately refused to be marginalized. After Icaza's definitive treatment, however, the indigenist novel began to lose its vitality, although one acknowledged master of the genre, Ciro Alegría (Peru, 1909–67), did not produce his first novel, *La serpiente de oro*, until 1935, and his world-famous *El mundo es ancho y ajeno* until 1941.

Although most of its development came after the period under consideration, the urban novel began to evolve in Spanish America in the 1920s and to reflect the disorientation of significant sectors of society in the face of rapidly changing circumstances. An early example was *Un perdido* (1917) by the Chilean Eduardo Barrios (1884–1963). *Un perdido* gave a petty-bourgeois gloss to the urban alienation theme dramatized by Cambaceres through the aristocratic protagonist of *Sin rumbo* thirty years before (see above). The outstanding exponent of this line was Roberto Arlt (Argentina, 1900–42), whose *El juguete rabioso* (1926), *Los siete locos* (1929), *Los lanzallamas* (1931) and *El amor brujo* (1932) conveyed a tortured, sordid yet fantastic world of almost expressionist horror, the first reminiscent of Gorky, the later works of Dostoyevsky and Céline, anticipating such typically Argentine novelists as Marechal, Mallea and Sábato. Closely associated with the Boedo social-realists, Arlt's own style burst all limitations; instead of providing typological case studies of workers like, say, Leónidas Barletta (1902–1975) in *Royal Circo* (1927), he used characters like pimps, prostitutes, embezzlers, murderers and lunatics as grotesque metaphors for the impact of capitalism as creator of the urban nightmare. His reputation continues to grow. Together with Barletta, Samuel Eichelbaum (1894–1967), Armando Discépolo (1887–1971), and Francisco Defilippis Novoa (1891–1930), Arlt also contributed to the continuing vigour of Argentine drama in the 1920s.

In Brazil, the century had begun dramatically with *Os sertões* and *Canaã*. Euclides da Cunha (1866–1909), an ex-soldier and engineer from Rio, was sent by a newspaper to cover the campaign against the messianic uprising of *sertanejos* at Canudos in 1896. The result, *Os sertões* (1902), was a powerful synthesis of history, geography and sociology, and a remarkable interpretation of the relation between man and environment in a narration of astonishing force and conviction. Although he too was blinded partly by the racial ideologies of mechanistic Positivism, Da Cunha argued fervently for the development and full integration of the north-east into the national economic, political and educational system, catalysing a process of self-analysis and public debate which came to see the *caboclo*, and in particular the *sertanejo*, as the bedrock of Brazilian national identity. This process led directly both to 1920s *modernismo* and to the regionalist movement launched by Gilberto Freyre after 1926 (see below). José Pereira da Graça Aranha (1868–1931) was himself from the north-east, but set his novel *Canaã* – about the differing attitudes of two German immigrants – in the south, target of most immigration and future economic development. Graça Aranha took a pessimistic view of Brazil's existing racial stock and placed his hopes in the new miscegenation. In general, however, novelists before 1918 were disappointingly unable to produce works relevant to Brazil's national problems. Although both Brazilian romanticism and naturalism had been more complete and more 'European' than their Spanish American equivalents, the late arrival of abolition and the republic meant that a number of historical tasks already completed elsewhere had not yet been carried out by Brazilian artists who were overwhelmingly resident in the coastal strip of an immense country which contained, in the *sertão* or the Amazon, for example, some of the most forbidding territories to be confronted anywhere in the continent. Whilst Brazil had continued its coherent but excessively respectful parnassian and symbolist movements, Spanish America undertook the road to true modernity through the continental movement of *modernismo*; and although Brazil produced more authentic naturalist novels than all the Spanish American republics combined, they remained at the level of socio-biological case studies, distanced from characters conceived as specimens with grave 'character' defects – often racial in origin – rather than products of a specific history and social structure. Euclides da Cunha shattered this illusion, but it took many years for the impact to be reflected adequately in fiction. Henrique Coelho Neto (1864–1934), Brazil's most prolific writer, produced numerous rather ornate stories about the *sertão*; João Simões Lopes Neto (1865–1916), published regionalist works like *Contos gauchescos* (1912) or *Lendas do sul* (1913); and Afonso Arinos (1868–1916), the anachronistic, almost picturesque stories in *Lendas e tradições brasileiras* (1917). More interesting was Afonso Henriques de Lima Barreto (1881–1922), mulatto author of bitter iconoclastic works depicting the frustrated inhabitants of suburban Rio in a style reminiscent of Machado, if less balanced. His best novel was *Triste fim de Policarpo Quaresma* (1915).

The writer who began to tie loose ends and weave a new regional pattern was the turbulent José Bento Monteiro Lobato (1882–1948), later recognized both by Oswald de Andrade, a leader of the 1922 modernist movement, and Gilberto Freyre, founder of the 1926 regionalist movement, as a precursor. Lobato called for a nationalist, quintessentially Brazilian art in all genres, pouring scorn on the mimetic quality of most contemporary works. His first book of short stories, *Urupês* (1918), set in his native São Paulo, not only renovated literary language but revealed a new attitude to the *caboclos* of the interior through the affectionately but critically drawn character 'Jeca Tatu', the indolent and illiterate yokel who was the unknown popular soul of Brazil.

In 1928 three fundamental works appeared. One, Mário de Andrade's *Macunaíma*, a fictional compendium of culture traits reminiscent of Villa-Lobos, properly belongs to our discussion of the avant-garde (see below). The second, *Retrato do Brasil*, by Paulo Prado (1869–1943), typical of that era of soul-searching and national characterology, with its memorable view of the Brazilian people as 'a sad race, the product of the fusion of three sad races', defined the Brazilian as melancholy, sensual and envious, and has been called 'the ugliest portrait Brazil could receive from one of her sons'.[22] The third was the first true regionalist novel of the kind then appearing in Spanish America, *A bagaceira*, by José Américo de Almeida (b. 1887). As ideologically incoherent as Gallegos's Venezuelan classic *Doña Bárbara* (1929), it traces the transition between the patriarchal world of the old sugar plantations and the new capitalist *usinas*, with the same ambivalence as Gilberto Freyre's *Casa grande e senzala* (1933) or Lins do Rêgo's novels (see below).

Almeida's work was prelude to a remarkable flowering of regionalist fiction which, in a characteristic dialectical leap, took the Brazilian version in just a few years to a level of universality well beyond that of the Spanish American novels which had only recently seemed so advanced. The explanation lies not only in the different inner rhythms of Brazil's literary advance, but in the specific nature of the historical conjuncture: the complex yet coherent interrelation between *modernismo* (itself far more Americanized in Brazil: based in São Paulo, not Paris) and regionalism, which, given the nation's vast proportions, contrasted a nativist movement based in the north-east with a vanguard movement based in São Paulo and Rio; and the fact that, starting later than in Mexico or Argentina, it accumulated all the experiences of the 1920s. The early 1930s saw the emergence of a compact group of social-realists, based mainly in the north-east, comparable to but even more accomplished

[22] Quoted by Azevedo, *Brazilian Culture*, 118.

than the Ecuadoreans. The first, *O quinze* (1930), by Rachel de Queirós (b. 1910), daughter of a plantation owner, re-enacted the tragic drought of 1915 and the suffering of the rural poor, particularly the women. In 1931 Jorge Amado (b. 1912), from Bahia, published *O país do carnaval*, an important adolescent expression of that generation's search for national values and personal meaning in a corrupt, superficial and unjust society. Amado, later to become Latin America's best known communist narrator, then wrote two short pamphleteering novels, *Cacau* (1933), about life on the cocoa plantations, and *Suor* (1934), on the condition of the urban poor and the workers' struggle. In 1935 *Jubiabá* appeared, on the culture of the Bahian negroes, and in 1942 his masterpiece, *Terras do sem fim*, a historical reconstruction of the rise and fall of the cacao estates.

José Lins do Rêgo (1901–57), a plantation owner's son from Paraíba, turned his family's history into one of Brazil's great fictional monuments, the 'Sugar-Cane Cycle', with *Menino de engenho* (1932), *Doidinho* (1933), *Bangüê* (1934), *O moleque Ricardo* (1934) and *Usina* (1936). In its passionate complexity, condemning the injustice of the plantation system whilst implicitly lamenting its passing, this is one of the most compelling documents of Brazilian social history, with its characters José Paulino, the old patriarch, Carlos, his grandson (a largely autobiographical depiction), and Ricardo, the black boy who goes to the city to seek his fortune. *Pedra Bonita* (1938) is a novel on a theme similar to *Os sertões*, whilst *Fogo morto* (1943), his masterpiece, returned to the subject matter of his first works.

The other great north-eastern writer of the period was Graciliano Ramos (1892–1953), son of a rural judge, Brazil's finest stylist since Machado de Assis. His pessimistic, heavily ironic yet austere prose created a whole new way of perceiving the world-view of the inhabitants of the north-east, similar to the later Mexican novelist Juan Rulfo. No regional novelist from the continent so perfectly fused the sociological and psychological dimensions as Graciliano Ramos did in *Caetés* (1933), *São Bernardo* (1934), *Angústia* (1936) and *Vidas sêcas* (1938).

Poetry

Graciliano Ramos constrained narrative prose to almost impossible spareness, reflecting the anguish of his inarticulate characters and refusing the reader the satisfactions of wordy 'literariness' to escape from the bleak realities of the subject matter. As usual, poetry had been embarked on this process long before fiction – always concerned more with the world outside than the means of signifying it. The shift to prosaic, everyday language in Latin American poetry, known variously as *sencillismo, prosaísmo, exteriorismo* or *antipoesía*, is often thought to be a quite recent phenomenon; so that when it did emerge – the 1920s, the 1930s or even later – it was a belated reaction against modernism accentuated by and coinciding with a reaction against the new avant-garde. It seems more exact, however, to consider it as an extension and re-emergence of traditional *tono menor* poetry, remembering Bécquer's contribution to modernism itself, José Asunción Silva's deliberately ingenuous childhood reminiscences, Martí's *Versos sencillos*, González Prada's *Baladas peruanas*, or even Amado Nervo's rather flat poetic mode. It follows that this poetic line is part of the regionalist impulse, whereas the avant-garde is a dialectical continuation of the dominant modernist mode. That this dominant current made all others invisible whilst it was in full flood only proves how coherent, all-embracing and historically significant it was. Yet even before González Martínez called on poets to wring the modernist swan's neck, Darío had signalled, as we have seen, his own weariness with *fin-de-siècle* postures when he moved ('Yo soy aquel que ayer no más decía . . .') from his earlier artifice and escapism to the simpler, fresher style which followed *Cantos de vida y esperanza* in 1905. Thus some view *prosaísmo* as an anti-*modernista* reaction, others as a transitional second, or third, phase of modernism itself, whilst ignoring all those poets in the early 1900s whose innovatory, conversational approach makes them precursors of a line of composition which has grown increasingly important, linking inevitably to rural folklore, urban popular music and the political song movements of recent times.

Ramón López Velarde (Zacatecas, 1888–1921) originated this poetic mode in Mexico. Like Lugones, he used a familiarity with European innovations to achieve artful simplicity in poetry about provincial life, the anguish of catholic belief for a man not only sentimental but sensual, family life, love and death. This was a new provincialism: earlier poets had been marooned in their regional world, limited by ignorance of life outside; now some, despite experience of other places, chose to write specifically provincial, even parochial verse, rather as Antonio Machado was doing in Spain at this time. López Velarde's collections were *La sangre devota* (1916) and *Zozobra* (1919), though many poems appeared posthumously, including his affectionate portrait of Mexico, 'Suave patria', completed shortly before his death and now one of the country's best loved poems, which feels as if it had been composed in the mid-morning sunshine on the veranda of a small-town bar.

Even more spontaneously conversational was the Colombian Luis Carlos López (1883–1950), another poet whose reputation is steadily emerging from the shadow of modernism. *De mi villorrio* (1908), *Posturas difíciles* (1909), *Varios a varios* (1910) and *Por el atajo* (1920) collected apparently simple poems about everyday life in Cartagena, based on the ironic counterpointing of dreams and reality, past glories and the humdrum flow of the present. In Argentina Evaristo Carriego (1883–1912) was perhaps the most characteristic serious poet influenced by tango culture in the early age of Argentinian urban folklore, with *Misas herejes* (1908), including the appropriately entitled 'El alma del suburbio', and 'La canción del barrio' (posth., 1913). Similar were Baldomero Fernández Moreno (1886–1950) and the more explicitly political Boedo poets Alvaro Yunque (b. 1889), Gustavo Riccio (1900–27) and César Tiempo (1906–80), who once also wrote under the name Clara Beter to make his poems on themes like prostitution more convincing.

More a social phenomenon themselves than producers of social poetry were the women who came to prominence in the early twentieth century and introduced new concerns into the male-dominated literary world. The first was Delmira Agustini (1886–1914), who conveyed passion, eroticism and every aspect of human love with a frankness and audacity astonishing for the times. Shortly after *Los cálices vacíos* (1913) appeared, she was murdered by her husband, who then killed himself. Hardly less dramatic was the life and work of the Argentine feminist, Alfonsina Storni (1892–1938), whose poetry treats the problems of a woman with normal sexual desires who resents submitting to the social conventions of a masculine world. An actress, teacher and journalist, her poetry in *La inquietud del rosal* (1916) and *Ocre* (1925) makes uncomfortable reading for both women and men. She committed suicide on discovering that she had an incurable disease. By contrast Juana de Ibarbourou (Argentina, b. 1895) married an Uruguayan army captain with whom she lived somewhat aridly until his early death. A very beautiful woman, her poetry was implicitly addressed to men, inviting their desire whilst professing the conventions of decent catholic society. During each phase of her life she wrote fresh, ingenuous poetry that perfectly combined the sensual and spiritual aspects of the Latin wife and mother. Perhaps because no one else had made fine poetry out of satisfaction with her imposed social condition, Ibarbourou became known as 'Juana de América' after 1929.

The other great female poet of the era was Gabriela Mistral (1889–1957), a Chilean teacher who in 1945 became the first Latin American to win the Nobel Prize. Still a young woman when her fiancé committed suicide, Mistral could never bring herself to marry, though she longed to have children. Her earliest works, *Desolación* (1922) and *Ternura* (1924), convey her feelings of frustrated motherhood, and vainly seek consolation in nature and religious contemplation. She later joined the consular service and became a roving cultural ambassador concerned with the care and education of the world's children. A fervent Americanist identified specially with Bolívar and Martí, she considered herself essentially Indian, despite her Basque ancestry, but wrote austere, disenchanted poetry shorn of all rhetoric and irony, coinciding therefore with the simpler, unpretentious current of poetry that has gradually become dominant in Latin America through the work of Vallejo, Bandeira, Parra or Cardenal.

THE 1920S AVANT-GARDE

After modernism, poetry either became simpler, more conversational and even prosaic, or much more playful, yet complex, hermetic and experimental under the impact of the European avant-garde. This parting of the ways was a phenomenon of great historical importance, for whereas previously it was possible to see a divorce between prose and poetry, naturalism and modernism, accentuating a tendency initiated but by no means completed by romanticism, what now emerged was the same bifurcation, not merely between poetry and prose but within each of the two forms of literary expression: prosaic poems and poetic narratives now became regular phenomena. And just as modernism had developed above all in poetry – always more flexible and adaptable – rather than prose, where the *crónica* and occasional short novel were much less successful vehicles, so in the 1920s the avant-garde novel was much slower to develop than avant-garde poetry, which in that era sees a small number of Latin Americans, such as Huidobro, Bandeira, Vallejo, Neruda and Guillén, emerge to international significance; whereas the vanguard novelists and short story writers who were actually products of the same historical transformation, like Asturias, Borges, Carpentier and Marechal, followers conscious or otherwise of Joyce, Proust, Faulkner and Kafka, made no international impact until long after the Second World War. If this is not understood, the 1920s, with their almost vertiginous profusion of writers and movements, corresponding more closely than at any time before or since to parallel developments in the other arts, can mistakenly appear to descend into chaos and incoherence.

To understand the Latin American avant-garde means returning to Paris, where a new generation identified their youth with that of the century, their modernity with the aesthetic revolution in poetry, music and the plastic arts, their revolt with the social revolutions of Mexico and the U.S.S.R. *Modernismo* now seemed crepuscular, autumnal, pseudo-aristocratic, a rhetorical vehicle for old men who had turned their faces against the new era of revolutionary change flowing from New York, Moscow, Berlin, Paris and Mexico. Other old men had led young Europeans in their millions to their deaths in the war, but in the process had destroyed their own patriarchal world. Now, in the age of cinema, radio, recorded music, automobiles, aeroplanes, transatlantic liners, Hollywood and *Proletkult*, came the moment of youth, the young artist as athlete or student revolutionary. For the first time in a century it was young men who were producing the dominant ideas and ideologies.

Evidently *modernismo*, now rejected, had helped prepare the ground in Latin America for the assimilation of these developments. Cosmopolitan and internationalist, it had spawned literary circles, *tertulias* and *veladas* in every major Spanish American city, putting Latin American writers in regular contact for the first time in several generations, establishing cultural networks between each of the American capitals and Paris, capital of them all; it was itself an avant-garde movement in its day, anticipating the world to come; was a poetry of the senses, completing a long process in Western literature which allowed the avant-garde to fuse ideas, emotions and sensations into one artistic construct for the first time; brought all the arts into fruitful communication, thereby allowing clear perception of the specificity of each and hence their possibilities for integration (seen most clearly in Mexico and Brazil); and began the appropriation – rather than mere imitation – of European culture, which *vanguardismo* would complete whilst simultaneously incorporating the very different modes of primitive art and culture and the American way of life. Given developments in travel and communications, even petty-bourgeois intellectuals could dream of following Darío and Gómez Carrillo to Paris, assisted by favourable exchange rates through the 1920s until the slump put an end to the *années folles* and sent them back, poor Cinderellas, from the city of light to the gloom of the authoritarian 1930s.

Mexico in the 1920s became what it has remained, the most representative Spanish American republic, home of cultural nationalism and *Latinoamericanismo*, with a Third World ideological orientation before the concept was invented. Only the Spanish Civil War and Cuban Revolution can compare with the impact of the Mexican Revolution on Hispanic art, culture and thought in the 1920s and since. Before it a group of young intellectuals and artists had founded the *Ateneo de la Juventud* (1909), whose orientation was essentially anti-Positivist, at a moment when Bergson's neo-idealism was sweeping deterministic ideologies away. The movement included many who would play key roles in constructing Mexico's new national culture in the post-revolutionary period: Antonio Caso, Alfonso Reyes, José Vasconcelos, Enrique González Martínez, Martín Luis Guzmán, Diego Rivera, Jesús Silva Herzog and the great Dominican literary historian, Pedro Henríquez Ureña.

During the Revolution writers survived as best they could, as we have seen. Afterwards many young writers succumbed without hesitation to the siren song of the cosmopolitan avant-garde. *Estridentismo*, an aggressive mixture of Spanish *ultraísmo*, Italian futurism and vague revolutionary theory, was led by Manuel Maples Arce (1898–1981), Germán List Arzubide (b. 1898) and the Guatemalan Arqueles Vela (1899–1977), author of *El café de nadie* (1926). A succession of little magazines came and went, most notably *Ulises* (1926–8) and *Contemporáneos* (1928–31), gathering young *vanguardistas* into relatively coherent groups within the general aesthetic and political anarchy of that effervescent time. Writers included Jaime Torres Bodet (1902–74), later a great educationalist, and an important poet and critic; Salvador Novo (1904–74), a talented, whimsical poet best known as a tireless social and literary critic in numerous newspapers and magazines, renovator of the *crónica* and modernizer of Mexican culture through his humorous importation of United States culture; Gilberto Owen Estrada (1905–52), founder of *Ulises*, connoisseur of Joyce, Proust, Eliot, Pound and the other 'sacred monsters' of European Modernism; Jorge Cuesta (1903–42), and two brilliant poets, Xavier Villaurrutia (1903–50) and José Gorostiza (1901–1973); and the editor of *Contemporáneos*, Bernardo Ortiz de Montellano

(1899–1949), who saw it as his mission, in the aftermath of the Revolution, to maintain literature's contribution to Mexico's spiritual education and cultural intelligence, producing one of the most sophisticated, witty and innovative magazines of the avant-garde era.

The most influential figure of the period was José Vasconcelos (1882–1959), rector of the National University in 1919, education minister in 1921, promoter of cultural missions and muralism, author of *La raza cósmica* (1925), *Indología* (1926) and *Ulises criollo* (1935); though in the 1930s this champion of *mestizo* culture turned violently to reactionary *hispanidad*. Meanwhile, *Perfil del hombre y la cultura en México* (1934) by Samuel Ramos (1897–1959), became the point of departure for all later explorations of *Mexicanidad*. In Paris Alfonso Reyes (1889–1959), perhaps Latin America's most complete man of letters, was representing his country, a central figure in the network of relations established between Latin America, French and Spanish intellectuals which was to be so important in the next thirty years. One of the great prose stylists and cultural critics of the century, his own literary creations, though never less than exquisitely tasteful and acutely intelligent, failed to achieve the resonance of his essays. *Visión de Anáhuac* (1917), an evocation of Mexico itself, and *Ifigenia cruel* (1924), are perhaps the most memorable.

Cuba's tragic destiny, which forged a succession of great moralists and patriots culminating in Martí, the 'apostle', and Enrique José Varona (1894–1933), the 'Prospero of America', who exerted an incalculable moral and intellectual influence on Cuban national life and culture over several decades and whose reorganization of Cuban education after 1898 paved the way for the outstanding generation of intellectuals and artists of the 1920s, saw Spanish colonialism give way to the Platt Amendment and the Big Stick. Mexico, Haiti, the Dominican Republic and Nicaragua each received short or long visits from the marines in the first thirty years of the century, and the 1920s saw the whole Caribbean zone subject to the unholy alliance between U.S. capital and local dictatorships, as expounded in Luis Araquistáin's *La agonía antillana* (1928) or the celebrated novel *Generales y doctores* (1920) by the Cuban Carlos Loveira (1882–1928). Cuba in the 1920s underwent feverish political and cultural ferment. Haya de la Torre's arrival in 1923 from Peru inspired Cuban students led by Julio Antonio Mella (1905–29) to found the José Martí Popular University, whilst Mariano Brull (1891–1956) formed the Grupo Minorista of young artists and intellectuals to campaign for a renovation of the national culture. Its principal members were Jorge

Mañach (1898–1961), José Tallet (b. 1893), Juan Marinello (1898–1977), Raimundo Lazo (1904–76), Alejo Carpentier (1904–80), Eugenio Florit (b. 1903), Emilio Ballagas (1908–54) and Rubén Martínez Villena (1899–1934). Their opposition to the Machado dictatorship made them more cohesive than their varied ideologies would normally permit, although Cuba's agonizingly unresolved condition eventually produced violent schisms. Their main organ was the *Revista de Avance* (1927–30), a vanguard review with a continental profile comparable to that of *Repertorio Americano* (1920–58), edited by the Costa Rican Joaquín García Monge (1881–1958). The North American threat provoked a Hispanicist revival in Cuba, where Góngora's rehabilitation was also especially enthusiastic, but *Afrocubanismo* was the guiding thread in 1920s culture, from Fernando Ortiz's pathbreaking ethnological work through Tallet's poem 'La rumba', Ballagas's 'Canción para dormir a un negrito', and culminating in Nicolás Guillén (1902–89), whose *Motivos de son* (1930), *Sóngoro Cosongo* (1931) and *West Indies Ltd* (1934) were classics of the genre combining black themes and rhythms with a Hispanic tinge reminiscent of Lorca's *Romancero gitano*, and underpinned by a militant anti-imperialism. Carpentier's first notable literary work, *Ecue-Yamba-O* (1933), was also an exploration of black culture. Except for Guillén, most writers of 'black' literature were white men, including the Puerto Rican Luis Palés Matos (1898–1959).

In Peru the intellectual and cultural scene was equally agitated. Here the precursor figures were González Prada, and the ambiguous figure of Abraham Valdelomar (1888–1919), a mulatto, the self-styled 'Conde de Lemos', whose persona was modelled on Wilde and D'Annunzio and who led the young artists and intellectuals grouped round the magazine *Colónida* in 1916 as Peru emerged reluctantly from the *belle époque*. Valdelomar talked openly of homosexuality, cocaine, heroin and revolution, scandalizing the susceptible Lima bourgeoisie but dazzling young provincial intellectuals. The heirs of González Prada were Víctor Raúl Haya de la Torre (1895–1980) and José Carlos Mariátegui (1894–1930), editor of the legendary *Amauta* (1926–30). Having begun as a *colónida*, or literary aesthete, Mariátegui became politically committed during a visit to Europe and in 1923 took over as editor of the journal *Claridad* from Haya who founded the Alianza Popular Revolucionaria Americana (APRA) a year later. In 1928 Mariátegui's *Siete ensayos de interpretación de la realidad peruana* appeared, a landmark in Latin American Marxist thought and a fundamental interpretation of Peruvian history and culture still debated to this day. *Amauta* was close to an *aprista* position at first, evolved towards a communist one thereafter, but always published cultural and political material from a wide range of sources, and remains essential reading on Peru's unresolved debates on nationalism, Americanism, *aprismo*, socialism, communism and indigenism. Most contemporary intellectuals contributed, including Haya and Mariátegui themselves, Luis E. Valcárcel (b. 1893), author of the influential indigenist *Tempestad en los Andes* (1927), Carlos Oquendo de Amat (1909–36), author of *Cinco metros de poemas* (1929), José Diez Canseco (1904–49), best known for *Estampas mulatas* (1930) and the urban novel *Duque* (1934), Martín Adán (b. 1908), author of the novel *La casa de cartón* (1928), Luis Alberto Sánchez (b. 1900), Peru's outstanding literary historian, and the indigenist painters José Sabogal and Julia Codesido (b. 1892).

Meanwhile in Europe César Vallejo (1892–1938), from the northern sierras, was writing the works which would make him one of the greatest of all twentieth-century poets, testifying to his long march to a communism wracked to the last by the unanswered spiritual questions which his traditional catholic childhood had posed. *Los heraldos negros* (1918), although not free of modernist influence, was already unlike anything written before, and *Trilce* (1922), composed partly in prison, was a unique and almost incredible achievement for one from his background who had never even left Peru. Their combination of surreal imagery, typographical and linguistic innovation, fractured and crippled syntax, disgust with life as it is and longing for future solidarity, place them among the most painful, disorientating and moving of all modern poems. His contribution to subsequent poetry in Latin America is incalculable. He left for Paris in 1923, never to return, visited Russia and Spain during the Civil War. His *Poemas humanos* and great Spanish Civil War poems appeared only after his death. In 1931 he published *El tungsteno*, a socialist realist novel on the ravages of capitalism and imperialism in the mining sierras of Peru.

In Chile the most visible literary and intellectual movements were the Grupo de Montparnasse in the plastic arts, and the literary circle, 'Los Diez'. Pedro Prado (1886–1952), author of the autobiographical novel *Alsino* (1920), provided an old colonial residence in the city centre for the group, with which Eduardo Barrios and Gabriela Mistral were also associated. The Chilean mainstream, then as now, was realist, in an era which saw the rise of Recabarren and Alessandri, strikes in the dock and nitrate sectors between 1907 and 1918, and the political martyrdom of the poet Domingo Gómez Rojas (1896–1920). 'Los Diez' were in effect attempting to stem the leftist, objectivist tide. Writers like Augusto d'Halmar (1880–1950) and Eduardo Barrios had written early naturalist novels but diverged from the movement when the realist mode became implicitly political, as in the famous novel *El roto* (1920), by Joaquín Edwards Bello (1887–1968), about the Santiago lumpenproletariat.

Chile at this time saw the emergence of a succession of brilliant poets without equal in Spanish America. Vicente Huidobro (1893–1948) was possibly the most important Latin American poet of his era, though critics still disagree both about his excellence and his influence. His doctrine, *Creacionismo*, evolved from his 1914 manifesto, *Non serviam*, which rejected all reflectionist interpretations of art, which should not imitate reality but create it. Like Darío, he travelled from Santiago to Buenos Aires (in 1916), and from there to Paris and Madrid, winning converts and imitators on his way, although his militant insouciance was resented and his influence frequently denied, then and since. He joined Apollinaire's celebrated *Nord-Sud*, working with Reverdy, Tzara and Jacob. Much of his poetry was written in French, including the first important collection *Horizon carré* (1917), immediately remarkable for its bizarre associations, original images and astonishing ability to poeticize modernity and the new, as it were, on the wing. Part of *Altazor, o el viaje en paracaídas* (1931), perhaps his greatest achievement, reads: 'Here lies Altazor, skyhawk struck down by altitude./ Here lies Vicente, antipoet and sorcerer'. The remarkable *Mío Cid Campeador* (1929), half-novel, half-whimsical essay, was dedicated to Douglas Fairbanks, and Chaplin was another emblematic figure. Huidobro's influence on the Spanish ultraist movement after 1921 was considerable, and, later, on the Brazilian Concrete Poetry movement of the 1950s. The true nature and extent of his historical influence remains to be clarified.

Another Chilean who came to attention in the 1920s was later to become the best-known Latin American poet of all time, Pablo Neruda (1904–73). His *Veinte poemas de amor* appeared in 1924, as fresh and youthful as the poet himself, and have never lost their popularity. In 1927 he began six years in the Far East, undergoing existential anguish and a persistent nihilism which only the poetic act itself seemed able to assuage. So intuitive was his composition at this time, verging on a native surrealism, that readers felt they were witnessing the evolution of a soul in progress. Contact with Spain after 1933 produced a complete change towards an explicitly political humanist poetry, but we must leave him in Asia during the World Depression, aghast at the spectacle of alienated existence in the dark hours of late European colonialism.

Across the Andes, it is prose writers who have stood out and poetry has traditionally taken second place. Buenos Aires in the 1920s, at the height of its splendour and historical promise, was home to one of the richest artistic experiences of the period, attracting a succession of foreign celebrities such as Ortega y Gasset, Keyserling and Waldo Frank. Argentina was one of the richest nations in the world, and did not feel much like a victim of imperialism; its population was largely European and so, accordingly, was its culture; it appeared to have liquidated the age of caudillos and dictators sixty years before; although always super- ficially turbulent and polemical, its literary development since *Facundo* had been more organic and less convulsive than elsewhere; it had the most vigorous theatre in the continent and a convenient unifying nationalist myth in the gaucho of the pampas. It exercised enormous cultural patronage through great newspapers like *La Nación* and *La Prensa*, enjoyed a range of widely read cultural reviews, like *Nosotros*, and had a flourishing concert, exhibition and opera life. National culture here, it seemed, was not in need of discovery or exploration; as in the United States, the road ahead was clear.

The young vanguard writers collaborated on two now legendary magazines, *Proa* (1922–5) and *Martín Fierro* (1924–7), whose titles condense the two characteristic currents; an avant-garde, futuristic and cosmopolitan form, and a nativist or nationalistic content. Beyond was the overtly committed social realist stance of the Boedo writers. Many writers took up all three postures in turn. A founder of *Proa*, involved in most innovations in those days, after returning from Europe as an ultraist, was Jorge Luis Borges (1899–1986), whose homecoming was similar in its importance to Echeverría's in 1825. Argentina's great man of letters at the time was Lugones, but the young generation considered him an anachronism and carried out the inevitable paricide. A secret mentor of the young iconoclasts was Macedonio Fernández (1874– 1952), who wrote little, but smoked, played guitar and philosophized, and, like Xul Solar or the Spaniard Gómez de la Serna, impressed his youthful companions with the example of his lifestyle and mentality. His only significant publication in the 1920s was *No toda es vigilia la de los ojos abiertos* (1928), but as Borges, his direct heir, once said, he was really an 'oral writer' at a time when café life reigned supreme. Borges may have been prompted by Macedonio's bizarre whimsicality and maverick reclusion to retire from his own frenetic activity of the 1920s and become the eccentric of the late 30s and after. Curiously enough, although the literary packaging is experimental, Borges's 1920s works are primarily localist, *Fervor de Buenos Aires* (1923), *Luna de enfrente* (1925) and *Cuaderno de San Martín* (1929). Only later would he repudiate those early works and become the writer of *ficciones* and *inquisiciones* we know today; but even in the 1920s we see the peculiar mix of the fantastic and the real, the geometrical and the deconstructionist, which would make him the most influential Latin American writer of the century. His fake seriousness, his solemn undermining of solemnity and academicism, his rigorous assaults on philosophical rigour, are in reality a Latin American strategem for fending off cultural imperialism, though Borges himself would never agree to see it this way; but he is the cardinal figure for any assessment of the evolution of Latin American literature from a regional–cosmopolitan dichotomy to a persuasive universal identity, without whom no *nueva novela* writers such as García Márquez could have emerged. He was also a vital element in the success of *Sur* (1931–70), the cultural magazine edited by Victoria Ocampo (1890–1979).

Two other writers associated with *Proa* and *Martín Fierro* were Oliverio Girondo (1891–1965), the playful, provocative author of *Veinte poemas para ser leídos en el tranvía* (1922) and *Calcomanías* (1925), ranging from ultraism to surrealism; and Leopoldo Marechal (1900–70), later a catholic and a Peronist and the author of the gargantuan *Adán Buenosayres* (1948), but in the 1920s avant-garde author of *Los aguiluchos* (1922), *Días como flechas* (1926) and *Odas para el hombre y la mujer* (1929).

The apotheosis of Modernism in Brazil did not all come to pass in the seven days of the Semana de Arte Moderna in São Paulo in February 1922, as some histories suggest, but that event did bring into focus a cultural explosion whose range and depth is rivalled only by the contemporary Mexican experience. Its precursors were Da Cunha and Lobato, foreshadowing the new regionalism, and the cosmopolitan Graça Aranha, who returned to Brazil to lend support, resigning from the Academy in a famous gesture in 1924 when it turned its face against the new wave. Whereas Spanish America had already begun to achieve a cultural synthesis – albeit artificial and partly illusory – through its own earlier *modernismo*, Brazil still had that task to undertake. Participants in the great unifying Week were Mário de Andrade (1893–1945), Oswald de Andrade (1890–1954), Ronald de Carvalho (1893–1935), Guilherme de Almeida (1890–1969), Menotti del Picchia (b. 1892), Sérgio Milliet (1898–1966), Raul Bopp (b. 1898), Manuel Bandeira (1886–1968), Ribeyro Couto (1898–1963), the painters Di Cavalcanti, Malfatti, Amaral and Segall, the sculptor Brecheret, the composer Villa-Lobos and many others. It was not accidental that the scene was São Paulo, Brazil's New York in the tropics, the most futuristic city in Latin America: the event set out to explore and synthesize modern art and, simultaneously, to explore and synthesize Brazil.

As in Mexico, it was the plastic arts which opened Brazilian consciousness to the nature and meaning of modernity. Malfatti's famous 1917 exhibition and Brecheret's sculptures took young artists into the world of cubism, futurism and expressionism before they had even heard of Cézanne, and they, like Oswald de Andrade and Manuel Bandeira, who had travelled back from Europe shortly before the war, were viewed with the reverence once accorded to religious pilgrims on their return from some holy shrine. Or so said Mário de Andrade, by 1922 the central figure in the movement, remarkably so since he, unlike the others, had never left Brazil. He perceived with astonishing lucidity what Brazil's cultural condition really was and what had to be done about it. No Latin American thinker of the time was more far-sighted than this remarkable poet, novelist, critic, musicologist, folklorist and professional iconoclast; and no one did more than he to acclimatize humour as an essential ingredient of Latin American artistic culture, even if, as he remarked, it was often like 'dancing on top of a volcano'. Yet although he often conceded that *modernismo* was more a destructive than a constructive movement, he insisted that it was at bottom a spiritual response to the horrors of the Great War which had made him a poet. His first poems, *Há uma gôta de sangue em cada poema* (1917) were followed by *Paulicéia desvairada* (1922), about São Paulo, inspired by Verhaeren's *Villes tentaculaires*. Under the slogan 'no more schools', he set to 'saving Brazil, inventing the world'. His novel *Macunaíma* (1928) was Latin America's first example of what is now called 'magical realism', a mythological narrative, at once epic and humorous, in which the Brazilian culture hero of the title stitches together with his own travels and adventures the disparate pages of Brazil across time and space. The novel, which appeared two years before Asturias' *Leyendas de Guatemala* (1930), and five years before Carpentier's more timid *Ecue-Yamba-O* (1933), is a paradigm in its effort to fuse European avant-garde forms and Latin American primitivist contents, a gesture which only became possible in the 1920s, which presupposes the integration of all the arts and depends, above all, on an educated awareness of the potential for relating universal mythology and anthropology with localist folklore.

The Brazilian 1920s was a great age of manifestos. Mário himself began the trend with his foreword to the first number of *Klaxon*, a modernist magazine which appeared in São Paulo after the 1922 Semana. In 1924 Oswald de Andrade, whose contribution to the movement was hardly less substantial than Mário's issued the *Manifesto Pau-Brasil*, inspired by Tarsila do Amaral's paintings, calling for fresh, spontaneous art 'seen through free eyes', executed with the agility of jungle monkeys and intended, like Brazil-wood itself, for export only. Like Mário, Oswald urged an end to academies and schools, declared the cinema the most relevant of the arts, and asserted that 'the whole of the present is to be found in the newspapers'. In 1928 he published the famous *Manifesto Antropofágico*, inspired by Tarsila's *Abaporu*, and, in addition to the famous 'Tupi or not tupi, that is the question' – a frivolous approach to nativism inconceivable in Mexico or Peru at the time – declared that the new movement would cannibalize European culture and undertake the permanent transformation of 'taboo into totem', revealing how important was Freud's role and that of surrealism in allowing Latin Americans from this time to accept their own native 'barbarism'.

Whilst the two terrible twins (who were not related) were translating Brazilian culture into European and vice versa (the import–export business, as Oswald saw it), other intellectuals were attending to the dialogue between the regions and the Rio-São Paulo axis, at the moment where the regional and the national at last became definitively superimposed. In 1926 Gilberto Freyre announced his historic *Manifesto Regionalista*, and in 1929 the ultra-nationalist *Manifesto Nheengaçu Verde Amarelo* was launched, denoting with its name the colours of the Brazilian flag. Though considering such movements retrograde, Mário de Andrade later confessed that he and the other modernists had, in the last analysis, been 'abstentionist', since politics was the very foundation of modernity. Rather than the first of the new, as they had imagined, they were the last of the old, 'children of a moribund civilization'. Perhaps he was unduly hard on himself: Modernism, truly anti-academicist, had effected the first authentic fusions of Brazilian and European forms and contents, and achieved artistic dialogue between erudite and popular culture, as did Asturias, Borges, Carpentier, Vallejo, Neruda and Guillén in Spanish America. However, the Brazilian movement also strayed closer to mere exoticism than most Spanish American versions, and there are times when Mário and Oswald, Villa-Lobos and Cavalcanti resemble sympathetic and enlightened foreigners gazing at their country.

Nevertheless, the impact on Brazilian poetry and language was remarkable. All literary conventions were abolished: beauty, tranquility and sentiment gave way to dissociation, violence and directness. Most resolutely anti-poetical of all was Oswald de Andrade, whose *Pau-Brasil* (1925) and *Caderno do aluno de poesia Oswald de Andrade* (1927), once routinely dismissed by critics, now appear revolutionary. Manuel Bandeira spent the First World War in Zurich, like Borges, Tzara, Joyce and Lenin, and remains the most generally admired, if not the most typical of the *modernista* poets. His *Carnaval* (1919) foreshadowed its moods and attitudes, both affectionate and ironic, to national culture. He became increasingly realist and anti-poetical by the 1930s. Ronald de Carvalho did not live long enough to become a truly great poet (dying in 1935 aged 42), but was well respected, after his early *Poemas e sonetos* (1919), *Epigramas irônicos e sentimentais* (1922) and *Toda a América* (1926). He was more familiar with Spanish America than any other Brazilian writer of the period. Raul Bopp was the author of the uncompromisingly primitivist *Cobra Norato* (1931), the result of a visit by the writer, a native of Rio Grande do Sul, to the Amazon jungle. The circle of Brazilian regional culture, already traced by Villa-Lobos in music, was now effectively complete in literature as well, after Mário's cinematographic novel and Bopp's symphonic poem. Brazil, like Latin America as a whole by 1930, was now more inside the twentieth century than outside it. Modernity, for good or ill, had been achieved.

A NOTE ON THE EARLY YEARS OF THE CINEMA

The first thirty years of the century coincided with the early years of the most modern and visual of all the arts, the cinema. It was the age of the silent movie. The birth of a new art form gave Latin America the opportunity to get in at the beginning, and the region quite quickly developed thriving national industries and one of the largest audiences in the world. Films by the Lumière brothers had appeared in Mexico City, Havana, Buenos Aires and Rio only months after the first showings in Paris in 1895, the Mexican poet Luis Urbina lamenting, despite his bedazzlement, that the new invention lacked colour and sound. Newsreels, *actualidades,* were inevitably predominant in the first twenty years to 1914, with views of European and South American capitals and state ceremonial occasions typical of the earliest period. Some historical footage from the continent, such as the hazy scenes of the Spanish American War or the arrival of Madero in Mexico City, is familiar to all students of the cinema's pioneering period. One of the earliest examples of all was a film of brief scenes (*vistas*) of Guanabara Bay, shot appropriately from on board the French liner *Brésil* as she steamed into Rio in July 1898. It was France, indeed, which was most closely associated with the early production and distribution in Latin America. The Pathé Company dominated the foreign share of the market up to 1914, with branches in Rio, Mexico City, Buenos Aires and Havana. The First World War, however, paralysed the efforts of European filmmakers. After 1914 the United States came to control some 95 per cent of the Latin American market – with profound long-term consequences for Latin American cultural development.

In the pre-war period the leading republics had each begun to produce the occasional feature picture. The first man in Mexico to make a primitive fiction film was Salvador Toscano Barragán (1872–1947), in 1898, with the first of many film versions of that nineteenth-century romantic staple, *Don Juan Tenorio.* In 1908 Felipe de Jesús Haro produced the first Mexican scripted feature, *El grito de Dolores*; in 1910 a second feature, *El suplicio de Cuauhtémoc,* appeared. In Argentina, too, the first feature film was on a nineteenth-century historical topic, *El fusilamiento de Dorrego* (1908), directed by an Italian, Max Gallo, who had originally gone to Buenos Aires, ironically enough, to stage operas. In 1915 there was violent controversy in the Argentine capital when two films appeared on the Rosas era, one from Hollywood entitled *El capitán Alvarez o bajo la tiranía de Rosas,* which gave the American ambassador at the time a grotesquely distorted leading role, and the other Max Glucksmann's *Mariano Moreno o la Revolución de Mayo.* This juxtaposition gave rise to one of the earliest examples of Latin American protest against the 'Hollywood' version of the history of the southern republics. The titles of both films reveal that the cinema was still very much immersed in the conventions of romantic theatre, a concept of drama which was itself at least seventy years out of date. Needless to say, the temptations of melodrama were accentuated by the absence of language from the movies, but there is little doubt that this technical limitation had stylistic and even thematic implications which encouraged the popularity of exotic themes in general, and in particular those involving 'Latin' passion. Adolfo Urzúa Rozas produced the first feature in Chile: *Manuel Rodríguez* (1910). The first true Brazilian feature film, characteristically, was sociological rather than historical in orientation. *Nhô Anastácio chegou de viagem* (1908) was about a *caipira*, or yokel, visiting Rio for the first time. A few years later in Argentina, another rural film, *Nobleza gaucha* (1916), by Martínez y Gunche Cía, achieved that country's greatest film success of the era. In Chile Latin America's first woman film-maker, Gabriela Bussenius, produced *La agonía de Arauco* (1917), about the exploitation of the Indians by ruthless capitalists. In 1908, the same year as *Nhô Anastácio*, *Os estranguladores* appeared in Brazil, the first of many Latin American films of the era to portray 'sensational' crimes on the North American model. The leading exponents in Brazil were the Botelho brothers. In Chile in 1916, the Argentinian Salvador Giambastiani produced his controversial picture, *La baraja de la muerte*, about a local society murder case, whilst in Mexico in 1919, the great pioneer Enrique Rosas and the Alva brothers produced *La banda del automóvil gris*, a gangster film generally recognized as the outstanding Mexican production of the silent era.

The Brazilian case was perhaps the most interesting at this time, since it is there that the most vigorous autochthonous cinema developed. In Brazil also one can see most clearly the cinema's tendency to reproduce, in an extraordinarily condensed and foreshortened time-scale, the historical development of the novel in the national period. Many of the early Brazilian films, indeed, were actually based on novels, especially such popular romantic works as Taunay's *Inocência* (1914) and Alencar's *A viuvinha* (1914), *Iracema* (1917), *Ubirajara* (1919), all transferred to the screen by Luís de Barros. Alencar's best-known work, *O guarani* was filmed by Antônio Botelho in 1920. Shortly after, films based on naturalist works like Azevedo's *O mulato* appeared, followed by similar social dramas such as *Exemplo regenerador* (1919), *Perversidade* (1921), *A culpa dos outros* (1922), and the masterpiece *Fragmentos de vida* (1929), all by the Italian immigrant Gilberto Rossi and his collaborator José Medina. The greatest Brazilian film-maker of the era, however, Humberto Mauro (1897–1983), from Minas Gerais, was, like Portinari, Lins do Rêgo or Villa-Lobos (with whom he worked on *O descobrimento do Brasil*), one of the great Brazilian artistic masters of the era and the principal forerunner of critical realism in the Brazilian cinema. He directed a number of films, from *Valadião, o cratera* (1925), on banditry in Minas, through *Tesouro perdido* (1926) and *Sangue mineiro* (1930), to his masterpiece, the classic *Ganga bruta* (1933), a stunning synthesis of expressionist, lyrical romantic and documentary realist techniques not dissimilar to Graciliano Ramos's later novel *Angústia* (1936). In 1934 Mauro produced the rather more sentimental *Favela dos meus amores*, thereafter to become enveloped, like other Brazilian and Mexican artists of the era, in bureaucratic diversions. Other notable Brazilian films of the period included *São Paulo: sinfonia de uma metrópole* (1929), by Adalberto Kemeny and Rodolfo Lustig, and Mário Peixoto's now legendary avant-garde silent movie *Limite* (1929), Brazil's equivalent to *Un chien andalou*, on the conditionings which limit human freedom.

It was in the 1920s that the manufacture and exhibition of moving pictures became the United States' largest industry. The United Artists Corporation, founded in 1919, undertook an aggressive marketing penetration in Latin America.[23] Wherever the film went, trade followed; and much else besides. Film magazines proliferated and Sunday supplements were full of news and pictures of Hollywood stars. Hispanic cultural forms like the *zarzuela* or the bullfight appeared suddenly old-fashioned and fell into decline, as the North Americanization of Latin American culture and misrepresentation of Latin American realities went on apace. The demonstration effect began to stir even the smallest towns and villages, beginning – it was said – with the imitation of crimes and sexual mores seen in movies from the United States.

Nowhere was this impact more dramatic, nor more resented, than in Mexico. There, the pre-1910 tradition of historical film dramas was continued during the Revolution. In 1914 an important documentary about the *zapatistas*, *Sangre hermana*, was widely exhibited, and in 1916 a Yucatecan company produced *1810 o los libertadores de México*, the country's first full-length film. As in Brazil, many popular nineteenth-century novels were filmed: in 1918 alone, for example, the romantic classics *María* and *Tabaré*, and the naturalistic *Santa*, were all filmed, and by the late 1930s many of Mexico's best-known novels had been turned into film scripts. But in the early 1920s, while Mexico was producing perhaps ten movies a year, Hollywood's annual output of five hundred features was saturating the international market and, quite incidentally but all the more insultingly, routinely purveying an image of the Mexican either as 'greaser' or as a dangerously uncontrollable and wild-eyed

---

[23] See G. S. de Usabel, *The high noon of American films in Latin America* (Ann Arbor, Mich., 1982) for a comprehensive analysis.

revolutionary. (When talking pictures arrived, further insult was added to injury when Mexican characters were heard speaking in accents from Madrid or Buenos Aires.) It was at this point that a Mexican self-image, equally caricaturesque, began to be built in opposition to such external characterizations. The Mexican revolutionary governments of the 1920s, although frequently responding to insults with censorship and expropriation, shared little of the awareness of Lenin and Lunacharsky of the cinema's political potential. The key film-maker of the era was, in fact, the rather stolid Miguel Contreras Torres, an ex-soldier who did perceive the importance of building a new historical tradition based on revolutionary myths, with films such as *El sueño del caporal* (1922), *De raza azteca* (1922), *Fulguración de la raza* (1922), *Almas tropicales* (1923), or *Atavismo* (1923). All of them were suffused by a rather double-edged patriotic fervour, with a unifying impulse which anticipated the great nationalist cinema of the 1930s in Mexico. Other leading film-makers were Jorge and Carlos Stahl, who began a series of works with *La linterna de Diógenes* in 1925. Gamboa's *Santa*, already filmed in 1918, became the first talkie in 1931, starring Lupita Tovar as the country girl who becomes a city prostitute, and a Mexican myth. Meanwhile Mexican actors like Antonio Moreno, Ramón Novarro and, above all, Dolores del Río, were beginning to star in Hollywood movies in heart-throb roles in the era of Valentino and *El Zorro*. In contrast, Eisenstein arrived in 1930 to begin *¡Que viva México!*. His obsessively hieratic and meticulous 'expressive realist' style had a lasting impact on Mexican cinema, and was appropriated by populist film-makers such as Emilio 'El Indio' Fernández and his collaborator, the great cameraman Gabriel Figueroa, to communicate a dramatic 'national essence' in a succession of monumental movies.[24]

As in Brazil, it was in 1933 that Mexican cinema began to find its defining national style. Arcady Boytler's *La mujer del puerto*, based on a Maupassant story and similar in many regards to Mauro's *Ganga bruta*, was the first truly outstanding Mexican cinematographic production. Even more important historically, however, was Fernando de Fuentes's *El compadre Mendoza*, released in the same year, a subtle satire on the way in which the landowning class had managed to survive the Revolution and build new alliances, a perspective not altogether dissimilar to that of the novelist Martín Luis Guzmán and implicitly critical of the post-revolutionary order. With already characteristic subtlety, the govern-

[24] See J. Ayala Blanco, *La aventura del cine mexicano* (3rd edn, Mexico, D.F., 1985), 34–42.

ment was moved to begin to subsidise this new style of cinema. In 1934 Zinnemann's *Redes* and Navarro's *Janitzio*, two scripted fictionalized documentaries, were financed by the Ministry of Education, with music by Chávez and Revueltas, the film technique itself a mixture of Eisenstein, Murnau and Flaherty, and with Emilio Fernández in the cast. In 1935 the Cárdenas government subsidized Fernando de Fuentes himself, and he produced the serious, disillusioned and again implicitly condemnatory *¡Vámonos con Pancho Villa!*. Incongruously yet appropri- ately enough, this was followed in 1936 by his celebrated *Allá en el Rancho Grande*, starring North America's favourite Mexican Tito Guízar, a film that was picturesque, melodramatic and self-indulgent, but the solution to many nationalist contradictions and the prototype of many essentially conservative *comedias rancheras* to come: the consecration of the Mexican as *mariachi* for the tourist trade, both to attract foreign visitors and to export a new brand of Latin movies to the rest of the continent.

CONCLUSION

In retrospect, it is easy to see that the 1920s and early 1930s, the age of the avant-garde and of modern art, were less a beginning than an end, and not only in Latin America. Although the artistic expression of the period shocked both the complacent bourgeoisie and the man in the street – himself a 'modern' phenomenon – and appeared to confront them with something either entirely new or threateningly alien, it was in reality the climactic moment of Western development since the Renaissance. Modernity was not, despite appearances, a new phase – one which might, implicitly, last for ever ('this is it', 'we've arrived') – but the end of the previous one, not a departure but a climax, a finale. Since that moment we have not known exactly where we are going, or what to say about it, which is why terms like post-modern have been coined, to indicate perhaps the current sense of a vision lost, or rather of an illusion recognized.

In the 1930s, following the slump, when fascism in Europe rose to challenge communism and culminated in the Second World War, the avant-garde itself rapidly lost momentum and gave way to movements dominated by the socialist realist doctrine: objectivist, documentary and sociological. In Spanish America, as a result, and by way of illustration, the only universally acknowledged historic narrative of the 1930s was Icaza's *Huasipungo*. This was an age of politics, not of poetry.

It was during the inter-war period, though most acutely up to 1930, that Latin American culture became at once more complicated and more coherent than ever before. Leading artists and major cities at last caught up with European trends, modes and models at precisely the moment when the United States, their continental neighbour, rose to economic, cultural and eventually political supremacy. Latin America became 'American' as it became modern, but its new American identity was a continental one which at once unified the Latin American nations themselves as never before, yet also incorporated concepts which aligned the new national cultures with United States patterns. In that sense, paradoxically, Latin America became truly modern earlier than the great European nations, whilst, of course, also remaining overwhelmingly underdeveloped. The dramatic tension and contrast determined by such historical contradictions began to give Latin American artists, who before the First World War had found it so difficult to *see* even their own national realities, a vision at once cosmopolitan, continental and national which has characterized Latin American art since that time. Painters like Rivera, Torres García or Portinari, musicians like Chávez and Villa-Lobos, architects like Costa, Niemeyer and Villanueva, novelists and poets like Vallejo, Huidobro, Mário de Andrade, Borges, Carpentier, Asturias and Neruda, were able, in the age of mass culture, to use the dynamic relationship between modern city and 'traditional' – slower moving – countryside, between their own American reality and European models, to develop distinctive forms of art which rank with the most important of the century.

Part Two

3

NARRATIVE SINCE *c.* 1920

INTRODUCTION

There are many ways in which one can try to encapsulate the process of Latin American fiction, but no point of departure is ultimately more persuasive, given the material conditions of Latin America's historical experience, than the distinction between an Americanist and a 'universalist', or 'cosmopolitan', orientation. The Americanist impulse can be traced from the earliest days of Latin American independence, when it took on both a nationalist and an anti-colonial ideology and rhetoric. The cosmopolitan impulse, equally strong, corresponds to a permanent desire to know and understand the global culture within which and against which the Latin American nations have had to define themselves. At the present time, in an era of 'pluralism', when even the existence of a recognizable and reasonably homogeneous 'Latin American' entity is questioned, such generalizations are not infrequently challenged, but this distinction remains profoundly persuasive as a conceptual tool. It applies within and between periods, and it applies within and between the forms and contents of literary works. To explain why one tendency or the other predominates at any particular time is not easy, but the phenomena themselves are not difficult to identify.

Similarly, although there is little agreement among critics and historians as to the detailed periodization of Latin American narrative in the twentieth century, the task inevitably becomes easier the more broadly the picture is focused. For the purposes of this history within a history, therefore, it seems appropriate to identify two literary eras, separated by the Second World War. The first, from approximately 1915 to 1945, the period between the two world wars, is that of the Latin American social novel (extending the earlier traditions of *costumbrismo, realismo* and *natura-*

lismo, and embracing *regionalismo,* the *novela de la tierra, indigenismo* and other similar trends). Within this period, 1930 sees a transitional moment, when patterns and options established in the 1920s become temporarily hardened as the social congeals into the political and the merely playful slides into the fantastic and the metaphysical. The second era, from the late 1940s to the present, is the age of the Latin American 'New Novel' (extending the discoveries of the international avant-garde, including Anglo-American 'Modernism', and incorporating *realismo mágico, literatura fantástica* and other experimental currents). Unmistakable signs of the 'New Novel' can be detected as early as the 1920s (Mário de Andrade, Asturias, Carpentier, Borges), whilst respectable versions of the social realist novel continue to be written to the present day. Fusions and hybridizations are equally frequent. In general, however, the historical dividing line – the mid-forties – is quite clear both in Spanish America and in Brazil.

The realist mode had been manifested in historical novels and in what critics call *costumbrista* fiction during the romantic period (the early and middle decades of the nineteenth century) and in naturalism à la Zola after the 1880s. In neither case was there any great sense of a continental dimension in the works produced. On the contrary, in the first period – after a brief Americanist moment following independence – the essential thrust in most countries was national, if not nationalist, and from the 1870s the rather scientistic and positivistic naturalist movement viewed national problems from an essentially objective, although progressive universal perspective – an internationalism without politics, so to speak. Paradoxically, it was Darío's *modernista* movement, usually accused of 'cosmopolitanism' and of psychological enslavement to France, which transformed the linguistic culture of Spanish America (the Brazilian case was somewhat different) and gave it a unifying cultural identity which has persisted until the present time. It was this sense of identity which, after the humiliation of Spain in 1898 and the affirmation of Mexican nationalism after 1917, allowed the social realists of the 1920s to produce works which may not have attained 'universality' but which unmistakably offered versions of the national and the continental combined in unified literary discourses and images. (The same phenomenon would be seen in Brazil in the 1930s.) This achievement, evidently the product of important philosophical and ideological shifts, could not of course have come about without equally important shifts in the class character of those who wrote and those who read fiction, not to mention their respective attitudes to those of their compatriots who could do neither but who were increasingly the subject matter of those works.

Much of the momentum was external. Latin America's integration into the world economic system after 1870 had not only brought about significant alterations in the continent's economic, social and political condition but had also brought the region closer to the attention of Europe and North America than at any time since the independence era; and outsiders invariably saw Latin Americans, as they do to this day, as one large international group of cultures rather than as the separate cluster of nationalities which Latin Americans tend themselves to perceive. The very concept of 'Latin' America – a French invention, for reasons which are obvious – was only fully asserted in the early years of the twentieth century, at a time when so many members of the Latin American ruling class were spending long sojourns in the French capital, with occasional sorties to Madrid. Once Spain's gender had changed after 1898 – from patriarchal conqueror and oppressor to defeated mother country – it became possible to view cultural questions rather more coolly and the occasional upsurges of 'Hispanidad' were usually temporary symptoms of resistance to French culture rather than the conservative enthusiasms they seemed at first sight to signify.

Spain's historic surrender and expulsion had liberated Cuba and Puerto Rico, and to that extent was welcomed in the sub-continent. Certainly it removed a heavy emotional burden from the Spanish American psychology, and matters were in a rather brutal way simplified when the United States moved to fill Spain's traditional role as imperialist oppressor. The 'Hispanic' became accessible again as Spain (and, for Brazil, Portugal) now represented Latin America's European source of tradition and history (Iberian America), whilst France continued to act as a more modern and plural version (Latin America) and the United States stepped in to provide a much more genuinely alien, genuinely external enemy, both objectively and subjectively (the Other America rather than Pan-America). The way was clear for Spanish Americans to search anew for their cultural identity, as they had between about 1780 and 1830, and as the Spaniards were already doing through the introspective meditations of the Generation of 1898. The greatest precursor of this quest was undoubtedly the Cuban revolutionary poet José Martí (1853–1895), the 'Apostle' (of Cuban independence, obviously, but also of cultural nationalism and, above all, of the cultural unity of 'Our America').

The most influential expression of such a quest, however, was that

of José Enrique Rodó (1871–1917), whose essay *Ariel* (1900), elitist
and Hellenistic as it was, nevertheless questioned the cultural value of
North American civilization almost at the very moment that the United
States began its irresistible rise, first to hemispheric, then global
supremacy. Rodó's rhetoric influenced a whole generation of Spanish
American students and intellectuals and acted as a unifying force which
put an end to Positivism and ranged the whole of Latin America as one
cultural and spiritual entity against the Anglo-Saxon colossus of the
north. Over the next two decades numerous other thinkers developed
these themes in an increasingly less abstract way than had Rodó, and
although it would be many years before the force of nineteenth-century
positivism and biologism – with their racial interpretations of Latin
American identity – were finally swept aside, the ideological impact of
the social sciences and the political impact of the embryonic workers'
movements exerted an increasing influence on the democratic tenor of
narrative itself.

The Spanish American independence centenaries clustered around
1910, coinciding in Mexico with the start of the Revolution, provided
the clearest possible focus for such debates, and it became apparent as
each new anniversary was celebrated that nationalist affirmation was being asserted against a continental dimension, each national identity
viewed within a family context (Brazil, which had declared its independence in 1822, of course being the most problematical member of such a
family group). Especially noteworthy was the work by the great Argentine literary historian Ricardo Rojas, *La restauración nacionalista* (1910),
but there were numerous other works in the same vein such as Manuel
Ugarte's *El porvenir de América Latina* (1910) and Francisco García Calderón's *Les Démocraties latines de l'Amérique* (1912). More negative positivist-
inspired works such as Alcides Arguedas's *Pueblo enfermo* (1909), whilst
also influential, were gradually losing their conviction, and Spengler's
Decline of the West (1918), coinciding with the end of a futile war in
Europe, effectively liquidated the problem of Latin America's racial inferiority and cultural backwardness almost at a stroke – at least in theory.
Henceforth, the principal problems to be confronted by Latin American
fiction, which had never had to consider the historically specific moral
dilemmas which consumed the nineteenth-century European 'realist'
novel, were social, economic and political in character, not biological and
psychological. Thus within the general perspectives of nationalism and
Americanism, the avenues of anti-imperialism, socialism and even com-

munism began to open up, though communist ideology and politics would only become both widely attractive and apparently feasible after 1945 when Latin American writers became capable of also attaining 'universality'.

REGIONALISM: LATIN AMERICAN NARRATIVE BETWEEN THE WARS

The story of the Latin American novel in the early decades of the twentieth century appears, in retrospect, as the story of a mapping, a narrative of fields, paths and horizons, in which knowledge, progress and development were seemingly no longer problematical, the only frontier the line between present and future, the known and the knowable, the developed and the as yet undeveloped. They were often written by men and women who originated in the provinces and moved to their national capital. And if, as frequently occurred, such novels and stories were records of failures, they tended to be confirmed only on the last page as if to emphasize their imminent resolution. They abound with images of open doors and open books, deeds waiting to be done and histories waiting to be written.

The classic expression of a savage, untamed America is to be found in the works of the Uruguayan Horacio Quiroga (1878–1937). His short stories, bridging the gulf between *modernismo* and *telurismo*, between Poe, Kipling and Conrad, provided an image of the struggle of man against nature and – though to a lesser extent – against his fellow man which fused the gothic and the epic, fantasy and realism, in a mix which foreshadowed not only his more direct successors in the 1920s and 1930s but also the so-called 'magical realists' of later generations. Quiroga, whose own life was marked by a succession of tragedies, had visited Paris at the height of *modernismo* at the turn of the century, but had been unable to 'triumph' there, felt out of place and exiled himself to Misiones, the wild frontier area in northern Argentina. His tales of horror and savagery, in such collections as *Cuentos de amor, de locura y de muerte* (1917), *Cuentos de la selva* (1918), *El salvaje* (1920), *Anaconda* (1921), *El desierto* (1924) and *Los desterrados* (1926), are more natural than social, more individual than collective, but provide the earliest and most authoritative example of a modernization of the genre which opened up entirely new paths in the Latin American short story and in fiction as a whole.

The best known of all Latin American novels about the jungle is *La vorágine* (1924) by the Colombian writer José Eustasio Rivera (1888–1928), whose only other major work was a collection of *modernista* poems entitled – somewhat ironically in view of the tenor of his later novel – *Tierra de promisión* (1921). *La vorágine* is a complex and heterogeneous work, which critics have traditionally called contradictory, though the passage of time has shown that its contradictions were only too well understood by the author and are those of Latin America itself (or, rather, its intellectuals), torn between the 'backward', autochthonous world of primitive nature and the apparently unattainable models of metropolitan development. Rivera's hero Arturo Cova is an anachronistic romantic idealist ('Ah, jungle, mistress of silence, mother of solitude and mist! What evil spirit left me a prisoner in your green dungeons?'), who feels the call of a wild nature of which he has no knowledge or understanding, in an age of capitalist development. His absurd, overblown rhetoric, like a Latin popular song of betrayal and despair, pervades the entire narrative ('Before I fell in love with any woman, I gambled my heart with Destiny and it was won by Violence'); but it soon becomes clear that the desired space of Cova's imagination has already been occupied by the most brutal realities, to which he is fatally slow to adapt. The vortex of the title, which represents the heart of darkness, the vast Amazon forest, is itself a partly romantic concept (the wilds of nature), but one negated by the realities of the Darwinian struggle for survival in a jungle conceived as a barbarous world of free competition in the age of primitive accumulation. Rivera put his experience as a boundary commissioner for the Colombian government to good effect and produced a novel whose denunciation of the brutal labour practices on the rubber plantations caused a national outcry after the book's publication. His insights showed the land as not merely a remote and mysterious natural landscape but as an economic and political arena, the workers as real people rather than biological impulses, and woman as a creature potentially equal to the males who made the grand gestures of history and wrote the idealized novels. The last line of *La vorágine* is possibly the most quoted in Latin American literature: 'Los devoró la selva!' ('The jungle devoured them.')[1]

There is a traditional (primordial?) kind of logic in beginning with those writers who evoked the mystery and romance – or horror – of the American forests. But few critics would dispute that the true point of departure of

---

[1] All translations are the author's unless otherwise noted. For this reason it has not been thought appropriate or necessary to reference the – very brief – quotations from the texts themselves.

twentieth-century narrative is the so-called 'Novel of the Mexican Revolution', a fictional sub-genre which inaugurates the new wave of social and regionalist fiction of the 1920s, just as the Mexican Revolution itself set the political agenda for much of Latin America after 1917. *Los de abajo* by Mariano Azuela (1872–1952) was the first important novel of the Mexican Revolution and, indeed, the greatest of them all. Its implicit project – political liberation opening the path to modernity – although frustrated, dominated the entire 'regionalist' wave of the 1920s and the 1930s. (Azuela had in fact also composed the very first narrative of the Revolution itself in 1911, with *Andrés Pérez, maderista,* an embittered fictional account of his own early experiences in the conflict.) Although written and serialized in 1915 while the Revolution was still under way, *Los de abajo* was not widely read or acknowledged until 1925, at precisely the moment where other major social novels were coming to critical attention across the Latin American continent.

Ironically enough, Azuela never truly understood the real political issues at stake in the Revolution but he viewed it with a sincere and critical eye. He did not pretend to narrate from the peasant point of view and was careful only to enter the consciousness of middle-class characters like himself; still his title emphasized that the peasant was the principal protagonist of the novel as he was of a historical rebellion expropriated by the rising agrarian and industrial middle sectors. The narrative shows the brief triumph of the primitive revolutionaries – 'A whirlwind of dust, swirling along the highway, suddenly broke into violent hazy masses, swelling chests, tangled manes, dilated nostrils, wild eyes, flying legs and pounding hoofs. Bronze-faced men, with ivory teeth and flashing eyes, brandished rifles or held them across their saddles' – and their tragic defeat – 'At the foot of the carved rock face, huge and sumptuous as the portico of an old cathedral, Demetrio Macías, his eyes fixed in an eternal gaze, keeps on pointing with the barrel of his gun.' Through the intense, almost cinematographic dynamism of its prose, the candid acknowledgment of the gulf between city and country, mental and manual labour, intellectuals and peasants, *Los de abajo* was in many respects more 'modern' than many of the regionalist narratives which followed it in subsequent decades. However, in later life Azuela himself, although a prolific novelist, never came close to matching, at leisure, what he had achieved in the heat of battle.

Azuela's principal literary competitor was Martín Luis Guzmán (1887–1976), a general's son who joined the revolution and sided, like Azuela, with Pancho Villa. *El águila y la serpiente* (1926) is a compelling documentary narrative inspired by Guzmán's personal experience of the leading protagonists of the insurrection. His unforgettable portraits have given permanent shape to the historical image of the conflict. Villa approximated most closely to the Mexican national self-conception at the time, and his legendary exploits dominate the fiction of the Revolution. Zapata's more mythical, Indian presence was slower to evolve, and the only major novel to convey his story was *Tierra* (1932) by Gregorio López y Fuentes (1891–1966), which thereby helped to mould the tragic persona of another national hero ('The news, like a hungry dog, goes diligently from door to door. It is passed on in whispers, in huddled groups, by men at the plough and women at the well. He has been seen. So it's true, he's not dead . . . ').

If the jungle provides the most dramatic and intense version of the natural world which is the context of American social and economic reality, the Indian is America's original autochthonous inhabitant. Azuela's protagonist, Demetrio Macías, is himself a 'full-blooded Indian' whose endeavour is, however, precisely to become something more than a mere extension of the landscape. Nineteenth-century literature had seen numerous noble but exotic savages safely consigned to the forests of the past, most notably Alencar's *O Guarani* (Brazil, 1857), Mera's *Cumandá* (Ecuador, 1879) and Zorilla's *Tabaré* (Uruguay, 1879). These were romantic, 'Indianist' works. Even the best known novel about the Indians of the Andean sierras and the acknowledged precursor of twentieth-century 'Indigenism', Clorinda Matto de Turner's *Aves sin nido* (Peru, 1889), betrays through its cloying title the fact that the work remained profoundly romantic despite its militant intentions.

The most important work of early twentieth-century *indigenismo* is *Raza de bronce* (1919), by the Bolivian Alcides Arguedas (1879–1946), whose pathbreaking status seems all the more extraordinary when it is recalled that an early version entitled *Wata Wara* appeared in 1904, five years before his apocalyptic socio-historical essay *Pueblo enfermo*. As a member of a powerful landowning family from the Bolivian *altiplano* who was also an assiduous traveller to Paris, Arguedas registered in his novel the horrifying brutality on Bolivian haciéndas, which nevertheless continued up to the Revolution of 1952 (and even longer in Peru). Like Quiroga and Rivera, Arguedas had taken part in the *modernista* movement and was now recanting the errors of his own escapist past. Thus *Raza de bronce* not only conveyed the plight of the *pongos* but also satirised the merely self-indulgent efforts by so many 'modernist' writers to exalt Latin American landscapes. His own striking descriptions of the unforgettable panoramas of the Bolivian Andes were based on extensive personal experience. The combination provided one of the earliest examples of the portrayal of the Indians as 'beggars on golden stools'.

This historical moment also saw the golden age of Latin American equivalents of the 'western': tales of Mexican *vaqueros,* Venezuelan *llaneros,* Chilean *huasos,* Argentine, Uruguayan and Brazilian *gauchos.* The man on horseback is an ambivalent but uniquely potent figure in Hispanic culture, given the long tradition of knight errantry and aristocracy, crusades and conquests, hunting and cattle herding, not to mention more elemental associations between taming and mounting horses and the physical domination of nature and even of women. The horse, in other words, focuses a complex network of symbols – power over the land, social status and privileged mobility – whose force is far from spent.

In 1926 yet another former *modernista,* the Argentine landowner Ricardo Güiraldes (1885–1927), who, like Arguedas, had spent much of his life in Paris, published what for many critics is the greatest regionalist work of the century, *Don Segundo Sombra.* Alone among the exalted works of the period, this bittersweet novel about the gaucho spirit of the pampas looks back unashamedly to the golden past rather than the beckoning future, to a time when there was no immigration and little urbanization, when the pampa was unfenced and the gauchos rode free like knights of the purple plain (to interphrase W. H. Hudson and Zane Grey). Since the novel's nostalgic vision communicates the essential structure of feeling of Güiraldes's entire oligarchical generation, it is not surprising that this great land of the future should have become the land that never was. The novel is narrated through a screen of nostalgia, artfully combining the Parisian forms of symbolism and impressionism with the epic spontaneity of life on the endless pampas. The story is told by Fabio Cáceres, a once poor and illegitimate country boy who through the whim of fate is educated by a legendary gaucho figure, the eponymous Don Segundo, from the age of fourteen to twenty-one, until he discovers, like Argentina, that he is, after all, heir to great wealth and responsibility (and, accordingly, not really illegitimate at all). He resigns himself to his new station but longs for the life he has lost with Don Segundo, one of the first heroes in the Americas to ride off into a cosmic twilight in the last scene of the text. The novel gazes back on spontaneity from reluctant immobility, innocence from knowingness, beginnings from a premonition of the end (Güiraldes died soon after its publication), and its conclusion is suitably elegiac: 'Concentrating my will on carrying out the smallest acts, I turned my horse and, slowly, rode back to the houses. I went as one whose life-blood was ebbing away.' The work became an instant classic, fit for every schoolboy, and far less discouraging ideologically than José Hernández's more sober epic poem *Martín Fierro* (1872) a half century before. To that extent it may be considered one of the most troubling art works in Latin American history.

In 1929 the Venezuelan Rómulo Gallegos (1884–1969) produced what seemed to be exactly the novel Latin American fiction had been crying out for in that new era of progress and enterprise after the First World War: *Doña Bárbara*. Güiraldes had exalted stoicism and fatalism in the face of Life, since History was no more than illusion. The trail was for riding, life being a river that flows inexorably into the sea of death, but the horizon for Don Segundo and Fabio, rather like Fitzgerald's *The Great Gatsby* from the same era, is a mere pampa mirage. Not so for the Venezuelan, who wrote about his own country's plains, the *llanos* or savannahs. Although not remotely as sophisticated as Güiraldes, with his Paris-constructed aesthetic consciousness, Gallegos must still be counted the greatest regionalist novelist in Spanish America taking his oeuvre as a whole. Güiraldes longed for the past, so he mendaciously idealized one of the working classes, Don Segundo Sombra (whose description was based on one of the family's hired hands). Gallegos, from the aspiring middle classes, looked to the future, so the hero of *Doña Bárbara* is a compromise figure, a member of the ruling landowning class but invested with the characteristics of the rising professional and industrial bourgeoisie and also capable of inspiring the masses through his personal charisma and educating them through his enlightened knowledge and passion for 'cultivation'.

Doña Bárbara's characterization was wooden and its action somewhat stiffly narrated, but the novel's importance lies in its breadth of vision and the infinitely layered symbolism inspired by Sarmiento's earlier epoch-making *Facundo: civilización y barbarie* (Argentina, 1845). Although short on psychological realism (he had almost no personal experience of the Llanos or their inhabitants), Gallegos updated Sarmiento's problematic to see it in terms of development, one of the grand themes of Latin American history. Moreover, he set it in the context of a Latin American cultural process viewed in terms of the great debates of Western history (spirit, matter), Latin American history (Spaniards, Indians) and universal history (male, female). He was undoubtedly the first novelist in the continent to perceive the full importance of this – now standard – Americanist conceptual framework, however simplistically dramatized in the struggle between the progressive landowner Santos Luzardo and his ruthless adversary the female caudillo Doña Bárbara (a covert symbol for the regime of Juan Vicente Gómez, effective dictator of Venezuela from 1908 to 1935 and himself the heir to a whole century of 'barbarous' caudillo figures). Interestingly enough, Santos discovers that what is needed is not so much an enlightened democracy as a somewhat steelier 'good *caudillismo*'; but Gallegos himself did not put this into practice when he became President in the last months of the post-war democratic *trienio* (1945–8).

For Gallegos, at any rate, as for Santos Luzardo, the *llano,* symbol of Venezuela's future, is a field for action, not for aesthetic or nostalgic contemplation, and his image of it stands as a symbol of the perspective of an entire generation of optimistic, democratic Americanist politicians: 'Plains of the *llano,* one and a thousand trails . . . Great land lying open and outstretched, made for work and grand deeds: all horizons, like hope; all paths, like will.' Fifty years ago this was the most admired novel in Latin American history. Then, twenty-five years ago, as the flood-tide of the 1960s 'Boom' washed all else away, it fell into disrepute and Gallegos was deemed to be less the novelist of underdevelopment than an embarrassingly underdeveloped novelist, whose work was as devoid of real people as the vast empty savannahs he depicted. Yet the visionary Gallegos was always more subtle than his detractors would allow. Few of the other novelists shared so confidently in his belief in capitalist development and incorporatist politics, but it is this, precisely, which makes him the most significant representative in literature of the dominant economic and political ideologies of the coming era: developmentalism and populism. Yet Gallegos also learned and changed. Míster Danger, the North American who longs to rape nubile Venezuela (Marisela) in *Doña Bárbara,* simply makes a run for it when confronted by Santos Luzardo's heroic resolution. Such later works as *Sobre la misma tierra* (1943) would take imperialism more seriously. And whereas in *Doña Bárbara* a repressed and repressive Santos prohibits the erotic antics of Venezuelan folklore when his peons dance around the camp fire, the almost Homeric *Cantaclaro* (1934) is notable for its tolerant and indeed exultant response to Llano traditions. Similarly, whereas Doña Bárbara's original sin was her Mestizo origin, the protagonist of *Canaima* (1935), Marcos Vargas, is a young man of great promise who immerses himself in an Indian jungle community in order to create a new, mixed culture. By this means Marcos, and his creator, were pointing the way beyond the regionalist novel to the more complex – indeed, labyrinthine – fiction which was to give Latin American narrative its worldwide reputation and focus.

It should be repeated that these 'novels of the land', as they came to be called, at first approvingly and later deprecatingly, were by no means the only fiction written in Latin America in the period from 1915 to 1945. There was a good deal of urban fiction, both within and outside the social realist genre, and there were avant-garde works by writers like Macedonio Fernández, Borges, Onetti and others, along with numerous other trends. But 'Americanism' was the banner of the era and the novel of the land gave the image of the continent – still undiscovered, uncompleted, largely unknown, but now aggressively emergent – that most foreign readers and indeed most Latin Americans wished to see. Like the earlier *costumbrista* fiction, it was a special form of knowledge, but also now a form of political assertion as incipient industrial capitalism brought new classes to the scene and the problem of the land and agrarian reform signalled vast social transformations and forms of class conflict previously unknown in the continent. In poetry also, Pablo Neruda, by far the best known poet of the era, took this politically motivated Americanist theme to its highest and literally its most monumental point with his epic *Canto General* (1950), whose best known section, 'Alturas de Macchu Picchu', was composed in 1945.

The 1930s

By the early 1930s a new wave of disillusionment was sweeping the sub-continent, against an international background as sombre as the modern world would ever know. Writers now gave less attention to grand historical symbols and focused more closely on their characters, albeit from a socio-logical and economic rather than a psychological standpoint. In every Latin American republic the triumphalist faith in development and moderniza-tion typical of the years after 1918 had evaporated, and political ideologies now began to separate intellectuals and artists in new and painful ways. Under the influence of international movements like communism and fascism, literature, like politics and economics, became more program-matic. The pseudo-scientific, objectivist realism of late nineteenth-century

naturalist writing now became transmuted into a more sociologically critical form of realism, as writers incorporated the perspectives of socialism
and, though much more gradually, of psychoanalysis. The somewhat vague
and idealistic humanist slogans of the 1920s, typical of the great symbolic
narratives discussed above, were transformed with revolutionary force into
the more ideologically explicit forms of commitment characteristic of the
1930s. In sharp contrast to this politically overdetermined 'realism', non-
socialist writers withdrew into 'philosophy', fantasy or the new Catholic
existentialism, as the aftermath of 1929 and the collapse of international
trade turned the 1930s into another moment of relative isolation in Latin
America.

Both in politics and literature, then, the main story of the 1930s was one
of radical assaults on a conservative status quo whose response was authoritarian retaliation; and the outward-looking Americanist works of the
1920s were succeeded in each republic – paradoxically, given the growing
internationalist influence of world communism – by another period of
national introspection. At the same time the committed, ideologically
explicit works which now appeared in most countries were matched by a
growing tendency towards essays written by *pensadores* consumed, in the
wake of Spengler and visits by other foreign luminaries like Keyserling,
Waldo Frank and Ortega y Gasset, with national character and the metaphysics of the Mexican, Argentinian or Brazilian 'mode of being in the
world'. The early phases of this process were marked by the influential
Argentine magazine *Sur* (1931–76), many of whose pages were devoted to
such continental self-analysis. These metaphysical tendencies were prolonged well into the mid-1950s, by which time the rising middle sectors
had begun to forge their own more specific cultural identity, with new
university systems, the growth and influence of the social sciences, and a
redefined insertion of the professions into the life of the continent.

In tracing these conflicting trends, it is important to keep in mind that
regionalism is in essence merely the other face of literary nationalism.
During this specific period, in fact, it signalled the need for national
integration. Nowhere was this more true than in Brazil, the huge
Portuguese-speaking republic, almost a continent in itself, which is separated from Spanish America by language, a distinct historical experience,
and the special influence of African culture. The regionalist impulse was
uniquely important in Brazil for the very reason that national synthesis
was still so far from being achieved. Rio de Janeiro's elegantly classical
nineteenth-century movements had been predictably superseded in the

early decades of the twentieth century by São Paulo's various forms of modernism, but it was much more of a shock to the literary system when, in the 1930s and 1940s, the centre of gravity was once more displaced to the apparently decaying Northeastern periphery to produce one of the golden eras of Brazilian narrative.

The great precursor of this historic shift was *A bagaceira* (1928) by José Américo de Almeida (1887–1980). Like *Doña Bárbara*, Almeida's novel portrays the modernization of the hacienda (*fazenda*) system, in this case that of the Brazilian sugar plantation or *engenho*. Almeida, who had trained as a lawyer, shared other attributes with the Venezuelan writer, including a lifelong commitment to represent the image of the people and to campaign on their behalf. He was closely associated with the *tenentes* movement of the 1920s, a leader of the 1930 Revolution and a minister of public works under Getúlio Vargas between 1930 and 1934. Later writers would have less comfortable relations with state power. *A bagaceira* was set in the sugar belt between the droughts of 1898 and 1915, depicting not only the permanent menace of nature but also the transition from labour-intensive to machine-based cultivation. It was characteristic of an entire sociological line in Brazilian fiction – still heavily influenced by Comtian Positivism and Zola's Naturalism – and its very title recalls those of other famous narrative works of the late nineteenth century. The somewhat melodramatic story follows the relationship between a beautiful refugee from the drought, Soledade, and an idealistic young student, Lúcio; and between Lúcio and his father the sugar baron, who eventually robs him of both his woman and his dreams of social progress. For all its self-evident imperfections, *A bagaceira* undeniably inaugurated a new complex of subjects such as the sugar mill, the drought, the *retirante* (migrant refugee) and the bandit. After 1930 these became stock themes to which a whole generation of younger Brazilian writers would turn.

A redoubtable woman, Raquel de Queirós (b.1910), was the first writer to profit from Almeida's pioneering example. She was a judge's daughter, and a qualified teacher by the age of fifteen. Her first novel *O quinze* (1930) began precisely where *A bagaceira* had ended, with the horrific *sêca* (drought) of 1915 which had devastated the entire Northeastern territory and had thrown countless desperate refugees into a hopeless search for food, water and work. Queirós's novel was strikingly sober, almost neo-realist (like many novels written by Latin American women), made effective use of everyday language and gave sympathetic insight into the individual aspects of social situations, above all the condition of women. *O quinze* was followed by three further novels before the young writer was twenty-eight, after which she turned her back on narrative fiction and opted for the theatre and for documentary endeavours of various kinds. It was at this time that she became, first, a Communist Party activist, and then, in 1937, a Trotskyist, for which she was rewarded with three months in prison around the time her third novel, *Caminho de pedras,* appeared. In later years she became something of a national institution and, like her mentor Gilberto Freyre, a much more conservative figure preoccupied with semi-eternal folkloric and popular traditions rather than with more immediate social concerns.

Another prodigy, similar to Queirós both in his equally precocious literary career and in his political militancy, was Jorge Amado (b.1912), the son of a merchant turned coffee planter, who was educated in Salvador and Rio. Amado was to become Brazil's best known twentieth-century novelist, and in 1931, at the age of nineteen, produced his first novel *O país do carnaval,* the expression of a lost generation looking for some nationalist ideal in the midst of stagnation and moral despair. After this polemical start he produced a series of more overtly committed novels, with a carefully calculated combination of socialist and populist ingredients. The first of them, *Cacau* (1933), exposed the inhuman condition of workers on the cocoa plantations of Ilhéus, and was followed by a sequence of urban novels set in Salvador, including *Suor* (1934) and *Jubiabá* (1935). Amado's political odyssey during these years obeyed a complicated and sometimes contradictory itinerary, and he was jailed on several occasions between 1937 and 1942. He had used the 1930s to travel the length and breadth of his own vast country and much of Latin America besides, and he soon began to win an international reputation. Perhaps his greatest novel, *Terras do sem-fim,* appeared in 1943 a work of great conviction and uncharacteristic sobriety which develops themes and characters first outlined in *Cacau* and paints the decline of the old rural *coronéis* on a vast temporal and geographical canvas. It is the most profoundly historical of all the Brazilian novels of this most notable era, to which, in a sense, it puts an end. Amado subsequently joined the Brazilian Communist Party and went into exile when the party was banned in 1947. He travelled extensively through Eastern Europe and elsewhere and produced books which rather crudely followed the party line with titles like *O mundo da paz* (1950) and *Os subterrâneos da liberdade* (1954). After the 1956 Soviet thaw he turned to a different kind of writing, composing a series of works calculated to appeal to a much wider popular audience in the capitalist West, the first of which was *Gabriela, cravo e canela* (1958), a worldwide bestseller. It would be difficult to deny that his almost embarrassingly sexual female protagonists have offered a more independent image of Latin American women than most traditional novels, though it could be argued that they merely substitute one form of exploitation for another. This later phase, which for some readers shows the real Amado – more sentimental than ideological, more voluptuous than passionate, and inherently colourful and picturesque – has made him as successful in the capitalist world since the 1960s as he was in the Communist world in the 1950s, and by far the most marketable Brazilian novelist of all time.

A rather different case was José Lins do Rego (1901–57). He had spent his childhood in the big house of one of his maternal grandfather's sugar plantations in the state of Paraíba, and he built a narrative world around this early experience. He studied law in Recife, where he was part of a literary circle including Gilberto Freyre and José Américo de Almeida. He remains identified above all with his *Sugar-Cane Cycle* of 1932–36, which effectively provided a literary illustration of Freyre's influential historical essay *Casa-grande e senzala* (1933). *Menino de engenho* (1932), *Doidinho* (1933), *Bangüê* (1934), *O moleque Ricardo* (1935) and *Usina* (1936), inspired by the plantation of his legendary grandfather Coronel Zé Paulino, mark out the successive phases in a Brazilian quest for lost time as the young central character, Carlos, is educated and socialized during a period in which slavery and plantation life are giving way to the mechanized practices of the sugar mill. In these works Lins do Rego effects an unforgettable fusion of emotional memoir and historical document, at one and the same time tragic and dispassionate, bearing witness to an era and a culture, albeit from the standpoint of the declining ruling class. Some years later *Fogo morto* appeared (1943) and provided a still more historically distanced appraisal of the decadent old order. It proved not only a delayed culmination of the literary sugar cycle but also Lins do Rego's greatest novel.

Another writer from the region was to achieve even greater acclaim than Lins do Rego: indeed Graciliano Ramos (1892–1953) was to be recognized, in due course, as Brazil's most outstanding literary stylist since Machado de Assis half a century before him. Ramos's father, a storekeeper, took the family to live in Palmeira dos Indios, Alagoas in 1910 and much later became its prefect from 1928–30. Graciliano, the eldest of fifteen children, began writing his first novel, *Caetés,* in 1925, but did not complete it for publication until 1933, by which time he was living in Maceió (Alagoas) and meeting other writers such as Queirós, Amado and Lins do Rego. He published a second novel, *São Bernardo*, in 1934. Its outstanding technical achievement made it one of the first novels from Latin America to convey through a first-person narrative the world view of an uneducated anti-heroic protagonist. A self-made land-owner, Paulo Honório, narrates with economic starkness the violent story of his disastrous marriage to a schoolteacher. Ramos was imprisoned in 1936 for alleged subversion, was subjected to brutal maltreatment, and spent a year inside, adding to his inherently pessimistic cast of mind. (*Memórias do cárcere*, a bitter and unforgiving memoir of his stay in prison, was published in 1953.) His masterpiece *Vidas sêcas* appeared in 1938, conveying the bitter experience of a family of illiterate refugees fighting to survive almost impossible odds in the natural and social desert of the Northeast. With its almost matchless linguistic and conceptual austerity reflecting the barren lives of its repeatedly humiliated *sertanejo* protagonists, this novel remains one of the most affecting literary works to have come out of Latin America. *Vidas sêcas* is an early Third World classic, one of only a few works to have found original solutions to the challenge of communicating illiteracy and inarticulateness with sensitivity, tact and precision. Eventually the desperate trekkers decide to abandon the hopeless conditions of the countryside and migrate to a new – though possibly equally hopeless – life in the city ('They would come to an unknown and civilized land, and there they'd be imprisoned . . . The Sertão would keep on sending strong, ignorant people, like Fabiano, Missy Vitória and the two boys'). (Many years later, in his depressing novel *Essa terra*, 1976, Antônio Torres would show that things had not changed much.)

After the novel of the Mexican Revolution, the novel of the Brazilian Northeast is one of the most important regional sub-genres in Latin America. More surprisingly, perhaps, a similar wave of socially and politically committed works appeared in Ecuador during the same period. After Alcides Arguedas's *Raza de bronce* in 1919, Indian-orientated social realist works appeared in many Spanish American republics in the 1920s; yet most writers, like the rural judge Enrique López Albújar (1872–1965) in Peru, for example, despite the vehemence of his portrayals, still saw the Indians as inherently inferior, irrational and superstitious (*Cuentos andinos*, 1920). In that sense his work may be compared directly with that of his Bolivian contemporary. Indian integration seemed unlikely, if not impossible, to such people, then as now. In Ecuador, however, a generation of young writers with different perceptions, known as the Grupo de

Guayaquil, appeared. They included Joaquín Gallegos Lara (1911–47), in whose garret they assembled, Enrique Gil Gilbert (1912–74), Demetrio Aguilera Malta (1909–81), whose work would later take on a 'magical realist' orientation, José de la Cuadra (1903–41), a short story writer of a power to match Horacio Quiroga, and Alfredo Pareja Diezcanseco (b. 1908): 'five in one fist', as Gil Gilbert would later say at Cuadra's funeral. In 1930 the first three published an epoch-making joint work, *Los que se van,* subtitled 'Cuentos del cholo y del montuvio'. It caused a sensation because of its violent subject matter and shocking, popular language.

In 1934, inspired in part by his colleagues from the tropical coast, the highlander Jorge Icaza (1906–76) launched a literary missile entitled *Huasipungo,* one of the most hotly debated works in the history of Latin American narrative. He had worked as an actor and playwright in a theatre company during the 1920s and published his first narrative work, *Cuentos de barro,* in 1933. His definitive claim to fame, however, was established in the following year and coincided, fittingly, with Zdhanov's intervention in the writers' congress in the USSR and the subsequent imposition of 'socialist realism' in the Communist world. The novel's title refers to the *huasipungos* or plots of land farmed by the Indians on feudal estates until the Liberal reforms of 1918. It is perhaps the most brutally laconic and deliberately offensive novel ever published about the condition of the Latin American Indians and the shameful realities of the hacienda system which prevailed from the colonial period to the present century. The question it raises perennially in the mind and conscience of each reader is: what exactly are we offended by as we read it? Icaza interprets everything according to the base-superstructure distinction of vulgar Marxism and traces the implacable logic of the semi-feudal socio-economic system on the basis of one case study, the building of a road through the hacienda by a North American lumber company. Icaza's position is that it is difficult to be human when subjected to inhuman treatment. The higher one's social class, the more 'worlds' one has available. His Indians have only one available world, as the Ecuadorean novelist is at pains to show us ('He searched for some mental support but found everything around him elusive and alien. For the others – mestizos, gentlemen and bosses – an Indian's woes are a matter for scorn, contempt and disgust. What could his anguish over the illness of his wife possibly signify in the face of the complex and delicate tragedies of the whites? Nothing!').

Viewed across the decades, it may seem almost incredible that at the same time that Icaza and his contemporaries were writing such works in

Ecuador and elsewhere, Jorge Luis Borges and his circle in Argentina were, as we shall see, writing their complex and labyrinthine literary inquisitions. There could hardly be a clearer example of what the concept of uneven development might mean as applied to cultural expression. Of course there is nowhere in Latin America where the relation between literature and society has been more direct, or more turbulent, than in the Andean republics of Peru, Bolivia and Ecuador, mainly due to the unavoidable connection between three great historical problematics: the national question, the agrarian question and the ethnic question. Peruvian cultural expression, in particular, often has a raw and unmistakably bitter flavour unlike that of any other country. There in the 1920s Víctor Raúl Haya de la Torre and José Carlos Mariátegui elaborated the two ideological alternatives to conservative or liberal rule in the continent: populism (Aprismo) and communism.

Aprismo was the creed of Ciro Alegría (1909–67), the most important Peruvian indigenist novelist of the entire regionalist era. He had spent much of his childhood on his grandfather's hacienda close to the River Marañón in Huanachuco. Living in Lima, years later, Alegría reneged on his background, joined Apra and was imprisoned during the events of 1932. After escaping from jail and being rearrested, he went into exile in Chile in 1934, where he fell ill with tuberculosis, became paralysed and lost the faculty of speech, before writing two episodic novels *La serpiente de oro* (1935), about the boatmen of the Marañón, and *Los perros hambrientos* (1938), about the Indian and Cholo peasants of the high cordilleras and their struggle against both nature in all its cruel indifference and Peruvian society in all its brutal hostility. However it was his next novel, *El mundo es ancho y ajeno,* which gave him his continental reputation. It was written in four months in 1940 for a Pan-American competition announced by the New York publishers Farrar and Rinehart. Like *Los perros hambrientos* it has a tone of classical authority and a simple grandeur reminiscent of Gallegos's best work and with a similar nineteenth-century conception. Using a vast historical, geographical and social canvas, this later work portrays a free community of Indians in northern Peru between 1912 and the 1930s, focusing on their mayor, Rosendo Maqui, once considered one of the great character creations of Latin American fiction ('The Indian Rosendo Maqui crouched there like some ancient idol, his body dark and gnarled like the *lloque* with its knotted, iron-hard trunk, for he was part plant, part man, and part rock. It was as if Rosendo Maqui were cast in the image of his geography; as if the turbulent forces of the earth had fashioned him and his people in the likeness of their mountains'). The novel ends like almost all indigenist novels: the Indians are robbed of their land by a cruel and unscrupulous landowner and obliged to wander the earth, only to discover with increasing desperation that although Peru is broad it has become alien, and that neither pacificism, banditry nor socialist insurrection seem likely to modify their historical destiny. Alegría won the New York competition, and was warmly lauded by John Dos Passos, a member of the jury, making the Peruvian novelist one of the two or three best-known Latin American writers of this period.

El mundo es ancho y ajeno is ambitious, panoramic and the only one of the great regionalist works to have a genuine historical framework, as we follow the epic quest for land and justice to the jungles and the rivers, the mines and the cities, among the bandits and the trade unionists. The book will endure as a great, if sometimes clumsy monument to the indigenist doctrine of an entire epoch. It is majestic despite its unevenness and moving despite its sentimentality, and it does provide the reader with a means by which to imagine the experience of the Andean Indians.

Urban Themes

No simple formula can illuminate the relation between country and city in Western history. Whatever our desires, no society has ever been free to choose between these two political and economic alternative realities nor between the different lifestyles which they have conditioned – although artists and intellectuals have often liked to imagine that they could – because it is precisely in the historical dynamic between the two milieux that social meaning has existed. From the very beginning writers from Latin American city environments were acutely conscious of the provincial and possibly caricatural status of their own neo-colonial and dependent cities compared to the world's great metropoli of past and present: theirs were parasitic enclaves, comprador corridors between city and country. Life in those increasingly ugly conurbations seemed somehow even more absurd than in European cities, whose existence was justified by the whole weight and authority of European history, however alienating the urban experience as such might seem to any given inhabitant of those places.

It was the Cuban writer Alejo Carpentier who in a memorable essay asserted that it was the mission of Latin American artists to do for their cities what Balzac had done for Paris, Dickens for London and Joyce for Dublin. He acknowledged that he and his contemporaries had an especially difficult problem, since not only were their readers ignorant of the context of their literary recreations but these were in any case cities 'without style' or, perhaps, with 'a third style, the style of things that have no style'.[2] Ironically enough, at the very time that Carpentier was writing, around 1960, the urban novel was finally beginning to prevail. However, given the subcontinent's involuntary role in Western mythologies, it seems likely that Latin America's fate may be always to represent the 'country' to Europe's 'city', and that, given its landscapes and state of development, novels of the land may continue to be important for longer than we think – or, perhaps, for as long as we can imagine.

In fact urban novels like those which had been written by Balzac and Dickens did not appear in Latin America until late in the nineteenth century, by which time Zola was the dominant influence, though few of his imitators at that time had his grasp of detail or social motivation. Latin American capitals were very small and largely provincial in character until well into the present century. The most notable exception to the general picture was Brazil, where the mulatto writer Joaquim Maria Machado de Assis (1839–1908) became Latin America's only truly great novelist in the century after independence and one of the undoubted masters of the genre in the Western world. The key to his achievement lay in finding a humorous, parodic, iconoclastic form with which to negotiate the difficulties of living in an intranscendent semi-colonial city, long before the similar twentieth-century solutions improvised by such 'postcolonial' writers as Borges or Naipaul.

Between the two world wars, however, there were few such humorous responses to the experience of Latin American cities. An early protest novel about the woes and injustices of urban existence was *Triste fim de Policarpo Quaresma* (1915) by Alfonso Henriques de Lima Barreto (1881–1922), another Brazilian mulatto who was in many respects the successor to Machado de Assis. In 1917 the Chilean Eduardo Barrios (1884–1963) followed this example with another novel of urban alienation and despair, *Un perdido,* in which the hopeless loser of the title is unable to discover meaning or satisfaction in life in twentieth-century Santiago. In the 1920s the Argentinian novelist Roberto Arlt (1900–42), now belatedly considered one of the most significant writers of the continent, gave an early indication

---

[2] Alejo Carpentier, 'Problemática de la actual novela latinoamericana', in *Tientos y diferencias* (Havana, 1966), p. 15.

of the extent to which Latin American fiction, particularly in Buenos Aires and Montevideo, would be able to echo or even anticipate European currents of nihilism and absurdism. This was because for writers or protagonists with a European mentality and European nostalgias, Latin America was either a nowhere land or a caricature. Arlt produced a remarkable sequence of urban horror tales, *El juguete rabioso* (1926), *Los siete locos* (1929) and *Los lanzallamas* (1931). Like the rural Quiroga before him, Arlt constructed his reality somewhere between alienation, madness, depravity and criminality, with neither the author nor the characters able to distinguish satisfactorily between these elements of the existential analysis. His is a world without transcendence, in which the bourgeoisie's official ideology of honour, hard work and decency is contradicted everywhere by reality and the only means of self-affirmation are crime or madness. The tradition is that of Dostoyevsky and originates in Argentina with Eugenio Cambaceres (1843–88), and goes on through Onetti, Marechal, Sábato and many others. It was somehow fitting though also ironic that Arlt was for a time Ricardo Güiraldes's secretary, for it was Güiraldes whose *Don Segundo Sombra* bade a sorrowful farewell to the gaucho era and indeed to literary concentration on the rural sector as a whole, whilst the clearest sign that in Argentina at least the age of urban fiction had definitely arrived was the appearance of Arlt's literary provocations.

It has become a commonplace of Latin American historical criticism to say that the New York prize awarded to *El mundo es ancho y ajeno* in 1941 should have gone to another competitor, the Uruguayan Juan Carlos Onetti (1909–94). Ciro Alegría was the last of the old-style 'regionalist' authors, rooted in the land, whilst Onetti was the first and perhaps the most important of a quite new generation of novelists routed through the cities. His first novel, *El pozo,* appeared in 1939, and shows that writers in Montevideo or Buenos Aires had no need to read Céline, Sartre or Camus to know that they were alienated or anguished. Onetti's fiction begins where Arlt left off, though Onetti always achieves the necessary distance from his materials to be able to impose the delicacy and coherence of art on even the most sordid and contradictory reality. *El pozo* tells the story of Eladio Linacero, a university-educated journalist frustrated but also mediocre, who shares a room like a prison cell with an ignorant Communist militant ironically called Lazarus, and vainly longs to become a writer. Outside the drab and depressing city which Montevideo has become lies a Uruguay without history: 'Behind us, there is nothing: one gaucho, two gauchos, thirty-three gauchos.' This is sacrilege: these 'thirty-three gauchos' were the symbolic heroes of Uruguay's liberation struggle. Clearly we have travelled very far from Gallegos and the other Americanists by this point. Latin America is a continent with nothing worth writing about beyond the writer's own anguish, and Onetti ends his work with a statement of existential bankruptcy: 'This is the night. I am a solitary man smoking somewhere in the city; the night surrounds me, as in a ritual, gradually, and I have no part in it.' Despite the gloom, Onetti is always more concerned to communicate a vision than to make a point, elaborating a picture not only of city life (Montevideo, Buenos Aires and his invented community of 'Santa María') but also of reality and consciousness themselves as labyrinthine, a tissue of perceptions and motives impossible to disentangle and clarify, with the effort to do so ending always in weariness, boredom, frustration and defeat. Later works by Onetti include *Tierra de nadie* (1941), *La vida breve* (1950), *Los adioses* (1954), *El astillero* (1961), generally considered his masterpiece, *Juntacadáveres* (1964), *Dejemos hablar al viento* (1979) and *Cuando entonces* (1987).

Undoubtedly, Onetti inaugurates the mature phase of Latin American urban fiction with his disturbing, world-weary narratives. As mentioned, this is a line of fiction particularly common in the River Plate, where the Argentine Eduardo Mallea (1903–82) gave it a somewhat portentous philosophical orientation from the 1930s to the 1950s (see especially *Todo verdor perecerá*, 1941), whilst the Uruguayan Mario Benedetti (b. 1920) concentrated more closely on the social and historical determinants of that same grey, heavy despair during the 1960s and 1970s. His best known works include *Quién de nosotros* (1953), *Montevideanos* (stories, 1959), *La tregua* (1960), *Gracias por el fuego* (1965) and *Primavera con una esquina rota* (1982). One of the most apocalyptic of such writers was Ernesto Sábato (Argentina, b. 1911), author of *Sobre héroes y tumbas* (1961). Even Onetti lacks the nightmarish note characteristic of Sábato's fiction, which also includes *El túnel* (1948) and *Abaddón el exterminador* (1977). Sábato's almost Dostoyevskyan work is at once a meditation on the condition of mankind in the twentieth century and on the development of Argentina from the time of Rosas to the time of Perón, viewed as a family history of criminal depravity. For him Buenos Aires is a home to nightmares, built on a vast sewer: 'Everything floated towards the Nothingness of the ocean through secret underground tunnels, as if those above were trying to forget, affecting to know nothing of this part of their truth. As if heroes in reverse, like me, were destined to the infernal and accursed task of bearing witness to that reality.'

Thus from the time of Roberto Arlt fiction was gradually moving to the metropolitan realm and away from the rural, though the latter continued to dominate until the late 1950s. In the cities, symbolic prisons, writers often found themselves in trouble with the authorities and much narrative fiction was devoted to prison themes in the 1930s and 1940s (whereas in the 1970s and 1980s themes of exile or 'disappearance' tended to be more frequent). There is indeed a sense in which for all Latin American writers, regardless of ideology, the literary act is always also a political one.

This traditionally strong emphasis on social and political themes only added to the difficulty which women writers, already condemned as second-class citizens to confrontation with a virulently patriarchal society, experienced in the early decades of the century. Interestingly enough, most of the women writers well known to the twentieth century, like Sor Juana Inés de la Cruz (Mexico, 1648–95), Gertrudis Gómez de Avellaneda (Cuba, 1814–73), or Clorinda Matto de Turner (Peru, 1854–1909), were involved in some form of literature of protest. But in the early twentieth century conditions were not favourable to this kind of activity by women, though there were notable exceptions such as Raquel de Queirós, discussed above, or Chile's valiant regionalist novelist Marta Brunet (1897–1967), whose career began as early as 1923 with *Montaña adentro*. Normally, however, women novelists were limited both by experience and by expectation to more domestic varieties of writing (and, of course, to the short story, a form particularly accessible to minority and disadvantaged writers of all kinds). Thus, for example, even though the delightful *Las memorias de Mamá Blanca* (1929) by Teresa de la Parra (Venezuela, 1891–1936), is set on an hacienda in the countryside, it has a light and intimate tone quite different from the kinds of regionalist writing then in vogue. (Her *Ifigenia. Diario de una señorita que escribió porque se fastidiaba,* 1924, is an excellent example of the nascent feminist consciousness emerging in those years.)

The gradual shift of emphasis to the cities, which has marked the whole of the twentieth century, has undoubtedly favoured the equally gradual emergence of women writers, above all perhaps in the River Plate area. In Argentina the wealthy Victoria Ocampo (1890–1979), through her literary salon, her patronage and her magazine *Sur,* brought together and encouraged a whole generation of Argentine literati, as well as putting them in touch with writers and developments from abroad. Her series of ten volumes of *Testimonios* (1935–77) are her most widely read works. Silvina Ocampo (1906–93), Victoria's sister, was married to the writer Adolfo Bioy Casares but was also one of Argentina's best known short story writers in her own right, with collections including *Viaje olvidado* (1937), *Autobiografía de Irene* (1948), *La furia* (1959) and several others. All were marked by a delicate but insistent sense of the perverse and the fantastic. Meanwhile in Chile María Luisa Bombal (1910–80) wrote two novels not much noticed at the time but which have since been recognized as milestones in the development of women's writing in Latin America, *La última niebla* (1934) and *La amortajada* (1938), both suffused by an intensely subjective mode of perception, a tormented vision from within. For women, too, the theme of imprisonment was a constant referent, though not at the hands of the state but by courtesy of their own fathers and husbands.

MODERNISM: FROM THE NEW NOVEL TO THE 'BOOM'

El mundo es ancho y ajeno (1940) was the last great regionalist work, though similar novels continued to be written and the social realist mode has persisted through a whole series of formal and ideological transformations up to the present day. Our task now is to travel back again in time to the 1920s to search for the origins of the 'Latin American New Novel', usually associated with the 1950s or even considered synonymous with the 'Boom' of the 1960s. Closer analysis will reveal that Latin America has taken a far more important part in twentieth-century Modernism (and Postmodernism) than even the most nationalistic Latin American critics tend to assert. The truth is that the only really persuasive description for Latin America's most distinctive line of fiction since the 1920s is, precisely, 'Modernism' in the European and North American sense, and it is important to ask why it has been more persistent in the new continent than in either Europe or the United States. Clearly, despite the technical fertility of Joyce, Proust, Woolf or Faulkner, European and North American Modernism has no system, no theory, except as a 'sign of the times'. Latin American writers, however, regardless of their politics, were always pulled in two directions and learned to balance different realities and different orders of experience and thereby to find their way into history as well as myth. Indeed, the essence of what has been called 'magical realism' (itself a form of Modernist discourse), is the juxtaposition and fusion, on equal terms, of the literate and pre-literate world, future and past, modern and traditional, the city and the country: or, to put it another way, the fusion of *modernista* and *naturalista* elements, radically updated, in one unifying discourse. This requires the application of indirect narration and the treatment of folk beliefs, superstitions and myths with absolute literalness. Joyce and Faulkner showed the way, and both were from marginal regions with something of the bi-culturalism required, but neither of them needed to formulate this as an explicit part of their system or project; whereas in Latin America all narratives, inevitably, bear the imprint of their origins in their structure, because all Latin American writers are from the 'periphery'.

As we have seen, most novels about Latin American cities concentrate on the negative, repressive aspects of the urban experience and rather few celebrate it as any kind of liberation from nature. In that sense the romantic impulse remains very strong in the subcontinent. The city is a world of alienation, reification, exchange values, consumption and exhaustion, contrasted negatively with the cosmic fertilization and global significance of the indigenous world which preceded it. Yet the great regionalist novels of the 1920s and 1930s also go well beyond the romantic obsession with mere landscape or mere spirituality, and so terms like 'novel of the land' or 'regionalist novel' are unsatisfactory and perhaps even misleading. These works were 'regional' not in the sense that they were 'subnational' but precisely because, from this moment, Latin America was conceived as one large though not yet integrated nation made up of numerous 'regions' (the twenty republics). Put another way, it is not so much a regionalist spirit as a nationalist and Americanist ideology which conditions and structures the novels of Latin America's first important narrative moment, integrating the country and the city within one nationhood and connecting each of these within an Americanist supranationhood or continental vision. (Of course this is not the same as identifying Latin America's place within world culture, a process which the *modernistas* had tentatively initiated, albeit on unequal and semicolonial terms: that more global literary-historical achievement – one which ended an entire cultural era – began at the same time as the novels studied thus far were being written, but was undertaken by a different kind of writer and, although likewise initiated in the 1920s, was only completed in the 1960s and early 1970s.) Regionalism and Americanism, then, are two sides of the same impulse and the concept 'novel of the land' was actually a symbolic designation: the 'land' is not so much the telluric earth as the American continent itself as a field of endeavour and object of meditation, with individual works alternating within the semantic field marked out by these two poles: region and continent.

Seeing this, we can understand why the capital cities depicted in the novels mentioned above are not usually imagined as capitals of that regional, American interior. Instead, they are European enclaves, treacherously conspiring or weakly collaborating in the exploitation of natural raw materials, or – like Lima, Rio de Janeiro and Buenos Aires – with their backs turned on the regions and gazing out longingly over the ocean that leads back to Europe. Naturally some writers have always argued that cosmopolitanism is an unavoidable and in any case desirable reaching out to the world, a wish to integrate Latin America into the universal order of things, to take its place among the cultures, recognizing and being recognized. This is a process of discussion whose end is not in sight.

Thus each of the regionalist works takes up the debate initiated by Domingo Faustino Sarmiento and Euclides da Cunha on the national question. Are these territorial entities really nations? What sort of community is a nation? How do regions smaller and larger than the nations relate to them? If these countries are not yet nations but nationhood is the project, how is it to be achieved? And to what extent might Latin America be conceived as a unified plurality which only makes sense at the level of the continent and therefore only makes unified writing possible from a continental perspective? The narrative fiction of the nineteenth century had symbolically founded nations and established the identity of the governing classes. Naturalist novels had examined the pathology of the lower classes and been disappointed by what they saw. In the 1920s 'regionalist' fiction looked again and took a more positive view, not only of the lower classes, but of the possibilities for a constructive relationship between the rulers and the ruled. The interior now was not only a field for imagination and romance, but for epic and social exploration, for knowledge and definition. Thus writers embarked on the journey from capital to interior, only to realize that the future was not after all clear: first, because everything was more complicated than had been thought, not least because alliances with the workers involved commitments which might not always suit the interests of the volatile petty bourgeoisie; and secondly, because the road still appeared to lie through Europe, whether capitalist or socialist. Thus to the chain from capital to village is added the journey from there back again to the capital and across the seas to Europe – and then back again to the village, with all those newly assimilated experiences within the writer's consciousness. This indeed is the fundamental explanation of what I have called elsewhere the 'Ulyssean' writer and the growth of the 'Ulyssean' novel,[3] inaugurated and given definitive form by perhaps the greatest of all twentieth century Modernist writers, James Joyce. He was not, at first sight, what young Latin American artists ought to have been looking for in the 1920s, and yet, avant-garde seductions aside, the Irishman and his Latin American admirers had a number of things in common which facilitated his influence: for example migrations and exile; Catholicism, its traditions and repressions; and the counter-conquest of an alien, imperial language.

None of these factors apply in the same way to the other great model, William Faulkner. Of course there would have been no Faulkner without Joyce, and we will recall that Faulkner learned from the Joyce who had written *Ulysses* and not from the one who went on to write *Finnegans Wake*. Still, Faulkner and his compatriot John Dos Passos were more accessible models in the Latin America of the thirties, forties, and fifties, whilst Joyce would finally exert his full impact only in the 1960s and 1970s. This is not really so surprising: what Faulkner, and to a lesser extent, Dos Passos, actually permitted, was the renovation and restructuring of the Latin American social novel through the next thirty years, whereas, despite the admiration he inspired in a generation of young Americans in Paris, Joyce's impact on most authors – if not, crucially, on the most important of them – remained largely fragmentary or superficial except in poetry and was only generally assimilable in the 1960s, the age, indeed, of the final flowering of Latin American Modernism in the form of the 'Boom' novel.

The bridge to Modernist developments in narrative was, indeed, avant-garde poetry. In that, at least, the continent was already fully modern, in the sense that many poets – Vicente Huidobro, Jorge Luis Borges, Oswald de Andrade, Manuel Bandeira, César Vallejo and Pablo Neruda – were writing poetry as 'up to date', innovative and recognizably twentieth-century as anything being produced in Europe, the Soviet Union or the United States.

The novel, however, is always slower to mature (in the end it is always a historical, retrospective genre, which needs time to focus) and in the 1920s there emerged in literature, broadly speaking, a contrast between a poetic expression whose dominant mode was cosmopolitan, produced by international experience and orientated in the same direction, and the

[3] See Gerald Martin, *Journeys through the Labyrinth: Latin American Fiction in the Twentieth Century* (London, 1989).

various forms of 'nativist' fiction – regionalist, Creolist, telluric, indigenist, etc. – examined above, which, because they lay somewhere between realism and naturalism, we are calling social realism. Its impetus had been both shaped and accelerated by the Mexican Revolution, and at that time was thought, not entirely paradoxically, to be the most innovative as well as the most typical current in Latin American literature, at a moment when few would have imagined that Latin Americans might participate in cultural discoveries and developments on equal terms. Equally strikingly, the novelists who were closest to the poets were young avant-garde writers like the Brazilian Mário de Andrade with his pathbreaking novel about the Brazilian culture hero *Macunaíma* (1928), the Guatemalan Miguel Angel Asturias, author of the quasi-ethnological *Leyendas de Guatemala* (1930), the Argentine Jorge Luis Borges, who was already intermingling literature with criticism in quite new ways, and the Cuban Alejo Carpentier, with his Afro-American *Ecué-Yamba-O* (1933). It was these writers who would lead the way into the future. Joyce had mapped the route to the great labyrinth of modernity and had effectively ordained the literary systematization of Modernism. Once seen, this labyrinth could not be ignored and had to be traversed. In the case of the Spanish American trio just cited, the full dimensions of their talents would not become apparent until the 1930s and – due to the nature of the 1930s and the intervention of the Second World War – would only become visible after 1945; and even then, only relatively so, because it was not until the 1960s that the complex interaction between Latin American and international conditions of education, readership and publishing combined to produce a situation in which the achievements of Latin American art could be relatively quickly and generally recognized.

In the 1920s, many young Latin American intellectuals and artists were in Paris at the same time as Joyce (and Picasso and Stravinsky). At the moment when the pre-war *modernista* movement, already fading autumnally in the last years of the *belle époque,* was giving way to the avant-garde of the *années folles,* these young writers, who had made the pilgrimage to Paris aided by the plunge of the franc, began to found and participate in a succession of new and exciting magazines with futuristic titles – *Proa* ('Prow': in his 1925 review of *Ulysses* in that same magazine Borges said that Joyce himself was 'audacious as a prow', in other words, an avant-garde explorer and adventurer) in Buenos Aires; *Revista de Avance* in Havana; *Contemporáneos* in Mexico; *Imán* in Paris itself – in all of which the name of Joyce would appear, usually as a rather distant, almost mythological referent.

Astonishingly, in view of his later trajectory, it was Borges who first appreciated the true significance of Joyce, and who became not only the pioneer translator of the famous last page of *Ulysses* but also saw that work as a 'wild and entangled land' into which only the most foolhardy would venture.[4] Borges's initial enthusiasm was soon renounced, just as he would in due course also dismiss his own avant-garde moment – *ultraísmo* – , his localist *Fervor de Buenos Aires,* his 'too vulgar' story 'El hombre de la esquina rosada', all plots requiring social or psychological realism, all wilful obscurity and linguistic experimentalism. He would later describe *Ulysses* itself as 'a failure', a work of microscopic naturalism with, paradoxically, 'no real characters'. Yet whenever Borges wished to explore the nature of literary language, he turned to Joyce's example, just as he did whenever he wished to discuss translation, comparativism, literary purity, artistic devotion, or totality. Moreover Borges, one of the writers who made possible the concept of 'intertextuality', frequently named Joyce as a key innovator of the phenomenon.

Many young Latin American poets sought to make use of Joyce's example in the 1920s, but were mostly unprepared for the task. It has not been much noticed that the reason for this is that Joyce was on his way past Modernism to what is now called Postmodernism. Thus in the 1930s it was Faulkner and Dos Passos who more clearly showed how to apply the new Modernist techniques to narrative fiction and thereby provided the means for updating the social or regionalist novel. The point, however, is that Joyce's influence began before either, was more widespread if not more powerful, and grew slowly but surely to a crescendo in the 1960s and 1970s. Moreover, in a few literary milestones of the following era – Asturias' *El señor Presidente* (1946) (see below), *Al filo del agua* (1947) by Agustín Yáñez (1904–80), considered by critics one of the great transitional works of Latin American fiction and a precursor of the 'New Novel', and Leopoldo Marechal's *Adán Buenosayres* (1948) (see below), the particular combination of interior monologue and stream-of-consciousness techniques with other devices, especially wordplay and myth, made critics correctly conclude that these historically fundamental works were more Joycean than Faulknerian. Not until 1945, four years after Joyce's death, was *Ulysses* available at last to those who could read neither French or English, when the first translation appeared in Buenos Aires.

---

[4] Jorge Luis Borges, 'El *Ulises* de Joyce', in *Proa* (Buenos Aires), 6 (January 1925), 3.

Many years later the great 'Boom' of Latin American fiction – itself now mythologized, its writers living legends – produced an emphatic shift of gravity to the urban realm, with the emergence and consolidation of its 'big four' – Cortázar, Fuentes, García Márquez and Vargas Llosa – followed by others like Lezama Lima, Cabrera Infante and Donoso. In an article on these new Latin American novelists in 1977, Emir Rodríguez Monegal, the influential Uruguayan critic, made a striking retrospective assessment of the Irish writer's influence: 'Joyce's achievement was to be imitated in many languages. Slowly, and through many successful works . . . *Ulysses* became the invisible but central model of the new Latin American narrative. From this point of view, Cortázar's *Hopscotch*, Lezama Lima's *Paradiso*, Fuentes's *Change of Skin* and Cabrera Infante's *Three Trapped Tigers*, are Joycean books. Whether or not they are obviously Joycean, they do share the same secret code. That is, they agree in conceiving of the novel as both a parody and a myth, a structure which in its topoi, as much as in its private symbols, reveals the unity of a complete system of signification.'[5] An equally decisive accolade was later paid to Joyce by the Mexican novelist Fernando del Paso, author of the Ulyssean novel *Palinuro de México* (1977): 'I consider that *Ulysses* is a sort of sun installed at the centre of the Gutenberg Galaxy, which illuminates not only all the works which followed it but all of universal literature that preceded it. Its influence is definitive and unique in modern Western literature . . . *Finnegans Wake* is a comet of great magnitude moving away from us at the speed of light, in danger of becoming lost for ever. But there is also the possibility that it will return one day and be better understood.'[6] This explains convincingly why the Joycean paradigm has been so attractive in Latin America. Viewed from this long perspective, however, it becomes obvious that Latin America as a whole, despite its post-colonial status, took less time to assimilate Joycean writing than a number of the English-speaking literatures for which such assimilation was easier and, moreover, assimilated it more completely. The same cultural factors which have made Latin America a hospitable environment for Joycean or 'Ulyssean' novels to flower are factors which, in turn, have allowed Latin American narrative to return the favour and influence a whole succession of European and North American works in the postmodern period since the 1960s.

---

[5] Emir Rodríguez Monegal, 'The New Latin American novelists', *Partisan Review*, 44 1 (1977), 41.
[6] Quoted by R. Fiddian in his 'James Joyce y Fernando del Paso', *Insula* (Madrid), 455 (October 1984), p. 10.

Myth and Magic: The Origins of the Latin American New Novel

After the social realism of the 1920s and 1930s, much of the narrative fiction of the 1950s, 1960s and 1970s has been given a more seductive name: 'Magical Realism'. When the label was given above all to Miguel Angel Asturias and Alejo Carpentier, as it used to be, together with one or two like-minded writers like Venezuela's Arturo Uslar Pietri and Ecuador's Demetrio Aguilera Malta, the term, although problematical, was in some ways attractive and acceptable. Now that, like the concept 'baroque', it has become an almost universal description of the 'Latin American style' – exotic and tropical, overblown and unrestrained, phantasmagorical and hallucinatory – it may seem so ideologically dangerous that it should really be rejected. And yet writers as influential and prestigious as Italo Calvino, Salman Rushdie, Umberto Eco and even John Updike have acknowledged its influence and allure, and so it seems possible that it has been at least partly 'decolonized'.

It has not been sufficiently understood that its origins lie in the surrealist movement of the 1920s, the most important avant-garde system coinciding historically with Modernism. Surrealism was never a significant influence in either Britain or the United States, both of which were far too empirical for such schemas at that time. Its emphasis upon the unconscious, and therefore the primitive, its insistence that there was a world more real than the visible 'reality' of commonsense and positivism, the idea that art is a journey of discovery involving free association and the liberation of the repressed, were all tailor-made for Third World interpretations and applications, and therefore for cementing the growing cultural relationship between France and Latin America following independence and the declaration that what the British persist in calling 'South' America was actually 'Latin'. Moreover, this relationship in which, instead of superordinate to subordinate, imperialist to colonial, France exchanged her rational civilization on equal terms (she had no large colonial axe to grind in Latin America) with the New World's supposed instinctual barbarism, was ideally suited to the interests of both sides.

The more convincing and less ideological justification for this most controversial of literary terms – magical realism – is that the 'magic' derives from the cultural sparks which fly from the juxtaposition and clash of different cultures at different levels of development, but this seems not to be the explanation for its attraction. In the era of Hollywood stars, Coca Cola and the intensifying fetishism of commodity exchange, it ought not to be too difficult to understand why 'magic' realism would give us pleasure and conciliate a number of painful contradictions. However in the end it is myth, the universal currency of communication through translation and transformation, which is the only unifying factor between, say, Andrade, Asturias, Borges, Carpentier and García Márquez, who, in other terms, are quite different kinds of novelist. To that extent, it would have been more logical to go for the concept of 'mythical realism'. Either way, one of the crucial features insufficiently stressed in most discussions is the question of the collective dimension characteristic of all magical realist writers, in contrast to the almost inveterate individualism of most kinds of fantastic writing.

Although rarely acknowledged as such, it is almost certainly the case that Mário de Andrade (1893–1945) was the first example, together with Miguel Angel Asturias, of this phenomenon in Latin American literature – thanks largely to his fertile relationship with Brazil's own 1920s *Modernista* movement. Interestingly enough, Andrade had never been abroad when he wrote *Macunaíma* (1928), a key text of the famous 'anthropophagous' movement, and most of what he knew about Brazil had come from books. Certainly what followers of Bakhtin would now call the 'carnivalization' of Latin American literature and the development of the 'polyphonic novel' began with *Macunaíma,* as is indicated by Mário's humorous explanation of his work: 'The Brazilian has no character because he has neither a civilization of his own nor a traditional consciousness . . . He is just like a twenty year old boy.' The eponymous hero travels around Brazil, from the primitive to the modern and back again, as Andrade whimsically confronts such previously unexplored themes as tribalism, totemism, sacrifice, cannibalism and – of course – magic. Oswald de Andrade, challenging the incomprehension with which the novel was greeted, said: 'Mário has written our *Odyssey* and with one blow with his club has created the cyclical hero and the national poetic style for the next fifty years.'[7] Towards the end of the novel there is an intriguing incident as the hero loses consciousness in a battle with a giant, and the narrator announces: 'Macunaíma got into the canoe, took a trip to the mouth of the Rio Negro to look for his consciousness, left behind on the island of Marapatá. And do you think he found it? Not a hope! So then our hero grabbed the consciousness of a Spanish American,

---

[7] Quoted by Haroldo de Campos, '*Macunaíma:* la fantasía estructural', in Mário de Andrade, *Macunaíma* (Barcelona, 1976), p. 11.

stuffed it in his head, and got on just as well.' Perhaps this was the moment when Brazil began to become part of Latin America. At any rate, Mário de Andrade was one of the first writers in the Third World to dare to take not only myth but also magic seriously and unapologetically, as a system of ideas and practices for working on the natural world as an alternative to Western science and technology.

The young Alejo Carpentier's brief novel *Ecue-Yamba-O* ('Praise be to Ecue') was published in 1933, though its first version was signed 'Havana Prison, 1–9 August 1927'. He was later reluctant to see the work republished. He felt that although it was based partly on people he had known as a child, he had failed to grasp either the essence of their psychology and way of life or the linguistic medium needed to convey it. He only relented at the very end of his life, when a clumsily produced pirate edition appeared. While it is undoubtedly true that Carpentier's novel on the culture of Cuba's Black population was more interesting for what it promised than for what it achieved, its project was similar to *Macunaíma* and to Asturias's *Leyendas de Guatemala*. Of course he and Asturias were both from small countries with large ethnic populations which made the question of a unified national identity more than usually problematical. Both were closely associated with the Surrealists in Paris in the 1920s; both knew of Joyce, both believed in the power of myth, metaphor, language and symbol, both were Freudian in orientation, Marxisant and revolutionary by instinct. They would each, from that moment, through the dark hibernatory age of the 1930s and 1940s – a fertile, global unconscious for both of them – gestate these ideas and in due course, around 1948, each would start to talk of 'magical realism' (Asturias) or 'the marvellous real' (Carpentier).

As an active member of Cuba's 1923 Generation, Alejo Carpentier (1904–80) was involved in efforts to revolutionize national culture and to confront the dictatorship of Gerardo Machado. The guiding thread of the search for identity was Afro-Cubanism, the quest to integrate the Black experience into Cuba's national self-expression, underpinned by the pathbreaking folkloric and ethnological work of Fernando Ortiz (1881–1969), one of Latin America's most original thinkers. Stories by Carpentier inspired compositions by the Mulatto composer Amadeo Roldán, and Carpentier subsequently became a leading authority on Cuban music in his own right. *Ecue-Yamba-O* includes several attempts to recreate the intense experience of Afro-Cuban music; and although it would be effortlessly surpassed by Carpentier's own *El reino de este mundo* (1949) almost two decades later, it was undoubtedly one of the first important attempts to characterize the Black presence in narrative.

By 1928 Miguel Angel Asturias (1899–1974) had almost completed his first major book in Paris, where he was studying ethnology at the Sorbonne. Early public readings took place in the year that *Macunaíma* was published. These *Leyendas de Guatemala* (1930), still virtually un-studied to the present day, are one of the first anthropological contribu-tions to Spanish American literature. Like Andrade, who called for an American 'cannibalization' of European culture, Asturias thought attack the best form of defence and communicated a radically different vision, revealing a Latin American world as yet unimagined. Asturias's small country had behind it what Andrade's huge one lacked: a great native civilization. Thus the second part of his integrative strategy was to relate the 'primitive' (we were all 'Indians' once upon a time, in the tribal era) to the classical maize-based civilizations of the Pre-Columbian era: Mayas, Aztecs, Incas. All were earth, maize, sun and star worshippers, space men. In Asturias's fiction the pre-human forces and creatures of native myth are given new life, and the Indians themselves are inserted into that landscape: the Spaniards here are very late arrivals.

Asturias's next major work was one of the landmarks of Latin American narrative, which, in the post-Second World War period, confirmed the rise of urban fiction which had already been signalled in Argentina and Uruguay. Ironically enough, the novel in question, *El señor Presidente* (1946), was about a very small capital city, that of his native Guatemala, and it was set in the period of the First World War, before the process of Latin American modernization had become generally visible. Asturias's entire life until the age of twenty-one had been overshadowed by the fearsome dictatorship of Manuel Estrada Cabrera (1898–1920), and his own father's legal career was ruined by the tyrant. This novel, in which every action and every thought is in some way conditioned by the real dictator and his mythological aura, reflects the horizons of Asturias's own childhood and adolescence ('A monstrous forest separated the President from his enemies, a forest of trees with ears which at the slightest sound began to turn as though whipped up by the hurricane wind . . . A web of invisible threads, more invisible than the telegraph wires, linked each leaf to the President, alert to all that went on in the most secret fibres of his citizens.'). From that darkness, that imprisonment (not only the dictator-ship, but also Hispanic traditionalism, semi-colonial provincialism, Ca-tholicism and the Family), Asturias travelled to Paris, 'City of Light', to undertake his cultural apprenticeship to the twentieth century, in a capital which offered perhaps the most remarkable array of ideas, schools and personalities gathered in one Western city since the Renaissance. The contrast between that light and the earlier darkness, perceived retrospectively and at first unconsciously, gives the novel its peculiar dramatic dynamism. Many readers have also found something characteristically Latin American in its contrast between imprisonment and freedom, reality and utopia. It was in the 1920s and 1930s, then, in the transition between the 'novels of the land' and the new 'labyrinthine' fiction, between 'social realism' and 'magical realism', that the liberation of Latin American fiction began.

In 1967 Asturias would become the first Latin American novelist to win the Nobel Prize. Yet even he was not to be the most influential narrator from the continent. That honour goes, undoubtedly, to Jorge Luis Borges (1899–1986), one of those rare literary phenomena, a writer who literally changed the way in which people see literature and, accordingly, the world. An almost indispensable point of reference in the era of Postmodernism, Borges – whose mature work is, effectively, a critique of Modernism – has influenced even the most influential of contemporary thinkers, like Michel Foucault and Jacques Derrida, as well as almost all his literary successors in Latin America. Yet although he had been a leading avant-garde poet in the 1920s, Borges was never any kind of revolutionary in the usual meaning of the word. He was never interested in magic, nor in the primitive, nor in Freud, and certainly not in Marx. Joyce was an early fascination, but not a model to be imitated. Yet if Andrade, Asturias and Carpentier brought about the opening to myth, oral expression and popular experience which was to allow the exploration of Latin American culture from the 1920s and thus to provide the essential basis for the 'New Novel', it is Borges, unmistakably, who supplied the sense of precision and structure which permitted the inter-textual systematization of that culture and the creation of the Latin American literature in which, ironically, he never believed. He was, indeed, universal, but in a uniquely Latin American way.

Borges had been a leading participant in the youthful Hispanic avant-garde, prominent in the 'Ultraist' movement in the 1920s and a tireless cultural animator and contributor to little magazines. At the same time his early poems entitled *Fervor de Buenos Aires* (1923) demonstrate that he too was at that time torn between the cosmopolitan lure of Europe and travel, on the one hand, and nostalgia for the local and the picturesque on the other. Needless to say, the pleasures and pains of both are heightened, for the 'Ulyssean' writer, by the contrast between them, which can only be fully experienced in the labyrinth of time, space and memory. But in the 1930s the still young writer renounced both nativism and the avant-garde as infantile disorders and began to effect a long, slow revolution, first in Latin American fiction and eventually in Western literature as a whole. For some critics the publication of his *Historia universal de la infamia* in 1935 marks the birth of 'magical realism' in Latin America. But this honour, as we have seen, must go to Andrade, Asturias and Carpentier, all writers with more convincingly 'native' cultures than that of Borges's disappearing gauchos. Indeed, the attraction of the gaucho for Borges was that of the Western gunslinger for certain North American ideologies: his insistent individualism. Nevertheless Borges's *Historia universal,* a distant relative of Kafka's work, does mark the birth of Latin America's distinctive tradition of 'fantastic literature', a tradition most firmly rooted precisely in Argentina and Uruguay. For example, *Museo de la novela de la eterna* by Argentine Macedonio Fernández (1874–1952), an influence on the artistically dehumanized writings of both Borges and Cortázar, though not published until 1967, was conceived in the 1920s and written in the 1930s. And Adolfo Bioy Casares (b. 1914), Borges's close friend and collaborator, was himself an outstanding narrator of both short stories and novels such as *La invención de Morel* (1940) or *El sueño de los héroes* (1954).

The two styles – 'magical realism' and 'fantastic literature' – were by no means the same, but certainly overlapped and both took on characteristically Latin American features, not least in their obsessive dualism. The tropical magical realism, centered on the Caribbean and Brazil, specifically set out to fuse an elemental but 'fertile' native culture with the more – but also less – knowing gaze of European consciousness; whereas the labyrinthine metaphysic of fantasy emanating from the River Plate, in the absence of such an alternative culture, fused the local reality, perceived as drab and second-rate, with a fantastic dimension which was really, perhaps, a sign for the superior 'meta-consciousness' of the Europe by which Argentinians and Uruguayans felt they were inevitably defined and to which they hopelessly aspired. Borges's whole endeavour would be to resolve this tension through a strategy of relativization and redefinition. Through this endeavour he quite literally changed the world.

At the end of the 1930s Borges prepared a landmark collection, the *Antología de la literatura fantástica* (1940), in collaboration with Bioy Casares and Silvina Ocampo; and then came his two incomparable collec-

tions of stories *Ficciones* (1944) and *El Aleph* (1949). After that, and once
he had collected his essays in *Otras inquisiciones* (1952), rather like some
precocious scientific experimenter, Borges's work was effectively at an
end. He continued of course to write poems, stories and essays, despite
increasing blindness, but never again with the revolutionary force of his
work in the 1940s. Later writers like Carlos Fuentes came to suggest that
without Borges there would not even have been a 'modern' Latin American novel, which is clearly untrue but nevertheless a remarkable claim
given his years as a political outcast and the fact that he never felt
remotely tempted to write anything as vulgar as a full-length novel. He
did, however, compile his own eccentric catalogue of books, writers and
ideas in order to chart his own course through Western literature, demonstrate that its central themes are really no different from those of the
Orient, and thereby justify his fundamental belief that 'universal history
is the history of a few metaphors.'[8] For this purpose he invoked the spirits
of Poe, Croce, Shelley, Schopenhauer, Kafka and Hawthorne, among
others, to support Carlyle's belief that 'history is an infinite sacred book
that all men write and read and try to understand and in which they too
are written'.[9] Borges then deduced what may be the key to an appreciation of his influence, namely the idea that all writers are many writers and
that 'each writer creates his precursors' – that is, 'each writer's work
modifies our conception of the past as it will modify the future'.[10] This
approach in the brilliantly inventive essays of *Otras inquisiciones* allowed
him to make such provoking statements as that Chesterton 'restrained
himself from being Edgar Allan Poe or Franz Kafka', or that, regarding
two versions of a certain tragic history, 'the original is unfaithful to the
translation'.[11]

Borges has, almost single-handed, revolutionized our ability to think
about reading and writing. In real respects he has demystified these
processes and even more profoundly the concepts of authorship and originality by emphasizing the artifice of art. This is the more extraordinary
when one considers that reading and writing is what writers and critics
are supposed to be meditating on all the time, yet it took a sceptic like
Borges to see through the myths which have prevailed since romanticism.

---

[8] Jorge Luis Borges, 'Pascal's Sphere', in *Other Inquisitions, 1937–52* (London, 1973), pp. 73–4.

[9] Borges, 'Partial Enchantments of the *Quijote*', in *Other Inquisitions*, p. 46.

[10] Borges, 'Kafka and his Precursors', in *Other Inquisitions*, p. 108.

[11] Borges, 'On Chesterton', in *Other Inquisitions*, p. 84; 'About William Beckford's *Vathek*', in *Other Inquisitions*, p. 140.

Almost equally as important is his approach to influences and his demonstration – despite himself – of the materiality of thought, language, literature and culture. The implications for a post-colonial literature are far-reaching. Moreover, since he was, despite everything, a Latin American, his revolutionary effect on literature and criticism has enormously advanced the international image and reputation of Latin America and its participation in Western culture. A whole swathe of twentieth-century writing from Kafka, Pirandello and Unamuno to Calvino, Kundera and Eco (not to mention Cortázar and García Márquez) only makes the kind of unified sense it currently does thanks to the meaning which Borges's way of seeing retrospectively confers on these writers whilst also linking them backwards to their great distant 'precursors', as mentioned above. In Latin America itself this gives confirmatory legitimacy to a certain form of cosmopolitanism, which has been necessary for cultural communication and even survival, a certain way of being in and out of, part of and separate from Western civilization, and at the same time a global approach to culture, knowledge and other people and other nations which is somehow wholly appropriate to the continent which completed humanity's knowledge of the world.

Andrade, Asturias, Borges and Carpentier made these decisive contributions to Latin American culture in this century, in the transition between a traditional and a modern world, and between Europe and Latin America. They were the great cultural bridges, effective intermediaries between two worlds, and thus the first 'Ulyssean' narrators, travellers through both time and space. When Andrade, Asturias, Borges and Carpentier began to write, in the mid-1920s, Latin America had barely begun to experience modernity, whereas the writers who attained celebrity and wrote their greatest works in the mid-1960s had grown up with it all their lives and absorbed the new pace and variety of contemporary urban experience without even thinking about it. For them, indeed, the city and its inhabitants were the primary reality and it was the country-side which was abnormal. For the earlier generation the motor car, airplane, gramophone, cinema and radio were all new experiences to be absorbed after childhood, but modernity as a whole and life in a great modern conurbation were recent enough in origin to be perceived as essentially non-American experiences. In that sense, indeed, 1920 was really the last moment where the divorce between modernity and underdevelopment could ever be quite so visible and quite so culturally shocking in the Latin American environment.

The New Novel

The 'New Novel', which in retrospect began its trajectory at the end of
the Second World War, followed the different paths marked out by the
writers who had undergone the 'Ulyssean' experience in the 1920s, above
all Asturias, Borges and Carpentier. It is perhaps surprising, at first
sight, that the most important novels to emerge during this period,
following another great war, should again have been 'regional' or even
'telluric' in orientation. Not until the 'Boom' itself in the 1960s were
Latin American writers able regularly to produce great works of urban
fiction in response to the growth of a well-educated, middle-class audience and the increasing concentration of the population in large cities.
One might say, oversimplifying inevitably, that the post-war era was the
moment in which the Faulknerian impulse predominated in Latin American fiction and that the Joycean mode would only fully crystallize in the
1960s, after the publication of Cortázar's *Rayuela* in 1963.

Of course even William Faulkner was a 'Ulyssean' writer in both senses
of the word. Longing for adventure he had travelled the world – first in his
imagination and then, briefly, in reality – and had returned, 'weary of
wonders', as Borges would put it (in his poem 'Ars Poetica'), to perceive
that 'Art is that Ithaca, of green eternity, not of wonders', and thus to make
a new world, Yoknapatawpha County, Mississippi, out of his original
world. And he was also a Modernist, Joycean writer, who was inspired by
the Irishman's unrivalled exercise of formal freedom and adapted the interior monologue and stream-of-consciousness to his own historical purpose.

Yet again it was Borges, never a lover of long fiction, who made the
most ironic but also the most significant contribution to Spanish American
consciousness of Faulkner by translating *The Wild Palms* in 1940, the year
after its first publication, just as he had translated the last page of *Ulysses* in
1925. *The Wild Palms,* with its juxtaposition of distinct realities, is the
precursor of a narrative line which would culminate in Vargas Llosa's *La
Casa Verde* in 1966. Faulkner's domain is the unfinished, traumatized rural
environment of the American South, an accursed land like the lands of
Juan Rulfo, João Guimaraes Rosa and Gabriel García Márquez. Faulkner's
characters are Black, Red and White, rich and poor (though usually the
former declining into the latter), portrayed over 300 years but particularly
since the early nineteenth century, all struggling to discover a destiny and
assert an identity which can never be forged collectively against a bitter

and tragic history of violation, extermination, slavery and civil war, and a legacy of guilt, despair and solitude. It is this nexus of themes and techniques – miscegenation and its contrasts and juxtapositions foremost among them – which makes Faulkner such a formidable influence on the Latin American New Novel. Like Faulkner, then, the leading Latin American writers were by the 1940s citizens not only of their own lands but of the world, and they looked on their continent and its culture with a radically transformed gaze, mapping the cultural landscape through their geographical, social and historical explorations. It was, in short, a process of internalization of Latin American history.

Many critics would agree that the first page of the New Novel – indeed, for one critic the first page of the 'Boom',[12] was the magical, incantatory opening of Asturias's *El señor Presidente*: 'Boom, bloom, alumbright, Lucifer of alunite! The sound of the prayer bells droned on, humming in the ears, uneasily tolling from light to gloom, gloom to light'. And the first work which decisively united the concept of the New Novel with that of magical realism was the same author's *Hombres de maíz* (1949). Ariel Dorfman perceived its importance as early as 1968: 'Although its origins fade into remote regions and its socio-cultural coordinates are still disputed, the contemporary Spanish American novel has a quite precise date of birth. It is the year 1949, when Alejo Carpentier's *El reino de este mundo* and Miguel Angel Asturias's *Hombres de maíz* saw the light of day. The latter, both the fountainhead and the backbone of all that is being written in our continent today, has met with a strange destiny, like so many works that open an era and close off the past.'[13]

The opening of the later novel was as strange and dramatic as that of *El señor Presidente*. Asturias was trying to imagine the world of Maya culture through his sleeping indigenous protagonist, Gaspar Ilóm, 'buried with his dead ones and his umbilicus, unable to free himself from a serpent of six hundred thousand coils of mud, moon, forests, rainstorms, mountains, birds and echoes he could feel around his body'. No novel has more profoundly explored the hidden labyrinths of Latin American cultural history. Asturias even has an unconcealed affection for – and much more direct knowledge of – the peasant, Mestizo culture which helped create him but which, as part of the Western heritage, he questions and even deplores, so

---

[12] William Gass, 'The First Seven Pages of the Boom', *Latin American Literary Review*, 29 (Pittsburgh, PA., 1987), 33–56.

[13] See Ariel Dorfman, '*Hombres de maíz*: el mito como tiempo y palabra', in his *Imaginación y violencia en América* (Santiago, Chile, 1970), p. 71.

that folk culture from the European side is as well represented as the myths and legends of the contemporary Indians and their pre-Alvaradian ancestors. The narrative's point of departure, the resistance of Gaspar Ilóm at the beginning of the century, is based on a real historical incident. This was itself representative of a historical process which still continues both in Guatemala and Latin America generally – a process whose chain-like structure is also visible in *Raza de bronce, Huasipungo, El mundo es ancho y ajeno,* José María Arguedas's *Todas las sangres* (see below) and Vargas Llosa's *La Casa Verde* (see below), namely that of the native Indian, uprooted from his culture and ejected from his homeland by the typical processes of Western capitalism and culture, who either rebels or sets out defeated on the road to loneliness and alienation. Clearly, in that sense this is a retrospective, assimilative work, a panoramic examination of a historical landscape, a meditation by a city man on the origins of a national and continental culture and on the theme of cultural loss ('Who has never called, never shouted the name of that woman lost in his yesterdays? Who has not pursued like a blind man that being who went away from his being, when he came to himself . . . ?'). Other authors who have written about the contemporary Maya Indians are the Guatemalan Mario Monteforte Toledo (b.1911), with *Anaité* (1940) and *Entre la piedra y la cruz* (1948), and, above all, the outstanding Mexican writer Rosario Castellanos (1925–74), with *Balún Canán* (1957) and *Oficio de tinieblas* (1962). *Balún Canán* is indeed the most important novel from the Maya region after Asturias's *Hombres de maíz,* though it is only one of a number of varied works by Castellanos, whose pioneering feminist approach to Latin American social relations gives all her work, fiction, poetry and theatre, a truly radical cutting edge.

The year of *Hombres de maíz,* 1949, was also the year when Alejo Carpentier, in the prologue to *El reino de este mundo,* wrote what is effectively the great magical realist manifesto, his essay on 'Lo real maravilloso'. This novel, a small literary jewel, deals with the slave revolts in eighteenth-century Haiti and ends with a classic meditation: 'In the Kingdom of Heaven there is no grandeur to be won, inasmuch as there all is an established hierarchy, the unknown is revealed, existence is infinite, there is no possibility or sacrifice, all is rest and joy. For this reason, bowed down by suffering and duties, beautiful in the midst of his misery, capable of loving in the face of afflictions and trials, man finds his greatness, his fullest measure, only in the Kingdom of this World.'[14] French-speaking

---

[14] Alejo Carpentier, *The Kingdom of this World,* trans. Harriet de Onís (London, 1967), p. 149.

Haiti itself has produced a number of novels which might conveniently be placed within a broadly magical realist definition. They would include *Gouverneurs de la Rosée* (1944) by Jacques Roumain (1907–44), *La Bête de musseau* (1946) and *Le Crayon de Dieu* (1952), both written jointly by the brothers Philippe-Thoby and Pierre Marcelin, and *Compère Général Soleil* (1955) and *Les Arbres musiciens* by Jacques Stephen Alexis (1922–61).

Other Spanish American writers often considered magical realist are the Venezuelan Arturo Uslar Pietri (b.1905), a close friend of both Asturias and Carpentier in Paris in the 1920s and one of the theoreticians of the movement, author of *El camino del Dorado* (1947) and *Oficio de difuntos* (1976); and the Ecuadorean Demetrio Aguilera Malta (1909–81), author of *Don Goyo* (1933) and *Siete lunas y siete serpientes* (1970). In the 1950s there were a number of variations on these magical realist models. By far the most successful was *Pedro Páramo* (1955) by the Mexican Juan Rulfo (1918–86). Rulfo has the extraordinary distinction of having written not only this, the most widely admired Mexican novel of the century, but also *El llano en llamas* (1953), some of the continent's most compelling short stories. His work gives him a close literary kinship with the Brazilian Graciliano Ramos. *Pedro Páramo* is a novel in which recognizable European motifs like the Oedipal, Thesean and Dantean quests are perfectly subordinated to the requirements of a metaphorical presentation of the colonized, feudal heritage of a whole country, a whole continent, unified by the power of myth ('I came to Comala because they told me my father lived here, one Pedro Páramo. My mother said so. And I promised her I'd come to see him as soon as she died. I squeezed her hands as a sign that I would do it; because she was about to die and I was in a mood to promise anything'). Rulfo's novel operates on both the national (Mexican/Latin American) and individual (universal) planes, and once again a critical vision compatible with the new Marx and the new Freud underpins the entire narrative. Without such a framework it becomes indecipherable and spirals away into labyrinths of 'magic' and 'mystery' ('This town is full of echoes. You would think they were trapped in the hollow walls or beneath the stones'). As the design for his novel, Rulfo – who, mysteriously, never managed to write another – dreamed up a brilliantly simple conception, worthy of Kafka: all the characters in the novel are dead when it begins and the town they inhabit, Comala, is a dead town where the air is full of tormented souls wandering in search of a redemption which, to judge from their terrestrial experience, is unlikely ever to come. Yet, as in all true magical realist works, it is social relationships which govern this apparently most ethereal of novels. This is of great importance, since *Pedro Páramo,* perhaps even more than García Márquez's *Cien años de soledad,* has been used time and again to justify the belief that Latin America is magical, mysterious and irrational – this is precisely what magical realism is *not* about – and that its literature celebrates this strange 'reality'; whereas for half a century most important writers have been attempting to carry out deconstruction of the myths elaborated over the previous 450 years. It has been said that this novel is pessimistic. Certainly Rulfo himself was, and it is difficult to see any other conclusion for a book reflecting the experience of the Mexican peasants in the past century. Yet Pedro himself is finally murdered: the Revolution may be shown – as in Azuela – to be confused, cynical or opportunistic, but in however indirect a way one of the landowner's illegitimate sons does take his revenge and the pile of barren rocks which is Pedro's regime does finally come crashing down: 'Pedro . . . leaned on Damiana Cisneros's arms and tried to walk. After a few paces he fell, pleading inside. He hit the earth and began to crumble like a pile of stones.' Two other writers who have examined the rural landscapes of post-revolutionary Mexico are his fellow Jaliscan Juan José Arreola (b. 1918), author of *La feria* (1963) and Elena Garro (b.1920), author of the novel *Los recuerdos del porvenir* (1963), a startlingly original revisionary work about the aftermath of the Mexican Revolution.

At this moment in literary history Brazil was, for once, quite closely in step with events in Spanish America. In 1956 the Brazilian João Guimarães Rosa (1908–67) produced *Grande sertão: veredas* (*The Devil to Pay in the Backlands*), one of Brazil's most important novels, again set in the unyielding, mysterious, exasperating and apparently eternal barren wastes of the Sertão, in this case that of Minas Gerais. The work has been compared with *Gargantua and Pantagruel, Don Quijote, Ulysses* and *Cien años de soledad.* Rosa was the writer who in 1946 turned Brazilian fiction away from social realism (as Asturias and Carpentier were doing in Spanish America), with his first collection of stories, *Sagarana.* In 1956, the same year as *Grande sertão,* the even more challenging narratives of *Corpo de baile* appeared. Later collections were *Primeiras estórias* (1962), *Trifle (Terceiras estórias)* (1967), and *Estas estórias* (1969). The Portuguese title of *Grande sertão* suggests the same concept of the field and the paths as in Gallegos's *Doña Bárbara,* that great telluric labyrinth in which the plain may represent both life itself (individual and universal) and the book which recreates it. In conception, however, it is much closer to another novel by Gallegos *Cantaclaro* (1934) – though the difference in sheer erudition and literary panache is evident — or to the Argentine Leopoldo Lugones's *El payador* (1916), a treatise on the gaucho 'minstrels'. Rosa makes no allowances for the reader in terms of the novel's hermeticism and reliance upon dense layerings of imagery, symbolism and regional vocabulary. The story is narrated by one Riobaldo ('dry river'), a former cowboy and bandit from the Sertão, now a landowner, who addresses some unknown interlocutor — the writer? the reader? the devil? — as he recalls his adventures and perplexities over a long and passionate life riding the great plains at the end of the last century: 'You, sir, knew nothing about me. Do you now know much or little? A person's life, all the paths into its past: is it a story that touches upon your own life at all, sir?'[15] If the novel is about Brazil, then it underscores the impossibility, recognized by so many Brazilian writers, of ever going beyond the concept of the nation as an irreconcilable plurality; if about man's condition in the world, then it underlines that Western man's destiny is to arrive forever at a crossroads, torn always between impossible choices and dualities, good and evil, male and female, objective and subjective, history and myth, in a world which, like fictional stories, is ultimately impossible to interpret. More clearly than other writers, Rosa shows just how much the Latin American novel of its era was forced to reconcile the requirements of the twentieth-century Modernist text with the impulse of romance, a medieval genre which is still surprisingly relevant in a world of loose ends, a still unwoven social and historical reality where more things are unresolved than identified, and where messianic movements promising transcendent meaning, the triumph of good over evil and imminent or eventual salvation are still invested with immense force.

A reading of this remarkable Brazilian novel prompts the reader to reflect again that this vast country — Lévi-Strauss's 'sad tropics' — remains dominated in its own consciousness by the 'three sad races' — the Portuguese, with their *saudade,* still missing Europe; the Africans, liberated from slavery only a century ago, longing for their magical past; and the Indians, staring into space, pining for their long-lost cultural universe. Thus far the combination has failed to produce a successful democratic society, but capitalism has taken firm root through the efforts of outsiders, including optimistic immigrants from all over the world. Little wonder that the largest republic in the region offers the perplexing image

15 J. Guimarães Rosa, *The Devil to Pay in the Backlands,* trans. J.L. Taylor and H. de Onís (New York, 1971), p. 482.

of a country with a national identity that strikes outsiders as unusually distinctive, whilst Brazilian artists and intellectuals themselves continue to insist that this most extraordinary of nations somehow remains a mystery unto itself.

An equally unique literary phenomenon was Peru's José María Arguedas (1913–69) whose early indigenist works, *Agua* (1935, stories) and *Yawar Fiesta* (1941), were contemporaneous with the works of Ciro Alegría. He is now considered perhaps the greatest indigenist novelist of the continent, mainly due to *Los ríos profundos* (1958) and *Todas las sangres* (1964). Although the interest of his works is in some respects circumscribed by their strictly Americanist orientation and, it must be said, by some limitations of technique, Arguedas is today counted among the most important Latin American novelists this century. *Los ríos profundos* is largely autobiographical. Arguedas lost his mother early and suffered rejection from his own family, living for much of his childhood among Quechua Indians. Quechua, indeed, was his first language and one of the fascinations of his writing is the relationship between the Spanish in which it is mainly written and the Quechua thought patterns and structures which lie beneath. Arguedas's classic explanation of his literary endeavour was as follows: 'I tried to convert into written language what I was as an individual: a link, strong and capable of universalizing itself, between the great imprisoned nation and the generous, human section of the oppressors.'[16] Angel Rama concluded that Arguedas's paradoxical solution was to make himself 'a white acculturated by the Indians',[17] and this is the problematic worked through by *Los ríos profundos* ('Fleeing from cruel relatives I threw myself upon the mercy of an *ayllu* where they grew maize in the smallest and most delightful valley I have known. Thorn bushes with blazing flowers and the song of doves lit up the maizefields. The family heads and the ladies, *mamakunas* of the community, looked after me and imbued me with the priceless tenderness which fills my life.'). The strength of *Los ríos profundos* lies in its juxtaposition of two worlds, its uniquely poetic approach to the realm of nature, and its innovative conception of language and myth in a narrative tradition previously dominated by the conventions of the European bourgeois novel.

Arguedas's longest work, *Todas las sangres,* is probably the last of the great indigenist narratives (though the novels of another Peruvian, Manuel

---

[16] J.M. Arguedas, 'No soy un aculturado' (1968), from the appendix to his posthumous novel *El zorro de arriba y el zorro de abajo.*

[17] Angel Rama, *Transculturación narrativa en América Latina* (Mexico, D.F., 1982), p. 207.

Scorza, are also remarkable – see below). It is an appropriate sequel to *El mundo es ancho y ajeno* (though published, ironically enough, in the midst of the 'Boom'). If *Huasipungo* is the classic of vulgar Marxism, *Todas las sangres* is the classic of dialectical materialism. It would appear to be set in the 1950s, in the period shortly before the Cuban Revolution and, in Peru, the foundation of the Apra Rebelde led by Luis de la Puente Uceda and the peasant upheavals in the valley of La Convención and Lares led by Hugo Blanco. It presents a kind of microcosm of Peruvian history by detailing the social transformations taking place around the small town of San Pedro when the old patriarchal landowner Don Andrés dies and curses his two sons, Bruno, a reactionary religious fanatic who wishes to maintain the feudal system yet eventually assists the Indians in their uprising, and Fermín, a ruthless modernizing capitalist, a member of the new nationalist bourgeoisie, who owns the local wolfram mine and is involved in a desperate struggle with a foreign multinational company. Bruno's hacienda and Fermín's mine dominate the otherwise decaying local economy, where the gentry are in decline and the Cholos scrape to make a living. Nearby are two free Indian communities, the prosperous Lahuaymarca and the poor Paraybamba. Within these social sectors the widest possible range of ethnic groups, classes and fractions of Peru is represented. This is a story which has been told many times in Latin American social realist literature, but never with such a sense of contradiction, mastery of detail and dynamic movement. The principal protagonist is Rendón Willka, an Indian who was exiled from the community as an adolescent for standing up for his rights at school. On his return eight years later Willka is an indigenist militant, a kind of Christ figure, one of the most complex and attractive character creations in Latin American fiction, a man who knows both of Peru's component social parts and thus has insight beyond that of the other characters. When Willka cries out shortly before the end of the novel that the Indians have 'found their country at last', he is not talking about the neo-colonial, capitalist state which has been developed – or, rather, underdeveloped – since Peru gained its formal independence in the early nineteenth century. Rather he looks forward to a new, genuinely plural society when 'the Peruvian' has finally managed to emerge from the ethnic labyrinth of blood and cultural conflict.

All the novels discussed thus far have left the novelist himself, and his natural habitat – the city – out of the frame. That is why consideration of another novel by Alejo Carpentier, *Los pasos perdidos,* has been delayed until now, although it was published in 1953. It remains his most important work despite the attractions of the even more ambitious *El siglo de las luces* (1962), a great historical novel about the independence movements of the Caribbean in the eighteenth century, *El recurso del método* (1975) and *Consagración de la primavera,* his celebration of the Cuban Revolution (1978). *Los pasos perdidos* is the most programmatic of all novels about the relationship between Latin America (above all the Caribbean and Venezuela) and 'Europe' (above all Spain and France), and between Latin America and 'modernity' as represented by the United States. In that sense it is an indispensable cultural document of Latin America's twentieth century. The title echoes Breton's Surrealist project, though the search for lost time and primitive roots actually takes place against a later Gallic background, that of post-war existentialism, in which a sometime Latin American, living in self-inflicted exile in New York, is nevertheless imbued with the absurdist ideas of Camus, though with none of the rebellious voluntarism of Sartre. The anonymous protagonist is a musician, a scholar and artist living an existence of utter alienation from both true values and from his Latin American cultural origins, selling his art in the capitalist market place by writing the music for advertising films. Once the narrator arrives in the jungle he falls in love with a Latin American Mestizo woman, a mixture of the continent's three great ethnic groupings, and forgets his North American wife and French mistress, giving himself over to a spontaneous eroticism which is also a cosmic ritual. This return to the maternal realm of nature stimulates him to write a long-cherished symphony based on Shelley's *Prometheus Unbound,* only to find that in order to obtain the materials to complete it – not to mention seeing it performed – he must return to the alienating civilization from which he has so recently escaped ('Today Sisyphus's vacation came to an end'). When, after a frustrating time in New York, he tries to journey back once more to the little jungle community, he finds that the waters of the river have symbolically risen and he cannot find the way through the labyrinth of trees and water. The conclusion is that there is no turning back because artists and intellectuals are, first and last, the antennae of the race: their realm is the present and the future.

The 'Boom'

Between the Second World War and the 1960s, as we now see, the 'New Novel' was beginning its remarkable rise to world attention, virtually unnoticed at first, with each new achievement in some part of Latin America remaining unrelated by either writers or critics to what was going on elsewhere. Economically and politically a different age seemed to be dawning and in the post-war years and again in the late 1950s there was much optimism that the Latin American middle classes, with liberal democratic regimes to represent them, might be on the verge of some new era of political stability as well as real economic expansion. The book which first reflected this changing and essentially urban reality was *La región más transparente* (1958) by Carlos Fuentes (b.1928), a novel about Mexico City and Mexican identity which now, with the benefit of history, appears clearly as the first novel of the 'Boom' and thus the signal of the developments that were shortly to occur in Latin American narrative. Paradoxically, of course, these developments became visible at the very moment that the Cuban Revolution was about to transform the whole perspective of Latin American history by proclaiming a Third World, anti-urban and anti-bourgeois ideology.

La región más transparente may have provided the early signs, but no one doubts which work effectively inaugurated the new movement by continuing the interrogation of Latin American identity which Carpentier had pursued in *Los pasos perdidos*. That novel was *Rayuela* (1963) by the Argentine Julio Cortázar (1914–83). Cortázar's achievement lies, first, in having updated and synthesized the twin traditions of 'Joycism' and Surrealism which were the legacy bequeathed by Andrade, Asturias and Carpentier from the 1920s; and second, in having fused them through an intense reading of the ideas and forms explored before him by his compatriot Borges. No other novelist and no other work so comprehensively embody this triple heritage. Cortázar's first novel, *Los premios* (1960), about an allegorical journey on a European cruise liner – tickets won by lottery and going nowhere – was already a rather timid fusion of Joyce (in structure and linguistic texture), Kafka (in theme and symbolic design), Borges and other Modernist currents. Its culminating moment, when the passengers capture the bridge, only to discover that no one is navigating the ship, is one of the great defining moments of Latin American literature, anticipating not only the vision of Postmodernism as a whole – of which the Argentine writer's own story 'Blow-Up' ('Las babas del diablo') was an early path-finder – but also the 'Boom' writers' overwhelming sense of cultural emancipation from 'Europe' ('It was true, now he came to think about it: the bridge was entirely empty but . . . it didn't matter, it hadn't the slightest importance because what mattered was something else, something that couldn't be grasped but was trying to show itself and define itself in the sensation that was exciting him more and more.'). Cortázar's emphasis upon sensation, spontaneity, imminence and the primacy of experience over conceptualization is one which characterizes Latin American fiction from its romantic origins in the early nineteenth century to its Surrealist designs in the early twentieth century.

It has been argued that *Rayuela* was to Spanish American fiction in 1963 what *Ulysses* had been for European and North American literature as a whole in 1922. Certainly it was a major point of crystallization and particularly significant for its timing – published early in the sixties. Moreover, its very structure is a comparison of two cities, moving from an exploration of art and its media and institutions in the first part, 'Over There', to an analysis of consciousness and language themselves in the second 'Over Here'. There are many quite tangible Joycean influences, but Cortázar's work also invokes Surrealist concepts not present in Joyce and existentialist considerations which post-dated him. Much of *Rayuela* also explores, tragicomically, the obscure and often sinister motives which lie behind the most frivolous or inconsequential behaviour, in a way reminiscent of Borges in stories like 'El Aleph'. Most of all, though, Cortázar's unique place in contemporary narrative is due to his simultaneous exploration and incarnation of the international avant-garde and its special concerns.

Rayuela, unmistakably, was the novel most admired by the other writers of the 'Boom', the one which made it visible and recognizable, the work situated at the other pole from *Cien años de soledad,* with which the literary firework show reached its grand crescendo in 1967. Yet despite first impressions to the contrary, *Rayuela* is really a variant of the conceptual model underpinning *Hombres de maíz, Pedro Páramo,* the later *La Casa Verde* and, indeed, *Cien años de soledad* itself, a work which rejects the rationalistic logocentrism of European civilization and posits a return to the natural, authentic world of America. Whether America – least of all Argentina, least of all Buenos Aires – can convincingly be considered in any sense spontaneous or natural is a questionable point, but the essential thrust of this position is that it is by definition newer, younger and more spontaneous than Europe or North America (which has on the whole – jazz apart – sacrificed spontaneity for mechanization), no matter how unspontaneous it may actually be on its own terms. This posture turns Europe's constant use of Latin America for catharsis to America's advantage, inverting the Surrealism which so influenced Asturias, Carpentier, Neruda, Paz and Cortázar himself, as if to suggest that Europeans irremediably approach Surrealism from the wrong side, whereas the Latin Americans can always come from the fertile maternal darkness of autochthonous America into the dazzling light of rational knowledge, and then, with their new knowledge aboard, can plunge back into the night and the underworld once more, as the earth itself does, growing, changing, advancing dialectically to the rhythm of the whole universe.

Cortázar, despite his age and his subsequent decision to take French citizenship, was the key writer of the youthful 1960s, though, in the climax to the 'Boom', what actually happened was something quite complicated. The Argentinian writer marks the moment where Joyce rules, but the other major novelists who seized that particular historic opportunity – Fuentes, Vargas Llosa and García Márquez – were all already Faulknerian writers, and their greatest works, written during the 'Boom', are recognizably in Faulknerian vein. Nevertheless, each of them also has an unmistakable additional element, and this is the labyrinthine, historical-mythological national quest motif which Joyce initiated in the 1920s and which Asturias, Carpentier, Guimarães Rosa and Cortázar had been elaborating progressively since the 1920s. Nothing written since has yet superseded those great works, the culmination – for the time being – of 400 years of Latin American cultural development and – possibly false – consciousness. Like Joyce in the First World, they seem for the moment to have put an end to the possibility of further developing the novel as we know it. The current moment seems to be one of assimilation at best, exhaustion at worst.

At any rate, the overtly Modernist works of the 1960s were swiftly perceived as a 'Boom', which moved rapidly towards a climax with *Cien años de soledad* and then shattered into the twinkling fragments of the 'Post-Boom' – or perhaps Postmodernist – novels of the 1970s. It was a confused and contradictory moment, marked deeply by the Cuban Revolution, which at first was itself so pluralist that writers like Cabrera Infante were able to publish extracts from Joyce as well as Trotsky – both were later effectively proscribed – in revolutionary arts journals like *Lunes de Revolución*. The sense of diverse ideological alternatives offered by Cuba and the various social democratic experiments of the day, combined with the new cosmopolitanism bred by a consumption-orientated capitalist boom and an expansion of the Latin American middle classes – buyers and consumers of novels – created a period of intense artistic activity throughout the sub-continent. If there was an overall shape to it in literature, however, that shape was for several years to come a Joycean and

'Ulvssean' one, but a Joycean one which wished not only to superimpose history over myth as abstract categories, but a specifically Latin American history involving the quest for identity and cultural liberation.

Speaking in the 1980s of the 1960s, which he compared explicitly with the 1920s, Perry Anderson identified the perspective for artists and intellectuals as an 'ambiguity – an openness of horizon, where the shapes of the future could alternatively assume the shifting forms of either a new type of capital or of the eruption of socialism – which was constitutive of so much of the original sensibility of what had come to be called Modernism'. After asserting that Modernism lost its creative thrust after 1930, Anderson continued: 'This is not true, manifestly, of the Third World. It is significant that so many of . . . the great Modernist achievements of our time should be taken from Latin American literature. For in the Third World generally, a kind of shadow configuration of what once prevailed in the First World does exist today.'[18] *Ulysses* was the supreme literary product of a peculiarly fertile, highly charged conjuncture, at the moment where the old European regime really was – or so it seemed – finally about to be laid to rest, and where some new modern world – which might be either communist or capitalist – was imposing itself with a speed and vigour the mind could barely encompass, due to a confluence of forms which Anderson summarizes as follows: 'European Modernism in the first [thirty] years of this century thus flowered in the space between a still usable classical past, a still indeterminate technical present, and a still unpredictable political future. Or, put another way, it arose at the intersection between a semi-aristocratic ruling order, a semi-industrialized capitalist economy, and a semi-emergent or insurgent, labour movement.'[19] Suddenly, Latin American writers of the period, above all in the 1920s, were able to take a step back, gain perspective and write works which were no longer, in their one-dimensional 'realist' historicity, secret metaphors for their own terminal lifespan, but metaphors for the whole of human experience since the earliest times. It was of course the development of the social sciences, especially ethnology, which had made such a development possible, viewed from the standpoint of a Western civilization whose own belief systems were in a state of disarray, at once underlining the relativity of culture and making mythology and mystification ever more alluring to the – reluctantly – profane mind of

[18] Perry Anderson, 'Modernity and Revolution', *New Left Review,* 144 (1984), p.109.
[19] *Ibid.*

capitalist consciousness. Only in Latin America, however, due to its specific bi-cultural circumstance, was the magical reconciliation of myth and history regularly performed.

La región más transparente remains perhaps the single most evocative novel about twentieth-century Mexico City. For many people, however, *La muerte de Artemio Cruz* (1962), written partly in Havana at the very beginning of the 'Boom', is probably Carlos Fuentes's outstanding literary achievement. It is also, appropriately enough, seen as the work which effectively puts an end to the cycle of novels of the Revolution (for some critics they ended in 1917, when the Revolution itself ended; for others in 1940, when Cárdenas left office; for others after the Tlatelolco massacre of 1968; whilst for others, ironically enough, they will only come to an end when the ruling Partido Revolucionario Institucional (PRI) ceases to hold power). It is, intriguingly, a vision of the legacy of the Mexican Revolution seen from the standpoint of the then still youthful Cuban Revolution, at a moment when writers like Fuentes and even Vargas Llosa supported it more or less unequivocally. Possibly more than any other Latin American novelist, Fuentes has pursued the theme of identity, which in Mexico since the Revolution has at times taken on the proportions, among intellectuals at least, of a national obsession. (The paradigm is Octavio Paz's *El laberinto de la soledad,* first published in 1950.) *La muerte de Artemio Cruz,* like most of the novels of this era, is retrospective (the character, on his death bed, looks back over his own life and over the history of Mexico and its Revolution: these are the same and the book is their story), and of course labyrinthine. Men quest into the future and then into the past, and novels shadow those quests in ways which, in the twentieth century, are increasingly complex. Fuentes's novel is the most straightforwardly labyrinthine of all ('Chaos: it has no plural.'). We see this most clearly when the author confronts his character overtly half-way through the novel: 'you will decide, you will choose one of those paths, you will sacrifice the rest; you will sacrifice yourself as you choose, ceasing to be all the other men you might have been'. Artemio Cruz, to the extent that can be imagined outside of the novel, is, like Rulfo's Pedro Páramo, a cynical and callous man, though in his heart of hearts he has the same sentimentality and even the same beautiful dreams as his predecessor. As Cruz is finally wheeled into the operating theatre for heart surgery, the novel seems to exonerate him, rather surprisingly, by beginning its ending on a note of absolute fatalism: 'On your head will fall, as if returning from a long journey through time, without beginning or end, all the promises of love and solitude, of hatred and endeavour, violence and tenderness, love and disenchantment, time and oblivion, innocence and surprise . . . In your heart, open to life, tonight.' It is important nevertheless to do justice to the audacity and complexity of this novel, its often brilliant writing, its superb evocation – precisely in and because of its contradictions – of contemporary Mexico, and its ability to give the reader the opportunity to meditate on the Revolution, the meaning of power and the difficulty of making choices in the actually existing world. Like Azuela's, Fuentes's negative judgement on Mexican history merges with a hymn to his turbulent and contradictory country, creating a curious bitter-sweet tension all its own: 'your land . . . you will think there is a second discovery of the land in that warrior quest, that first step upon mountains and gorges which are like a defiant fist raised against the painfully slow advance of road, dam, rail and telegraph pole . . . you will inherit the earth'.

Fuentes, it is worth remarking, was the most clubbable of the 'Boom' writers. Not only did he launch the entire bandwagon and then do everything possible to publicize it; he also associated the Spaniard Juan Goytisolo with the movement and effectively invited in the novelist generally agreed to be the fifth member of the 'Boom', the Chilean José Donoso (1924–96). Donoso's first novel, *Coronación* (1955), had been social realist, but the 'Boom' encouraged him to branch out and he produced a series of works like *Este domingo* (1966), *El lugar sin límites* (1967), and then, in 1970, his *El obsceno pájaro del noche,* at once gothic and surreal, one of the outstanding literary creations of the era. Subsequent works by Donoso include *Casa de campo* (1978), *La misteriosa desaparición de la marquesita de Loria* (1980), *El jardín de al lado* (1981) and *La desesperanza* (1986), which takes a critical look at the Pinochet period.

Despite the critical success of *El obsceno pájaro,* Donoso never quite managed to turn the Boom's big four into a big five. Mario Vargas Llosa (b. 1936) was a member from the very beginning and has remained one of Latin America's most widely admired and controversial novelists up to the present. With the passage of time *La Casa Verde* (1966) seems to become an ever more compelling representation of the lives, dreams and illusions of ordinary Latin Americans, and the fact that its author wrote it at the age of thirty, and – following the success of the also admirable *La ciudad y los perros* (1963) – under pressure of immense audience expectation, makes the achievement all the more remarkable. Nevertheless, despite the acclaim with which it was greeted, it has not been as popular with readers and critics as other novels by Vargas Llosa. The book is effectively in two halves, the one corresponding to events which take place in the jungle, around the mission and garrison of Santa María de Nieva, and the other to the city of Piura on the edge of the northern desert, near the coast, which happens to be the first city founded by the Spaniards on their arrival.

Vargas Llosa's achievement is all the more astonishing since the Amazon, apart from its sensationalist possibilities – so difficult to realize in fiction – does not at first sight appear to be ideal material for his complex Faulknerian techniques. The world he depicts is a male one, and the most cherished fantasies are masculine: the realm of nature is seen only too clearly as an ideological construction which provides both a justification of masculine domination and an ever available means of escape from the class hierarchies of an unjust social order. Bonifacia, the Indian teenager, is known as 'Jungle Girl'; Lalita the jungle sex slave is obviously related to Nabokov's Lolita; and the theme reaches its climactic moment with the musician Anselmo's passion for Toñita, the Latin American dream girl, beautiful, adolescent, blind and mute, but capable of feeling and hearing, and therefore a receptive instrument – like a harp – in the hands of the male, who can use her for any kind of fantasy and therefore as an effective aid to his own masturbatory desires. The vision of Anselmo in his tower – explorer, conquerer, exploiter, creator of fantasies and fountainhead of myth (from epic hero to popular street singer) – is one of the most complete and radical presentations of the patriarchal complex, presented by Vargas Llosa with an almost perfect blend of ambiguities which at once holds, recreates, exposes and subverts. This is an unusual achievement in Latin America where, on the whole, the partisan character of narrative psychology – based on a largely unmediated and none too subtle real history of violence and repression – leads most novelists into presenting villains as villains even unto themselves. Like Rulfo, Vargas Llosa shows us a far more human and thus tenacious social and psychological reality, without in any way underplaying its lamentable and despicable aspects.

After *La Casa Verde* Vargas Llosa brought us, in *Conversación en la Catedral* (1969), Latin America's most complete and desolate picture of one of its great cities, with their penthouses and shanty towns, beggars and plutocrats, and the injustices, squalor and almost incredible contradictions which link them together: 'from the doorway of the *Crónica* Santiago looks down Avenida Tacna, without love: cars, uneven and faded buildings, the skeletons of neon signs floating in the mist of a grey noon.

At what precise moment had Peru fucked up? . . . Peru fucked up, Carlitos fucked up, everyone fucked up. He thinks: there is no solution'. Six hundred pages later, as the novel ends after an unceasing stream of sordid and violent events, passing frequently through brothels and prisons, the reader realises that the author agrees with his character about 'Lima the horrible': there is no solution. By now, however, for all this novel's mesmeric brilliance, it was becoming clear that Vargas Llosa was really lamenting the human and social condition rather than specific societies, and that like Borges and so many others before them he was saying that society was everywhere corrupt, but even worse – hopeless – in the place he had been cursed to be born in. For this reason, ironically, his most successful works in the future would not be his ideologically overwritten political fiction but his humorous and satirical works like *Pantaleón y las visitadoras* (1973), about a military operation to organize a brothel in the Amazon, and the uproarious *La tía Julia y el escribidor* (1977), about the writer's own early marriage to his aunt, conceived as one among many Latin American soap operas.

The 'Boom' reached its climax in 1967 with the publication of its most famous literary manifestation, *Cien años de soledad* by the Colombian novelist Gabriel García Márquez (b.1927). If the opening to Asturias' *El señor Presidente* is the boom-blooming first page of the 'New Novel', it is arguable that García Márquez's first sentence retrospectively provides the first page of Latin American narrative as a whole: 'Many years later, as he faced the firing squad, Colonel Aureliano Buendía was to remember that distant afternoon when his father took him to discover ice. Macondo at that time was a village of twenty adobe houses, built on the banks of a river of transparent water that ran along a bed of polished stones, which were white and enormous like prehistoric eggs. The world was so recent that many things lacked names, and in order to mention them it was necessary to point one's finger'. This innocent, fairy-tale beginning has the transparency of the great works of childhood, like *Robinson Crusoe, Gulliver's Travels* or *Treasure Island*. Almost anyone can understand it and yet this remarkable book, despite its limpidity, is also one of the most deceptive and impenetrable works of contemporary literature, a worthy successor to those other children's works for adults, *Don Quixote, Gargantua and Pantagruel, Tristram Shandy* and *Alice through the Looking Glass*. It is of course the novel which, more than any other, was taken to confirm the historical demise, not only of social realism, but of the kinds of Modernist works which, despite their experimental aspects, nevertheless sought to produce what sceptical post-structuralist critics sometimes call 'cultural knowledge', and therefore to herald the arrival of the linguistically inclined, experimental or Postmodernist novel. Yet *Cien años de soledad* contains a greater variety of carefully encoded material relating to the positivistic orders of social psychology, political economy and the history of ideas than almost any other Latin American novel that comes to mind. Thus Angel Rama's verdict on García Márquez's early works is equally applicable to *Cien años de soledad:* 'I do not believe any other novelist has so acutely, so truthfully seen the intimate relationship between the socio-political structure of a given country and the behaviour of his characters.'[20]

This crucial question – how magical and how realist is García Márquez's writing? – is relevant to all his fictional production. In *La hojarasca* (1955), *La mala hora* (1962), most of the stories of *Los funerales de la Mamá Grande* (1962) or, quintessentially, *El coronel no tiene quien le escriba* (1958), the basic narrative conventions are those of critical realism, with implicit but perfectly straightforward economic, social and political – that is, historical – explanations for the psychological motivations of each of the characters (Angel Rama speaks of 'a pronounced social determinism'). By contrast the later *El otoño del patriarca* (1975), an extraordinary linguistic achievement, is nevertheless characterized by a weakness for hyperbole and the grotesque (though one should add, in justice, that for a number of critics – and for García Márquez himself – this is the Colombian's supreme achievement).

In *Cien años de soledad,* as in most of García Márquez's work, Latin America is a home of futility and lost illusions. Nothing ever turns out as its characters expect; almost everything surprises them; almost all of them fail; few achieve communion with others for more than a fleeting moment, and most not at all. The majority of their actions, like the structure of the novel as a whole (and of course its first chapter), are circular. Ploughers of the sea, they are unable to make their lives purposive, achieve productiveness, break out of the vicious circle of fate. In short, they fail to become agents of history for themselves; rather, they are the echoes of someone else's history, the last link in the centre–periphery chain. The only explanation possible is that these characters are living out their lives in the name of someone else's values or someone else's dreams. Hence the solitude and distance, those recurrent themes of Latin Ameri-

---

[20] A. Rama, 'Un novelista de la violencia americana', in P.S. Martínez (ed.), *Recopilación de textos sobre García Márquez* (Havana, 1969), pp. 58–71 (p. 64).

can history: it is their abandonment in an empty continent, a vast cultural vacuum, marooned thousands of miles away from their true home. Conceived by Spain in the sixteenth century (the stranded galleon, the buried suit of armour), the characters awaken in the late eighteenth-century Enlightenment (magnet and telescope are symbols of the two pillars of Newtonian physics), but are entirely unable to bring themselves into focus in a world they have not made.

A number of critics have recognized the strike against the Banana Company and the ensuing massacre as the central shaping episode of the entire novel. The memory of this event is the secret thread which leads the reader, if not the characters, out into the light at the end of the labyrinth. García Márquez was born in 1927, eighteen months before the historic massacre took place. In the novel the Banana Company has brought temporary prosperity around the time of the First World War, but as profits are threatened in the mid-1920s the workers begin strike action, and the authorities respond with brutal violence, which they then deny: 'In Macondo nothing has happened, nor is anything happening now, nor will it ever.' All history and all memory are comprehensively blotted out by the rain which lasts four years, eleven months and two days, and which recalls the previous 'plague of insomnia' in chapter 3, significantly provoked on that occasion by the suppression of Colombian Indian history. Now proletarian history was to be erased. In this instance, however, despite assiduous efforts by Colombia's official historians to make even the memory of the murdered strikers 'disappear', it was not to be so easy. The massacre was perpetrated by troops under General Carlos Cortés Vargas at the Ciénaga (Magdalena) railway station on 5 December 1928, in direct connivance with the United Fruit Company. The conservative government of Miguel Abadía Méndez (1926–30) reported that a mere nine strikers were killed and, like all succeeding regimes, set about suppressing the true story. After some tempestuous parliamentary debates in September 1929, almost nothing of importance concerning these events appeared in Colombia in the forty years up to the publication of *Cien años de soledad*.

García Márquez shows us that the true history of Colombia and of Latin America is to be established not by the great patriarchs but by members of the younger generation, that of the writer himself (through the two characters called Aureliano Babilonia and Gabriel), who finally come to read and write the real history of the continent. They do so by deciphering the magical reality and labyrinthine fantasies of the previous one hundred years of solitude, this very novel, which is their world, and in which so many other characters have been bewitched and bewildered. Hence the mirror/ mirage ambiguity on the last page. There we find the apocalyptically named Aureliano Babilonia 'deciphering the instant he was living, deciphering it as he lived it', or, as the Mexican philosopher Leopoldo Zea would no doubt argue, negating the past dialectically in order to become, in Octavio Paz's phrase, 'contemporary with all men'. Thus Aureliano breaks out of false circularities, meaningless repetitions, the prehistory before the dawn of true historical consciousness. His reading literally puts an end to one hundred years of solitude, to *Cien años de soledad,* and turns the reader who is reading about him back into the history outside the book. How, one wonders, can critics argue that the 'Boom' writers wilfully detached themselves and their works from Latin American history?

Thus the 'Boom' of the Latin American novel that was heralded by *La región más transparente* in 1958 and announced by *Rayuela* in 1963 climaxed with *Cien años de soledad* in 1967; and the latter, as text, is perfectly aware of its own literary-historical significance, one whose implicit claim is that the 'Boom' itself is proof of the impending transformation of Latin America, of the end of neo-colonialism and the beginning of true liberation. The inter-textual references to Alejo Carpentier's *El siglo de las luces, La muerte de Artemio Cruz, Rayuela* itself and *La Casa Verde* are clear signs of this, in contrast with the work of a writer like Borges, whose textual references are either to Argentina itself, or, much more often, to literatures outside Latin America. The sense of euphoria in the novel, and particularly in its final pages, is palpable. García Márquez had even, momentarily, found a means of reconciling his underlying intellectual pessimism about the human condition with his wilfully optimistic conception of the march of history. Truly he appeared to have liberated the Latin American literary labyrinth. And this, surely, is one of the grandest of historical illusions.

POSTMODERNISM: FROM 'BOOM' TO 'POST-BOOM'

Each of the great 'Boom' novels of the 1960s was about some kind of quest and about the nature of Latin American identity; each also provided a metaphor for the course of Latin American history; they were also linguistically exploratory and structurally mythological: labyrinthine, preoccupied with consciousness, obsessed with the woman both as muse and materiality. In short, they were Joycean, Ulyssean works, products of patriarchal idealism inspired by and dedicated (though only rarely addressed) to Penelope, the Other, the world of matter, the female, the people, the nation, Mother America. The true story of the 'New Novel', then, is of a moment in Latin American history when the Joycean narrative became both generally writable and also unavoidable.

Then politics took a decisive role in developments. In Europe in the 1920s the key contradiction had been that which existed between the bourgeois liberal democratic systems of the advanced capitalist world and the communist ideology made feasible as a historical threat or promise by the October Revolution. These movements seemed to many writers at first to be going in roughly the same direction but at different speeds and with different priorities, and between them they allowed for the extraordinary explosion of the avant-garde in the period after the First World War. At the same time the spectre of the dictatorship of the proletariat produced a rapid tactical extension of the franchise, especially to women, in the more advanced and stable capitalist states, such as Britain, the United States and France, and the rise and triumph of fascism in Italy, Germany and Spain. As the 1929 Depression began to bite and with Soviet attitudes hardening, choices came to seem less free and literature was forced to divide into two camps, to the artistic detriment of both. In Latin America the economic expansion of the 1950s and 1960s, combined with the threat and lure of the Cuban Revolution – at first hastily matched, just as in Europe in the 1920s, with a promised extension of bourgeois democracy (the Alliance for Progress, Frei and Belaúnde et al.) – created for bourgeois liberal writers, in a new cosmopolitan era of consumer capitalism, a perspective of change, progress and apparently infinite choice – a benevolent labyrinth – which dazzled them and produced the fertile contradictions so characteristic of Latin American novels of the 1960s. Then, as the true intentions of Cuban socialism gradually took shape out of the mists of ideology and propaganda (Castro's declaration that he was a Communist, the USSR connection, the guerrilla struggles on the mainland, the Cabrera Infante and Padilla affairs), conflicts began to emerge and the stream of protest letters from Latin American writers on the subject of intellectual conscience were merely the outward sign of the fact that writers were no longer 'free' to imagine and to create whatever they liked, because reality was closing in on them once again. And once again they were forced, as writers had been in the 1930s, to choose, like Fuentes's Artemio Cruz. After the death of Che Guevara in the mountains of Bolivia in 1967 and other setbacks for guerrilla struggle in

Latin America, Cuba began to batten down the revolutionary hatches and the – probably inevitable – trajectory between Castro's *Words to the Intellectuals* (1961) and the 'Padilla Affair' (1971) was completed. Elsewhere, a more overtly violent repression swept a continent in which film was able to record much more immediately than literature the horror of all that was going on, particularly in Argentina, Chile and Bolivia. In the face of this situation, some writers spoke left and wrote right, sustaining the contradictions of their situation ever more acutely, well into the new era. That era itself, however, belongs to yet another 'new novel' (à la française), none other than the 'Post-Boom' novel, which we should probably call late-Modernist or even Postmodernist. In the transition between the representative works of the 'Boom', and the developments of the 1970s, lies the moment where Latin America (meaning of course its novel-writing middle sectors) 'caught up' with Europe and finally produced equivalent, if still specifically Latin American, narrative forms to those being produced contemporaneously in Europe and the United States.

Paradoxically enough, it was in Cuba, always open to the lure of the baroque, broadly conceived – it was in Havana that the 1920s Góngora revival was most enthusiastically celebrated – and at the same time especially vulnerable to North American popular culture, that Joyce's specifically linguistic lessons seem to have been easiest to learn. The *Orígenes* group, organized around the large figure of José Lezama Lima and younger men like Cabrera Infante, had been experimenting long before the 1960s with language, parody, satire and other forms of humour. Thus Lezama Lima's *Paradiso* (1966) and Cabrera Infante's *Tres tristes tigres* (1967) were by no means surprising products of the Caribbean island, and both were specifically applauded by Cortázar himself. Other important Cuban proponents of the new vogue were Severo Sarduy, later a member of the *Tel Quel* circle, and Reinaldo Arenas. It must be said at this point, however, as the Cuban cultural commissars were soon to say from their own more dogmatic standpoint, that while the technical focus of the new fiction appeared immeasurably widened, its social relevance, with some notable exceptions, was becoming inexorably narrower. The Joyce of *Dubliners* and *Ulysses* was, when all is said and done, *also* a social observer applying new techniques to traditional everyday materials and by that means revolutionizing the realist novel. Many of the younger Spanish American writers of the sixties and seventies were interested only in selected aspects of the Joycean 'package', or in the somewhat whimsical works published by Cortázar after 1963, such as *Vuelta al día en ochenta mundos* (1967), *62/Modelo para armar* (1968) and *Ultimo round* (1969). *Libro de Manuel* (1973), which decisively marks Cortázar's turn to commitment, was far less influential.

Typical of the new mood were the young Mexicans of the *Onda*, or 'new wave', for whom Joyce was the great experimentalist of the twentieth century, not its exemplary craftsman. Some of them tended to use him and Cortázar less as an influence or an inspiration than as a pretext for engaging in 'semi-automatic' experiments that in reality had more to do with Surrealism or psychedelia. A reluctant precursor of such young writers is Salvador Elizondo (b.1932), author of the pathbreaking French-style *Farabeuf* (1965), similar in conception to Cortázar's 'Blow-up'. Elizondo has written a number of articles on and around both Joyce and Borges, in addition to his pioneering translation and commentary of the first page of *Finnegans Wake*. *La Princesa del Palacio de Hierro* (1974) by Gustavo Sainz (b.1940) may be construed as one long homage to the Molly Bloom soliloquy, whilst in his *Obsesivos días circulares* (1969 and 1978) the narrator is trying to read *Ulysses* itself throughout his narrative, failing ever actually to achieve this objective because life – in its most incoherent and absurd contemporary forms – keeps getting in the way. What such works implicitly question, in the age of pop and television advertising, is whether 'Literature' can have any meaning or function for us now: Joyce brought the novel to an end, perhaps, but this was only the sign of a wider cultural and social malaise – we would like to be his equals, but civilization itself appears to be saying that the gesture would be futile. This dilemma is at the heart of the postmodern conundrum.

The potential confusion, complexity and bitterness of these conflicts in the Latin American situation was exemplified by the lamentable debate in 1969 between two emblematic figures, Julio Cortázar himself, the cosmo-politan icon, and José María Arguedas, perhaps the greatest nativist novel-ist this century and the last of the great regionalist writers. Cortázar was at that time in self-imposed exile from Latin America, working in Paris as a translator for international organizations, whereas Arguedas, as we have seen, was a Quechua-speaking novelist, brought up among and for a time by the Indians of the Peruvian sierras. He never resolved his traumas and inner conflicts, which were those of Peru as a whole, but in 1964 had produced his own supreme achievement, *Todas las sangres,* at the very moment when such writing appeared to have been definitively superseded by the new novel. Cortázar's reply to Arguedas's critique of the 'Boom' as a cosmopolitan betrayal of the real Latin America was published in *Life* magazine. Arguedas reprinted his views in the 'First Diary', corresponding to May 1968, of his posthumously published novel, *El zorro de arriba y el zorro de abajo* (1971) – generally considered, ironically enough, Arguedas's first effort at self-referential fiction. Arguedas, genuinely shocked by Cortázar's self-conscious sophistication and pretensions to professionalism, exclaimed that 'writing novels and poems is not a profession'. Arguedas presented himself as indigenist, provincial, Peruvian and American, deriding Cortázar's 'brilliance, his solemn conviction that one can understand the essence of one's own nation from the exalted spheres of some supranational perspective'. As his erratic diatribe developed, Arguedas linked Joyce, Cortázar and Lezama Lima together as purveyors of an elitist literature born of the corrupt cities, and declared himself proud to be among those 'marginalized' by the new writing. Cortázar's reply to his adversary's comments was typically dazzling, and he made some telling points; but to accuse a writer from Arguedas's background of a bad case of inferiority complex was not one of the better ones.[21] It has to be said also that Cortázar, like other defenders of the 'New Novel', offered no strategy for reconciling the demands of the regional and the national, still less of the regional and the supranational, while the concept of class was not mentioned once in twenty pages of discourse. In the most brutal of ironies, Cortázar later managed to maintain his support for the Cuban Revolution (sorely tested but decisively reasserted in May 1971), wrote *Libro de Manuel* in the early 1970s, and became one of the most active and effective campaigners for the Allende regime in Chile after 1970 and for the Nicaraguan Revolution after 1979; whilst Arguedas, for his part, committed suicide in November 1969, shortly after their bitter polemic.

After Arguedas's death, the other great representative of the regionalist current still alive at the time was Augusto Roa Bastos (Paraguay, b.1918), with whom he had much else in common. Roa had written one of the most interesting novels of the late 1950s, *Hijo de Hombre* (1959), which was almost a premonition of the literary and political future. The work is all the more interesting in retrospect, since it was one of the very last of the recognizably pre-'Boom' novels by an author who was in due course to write one of the most remarkable 'Post-Boom' works, *Yo el Supremo* (1974). His first novel, like that of Arguedas, dealt with a bi-cultural and indeed bi-lingual society; and also, like Arguedas's, it painted a moving picture of oppression and suffering, matched by heroic

21 J. Cortázar, 'Un gran escritor y su soledad: Julio Cortázar', *Life en Español*, 33/7 (Mexico, D.F., 1969), 43–55.

powers of resistance on the part of the usually anonymous poor, and raised the question of commitment in a form which pointedly confronted the reader himself with inescapable dilemmas. Whilst never committing absolutely to any specific ideology, Roa's concerns are uniquely those of the Latin American Left as a whole during the period from the 1950s to the 1980s. A long-time supporter of the Cuban Revolution, Roa took his novels closer than those of any other major writer to the debates of Fanon, Mao, Castro, Guevara and Liberation Theology. *Hijo de hombre* tells the dramatic story of two Paraguayan communities, lost in the outback, over a period of three decades from the early 1900s to the time of the Chaco War with Bolivia and its aftermath in the 1930s. The novel juxtaposes two views of Christianity, that of the official Church and that of the Indian peasants who interpret Christ's torment as a reflection of their own agony: 'This was the ceremony which gave us villagers of Itapé the name of fanatics and heretics. The people of those times came year after year to unnail Christ and carry him through the town like a victim they wished to avenge rather than a God who had wanted to die for men's sakes.'

Roa has often said that the people have a capacity for heroism and self-sacrifice which is in itself utopian and carries the seeds of the future. Their concrete experience and beliefs should be the first, if not the last, concern of the Latin American novelist. Thus although he does not share the messianic Christianity of his desperate peasant characters, he presents it with respect and indeed underlines its socio-economic content. In this regard, as Roa himself modestly pointed out, he anticipated the development of the Church militant which was to be such a force in Latin America in the coming years. His insistence in *Hijo de hombre* on his old kind of 'zero degree writing' – the writing of hunger – makes his work the logical culmination of a Marxist, and hence internationalist focus, which had been developing from Icaza's vulgar and Arguedas's dialectical 'Old Left' perspectives to the kind of Third-Worldist 'New Left' vision we glimpse in *Hijo de hombre* itself. At the same time, however, Roa recognized the inevitability of taking up the challenge of the new whilst resisting its temptations, and the result was *Yo el Supremo* (1974, see below), as fearsomely complex, self-referential and meta-textual as anyone could require whilst reaffirming the previous collective tradition in new ways in the face of a much more complex world.

After *Cien años de soledad* and the high-point of the 'Boom', the hardening of the Cuban Revolution, the Chilean coup of 1973 and other such revolutionary reverses coincided with a sense of voluntarism and surfeit on the part of authors who were now in many cases wanting to write big novels rather than proving able to write great ones. Needless to say, Latin American fiction has continued to produce large numbers of outstanding works, and remains perhaps the most fertile body of narrative in the world today, whilst publicity and sales have continued on an ever upward trend. Nevertheless, most readers would agree that the works of the past two decades do not quite match the old ones in scale and perspective, and the genre has not developed very far beyond its state in the mid-seventies. What we have seen has been more of a repositioning than an advance.

Curiously, most of the novels to be examined in this section are exclusively urban, with cities viewed as Dantean infernos (this was Asturias's original conception for *El señor Presidente*). The more usual approach is parody, though mixed often enough with a tragic vein; when this becomes extreme, as it has towards the century's end, then an apocalyptic note becomes increasingly apparent. The first, and in some ways the most impressive, of Latin America's wilfully wayward blockbusters, was published at the end of the 1940s, when Asturias, Carpentier and Borges were at the peak of their creativity. *Adán Buenosayres* (1948) by the Argentine Leopoldo Marechal (1900–70), was a monstrous construction of almost 800 pages set, significantly enough, in the 1920s, and specifically addressed to readers in the Argentine capital itself. It is undoubtedly one of the great neglected works of Latin American Modernism, partly due to its Catholic framework and partly due to Marechal's fervent support for Peronism at a time when most other artists and intellectuals – such as his close associate of the 1920s, Borges – were in opposition. It is also the most obviously Dantesque of all Latin American novels, since the Inferno itself appears to be situated not far below the streets of Buenos Aires, and it was the first Latin American novel to attempt a close approximation to what Joyce had done for Dublin. Such a project, however, did not emerge naturally from Latin America's historical experience and Marechal lacked the lightness of touch to compensate for the novel's structural weaknesses.

In Brazil, Erico Veríssimo (1951–75) also set out to produce grand novels on the scale, and with some of the characteristics, of Tolstoy, Joyce and Proust, though legibility was always a primordial objective of his work. Nevertheless, he was also concerned with self-referentiality, the role of the writer and the function of fiction. His best known works are *O resto é silencio* (1942) and his largest project, the three-volume *O tempo e o vento* (1949, 1951, 1962), a historical epic about the people of his home state of Rio Grande do Sul. In this novel also the city predominates, both in subject matter and in structural presentation, and Veríssimo has little interest in the world which lies outside. Nevertheless, his experiments with simultaneity and multiplicity on the lines of Dos Passos, Huxley and Woolf – so well suited to Latin America's pluralist realities – predate those of Fuentes and Vargas Llosa by many years.

In 1966, at the height of the 'Boom', José Lezama Lima (1910–76) produced his astonishing novel with the Dantean title of *Paradiso* (1966), mixing both classical and Catholic imagery and achieving the remarkable double coup of offending both the Catholic Church and the Cuban Revolution through its approach to eroticism in general and homosexuality in particular. Lezama had been writing the work since 1949, just as Marechal had been composing his novel since the 1920s (indeed, both are set mainly in that decisive decade). Where Dante's patriarchal vision implies that the ideal woman can never be found on earth, and not finding her will always cause torment, Lezama's very title opts for unambiguous fulfilment, and it may be that sexual inversion and its consequent democratization of gender relations is here proposed as one key to future social transformation. The initials of the undoubtedly autobiographical protagonist José Cemí give the clue to the novel's conception of the child as holy infant constituted through sensuality and language within the trinity completed by his mother and father. For a Cuba undergoing the seemingly unavoidable puritanical backlash consequent on revolutionary consolidation, with its historically masculine gestures, Lezama's book appeared a somewhat provocative way of celebrating the city of Havana, whose traditions of sinfulness the authorities were keen to put behind them. The book has now been thoroughly rehabilitated, but its hermeticism, allusiveness and complexity have ensured that it will never be read by more than a few highly educated readers and scholars.

Guillermo Cabrera Infante (b. 1929) is, by general consent, with *Tres tristes tigres* (first version 1964, definitive 1967), author of the first Latin American comic classic with its hilarious vision of three hangers on and around in pre-revolutionary Havana. The novel has a similar theme to that of Edmundo Desnoes's *Memorias del subdesarrollo* (1967), which criticizes the posture of the petty-bourgeois intellectual, but when it transpired that Cabrera, like his characters, preferred unrepentantly to go on being a 'sad tiger' even after the Revolution, the Cuban authorities rapidly lost patience with this born iconoclast and in due course he went into exile.

This was a pity, though perhaps an inevitable one, since at that time Cabrera was one of the most talented writers of the new wave. His linguistic exuberance makes comparison with Lezama (as well as Carpentier and Sarduy) inevitable, but there is one major difference: where Lezama's work relies heavily on a Greek and Roman Catholic philosophical background, Cabrera Infante turns to popular – indeed, Pop – culture, and was the first to introduce the mass media into his fiction as a solid proposition and without parody or apology. On the contrary, it was educated or official culture which seemed to him to be risible. Cabrera's most ambitious work, *La Habana para un infante difunto* (1979), appropriately translated as *Infante's Inferno,* is also a major novel by any standards, not least in length, and an important biographical document. It is in effect an almost interminable sexual odyssey, with Cabrera, writing from London, recalling his early erotic experiences as an adolescent and as a young man in the tropical fleshpots of old Havana. Here too, as in *Tres tristes tigres,* nostalgia is a pervasive and ultimately perverse shaping emotion.

Fernando del Paso (b. 1935) is a Mexican writer who has tried harder than most to reconcile avant-garde literature with political writing, beginning with *José Trigo* (1965), which is based in part on the critical railway workers' strike in the late 1950s. In 1977 however he produced a huge novel, inspired directly by James Joyce's *Ulysses* and Rabelais's *Gargantua and Pantagruel,* as well as by chivalresque and picaresque fiction, entitled *Palinuro de México.* The echo of *Adán Buenosayres* is obvious in the title, as well as the fact that Palinuro, like Adán, is dead before the work starts. (The last chapter of *Paradiso* likewise relates the death of Cemí's alter ego, Oppiano Licario, and Cabrera's title, 'Havana for a Dead Infante' suggests an equally apocalyptic conception of the meaning of these colossal literary self-projections). Ironically enough, the weakness of Del Paso's work is the opposite of Lezama's, namely that the linguistic texture itself is perhaps insufficiently demanding to stretch the reader's consciousness to the dimensions required by Del Paso's 'Ulyssean' perspective. Thus although Del Paso is an entertaining and knowledgeable writer, and although the novel's fictionality fuses with Mexico's recent reality when Palinuro dies at the 1968 Tlatelolco massacre (in a section entitled 'Acta est Fabula: The Comedy is Over'), the narrative ultimately fails to achieve historical transcendence and is more of a Joycean improvisation than a successful 'Ulyssean' novel. Del Paso's latest work is another monster production, *Noticias del imperio* (1987), about the episode involving the imposition of Emperor Maximilian and Queen Carlota of Mexico in the nineteenth century. It is considered by a number of critics to be one of Latin America's most accomplished historical novels.

The biggest of all Latin American novels thus far is Carlos Fuentes's *Terra Nostra* (1975), gargantuan both in length (almost 900 pages) and ambition. Its title makes plain an intention which we see, in retrospect, was also that of Marechal, Lezama, Cabrera and Del Paso, namely to lay claim to a territory and its history through a literary reconstruction which identifies that temporal space with the life of its author. Fuentes's ambition is the greatest of all, since his work is not only *not* confined to a capital city, or even a capital and its country, but lays claim to the whole of Latin America and Spain, that is to the whole Hispanic region over the whole of its history; indeed, it is really more ambitious even than this because it also whimsically modifies that vast history and invents its own variants. This is magical realism with a vengeance: the vengeance of Latin American culture against its Spanish paternity, the culmination of almost a century of literary parricide.

Fuentes, perhaps the most inherently talented writer of the past thirty years in Latin America, has consistently changed his literary style, and the title of his 1966 novel *Cambio de piel* is suggestive in this regard. Other novels include *Las buenas conciencias* (1959), the brief gothic classic *Aura* (1962), *Zona sagrada* (1967), *La cabeza de la hidra* (1978), *Gringo viejo* (1988) and *La campaña* (1992), the first of a trilogy of historical novels about the nineteenth century independence struggles. *Cristóbal Nonato* (1987) was one of a series of activities the endlessly self-circulating Fuentes undertook in honour of the forthcoming 1992 celebrations. Long before this, however, *Terra Nostra* was clearly intended as the Latin American novel to end all Latin American novels, a blockbusting total novel at the end of fiction, of the century, and, symbolically – given its apocalyptic overtones – of the world. In the process Fuentes playfully rearranges half a millennium in the history of Spanish and Latin American history, and begins by marrying Elizabeth Tudor of England to Philip II of Spain. Then Spain's historical figures, from Philip and Cortés to Franco, intermingle with such Spanish literary figures as Celestina, Don Quixote and Don Juan, plus a host of Latin Americans – not to mention other literary and historical characters drafted in as required from the whole of Western culture, including most of the writers of the 'Boom'. Sadly many critics have considered this work a failure, but it is certainly a grandiose one by a writer with more creative energy than most others could even dream of marshalling.

At this point our historical narrative runs into a problem. Despite its heading, 'Postmodernism', this third section has taken a quite orthodox course up to now. Granted, other writers would not necessarily agree in detail with either its preconceptions or its conclusions, but this has been a narrative with a central thematic and a developing plot, and one which incorporates a large number of authors and works which are, for the most part, 'canonical': that is to say, they would have been included by almost any other literary historian in the field. Thus although no other writer would have told the story in quite the same way, few traditional critics would strongly disagree with the fact that Mário de Andrade, Asturias, Borges and Carpentier were names to reckon with, if not the major precursors of the 1960s 'Boom', followed by Rulfo, Guimarães Rosa, Arguedas and Roa Bastos (this group is slightly less immovable); and probably no one in the entire critical world would disagree that the four great leaders of the 'Boom' itself were Julio Cortázar, Carlos Fuentes, Mario Vargas Llosa and Gabriel García Márquez.

But for the period 1975 to the present there would be no such agreement, and the problem is not only one of proximity and historical perspective. There is no consensus as to the important movements, authors or works. Now this may well be in part because no one has emerged to challenge the pre-eminence of the 'Boom' writers themselves. Indeed, Fuentes, Vargas Llosa and García Márquez remain overwhelmingly the most important and prestigious living writers (Cortázar having died in 1983). They have moved into middle age and – in literary terms – relative decline, though they have continued to write as energetically as before. But even as they continue to make grand literary gestures – Fuentes's *Terra Nostra* (1975) and *Cristóbal Nonato* (1987), Vargas Llosa's *La guerra del fin del mundo* (1981), García Márquez's *El amor en los tiempos del cólera* (1985), all major novels – the results are somehow slightly disappointing, essentially voluntarist works, there because the audience and the writers willed them, but perhaps not truly from the heart. The best of them is *El amor en los tiempos del cólera* – an international best-seller, moreover – but it is fair to point out that if that novel succeeds it is in part because it dramatizes our sense of a typically Latin American heroic failure. Its theme, after all – a man who waits more than half a century for the woman he loves – was one for the late 1980s: a brief, belated, totally private and largely symbolic triumph in the face of hopeless odds. But much more important, and a problem of a quite different conceptual order, is the fact that the whole concept of the canon, of an author, a work, a writing and acting subject, and even 'literature' itself have all been 'de-centred', 'deconstructed' or 'placed under erasure', to use just a few of the critical terms which have emerged in the past twenty-five years. This means that the study of texts and discourses has been revolutionized in unprecedented ways and to an unprecedented degree, and it also means that the kinds of (literary) texts being produced has undergone an equally radical change, both in response to the same global transformations in cultural production which have altered critical writing and in response to changing critical expectations themselves. If one introduces back into this already complex problematic the long-standing problem of the extent to which Latin American cultural production is generated from within Latin American society itself and to what extent it is over-determined by 'external factors' (if these can be said any longer to exist) – that is to say, what we have earlier called the phenomenon of uneven development – then the theoretical problems confronting us are of a truly intimidating complexity.

This is not the place to examine this new problematic in any detail but its existence is worth noting. If we were to judge contemporary writers by the criteria used in mapping the narrative history thus far, few would seem to merit a whole page or even a paragraph rather than a line or two. However, history – even contemporary history – must be written, and what follows is a compromise – and in every way a provisional one – between the traditional history of authors and works and the new history of subject positions, discourses and texts. This is partly, on the positive side, an attempt to maintain a certain level of narrative coherence whilst responding to the changed cultural and critical situation; equally, and more negatively, its caution is explained by the uneasy feeling that this really is a less creative moment in Latin American narrative, that it will be recognized as such in some not too distant future, and that in that not too distant future we may again, despite everything, be back in a world, however much transformed, of more or less great authors and more or less canonical works. For the moment, at any rate, the Postmodern phenomenon has sharpened the distinction between the earlier narrative mode of literary history – more or less what the reader has experienced thus far – and what is often termed the 'encyclopedic' mode, which, for theoretical reasons, challenges the traditional division between elite and popular culture, eschews linearity and closure, and stresses particularity, contingency and randomness. In an age when 'grand' or 'master' narratives have fallen into disrepute, critics argue that it is contradictory to construct a literary history of the old kind.

Textuality, then, is the watchword, in an era where reality itself is deemed increasingly 'fictitious', because explicitly 'constructed' and therefore relativized. All previously existing certainties have been dissolved and the globalization of the mass media has annulled distance, divorcing the signifier from the signified, so that the problem of representation has come to dominate theoretical debate in the new era of detotalization and detemporalization. That is why nothing is clear in this present cultural panorama. There is little agreement about what Postmodernity is or when it began. Was it in the 1980s, when most critics and even the press began to talk about it? In the 1970s, when the oil crisis made it clear for the first time that neither the capitalist West nor the communist East was able to control the post-colonial 'Third World'? Or in the 1960s, the age of (illusory) revolution, both political and cultural? It may be a simplistic view, but perhaps Modernism reached its peak shortly after the First World War, completing not only the process initiated by the capitalist-imperialist scramble in the last quarter of the nineteenth century but also the era of European, and indeed Atlantic, hegemony. Postmodernity corresponds to the period after the Second World War (television, electronic music, computers, space exploration) and coincides with the completion of the rise to world dominance of the United States and the beginnings of the shift of the centre of gravity to the Pacific. Postmodernity and its cultural creature, Postmodernism, became dominant in the late 1950s and early 1960s, but their origins lay in the transformations of everyday life which began in the 1920s and which were reflected at that time in the international avant-garde movements and in the writing of Modernist authors like James Joyce and, indeed, Jorge Luis Borges. For this historian, then, as will have become clear above, the 'Boom' of the Latin American narrative completed the assimilation of Modernist procedures and also inaugurated the transition to what we now call Postmodernist modes of writing. Cortázar, Fuentes, García Márquez and Vargas Llosa are all writers who undertook that transition.

As we have seen, the 'Boom' was effectively bust by the time *Yo el Supremo* and *Terra Nostra* appeared in 1974 and 1975 respectively. It had been the culmination of fifty years of steady and coherent development in Latin American narrative, and in that sense was more of a climax than any kind of rupture with the past. In other words, it marked a particular stage in the process of modernity. It also signalled the moment when Latin American literature became integrated within the international 'mainstream' (to quote Luis Harss).[22] At the same time, however, the conjuncture which the 'Boom' represented saw the completion of one development – Latin American Modernism – and the beginnings of another – Latin American Postmodernism. Here the great precursors once again were Asturias, in whose early works much of Severo Sarduy and the Mexican new wave can be found in embryo, but above all Borges, who has revolutionized our understanding of the relations between texts, especially the relation between 'literature' and 'criticism'. The great instigator, however, was Julio Cortázar, whose *Rayuela*, like the 'Boom' itself, was trebly significant – in its own right, as a climax to Modernism, and as the point of departure for Postmodernism. It is surely no coincidence that Cortázar's works were produced from Paris in the late 1950s and early 1960s. This was not only the moment of the *nouveau roman* and the *nouvelle vague* but also of the *nouvelle critique*. As mentioned above, and each in their different ways, the great French theorists – Barthes, Derrida, Foucault and Lacan – were undermining the notions of the subject, the author and the work. The implications were revolutionary and their effects are still with us today, not only in literary criticism but in creative writing itself.

That said, it is difficult to find fixed patterns in the narrative fiction of Latin America over the past twenty years, and we shall have to settle for trends. Here the theoretical problems mentioned above and mere pragmatism come together in unholy alliance. For most of the period serious writers have been paralysed by the horrors and reverses of the continent's recent history. Ironically enough, the absence of a stable centre for Latin American culture – unless Paris is thought to play such a role – has had a decisive and possibly beneficial effect on the idea and the possibility of a 'Latin American Literature' and the particular 'Ulyssean' shape it has taken during its voyage into the mainstream. In a Postmodern era of pluralism, multi-culturalism and shifting identities, Latin America may even be considered a paradigm for future developments in the realm of cultural critique.

Women's Rites

It is appropriate to begin with a brief survey of female writing and feminist writing, because its definitive irruption and apparent normaliza-

---

[22] Harss's book *Los nuestros* (1966), whose English version was entitled *Into the Mainstream* (New York, 1967), was a collection of conversations with Latin American authors which set many of the terms of critical debate about Latin American narrative from the late 1960s onward.

tion is without doubt the single most important phenomenon of the 'Post-Boom' era. The assumption by women of their own representation has inevitably put an end to the version of the great Latin American myths which reached their patriarchal apotheosis with the 'Boom' itself.

Progress in the twentieth century has been arduous for women writers. Even in poetry women have had to take a back seat, with only the Uruguayan writer, the significantly beautiful Juana de Ibarbourou, and the Chilean Gabriela Mistral (the first Latin American to win the Nobel Prize, in 1945) able to claim continental recognition until the very recent past. Nevertheless, in many countries, above all Argentina (Victoria and Silvina Ocampo, Beatriz Guido, Silvina Bullrich, Marta Traba, Luisa Valenzuela, and many others), Uruguay (Cristina Peri Rossi), Chile (Marta Brunet, María Luisa Bombal, Isabel Allende), Brazil (Raquel de Queirós, Ligia Fagundes Telles, Clarice Lispector, Nélida Piñón) and Mexico (Nellie Campobello, Elena Garro, Rosario Castellanos, Elena Poniatowska, Luisa Josefa Hernández), much excellent writing has appeared and opportunities for women are gradually increasing. In the 1980s and 1990s a few women became almost as well known as the best known men, though none has yet become the best known novelist or poet of their country. Similarly, in literary criticism women have begun to make their mark, and this is perhaps an especially significant phenomenon. They include Ana Pizarro, Beatriz Sarlo, Josefina Ludmer, Silvia Molloy, Sara Castro Klarén and Margo Glantz.

Elena Poniatowska (b. 1933) is one of Latin America's most remarkable narrators. Outside of Paz and Fuentes, she is probably the most important writer in Mexico today. Her father was a French-Polish émigré aristocrat, her mother the daughter of a Mexican landowning family which fled the country during the Revolution. In later years she strove conscientiously to integrate herself into Mexican national life, and today is possibly the country's best known journalist and arguably Latin America's most important producer of documentary narrative. *La noche de Tlatelolco* (1971) is the single most influential record of any kind of the 1968 massacre, in which her brother Jan died. And *Nada, nadie* (1988) is a truly moving testimony to the experience of the 1986 earthquake. Thus Poniatowska has produced the most lasting memorials to the two most significant events of Mexican history in the last two decades, the Tlatelolco affair and the great earthquake, as well as a series of other works such as *Querido Diego, te abraza Quiela* (1978), *Lilus Kilus* (1976) and *La flor de lis* (1988), something like a fictionalized autobiography. (Another child of émigré parents, Margo Glantz (b. 1930), has made a similarly wide-ranging contribution to fiction and literary criticism: *Las genealogías,* 1981, is an outstanding contribution to women's autobiographical writing).

Poniatowska's documentary novel *Hasta no verte Jesús mío* (1969) is perhaps the most substantial example of Latin American documentary fiction and gives the fullest picture of its protagonist, Jesusa Palancares, a woman born in the interior, who took part in the Revolution and lived for more than forty years in Mexico City. Jesusa's view of the world excludes politics, and she has little sympathy for her fellow women (all 'soft touches'), but the political impact of the book is considerable. It is principally concerned with the endless work Jesusa has done throughout a long and lonely life, and her reflections on that and her other personal experiences. The combination of its artful construction and compelling story makes most social realist fiction seem artificial. In 1993 Poniatowska completed a favourite long-term project, *Tinísima,* a huge documentary novel about the photographer Tina Modotti, political activist in the 1920s and 1930s, sometime lover of Julio Antonio Mella, and feminist icon.

Brazil's most celebrated woman writer was Clarice Lispector (1925–77), author of *Laços de família* (1960), *A maçã no escuro* (1961), *Legião estrangeira* (1964), the stunning *A paixão segundo G.H.* (1964), and several other works of fiction and chronicles. Comparisons are often made with another Brazilian novelist with a penchant for intimate tales, Autran Dourado (b. 1926), author of extraordinary novels like *O risco do bordado* (1970), and the scintillating *Os sinos da agonia* (1974) about colonial Ouro Preto. One of a remarkable generation of Latin American women writers from East European backgrounds – including Elena Poniatowska, Margo Glantz, Alina Diaconú, Vlady Kociancich, Alejandra Pizarnik – Lispector was two months old when her Ukrainian parents arrived in Brazil. She was to become best known for her extraordinary explorations of feminine subjectivity, above all the way in which women are entrapped and isolated in a private world of helpless rage and frustration which they often conceal even from themselves. Lispector's best known novel was her last, the very brief *A hora da estrêla* (1977), which later became a successful film. It tells the story of the pathetic Macabéa, a half-literate typist from the country who comes to work in São Paulo, feeds spiritually on a diet of radio commercials and quiz shows, and ends up killed by a fast car just as she begins to dream of a Hollywood-style happy ending for herself. The French feminist theorist Hélène Cixous has suggested that Lispector's writing constitutes the most important body of fiction accumulated by any woman writer in the contemporary era, and not just in Latin America.

By far the most successful Latin American woman writer with the international reading public is the Chilean Isabel Allende (b. 1942), author of *La casa de los espíritus* (1982), *De amor y de sombras* (1984), *Eva Luna* (1987) and the very disappointing *El plan infinito* (1992), set in the United States. A work of world renown, *La casa de los espíritus* has also met with controversy: many critics have accused the writer of plagiarizing García Márquez or have asserted that the book is little more than an amateurish sentimental romance. Yet there is little doubt that it has brought the horrors of the Chilean coup to the attention of as many people as Costa-Gavras' film *Missing,* whose intentions were similar. There is a parallel recent endeavour from Brazil, *A República dos sonhos* (1984) by Clarice Lispector's best known successor, Nélida Piñón (b. 1935). Piñón, like Lispector, began by writing allusive, suggestive fiction, confirming the movement away from social realism after the 1940s; but she too, in the face of the military oppression of the 1960s and 1970s, has evolved towards a more historical mode. *A República dos sonhos* returns with a vengeance to the theme of Brazilian identity, in this case from the perspective of a woman whose grandparents migrated to Brazil from Galicia in Spain and made their fortune, despite the new land failing to turn out as the utopia of the deliberately ambiguous title. Piñón's very long book alternates between an insider and an outsider view of Brazil and again combines a personal and family saga with the history of the country.

It is not only men who are lured by the seductive force of fantasy in the River Plate region. As mentioned above, Silvina Ocampo (1906–93), sister of Victoria, was one of the pioneers of the genre, also worked by Onetti and Cortázar, in which the fantastic seeps uncannily out of everyday experience. More recently the Uruguayan writer Cristina Peri Rossi (b. 1941), in exile since 1971, has established a wide reputation for her ability to combine the fantastic, the erotic and the political in both short stories and novels, including *El libro de mis primos* (1969), the much admired *La nave de los locos* (1984), about the virtues of exile, *Una pasión prohibida* (1986), *Cosmoagonías* (stories, 1988) and *Solitario de amor* (1988).

The Argentine Luisa Valenzuela (b. 1938) is another exile who lives in the United States and has written one of the most vivid and original novels about the period following Perón's return in 1973. Its title, *Cola de lagartija* (1983), comes from one of the many instruments of torture recently invented in the Southern Cone. Valenzuela's previous works include *Cambio de armas* (1977; published 1982), which explores the more disturbing aspects of male-female relations against the background of the prevailing military repression, and *Aquí pasan cosas raras* (1979). *Cola de lagartija* however is a much more hypnotic novel, focused on the almost incredible figure of José López Rega, the self-styled minister of social welfare of President Isabel Perón (1974–6). He is portrayed as an insane Svengali committed to an atavistic crusade involving the most hideous impulses and blood rituals. Valenzuela's surrealistic language is reminiscent of the only extant prose work by the Argentine poet Alejandra Pizarnik (1936–72), *La condesa sangrienta* (1968).

Valenzuela has found a sisterly though even more disconcerting voice in the Chilean Diamela Eltit (b.1949), author of *Lumpérica* (1983), *Por la patria* (1986), *Cuarto mundo* (1988) and *Vaca sagrada* (1992). Eltit remained in Chile after the Pinochet coup, and like a number of Argentine novelists contrived a line of fiction designed to be subversive yet illegible to the powers that be. Her perspective is provocative and aggressive, an intimidating example of an implicitly feminist work which aligns itself with every other form of marginalization. Eltit's work promises to develop in directions as radical as anything yet produced by a Latin American, whether male or female.

Other notable recent works by women writers are *Papeles de Pandora* (1976) and *Maldito amor* (1986) by Rosario Ferré (Puerto Rico, b. 1938); Postmodern pastiches of genre fiction by Ana Lydia Vega (Puerto Rico, b.1946), like *Pasión de historia* (1987) or *Falsas crónicas del sur* (1991); the bolero-based *Arráncame la vida* (1985) by Angeles Mastretta (Mexico, b. 1949); *Como agua para chocolate* (1989) by Laura Esquivel (Mexico, b.1950), a 'novel in monthly instalments, with recipes, love affairs and home remedies' which became a runaway international best-seller following the success of the movie adaptation; *Ultimos días de William Shakespeare* (1984) by Vlady Kociancich (Argentina, b. 1941); and *La mujer habitada* (1990), a work both political and magical realist by the well-known Nicaraguan poet Gioconda Belli (b. 1948). Among new writers emerging across the continent there seem to be as many women as men.

Popular Culture and Pastiche

One of the aspects of Postmodernism agreed upon by most observers is that its cultural vehicles seek to reduce or abolish the gulf between 'high' and 'popular' culture. For many historical reasons, this is a trend well suited to Latin American cultural realities and popular culture has indeed been an increasingly influential source of material for Latin American writers since the transition from rural to urban fiction in the 1940s and 1950s. Cortázar's enthusiasm for jazz was an early antecedent of the shift. Mexico City became an influential cultural axis of the ensuing period and had its own mini-boom. In the swinging sixties that 'new wave' of hip young writers known as the 'Onda' emerged, centred on Mexico City's fashionable 'Pink Zone'. The movement involved a curious mixing-in of United States beat, pop and psychedelic culture with Latin American literary ingredients like the works of Borges, Cabrera Infante, Sarduy and above all Cortázar's quintessentially 1960s mode. Inevitably, the new wave struck a series of profoundly ambiguous postures both towards the idea of consumer capitalism in general and the Mexican state in particular. It has to be admitted that the 'Onda' appears to have produced no historically transcendent works, but then it is a tenet of Postmodernism that words like 'transcendent' should be despatched to the critical dustbin. 'Onda' writers were young, cosmopolitan, anti-establishment and mainly male, purveyors of a narrative literature apparently grounded in the pleasure principle though rarely far from political despair. Thus although few of them were overtly militant, they were often aggressively proletarian in their vocabulary and cultural tastes. Leading writers included José Agustín (b. 1944), writer of acid-rock novels like *La tumba* (1964), *De perfil* (1966), *Inventando que sueño* (1968) and *Se está haciendo tarde* (1973); Gustavo Sainz (b. 1940), author of *Gazapo* (1965), *Obsesivos días circulares* (1969) and *La Princesa del Palacio de Hierro* (1974), both mentioned above, and *Compadre Lobo* (1978); and Parménides García Saldaña (1944–82), author of another rock-and-roll novel *Pasto verde* (1968). At some distance from their wilder contemporaries were Juan García Ponce (b. 1932), mainly a short-story writer but later also author of a hugely ambitious socio-erotic novel, *Crónica de la intervención* (1982); and José Emilio Pacheco (b. 1939), an outstanding poet but also author of *Morirás lejos* (1967), *El principio del placer* (stories, 1972) and many other works.

Outstanding among the writers who fuse popular speech and popular culture into elusive avant-garde concoctions was the Cuban Severo Sarduy (1937–92), self-exiled from the revolutionary island after 1960. Sarduy joined the *Tel Quel* group in Paris and produced a series of dazzling linguistic exercises such as *Gestos,* (1963), *De dónde son los cantantes* (1967), *Cobra* (1975), *Maitreya* (1978), *Colibrí* (1982) and *Cocuyo* (1990). For some critics the colourful literary miscegenations of Sarduy make him one of the most important of recent Latin American writers, though a comparison with the apparently similarly intentioned novels of Argentina's Manuel Puig may lead to the conclusion that the Cuban's work, however alluring, remained external – literally – to the recent history of the continent. A younger writer, Eliseo Diego, (Cuba, b. 1951), has written *La eternidad por fin comienza un lunes* (1992), reminiscent of Sarduy in its neo-baroque precision but more substantial in length and ambition.

Manuel Puig (1932–90) seems, by common consent, to be the most important writer to have emerged out of the confused and confusing process of Latin American fiction since the 'Boom'. His work fuses the sort of pop Postmodernism characteristic of Cortázar with the dialectical self-awareness of a Roa Bastos. Puig distances that which entraps and seduces him through irony and the techniques of the new journalism. His uniquely focused problematic includes mass and popular culture, Hollywood movies, TV soap operas and advertising, power relations and sexuality: in short, he surveys the tragic banality and alienation of life inside the capitalist cultural labyrinth with almost Brechtian ruthlessness. His major novels are *La traición de Rita Hayworth* (1968), *Boquitas pintadas* (1969), *The Buenos Aires Affair* (1973), *El beso de la mujer araña* (1976), *Pubis Angelical* (1979), *Maldición eterna a quien lea estas páginas* (1980), *Sangre de amor correspondido* (1982) and *Cae la noche tropical* (1988). These almost perfect pastiches bring us close to the real world which so many Latin Americans actually inhabit, a media labyrinth with no way out. As long ago as 1969, Carlos Fuentes remarked that melodrama was 'one of the bases of Latin American social life . . . When one lacks tragic consciousness, a sense of history or of oneself, melodrama supplies them: it is a substitute, an imitation, an illusion of being.'[23] No one has given a better insight into this phenomenon than Puig.

El beso de la mujer araña, made into a famous film, is perhaps Puig's most important novel. It brings together, in a prison cell, a homosexual and a revolutionary militant to create one of the most provoking and illuminating episodes in contemporary fiction. Half the novel, presented mainly through dialogue like a radio drama, is taken up with the stories told by Molina, the lower middle-class gay, to Valentín, the revolutionary activist from an upper-bourgeois background. These stories are not Molina's own, but are his immensely detailed recollections of second-rate

[23] Carlos Fuentes, *La nueva novela hispanoamericana* (Mexico, D.F., 1969), p. 47.

movies he has seen and loved. The other half of the novel is taken up with conversations between the two men outside of these personalized film narratives, the occasional interior monologue, and such documentary materials as prison reports and footnoted extracts from psychoanalytical and behaviourist theories of homosexuality. The overall effect is stunning in lucidity and dialectical impact. It seems safe to say that no one, anywhere, has written texts which are more radical, subversive or deconstructive than Puig, as he both registers and contributes to the extraordinary narrativization of existence in the postmodern era.

Puig's books often seem frivolous and even light-hearted, but they are deadly serious. Other popular, populist and popularizing novelists who have perhaps tried harder to be simply entertaining are Luis Rafael Sánchez (b. 1936), of Puerto Rico, author of the rumbustious *La guaracha del macho Camacho* (1980) and *La importancia de llamarse Daniel Santos* (1989), a fictional biography of the famous bolero singer; Mempo Giardinelli (Argentina, b. 1949), best-selling author of *¿Por qué prohibieron el circo?* (1976), *La revolución en bicicleta* (1980), *El cielo con las manos* (1982) and *Luna caliente* (1983); and Marco Tulio Aguilera Garramuño (Colombia, 1949), writer of provocative erotic fictions like *Breve historia de todas las cosas* (1975), *El juego de las seducciones* (1989) and *Los grandes y los pequeños amores* (stories, 1990). A quite different kind of postmodern phenomenon, reminiscent of Conrad and Greene but flatter and less melodramatic, is the remarkable Alvaro Mutis (Colombia, b. 1923), friend of García Márquez and author, in his sixties, of a stream of haunting novels about a wandering seaman, Maqroll the Lookout: they include *La nieve del almirante* (1986) *Ilona llega con la lluvia* (1988), *La última escala del tramp steamer* (1988), *Un bel morir* (1989), *Amirbar* (1990), *Abdul Bashur, soñador de navíos* (1991). Mutis has also written many stories and poems.

Politics and Testimony

Overtly socialist committed writing of the kind going back to Icaza and beyond was already out of fashion by the time of the 'Boom'. The Peruvians Arguedas and Scorza had really marked its outer limits – and desperation – even before the Sendero Luminoso movement propelled their country into a hyper-reality beyond the reach of literary expression. Since the mid-1960s, however, the old social novels have been replaced by a more overtly political kind of writing.

In Mexico the experimental vogue of the alienated 'Onda' generation was brutally interrupted by the events of 1968 and the Tlatelolco massacre in the wake of the student movement. For the next decade and beyond many Mexican novels would be marked by these events: *Los días y los años* (1971) by Luis González de Alba, really more of a 'testimonio'; *El gran solitario de Palacio* (1971) by René Avilés Fabila; *La Plaza* (1971) by the best-selling Luis Spota, implicitly supportive of the government position in the dispute; *Juegos de invierno* (1974) by Rafael Solana; *El infierno de todos tan temido* (1975) by Luis Carrión; *Los símbolos transparentes* (1978) by Gonzalo Martré; *Si muero lejos de ti* (1979) by Jorge Aguilera Mora; *Al cielo por asalto* (1979) by Agustín Ramos; *Manifestación de silencios* (1979) by Arturo Azuela, grandson of Mariano; *Pretexta* (1979) by Federico Campbell; *Muertes de Aurora* (1980) by Gerardo de la Torre; *El león que se agazapa* (1981) by Norberto Trenzo; *Los octubres del otoño* (1982) by Martha Robles; *Héroes convocados* (1982) by Paco Ignacio Taibo; *Esta tierra del amor* (1983) by David Martín del Campo; and *Los testigos* (1985) by Emma Prieto, among many others. José Revueltas (1914–76), one of Mexico's most influential novelists of the last half century with works like *El luto humano* (1943) and *Los días terrenales* (1949), found himself incarcerated as an 'intellectual instigator' of the movement and wrote the brutal prison novel *El apando* (1969) by way of response. On a more recent episode, Carlos Montemayor (b.1947) has written *Guerra en el paraíso* (1991) about the guerrilla campaign led by Lucio Cabañas in the 1970s.

An upsurge of committed fiction from a socialist or communist perspective might have been expected in Cuba. The fact is, however, that while there have been as many novels and short stories as one might expect from a country of Cuba's size, and many of them interesting and accomplished, rather few of them have been about the post-revolutionary era as such, and none of those can be ranked unequivocally among the great Latin American classics. Indeed, the best known works have been non-revolutionary, such as *Tres tristes tigres* or *Paradiso*. Nevertheless, there have been many interesting novels: *Memorias del subdesarrollo* (1965) by Edmundo Desnoes (b. 1930), *Los niños se despiden* (1968) by Pablo Armando Fernández (b. 1930), *Canción de Rachel* (1969), an early testimonial novel by Miguel Barnet (b. 1940), *La última mujer y el próximo combate* (1971), a socialist equivalent of *Doña Bárbara* by Manuel Cofiño (b. 1936), *El pan dormido* (1975), a historical novel set in Santiago de Cuba by José Soler Puig (b. 1916), *El mar de las lentejas* (1979) by Antonio Benítez Rojo (b. 1931), and *De Peña Pobre* (1979) by Cintio Vitier (b.

1921), an ambitious panoramic work spanning the period from the 1890s to the 1970s and uniting the writer's Christian point of departure with his Marxist present. Perhaps Carpentier's *Consagración de la primavera* (1978) is the closest to an approved revolutionary text, integrating the past with the present, from 1920s Paris and Moscow to 1960s Havana and a window on the future. Like so many other novels, however, it ends at the moment of revolutionary triumph and the inauguration of a new socialist culture. As for the failure of works by younger writers to find success, political anxieties might seem the most obvious explanation (in his *Words to the Intellectuals* in 1961 Castro had declared 'Inside the Revolution, everything; outside the Revolution, nothing', and Article 38 of the 1976 constitution specifies that 'Artistic creation is free so long as its content is not contrary to the Revolution'), but an equally persuasive one is that writing fiction seems a solitary, unheroic and unassertive activity in comparison with film and television, poetry and song, art and dance.

The most important of the dissident Cuban novelists was Reinaldo Arenas (1943–92), whose early works, written from within the Revolution, were *Celestino antes del alba* (1967) and the celebrated *El mundo alucinante* (1969), a magical history of the life of Fray Servando Teresa de Mier in Mexico's pre-independence period. Had he been born outside Cuba, Arenas, who happened to be homosexual, would probably have become one of the most successful Latin American exponents of the magical realist manner, but fate decreed that he was to live in a country where the social realist – or, indeed, socialist realist – mode would dominate, and little by little he found this and other restrictions on his personal freedom not only unacceptable but quite literally intolerable, as the stories of *Con los ojos cerrados* (1972) began to show. In 1980 he took refuge in the United States and published *El palacio de las blanquísimas mofetas* and *La vieja Rosa,* and then, in 1982, launched his most substantial novel, *Otra vez el mar.* It tells the story of a disillusioned revolutionary poet and his wife, whose marriage falls to pieces at the same pace as their revolutionary commitment.

Jesús Díaz (b.1941) is a quite different case. He fought as a high-school student against Batista, became leader of those same students after 1959, took part in the Bay of Pigs campaign, founded the magazine *El Caimán Barbudo* in 1966 and won the Casa de las Américas prize that same year with his short stories *Las años duros.* In 1969 to 1970 he participated physically in the ill-fated campaign to harvest 10 million tons of sugar and then prepared a first version of *Los iniciales de la tierra* at the height of the hard-line response to the Padilla affair in the early 1970s. The book was not well received and was not published. Díaz was by then working in the Cuban Film Institute (ICAIC) and became a successful director. He also produced a further short story collection, *Canto de amor y de guerra* (1978), and an important documentary work, *De la patria y el exilio* (1979), based around a film he made on the same subject. However *Los iniciales de la tierra* is in a sense the distillation of his life thus far, and is probably the most important novel written from within the Revolution by a writer who has lived through 'the hard years' (to quote his short story title). Yet Díaz, too, became detached from the Revolution in 1992, and published his latest novel *Las palabras iniciales* (1992) outside of Cuba.

It is in Central America in particular that the tradition of revolutionary literature has been maintained. Such classics as *Mamita Yunai* (1941) by the Costa Rican Carlos Luis Fallas (1911–66) and Asturias's *Trilogía bananera* have been followed by *Cenizas de Izalco* (1966) by the Salvadorean Claribel Alegría (b. 1924) and her North American husband Darwin T. Flakoll, on the 1932 uprising in El Salvador in which 30,000 peasants were massacred; *¿Te dio miedo la sangre?* (1977) and *Castigo divino* (1988) by the Nicaraguan Sergio Ramírez (b.1942), a leading Sandinista politician; the inspiring *La selva es algo más que una inmensa estepa verde* (1981) by another revolutionary novelist, Omar Cabezas (Nicaragua, b. 1950); an outstanding sequence of novels by Manlio Argueta (b.1935) of El Salvador, including *El valle de las hamacas* (1970), *Caperucita en la zona roja* (1977), *Un día en la vida* (1980) and *Cuzcatlán, donde bate la mar del sur* (1986), which provide brilliantly focused solutions to the problems of writing about peasant characters at a time of repression and revolution.

Writing political novels did not mean eschewing experimentation and complexity. In Peru Alfredo Bryce Echenique (b.1939), author of the long psychological novel *Un sueño para Julius* (1970), published *La vida exagerada de Martín Romaña* in 1981. It tells the story of a young Peruvian in 1960s Paris delegated by an extreme left group to write a socialist realist novel about the Peruvian fishing unions. Instead, the protagonist, who frequently curses the well-known novelist Bryce Echenique, writes an experimental work on an intranscendent subject in which its own author makes frequent appearances. Already in 1978 Manuel Scorza (1928–83), the last of the true indigenist novelists, had included himself and some of his own articles and documents in *La tumba del relámpago*, the culmination of his five-part series, *La guerra silenciosa*, about the Indian struggle for survival in the high sierras and their unsuccessful battle against the Cerro de Pasco Mining Company. In *La danza inmóvil* (1983), published in the year of his tragic death, Scorza went even further by writing a novel on Bryce's theme, but one which moved in exactly the opposite direction (it is also eerily reminiscent of Régis Debray's later *Masks,* whose format it also inverts): a writer in Paris, member of a Peruvian guerrilla movement, falls in love with a beautiful Parisian bohemian as he tries to write a story about a guerrilla in which he ransacks the styles and motifs of Cortázar, García Márquez and the rest. Scorza effectively dramatizes the forking paths open to Latin American writers today and emphasizes hilariously the seductions and temptations to which they are subject, thereby making a most incisive comment on self-referentiality and inter-textuality from the revolutionary Left. Finally in 1984, Peru's best-known writer, Mario Vargas Llosa himself, who had already played these games in *La tía Julia y el escribidor,* published *Historia de Mayta,* about a Trotskyist guerrilla of the 1950s. In this, a well-known novelist whose curriculum vitae appears to coincide precisely with that of Vargas Llosa, attempts, in an apocalyptic near future, to unravel the story of Mayta against a terrifying background of social dislocation. *El hablador* (1987) repeats the gesture.

Since the 1970s literature in Chile, Uruguay and Argentina has had to come to terms with a series of shattering political experiences. In Chile the accomplished metaphysical experiments of Donoso's *El obsceno pájaro de la noche* published in 1970, the year of Allende's election, were soon to seem frivolous. After Allende's overthrow in 1973 Antonio Skármeta (b. 1940), with *Soñé que la nieve ardía* (1975) and *Ardiente paciencia* (1985), and Ariel Dorfman (b. 1942), with *Viudas* (1981) and *La última canción de Manuel Sendero* (1982), among others, made the Chilean exile response to the coup. In Uruguay, which also fell into the hands of the military in 1973, Carlos Martínez Moreno's *El color que el infierno me escondiera* (1981) was a striking equivalent. In Argentina, where hysteria and philosophical pessimism have long been a staple ingredient of the national narrative mix (Arlt, Sábato), the decade 1973–82, and especially the period after the military coup of April 1976, was horrifying enough to make even the most optimistic despair. An army which represented the sacred values of the fatherland and its history attempted once again to impose unity on its own terms, this time by eliminating all those who saw things differently – writers among them. In 1976 Haroldo Conti (1925–76), author of the excellent *Mascaró, el cazador americano* (1975), who was awakened to his Latin

American identity by a visit to Cuba, disappeared; followed a year later by Rodolfo Walsh (1927–77), whose best known work was the documentary *Operación masacre* (1957), an early exposé of military repression. Walsh vanished shortly after sending an 'Open Letter' to the military denouncing the policy of disappearances. After that writers knew what to expect if they told the truth and published it inside Argentina.

Numbers of Argentine novelists, inside and outside the country, began to seek new ways of projecting what was going on inside its borders. Among the most interesting works were Puig's *El beso de la mujer araña* (1976); *El trino del diablo* (1974) by Daniel Moyano (b. 1928), another novel anticipating what was to come; *Cuerpo a cuerpo,* (1979) by David Viñas (b. 1929), on the military and their proletarian opponents over the past century, with the history of Argentina conceived as a war of conquest and extermination; *No habrá más penas ni olvido* (1980) by Osvaldo Soriano (b. 1943), on the absurd contradictions of Peronism; *Respiración artificial* (1980) by Ricardo Piglia, which works back through an authoritarian past to try to discover what had gone wrong in Argentina and indeed in his own family (the first words are: 'Is there a history?'); *A las 20.25 la señora entró en la inmortalidad* (1981) by Mario Schizman (b. 1945), on recent history viewed through the eyes of a bemused Jewish family; *La vida eterna* (1981) by Juan Carlos Martini, on symbolic struggles for power among prostitutes and pimps; *Conversación al sur* (1981) by Marta Traba (1930–85), a widely diffused dialogue of resistance among ordinary women; *Nada que perder* (1982) by Andrés Rivera (b. 1928), a reconstruction of the life of a union leader; *Hay cenizas en el viento* (1982) by Carlos Dámaso Martínez, on teachers turned undertakers burying murdered workers; *Cola de lagartija* (1983) by Luisa Valenzuela, discussed above; *Recuerdo de la muerte* (1984) by the ex-Montonero Miguel Bonasso, written in exile in Mexico, a more straightforward realist encapsulation of the 'dirty war', and in particular the efforts of the guerrillas and the counter-attack by the military, but a novel that also mixes dramatized fictional reenactments with documentary evidence, especially relating to repression and torture; and *La novela de Perón* (1985) by Tomás Eloy Martínez, who applied similar techniques – the interweaving of fact, documents and fiction – to an exploration of the central protagonist of the last half century in Argentina, General Juan Domingo Perón. All these novels are covertly or overtly political, most interweave the chronicle and journalism with narrative fiction. Many are obsessed, on the one hand, with documents of every kind (especially those that are falsified to distort reality and those that inadvertently falsify it in the first place), not least with legal sentences and death certificates, and on the other hand, with the almost ungraspable realm of memory or oral history. Above all, they are concerned with the nature of power, politics and reading and their interaction in Argentine history. It is worth noting that this is precisely the problematic carved out by Augusto Roa Bastos, who was still resident in Argentina when Perón made his fateful return in 1973. To that extent his *Yo el Supremo* is also an Argentine novel.

Perhaps the most important development in political writing, however, is a phenomenon centred on Latin American documentary narrative, a genre which in a sense has replaced the old journalistic 'chronicles' and the social realist novel (both of which still survive), though of course its roots go back to Sarmiento and Da Cunha – some would say to the first chronicles at the time of discovery (though others might counter that these were examples of 'magical realism' and that the Spanish picaresque novel is the true ancestor of the documentary). Its antecedents also include works by anthropologists and sociologists: Gilberto Freyre's *Casa grande e senzala* (1933), Ricardo Pozas's *Juan Pérez Jolote* (Mexico, 1956), the life of a Tzotzil Indian, and Oscar Lewis' enormously influential *Children of Sanchez* (1961) about the Mexico City slums and *La Vida* (1965) on prostitutes in Puerto Rico. From the late 1950s, as the social realist novel began to seem both patronizing and anachronistic, documentary works began to take a more overtly political and 'testimonial' turn, with Walsh's *Operación masacre* in 1957 perhaps the first of a series of committed, partly fictionalized – or merely narrativized – texts which have established an important and compelling tradition: Carolina Maria de Jesús, *Quarto de despejo* (1960), on a woman's life in the São Paulo slums; Miguel Barnet, *Biografía de un cimarrón* (Cuba, 1966), about an ex-slave; Domitila Chungara, *Si me permiten hablar* (1977), about oppression in the Bolivian mining camps; *Me llamo Rigoberta Menchú* (1985) by the Quiche Indian woman who won the Nobel Peace Prize in 1992; plus a whole series of harrowing prison memoirs by writers like Hernán Valdés, *Tejas Verdes: diario de un campo de concentración en Chile* (1974), Jacobo Timerman (b. 1923), *Preso sin nombre, celda sin número* (Argentina, 1981), and Alicia Partnoy's *La escuelita* (Argentina, 1986). Gabriel García Márquez himself returned to the documentary mode with *La aventura de Miguel Littín, clandestino en Chile* (1986).

Towards 1992 and Beyond: The New Historicism

Consciously or unconsciously, Western writers and intellectuals have been thinking in terms of anniversaries, apocalyptic premonitions and concepts like the 'End of History' as the twentieth century has approached its end and a new millennium appeared on the horizon. The fashion for great commemorations probably began in the last quarter of our century with the United States bicentenary in 1976 and went on, somewhat incoherently, through Orwell's 1984 to Robespierre's 1989. Little did anyone imagine that in the year when the French Revolution was commemorated we would also witness the end of the Russian Soviet Revolution and with it, apparently, the end of the Cold War. That the Gulf War against Iraq should take place so soon afterwards, reviving the spectre, against a background of growing Islamic fundamentalism, of a return to the West's greatest battles at the dawn of the modern era seemed to be one of History's most sombre ironies. All of this tended to undermine mental and emotional preparations for what in the eyes of many was the greatest commemoration of all, namely the 500th anniversary of the so-called 'discovery' of the so-called 'New World' in 1492, although this celebration was already in trouble before its time arrived, in view of the objections of the American native peoples and their sympathizers, prompting Spain's euphemistic retitling of the year's events under that unconvincing slogan 'Encounter of Two Worlds'.

No one could have foreseen the confused and radically altered global panorama confronting thoughtful observers in 1992. And yet it might be said that Latin American writers and historians were, deep down, already prepared for such confusion and anti-climax: prepared for it precisely by the 500 years of Latin America's previous history of hopes turned to illusions, triumphs turned to defeats. It seemed in retrospect that the continent was invented on a single day, by Columbus, five centuries ago, and that each republic, or fragment of the whole, was constantly making new beginnings only to find, 'many years later', that the route embarked on was yet another illusion. The difference now, of course, was that for the first time in its history, Latin America, always a 'land of the future', no longer had much faith in that future, was no longer, after the disillusionment of the 1970s and 1980s, producing new futures in which to believe. The fact that it shares this condition with the rest of the Western world is not much consolation for a continent built upon the concept of providential transformation.

This is no doubt why a region where the historical novel had never previously flourished has for the past twenty years begun to produce a succession of important and compelling historical narratives. The 'Boom' writers had used the apparently mythologizing structures and techniques of European Modernism against the grain, used them precisely to prevent their readers from mythologizing and to force them, somewhat arrogantly, to gaze on the new – perhaps pre-revolutionary – dawn. Now, older and wiser, those same writers were forced to recognize their own illusions and to gaze back upon a different, reinterpreted history. The disappointments, bitter ironies and regrets involved explain why parody and satire condition much of the writing which has appeared during this period. Here, as in so many other ways, the great precursor is undoubtedly Carlos Fuentes with *Terra Nostra* (1975) and he continued the trend with *Cristóbal Nonato* (1987), a novel which – taking its cue from Salman Rushdie's *Midnight's Children* – parodies both the idea of the discovery and of its celebration. *Terra Nostra* had appeared, significantly enough, at the same time as the three dictator novels always now linked together: Roa Bastos's *Yo el Supremo* (1974), Carpentier's *El recurso del método* (1975) and García Márquez's *El otoño del patriarca* (1975). Although each of those novels looked back at a distant past, it was obviously the desperately disappointing and disillusioning turn of events in the continent between the mid-1960s and mid-1970s which prompted their choice of theme and their meditation on Latin American history.

Of course the stereotypical representation of Latin America as a continent with an addictive taste for dictatorship is a travesty of its historical reality. Since the period of revolutions after 1810 it has been a region of liberal democratic constitutions on the European or North American models. It is precisely in the tension between this aspiration and reality, viewed both as a national and continental problem, as well as an individual one, that much of the force of the theme is concentrated, from *Facundo* (1845) and *Amalia* (1851) through *El señor Presidente* (1946) to the present. There have been innumerable novels about individual dictators, or about the problems of dictatorship, *caudillismo, caciquismo,* militarism and the like. Few of them have managed successfully to unite the specific instance – Francia, Rosas, Estrada Cabrera, Gómez, Pinochet – with the more universal concerns of tyranny, power and evil. The first important works were inspired by Argentina's Rosas. Sarmiento's *Facundo* examined the themes of civilization and barbarism, dictatorship and power, based on the case study of Facundo Quiroga and his relation to Rosas. José Mármol's *Amalia* conceived the problem, as Asturias's *El señor Presidente* later did, partly as a problem of the state, manifested through the will of some Monstrous Personage, violating the ordinary individual's privacy, both of home and of consciousness.

During the 1950s and 1960s, however, neither the dictator novel, nor its more general associate the novel of urban alienation, received much attention, because this again appeared to be a time of 'apertura', when the people were on the move and development seemed to provide the answers to the great problems of the continent and its future. In a directly sociological sense, the 'Boom' itself was associated with the transition to liberal democracy which had seemed to be evolving since the Second World War, along with industrialization, urbanization, and the growth of the middle sectors. Then came revolution in a small Caribbean republic, the rise and fall of liberal perceptions of Cuba between 1959 and the late 1960s (culminating abruptly in the events of 1971, the so-called 'Padilla Affair'), the growing gulf between Left and Right, with the gradual disappearance of the political centre, the struggle between guerrillas and military juntas, and the gradual reassertion of pessimism, disillusionment and despair associated in the end with the defeat of left and popular governments almost everywhere in the continent until the – in a way anomalous – triumph of the Sandinista guerrillas in Nicaragua in 1979.

In a sense, both García Márquez in *El otoño del patriarca* and Carpentier in *El recurso del método* aimed at easy targets – firing at the Right from the Left – whereas in *Yo el Supremo* Roa Bastos made a critique of the Left (for that is where he situated his protagonist Francia) from within the Left itself. Moreover, Roa's novel implicitly compared the past with the present, whilst there was little evidence at the time that the novels of Carpentier or García Márquez had much contemporary relevance – though with the passage of the years their parodic perspective is coming to seem more prescient. Perhaps the most immediately striking thing about them, however, was that their dictators were not even historical figures, but composite and essentially imaginary ones, and that they broke the tradition whereby the characterization of the dictator is oblique or in other ways problematical, without any obvious advantages accruing from such a risky venture. In short, they appeared to evade the challenges of the era – one of the bleakest periods in Latin American history – and they also ignored

Lukács' recommendation that great men, even fictional ones, should be left off-stage when historical interpretation is involved (as Vargas Llosa had decided to do with Odría in *Conversación en la Catedral*), both entering the minds of their dictators at will.

Yo el Supremo seemed a work of a different order. Like Sarmiento's *Facundo,* it has a clear Latin American specificity. While it is unmistakably a novel about dictatorship both as a universal and as a Latin American problem, it takes its concrete force from, and continually returns to, the life and works of José Gaspar Rodríguez de Francia, the supreme and perpetual dictator of Paraguay from 1814 to 1840; and although it considers the function and meaning of writing in Western history as a whole, and the roles and duties of the Latin American writer since Independence, it cannot be separated from the predicament of one specific writer, Roa Bastos himself in the early 1970s, confronted with the dilemma of what to write, for whom to write, and whether in any case writing is anything other than an irrelevant or even cowardly thing to do in a continent where dictators are everywhere in power and where the great mass of the population is illiterate and condemned by uneven development to a consciousness anterior to that which has historically produced the novel as a literary form. Its central question, put starkly, is this: does the practice of writing fiction have anything at all to contribute to the process of national and continental liberation? Or is the writer condemned, perhaps fatally, to be on the other side? It is difficult to escape the conclusion that the novel was addressed above all to Roa's friends in Cuba, who were similarly trying to force the hand of history in the face of an imperialist blockade, while the relation of an austere individualist leader to a revolutionary collectivity was similarly being worked out.

It is impossible to understand the full dialogical significance of *Yo el Supremo* without first recognizing that it contains an implied critique of the Latin American 'New Novel', and second, and still more important, that it is structured around two great presences and two great absences. The presences are Francia, the all-powerful supreme dictator, the man who is everything, whose every thought and action is translated at once into objective reality, and whose audience is absolutely certain; and Roa Bastos himself, the 'compiler' of the book, alluded to within it as a fugitive and a traitor, a writer of fictions and fables, a man whose impact on his country is negligible after thirty years of exile, and whose audience, like that of all novelists, is wholly indeterminate. The two great absences are Stroessner, then (and until 1989) dictator of Paraguay and an

example of one of the worst kinds of Latin American tyrant; and Fidel
Castro, who may well have been the contemporary version of Francia in
Roa Bastos's conception. The following, at any rate, is the nub of Roa
Bastos's last judgement on his dictator: 'You turned yourself into a great
obscurity for the people-mob; into the great Don-Amo, the Lord-and-
Master who demands docility in return for a full belly and an empty
head . . . No, little mummy; true Revolution does not devour its children. Only its bastards; those who are not capable of carrying it to its
ultimate consequences. Beyond its limits if necessary.'[24] The Paraguayan
writer's anxieties that Cuba's Revolution was heading for the same end as
Francia's led him neither to renounce socialism nor to counsel despair, but
to renew old questions and resuscitate earlier debates in preparation for
the new historical period to come. In 1992 Roa published his long-
awaited sequel *El fiscal,* which relates to Paraguay's long succession of
dictators after Francia.

   In Brazil, the military coup of 1964 interrupted the normal development of narrative fiction before the 'Boom' in Spanish America could
really make its impact felt. Thus little overtly political or historical
writing has been possible until quite recently. Significant exceptions were
two valiant novels by Antônio Callado (b. 1917), linking country and
city, *Quarup* (1967) and *Bar Don Juan* (1971), and *Gálvez, imperador do
Acre* (1975) by Márcio Souza (b. 1946), a satire which cost him his job in
the civil service. Other works like *Zero* (1974, though banned in Brazil)
by Inácio de Loyola Brandão (b. 1936), *A festa* (1976) by Ivan Angelo (b.
1937), *Mês de cães danados* (1977) by Moacyr Scliar (b. 1937), *Em câmara
lenta* (1977) by Renato Tapajos (b. 1943), *A grande arte* (1983) and *Buffo
and Spalanzani* (1985) by Rubem Fonseca (b. 1925), were also novels
which in a variety of ways – usually implicitly – attempted to explain
Brazil's lurch into authoritarianism. (Also worthy of note is the remarkable novel *Maíra,* 1979, about the Amazon Indians by the well-known
anthropologist and politician, Darcy Ribeiro). Nevertheless, since Mário
de Andrade's formidable *Macunaíma,* no one had felt able to attempt a
grand work uniting the whole of Brazilian history and culture in one big
narrative work. In the mid-1980s, however, João Ubaldo Ribeiro (b.
1940), whose *Sargento Getúlio* (1971) was already widely admired, wrote
perhaps the most ambitious novel in the history of Brazilian narrative,
Viva o povo brasileiro (1984). This work of almost 700 pages covers the

[24] A. Roa Bastos, *I the Supreme,* trans. Helen Lane (London, 1987), p. 423.

entire period from the Dutch occupation in the first half of the seventeenth century to the late 1970s, and although centred on the fertile
coastal strip around Bahia, it is clearly intended symbolically to embrace
the whole of Brazil. The opening lines of the narrative proper return us
tongue in cheek to the anthropophagous theme of the 1920s: 'The
Capiroba enjoyed eating Dutchmen.' It ends with a storm blowing in
from the ocean: 'No one looked up and so no one saw, in the midst of the
storm, the Spirit of Man, lost but full of hope, wandering above the
unilluminated waters of the great bay.' Ribeiro writes in an apocalyptic,
sometimes overbearing tone, but it is refreshing to have a novel conceived
for once on Brazil's own massive scale.

It was, of course, in Spanish America, and Spain itself, more than in
Brazil, that novelists began to reflect on the beginnings and ends of both
the colonial experience and the emancipation period of the early nineteenth century. Thus there have been several works about Columbus,
including Alejo Carpentier's *El arpa y la sombra* (1980), the outrageous
and disconcerting *Los perros del paraíso* (1983) by the Argentine Abel Posse
(b. 1936), surely one of the most remarkable of all Latin American
historical novels, and *Vigilia del almirante* (1993) by Augusto Roa Bastos.
Abel Posse also turned to one of the most ambiguous and troubling
figures of the colonial period, the rebel Lope de Aguirre, in *Daimón*
(1978), as did the veteran Venezuelan Miguel Otero Silva (1908–85),
campaigning author of *Fiebre* (1939), *Casas muertas* (1955), *Oficina no. 1*
(1960) and *Cuando quiero llorar no lloro* (1970), in *Lope de Aguirre, príncipe
de la libertad* (1979). *El entenado* (1983) by Juan José Saer (Argentina, b.
1937) is another novel set in the sixteenth century, whilst the same
author's *La ocasión* (1988) recreates life on the Argentine pampa in the
nineteenth century. Mario Vargas Llosa's *La guerra del fin del mundo* (1981)
provided a brutally ironic commentary on the late nineteenth century
confrontation between 'civilization' and 'barbarism' at Canudos in Brazil,
so memorably registered in Da Cunha's *Os sertões* at the time. In 1987
Fernando del Paso published *Noticias del imperio,* his ambitious portrait of
Maximilian and Carlota in Mexico following the French intervention.
And in 1990 Carlos Fuentes, whose *Gringo viejo* (1985) had told the story
of Ambrose Bierce in Mexico during the Revolution, turned back to the
emancipation period with *La campaña* (1990), announced as the first of a
trilogy of novels about the independence campaigns across the continent.

It is appropriate, however, to end with the image of one great Latin
American icon, Simón Bolívar, as fashioned by another, Gabriel García

Márquez. In 1989 García Márquez returned to his obsession with power and confronted the grandest political myth in the history of Latin America, that of Bolívar. *El general en su laberinto* is about the defeated hero's last journey towards his early death. It is, one might say, the 'Autumn of Another Patriarch' with a similarly incestuous relation between author and character. In his acknowledgments following the body of the text García Márquez confesses his own 'absolute lack of experience and method in historical research', but he shows little hesitation, in an age of parody and scepticism, in painting his late twentieth-century portrait in the boldest of colours, turning Bolívar, almost inevitably, into a character from the writer's own historical gallery. Like the protagonist of *El coronel no tiene quien le escriba,* endlessly waiting for his pension, Bolívar spends much of the novel waiting for a passport (though possibly hoping that it will never come). Like the Patriarchal Dictator wandering through the labyrinthine corridors of his autumnal palace, Bolívar wanders through the wintry labyrinth of his staggering decline and fall. And like all García Márquez's novels, the work is about defeat, not victory, about disillusionment, not the apotheosis of an idea. Bolívar is shown as a man who has succeeded in his great task as liberator of a continent but failed in the even greater endeavour of uniting it; and as a man who, mightily fallen, somehow retains his courage and greatness of spirit in even the most desperate and humiliating circumstances, at the end of his 'mad chase between his woes and his dreams'. Evidently García Márquez believes that this is an equally great aspect of the Liberator's character. Perhaps Bolívar's ultimate grandeur lay in his becoming an ordinary Latin American in his last months, the predecessor of all those other magnificent failures who struggle through the pages of Latin American fiction in the arduous kingdom of this world? Be that as it may, Columbus and Bolívar, as well known for their failures as for their successes, live once again in the pages of contemporary Latin American fiction.

Despite numerous efforts to characterize the 'Post-Boom' novel, it seems clear that we are not yet in a position to do so. For the moment at least, the 'Post-Boom' narrative is, quite simply, the novels which have appeared since the mid-1970s, and efforts to demonstrate radical new departures are usually just grist for the academic mill which rarely manage to propose entirely convincing formulations. One of the major phenomena, undoubtedly, is the accumulation of a body of determinedly self-referential fiction on a scale unseen in other parts of the world. This would seem to confirm the thesis that Latin America's historically dualist experience continues to magnify in intensity the intellectual's paradoxical self-awareness of his or her responsibility to the objects of their contemplation and representation. It has also facilitated the return of social realism under another guise, through an ideologically self-conscious mode of enunciation which mitigates some of the technical and philosophical inadequacies of earlier exponents of the genre. Nevertheless, despite such striking phenomena as the emergence of an important new generation of women writers, the narrowing of the gap between 'high' and 'popular' art, and a return in many cases to a simpler, more accessible mode of narrative discourse, the fact remains that the best known writers today are those who made the 'Boom' of the 1960s. Clearly we shall be well into the next century before the shape of Latin American fiction takes on some decisive new form.

4

POETRY, *c.* 1920–1950*

INTRODUCTION

Before the blossoming of narrative in the second half of the twentieth century poetry occupied a pre-eminent position and role in the world of Latin American literature. Before Borges, the short-story writer, interest and attention focused more on Borges as a poet; or on the Peruvian poet, César Vallejo, and the Chilean poet, Pablo Neruda, whose *Canto general* burst upon the scene in 1950, dividing the century into equal halves and becoming the prime testimony of Latin American consciousness. The Nobel Prize for Literature was awarded to the Chilean poet, Gabriela Mistral in 1945, more than two decades before the Central American novelist Miguel Angel Asturias, in 1967; it was awarded to Neruda himself, in 1971, more than a decade before the Colombian novelist, Gabriel García Márquez, in 1982. With the help of these four representative names, it is possible to observe a swing from poetry to narrative prose in the central forces that shape the literary process. The first half of the twentieth century is in fact characterized by the special relevance of poetry; without this antecedent and example, the emergence of narrative would be incomprehensible.[1]

Although from Vasconcelos to Paz and from Mariátegui to Salazar Bondy the essay also contributed to the development of Latin American cultural identity, it was poetry that first crossed national frontiers, formulating a global reality which reached the Spanish world as a whole. This

---

* Translated from the Spanish by Anthony Edkins.
[1] Borges conceived his stories as poetic pieces; time and again Cortázar reminded us that his narratives were built with structures of images; the relationship between Onetti – or, at least, the Onetti of *La vida breve* (1950) – and Neruda's *Residencias* is evident; and so on.

situation had existed since Rubén Darío (Nicaragua, 1867–1916), whose
most mature poetry – the poems in *Cantos de vida y esperanza* (1905) –
was in one way a search for a cultural definition of the Spanish-speaking
peoples. Although in conceptual terms the result did not go beyond the
idea of 'Latinity' (which appears in the ode 'To Roosevelt', for example,
and in other poems of the same collection), his words were to find a very
wide dissemination, due to a historic moment of Pan-American significance: the beginnings and the subsequent aggressive consolidation of
U.S. domination over Latin America.

What Darío represented at the beginning of the century, with his
wanderings in France, Spain and Majorca (as if to give active proof of his
loyalty to the Latin and Mediterranean world), was repeated later by the
Chilean Vicente Huidobro (1893–1948), whose work and personality
followed the transatlantic course mapped out by the Nicaraguan poet.
Between 1918 and 1924, during the years after the First World War
Huidobro constantly crossed the Pyrenees to preach the good tidings of
the Parisian avant-garde in the literary cafés of Madrid. He sowed the
avant-garde and reaped ultraism. Indeed, his influence was to be far from
negligible on the young iconoclasts who were then looking for ways and
ideas to renovate poetic life in the old metropolis. Then, in the mid-
thirties and on the brink of the Spanish Civil War, the presence of Neruda
among the great poets of the so-called Generation of 1927 strengthened
the links between both cultural hemispheres. This provides a key – a
partial key, but no less crucial – to the historical leaning of this poetry.
Faced with the consuming crisis of the conflict that was going to initiate
the débâcle of the Second World War, leading Latin American poets,
regardless of personal or national differences and subsequent divergences,
presented a united front. Alongside the many intellectuals and writers
who fought in the trenches or were alert to what was going on, the
participation of Vallejo, Neruda, Nicolás Guillén, González Tuñón and
even the young Octavio Paz emphasizes the cohesion that existed among
them.

This group of poets was 'at one with its time' in its thinking and in its
output. Such an encounter between poetry and history would not repeat
itself – not, at least, to the same degree and with the same passion. 1936
and its adjacent years marked a high point in Latin American consciousness which, along the highways of Spain and the rest of Europe, began to
comprehend the forces of chaos and negation. Latinity ceased to be sacro-

sanct. People saw that it was not immune to a barbarism that proceeded from its own tradition.[2]

In fifteen-year periods with regular intervals – 1905, *c.* 1920, *c.* 1935, 1950 – the poets' self-imposed cultural task coincided with a historical praxis of the first magnitude. The appearance of the *Canto general* in 1950 came at the beginning of the Cold War, which had brutally broken up the framework of alliances in force at the end of the Second World War, insinuating a repressive spirit into every corner of the subcontinent. It was not by chance that the *Canto general* was published simultaneously in Mexico and Chile, albeit clandestinely in the latter, the poet's own country. Poets were no longer fighting away from home; they had to fight to preserve their own habitat. In the scenario of bonfires and shadows which Neruda's great book unearths, we are able to notice an intensification of the poetic and critical perception of the continent. Between Darío's ode 'To Roosevelt' and the section of the *Canto general* devoted to Lincoln – 'Que despierte el leñador' (Let the wood-cutter awaken) – the distance travelled is very great. Between the *Canto a la Argentina* (1910) – a breviary of progressive liberalism – and the dictatorial hell that is the focal point and nucleus of 'América, no invoco tu nombre en vano' (America, I do not invoke your name in vain), the distance is immeasurable. What had been a moment of U.S. expansion at the beginning of the century had now become an iron structure of domination. The *Canto general* had to respond to such a challenge by forging new weapons of consciousness.

The pages that follow aspire to describe this projection of Latin American poets and to determine the value of their contribution within the chronological framework which, broadly speaking, spans the century from its first decades until a little after 1950. To sketch a view of half a century of poetry is an almost impossible task. A complete list of poets should not, therefore, be expected. We are more interested in pointing out the strengths and general importance of this poetic development, and in combining an approach to its peaks with a description of the 'spirit of the valley' – a Taoist metaphor which, in these days, seems appropriate. On the other hand, bearing in mind that this is a contribution to a history of Latin America we shall also consider its historical dimension, that is, where it runs parallel with, or counter to, corresponding collective pro-

---

[2] Alejo Carpentier, who had already ironized the ideology of Latinity in *El recurso del método* (1974) composed a gigantic frieze of the period in one of his last novels, *La consagración de la primavera* (1978).

cesses, without losing sight of the specifically poetic properties of what is being studied (its aesthetic distance, as traditional jargon has it). Finally, because the cultural categorization of twentieth century Latin America is still in its infancy, it is preferable to dispense with a systematic formulation and to rely on a more modest approach, a purely heuristic outline. We shall talk, therefore, about decades, moments, phases, intervals of time, and so on. We shall seek to explain, after examining some aspects of literary *posmodernismo**, which will serve as a transition to the avant-garde: 1) the nationalist character common to the avant-garde of the twenties; 2) the moment of the intensification of American reality by means of the essential works published by Vallejo and Neruda during the thirties; and 3) a significant bifurcation in poetic tendencies from the end of the Second World War.

Prior to the 1920s, the poetry panorama is, essentially, characterized by the exhaustion of the *modernista* formula. *Modernismo* and Parnassianism-Symbolism, in spite of all their limitations, at least meant a certain dawning awareness of progress, hope and the future, among the enlightened elites of Spanish America and Brazil. The growing mimicry of the first of these movements and the academicism of the second are extinguished at precisely the same time as the Latin American nineteenth century, that is, at the end of the First World War. (Nevertheless, there are echoes of this dawning consciousness, which curiously bring together some important later essayists, including Vasconcelos and Mariátegui.)

Some time ago, the critic of Spanish origin, Federico de Onís, conceived a chronological ordering of poetry written before and after Darío which, although debatable as to detail, can serve as a point of departure.[3] Taking Darío's *modernista* work as a centre point, he distinguished a pre-*modernista* phase, placed approximately between 1882 and 1888, and then a *posmodernista* stage and one that was ultra-*modernista*. This last essentially coincides with what we call today the avant-garde or vanguardism. It is quite obvious that the first heading was too narrow to classify personalities with the range of a José Martí (1853–95) as forerunners. However, the most problematic stage of this chronology is the *posmodernista*.

---

* *Translator's note: Posmodernismo* and *modernismo* in this essay refer to Spanish literary movements. The terms have been left in Spanish to avoid confusion with Postmodernism of current critical usage.
[3] Federico de Onís, *Antología de la poesía española e hispanoamericana (1882–1932)* (Madrid, 1934), 'Introduction'. The author has the peak of Darío's modernism coincide with *Prosas profanas* (1886) and places the starting point of Postmodernism in 1905.

At present there is an undeniable tendency to reject the validity of that idea. The Mexican critic and poet, José Emilio Pacheco, a distinguished poetry scholar, flatly rejects it.[4] Pacheco is right to point out that *modernista* and *posmodernista* themes and styles are indiscernible in Darío's work until the point where it incorporates and subsumes them, making the abovementioned distinction irrelevant, when not entirely useless. What has come to be called *posmodernismo,* Pacheco argues, is one more aspect of the internal dynamism of *modernismo.* Therefore there is no need to make it a separate category.

There is a great deal of truth in this point of view. Nevertheless, it is possible to examine *posmodernismo* in two of its conditions: as a preliminary phase of individual poetic development; and as an orientation of *modernismo* towards the respective national realities from which the authors proceed – and especially towards their rural surroundings. Those national elements which then began to introduce themselves – *posmodernismo*'s rural approach within a predominantly cosmopolitan and at times exclusively urban *modernismo* – were what, in my opinion, justified the idea's raison d'être. National variable; region; rural landscape; also province – this series not only coherently counterpointed the emphasis on the great metropolis (Darío's cosmopolitan city), it also helped to fashion a tone of lasting resonance in subsequent poetry. In a certain sense, the subjectivity of Latin America's great poetry is closer to the *posmodernista* spirit than to the voice of Darío, even when his notable 'Nocturnos' are taken into account.[5] We have only to think of the question of tempo, so closely linked to tone and poetic subjectivity in general. This natural sympathy with the inwardness of the country created an oasis of the ordinary, a slow village rhythm, which was often at the opposite extreme to the *modernista* attitude – one much more aware of the actual moment and the seduction of the present. Sedimentation, then, not vibration, was the characteristic of this tempo. Archaism, anachronism, the traces and remains of a 'history' behind History were noticeable in that sensibility. This village tone sounded in the simple, luminous poems of Abraham Valdelomar (1888– 1919), the Peruvian of the *Colónida* group, in which Mariátegui too participated around 1916; and it also found a strong, persistent echo in the Mexican, Ramón López Velarde (1888–1921), whose rural and provin-

---

[4] See, among his other publications, *Poesía modernista: una antología general* (Mexico, D.F., 1982), in particular, p. 12 et seq.
[5] This does not mean ignoring Darío's enormous influence. This influence was central in subsequent poetry, but it did not fundamentally affect tone or similar elements.

cial stamp – highly refined, of course – was duly noted by poets such as Neruda and Paz. In a brief, concentrated output (*La sangre devota,* 1916; *Zozobra,* 1919; and a poem of 1921, 'La suave patria') López Velarde called woman 'flor del terruño' (flower of the native soil), praised places and landscape in the province, and ended by unmasking 'la carreta alegórica de paja' (the allegorical wagon of straw) behind the official pomp of the nation and the state. Intimacy, then, peopled by echoes which began to be indigenous; the turning of the poet on himself to find himself inhabited by an earlier time that was colonial and passive.

It is a fact of incalculable consequences that, in the main, *modernismo* blocked observation of Latin America's agrarian hinterland. Country life which, in a poem like *Martín Fierro* (1872 and 1879), had displayed such strength, was sidestepped by the new aesthetic hierarchies that modernism imposed. At the most, it was converted into an alternative, but always subordinate, discourse, as happened in Argentina. When Darío inclined towards the countryside, when he looked out beyond the city (as he did on rare occasions), either he dealt with an offbeat mirage ('Del campo' in *Prosas profanas* anticipated the 'platonization' of which the gaucho would be the object in Ricardo Güiraldes, *Don Segundo Sombra,* 1926), or he restored the contours of a childhood Arcadia ('Nicaragua natal' in the ending of his *Cantos*). The enlightened groups who came together in *modernismo* (lawyers, artists, journalists) were unreservedly in the Sarmiento mould and did not understand the earthy agrarian or pastoral root that was fundamental to the richness of South America, about which they were so determined to sing. This began to change with the poets who were linked to *posmodernismo,* at first slightly, but in a direct, frontal manner as the century advanced.

Of course, the range was extremely wide and made room for infinite gradations. There was the grandiloquent attitude of the Peruvian José Santos Chocano (1874–1934), who turned the jungles of his *Alma América* (1906) into small plots of universal exoticism. It costs us an effort to read Chocano seriously today, but he had an enormous influence in many parts of Latin America. His trips to Puerto Rico aroused such enthusiasm in cultural and academic circles, no doubt due to his hispanophile, conservative position.[6] And not only there; his voice was imitated and his example followed in Mexico and Chile. Quite early on also, there was the

[6] See Arcadio Díaz Quiñones, *El almuerzo en la hierba. Lloréns Torres, Palés Matos, René Marqués* (Río Piedras, 1982), pp. 47 ff.

rough poetry of the Chilean Carlos Pezoa Véliz (1879–1908) who aggressively grafted *modernismo*'s sumptuary prospect on poverty's outlook. Bourgeois ostentation vanished in his plebeian poetry, giving way to the big city's poorer quarters, to the spaces frequented by life's defeated people. No longer the exotic jungle; instead, the appearance of dusty, grey parks in the bowels of the cosmopolitan city. Pezoa died too young to consolidate this poetic approach, but he did also leave a handful of peasant poems which went back to a folk tradition close to gaucho poetry. Furthermore, there was a whiff of spiritualistic agrarianism running through Spanish-American poetry around 1915, which was in closer harmony with *modernismo*'s aesthetic preferences. This was due to the influence of Rabindranath Tagore, who was translated from the English by Juan Ramón Jiménez and his wife, Zenobia Camprubí. This doubtless edifying agrarianism of the Bengali poet half-opened poetry's doors onto a space that was the background and backdrop of Latin American cities. Its concentration on the series of orchards, estates, vineyards and mountain ranges (i.e. latifundia), which were the real 'beyond' of the region's towns and capital cities, was *posmodernismo*'s salutary contribution.

As if miraculously, pictures of rural life began to bud – to abound, even. They were made aesthetic of course, but were responsive to work and activities that, until then, had not been considered worthy to enter the world of poetry. This was an extension of the repertoire, a stretching of the canon, which would necessarily set about making new expressive forms and – why not? – permitting a growing sensitivity towards 'the other', towards what *modernismo* had left outside. In this respect and without any hesitation, *posmodernismo* was clearly extra-modernista. As the countryside did not fit into a sonnet – and even less into the euphonies and preciousness of the prevailing fashion – it became necessary to devise small cycles (triptychs, pictures in series) which took account of the successive processes of farming and the complex reality that was being contemplated. Descriptions sketched the contours of a rural scene, allowing us to imagine what was lacking: the oligarchic context that made the experience possible. This is what we can see in Chilean *posmodernistas* such as Manuel Magallanes Moure (1878–1924) and Pedro Prado (1886–1952) – particularly in the latter's early work. The same motifs, but with greater depth and elaboration, are found in the Vallejo of *Los heraldos negros* (1918), his first book of poems; in the earliest work of Gabriela Mistral (1889–1957), a woman of peasant origin who lived the greater part of her life, before leaving Chile in 1922, in rural or provincial places; and in fragments of the Uruguayan Julio Herrera y Reissig (1875–1910), who in this way built a bridge for the invasion of the avant-garde (particularly in *Los éxtasis de la montaña*, 1904–7). Both fashions came together and merged in the Argentine Leopoldo Lugones (1874–1939) of *Lunario sentimental* (1909) and *El libro de los paisajes* (1917).

THE 1920S: AVANT-GARDE AND NATIONALISM

If it were necessary to choose a distinctive characteristic of the avant-garde movements that occurred in Latin America in the period between the two world wars, perhaps the most definitive would be the close connection between nationalism and internationalism which they promoted and put into practice. There was a subtle combination of both dimensions, as if international influences were put to the service of national lyric poetry and, complementarily, as if the nationalist design could not be fulfilled without constant appeal to exogenous forces. A cultural parable through which the Latin American recognized himself *thanks to and in contrast with* the European world; and a central paradox of vanguardism, which was very probably expressing the real contradictions that often flower on the field of political battle. It was the exceptional atmosphere of the twenties, whose emotional mood fluctuated incessantly between exaltation and misery, between the poles of optimism and depression. In the internal logic of the subcontinent's literary processes, especially poetry, we have to see the nationalist consciousness the avant-gardes expressed as a potentiality, a greater degree of the *posmodernismo* national sensibility. However weak and partial this was, the radius of its vision was provincial – of the interior. The international ferment granted poetry at that time an incredible familiarity with the fate of its own country: in the case of Argentina, confidence; concern and enquiry in the case of Brazilian modernism. In the Caribbean, the area's regional peculiarity won through; while in Mexico some poets participated in elaborating an Iberian-American creed. There are, I would suggest, few places in the world where it would have been possible to title books of poetry as follows: *Argentina* (1927) by Ezequiel Martínez Estrada; *Raça* (Race) (1928) by Guilherme de Almeida; *Canto do Brasileiro* (Brazilian Song) (1928) by Augusto F. Schmidt; *A República dos Estados Unidos do Brasil* (To the Republic of the United States of Brazil) (1928) by Menotti del Picchia.

Argentina

The poetry produced in Argentina during the Radical ascendency (1916–30) included work by Jorge Luis Borges (1899–1986), Oliverio Girondo (1891–1967) – possibly the poet with the most authentic avant-garde spirit – and many others (Martínez Estrada, Marechal, Molinari etc.). Later, all of them were to follow divergent paths and, around or after 1940, to complete outstanding works of great range. Nevertheless, if the diversity of their natures is left aside, what remains as a common denominator is a firm conviction about the nation's future, one in which – miraculously or deservedly – history has been tamed in the South Atlantic. They all had a blind belief in the Republic, with variations of course, but without real disagreement. There was an optimism that, in the light of subsequent events, is both ingenuous and frightening. It is impossible to understand the Argentine crisis of conscience, which increasingly grew from the military coup in 1930 until the dreadful dictatorship of 1976–83, without taking into account this complacent self-consciousness, which almost amounted to historical immortality. There was a meta-historical attitude setting the tone of this poetry, even in its most extreme avant-garde pirouettes.[7]

What, then, is the real basis of all this? An ideology accentuating the country's undoubtable achievements had been forming ever since the Independence centenary celebrations in 1910. It can most easily be seen at work in the essays of Ricardo Rojas. The 'tierra de promisión' (land of promise) – and doubtless it was for a huge mass of European outcasts (of whom Vincente Blasco Ibáñez, the Spanish novelist, spoke) had moulded the nation's collective ego. The enrichment caused by the war and the country's growing international role increased this aura of triumph, while butchery on a grand scale reigned in Europe and while, in the extreme north, Mexico gave the impression of being chaotic and lawless, Argentina was, *par excellence,* the most serious and responsible country, a model of well-being and civilization.

'Irigoyenism' did not shatter these convictions, rather, it extended and 'democratized' them. In spite of the Semana Trágica (Tragic Week) and a generally anti-worker policy, successive Radical regimes appealed to the

---

[7] Cf., for example, the *Odas para el hombre y la mujer* (1929) by Leopold Marechal, or the early poems of R. Molinari (*El imaginero,* 1927).

middle classes, to their sense of progress and responsibility, provoking an ideology of fusion and social amalgam. David Viñas has ironically recalled that the photographs of the period usually show Güiraldes and Arlt amicably together: the novelist of the ethos of the *pampa* and the novelist of the anguished city; Florida and Boedo;* a potential Right and Left which did not even conceive of the possibility of a future polarization.

That the crisis existed in embryonic form, can easily be verified by reading the numerous manifestations of critical thought, whether anarchist or socialist. José Ingenieros's work speaks for itself. And we have just mentioned Roberto Arlt, who comes closer to what we are expounding. In his narrative output, which began in the middle of the period we are discussing with *El juguete rabioso* (1926), the author perceived the underground currents of the crisis with unequalled lucidity.

However, this is not the case with poetry. To establish this rapidly, it is enough to turn to a book we have already mentioned, Martínez Estrada's *Argentina;* it gives us, though slightly exaggerated, a good example of what we are trying to describe. A short commentary will help us the better to understand, as a contrast, the singularity of *Fervor de Buenos Aires* (1923), Borges's undeniable masterpiece.

Argentina (Poesías) consists of two well-differentiated parts. The first includes a long poem with the same title, 'Argentina', which extends over several sections. This part closes with a Hymn dedicated to Argentina, in which the old political metaphor of the state as a ship is once again brought out from the dead and dusted: 'Argentina: tu nave reluciente' (your sparkling ship); 'tu nave triunfal' (your triumphant ship); 'velamen de oro' (golden sail); and so on. Malice and mockery aside, this book expresses the prevailing climate of those years with absolute ingenuousness; there is complete rapport between the poet and his society.

To do justice to Martínez Estrada, it should be added that his vision is weakly anti-Sarmiento, even in this part. There is a defence of the Indian which, however ambiguous Argentine indigenism seems after the pacification campaigns in the *pampa,* does not fail to stand out in a picture that is ideologically dominated by the alternative of civilization or barbarism.

But if the outward composition of this little book reveals the country's characteristic split, its second part abandons the hymn and begins to voice real concerns. It starts with 'La estancia' (the ranch) and ends with 'Buenos Aires', an extensive poem which gets watered down in 'Río de la Plata'.

Translator's note: Boedo is the name of a street in Buenos Aires where a group of left-wing writers used to meet; Florida is the name of another street where a group of more sophisticated writers met.

Everywhere, agrarian pictures in the *posmodernista* style – 'La oveja' (the sheep), 'Siembra' (sowing), etc. – keep filtering through; these, along with descriptions of indigenous realities (birds, trees, farm produce), lay the fragmentary foundations of a future national canticle. They were the materials and scaffolding of a building which soon would be seen to be cracked.

Fervor de Buenos Aires, the initial collection of Borges's poems, was one of Borges's best works, and a crucial contribution to this century's Spanish-American poetry. Its youthful awkwardness was patiently corrected throughout the author's life; he went on rubbing out, expurgating the old text, without spoiling his original intuitive creation in any way. The outcome – a reduced, always improved version – is the sum of some astonishingly rigorous aesthetic decisions; it perfectly captures the potentialities of the period.

The title is partly a subtle strategy, depending on a single letter. 'Fervor' (fervour) replaces 'hervor' (ferment), which brings too closely to mind the seething city and its crowds. While this is a naturalistic metaphor, extracted – *horresco referens!* – from transformations of matter, 'fervor' is associated with spiritual dispositions, coating and sublimating 'hervor'. From its title, then, this book transmutes a collective experience into a personal cult.

Inherent in the play with the language's articles, are some very simple stylistic expedients, which were skilfully described some time ago by Amado Alonso.[8] 'A' street in Borges – any old street – is soon shown as 'the' sought for and beloved street. And quite naturally, it ends up being 'street' without any article and with the purity and fullness of the unique. The absence of article in *Fervor* is precisely that, an indicator of fervour. This clever dematerialization renders the object weightless, prolonging it like an echo in the – fervent – intimacy of the subject.

There was a third poetic element determining Borges's vision of the city. It will have been noticed that his Buenos Aires was no longer the cosmopolitan city of yesteryear; it was an artifice of corners: districts, suburbs, fragments of remembered streets. A city imitating the province, viewed inwardly and crystallizing in a space equidistant from official centres and plebeian periphery. It was the 'platonization' of a Buenos Aires which had been and always would be. Borges accepted all this, writing in a prologue that he withdrew from later editions: 'My fatherland – Buenos Aires – is not the

[8] Cf. Amado Alonso, 'Estilística y gramática del artículo en español', in *Estudios lingüísticos (Temas españoles)* (Madrid, 1951), pp. 151–94.

expansive geographical myth these two words suggest; it is my house, the friendly *barrios*, those streets and hidden corners that are the well-loved devotion of my time . . . ' – 'A quien leyere' (To whoever reads).

A subjectivity *revises* the city. The verb is literal: the passer-by reads and deciphers this city with his eyes; his city and that of his forebears. He moves, he roams, he travels, he interprets. The city is a text: a spirit, in other words. Those who hold the key, those who know how to interpret it, how to read it, are trustees of tradition. The attitude is distant and can be calm, because this city is a long way off, more distant than history. Rosas is a bad memory, and he can be forgiven; the Independence epic (San Martín, our ancestors) is quite remote. Suddenly, however, we have these disturbing lines:

> Más vil que un lupanar
> la carnicería rubrica como una afrente la calle.
> Sobre el dintel
> la esculpidura de una cabeza de vaca
> de mirar ciego y cornamenta grandiosa
> preside el aquelarre
> de carne charra y mármoles finales. . .
> con la lejana majestad de un ídolo.

(Baser than a brothel/the butcher's shop marks the street like an affront./ Over the doorway/ the little sculpture of a cow's head/ with blind look and set of horns/ presides over the watercolour,/gaudy meat and bits of marble. . ./with the distant majesty of an idol.)

The brief poem – here in its more extensive version – was later reduced to five or six lines. In 'Carnicería' (Butcher's shop) everything is out of tune; ripples of bad taste shatter the friendly comfort of the streets: it is the reign of the 'charro' (ill-bred). No coincidence, then, that amid the spiritual fervour, such a place should be the centre of such sensations. A butcher's shop, a history of bloodshed, the Argentine economy, metaphysical hatred for the flesh as such – very Borgesian! From then on, *res* (head of cattle) was to be, for Borges, the reverse of *ser* (being).

Mexico

In Mexico under Obregón and Calles the country was trying to reconstruct its civic life after the armed revolutionary conflict. When the conquests of the revolution appeared to have taken hold, the Cristero uprising reopened the war. We are dealing here with the exact opposite of Argentina. Opposed to the serious, patrician countenance of Southern worthies were heroes who had wagered on history with weapons in their hands. We get plebeian images of peasants, shepherds, miners, in disorderly collective mobilization. Chaos versus order; the barbarism of here and now versus the eternal civilization ruling down there. Consequently, the poetry of Mexico of that time is very different from that of Argentina.

From the initial example of José Juan Tablada (1871–1945) up until the forming of the *Contemporáneos* group, the Mexican avant-garde assimilated varied cultural movements, aesthetics and ideologies. First of all, orientalism, a current that was to have greater persistence in Mexico than in other countries, from Tablada to Paz (*Ladera Este*, mainly the fruit of the poet's stay in India as Mexico's Ambassador), by way of the influential *Estudios Indostánicos* (1920), which Vasconcelos wrote in San Diego, California, during his years of exile. Second, Castilian poetry: the resurgence of the lyric on the Peninsula, which was then in full flood, very soon reached the Mexican high plateau, greatly contributing to twentieth-century poetry. Seen from without it is the poetry of Mexico that shows most affinity with the Castilian tradition. (Perhaps for this reason Paz highlights his French connection.) European influence in general was to have considerable impact on the work of, for example, Villaurrutia. This amalgam produced some of the continent's richest avant-garde poetry.

Considered as an expressive unity, the most important work of this period was written by the *Contemporáneos* group. Nowhere else was there so varied and homogenous a flowering (homogenous at the level of technical competence; varied in the range of individual works) as that produced by Xavier Villaurrutia (1903–50), José Gorostiza (1901–73), Carlos Pellicer (1898–1977) and other members of the group. *Reflejos* (1926), Villaurrutia's terse initial work, and *Nostalgia de la muerte* (1930), the high point of his lyrical development, along with Gorostiza's substantial *Muerte sin fin* (1939), allow us to bring this judgement to bear. In what follows, we shall also highlight a minor work taken from early on in Carlos Pellicer's poetic development, because it seems to us representative of the spirit of a certain Mexican avant-garde.

The perceptive critic, José Joaquín Blanco, has discerned a double orientation within the *Contemporáneos* group. Only one of them interests us here, namely, what could be called the group's Vasconcelos wing, which was more allied to ideals that were detached from the revolution itself and which viewed events through Latin American eyes, following the example of the man who was guide to the young in the post-revolution reconstruction phase, the ideologue José Vasconcelos. Between 1921 and 1924 Vasconcelos held the posts of Rector of the University of Mexico and Secretary for Public Education. And it was precisely in 1924 that Carlos Pellicer published his second book of poems, *Piedra de sacrificios. Poema iberoamericano,* a work which very competently synthesized this tendency. With a prologue by 'The Master' and epigraphs from Darío, the book has a very explicit opening: 'América, América mía'; it appeals to the 'great international Ibero-American family', as Vasconcelos does not fail to point out in his introductory remarks. In effect, this extensive poem, which is conceived symphonically, names people and places in different parts of the continent, using a kind of travelling cinematic approach – a quality also noticeable in Vasconcelos's main essays. Bear in mind that Vasconcelos's *La raza cósmica* (1925), along with its historico-philosophical introduction about American *mestizaje* (miscegenation), was also a travel book in which the Revolution's intellectual delegate conveyed his impressions of Argentina, Brazil and other countries. The cinematic approach, in other words, characterized Pellicer's images and style from then on.

In his desire for knowledge of the immense reality he had chosen to celebrate, Pellicer multiplied perspectives in order to sense and embrace the American land. The phrase 'Desde el avión' (From the aircraft) opens two stanzas, shaping an aerial vision that, a quarter of a century later, the *Canto general* did not scorn. Above all, there was a perspective in depth, which showed the poet's immersion in the Americas:

> Y así desde México sigo
> creyendo que las aguas de América
> caen tan cerca de mi corazón,
> como la sangre en las liturgias aztecas.

(And so from Mexico I continue/believing that America's waters/fall as close to my heart/as blood in Aztec liturgies.)

This is decisive, it is a site for the *canto;* a lyrical path par excellence, in which the poetic subject becomes identified with experience of the past. The indigenous element reflects this tension, sometimes reaching beyond the optimism of Vasconcelos.

Thus, in spite of obvious technical immaturity, Pellicer created a poem filled with enormous possibilities. One example will suffice: in the fragment to Carabobo, using a language of unusual vigour, he was on the point of rising above the traditional liberal hymn extolling national glories. Although the poem fails to fulfil its promise, it leaves with us a magnificent line, which condenses all the grandeur of Bolívar's expedition: 'Un gran viento desmantelaba el cielo' (A great wind uncloaked the sky). Instead of superficial discussion, where the poem is a gloss on the political discourse, nature as the site and sphere of historical conflicts is granted a voice.

Brazil

The character of the Brazilian avant-garde – the so-called *Modernismo* – is not an exception in the review we are conducting. On the contrary, the obsession with national identity would be bordering on caricature, were it not for the saving graces of humour and irony, so firmly etched into Brazilian literature. In Chapter 2 of this volume, Gerald Martin has described the cultural significance of the work and actions of the two Andrades, Mário and Oswald, leaders of the Brazilian modernist movement from its origins at the beginning of the twenties until its extinction in the mid-forties. The connection between creative motivation and preoccupation with national and ethnic identity acquired an exemplary standing in their work. With Mário (1893–1945), the writer who led the movement with *Paulicéia desvairada* (1922), we can witness a model development, one that transformed him into a veritable strategist of contemporary Brazilian culture. His novel *Macunaíma* (1928), a masterpiece with a strange primitivism, his poetry texts published during the twenties, and his illuminating research into music and folklore, served as the basis for a systematic exploration into Brazilian reality. And Oswald (1890–1954), the author of a series of novels spanning three decades, for his part, entitled his most relevant poetry collection *Pau Brasil* (1925). In it he attempted a historical survey, aimed at retrieving national origins. Although chronology, tone and spirit are very different, there is a similarity between this attempt and the semi-historical poems, based on chronicles and accounts of voyages, with which the Nicaraguan, Ernesto Cardenal, began his poetic work at the end of the forties.

The events that mark the development of Modernism can be outlined as follows: a climate of cultural renewal began to form with the plastic arts (the Malfatti exhibition in 1917) and other incentives as a background; and then, halfway through February, 1922, there was an explosion: São Paulo's Teatro Municipal put on three artistic festivals – one devoted to painting and sculpture, one to literature and poetry, and one to music. This rapidly spread from São Paulo to Rio, Belo Horizonte, and so on, but it encountered resistance in the north, where the intellectual views of Gilberto Freyre held sway. As we have said, 1922 was also the year in which *Paulicéia desvairada* appeared. Andrade wrote it after worriedly reading *Les Villes Tentaculaires* by the Belgian symbolist, E. Verhaeren. To compare Borges with Andrade at this point, and the Buenos Aires of the former with the São Paulo of the latter, is to go from the calm posture of the passer-by to the absolutely free, basically muscular attitude with which the Brazilian assaults his hallucinatory city. The book also had primitivist aspects which were to become more and more noticeable over the decade.

Within the framework we have suggested, the limit of this development is marked by the foundation of the *Revista de Antropofagia* (1928) and Oswald's 'Manifesto antropófago', which appeared in its first number. Primitivist postulates here reached a culminating point, coinciding and combining with the artistic-folkloric productions of the composer Heitor Villa-Lobos and Mário himself. A division in the modernist avant-garde between a socialist-leaning left and a Catholic, traditionalist right was beginning to take shape at the same time. It was as if the fascist sympathies of Italian Futurism and the Bolshevik orientation of a certain Soviet avant-garde had, by strange chance, coincided on Brazilian soil. In all events, the two tendencies shared a basic, common nationalism, which is emphasized by Wilson Martins in a study dedicated to this period: 'the nationalism, that in the guise of various avatars, would be one of the most imperious dogmas of Modernism and of Brazilian life then and to come'.[9] And he continues: 'Modernism preferred the nationalist course to cosmopolitanism, the course of primitivism to that of artifice, the sociological to the psychological, the folkloric to the literary, and . . . the political to the unpolitical'.

But, more important than the literary output generated during the years of the avant-garde – ephemeral in a world context – it must be remembered that during this time the contribution of two of the most important Brazilian poets of this century, Carlos Drummond de Andrade (1902–87) and Cecília Meireles (1901–64), was being prepared. From

[9] Wilson Martins, *The Modernist Idea* (New York, 1970), pp. 8, 94.

1925, the former was obviously part of the avant-garde climate, while the latter was influenced more by earlier symbolism and was as a general rule reserved when confronted by the appeals of the 'new'. These two, together with the significant figure of Manuel Bandeira (1896–1968), are possibly the most outstanding personalities in Brazilian poetry.[10]

Although Drummond's great poetic works were to come later (*Sentimento do mundo*, 1940; *A rosa do povo*, 1945), his first unique work – which falls within this chapter's chronological limits – signalled a clear distancing from the regional and nationalist concerns of the day. It did reproduce them, but with *detachment**, and with a quality of humour that was to be the hallmark of his poetry from then on.

Alguma poesia (1930) – the title is every inch an euphemism, if the surrounding enthusiasm and elation are taken into account – collected poems written by Drummond between 1923 and 1930. It was dedicated to 'Meu amigo Mário de Andrade'. With an obviously autobiographical axis invested with an uninhibited mythology of ad hoc angels – 'o anjo terto' (the hurt angel) of his birth, 'o anjo batalhador' (the champion angel) of the denouement – the poet's infancy was recalled and cyclical sections about Brazilian life were introduced. After sketches of Rio, Belo Horizonte and other places, he rounds off:

> E preciso fazer um poema sobre a Bahia.
> Ma eu nunca fui lá.

(It's necessary to write a poem about Bahia/But I was never there.)

There was an epigrammatic wit, which was not incompatible with potential profundity, such as that exhibited in 'Quadrilha'. The fate of several frustrated lives – about which Mistral sang with unparalleled understanding in her ballad 'Todos ibamos a ser reinas' (All of us were going to be queens) – was here reduced to a miniature, as if the form itself were ironising the poor living parables described. Perhaps Antônio Cândido is the critic who has best caught the peculiarity of Drummond's poetry: 'In truth, with him. . .Brazilian Modernism attained the transcending of the verse, allowing the manipulation of the expression of space without barriers, where poetry's magic flow depends on the overall shape of the poem, freely arranged, which he glimpsed in his descent into the world of words.'[11]

---

* *Translator's note:* In English in the original text.

[10] Vinícius de Moraes (1913–80), another outstanding figure in the Brazilian poetry of this century, was to start his output in the following decade, at the beginning of the thirties.

[11] Antônio Cândido, *Vários Escritos* (São Paulo, 1970), p. 122.

Without any doubt, Cecília Meireles is one of the greatest women poets in the Portuguese language. Her main peer in Spanish America was the Chilean poet Gabriela Mistral, with whom she had strong ties of friendship. Although her earliest work – which began with *Espectros* (1919) – was symbolist in style, she was later to find a voice of her own with her book *Viagem* (1939), which she herself chose to head a collection of her complete works. The clarity of these verses and their extremely clear notation of nature's most subtle moments make this poetry a fascinating experience. It could only have emerged, as she recorded herself, from the 'silence and loneliness' of her childhood; and – we in turn add – from the enormous hurt that surrounded her existence. If, in accordance with Gide's dictum, to be classical a work must be permeated with a *profound clarity,* then there is no poetry more classical than that of *Viagem* and Meireles's subsequent works. A fragment of 'Música' suffices to give us an idea:

> Minha partida,
> minha chegada,
> a tudo vento. . .
> Ai da alvorada!
> Noite perdida,
> Noite encontrada

(My departure,/my arrival,/the wind at full blast. . ./Oh dawn!/Night lost,/night encountered.)

The Andean republics

The avant-garde in Chile did not have any significant weight at this time. It can be reduced to Huidobro who published a slim volume, *El espejo de agua,* in 1916, Neruda's transitional poetry, one or two works by Angel Cruchaga Santa María (*La selva prometida,* 1920) and the emergent phase of two subsequently great poets, Humberto Díaz Casanueva (1908–92) and Rosamel del Valle (1900–63). In Ecuador, apart from Alfredo Gangotena (1904–44), who was a somewhat eccentric figure on the literary scene (the greater part of his books was written in French), the avant-garde as such could only claim the work – and the personality – of Jorge Carrera Andrade (1903–78). After publishing his first book, *El estanque inefable* in 1922, and leaving the country in 1928, Carrera Andrade published his first avant-garde collection, *Boletines de mar y tierra* (1930). He produced almost all his poetic work abroad, while working as an official connected with international organizations or Ecuador's diplomatic corps. The avant-garde in Colombia came into being a little after the period with which we are now concerned, halfway through the thirties. The *Piedra y Cielo* (Stone and Sky) movement, around which it coalesced, included three leading poets: Jorge Rojas (b. 1911), who undeniably inspired it; Arturo Comacho (1910–82); and Eduardo Carranza (1913–85).[12]

Cuba and Puerto Rico

In spite of differences in historical development, social structure and cultural traditions, Puerto Rico and Cuba are not too dissimilar, linked by the former's colonial situation and the neo-colonial domination suffered by the latter, which had begun to be consolidated under Gerardo Machado's dictatorship (1927–33). To begin with Cuba, there was an almost uninterrupted flow, embracing the work and activity of Rubén Martínez Villena, co-founder of Cuba's Communist party in 1925, the *Revista de Avance*, the research of Alejo Carpentier and the blossoming of Black themes in the poetry of Nicolás Guillén and Emilio Ballagas.

In effect, the first three books of Guillén (1902–89) registered an ascending curve of impressive significance, not only for the poetic possibilities that they offered, but more especially for their cultural implications for the Caribbean area and, therefore, for Latin America in general. In the field of poetry, it is probably Guillén who has contributed most to making Latin America aware that the African element is an essential ingredient of its ethnicity; that Africa, together with Europe and America, is the third continental angle in our historical triangle. To this end, the poet began to search through the Afro-Spanish cultural tradition so rich and abundant on the island; in particular, the traditional dance known as *son*. Underlying this were, doubtless, the interest in African cultures that had been starting to assert itself since the beginning of the century and, a little later, the impact of the North American Harlem Renaissance, and especially the work of Langston Hughes, the Black poet who visited Cuba in 1928. But, more than anything, it must have been the ethnographic, artistic and folkloric research, which was beginning to

[12] See the excellent anthology *Poesía y poetas colombianos* (Bogotá, 1985) edited by the Colombian poet Fernando Charry Lara and Eduardo Comacho's magnificent studies, especially *Sobre literatura colombiana e hispanoamericana* (Bogotá, 1978).

be carried out on the island, that contributed most to highlighting the Black cultural input: Fernando Ortiz's research, naturally, and the studies which later culminated in Alejo Carpentier's *La música en Cuba* (1946).

With *Motivos de son* (1930) Guillén achieved a powerful cultural synthesis; at heart, it rested on a very simple procedure: the translation of what already existed in the popular and musical area of the *son* to the level of poetry. The means were also simple, but extremely effective; they corresponded to the spirit of what he was attempting to combine. The Spanish octosyllable, as the basic metrical unit, was complemented with refrains, broken feet and repetitions, which exercised a polyrhythmic effect and ended up giving the poem an incantatory tone, one of magic trance. At the same time, ideological strategies were helping to overcome ethnic prejudice and to fight racism. In this way, the African theme, which, in colonial poetry (Caviedes, and others) was dealt with in terms of caste, acquired here a powerful form of cultural counter-effect.[13]

After a transitional work (*Sóngoro Cosongo. Poemas mulatos*, 1931) which immediately followed *Motivos de son*, but already displayed a greater social and political consciousness, *West Indies Ltd.* (1934) both strengthened this increasing scrutiny of the Caribbean arena and expressed an accusation against the foreign forces entrenched in the zone. The English title was a conspicuous indicator of linguistic alienation, economic exploitation and political colonialism. It portrayed not only the oppressor *establishment*,* but – with a very characteristic Guillén twist – also the servility and submission it engendered in dominated peoples. These were Guillén's beginnings. His later *El son entero* (1947), *La paloma de vuelo popular* (1957) and the splendid poetry written after the Cuban Revolution make him a pivotal figure amongst the poets of Spanish America and the Caribbean.

In the sphere of poetry, Puerto Rican nationalist aspirations crystallized in the century's second decade with the work of Luis Lloréns Torres (1876–1944). Allied with the island's intellectual elite at a time when the plantation owners were beginning to feel the loss of their economic power and social ascendancy at the hands of the imperial metropolis, Lloréns started to shape a Utopian vision of the Antilles within the framework of the concept of *hispanidad*.† He elaborated a

---

* *Translator's note:* In English in the original text.
† *Translator's note:* Literally, 'Spanishness'; as a political concept, it implies an almost mystical relationship between Spain and her former possessions.
[13] For this aspect in particular, see Jorge Ruffinelli, *Poesía y descolonización: viaje por la poesía de Nicolás Guillén* (Oaxaca, 1985), pp. 42 et seq.

programme of historical poetry centred on household gods and, using the *decimas** of popular tradition, he extolled the peasant, the island country-man who, it seemed to him, was invested with all the positive virtues of the race.

At the same time that Lloréns was producing the bulk of his poetic work, Luis Palés Matos (1898–1959), a native of Guayama, published his first book of lyrics, *Azaleas* (1915). From 1920, at least, he was trying to create an Afro-Antillian poetry. This took shape in *Tuntún de pasa y grifería* (1937), the fruit of a long gestation and also the subject of much subsequent rearrangement (1950, etc.). The book's basic intention – a contrast to Lloréns's White Hispanist assumptions – was to recover the Black half of the island, as well as to affirm and assess his condition as a mulatto; also – in response to the colonial situation – to fight against the attitude of stagnation and defeatism, which was widespread throughout the population. Because of the fairness of its voice and tone (it neither stops short nor goes beyond his country's historical potential); because of its taut structure – in effect, the Martí tradition: 'Tronco' (Trunk), 'Rama' (Branch) and 'Flor' (Flower), as if to create the fruit it were necessary to seek out the secret root; and because of its generous relationship with Puerto Rican nationality, *Tuntún de pasa y grifería* is a work without parallel in the Latin American poetry of this century.[14]

THE 1930S

The decade running from 1930 to 1940 was probably the most significant in the development of Latin American poetry. During this time, poetry reached its highest levels of revelation and expression. We have already mentioned the early works of Guillén and the mature works of Villaurrutia and Gorostiza in Mexico. In Chile the decade opened with *Altazor* (1931), an exceptional poem by Vicente Huidobro, and it closed, we might argue, with *Tala* (1938), the opus magnum of Gabriela Mistral up to that time. In the same period Pablo Neruda's *Residencia en la tierra* (1935) and César Vallejo's *Poemas humanos* (1939) appeared. Without doubt, these are two key books in the history of Latin American lyrical poetry.

---

* *Translator's note:* A form of Spanish poetry employing a ten-line, octosyllabic stanza rhyming: a b b a a c c d d c.
[14] See Díaz Quiñones, *El almuerzo en la hierba*, whom I follow and abridge.

Neruda

Pablo Neruda (1904–73), who was born in provincial Chile at the beginning of the century, began his literary career with *Crepusculario* (1923), a
still adolescent book pervaded by a melancholy that was very typical of
the student generation of the twenties. The youthful tone took more
coherent shape in *Veinte poemas de amor y una canción desesperada* (1924)
which, in addition to being quite an editorial coup amid the meagre
poetry offerings of that time, became a love breviary for many groups of
young people throughout the continent. From province to capital; from
Marisol to Marisombra* – as the poet was to say in his memories of *O
Cruzeiro Internacional* (1962) – from student autumn to the summer tides
of the south of Chile, these poems forged a sensitive, carnal experience
whose power resided in their ambiguity and the endless fluctuation they
set up between the intensity and vagueness of passion and desire.

With *Veinte poemas* the Nerudian subjectivity received its first ob-
jectivization in the world of amorous relationship. However, a different
landscape asserted itself in the books which followed: the prose poems of
Anillos (1926), the avant-garde narrative text *El habitante y su esperanza*
(1926) and also that same year his ambitious and sombre poem, *Tentativa
del hombre infinito*. This 'infinite man' who emerged into the Nerudian
world was a new form of poetic subject, a nocturnal, wintry shape that
went beyond the still aesthetic horizon of his earlier works. A strange,
painful experience of reality, in which everything displayed a threatening
face of adversity and resistance, had now become conspicuous. There was
an ultimate feeling of devastation on every page. And, oddly, it was the
rural note that predominated. Flooded countryside, uninhabited islands,
torrential storms seemed to preside over the undermined confines of
Neruda's new poetry. The poet was already on the road to his *Residencias*.

Four groups of poems can be established in *Residencia en la tierra*. This
classification – entirely chronological – only takes account of the different phases of the book's structure. Their coinciding with the writer's
geographical travels is by no means an exclusive criterion. More than anything, it emphasizes that the inclusion of new zones of experience represents a decisive element of poetic integration and an acceptable method of
ordering. The four groups are: 1) poems written in Chile, before the poet

---

* *Translator's note:* An untranslatable pun: *sol* means 'sun', *sombra* means 'shade'; Marisol is a girl's
name, Marisombra is a neologism invented by Neruda.

leaves his country (1925 or 1926–27) – in general, they present a violent, chaotic vision of nature and the world of men; 2) poems written in the East during his stay in different parts of Burma, Ceylon and Java (1927–32) – these poems, written in the middle of a colonial crisis affecting the Dutch and English domination in South East Asia, introduce us to the poet's daily oriental life, one of exile, poverty and despair; 3) poems written back in Chile on his return from Asia (1932–33) – they present pictures of bureaucratic labour, in other words, sterile exercises in a world of offices; poems such as 'Walking Around' and 'Desespediente' serve as good illustrations of this state of mind; finally, 4) poems written in Spain (1934–35), during the time of the Republic – these allow us a glimpse of a decidedly less pessimistic tone. The initial 'Galope muerte' opens up, at least partially, a quest for fertility, which seems to invade some pieces in *Cantos materiales,* chiefly 'Entrada a la madera' and 'Apogeo del apio'.

The poems in *Residencia en la tierra* are organized in an unusual way, far removed from the *posmodernista* composition of *Crepusculario* and the lyrical, sentimental tone of *Veinte poemas.* Divided into two *Residencias* – with the inclusion of five prose poems in the first – the book also offers another duality; a broad, solemn, almost ritual verse alongside poems in a minor key, concentrated miniatures. However, we are not given a dominant impression of variety, but rather one of homogeneity and intense, all-pervasive swell. Density, slowness, intensity are the values that preside over this Nerudian conception of form and language in *Residencia en la tierra.*

From a historical-spiritual angle, the *Residencias* signify the possibility of formulating new axiological hierarchies. Their obvious geological flavour gives clear warning of this. The 'tierra' (land/earth) of these *Residencias* are not only the planetary latitudes inhabited by the poet, but – also at a deep level – a kind of mineral coefficient. In the world of the *Residencias* and the polarizations of its imagination, the lower, the terrestrial, the nocturnal establish positive and supreme values, directly transmuting the axiological orientations implicit in all spiritualism.

At the same time, the subject that wanders through these poems turns out to be a strange mixture of contemporaneity and anachronism. Following very closely the historical avatars of a collective experience (with something of the explorer and a great deal of the colonial gentleman; and with partly the helpless citizen of the world, partly the impotent pioneer), the 'residential' personage is swathed in an enormous cosmic forbearance, as if resistance and passive warfare were the privileged resolutions of his soul. Signs are refreshingly inverted. As can be seen, we are not dealing with positive energy, capable of overcoming material obstacles, but with a current of contrary flow, in which a heroic 'patience' seems to be the only attitude possible in the face of such forms of devastation.[15]

From the foregoing it is apparent that the considerable influence of this poetry lies in the fact that Neruda seizes on the painful and traumatic collective experience of a society greatly scarred by historical impotence. If there is a poignancy in *Residencia en la tierra,* if we often reach the edge of desperation, it is because we are present at a history of destruction, of cataclysms, of blood spilt incessantly. With its restless images, with its stuttering syntax and language in general, it is a nightmare vision that we are taking by surprise. But this vision is only the transference of a very lucid consciousness of what characterizes the surrounding human world: oppression, poverty, the unshakeable shadow of immobility and death.

Vallejo

The case of César Vallejo (1892–1938) is slightly similar to that of Neruda, but fundamentally very different. Like Neruda, he began with a book of poems bearing a *posmodernista* stamp; like Neruda, he produced a significant avant-garde book at the beginning of the twenties. But these appearances are deceptive. In *Los heraldos negros* (1918) Vallejo was already making way – alongside many poems that are only echoes of *modernismo* – for a feeling of autochthony, expressed in Andean scenes and, above all, in an intense exploration of human suffering. The first poem, which gave its title to the book, was almost emblematic of pain the world over. Similarly, there was no avant-garde work – at least during the twenties – which could be compared with *Trilce* (1922) in terms of powerful effect. *Trilce* was a true *experimentum crucis* of the complex relationship between foreignness and a radical American consciousness. If the book is looked at from outside, the more obvious expedients of avant-garde poetry can clearly be seen, namely: orthographic violations, layout practices, broken syntax, and so on. But this is not the essential point. In a much stronger way than Neruda's *Tentativa, Trilce* contains a substantial local appeal, making it the first formulation of an endogenous avant-garde. The Peruvian landscape, the highlands, the suffering face of the entire country are

[15] On the subject of Nerudian 'patience', see the penetrating pages Alain Sicard dedicates to it in *La pensée poétique de Pablo Neruda* (Lille, 1977).

resoundingly assimilated in a tone of expression and a complex manner of feeling. 'Aventura y el orden' (Adventure and order) are here placed at the disposal of a deepfelt cause, which is nothing more than knowledge of self. *Trilce*'s vanguardism is definitely 'ours'; Mariátegui wisely saw that the essential 'indigenous voice' was flowering in Peruvian poetry.

Vallejo left the country in 1923, the year following the publication of *Trilce*. He left behind him the valuable work experiences of his youth (the mine and the sugar plantation), where he had been able to see at first hand the exploitation of many of his fellow countrymen. He had also left behind – a bleak memory – his brief but wrongful encarceration. He was never to return to Peru, spending the greater part of his life in Paris and Spain. His interest in the achievements of contemporary Marxism led him to travel on three occasions around 1930 to the Soviet Union, then in its full socialist construction stage. His social and political faith was strengthened by this experience; it fortified his militancy as a member of the Communist Party (in both France and Spain). The endless discussions among students of his work about whether Vallejo was 'Christian' or 'Marxist', a 'dialectician' or an 'existentialist', are ultimately senseless, however many examples are put forward. His Marxism was at once orthodox and original; and in his prose works he has left us pages which are both obscure and illuminating, but they are always governed by his poetic sensibility and imagination. There is a definite experience of suffering in Vallejo. It was originally moulded by religious forms and symbols, and later elucidated by means of social, political and historical categories. This tension, far from harming the coherence of his work, was extremely productive. It caused him to maintain a poetic discourse that was always faithful to the undergone experience – his and others. What Jean Franco has called 'his devastating attack on the individualized subject' is an integral part of the paradoxical design of possibly one of the most complex Latin American imaginations.

Soon after his return from the Soviet Union, Vallejo wrote a handful of poems which amounted to one of the first layers of his future *Poemas humanos* (1939) and which almost forms a separate group within this collection.[16] They are 'Salutación angélica', 'Los mineros', 'Gleba' and 'Telúrica y magnética'. According to Franco, the influence of the first of these can be underlined in this way: 'it proposes in an unequivocal fashion

[16] For the involved publication problems of *Poemas humanos*, see Americo Ferrari's concise note ('C. V. entre la angustia y la esperanza'), in César Vallejo, *Obra poética completa* (Madrid, 1982).

what will become a central issue in the 'Spain poems' – a poet-prophet who is not avant-garde or vanguard but, as it were, bringing up the rear. It is not the poet who produces a new consciousness but the militant'.[17]

In effect, 'Salutación angélica' (Angelic Salutation) uses a title with a Christian flavour in order to celebrate the birth of the 'Bolshevik' as the embodiment of the new man in the march of history. This, unlike the representatives of nations and specific states, overcomes and goes beyond 'el beso del limite en los hombros' (the limited kiss on the shoulders). The image of this man of the present who looks towards the future is devised in terms that are at once political slogans of the period and religious allusions:

> y aquesos tuyos pasos metalúrgicos,
> aquesos tuyos pasos de otra vida.

(and those metallurgical steps of yours,/those steps of yours of another life.)

Furthermore, at the poem's outcome, the Bolshevik triumph does not eliminate the situation of the poet and other peoples in other parts of the earth:

> me dan tus simultáneas estaturas mucha pena,
> pues tú no ignoras en quién se me hace tarde diariamente,
> en quién estoy callado y medio tuerto.

(your simultaneous heights greatly grieve me,/for you do know in whom I'm daily made late,/in whom I'm silent and half blind.)

This feeling of limits and of mutilation, centred in the domain of corporeal human nature, was to reach an impressive development in Vallejo's posthumous poems, particularly the fifteen pieces that made up *España, aparta de mí este cáliz*. The Spanish conflict, which sharpened the poet's already wounded sensibility to the point of an eminently lucid delirium, transported him to an intense meditation upon the body as the vehicle of human solidarity. For example, in 'Himno a los voluntarios de la República' (Hymn to the Republic's Volunteers), he wrote:

> ¡Constructores
> agrícolas, civiles y guerreros,
> de la activa, hormigueante eternidad: estaba escrito
> que vosotros haríais la luz, entornando
> con la muerte vuestros ojos;

---

[17] Jean Franco, *César Vallejo: The Dialectics of Poetry and Silence* (Cambridge, Eng., 1976), p. 168.

que, a la caída cruel de vuestras bocas,
vendrá en siete bandejas la abundancia, todo
en el mundo será de oro subito
y el oro,
fabulosos mendigos de vuestra propia secreción de sangre,
y el oro mismo será entonces de oro!

(Builders, farmworkers, civilians and soldiers,/of busy, ant-like eternity: it was written/that you would be light,/half-closing your eyes with death;/that, at the cruel fall of your mouths,/abundance will arrive on seven trays, everything/in the world will suddenly be made of gold/and the gold/fabulous beggars of your own blood's secretion,/the gold itself will then be made of gold!)

Eternity is here constructed anew with the active energy of the many; but what is stressed above all is a solidarity leaning towards the beyond, a posthumous solidarity which is rooted in the sacrifice of the combatants. A dialectical vision of death, in the end convergent (although not identical) with what Neruda expresses in 'Alturas de Macchu Picchu' (1946). In Vallejo, however, it is articulated within the paradigm of a Spanish Lazarus (see poem XII, 'Masa'): the corpse immortalized through collective achievement. The book's provocatively evangelical title attains an air of parable, in which human history is visualized through eyes of a miracle – the miracle of blood and death – unifying *España*'s dominant voices, namely the public oration and the religious sermon.

The *Poemas humanos,* then, suggest a powerful inversion of values, something that also happens in *Residencia en la tierra.* The body is no longer seen as the modern and classical *locus* of the individual and individualism; it is inhabited by elements of the community and society. Vallejo had already begun a tenacious deconstruction of the human organism in *Trilce.* The points of spiritualist privilege (eyes, brow) were substituted in *Trilce* by an overbearing invasion of the shoulder, the lower members, or the extremities. This tendency continued and grew even greater in his poetry of the thirties. Grey hairs and nails – those expendable remains of the flesh – become fossils of the family circle ('canas tías' (aunts with white hair), and so on); and the clothes that human beings dress in become the skin of other beings: each re-enacts his own life with the work and suffering of the great many as background. Thus, by means of this double avatar, images of the corporeal are extended and prolonged beyond the limits of the singular individual, integrating and *incorporating* signs of the collective, that is, the productive groups and society in general.

LATIN AMERICAN POETRY AT MID-CENTURY

As we come to the mid-century after the end of the Second World War, we see Latin American poetry consolidating its cultural importance on the continent. At the same time, it begins to reach an increasingly international audience. The decade's most memorable events were undoubtedly the Nobel Prize for Literature awarded to the Chilean poet, Gabriela Mistral (1945), and the publication of the *Canto general* in 1950. With its award, the Swedish Academy were honouring a body of work that, from its very beginnings, had been marked by pacifism and deep compassion for the suffering of the weak, ever the victims of this century's panorama of war. The prize was given for a work that was in full flow and which, to a high degree, summed up the trajectory we have been outlining so far. A poetry with an archaic slant that was both bitter and intense had followed the still provincial and rural verse of *Desolación* (1922). *Tala* (1938) was Mistral's characteristic contribution to the endogenous avant-garde and the Americanism of the thirties. At the time she received the Nobel Prize, Mistral was working on part of her last collection of poems (*Lagar*, 1954), which was to appear three years before her death in 1957.

With the *Canto general*, Neruda completed a poetic project that had absorbed him for nearly ten years, from 1938 until early 1949, when he had to leave Chile following persecution of the Communist party in his country. Begun in years of freedom and hope during the victory of the Popular Front, the book was finished under oppression, in clandestine circumstances within the shadow of exile. Neruda's stay in Mexico around 1940 and his journey to Machu Picchu in 1943 were decisive in expanding his project from the 'Canto general de Chile' (a part that remains as section VII of the whole) into, simply, the *Canto general*, American in source and scope. With fifteen vast sections, the book opens with an almost Utopian vision of the pre-Columbian world. It unfolds the collective American experience from the Spanish conquest up to the wars of the twentieth century, and it culminates with the complementary halves of a grandiose objective cosmography – 'El Gran Océano' (The Big Ocean) and an autobiographical elaboration 'Yo soy' (I am) – in which the poet's body and spirit are conceived as the product of his country's natural environment and the struggles of its people. It can surely be claimed that, by virtue of its epic dimensions and the structural variety of the poetic forms it embraces, this great Nerudian book is one of this century's fundamental works.[18]

In Argentina Borges – whose work, we have seen, was initiated within the framework of the avant-garde at the beginning of the twenties – undertook an appraisal of his own poetry by means of an anthology that he prepared and published in 1943 (*Poemas, 1922–1943*). It marked a significant point in Borges's trajectory, in that he re-orientated his work in a classical direction, almost purging it of avant-garde tendencies, while at the same time he injected it with a metaphysical air, which had not existed before as such and which could be accounted for as the result of the author's own stories influencing his poetry from within. From that time on, it became hard to distinguish the poet from the storyteller. Both poems and short stories were chosen by Borges for his underlying purpose of systematically excluding the novel, with all the dangers of 'realism' and the prosaic that, according to him, this genre carried with it. In Borges the poet a further facet of the author of *El Aleph* (1949) and his other stories will always be seen, confirming the immense distance that there is between his work and Latin American history. A distance that, whether or not a sign of persistent Buenos Aires cosmopolitanism, is also – paradoxically – a characteristic reaction to turning points in Argentina's history, and particularly to a specific view of universal history. In fact, deconstructing history, which appears to be the most obvious indicator of Borges's literary apparatus, is also the cover for one of the most refined philosophies of history ever undertaken by one of our men of letters. On the map of universal history, with commendable tolerance, Latin American culture co-exists with other civilizations forged by humanity throughout the planet over the centuries; but the common denominator of this history has always been violence (invasions, the incursion of nomadic tribes, and so on). Latin America also participates in this consubstantial violence. Tolerance is pluri-cultural and avoids every attempt at ethnocentrism; violence is ubiquitous and, in the interests of this same tolerance, it passes from culture to culture, it is culture itself *at work,** carrying and contributing to the fertile synthesis, transfer and movement of tradition, and so on. It can be noted that the

---

* *Translator's note:* In English in the original text.
[18] A significant detail for the relationship between literature and politics: when he died in Bolivia, Ernesto 'Che' Guevara was carrying a treatise on Calculus and a copy of the *Canto general* in his military rucksack.

butcher's shop, which appeared modestly in a corner of Borges's first book (see above), now becomes the symbol of a civilization built on barbarism. (His own experience of his country and the contemporary period, perhaps?)

In Mexico, Octavio Paz (b. 1914) first anthologized himself in *Libertad bajo palabra* (1949). Almost all his earlier poetry – *Luna silvestre* (1933), for example, and subsequent books, especially his poetry written in Spain – were excluded from his selection by Paz. He gave special emphasis to his surrealist phase in the forties. This had led him in 1943 to start editing the influential review, *El hijo pródigo*. His poetry – likeable when it has a symbolist slant – basically inherited the tradition created by the *Contemporáneos* group and it was to obtain its best results later with *Piedra del sol* (1957), *Salamandra (1958–1961)* (1962) and *Ladera Este (1962–1968)* (1969). However important Paz may be in Mexican literature – and his importance tends at times to overshadow the existence and value of other poets, such as Efraín Huerta, José Emilio Pacheco and the group belonging to *La espiga amotinada* – it seems fair to claim that his work is not that of an 'originator' in the proper sense nor does his poetry break new ground. His poetry is an echo – albeit a harmonious, refined echo almost always controlled by a painstaking competence – of his great predecessors in the first half of the century, particularly Villaurrutia and Gorostiza.

More names can be singled out in other parts of Latin America. Some poets reaffirmed or renewed their creative impulse. In Chile, for example, Humberto Díaz Casanueva, halfway through the decade, published one of his most mature poems (*Requiem*, 1945). Pablo de Rokha (1894–1968), a poet born on Chile's central coast, who brought a rural note and new forms of social poetry to the Chilean repertory, definitively affirmed his already prolific output in the same period. In Cuba, at the same moment that Guillén was giving a retrospective look at the whole of his output (the already mentioned *El son entero* of 1947), the entirely different work of José Lezama Lima (1910–76) was growing and developing. Following *Muerte de Narciso* (1937), he published several books of poetry in the forties, from *Enemigo rumor* (1941) to *La fijeza* (1949). It was a basically hermetic poetry, whose codes still need deciphering (and this is said in spite of Cintio Vitier's important critical contribution). Finally, special mention must be made of Eunice Odio (1922–74), the great Costa Rican poet who was to live most of her life outside her own country, mainly in Mexico, and who began her dazzling output with *Los elementos terrestres* (1947), but her work was practically unknown or ignored until it was posthumously rescued from oblivion and she was given the place she rightfully deserved.

As regards the national variations that are crystallized by mid-century, how can we give even a summary account of tendencies and the richness of poetic temperaments, so heterogeneous by any reckoning? The lack of symmetry with which the phenomenon expresses itself in the continent's different regions further complicates matters. A simple contrast between Peru and Ecuador is sufficient example. In the former, the tradition established by Vallejo was maintained in the work of Martín Adán (1908–85), Carlos Germán Belli (b. 1927) and many more. In Ecuador, the best literary talent seems to have been absorbed by narrative prose, under the influence of the great indigenist novel of the thirties no doubt.

The case of Colombia is particularly interesting. Between the main poets of earlier periods and the few important voices that can be found around 1950, there was considerable continuity; this gives the Colombian poetry of the present century a very clear profile. If there is anything that characterizes the work of José Asunción Silva (1865–96) – often limitingly considered to be a pre-*modernista* poet – it is his overwhelming musicality. The country's best critics have noted a similar musical gift in the varied and multifaceted work of León de Greiff (1895–1976) and in the frugal output of Aurelio Arturo (1909–74), which is more or less concentrated in one book (*Morada al sur*, 1963) and in a handful of poems. Rooted in Colombian regionalism, an Arcadian breath of fresh air impregnates the work of Arturo who, together with Eduardo Cote Lamus (1928–64) and Fernando Charry Lara (b. 1920), exemplify the best of Colombian poetry.

In spite of the existence of talented poets such as Líber Falco (1906–55), Roberto Ibáñez (b. 1907) and Juan Cunha (1910–85), it is evident that the most telling characteristic of the poetry of Uruguay is the strong feminine presence at its inception. No other Latin American country has ever had such an amount of splendid poetry written by women. Following in Delmira Agustini's wake are the numerous publications of Esther de Cáceres (1903–71), Clara Silva (1903–76), Idea Vilariño (b. 1920) and, a little later, Ida Vitale (b. 1938) and Circe Maia (b. 1932), two estimable present-day poets. The main star of this Pleiad was, of course, Sara Iglesias de Ibáñez (1904–71) who, from her *Canto* of 1940 to her posthumous poems of 1973, elevated and dignified the Uruguayan poetic imagination.

Along with the better known names of Antonio Arraiz (1903–62) and Vicente Gerbasi (1913–93), the figure of Juan Liscano (b. 1915) is dominant in Venezuela. He published two of his first books – *Contienda* (1942) and *Humano destino* (1949) – in the decade that here concerns us. The unhappy tone of the first and the eager exaltation of the second foreshadowed the powerful work he has since produced. Liscano is, without doubt, Venezuela's principal poet.[19]

The excitement provoked by the Argentine poetry of those years is curious. In contrast with the more powerful note of some nations' poetry – that of Peru and Nicaragua, for example – and perhaps because of the very dispersal of poetic energy encouraged by a somewhat external avant-garde, the Argentine lyric seems to lack a distinctive stamp. By virtue of its very variety, which includes a highly diversified regional poetry (in Rosario, Córdoba, Mendoza and Bahía Blanca), a cohesive force is apparently lacking. The individual poet and the group maintain a somewhat erratic relationship and fail to establish a harmonious tradition. This view is deceptive, however. There is no poetry more subtle, more intense or more complex than the work of Enrique Molina, Alberto Girri and Olga Orozco, whose output commenced precisely in the forties. This trio of writers – less publicized than their continental peers – is definitely of world standing.

Enrique Molina (1910–96) revealed a deep-felt reverence for the planet's beauty in a striking series of volumes, including *Las cosas y el delirio* (1941), *Pasiones terrestres* (1946) and *Costumbres errantes o La redondez de la tierra* (1951). At the end of his first book the Earth was 'this adorable planet' and in a later work he spoke of the 'nomadic brilliance of the world', placing on record his travels over the world's surface. At a much later date, *Monzón Napalm* (1968) was not only to carry this planetary geography to extremes, but also to give evidence of an intensification of Molina's historical consciousness, without substantially altering the aesthetic line he has faithfully followed since he commenced his work. Predominant in his poetry is a dignified, polished verse, with more pathos than Girri and, arguably, with less intensity than Orozco – a compact, well-ordered world which makes Molina's voice one of the most authentic in the Latin American poetry of today.

Alberto Girri (1919–91) and Olga Orozco (b. 1922) began their work in the same year, 1946, the first with *Playa sola* and the second with *Desde lejos*. Girri's poetic imagination, which was forged with *Playa sola* and *La*

[19] Consult the anthology prepared by René L. F. Durand, *Algunos poetas venezolanos contemporáneos* (Caracas, n.d.). J. Sánchez Paláez (b. 1922) and Guillermo Sucre (b. 1933), who began to publish at the beginning of the 1970s, should be added.

coronación de la espera (1947) is possibly one of the purest that exists in the Spanish-American world today. His autobiographical 'I' – with its past history, its psychological labyrinths, its intellectual tics – becomes lighter and more compact, until it turns into a completely lyrical 'I', inhabited only by the reverberations of time and the shifting mirage of material things. It is a poetry at once temporal and essential, which is situated in exact equilibrium between perception and image. Girri's poetry also establishes equidistance between anguish and desire on the one hand, and the subject's calmness and ultimate serenity on the other. In the slow swing of his verse, which is both sensitive and meditative, we can glimpse the secret yearning and transparent choreography of dreams.

Olga Orozco's *Desde lejos*, signalled this poet's mature entry into South American letters. *Desde lejos* was, above all, an evocation of woman's immediate concern: the family home, the grandmother's protective shadow, the southern landscape. But the forceful dimensions of the *pampa* wipe out all comforting trace and sow a wind of idolatry, an untameable climate of great devastation peopling the intimacy with nature's violent powers. Orozco's poetry, made out of pain and wisdom, with grand ritual and tiny gestures, lying between the soul's composure and the ever imminent verge of catastrophe, propagates the voice of one of the major spirits of the time.

The position of Nicaragua in the picture of Latin American poetry is truly exceptional. During the long night of the Somozas, which lasted half a century from the assassination of Sandino until the victory of the Sandinista Revolution, a group of poets was able to provide a bastion for resistance from both inside and outside the country, and to maintain it in spite of repression and torture. While Alfonso Cortés declined into madness in 1927, José Coronel Urtecho (1906–94) managed to survive long years of real internal exile, and Ernesto Cardenal (b. 1925) was able to create the revolutionary and evangelical experiment of Solentiname. Grouped together between Master and disciples were poets of the stature of Manolo Cuadra (1907–87), Pablo Antonio Cuadra (b. 1912), Joaquín Pasos (1914–47) and Ernesto Mejía Sánchez (1923–89). Directly or indirectly, sooner or later, they all participated in a poetic development with the following characteristics: early contact with the most renovative North American poetry (with Salomón de la Selva (1893–1958) as a forerunner in his *El soldado desconocido*, 1922); the crucial role played by José Coronel Urtecho in absorbing foreign influence, taking certain elements from Pound who, it should not be forgotten, was a stinging critic of 'usury' in the capitalist system, even if he did espouse Italian fascism; and the individual exposition of the works of the above mentioned poets. Both priest and poet, Ernesto Cardenal who became Minister of Culture after the Sandinista revolution in 1979 embodied the living movement from dictatorship to freedom, from his first historic poems, written during his stay in Mexico at the end of the forties, up to his decisive *Canto nacional* (1973).

From this overall picture it is easy to get the impression of a growing ideological polarization in the poetic tendencies of those years. More recent experience has come to confirm that, if not a polarization in the strictest sense, we are dealing with a bifurcation that expresses clearly defined options on a continental level which are, essentially, of a political and historical nature. These poets could not ignore the global conflict between capitalism and socialism and it strongly affected their poetry and the thinking that moulded their lives. On the one hand, a *Canto general* (1950) in the manner of Neruda and a *Canto nacional* (1973) in the manner of Cardenal, postulating resistance to political oppression and the creation of new ways of collective living; and on the other, 'orientalism' in the vein of Paz and historical-universal metaphysics *à la* Borges, advocating the status quo. A divergence and antithesis that does not exclude space for the expression of dreams, which surface in the poetry of Girri or Orozco. The obscure splendour these poets seek – sometimes blindly – is not opposed to that other, committed poetry, whose conscience and clarity make it see itself as companion of the social forces in ascendancy on the continent. The chiaroscuro of dreams dwells there as well. How could it be otherwise? The forms that give Latin American poetry of the first half century and subsequent years its exceptional vibrancy and recognizable authority in contemporary literature as a whole are the forms of history, nature and Utopia.

5

POETRY SINCE 1950

INTRODUCTION

By the 1950s Latin American poets were writing within the context of their own continental traditions. From Rubén Darío's break with the post-colonial Hispanic tradition in the 1890s, to the following generational break embodied in Vicente Huidobro's avant-garde poems in the 1920s and César Vallejo's experimental *Trilce* (1922), the desire to be as modern as possible by absorbing the latest modes from Europe continued to dominate Latin American poetry. A typical avant-garde poem from the 1920s refused to conform to metre as a definition of what was poetic (i.e. free verse), and sought a new kind of subjective sensibility through playing with syntax, punctuation, common sense, and obvious metaphorical associations, in order to express the novelty and originality of the 'romance' of technology ushered in by the cosmopolitan twentieth century. This typical avant-garde poem serves, at a formal level, as a mould that includes the Brazilian *modernistas* as much as the Mexican *estridentistas*. One of the most representative collections of this period was Carlos Oquendo de Amat's *5 metros de poemas* (1927).[1] A third wave of Latin American poets who wanted to 'make it new' were less Europeanized. Here the emblematic collection was Pablo Neruda's *Residencia en la tierra I y II* (1935), whose title was a proclamation of an earthy or materialistic position. Neruda idiosyncratically created a new generational style exploring telluric, or sensual, relations with the empirical world that did not apparently feed off culture. In 1930 Carlos Drummond de Andrade claimed that stupidity made poets sigh for Europe where in fact only making money counted. What emerged

---

[1] On Brazilian modernism, see John Nist, *The Modernist Movement in Brazil* (Austin, Tex., 1967); on the *estridentistas*, Luis Mario Schneider, *El estridentismo: una literatura de la estrategia* (Mexico, D. F., 1970). On Oquendo de Amat, Mirko Lauer and Abelardo Oquendo, *Vuelta a la otra margen* (Lima, 1970).

from these Latin American avant-garde traditions was that individual poets writing in the 1950s not only had a general Western tradition available through a proliferation of translations, but also fluid, emergent native Latin American traditions.

The Romantic seeking of originality over several generations, where poetry is an individual's coming to terms with an inner, subjective status, exploring multi-layered consciousness through language, must be counter-balanced by an equally crucial Latin American tradition that sees the poet's role as subservient to a social revolution, or to a more public persona. The starting point for this tradition would be Rubén Darío's public and denunciatory poems like 'Salutación del optimista' from *Cantos de vida y esperanza* (1905), or the nationalistic Brazilians like Manuel Bandeira, and passes through all the poets like Pablo Neruda or Nicolás Guillén, who reacted to the rising evil in Europe by changing their poetry to make it communicate immediately, to be understood by those who might not read, or buy, books of poems. This politicized tradition centres on César Vallejo's posthumous poems, on Neruda's post 1950s populist stance, and includes the Brazilianization at work in post 1920s Brazilian poetry.

As crucial as the traditions for poets beginning to publish in the 1950s was the social status of the poet. Here a poet's charisma, close to that of a shaman, in cultures in the process of defining themselves against Europe, and in relation to their neighbours, and shared histories, still seduced younger poets into wanting to become poets. At an anecdotal level, Manuel Bandeira had a sign outside his workplace saying that a parking space was reserved 'for the Poet'. Pablo Neruda was usually referred to simply as the 'Poet'. As living from poetry was impossible poets like Pablo Neruda, Vinícius de Moraes, João Cabral de Melo Neto, Octavio Paz, Jorge Carrera Andrade, Jaime García Terrés, Raúl Zurita, Juan Gustavo Cobo Borda, and Homero Aridjis, to mention a few, were given glamorous diplomatic posts. Others like José Lezama Lima, or Carlos Drummond de Andrade (thirty years in the Brazilian Ministry of Education), or César Fernández Moreno (at UNESCO), or Ernesto Cardenal (Minister of Culture in the Sandinista government in Nicaragua), have worked in bureaucracies. Poets in Latin America were and are rewarded for being poets in a continent with high levels of illiteracy, and little access to 'high culture'. Poets are asked to take part in debates, give opinions, be a conspicuous role model. Pablo Neruda's post-1950s poetry cannot be separated from his role in the Chilean Communist party, ending up as ambassador under Salvador Allende in Paris. Octavio Paz's public utterances, from his condemnation of the U.S. invasion of Santo Domingo in 1965 and the massacre of over 300 students in Tlatelolco in 1968, to his contested views on Cuba and Nicaragua, come from his respected status of 'poet'.[2]

As the publication of poetry lies outside the economics of the market-place for the vast majority, most poets begin by paying for their own editions. This presents enormous freedom for poets, and problems for a critic. A poetry press like Ediciones Ultimo Reino in Buenos Aires has a huge list of poets in print. Contemporary poetry presses proliferate. There is a history of Latin American poetry to be written around the status of these small presses and little magazines. Typical examples would be Victoria Ocampo's magazine *Sur* and its press, running from the 1930s to the 1970s, or Peruvian poet Javier Sologuren's one-man effort at publishing poets in his La Rama Florida press from the 1960s, or Octavio Paz's more prestigious Vuelta press.

Within this living dialogue between generations and traditions that can never be fossilized into a fixed tradition, the genre of poetry itself remains viable in Latin America. In advanced Western countries the poem has been forced into small presses, university presses, and creative writing departments. That poetry is not economically rewarding has affected the social status of a poet. Poets have become marginalized voices in a mass culture doped on TV and videos, with fewer and fewer readers of poetry outside Academe. Latin American poets are equally aware of this demise of poetry within society's values. They may ridicule the Romantic status of poet as special or visionary or social critic, but as they never submitted to the pressures of the commercial market continue to want to call themselves poets.

Finally, in Latin America, as in the late Eastern block countries, poets found a new role in hostile political situations, and became 'witness' writers, even guerrillas. They took a step beyond Neruda's position in 'Alturas de Macchu Picchu' (1946), that he would let the voiceless working class speak through him;[3] they actually took up arms for them.

In what follows I have chosen four loosely defined poetic traditions into which I group representative Latin American poets. These are the surreal-

---

[2] See Paz's poem 'Intermitencias del oeste (3)' in *Ladera este* (Mexico, D. F., 1969), his essay *Posdata* (Mexico, D. F., 1970), and 'En Santo Domingo mueren nuestros hermanos' from 'Viento entero' (1969).

[3] Neruda's 'Alturas de Macchu-Picchu': 'Yo vengo a hablar por vuestra boca muerta. . . . Acudid a mis venas y a mi boca / Hablad por mis palabras y mi sangre.'

ist and post-surrealistic tradition, the guerrilla and political poetry tradition, the concrete and neo-baroque tradition, and lastly the anti-poetry tradition.

SURREALISM AND POST-SURREALISM

Parisian surrealism condensed all the theories about liberation and writing in the air in the 1920s, and turned them into manifestos with codes, invoking anarchic and revolutionary theories from Charles Fourier to Trotsky, whom André Breton visited in Mexico in 1938. As an exploration of latent and repressed mind levels, offering a *technique* of self-liberation, a praxis, surrealism was by far the most influential artistic movement of the mid-twentieth century. From an early stage Spanish and Latin American painters were involved (Dalí, Buñuel, Picasso, Lam, Matta, Tamayo, and so on), even some poets who changed language and wrote in French like the Peruvian César Moro. But it was in the 1940s and 1950s that surrealism had a real effect on poets and painters, offering at worst facile metaphorical outpourings.

Embryonic surrealist groups grew up in Argentina around Aldo Pellegrini in 1928, and later in Chile around Braulio Arenas in 1938, but it was in Mexico and Argentina in the 1950s that surrealism threw up noteworthy poets. In the Mexico of the 1950s Octavio Paz (b. 1914), after eleven years abroad, and befriending the surrealist leader André Breton in Paris, challenged the official revolutionary orthodoxy in both polemical essays like *El laberinto de la soledad* (1950) and in poetry like *¿Aguila o sol?* (1951). Paz's surrealism incorporated a utopian belief in the transforming powers of art in a sterile political context of betrayal of revolutionary beliefs, and moral corruption. Paz opposed his finely evaluated surrealist beliefs against the PRI of the 1950s and 1960s. He reinterpreted Aztec myths, redefined the liberating action of poetry in changing consciousness, and offered an alternative revolutionary tradition that was immensely influential on writers like Carlos Fuentes and Juan Rulfo. Paz's presence in Mexican culture increased with his surrealist study of inspiration, and the role of a poet in society and history, in *El arco y la lira* (1956), and with long dense poems re-evaluating history and myth like *Piedra de sol,* (1957). His later less programmatic (and less surreal) works from India where he was Mexican ambassador like *Ladera este* (1969), or his poems about returning to Mexico after a nomadic life abroad in *Vuelta* (1976) and his many acute essays, have created a persona against whom it has been hard to fight for younger Mexicans. Paz almost single-handedly recast the Mexican poetic tradition along avant-garde lines with his anthology *Poesía en movimiento* (1966). Winner of the Nobel Prize for Literature in 1990, he remains today an excellent poet, running a powerful literary magazine *Vuelta,* and dominating Mexican cultural politics. The younger poet José Emilio Pacheco (see below) spoke for many when he said in 1966: 'His poetry and prose have ensured that my discovery of what I wanted to say could begin; they have illuminated me.'[4]

In Argentina, a surrealist nucleus resurfaced around a fine literary magazine *A partir de cero,* with three numbers appearing between 1952–56, and edited by poet Enrique Molina (1910–96).[5] This group opposed both the Peronist philistine neo-fascist cultural policies, as well as the cosmopolitan *Sur* magazine group around Victoria Ocampo, and Borges. Like Paz in Mexico, with whom they had contacts, Enrique Molina and Francisco Madariaga envisaged surrealism as an inner transformation, and a defence of the values of the imagination. They did not turn to political action. Enrique Molina's crucial book *Amantes antípodas* (1961) asserts surrealism as a rush of sensuous images suggesting Molina's erotic paradise as an island, or port, or childhood town (Bella Vista on the Paraná river) with degradation, and tropical decay, liberating the mind from utilitarian concerns (and language). Molina has constructed a theory of sensation (as opposed to intellect) as the only path towards understanding reality. He said to Danubio Torres Fierro: 'sensations alone can touch, smell, taste and affirm the diversity, the irreducible, infinite diversity of matter and beings.'[6] Poetry is a recreation of this sensational understanding through words evoking mental sensations. The opening poem of this collection defines poetry as 'sudor de instintos' [sweat of instincts] that changes the poet into a 'bestia inocente' [innocent beast]. Further poems describe journeys (Molina once worked as a merchant seaman) to white-hot, passionate places far away from overcrowded Buenos Aires. 'Etapa' [Stage] proposes a surrealist anti-family, anti-home ethic: 'Corrompidos por un esplendor de ríos y de grandes sorpresas hemos perdido para siempre la paciencia de las familias./ Fuimos demasiado lejos. Libres y sin

[4] Pacheco in *Confrontaciones: los narradores ante el público* (Mexico, D. F., 1966), p. 246. On Paz's surrealism, see Jason Wilson, *Octavio Paz* (Boston, 1986). On surrealism in Mexico, see Luis Mario Schneider, *México y el surrealismo (1925–1950)* (Mexico, D. F., 1978).

[5] On Argentine surrealism, see Graciela de Sola, *Proyecciones del surrealismo en la literatura argentina* (Buenos Aires, 1967).

[6] Danubio Torres Fierro interviews Molina in *Memoria plural* (Montevideo, 1986), p. 188. (My translation).

esperanza como después del veneno y del amor / nuestra fuerza es ahora
una garra de sol / los labios más infieles/ y apenas nos reconocemos por
esas extrañas costumbres de tatuarnos el alma con la corriente' (Corrupted
by a splendour of rivers and great surprises we have lost for ever the
patience of families. We went too far. Free and without hope like after
poison and love our force is now a claw of sun, the most faithless lips, and
we hardly recognize ourselves in this strange custom of tatooing the soul
with the current).[7] Molina's poetry does not develop much from the
1960s, despite an attempt at an anti US-in-Vietnam collection *Monzón
napalm* (1968). He himself derived his tropically metaphorical style from
Pablo Neruda's earthy 1930s poetry: 'I think that the greatest resonance
in my poetry has to be secretly identified with those poems by Neruda,
who is to me a colossal poet to whom I owe the atmosphere, the climate of
my poetry'.[8] Molina is also a painter, and exhibited in the surrealist show
in Buenos Aires in 1967. His surrealism is ethical, a 'compromiso total de
vivir la poesía'.[9]

Francisco Madariaga (b. 1927) is also a fine surrealist without ever
being orthodox to the Parisian school, following the mould of Paz and
Molina by attempting to apply his poetics to his own life. His first
collection *El pequeño patíbulo* appeared in 1954, followed by his two best
collections *Las jaulas del sol* (1960) and *El delito natal* (1963). His complete work was collected as *El tren casi fluvial* in 1987. His compressed,
telegrammatic poems are set in Corrientes, with dunes, lagoons and wild
nature, suggesting a landscape of passion, and total commitment to
intense life. Both Molina and Madariaga link mental life with marginalized, tropical places, writing what could be called a 'criollo' surrealism where metaphor is seen as the linguistic tool that unlocks the mind's
potential, and direct experience as more intense than culture.

The most extremist Argentine 'surrealist' poet is Alejandra Pizarnik
(1936–72) for whom poetry is an exploration of inner being cut off from
any references to some empiric outside. In her short poems, often in
prose, only the subjective counts. At the same time, these inner depths
resist words, so that Pizarnik's poetics are on the edge of silence. A short
poem from her fourth book, *Arbol de Diana* (1962, with a prologue by
Octavio Paz) outlines her endeavour: 'Por un minuto de vida breve/ única

[7] Molina, *Amantes antípodas* (Buenos Aires, 1961), p. 31.
[8] Horacio Salas interviews Molina in 'Vivir su poesía', *Análisis*, 477 (1970), p. 50. (My translation.)
[9] Molina's complete works appeared as *Obra poética* (Caracas, 1978) and *Obra completa* (Buenos Aires,
    1989). His sole novel is *Una sombra donde sueña Camila O'Gorman* (Buenos Aires, 1973).

de ojos abiertos / por un minuto de ver / en el cerebro flores pequeñas / danzando como palabras en la boca de un mudo' (For a minute of brief life, unique with open eyes, for a minute of seeing small flowers in the brain dancing with words in the mouth of a mute). Pizarnik enjoyed a reputation as a *poète maudite*, whose final suicide seemed to confirm the agony of her verse. At the heart of her work is an attempt to turn herself into a work of art. But there is a lack of music, a yearning for death and self-destruction that throws up images of mirrors, an intense narcissism, walls, rooms and loneliness. Her work has attracted cult readers to its risky plight, and pity for the poet's sense of being 'gagged' ('este canto me desmiente, me amordaza' (this song refutes me, gags me)), and exiled into a dull adult's world, like an Alice expelled from Wonderland, facing death: 'La muerte siempre al lado. /Escucho su decir. / Sólo me oigo' (Death always by my side I listen to its saying. I only hear myself).[10]

Marco Antonio Montes de Oca (b. 1932) is a Mexican poet whose surrealistic inspired poems try to trap the sensuality of an ever-changing reality through strings of metaphors. Championed by Octavio Paz, the prolific Montes de Oca collected his poems in 1987. His poetics are a search for 'tiempo vivo' (living time), for 'el vértigo maravilloso' (marvellous vertigo). An early collection *Fundación del entusiasmo* (1963) defines his work, for his poems enthusiastically celebrate life as in 'Atrás de la memoria' (Beyond memory) where the poet is born into 'la profunda felicidad /Que uno siente cuando conoce el aire' (the deep happiness that one feels when one knows air). His poetry explores inspiration, his own creativity. He wants to fly: 'Pido volar / En vez de ser ayudado por los vientos' (I demand to fly instead of being aided by the winds), where flying is believing that words have the magic to lift you out of mundane reality. Words are the 'llaves maestras de los pechos' (the master keys of our chests). His later work has passed through a 'concrete phase' (see below the section on concrete poetry), and then become more colloquial and disenchanted, but without abandoning his 'geiser' of rich metaphors so that Eduardo Milán could say about his complete poems: 'It is almost impossible to find in Latin American literature a body of work of such proteic intensity.'[11]

[10] Pizarnik, 'Los trabajos y la noche' (1965), in *Antología consultada* (Buenos Aires, 1968), p. 73. See Cristina Piña, *Alejandra Pizarnik* (Buenos Aires, 1991). Pizarnik's complete works appeared as *Obras completas* (Buenos Aires, 1990).

[11] *Fundación del entusiasmo* (Mexico, D. F., 1963), pp. 73 and 101. Montes de Oca's complete poems appeared as *Poesía reunida* (Mexico, D. F., 1971), and as *Pedir el fuego* (Mexico, D. F., 1987). Milán, *Una cierta mirada* (Mexico, D. F., 1989), p. 101. (My translation.)

Another Mexican poet, Homero Aridjis (b. 1940), also participated in the surrealistic adventure. There is a torrential quality to Aridjis's early poetry that suggests a litany, almost a lyrical narrative. *Mirándola dormir* (Watching her sleep) (1964) is the poet's meditation on a sleeping woman, borrowing magical insights from Octavio Paz's view of woman in *Piedra de sol* (Sun stone) (1957). The long poem incorporates dialogues, monologues and mind-flow sequences in long lines with repeated words and leitmotifs. Woman becomes all women, Eve and Bérenice, man's opposite without whom there is no revelation, no poetry. Aridjis's lyrical expansion reaches its climax in *Perséfone* (1967). In this erotic lyrical novel, without a plot or well-defined characters, Aridjis recreates the Goddess of the Dead and the Underworld, an insatiable amorous woman turned into a whore in a brothel. Aridjis privileges the gaze, and names erotic parts in a hypnotic litany. Several passages embody his theory of regenerative love pulling people back to their 'confused beginning' and origins, charting a descent into a more meaningful self. The men who arrive at the brothel 'had left their brains, hearts and teeth in a closet, had put on their sense at random and in haste, putting memory on their knees and souls in their genitals'. All the time Persephone, slightly absent and mysterious, controls this erotic ritual of self-knowledge.

Aridjis has also mastered the short lyric. In *Los espacios azules* (The Blue spaces) (1968), and especially in *Quemar las naves* (To Burn the Boats) (1975) and *Vivir para ver* (1977) we see how vision predominates in poetry celebrating light, this world, and the here and now. In 'Quemar las naves' Aridjis moves from Cortés's daring act of burning his boats, to impersonating several Mexican figures from Aztec deities to Emiliano Zapata. The poem 'Carta de México' (Letter from Mexico) captures Aridjis' sense of the haunting Mexican past: 'Por estas callejuelas/ ancestros invisibles/ caminan con nosotros' (Along these backstreets invisible ancestors walk with us), that ends with the sun shining on the poet's face, who will also become transparent. Aridjis is genuinely lyrical, not letting his intellect interfere with the poem's music. He tends to expand endlessly and rely on a piling up of images and repetitions to create sense.[12]

The surrealistic tradition privileges the word as capable of recreating

---

[12] Aridjis's complete poems *Obra poética, 1960–1986* (Mexico, D. F., 1988). See Emir Rodríguez Monegal's interview in *El arte de narrar* (Caracas, 1969). Aridjis's novels include *1492. Vida y tiempo de Juan Cabezón de Castilla* (Mexico, D. F., 1985) and *Memorias del nuevo mundo* (Mexico, D. F., 1988).

reality through the imagination. It relies on opening the mind's verbal sluice-gates to allow words to emerge beyond the self's control. Another surrealistic strand situates reality completely within language itself. A suspicious critical attitude to the inner thought processes is the theme of Venezuelan poet Rafael Cadenas (b. 1930). He writes a poetry of divided selves, of the mind's 'trampas'. 'Combate' from *Falsas maniobras* (1966) sets the poem solely in the arena of the poet's inner selves: 'Estoy frente a mi adversario. /Lo miro . . . lo derribo . . . Veo su traje en el suelo, las manchas de sangre . . . él no está por ninguna parte y yo me desespero' (I'm opposite my adversary. I look at him . . . knock him over . . . I see his suit on the ground, blood stains . . . he is nowhere and I get desperate). Cadenas's poems border on aphorisms and prose, there is no outer reality, yet the inner self barely exists; 'Tú no existes' (You don't exist) he writes about himself in 'Fracaso' (Failure).[13]

Argentine poet Roberto Juarroz (1925–95) began publishing in 1958, collecting his 13 books under the same title *Poesía vertical* (Vertical poetry). He also deals with inner verbal paradoxes, relating the slippery self to devious words, rather than to understanding current history, writing a poetry of 'ser' (being), of 'pensamientos' (thoughts). The consistent, solid self is dismantled in sudden inversions and enigmas. Breaking down automatic verbal associations, allows liberating insights to enter the mind, as he claims in his essay 'Poesía y realidad' (1987). In poem 2 of *Tercera poesía vertical* (Third Vertical Poetry) (1965), he plays with his false identity: 'El otro que lleva mi nombre / ha comenzado a desconocerme' [the other who carries my name has begun to unknow me], to end 'Imitando su ejemplo, / ahora empiezo yo a desconocerme. / Tal vez no exista otra manera / de comenzar a conocernos.' [Imitating his example I now begin to unknow myself. Perhaps there is no other way to begin to know yourself] Inside the self is a 'vacío' [emptiness], that is also the emptiness of the apparently solid outside world. Juarroz's nihilistic, quasi-Buddhist stance, depends on defying words. In Juarroz's work (as in Cadenas's) the process of writing (and reading) a poem is clearing the mind of its rubble so that reality appears as it really is: 'Bautizar el mundo/ sacrificar el nombre de las cosas/ para ganar su presencia' (To baptize the world, to sacrifice the name of things to win their presence). His creed is completely mentalist: 'La imaginación es la verdadera historia

---

[13] Cadenas, *Falsas maniobras* (Caracas, 1966), p. 15. Cadenas's first three books were collected in 1979. *Memorial* (Caracas, 1977) contains work from 1970–75. See José Balza, *Lectura transitoria sobre la poesía de Rafael Cadenas* (Caracas, 1973).

del mundo' (Imagination is the real history of the world). There is no local colour, no reference to South-American-ness.[14]

Many further names could be added to the Latin American surrealistic tradition, but all share an apolitical stance, a belief in the liberating power of the imagination, a trust in words as carrying hidden enriching meanings, and a belief that the world and history are distorted by the traps of language itself. In the 1950s and 1960s important literary magazines like Raúl Gustavo Aguirre's *Poesía Buenos Aires* (Argentina), Sergio Mondragón's *El corno emplumado* (Mexico), *El techo de la ballena* (Venezuela),[15] Gonzalo Arango and Jaime Jaramillo Escobar's *Nadaísmo* (Colombia), Miguel Grinberg's *Eco contemporáneo* (Argentina), amongst many others, develop surrealistic rebellion by incorporating the U.S. beat poets, jazz, and later the hippy movement, slowly to become politicized in the late 1960s.[16]

POLITICAL POETRY

The Cuban revolution offered a way forward for many Latin American poets concerned with the scandalous injustices of their continent; it was possible to combine impatience for change with a revolutionary poetics. The icon of the 1960s and 1970s, Che Guevara, who died in Bolivia with a copy of Neruda's *Canto general* in his backpack, was seen as a poet who renounced writing to act, a kind of Rimbaud. The Romantic purifying act that changes a political stalemate allowed a generation of Latin American poets to combine praxis with art, writing a literal poetry, often directly against the obscure, mentalist metaphors of the surrealists, whose writing changed nothing.

Salvadorean poet Roque Dalton (1935–75), one of Latin America's most charismatic guerrilla poets, was executed by a dissident wing of his own revolutionary party. In an interview with Mario Benedetti in 1969, Dalton labelled himself a 'nieto de Vallejo' (Vallejo's grandson).[17] Dalton,

[14] The first volume of Juarroz's complete poems appeared in Buenos Aires in 1993. See his 'Poesía y realidad', *Academia argentina de letras* (1987), 371–405.

[15] See Edmundo Aray: 'Se quiere encender petardos dentro de la literatura' and 'La búsqueda de investigación de las basuras' in 'La actual literatura de Venezuela', in *Panorama actual de la literatura latinoamericana* (Madrid, 1971), p. 124.

[16] An orthodox view of Latin American surrealist poetry is Stefan Baciu, *Antología de la poesía surrealista latinoamericana* (Mexico, D. F., 1974). Baciu uses 'parasurrealista' for surrealistic poets. See his 'Algunos poetas parasurrealistas latinoamericanos', *Eco*, (Octobre 1980), 591–601, which includes Juarroz.

[17] Mario Benedetti, *Los poetas comunicantes* (Montevideo, 1972), p. 33.

like many of his generation, had turned to César Vallejo's colloquial, posthumous poetry that did not shun personal emotions, contradictions, humour, irony, sarcasm or satire. Vallejo's 'human' poems broke with metre, and reached out to its audience by employing slang, and stressing the vitality of voice. Vallejo showed how a poetry of plain truth need not flinch from being circumstantial, and being immediately understood by a sympathetic reader. By adapting Vallejo's kind of poetry guerrilla poets could become witnesses to their age.

Another crucial factor in Vallejo's influence was that he showed that a political poet did not need to prove his political stance by promoting party doctrine. For Vallejo a socialist poet evidenced 'an organic and tacitly socialist sensibility'. Vallejo's revolutionary intellectual was some-one who 'fought writing and combating simultaneously'.[18] The most liberating consequence of Vallejo's lead was that subjectivity spread out-wards into public life so that 'love' and 'politics' were freed from alien-ation. The key term here is *sincerity,* and the sincerity of a poem was tested by the poet's actions.

As a poet Dalton came into prominence when he won the Casa de las Américas poetry prize in 1969 for *Taberna y otros lugares* (Tavern and other places). In the poem titled 'América Latina' we have the intercontinental Cuban view, and why art cannot achieve the necessary revolution, for the poet may face the moon, employ foreign words, scratch his little violin, but that does not stop him smashing his face against the 'harsh wall of the barracks'. In 1973 he had joined the guerrilla group Ejército Revolu-cionario del Pueblo (ERP) without relinquishing writing poems. In fact he also tape-recorded a long interview with a militant survivor of the 1932 Izalco massacre, published as *Miguel Mármol* (1974). But his sarcastic poems written in Cuba began with *El turno del ofendido* (1963). It includes a short poem titled 'General Martínez': 'Dicen que fue un buen Presidente / porque repartió casas baratas / a los salvadoreños que quedaron . . .' (They say you were a good president because you handed out cheap houses to the salvadoreans who remained) which illustrates Dalton's rhetoric of direct names, and the gruesome irony of free houses for the few peasants not killed by the army. Dalton returned to name Martínez when the ex-president was assassinated, in a long poem 'La segura mano de Dios' (The sure hand of God), written from Ahuachapán prison. This 1963 collection ends with a poem 'Lo terrible' confessing how Dalton had changed: 'Ahora

[18] César Vallejo quotations from Angel Flores (ed.), *Aproximaciones a César Vallejo* (New York, 1971).

la ternura no basta/ He probado el sabor de la pólvora' (Now tenderness will not do. I have tasted gunpowder). Again this symbol is literal, for only gunpowder will change all that Dalton records as evil and corrupt in his society. His *ars poetica* (1974) yokes real poetry with revolutionary action for poetry 'is not made of words alone'. The poem 'Historia de una poética' from *Poemas clandestinos* (1975) ends justifying his art for telling 'the plain truth'. Reading Dalton's words is to read the impressionistic, ironic diary of a combatant in the on-going Central American disasters.

The Argentine poet Juan Gelman (b. 1930) hit the headlines in his own country when he was sentenced to death by a faction of the Montonero guerrilla group to which he belonged. Later Gelman was not allowed to return to Alfonsín's democratic Argentina because of a pending arrest, despite the disappearances of Gelman's son and pregnant daughter-in-law. Following Menem's amnesty of the military, Gelman went into exile in Mexico in protest. Much of Argentina's turbulent history of the last thirty years can be read into Gelman's life and poems. He remains one of Argentina's more admired poets.

Gelman does not hide behind literary artifice. In his linked poems 'Carta abierta' (Open letter) he names his disappeared son, along with all the grim details. More importantly, Gelman's poetry both denounces existing social limitations, and offers a violent change. Gelman told Benedetti in 1971 that the Cuban revolution changed his feeling of impotence towards the Argentine communist party, fossilized in bureaucracy and Stalinism. He said: 'When we take power I think that the world will feel in a different way'; Revolution will usher in a new sensibility. Like Dalton, Gelman turned back to César Vallejo who 'profoundly influenced me both personally and in my poetry'. Like Vallejo Gelman does not separate politics from his deepest personal emotions. Real poetry is the consequence of ethical choices; 'el resultado de una manera de vivir' (the result of a way of living).[19]

All Gelman's emotive poetry is literalist. He stands against the surrealists – 'Te juro que no estoy haciendo surrealismo' (I swear I am not making surrealism). In 'Belleza' (Beauty) he mocks Octavio Paz, Lezama Lima and Alberto Girri as over-cultured symbolists, as idealist liberals. Poems do not end with poetic emotions, but lead to action: 'este poema / no se termina en estas páginas' (this poem does not end with these pages). The poet has no doubts about capitalism's egoism, about class society,

---

[19] Benedetti, *Los poetas*, pp. 224, 225, and 228.

about foreign intellectuals who do not understand Latin America, who do not know how a 'picana eléctrica' actually feels. He's working for the 'entierro del capitalismo' (burial of capitalism). Poet and revolutionary become synonymous.

From *Velorio del solo* (Funeral wake for the solitary man) (1961) Gelman establishes his guerrilla identity. The short poem 'Nacimiento de la poesía' links gun shots with words. In *Gotán* (1962, 'tango' respelt) Gelman evokes the erotic thrill of clandestine guerrilla activity in the Montoneros as 'como un hombre que entra temblando en el amor' (as a man who enters into love trembling). This book ends with Gelman's rebirth as the Guevarist New Man. *Cólera buey* (1967) links the guerrilla's 'bellas aventuras' (beautiful adventures), with 'tiros en la noche' (shots in the night). The poem 'Masacres de guerrilleros' (Massacres of guerrillas) ends with a boast 'por fin hay muertos por la patria' (at last people have died for their country). His next collection *Fábulas* (1971), eulogizes guerrilla groups. The topic of *Hechos* (poems written between 1974–78) is the clandestine life 'probando pistolas acomodando cargadores / los com-pañeros // parecen brillar inmortales o lejos de la muerte/ vivos/ en el esfuerzo de probar/ sin// pensar en la suerte adversa favorable' (trying out fitting charges the compañeros seem to shine immortal far from death alive struggling to prove settle without worrying about good or bad luck). Gelman has dispensed with punctuation, with metaphor. From exile in 1976 Gelman recalled 'la alegría de combatir', and guerrilla friends killed and 'disappeared' as he fights political apathy.

A name of a dead 'combatiente' that occurs often in Gelman's poetry is his poet friend Francisco 'Paco' Urondo, a Montonero leader killed in a shoot out in 1976. Urondo had written an essay *Veinte años de poesía argentina, 1940–1960* (1968), criticizing the poets before him for vague anti-Peronist stances, and a total lack of real political commitment. Urondo was one of the intellectual leaders of the 1960s and 1970s, becoming rector of Buenos Aires university after being released from prison under Argentina's caretaker president Cámpora in 1973. Urondo's choice of death rather than surrender became heroic for Gelman, and many others.[20] In a conversation with Roberto Mero, Gelman evokes this exemplary status: 'despite clandestinity, Urondo did not stop writing and

[20] On Urondo, see Jason Wilson, 'The poet as hero', *London Magazine* (February, 1987), 51–60; (trans. in *Culturas. Suplemento de Diario 16*, 128, 1987, iii–v and in *Hojas universitarias*, Bogotá, 4/32, 113–24).

finished a book of poems before he died. I repeat, this example is very important'.[21]

However, Gelman's poems are more than sincere reflections of a revolutionary out to change consciousness for they are crafted with suppressed punctuation, no capitals, lines ending with dashes, neologisms, gender changes, and slogans in a melancholic, colloquial and angry tone. Many of the poems are one long question. He ensured that poetry has been rescued from academic analysis, and literary history, to be read as a *testimonio* to a fanatic mind-frame that both fascinates and repels.[22]

Many poets took up arms to change their societies as quickly as possible, and to recover a sense of personal authenticity. The best known are Otto René Castillo, a Guatemalan poet, who joined Fuerzas Armadas Rebeldes (FAR) in 1966, was ambushed and tortured to death in 1967, the Nicaraguan Leonel Rugama (1950–70) who died under Somoza, and the Peruvian Javier Heraud (1942–63).[23] There are even more poets whose poems invoke a similar ideology but who did not become guerrillas, who just resisted under dictatorships. The Honduran poet Roberto Sosa (b. 1930) summed up the options: 'For Central American writers there is no road left but to be in favor of the oligarchies or against them.'[24]

When Ernesto Cardenal (b. 1925), the charismatic, ex-Sandinista minister of culture, and priest, began publishing his poems in the 1940s it was under two critical influences, one literary, the other political. As we had argued, literary surrealism had an enormous liberating impact in Latin American poetry for it seemed to combine personal freedom of expression within a revolutionary context. Cardenal first published poems in 1946 in free verse. However the ferocious political situation under the successive dictatorships of the Somozas made Cardenal reconsider the point of merely personal liberation in a written text. From this questioning emerged one of the constants of Cardenal's developing poetics: namely, the position of the poet's 'ego' is made secondary to the need to write a poem that urges action. By taking the *effect* of the poem on the reader as central to the poem's area of action, the more Romantic notion of the poem as the sincere expression of the poet's own inner world is relegated to the past.

[21] Roberto Mero, *Conversaciones con Juan Gelman. Contraderrota, Montoneros y la revolución perdida* (Buenos Aires, 1989), p. 120.
[22] Gelman's poetry was collected in 2 vols. as *Interrupciones* (Buenos Aires, 1988).
[23] See Mario Benedetti's anthology of assassinated guerrilla poets, *Poesía trunca. Poesía latinoamericana revolucionaria* (Madrid, 1980).
[24] Sosa interview in Sosa, *The Difficult Days* (Princeton, N.J., 1983), p. xi.

Cardenal discovered the means to carry out his new perception of the role of the poem in an illiterate country like Nicaragua through his reading, while studying at Columbia University in New York (1947–9), of Ezra Pound. Cardenal began translating Pound, aware that most of the Latin American poets of his generation were still looking towards French culture, especially surrealism. To Cardenal, Pound's *Cantos* with their incorporation of quotations, with the collage technique of confronting documentary texts with Chinese poems, and with their ambitious attempt to go beyond the limitations of an individual's private world, suggested a new technique Cardenal called 'exteriorismo', paying more attention to the outer than to the inner world.

The political context to Cardenal's poetry further drives the ego-obsessed Romantic out of the poems. In 1961 in Mexico Cardenal published his *Epigramas,* based, through Pound, on reading Latin and Greek poets. Cardenal developed a counterpointing technique of opposing the classical past (Caesar, etc.) with the Central American present (Somoza). By pretending to write love poems, he avoided direct political denunciation. His little poem 'Imitación de Propercio' (Imitation of Propertius) ends 'Y ella me prefiere, aunque soy pobre, a todos los millones de Somoza' (And she prefers me, poor, to all Somoza's millions). Through Pound, Cardenal also learnt that a poem must be clear, and immediately understood, as Cardenal said to his muse Claudia: 'Los he escrito sencillos para que tú los entiendas' ('I wrote them simply so that you will understand them).

For protest poetry to work on its audience it must be direct, immediately understandable, and in Latin America, readable aloud. Pablo Neruda had led the way in the late 1930s with his realization that a poem must be read aloud to spread beyond the confines of the printed word, and the few who can afford to buy books. All Cardenal's post-1950s poetry is narrative. It avoids the condensation of meaning in metaphors, and uses the syntax of prose.

In some ways Cardenal, by expanding what can be included in a lyrical poem, becomes the unofficial historian of Nicaragua, then Central America, and finally for the whole Latin American continent. In *Hora 0* (1960) there are poems with specific references to local revolutionaries like Adolfo Báez Bone or Sandino; he names places, dictators, characters from the past and the present that have no universal poetic appeal as such but represent his version of evil. This moral vision allows Cardenal to blend his Christian messianism (he was ordained in 1965 in Colombia) with his reading of Marx. *Salmos* (1964), combines the re-writing of the Biblical psalms with his critique of Somoza. This political-religious vein continues through the poems of *Oración por Marilyn Monroe y otros poemas* (1965) where in the title poem Cardenal mentions Monroe's last unanswered phone call and ends 'Contesta Tú el teléfono' (You (Lord) answer the phone). The title of that poem shows how Cardenal has moved beyond Pound to the pop-culture of the United States of the 1960s giving Marilyn Monroe, an Andy Warhol icon, a moral value. His criticism of US consumer culture flows from this stance.

In the collections *El estrecho dudoso* (1969) and *Homenaje a los indios americanos* (1969) Cardenal expands his poems into the history of the conquest of Central America, and catalogues the pre-Columbian Indian heritage, based on archival studies, incorporating voices and documents into the poems so that a reader actually learns about the forgotten past. A good example is 'Economía de Tahuantinsuyu' (Economy of Tahuantinsuyu) where Cardenal contrasts capitalist North American with Pre-Columbian uses of money where political truth and religious truth 'eran para el pueblo una misma verdad' (were but the one truth for the people). The poem that best draws together Cardenal's radical moral vision is his lament on the death of his Trappist poet mentor Thomas Merton (whose poems he translated into Spanish in 1963) which ends 'Sólo amamos o somos al morir./ El gran acto final de dar todo el ser. / o.k.' (We only love and we only are on dying [when we die]. The final act of giving all one's being. o.k.). Read in conjunction with the notes he was allowed to write during his stay at the Trappist monastery – see *Gethsemani Ky* (1960) – and few would doubt Cardenal's deserved position as a poet.[25]

Engaged poetry is defined by its political circumstances; it forces literal references on to the reader to remove doubt; it challenges a surrealist leaning on deep associations; it relies on voice and colloquialisms, and above all, its imperative is to communicate emotionally. A prime intention was to make poetry matter again in the struggle for social justice, and this still concerns younger poets.

CONCRETE AND NEO-BAROQUE POETRY

Poetry has always had a formal side despised by the post-Romantic poets to the extent that the Parisian surrealists, in their first surrealist mani-

---

[25] See Cardenal's *Antología* (Buenos Aires, 1971).

festo of 1924, claimed that anybody could be a poet and write poetry because poetry was the unconscious manifesting itself in surprising images. Throughout the twentieth century, metre has been slowly abandoned for a free verse that promised to mirror a free imagination. Against this belief many poets have argued that form and craft define the poem. There is an alternative tradition enshrining the poem as a game with words that goes back to the Golden Age master Luis de Góngora, and up to the Spanish poets clustered around Federico García Lorca who celebrated Góngora's tricentenary in 1925 with public acts in his homage.

This verbalist tradition mocks the literalist engaged poets, as well as those surrealists who believed in the magic qualities of words. Instead it asserts that poetry is purely verbal, and written, a game with a complete dictionary. Within the Hispanic tradition Góngora's *Soledades* (1612–17) defined poetic genius as making a reader creatively guess at metaphors. In the twentieth century this destructive playfulness was characterized by Vicente Huidobro in his polemical long poem *Altazor,* (1931) as provoking a 'cataclismo en la gramática' (cataclysm in grammar), and the 'simple sport de los vocablos' (the simple sport of words). Huidobro's seventh canto is nonsensical, neologisms perhaps imitating the new song that Huidobro's superman-poet hoped to write, beyond conventional Spanish.[26] César Vallejo's *Trilce* (1922), the title itself a neologism, also played with words so that a poem tended towards a visual object, with unexpected use of capitals, and no punctuation. Following Apollinaire's *calligrammes,* Huidobro had a poem called 'Moulin' (written in French) that was shaped like a windmill. During the same experimental period Juan José Tablada (1871–1945) also played with typography imitating a woman's eyes in the line 'rOstrOs de una mujer' where the capitalized O's look like 'her' eyes.

The most notorious group of poets who broke down the barriers between a poem and a picture were the pioneer Brazilian concrete poets grouped around the magazine *Noigandres* (a Provençal word derived from Ezra Pound), founded in 1952 by Augusto de Campos (b. 1931), and aided by his brother Haroldo de Campos (b. 1929) and Décio Pignatari (b. 1927). Concrete poetry was unofficially launched at an exhibition in São Paulo in 1956. Later a meeting with the Swiss-Bolivian Eugen Gomringer in Ulm, Germany, set up the international movement (which spread to Britain with Ian Hamilton Finlay). The Brazilian concretists are internationalists, and appear to begin from scratch in attempting to come

[26] Vicente Huidobro, *Obras completas,* Vol. 1, (Santiago, 1963), p. 393.

to grips with modernity, but they also look back to Mallarmé, Ezra
Pound, e.e. cummings, and rediscover Oswald de Andrade.

The term 'concrete' is opposed to 'abstract', that is, these poets isolate
the sign itself, the materiality of the word, its semantics not its phonet-
ics. An early Haroldo de Campos poem (1956) is word play 'O ãmago do
õmega' (Core of omega) where the pun leads to the heart of linguistic
matter. His 1979 poem 'Esboco para uma nékuía' (Sketches for a Nekuia)
has the word 'branco' (white) capitalized in a corner of an entirely white
page. The whole poem has isolated words drifting across the page's empty
white spaces so that the poem is understood pictorially first, without
metre, or much syntax. Haroldo de Campos accompanies the poem with a
learned note; he is professor of literary theory, a specialist on Poundian
ideogrammes, a translator of James Joyce's *Finnegans Wake*.[27]

Augusto de Campos's verbal-visual experiments are hard to reproduce
as he plays with typefaces, collages, and puns. 'Olho por ôlho' (eye for an
eye) is made of clippings of eyes in the shape of a pyramid or skyscraper.
'A rosa doente' (O sick rose), based on a short William Blake poem, curls
into the shape of a rose, using italic typeface. Décio Pignatari, a graphic
artist and professor of information theory, has an engaged concrete poem
from 1958 subverting a Coca-Cola advert, and moves in capitalized puns
from 'beba coca cola' (drink coca-cola) to 'babe' (to slobber), 'caco'
(pieces), 'cola' (glue), and ends 'cloaca' (sewer). Another Pignatari concrete poem has a US dollar bill with a face of Christ rather than Washington, with the title 'Cr$isto é a solucão' (Chri$t is the solution). Another is
a cine-poem with large single letters spelling 'ILFE', each one on a page,
forcing the reader to re-organize them into 'LIFE'.[28]

Despite their debt to technology, and their roots in a Brazil that had
just created Brasília out of nowhere in the style of Le Corbusier, the
concrete poets were seen as critical poets, especially of manipulation
through advertising. A later group round a magazine *Praxis* and led by
Mário Chamie (b. 1933) developed this critical visualized text. Chamie's
poem 'TV' is a good example of combining verbal games with a political
message. One positive aspect of these verbal experiments was to undermine automatic verbal opulence by objectifying single words. All the

[27] See Haroldo de Campos interview with Julio Ortega in *Syntaxis* 8–9 (1985), 15–32. Most of his
poetry was collected in *Xadrez de Estrelas. Percurso textual*, 1949–1974 (São Paulo, 1976).
[28] Augusto de Campos collected his poetry in *Viva vaia* (São Paulo, 1979), and again in 1986.
Décio Pignatari's collected poems can be found in *Poesia pois é poesia (1950–1975)* and *Poetc
(1976–1988)*.

major concrete poets moved on into further formal experiments playing with meta-texts, with neologisms, to Haroldo de Campos's 'Galactic' project finally published in 1985.

If there is an avant-garde still today in Latin America it follows from the kind of work the concretists were doing in Brazil, one of the few movements to cross out of Brazilian literature and attract poets like Octavio Paz, Severo Sarduy and Néstor Perlongher. It also pushed Hispanic poets to rediscover poets like Argentine Oliveiro Girondo (1891–1967) whose last book *En la masmédula* (1954), is one long attack on the word and syntax, creating a kind of ur-talk, stripping language of its expressiveness to make it just a material object, as Tamara Kamenszain has noted.[29] Equally crucial to this neo-baroque avant-garde is the role of Cuban José Lezama Lima (1912–76), whose complete works were published in 1970, and who wrote an opaque poetry based on obscure metaphors, that highlighted the sound of the word at the expense of sense, but densely allusive to literary history, whose point was that it mysteriously defied literal meanings.

Paris-based Cuban Severo Sarduy (1937–94) has broken the boundaries between prose and poetry, and in collections like *Big Bang* (1974) playfully mixes allusions to science and sex typographically, following the concrete poets. In his essay *Barroco* (1974), he quotes Lezama Lima to define Góngora's baroque strategies as the elimination of part of a term, ellipsis, in order to make the other part stand out. To suppress half the metaphor was to eliminate ugliness, and evil, by never naming it, saying something for something else. This is the peculiar feeling that reading Lezama Lima gives of half understanding the meaning. In this sense neo-baroque poetry is anti-realist, anti-literalist, and teasingly playful.

In Argentina the collection *Oro* (1975) by Arturo Carrera (b. 1948) can only read as a typographically inventive litany where the words and short phrases are not much more than the pure sound of an *escriba* (scribe) just writing, and the reader just using his eyes, displacing meaning continuously. In his later *Arturo y yo* (1980), mockingly re-creating childhood perceptions of the 'campo', one line can be converted into a poetics, 'el sonido puro que rapta el deseo' (pure sound that abducts desire). The sound of language wakes up secret desires, that cannot be defined except as 'gozo' (pleasure), anticipation of a meaning that never quite happens.

---

[29] Oliveiro Girondo, *Obras completas* (Buenos Aires, 1968). Tamara Kamenszain, *El texto silencioso: tradición y vanguardia en la poesía sudamericana* (Mexico, D. F., 1985), p. 19.

Argentine Néstor Perlongher (1949–93) takes this neo-baroque into politics with his *Alambres* (1987) that ends on the litany poem 'Cadáveres' (corpses) where, as Perlongher said in an interview, the references are omitted. The title of his latest book *Parque Lezama* (1990) is a pun on an actual plaza in Buenos Aires, and a tradition harking back to the poet Lezama Lima. The poem 'Danzig' opens in baroque Spanish with 'La rutilancia de las lentejuelas / en un rimmel de tan marmóreo transparente / el rebote de los ojares . . . ' Perlongher explained his subversions of meaning when he evoked his love of the word 'jade' in Spanish, which forced him to complete it by saying 'jadeo' (panting), where the first word jade contains a secret erotic charge.[30]

There are formalist poets writing against surrealist facilities, and political faiths, who turn to the craft of metres, and the defamiliarizing of pure pleasure in sounds. One of the best known is the Peruvian Carlos Germán Belli (b. 1927) who uses baroque Spanish syntax, allusions, and anachronisms in an expressionist attempt to capture contemporary anguish and 'carencia' (lack). His neo-baroque stance is not similar to Lezama Lima, but by colliding old forms with modern misery manages to capture the present in Peru. In his first collection *Poemas* (1958) the poem 'Segregación N.1' defines the area of his poetic explorations as an insignificant Peruvian faced with authorities: 'Yo, mamá, mis dos hermanos / y muchos peruanitos / abrimos un hueco hondo, hondo / donde nos guarecemos,/ porque arriba todo tiene dueño' (I, mother, my two brothers and many little Peruvians open a deep deep hole where we can hide because above everything has an owner), to end with a wonderful diminutive: 'y nosotros rojos de vergüenza, / tan sólo deseamos desaparecer / en pedacitititos' (and we red with shame only want to disappear into tiny little bits). The downtrodden bureaucrat-poet emerges questioning his body, his love-life, being a Peruvian, as in later collections Belli contorts his syntax, relies on deliberate archaisms, and hyperbaton. By *¿Oh hada cibernética* (O cybernetic fairy) (1962), he counterpoints the classic language of the Spanish Golden Age, with a black-humoured nihilism, as in 'Una desconocida voz . . . ': 'una desconocida voz me dijo:/ 'no folgarás con Filis, no, en el prado,/ si con hierros te sacan/ del luminoso claustro, feto mío;'/y ahora que en este albergue arisco / encuentro me ya desde varios lustros,/ pregunto por qué no fui despeñado, / desde el más alto risco, / por tartamudo o cojo o manco o bizco' (an unknown voice said to me You

[30] Luis Chitarroni interviews Perlongher in *La papirola*, 3 April 1988, 10–14.

will not couple with Filis in the field, no, not even if they take you out with irons from the luminous cloister, o my fetus).[31] In Belli's case the deliberate archaisms heighten the drama of coping with actuality. Belli collected his poetry under the significant title *El pie sobre el cuello* (1967) that perfectly describes his ironic view of the downtrodden poet today. When he presented this book in Lima Belli recalled his development: 'Like other Latin American poets I was dazzled by surrealism' so much so that he preferred the sound of words to their sense. Then he turned to baroque extravagance: ' . . . I try to dominate an atemporal syntax that is not of our time, based on hyperbaton and ellipsis. I deliberately affect my language with archaisms.'[32] In 1970 he published *Sextinas y otros poemas* where the verse form gives the title, a homage to formalism.

ANTIPOETRY

Several critics have seen in anti-poetry the style that matches the post-1950s period, for anti-poetry is a questioning of the value of poetry and of the inflated egos of poets from within the poems. Anti-poems correspond to what the critic Michael Hamburger called the 'new austerity' and arose out of 'an acute distrust of all the devices by which lyrical poetry had maintained its autonomy'. Anti-poetry as defined empirically by Hamburger is based on the urge to communicate as directly as prose; it seeks to reveal socio-political concerns without metaphors, and it uses humour and irony to deflate, to demythify.[33]

In Latin America anti-poetry is a reaction to the kind of self-restricted aestheticism embodied in Juan Ramón Jiménez's 'poesía pura' against which Pablo Neruda argued vehemently for a poetry that was 'impura', that desublimated art, that reeked of sweat and work and the street. But it was another Chilean, Nicanor Parra (b. 1914) who coined the term anti-poetry in his *Poemas y antipoemas* (Poems and antipoems) (1954). It is apt that 'poems' appears in this title as well, for a limited definition of anti-poetry in Parra's case was his reaction against his first lyrical, but never re-edited, collection *Cancionero sin nombre* (Song Book without a name) (1937). Anti-poetry is first of all, anti-lyrical poetry, because lyrical poetry does not capture the alienation and anguish of the age in its 'sweet music'.

[31] Belli, *El pie sobre el cuello* (Montevideo, 1967), pp. 16–17 and 45–6.
[32] Javier Sologuren, *Tres poetas. tres obras. Belli. Delgado. Salazar Bondy* (Lima, 1969), pp. 35–6.
[33] Michael Hamburger, *The Truth of Poetry. Tensions in Modern Poetry from Baudelaire to the 1960s* (London, 1969), p. 220.

Critic Fernando Alegría defined three elements in anti-poetry in an essay published in 1970. It narrates; it has humour; it uses colloquial language. He discovered a tradition that begins with the Mexican Ramón López Velarde, passes through César Vallejo, into Nicanor Parra, Gonzalo Rojas, and Ernesto Cardenal. Alegría summarised: 'anti-poetry which has been anarchic, an anti-rhetorical shawl, found a direct, violent language that restored a lost reality to man'.[34] Anti-poetry has been accused of not being political enough (by Roberto Fernández Retamar),[35] but its basic strategy was to make poetry more important through making it demotic.

Anti-poetry in Brazil also reflects a growing scepticism towards subjective lyrical poetry defined early on by Manuel Bandeira's urge to say 'as coisas mais simples e menos intencionais' (the simplest and least intended things), to the later works of Carlos Drummond de Andrade (1902–87) epitomized in his title *Lição de coisas* (Lesson of things) (1962). Drummond's return to simplicity appeals to his roots, in his family poems, and like César Vallejo, asking his mother 'e o desejo muito simples' (the very simple desire) to mend his soul. Direct, anti-metaphorical poems about tables ('A mesa', 1951), stones, apples. Earlier in 'Nosso tempo' (1945) Drummond had defined this new aggressive poet as somebody who 'declina de toda responsabilidade/ na marcha do mundo capitalista / e com sus palavras, intuicões, símbolos e outras armas / promete ajudar / a destruí-lo / como uma pedreira, uma floresta, / um verme' (declines any responsibility in the march of capitalist society and with his words, intuitions, symbols and other weapons promises to help destroy it like a stone, a flower, a worm). Drummond's 'No meio do caminho' (1930) ('In the middle of the journey', echoing Dante) selects the stone as brute evidence of existence.[36]

João Cabral de Melo Neto (b. 1920) takes up this 'stone' in his poem 'A educacão pela pedra' (1966) where the bare stone symbolises the sertão's dry hardness, and becomes a poetics 'para aprender da pedra/ a de poética, sua carnadura concreta' (to learn from the stone a poetics, its concrete flesh), and thus 'e no idioma pedra se fala doloroso' (in a language of stone one speaks painfully). Cabral de Melo Neto's *Duas aguas* (1956), can be seen as a watershed of this paring down of lyrical poetry in Brazil where his long poem 'Uma faca só lâmina' (1955) (Only the blade of a knife)

[34] Fernando Alegría, 'La antipoesía', *Literatura y revolucíon* (Mexico, D. F., 1971), pp. 204 and 240.
[35] Roberto Fernández Retamar, 'Anti poesía y poesía conversacional en América Latina', in *Panorama actual de la literatura latinoamericana* (Madrid, 1971), p. 342.
[36] See Carlos Drummond de Andrade's *Nova reunião*, 2 vols. (Rio de Janeiro, 1983).

ends with his poetics of 'the presence of reality' as more pressingly real than an 'image' of it. Like the Hispanic anti-poets, Cabral de Melo Neto had moved on to this distrust with lyrical aesthetics from surrealism's rebellion against organized social life.[37]

As early as 1948 Nicanor Parra sought 'a poetry based on facts and not combinations or literary figures. In this sense I feel closer to a scientist. I am against the affected form of traditional poetic language . . . '; and all this because he wants to trap 'modern life' in a poetry that coldly, scientifically, looked at contemporary man.[38] As a theoretical physicist (he became a professor, even wrote a textbook on relativity) Parra began writing anti-Neruda poems in England in 1948. Over his career as a poet he has progressively eliminated lyrical elements until he gave up writing poems, and in 'Artefactos' (1972) just copied down graffiti, or cut out bits from newspapers. Poetry to Parra, like to Drummond, was always outside the poet's subjectivity, in 'cosas' [things]. He refuses effusive and emotional reactions; he denies the ego its omnipotent place at the centre of personality. Many of his 1954 poems are about degradation, exhaustion, failure, hysteria. The poet 'es un hombre como todos' (a man like anybody else); there is nothing special about being a poet. The new anti-poetry is not humanistically uplifting; it does not teach people how they should be. Anti-poetry for Parra simply mirrors the absurdity of life ('la vida no tiene sentido' – life has no sense), that culture and thinking get you nowhere. Parra, like Drummond, takes a stone to invert aesthetics. To Manuel Durán he said in 1972: 'My personal experience is that the ugliest stone is superior to the most beautiful statue.'[39]

His self-portrait as a teacher summarises his world view in its sarcasms, and shifts of tone: '¿Qué me sucede? -¡Nada! / me los he arruinado haciendo clases: / La mala luz, el sol, / La venenosa luna miserable. / Y todo ¡para qué! / Para ganar un pan imperdonable / Duro como la cara del burgués / Y con olor y con sabor a sangre./ ¡Para qué hemos nacido como hombres / Si nos dan una muerte de animales!' (I have ruined my life teaching. The bad light, the sun, the miserable, poisonous moon. What is happening to me? Nothing. And all this, for what? To earn unforgiving bread as hard as a bourgeois's face and with the smell and taste of blood. Why were we born as men if they kill us like animals?). From a working-class background, brother to Chile's great folk singer Violeta Parra

[37] See João Cabral de Melo Neto, *Poesia completa, 1940–1980* (Lisbon, 1986).
[38] Parra in Huga Zambelli, *13 poetas chilenos* (Santiago, Chile, 1948), p. 79. (My translation.)
[39] Durán interviewed Parra in *Plural*, 6 (1972), pp. 10–13. (My translation.)

(1917–67), Nicanor Parra kept his distance from political parties, saw himself as a 'francotirador' (sharpshooter), was denounced by Cuba as the result of having had a cup of tea with Mrs Nixon in 1970, stayed independent in Chile under Pinochet, and whose black humour has not endeared him to any faction. As he said in 'Telegramas' (1970): 'Yo simplemente rompo los moldes' (I simply break moulds). His unpredictable amalgam of vulgarity, nostalgia, contradictions, humour and exaggerations is based on the persona of buffoon to society's serious intellectuals. Anti-poetry is a violent critique of existing society: 'mi postulado fundamental proclama que la verdadera seriedad es cómica' (My fundamental postulate is that true seriousness is comic). In his long poem 'Los vicios del mundo moderno' (The vices of the modern world) he stated: 'El mundo moderno es una gran cloaca' (the modern world is a sewer). His recent work impersonates a nineteenth-century religious crank called the 'Cristo de Elqui'.[40]

Within the Chilean national tradition Parra served as an antidote to the sensual dominance of Pablo Neruda's partisan poetry. Many excellent younger poets followed in Parra's wake of mocking and demythifying, especially Enrique Lihn (1929–88) who had edited a selection of Parra's poetry in 1952 and Gonzalo Rojas (b. 1917), who had emerged from the Chilean surrealist group. But anti-poetry travelled beyond Chilean frontiers. A good example comes with the Mexican poet Jaime Sabines (b. 1925) whose down-to-earth prosy poems stand out against the serious poetics of Octavio Paz. Sabines, like Parra, writes an urban, anguished poetry, where the poet is not protected by culture and education, what he calls the 'tufo de literato' (the stink of a literary man). In his poetry there are few cultural references, and the language is direct, communicative, vulgar, emotional and colloquial. Like Parra again he uses antithesis, paradox and opposites to provoke emotions, rather than metaphor and images. He too believes in reality: 'la realidad es superior a los sueños' (reality is superior to dreams). Nothing is especially poetic; he exploits bad taste, discards discretion. For Sabines the only answer to disease and death is sex: 'No hay más/ Sólo mujer' (there is nothing else. Only woman). He defines life: 'Uno nació desnudo, sucio / en la humedad directa,/ y no bebió metáforas de leche' (one was born naked, dirty, in direct humidity and did not drink metaphors of milk).

[40] Parra collected his poems in *Obra gruesa* (Santiago, Chile, 1969). Later work includes *Sermones y prédicas del cristo de Elqui*, (Valparaíso, 1979), *Hojas de parra* (1985), and *Chistes para desorientar a la poesía* (Madrid, 1989). For criticism on Parra, see Angel Flores and Dante Medina (eds.), *Aproximaciones a la poesía de Nicanor Parra* (Santiago, 1991).

Sabines began publishing with *Horal* (1950). His main collection *Tarumba,* appeared in 1956, and his collected poems *Recuento de poemas* in 1962, followed by *Nuevo recuento de poemas* in 1977. His street-wise poetics emerge in 'A estas horas, aquí' (At these hours, here): 'Habría que bailar ese danzón que tocan en el cabaret de abajo,/ dejar mi cuarto encerrado / y bajar a bailar entre borrachos./ Uno es un tonto en una cama acostado,/ sin mujer, aburrido, pensando, / sólo pensando' (I would have to dance this dance they're playing in the cabaret below, leave my stuffy room and go down and dance with drunks. One is a fool lying in bed, without a woman, bored, thinking, only thinking) where the colloquial voice speaks directly about experience.

A younger Mexican poet (and excellent fiction writer),[41] José Emilio Pacheco (b. 1939) began his writer's career working on the literary magazine *Estaciones* attacking Paz in 1957 for being 'contaminated' by Parisian surrealism. A few years later in 1961 Pacheco publicly declared that Paz's version of surrealism had led to his best poetry. Over those years Pacheco had been seduced into admiring Paz's version of what it meant to be a poet in post-revolutionary Mexico. However, as Pacheco has said, his generation grew up with cinema as the cultural model, and with the 1959 Cuban revolution as their version of 1960s liberation (more politicised than their European counterparts).[42] This has allowed Pacheco to move into an area of writing that is completely his own, distancing himself politically, and owing little to Paz.

The book of poems that heralded this change in tone was *No me preguntes cómo pasa el tiempo* (1969), where the title proclaims Pacheco's particular vision of life and art as grounded in inexorable passing time. Passing time is one of the great lyrical and emotional themes of poetry, and Pacheco explores this in fascinating ways. One strand that typifies his work is the stress on dismissing the traditional poet's ego. Pacheco has consistently refused to glorify himself, dislikes giving interviews, and places the poem above its creator the poet. He often impersonates a historical character, puts on a mask, and employs ironic set-phrases, leading critics to talk of his 'collage' technique.

Following this avoidance of his own ego Pacheco is a great respecter of the lyric tradition while at the same time affirming that nobody reads

---

[41] Pacheco's fiction includes *El viento distante* (Mexico, D. F., 1963); *Morirás lejos* (Mexico, D. F., 1967); *Las batallas en el desierto* (Mexico, D. F., 1981). Hugo J. Verani has compiled *La hoguera y el viento. José Emilio Pacheco ante la crítica* (Mexico, D. F., 1994).

[42] Pacheco in *Confrontaciones. Los narradores ante el público* (Mexico, D. F., 1966), pp. 246–8.

poetry any more, and that it has lost its cultural importance, thus affirming an ambivalent belief in the 'survival of the genre'. His poem 'Crítica
de la poesía' (Critique of Poetry) reveals this in brackets: '(La perra in-
fecta, la sarnosa poesía, / risible variedad de la neurosis, / precio que
algunos hombres pagan/ por no saber vivir. / La dulce, eterna, luminosa
poesía)' (The infected bitch, flea-bitten poetry, / a laughable variety of
neurosis, / the price which some men pay / for not knowing how to live. /
Oh sweet, eternal, luminous poetry.) In a confessedly post-Borgesian way
Pacheco is aware that poetry only happens in a written poem, that he is a
poet only when he writes a poem. This anti-Romantic stance remains
subversive today, and links Pacheco with the anti-poetry tendency.

Another consequence of Pacheco's exploring passing time is his sense of
relativity. The poet is a chronicler who comments on events from the
limitations of his period. Fashions change, and history accelerates (a title
of a short poem) so that passing time undermines any certainties, any
'truths'. Pacheco's poetry is littered with ironic references from the 1960s
youth culture (for example, in a wonderful poem called 'Kodak'), from
1960s political positions. As a chronicler he has commented on the
Vietnam war, on the massacre of students in Tlatelolco in 1968, on the
ecological disaster that is Mexico City, and most recently on the 1985
earthquake in that city. Just the titles of his collections confirm this
complex investigation into time and art from *Desde entonces* (1980), to
Tarde o temprano (1980), which collects his poetry from 1958 to 1978. In
1986 he published *Miro la tierra,* hinting at the way he coolly observes
life, followed in 1989 by *Ciudad de la memoria.* His distinctive voice is at
odds with the more literal and obvious politicized poets, as well as those
who still affirm the prestige and magic of art.

Another anti-poet who became a *cause célèbre* in 1971 was the Cuban
Heberto Padilla (b. 1930). In his second collection of poems *El justo tiempo
humano* (1962), written between 1953 and 1961 when he lived abroad in
the United States and in London, there is a sequence dedicated to William
Blake that contrasts his age with Blake's, but both share a fear of persecution by 'un inspector de herejías' (inspector of heresies), as if poets were
natural dissidents to any regime. This outsider pose ended for Padilla in
this book with his acceptance of a new role in revolutionary Cuba. In the
title poem he accuses himself: 'Tú soñador de dura pupila, / rompe ya esa
guarida de astucias / y terrores./ Por el amor de tu pueblo, ¡despierta!' (You
dreamer with the hard pupil, break your cunning shelter of terrors. For love
of your people, wake up!). Publication of poems in Cuba was a problem due

to the U.S. blockade and paper shortages but Padilla won the UNEAC (Union of Cuban Writers and Artists) prize for *Fuera del juego* (off-side; out of play) (1969). When the book came out his irreverent attitude got him in deep trouble. We find a few poems in praise of Castro's revolution, and others mocking revolutionary seriousness, especially concerning Russia. Padilla adopted a Parra-like irony, even iconoclasm, which jarred with revolutionary earnestness. Padilla was aware that art does not always conform, that it is immoral, and warns himself in a short poem: 'No lo olvides, poeta. En cualquier sitio y época / en que hagas o en que sufras la Historia,/ siempre estará acechándote algún poema peligroso' (Don't forget it poet. In whatever place or period in which you make or suffer history some dangerous poem will always be lying in wait for you). His anti-poetry poetics push him to speak the truth ('Di la verdad'). He defends the apathetic Lezama Lima, accused of being an 'observer', an apt description of all anti-poets. In the title poem Padilla mocks the poet's role in the new society by saying no poets fit. The poem ends: '¡A ese tipo, despídanlo! / Ese no tiene aquí nada que hacer' (that chap, sack him. He's got nothing to do here). In the ironic 'Instrucciones para ingresar en una nueva sociedad' (Instructions to enter the new society) Padilla looks at the good Russian communist as optimistic, obedient, sporty and always applauding.[43]

When *Fuera del juego* was published UNEAC slipped in a note declaring it disagreed with Padilla's counter-revolutionary ideology. Following this Padilla was detained, and finally in court repented ('I have committed so many mistakes') in an extraordinary speech that puts the sincerity of his poetry in doubt. In this speech he despises his poet's pose: 'Yo, bajo el disfraz de un escritor rebelde, lo único que hacía era ocultar mi desafecto a la revolución' (I, under disguise of a rebel poet, have only hidden my hostility for the revolution). He criticized his *Fuera del juego* as packed with 'bitterness' and 'pessimism'; he lamented complaining about Cuba to foreign friends (like Enzensberger), lamented being a friend to Lezama Lima, and praised the revolution for getting him work. The Padilla case polarized the intellectual world with luminaries like Sartre, de Beauvoir, Calvino as well as Europeanized Latin Americans like Cortázar, Paz and Vargas Llosa signing a letter condemning Cuba, published in several newspapers.[44]

---

[43] Quotations from Padilla, *El justo tiempo humano* (Barcelona, 1970), pp. 71 and 88; *Fuera del juego* (Buenos Aires, 1969), pp. 17, 41 and 56. Padilla's novel is *En mi jardín pastan los héroes* (Barcelona, 1981); his memoirs, *Autoretrato del otro: la mala memoria* (Madrid, 1989).

[44] See 'Documentos. El caso Padilla' in *Libre*, 1 (1971), 95–145. (My translations.)

When the Peruvian poet Antonio Cisneros (b. 1942) won the Casa de
las Américas poetry prize in 1968 for *Canto ceremonial contra un oso
hormiguero* (Ceremonial song against an ant-eater) he confirmed that a new
kind of poetry spoke to readers excited by Che, Mao and liberation
movements. Cisneros did not adapt surrealism, or modify Neruda or
Vallejo; he sounded different, wrote a narrative, mocking poetry with
sudden shifts, juxtapositions, collage quotations, and colloquialisms,
reminiscent of Ezra Pound, and U.S. beat poets like Allen Ginsburg.

At the heart of Cisneros's poetic lies a peculiar sense of being a stranger
in his own country, at odds with the official histories, and uncomfortable
with the rich Inca past (like the Mexican José Emilio Pacheco with his
Aztec past). His uneasy distancing from the conquistadores, and from
contemporary Lima society, allowed the poet to range through Europe
and European cultures with a similar sense of it not quite meaning
anything, illustrating Ezra Pound's 'botched civilization' from a Peruvian
point of view.

His best poems present him as a politicized hippy who mocks his own
bourgeois background and first marriage. He contrasts sordid power, and
a rotten past with ecstatic moments lying on his back in the sun, or
making love in the open. The old Inca sun becomes his point of reference,
whether in St James's Park or in Budapest where the poet – 'el gran
haragán' (the great layabout) – equates his years of exile, teaching in
European universities, with cold rain and silence. But although Cisneros
quotes from Leonard Cohen, and scatters his poems with 'piss' and 'shit',
he is not just a sun-loving hippy seeking new sensations and refusing to
work or think. His rebelliousness is more politicized (Cuba, guerrilla
sympathies), and toughens his poetry. He is not seduced by European
glamour. In a poem written from Southampton University he mocks
those who believe in the reality of their cars, and that where they are 'is
the world', where people are alienated by comfort, homes and a convenient forgetfulness. Life in rainy England leaves Cisneros shut 'entre mi
caja de Corn Flakes / a escribir por las puras / sin corona de yerbas ni pata
de conejo que me salven' (inside my box of Corn flakes / writing for the
heck of it/ without a crown of herbs nor a rabbit's foot to save me)'. When
Cisneros returned to live in Peru he continued his misfit's role of critic,
turning to a religious and radical ecological view of Peru's poor stranded
in 'an ocean of seaweed and jelly fish and a sandbank of shit'. Cisneros is
honest, his irony deflates many of his culture's myths. He said: 'My
country has a fabulous past but that culture does not belong to me

anymore, and I can only appreciate its remains like any stranger',[45] where he speaks not only for Peruvians, but for all Latin Americans faced with their severed past, and the realities of underdevelopment.

The same shift towards a literalist anti-poetry can also be discerned in Brazilian poetry. Ferreira Gullar (b. 1930, real name José Ribamar Ferreira) is a good example. His second collection *A luta corporal* (The bodily struggle) where he sought an honest, precise poetry about things, sometimes close to the avant-garde appeared in 1951 (in 1958 he joined the Concretists in *Noigandres*). From 1964 he opposed the military until he went into exile in 1971. On his return he published *Poema sujo* (Dirty poem) (1977) that sums up his intention at looking at the seamy side of urban life. His anti-poetry poetics are summed up in the opening of 'A vida bate' (Life strikes): 'Não se trata do poemas sim do homem / e sua vida' (This does not deal with poems but with men and their life). In 'A casa' the poet asks who speaks, and locates simple things like a coin, or a mouse: 'Fala / talvez o rato morto fedendo até secar' (Perhaps the dead mouse speaks, stinking until it dries up). Gullar's poetry of things is subversive, politicized. In 'Coisas da Terra' (Things of the earth) he writes: 'São coisas, todas elas, / cotidianas, como bocas/ e mãos, sonhos, greves, / denúncias/ acidentes do trabalho e do amor. Coisas, / de que falam os jornais / as vezes tão rudes / as vezes tão escuras / que mesmo a poesia a ilumina com dificuldade' (They are things, all of them, daily, like mouths and hands, dreams, strikes, denunciations, work or love accidents. Things that newspapers talk about at times so crude, at times so obscure that even poetry illuminates them with difficulty). In another poem 'Agosto 1964' the poet is 'fatigado de mentiras' (tired of lies) as he returns from work in his bus he says 'Adeus Rimbaud,/ relógio de lilazes, concretismo,/ neoconcretismo, ficcões da juventude, adeus,/ que a vida / eu a compro à vista aos donos do mundo. / Ao peso dos impostos, o verso sufoca, / a poesia agora responde a inquérito policial-militar' (Farewell Rimbaud. Clock of lilac, concretism, neo-concretism, fictions of youth, farewell, for life, I will buy on sight from the owners of the world. Under the weight of taxes, verse suffocates, and poetry now responds to a secret police inquiry).[46] This farewell to the grand lyric tradition has been

[45] Cisneros in L. Cevallos Mesones, *Los nuevos* (Lima, 1967), p. 14. (My translation.) Cisneros's other main books: *Commentarios reaies*, (Lima, 1964); *Agua que no has de beber* (Barcelona, 1971); *Como higuera en un campo de golf* (Lima, 1972); *El libro de Dios y de los húngaros* (Lima, 1977); *Crónica del Niño Jesús de Chilca* (Lima, 1982); *Monólogo de la casta Susana* (Lima, 1986) and *El libro del buen salvaje. Crónicas de viaje/Crónicas de viejo* (Lima, 1994).
[46] Gullar's complete poems in *Toda Poesia (1950–1980)* (São Paulo, 1989).

assumed by countless Latin American poets worried by what is actually happening in their societies.

CONCLUSION

Whether a poet retreats into his own privacy, and subjectivity, or whether he or she sacrifices the word for a cause, poets and poetry continue to matter in a continent where most poets pay for their own editions, and where poets still represent a symbolic position in society. Poetry continues to be the voice of exacerbated individuality. As historic tendencies and tastes change so too will forgotten poets, marginalized into irrelevancy for a time, emerge.

When it comes to poets writing after 1950 a critic has to choose between selecting poets on subjective criteria, and finding representative voices. However, only an eclectic position allows space for the differing responses to life and tradition that charge the best poems with value. To select names from the mass of poets writing in the 1970s and 1980s is a more dubious critical task. In an essay in 1989 I put forward Horacio Castillo, Ricardo Herrera, Juan Gustavo Cobo Borda, and Reynaldo Pérez Só as poets who speak for the chaotic present some call Postmodernism.[47] In a recent essay Juan Gustavo Cobo Borda chose Antonio Cisneros, Raúl Zurita, Eduardo Mitre, Darío Jaramillo and David Huerta as most likely to survive their period.[48] Eduardo Milán selected poets who question language itself like Haroldo de Campos, Roberto Echavarren, Néstor Perlongher, Arturo Carrera, or Emeterio Cerro as those experimenting beyond the poetics of the 1960s and 1970s.[49] Perhaps the most judicious way to evaluate contemporary poets is through the excellent anthologies by Julio Ortega (1987) and Juan Gustavo Cobo Borda (1985) that break down the barriers between Latin American countries.[50] The freedom that Latin American poets have attained today in relation to their own rich, and diversified, poetic traditions, yet often faced with distressing social and personal circumstances, is epitomized by Colombian poet Juan Gustavo Cobo Borda's dictum: 'Escribir como se nos dé la gana' (To write as we want to).

[47] See Jason Wilson, 'Después de la poesía surrealista', *Insula,* 47 (1989), 47–9.
[48] Juan Gustavo Cobo Borda, 'Latinoamérica en su poesía: 1930–1980', *Boletín cultural y bibliográfico,* XXVIII (1991), 34–53.
[49] Eduardo Milán, *Una cierta mirada* (Mexico, D. F., 1989).
[50] See Julio Ortega, *Antología de la poesía hispanoamericana actual* (Madrid, 1987); Juan Gustavo Cobo Borda, *Antología de la poesía hispanoamericana* (Mexico, D. F., 1985) See also José Antonio Escalona-Escalona, *Muestra de poesía hispanoamericana del siglo XX* (Caracas, 1985); Jorge Boccanera, *La novísima poesía latinoamericana* (Mexico, D. F., 1982).

6

INDIGENOUS LITERATURES IN THE TWENTIETH CENTURY

SOURCES AND INTERPRETATION

During the last half-century accounts of indigenous America have pointed to a deeper and wider coherence, and a greater resilience, than was formerly recognized in academic and official discourse, notably in mainstream Anglo-American social anthropology. As early as the 1950s, Claude Lévi-Strauss celebrated not just the coherence of American culture but its prime role in the 'cumulative history' of the planet, pointing to its distinctive achievement in such endeavours as plant genetics, medicine (anaesthetics, poisons) and mathematics. Since then scholarship has abundantly vindicated this view while drawing in further areas of common reference, like cosmogony and visual language.

In the matter of script, analysis has revealed characteristics common to the recording systems used in the two principal urban societies of the continent, Tahuantinsuyu or the Inca empire of the Andes, and Mesoamerica. Both the quipu of Tahuantinsuyu, whose logic and codes have been adequately described only in the last few decades, and the books of Mesoamerica are notable for their numeracy and their reliance on such principles as place-value notation. Mesoamerican script conventions have generally become more comprehensible thanks in part to high-quality reproductions of inscribed texts and superb facsimiles of the screenfold books and codices. The hieroglyphic script peculiar to the lowland Maya is now being successfully read according to phonetic principles (advocated by the Soviet scholar Yuri Knorosoz), which effectively link living Maya speech with signs shaped 1700 years ago.

The 'Mixtec-Aztec' or iconic script used elsewhere in Mesoamerica has also been elucidated through study of the principal literary genres associated with it, the ritual books discussed in K.A. Nowotny's grossly under-read *Tlacuilolli* (1961), and the histories or annals (*xiuhtlapoualli*). The patterning of space characteristic of the ritual texts has been fruitfully compared with current practices among the Huichol in Mexico, and the Pueblo, Navajo and other heirs of the Anasazi in the southwestern United States. In the deciphering of the annals, a breakthrough was made by Alfonso Caso when he assigned Christian dates to the life of the Mixtec hero Eight Deer (1001–63 AD) and several preceding generations; and re-examinations of texts from Metlatoyuca and Itzcuintepec now confirm the seventh-century AD Chichimec base date given or suggested in other texts from Cuauhtitlan, Chalco, Nepopoalco, Cuauhtinchan and Coixtlahuaca. Moreover, as they are increasingly deciphered, these inscribed and other early documents are being accorded a long-denied place in Mesoamerican literary history. At the same time, beyond Mesoamerica, the Taino of the Caribbean and the Moche of Peru, among others, have inspired analogous attempts to incorporate ancient inscription and design into the literary corpus.

In the case of recording systems which use verbal language itself, rather than a visual or tactile correlative, a major insight was gained by Marc de Civrieux in his work on the Makiritare Carib cosmogony *Watunna*.[1] In his introduction to the Spanish edition of this work (1970), Civrieux shows how memory of its considerable length is preserved in highly encoded chants, which are not readily intelligible in ordinary language. This model has important implications for the concept of 'orality', as this has been so liberally applied to native American literature since the days of Montaigne, especially by those structuralists working along lines set out by Claude Lévi-Strauss.

Closely akin to Civrieux in their approach, other anthropologists have in the last two decades developed decidedly literary techniques for dealing with native texts from all parts of the continent. Within the framework of discourse theory and ethnopoetics, Dell Hymes, Jerome Rothenberg, Dennis Tedlock, Joel Sherzer and others have come to place greater emphasis on visual presentation on the page, highlighting through typography such concepts as stress or pace in performance, and indeed text itself, paying attention above all to the notion of line, as in verse. Their efforts have brought startling new life to older texts that had been buried in

---

[1] For translations into Spanish, English and other major languages of the native texts discussed in this chapter, see bibliographical essays in *Cambridge History of Latin America* vol. X *Latin America Since 1930: Ideas, Culture and Society* (1995), pp. 591–99, reprinted in vol. XI *Bibliographical Essays* (1995), pp. 925–33.

amorphous prose, for example by the Bureau of American Ethnology, and are enhancing the reproduction of currently recorded texts.

Bringing this scholarly effort home, native Americans themselves have become increasingly articulate about their culture and their texts. They have recovered an authoritative voice of their own, especially when speaking from common ground. The shift is now being actively registered in the programmes and policies of the United Nations, the International Labour Organization and other major international bodies. It has resulted in radical changes in the approach of the Instituto Indigenista Interamericano in Mexico, as is made evident in the fiftieth issue of its publication *América Indígena* (1990). Only in this revised framework may we sensibly approach the literary production of native America, its world view and its resilience.

WORLD VIEW AND COSMOGONY

The literal bedrock of native thought, American cosmogony has in recent years acquired dramatic relevance for those interested in ecology and the possible survival of the human species. It is best approached from within, via certain native-language 'classics', which directly convey native world views and whose published alphabetic versions date from the sixteenth century to the present. The earliest of them emerged from the Spanish invasion of the urban cultures of Mesoamerica and Tahuantinsuyu, and include the *Popol vuh* and the Book of Chumayel of the highland and lowland Maya, the Nahuatl *Inomaca tonatiuh* or Legend of the Suns, and *Runa yndio*, the Quechua manuscript of Huarochiri. Today these narratives are supplemented by others from surrounding and intervening areas, like the Navajo *Dine bahane* from Anasazi, now the southwest of the United States, the *Tatkan ikala* from the Cuna islands off Panama's Caribbean coast, and the Huinkulche narrative of the Mapuche homeland that straddles the Andes between Argentina and Chile. From the rain forest, that last great bastion now under genocidal assault, come the Guarani *Ayvu rapyta*, the Carib *Watunna*, and extensive narratives by the Huitoto, Desana, Shuar and many others, all of them published for the first time in our century.

Common to these American versions of genesis is the scheme of world-ages, of plural creations which end in flood, eclipse and other catastrophes. The emergence of our human species is posited as a late though climactic event in the story of life forms and is threaded particularly through the long and hazardous line proper to vertebrates (fish, saurian, bird, monkey). Humankind's distinctive genius, Cain's, is to have learned how to feed itself, to have developed genetically the most nourishing and beneficent plants, first gourds and tubers like manioc and then beans and cereals. In the Anasazi and Maya texts the cereal maize is even held to be the substance of humankind, according to the doctrine that you are what you eat. In the moral terms of this scheme, the encounter with Europe and the West is most often diagnosed as regress to a less cultured age.

Deriving directly from the still vigorous practice of shamanism, the epic part of this cosmogony deserves special attention, also because it is the one that mediates in principle between the grand metamorphoses of creation, on the one hand, and specifically human history, on the other. The epic hero who braves the underworld and walks like the 'travellers' or planets into the sky is the prototype of the initiate shaman, the curer, the midwife and the psychopomp, bearer of the soul on its journey after death, as Mircea Eliade has shown in *Shamanism: Archaic Techniques of Ecstasy* (1964) and his other fundamental studies of shamanism. A kind of appendix to the Carib *Watunna*, 'Medatia' published in David Guss (ed.), *The Language of the Birds* (1985), is a version of such journeys and practices; the work of an apostate, it is without doubt one of the most powerful pieces of literature to have emerged from America this century.

Dealing in alterations of consciousness and sense perception, these epics also operate shifts between the dimensions of time: the four days of mourning on earth are four years for the spirit travelling beyond, just as a night may stand for a moon, in the midwives' count of nine, or for a year of migration history. Far exceeding Western linearity, just this understanding or articulation of time was enshrined in the great calendar systems of the continent, especially Mesoamerica, where indeed elements of it continue to inform lives among the Maya in highland Guatemala, for example, or the Mixe in Oaxaca.

Through these same recurrent shamanic ciphers, the whole world age scheme is also translated into territory, justifying native occupation of it on the cosmic scale. Hence, ritual Mesoamerican texts like the Féjérváry screenfold and the Aubin Ms. 20 establish the paradigm maps of the four quarters, usually orientated to east or west, and the geological quincunx, usually orientated to north or south. In Tahuantinsuyu, according to Guaman Poma, the same logic underlies the placing of the four huaca mountains – Pariacaca, Sauriciray, Vilcabamba, Coropuna – that guard Cuzco's huaca Pacaritambo, the place of emergence. Today these ritual maps continue to be made and used. Closely following the designs found in the Mesoamerican books, the Navajo make therapeutic sand and dry

paintings which also affirm territory, specifically the concept of the homeland Dinetai on the continental divide. Further, in identifying the four
mountains or landmarks that guard their place of emergence and Dinetai,
to northeast, northwest, southwest and southeast and to either side of the
continental divide, the Navajo quincunx finds perfect analogues among
the Cuicatec and the Mixe in highland Oaxaca, and even among the
Mapuche who until only a century ago held the southern Andean passes
between what are now Argentina and Chile. Thus placing and representing territory, ritually and in actual map designs, in itself not only remembers the homeland but inspires the reason and energy for its defence,
and even its recovery.

Particularly strong ritual geography of this kind has been shown to
characterize the Andes. Vast as it is, this area is held together in Quechua
terms by certain key concepts, like the legend of Inkarri whose head and
body – capital and four limb-provinces – wait to re-unite, or the female
anatomical landscape which places the head in Quito, the navel in Cuzco
(which is what cuzco means) and the uterus in Tiahuanaco, Copacabana and
the 'mother' lake Titicaca. Moreover, emerging from cosmogony the very
strata of geology are similarly construed along the whole length of the
cordillera, as reptilian monsters who had to be laid to rest yet who may
embody and prepare the way for cataclysmic change and political earthquake or revolution: Amaru in Quechua, Catari in Aymara and Kai-kai in
Mapuche. Indeed, as is well known, with the prefix Tupac, Amaru and
Catari named the leaders of the great native uprising in the Andes in 1780,
the former being an Inca name also used by a guerrilla group in Peru today.

While telling a story and naming their space in this way, these
cosmogonies construct the world as they construct themselves. In other
words they are complex literary artifacts, which reflect on their own
beginnings, argument and even ontology. And contrary to the Positivist
assumptions of older anthropologists, this order of sophistication tends to
be the greater the more 'primitive' its origin. Such is the case for example
with the remarkable Huitoto creation published by Konrad Preuss in *Die
Religion und Mythologie der Uitoto* (1921).

Since these texts are so consciously and finely articulated, it is important to note the process whereby they have ended up in alphabetic script
on the printed page. The optimum example here is the *Watunna* narrative
of the Makiritare or Soto Carib, first because it originates in that part of
America which effectively has remained least known and understood from
the outside. It was brought before Western eyes as a result of the Franco-

Venezuelan expedition that went in search of the true sources of the Orinoco as late as 1950, in the area that proved to coincide largely with Makiritare territory. Indeed, this geography is integral to the argument of the text, as it recounts the world ages centering itself on the western end of Pacaraima, the ridge that stretches from Roraima (the 'botanical el dorado' of South America as it has been called) towards Marahuaka, and the improbable Casiquiare canal that links the Orinoco and Amazon drainage systems. Then, once encountered, *Watunna* proved extremely difficult to transcribe and in fact parts and episodes are put together differently in the versions in Spanish (1970) and English (1980). The difference resulted from continuing discussion between the editor, Marc de Civrieux, and the Soto authors, about how to resolve the problem of reducing to a single linear sequence a text whose structure depends originally on dense poetic language and on cycles of performance. Similar issues have also surfaced in editions of Desana cosmogony, the main point of reference in Reichel-Dolmatoff's *Amazonian Cosmos* (1971), as well as studies by other Colombian anthropologists. Working with Berta Ribeiro, Umusin Panlon and other Desana shamans prepared their Brazilian version (1980) with the explicit purpose of correcting previous mistakes and misreadings. The first outsider to publish the Tupi-Guarani version of rainforest cosmogony on any scale, the German anthropologist Kurt Onkel, lived so long and intensely among the authors and bearers of these texts that he himself became Guarani and changed his name to Nimuendaju. The life of his successor, León Cadogan, took a quite similar course, a fact reflected in his handling of the core doctrine of '*ayvu rapyta*' or 'origin of human speech'.

In these and several other cases what is being defended is the integrity of the text itself, a concept for which little room has been traditionally left in mainstream anthropology, notably in structuralist approaches to American 'myth'. This approach was best exemplified in the four volumes of Lévi-Strauss's *Mythologiques* (1967–74) which, remarkable as they are in revealing intellectual coherence over wide geographical areas, deal only in synthesized units of myth, never allowing the concept of text or its integrity to function at all.

Taking such care in reproducing and editing native cosmogonies is by no means an idly literary matter: the whole system of shamanic apprenticeship, for one thing, depends on the prior existence of an authorized text. Cuna society, in this sense, acknowledges a hierarchy of sub-genres or 'ways' (ikala) – childbirth epics, funereal epics and so on – that derive from the major cosmogony *Tatkan ikala,* consigning all to notebooks in a special form of pictographic script. In other words, expressing things properly is essential in the whole process of native education that stems from such world views. Unequivocal statements on this point have recently been made by the Piaroa, neighbours of the Soto, and the Shuar, once better known as the dread head-shrinking Jivaro. In the last decade the Shuar have produced a whole series of textbooks in their language for use by children in schools, topics and moral lessons being drawn directly from the story of the world ages. In a similar vein, the Tzotzil and other highland Maya continue to read the eclipse as the warning against human exploitiveness issued previously in the *Popol vuh,* in a passage which prompted the Cuban novelist Alejo Carpentier correctly to identify American cosmogony as the only one in the world to have warned against the perils of machine technology.

At all events, as a live body of knowledge, cosmogony in this sense underpins nothing less than a philosophy of life, one which formulates in its own way such questions as the human spot in the environment, individual ambition within the collective, and substantive gendering (appealing to a dualism far more subtle than those Western binaries that oppose female earth to male fecundator, and so on). The cogency with which it does so exposes a certain absurdity in Leopoldo Zea's reaffirmation, at the XII Interamerican Congress of Philosophers in Buenos Aires in August 1992, of the idea that philosophy was born in America on 12 October 1492. This New World doctrine was openly endorsed as native American by no fewer than 120 American nations when they met at a conference in Quito in July 1990, in order to work out their common policy towards the Columbus quincentenary. Overriding local and other differences, they drew up a manifesto that made precisely this ecological reading of the world into a first political principle.

RESILIENCE AND MEDIUM

Recognizing formulations like these we can better hope to understand the tenacity of native literatures and cultures, against odds which elsewhere in the world have usually proved terminal. Rather than some pure 'primitive' superstition that necessarily fades before the 'civilized' advance, it is a question of beliefs and practices that can also absorb and adapt. At the brute economic level, ways of turning the intrusive economy to advantage have effectively been found, as in the world-famous and much-studied cases of the Navajo silversmiths and the Otavalo weavers, and the Cuna who market appliqué designs taken from the molas featured in their shamanic texts. In Mexico, the Huichol have similarly adapted dream maps and designs (*neirike*) traditionally incised on gourds, working them into vivid yarn-paintings sold in thousands to tourists; appealing ultimately to the same iconographic tradition and Mesoamerican visual language, the Otomi papermakers of Pahuatlan and the Nahuatl painters of Xalitla, Guerrero, have worked together to produce screenfold books and pages of *amate* or bark paper that they sell locally and internationally. The Cuna, Otomi and Nahuatl products are especially significant since they incorporate elements from the heart of cosmogony – the Cuna tree of life whence the ocean flood (*mu*) issues, the twelve lords of the underworld below Pahuatlan, or the communal harvests of Xalitla – and indeed for the outsider may serve as a first guide to that cosmogony, prompting enquiry into the anterior meaning of these texts, their proper message. At the same time, commercial reproduction has been set up so as not to vitiate native belief and education.

In all this, what anthropologists have termed 'acculturation' (since apparently they recognize only one culture, theirs) may sooner be evidence of inner resilience, the ability to choose from the foreign source and mould it for one's own purposes. In literature, a finely calibrated measure of this process is available in the study of translations that have been made into native languages since Columbus and which in recent decades have come to form part of conscious programmes of cultural renovation. Robert Laughlin, Neville Stiles, Carlos Montemayor and other field workers report the intense desire of native peoples to translate into and thereby strengthen their own languages, not just in the legal and political discourse but in poetry and fiction. The Zapotec version of Brecht's ode to study, published along with comparable pieces in the Tehuantepec literary review *Guchachireza,* is exemplary here. In tune with the Instituto Indigenista Interamericano's revised notion of literacy and education, native translators have also brought Western literary works into their languages through the educational and pedagogical programmes of such bodies as Proyecto Experimental de Educación Bilingue (PEEB) in Peru and Centro de Investigaciones y Estudios de Sociología y Antropología Social (CIESAS) in Mexico, while in Ecuador bilingual illustrated books in Quechua and Spanish, that re-tell traditional tales, are being produced for use in schools.

Bound up in all this is the question of medium and technology. While the classic industrial revolution indeed generally had a devastating impact on native society, today the more refined technology of the transistor and the microchip has proved less culturally predetermined and has been more readily turned to native advantage. The corpus of Quechua songs which has had so long a life in the Andes is now finding modes of survival and dissemination via transistor recordings, like those by the Rumi llajta group who also perform a version of the drama Apu Ollantay. The same is true in the case of the Embera-Chami and Chocó songs of Colombia, where ethnomusicology is being redefined for similarly immediate social, political and pedagogical ends. The Navajo in the United States, the Paez in Colombia and the Kayapo in Brazil are also known for the video-tape versions they have made of their experience, not least their ceremonies and songs. The Paez work with the Consejo Regional Indígena del Cauca (CRIC), a body that has suffered intense persecution in the last decade, and have focused on the annual encounter instituted in Toribio in 1987; the Kayapo are recognized as part of a 'grassroots' media movement that also includes the Nambikwara and the Xavante. Classic texts have also become the subject of film, in such cases as the Mendoza Codex (Tlacuilo), *Popol vuh* and *Watunna*. As for the computer, a recent essay by the Mexican Otomi (Ñähñu) writer Jesús Salinas Pedraza reveals how it has been a main aid to the redesigning of the Ñähñu alphabet and the production of the native-language texts hungrily demanded by villages throughout Otomi territory. In its novelty, this project has refined relationships and roles, notably that of the 'informant'. Traditionally the anonymous Indian who supplied data to the Western writer, from Bernardino de Sahagún in the sixteenth century to Robert Redfield in the twentieth, the informant here becomes the computer programmer who helps the native writer. Jesús Salinas also notes how the success of the Ñähñu project has led to collaboration with Indian groups elsewhere in Mexico, and beyond. Most recently (1991–), it has served as a model for the Quechua in Ecuador, and the Aymara in Bolivia (Aymara having been previously identified by some as the form of human speech closest to computer language).

Finally, a feature of recent decades generally has been the emergence of scholarship about native America published by native Americans, among them Luis Reyes (Nahuatl), Ramón Arzápalo (Maya), Petu' Krus (Tzotzil Maya), Salvador Palomino of the Consejo Indio de Sud America and Abdón Yaranga (Quechua) and Juan de Dios Yapita (Aymara). Nahuaspeakers in Tepoztlan, Morelos, have carefully edited the text of 'Ecaliztli

Tepoztecatl' (The Challenge of Tepozteco), the play performed annually in that town. Tzotzil scholars and writers associated with the Sna Itz'ibajom in San Cristobal de Las Casas since 1982 have explicitly confirmed their need to go beyond the old role of 'informant' and to become researchers in their own right.

MODERN AUTHORS

Collective authorship has undoubtedly been the norm in native literary production. Although the signatures of individual scribes (*u tzib*) are legible in certain hieroglyphic inscriptions of the Maya Classic period (300–900 AD), the post-Classic books are clearly the work of several hands, as are the post-Cortesian alphabetic transcriptions and adaptations known by the name Chilam Balam. The authors of the Cuauhtitlan Annals, one of the major histories in Nahuatl, discussed and agreed in committee the text we have today, while the native scribes who wrote in Latin out of courtesy to the friars typically used the first person plural (. . . *quod vocamus* . . .) in introducing their work. The same is the case with the first major collection of Quechua poems to be published in the original language, 'por unas parias': *Tarmap pacha huaray*, Tarma, Peru, 1905. This is just as much because of a social and political preference as it is because of the sheer nature of the texts themselves. What single individual could ever have dreamt of laying claim to a text so ingenious and all-encompassing as the *Popol vuh*?

In recent years, individually named native authors have nevertheless become more visible, partly because of Western cataloguing and marketing preferences, and partly for reasons internal to their culture. For these authors have chosen to occupy that hazardous space that lies between traditional community and the hail of insult from beyond the community. In other words, to work as a writer in this sense in a native American language of itself implies a major literary and political choice. In each case, forgoing a more likely market the writer gains a range of expression not necessarily available in imported languages like Spanish, Portuguese, English, French and Dutch. Even at the grammatical level, American languages cast gender and person differently, as we noted above. Nor is it easy to find equivalents for certain of those key concepts that have been defined over many centuries of experience in, say, agriculture, the field garden where many of the world's finest plants were first cultivated, lovingly invoked as chacra (Quechua), conuco (Carib), kol (Maya) and milpa (Nahuatl); or the philosophy that never fully divorces place from time, in the 'earth-moment' called pacha (Quechua), mapu (Mapuche) or neka (Cuna). Such notions of time and space derive from that American cosmogony of world ages, whereby previous creations inhere in our present and are constantly alluded to in everyday situations.

Again, choosing to write in the native language allows the author an attitude towards the official imported language of his or her country, either by exulting in autonomy and refusing to admit even a word of it, or by incorporating it dialectically for sarcastic or other ends.

Guarani playwrights, among whom Julio Correa (*Sandía Yvyvy*) and Tadeo Zarretea (*Mitá Reko Mará*) are well-known names, have long been a feature of the theatre in Paraguay, where moreover works in Spanish are commonly translated into that language. In Chile, a special position is occupied by *Nepey ñi güñün piuke* (*Se ha despertado el ave de mi corazón*) (1989) by the Mapuche poet Leonel Lienlaf. From the Mapuche heartland of Temuco, Lienlaf was only nineteen when he wrote the thirty-five poems in this collection, which belongs to the recent Mapuche literary renaissance (Sebastián Queupul, Martín Alonqueo, Elicura Chihuailaf; plus Victorio Pranao and others who have appeared in the 'Küme dungu' series of texts published in collaboration with the University of Temuco). Lienlaf is exemplary in drawing on the deeper Mapuche and native tradition while giving his lines an edge that is very much here and now. The mountain that saved people from the flood, Threng-threng, still serves as a promise of refuge when seen from a boat out at sea ('Boat Song'); and in Temuco, another mountain Nielol remembers the quite recent times when all the houses there were Mapuche. Yet in 'They tore the skin off his back' the wounds inflicted by the savage invasions of the late nineteenth-century, on both sides of the Andes, threaten even the idea of native coherence. Previous Mapuche versions of this violence are found in accounts of the life of Calfucura, hero of the pampa, and in the notable autobiography of Pascual Coña (1930). In what is perhaps the most intense and difficult poem of the collection 'Footsteps' (Rupanum), the experience of walking through Mapuche time, up to the intrusion of the 'cross' and the 'sword', coincides with feeling the growth of the tree. As such the analogy drawn between plant growth and human movement belongs to the wider native American tradition. In the epic section of the *Popol vuh* the fortune of the Twins as they pass through the underworld is paralleled by that of the maize plant left at home: the plant thrives as the traveller fares. The particular analogy with the tree recalls the tree cults of the Chilean Mapuche, evident in a host of place names (including Temuco itself), and in the east-facing tree-post or *rehue* which once centred every community. In cosmogony, each leaf of each tree tells its story.

The great power to the north in the old Mapuche world view, Tahuantinsuyu or the 'four districts' of the Inca empire lives on in the language of ten million or more speakers of *runasimi* or Quechua, in the Andean countries of Bolivia, Peru and Ecuador. Quechua even extends its literary presence into Andean Argentina while far to the north, in the Sibundoy valley of southern Colombia, the very dialect of the old capital Cuzco still records the 'Sayings of the ancestors' and the events of every day. Always pressing hard beneath the surface of the Hispanic culture imposed on these countries, Quechua runs unbroken through the Colonial and Independence periods and issues into the twentieth century in the Tarma anthology of 1905. Its particular strengths have been the drama and song that were so highly developed at the court in Cuzco, in cycles of kingship plays, and a repertoire of poetic modes that include the *wayno* and the *yaravi*. Even within the last few decades the tragedy concerning the death of the Inca emperor Atahuallpa at the hands of Francisco Pizarro was still being performed in the Bolivian Andes, evidence of a living dramatic tradition into which are now being fed works by such modern Quechua theatre groups as Yuyachkani. In the 1960s, Kilku Waraka (Andrés Alencastre) published poetry in Quechua which astounded José María Arguedas with its classical force.

Contemporary Quechua poets, enduring a civil war brought on by centuries of racist outrage against them, have turned especially to the *wayno,* the poetry of its words being matched in performance by that of its Andean music. A leader in the movement in question, Lino Quintanilla chose the *wayno* to celebrate the taking back of stolen peasant lands in Andahuaylas in 1972; urging resistance in his hometown Huamanga (Ayacucho) in another *wayno,* Eusebio Huamani decries the *sinchi* police, whose mottled green uniforms identify them as arrogant parrots that infest home and fields. A *wayno* of quite devastating power is 'Viva la patria' by Carlos Falconi, which like Lienlaf's 'Rupamum' uses the technique of incorporating Spanish words in order to deconstruct and ultimately revile them, to the extent that the 'patria' in question is exposed as vicious hypocrisy, an imposition both incoherent and insulting on all those who are not Latin or white.

The question of racial conflict and of identity within the nation state recurs in Mexico and the other countries that emerged from Mesoamerica, that other great urban focus of pre-Columbian times. And again, modern authors give their edge to the poetics and rhetoric of the old language, in this case the Nahuatl once spoken at the courts of Tenochtitlan and Texcoco. This recuperation may involve no more than re-stating the aesthetics and philosophy of 'flower-song' (xochi-cuicatl) or Nahuatl poetry itself, as this has been preserved for example in the sixteenth-century manuscript known as the Cantares mexicanos. Hence, Natalio Hernández Hernández's poem 'Our ancestral singers' (Nocolhua cuicate, 1987) delicately revives Nahuatl binary phrasing in invoking the old capacity to 'say and know', 'say and sing'. Or, as in a poem by Fausto Hernández Hernández, a traditional mode like the 'orphan song' (*icno-cuicatl*) may be employed to express the current predicament of children and families in Nahuatl-speaking Veracruz who have been abandoned by parents obliged to migrate to alien cities: the title 'Tototl' ([migrant] bird) can refer to either gender, women having in fact borne much of this burden, earning money as they can in the hope of eventually helping those they left behind. Other verse recalls the cadences of Nahuatl rhetoric and oratory. This aspect of Nahuatl has a long history of its own and in 1524 was superbly exemplified in the speech addressed by the Aztec priests to the Franciscan missionaries who wished to convert them to Christianity. In Luis Reyes's poem (1988) 'How many Nahua are we?' ('Keski nauamaseualme tiitstoke?'), there is the same flexibility of persona, from humble to self-assertive, the same dry irony and open sarcasm. Representing the non-Indians of Mexico is the coyote, the trickster, opportunist and scavenger whose pre-social instincts belong to a pre-human age, according to North American cosmogony in general: 'Four hundred years have taught us/ what coyote wants.'

Within Mesoamerica, the Nahuatl tradition is matched by that of the Maya, lowland and highland, among whose classics are numbered the Books of Chilam Balam and the *Popol vuh*. Indeed in the case of the lowland Maya it is possible to trace a continuous line from the hieroglyphic texts of pre-Cortesian times through the Books of Chilam Balam up to such modern authors as Dzul Poot, whose stories immerse us in the geography of the Chilam Balam towns, indicating its hidden but live significance for Maya speakers today. This view is borne out by the authors of Maya texts included in Allan F. Burns's *An Epoch of Miracles* (1983), which includes a salutary re-writing by Paulino Yama of the US archaeologist Sylvanus Morley's account of his dealings with the Maya at

Chichen Itza in 1934–5. Among highland Maya authors, the Quiché Victor Montejo has, like Rigoberta Menchú, documented the genocidal campaigns of the Guatemalan government of the 1980s, linking the resistance of the Maya to their cosmological beliefs (*The Bird who Cleans the World,* 1992). Writing in Tzotzil, Petu' Krus is the first native woman to have received the Chiapas prize for literature.

Then, in addition to Nahuatl and Maya, other Mesoamerican languages are now making their first true literary appearance, notably those which like Zapotec and Otomi (Ñähñu) belong to the most ancient Otomanguan family, scarcely known hitherto through alphabetic texts. In this respect, Carlos Montemayor's *Los escritores indígenas actuales* (1992), which gathers these new beginnings together, is a definite landmark. Distinguished yet unrecorded as a source language and a 'wild' style in the Nahuatl court poetry, Otomi is said to have been used by Nezahualcoyotl the poet-king of Texcoco (1402–72), when he composed his laments: now thanks in part to the computer, it is the vehicle of poems like Thaayrohyadi Bermúdez's 'Tsi Mahkitaa Lerma', a heartfelt ode to the 'father-river' Lerma, which passes on its ecological message by honouring of the old water gods. A counterpart to 'How many Nahua are we?', Victor de la Cruz's Zapotec poem 'Tu laanu, tu lanu' uses half-rhyme to ask 'Who are we? What is our name?'.

IMPACT ON LATIN AMERICAN LITERATURE

With regard to native precedent, the story of Latin American literature in this century has largely been one of recuperation and what Angel Rama called 'transculturation'. After decades of Indianism and indigenism, in which Indian characters tended to be little more than the hypothetical constructs of Romantics or social realists, native culture began to make a profound impact on Latin American literature, as classic texts at last became accessible thanks to scholarly translations and editions. The result has been a major case of intertextuality, a concept which however has most often been reserved in Latin American criticism just for the impact of Western and Old World literature.

The *Popol vuh* is a good example of this interaction. Alluded to in the *mundonovista* work of the Modernistas, like Rubén Darío's poems 'Tutecotzimi' and 'Momotombo' with their references to the creator 'Hurakan' and the proud military strength of the Quichés and Cakchiquels, this highland Maya text provided the only geographically recognizable episode in Salarrue's Atlantis fantasy *O-Yarkandal* (Cuzcatlán [San Salvador], 1929). It then became the decisive element in the work of Miguel Angel Asturias, who translated it (from Georges Raynaud's French) when in Paris and included whole passages in his *Leyendas de Guatemala* (1930). In 'Gaspar Ilóm' (1945), later the opening chapter of *Hombres de maíz* (1949), engagement with the Quiché text can be shown to have transformed completely Asturias's view of his compatriot Maya, curing him of the racism evident in his early thesis *El problema social del indio* (1923), and revealing to him the reasons for the military resistance to white invasion offered by Ilóm's prototype, who actually existed, in Cuchumatanes at the turn of the century. This literary conversion has in practice continued through the life of his son who adopted the name Gaspar Ilóm as the member of the URNG guerrilla forces. In tacit homage, Alejo Carpentier drew on and quoted Asturias's translation of the *Popol vuh* in *Visión de América* (1948) and in the novel which grew out of those essays, *Los pasos perdidos* (1953), which develops most fully his notions of a deeply rooted and autonomous American culture, 'lo maravilloso americano'. Carpentier's readings of the flood and world-ages have scholarly value, as has his remarkable intuition of the links between this Mesoamerican scheme and that of the South American rainforest. Even Jorge Luis Borges, hardly an *indigenista* by calling, turned to the *Popol vuh*, quoting it in the climactic moments of the Jaguar Priest's vision in 'La escritura del dios' (1949). In Amparo Dávila's short story 'El patio cuadrado' (*Arboles petrificados* 1977), an anthropologist tries to 'cross over' (in the terms of Borges or Cortázar) to the native American world represented here by the actual text of the Quiché play *Rabinal Achí*. In the 1960s Ernesto Cardenal began incorporating Quiché-Maya originals into his *Homenaje a los indios americanos* (1969) a work of continental range in which the *Popol vuh* cosmogony and its marvellous evocation of the beginnings of earthly life are directly linked to the creation dates of hundreds of millions of years recorded in the hieroglyphic inscriptions of the Maya ('Mayapan').

Of these examples, Asturias's 'Gaspar Ilóm' and Cardenal's *Homenaje* in particular alert us to a political reading of the *Popol vuh* which is also found in narratives like Virgilio Rodríguez Beteta's *Los dos brujitos mayas* (Guatemala City, 1956), with its highlighting of Xibalba's 'Halcones de la muerte' and 'Mansión tenebrosa de la Desaparición', and Rosario Castellanos's *Balún Canan* (Mexico, 1957). The catastrophic deaths accorded to the exploiters of this world and the epic struggle of the Twins against the power-mad cigar-smoking Lords of Xibalba have found especial resonance in popular literature in Mexico and Central America: these motifs inform consciousness-raising plays performed by La Fragua theatre group in Honduras in the 1970s and the Lo'il Maxil group in Chiapas in the 1990s, as well as the paintings of Juan Gallo in Chiapas, and of Juan Sisay, recently assassinated in Quiché, Guatemala; and they underpin the tenacity revealed in the autobiography of Rigoberta Menchú (1983). In Nicaragua, Pablo Antonio Cuadra read in the story of the Twins' mother Ixquic (Blood Woman), daughter of the Lords of Xibalba, a sign of the end of Somoza's bloody tyranny ('El jícaro', 1978). More recently, the Salvadorean author Manlio Argueta, currently in exile in Costa Rica, has updated Asturias's account of peasant resistance in El Salvador in *Cuzcatlán donde bate la mar del sur* (1986), where again the philosophy and world view inscribed in the *Popol vuh* are shown to be an irreplaceable sustaining force.

Likewise incorporated into Asturias's *Leyendas de Guatemala* and Cardenal's *Homenaje*, the Chilam Balam books of the lowland Maya have passed into Latin American literature having themselves been the focus of the centuries-old 'caste war' of Yucatan that ended effectively only with Lázaro Cárdenas's wise concessions of the 1930s. Just this role is made explicit in the revivalist novel *La tierra del faisán y del venado* (1934) by Antonio Médiz Bolio, translator of the Chilam Balam book of Chumayel; and in what has proved to be one of the best-selling Mexican novels ever, Ermilo Abreu Gómez's *Canek* (1942), named after the leader of the 1761 Maya uprising who looked forward to the nineteenth-century Caste War (1848) and back to the last leader of the independent Maya (1697), also Canek. The question of Maya historical consciousness and its articulation in hieroglyphic and later in alphabetic texts is developed in several of the poems in Cardenal's *Homenaje* ('Oráculos de Tikal', 'Katun 11 Ahau', '8 Ahau', 'Ardilla de los tunes de un katun').

Within Mesoamerica, the matching Nahuatl tradition of cosmogony exemplified in the Sunstone of Tenochtitlan, the Legend of the Suns and the Cuauhtitlan Annals has been generally a pervasive force in the work of Octavio Paz and Carlos Fuentes, while the epic story of Quetzalcoatl's descent to the underworld Mictlan, in its current rural versions, gave shape to Juan Rulfo's *Pedro Páramo* (1955). By far the most directly influential text in the Nahuatl corpus has, however, been the *Cantares mexicanos*, a collection of poetry initially from the court of Tenochtitlan which a recent translation by John Bierhorst (1985) suggests has similarities with the nineteenth-century Ghost Dance songs of the Sioux and other Plains Indians (a view hotly contested by the Mexican Nahuatl expert Miguel León-Portilla). Already in the sixteenth century, Ixtlilxochitl popularized the 'laments' of his ancestor Nezahualcoyotl (1402–72), the poet-king of Texcoco who belonged to the *Cantares* tradition and who was made even more famous by W. H. Prescott's *Conquest of Mexico* (London, 1843), as well as such Christianizing nineteenth-century Mexican poets as Juan José Pesado, Augusto Roa Barcena, Villalón, José Tercero. This century, the *Cantares* began to be read as testimony to the cultural wealth of the Middle America, the place that stretched from Rubén Darío's birthplace Nicaragua in the east to Mexico in the west and whose ancient coherence underlies modern political divisions. In the wake of the Mexican Revolution and the new translations by Angel María Garibay prompted by that event, the Cantares acquired greater resonance in the poetry of Octavio Paz, Marco Antonio Montes de Oca, José Emilio Pacheco, Rubén Bonifaz Nuño and Homero Aridjis, as well as that of the Nicaraguans Pablo Antonio Cuadra and Ernesto Cardenal.

In recreating the brilliant verbal images of the *Cantares*, both Cuadra and Cardenal go further in relating them back to their visual precedent in the screenfold books of Mesoamerica, like the Borgia Codex. These same ancient books are vividly reproduced in words in *Los perros del paraíso* (1987), by the Argentine Abel Posse, part of a 'trilogía americana' that in fact touches repeatedly on native American literature. And in modern Mexico they have become a notable resource for political satirists, for example the illustrated pages of *Quetzalcoatl no era del PRI* by Eduardo del Rios (RIUS), and the brilliant series of cartoons and narratives featured in *El Ahuizote* (a supplement of *La Jornada*), that provided a keenly irreverent response to the 1992 celebrations.

As for the other great urban focus of ancient America, Tahuantinsuyu, literary historians have amply reported the enduring vogue of the *yaravi*, a verse form that had its roots in the *haravek* of the Inca court in Cuzco and which was widely cultivated by the Spanish American Romantics and their successors, including the Nobel-prize winner Gabriela Mistral. Another court genre, the kingship drama, finds its way into the Bolivian novel *El valle* by Mario Unzueta (1962), which indeed preserves the Quechua perspective on Pizarro's murder of the emperor Atahuallpa. Published only within the last half-century, the Quechua narrative from Huarochiri *Runa yndio* gave title and shape to *El zorro de arriba y el zorro de abajo* (1971), the posthumous novel of José María Arguedas (who also

translated this text as *Dioses y hombres de Huarochirí;* 1966), and to Manuel
Scorza's *Garabombo el invisible* (1972), part of the quintet devoted to the
account of the Pasco uprising of 1962. Also published and transcribed
only in recent decades, Guaman Poma's account of the European destruction of Tahuantinsuyu, based as it was on *quipu* archives, has similarly
come to strengthen the cry for political change in the Andes, especially
the vivid page-drawings that have now become universal currency.

That part of America which has resisted invasion still in this century, the
rainforest of South America has also preserved a literary wealth that led
Italo Calvino, for one, to characterize it as 'the universal source of narrative
material, the primordial magma . . .'[2] Reflected in the poems and novels
of José de Alencar, Gonçalves Dias and the nineteenth-century Brazilian
Americanistas, the Tupi-Guarani cosmogony transcribed in *Ayvu raptya*
has subsequently entered a dialectic with western philosophy and religion
in Cardenal's *Homenaje* ('Los hijos del bosque de las palabras-almas') and in
novels by the Brazilian anthropologist Darcy Ribeiro (*Maíra*, 1976) and
the Paraguayan Augusto Roa Bastos (*Hijo de hombre*, 1961; *Yo el supremo*,
1974): *Maíra* and *Yo el supremo* both feature for example the hallucinatory
blue jaguar of solar eclipse. In an uncharacteristic gesture – given his
general demeaning of Indians in his novels of Peru and in his Brazilian *La
guerra del fin del mundo* – Mario Vargas Llosa borrowed the cosmogony of
the Machiguenga making it the centrepiece of *El hablador* (1987), and
showing how the very survival of these Arawak-speaking people on the
uppermost Amazon depends on their remembering their history and place
in the universe.

A last and special chapter in this record is that of the Carib texts from
the Pacaraima area defined in the great Makiritare Carib charter *Watunna*.
Working alone and mostly in ignorance of each other, many South American writers have drawn on the corpus epitomized by *Watunna* and contributed to previously by such visitors as Humboldt, Schomburgk,
Koch-Grünberg and Armellada, a story told in part in Carpentier's 'Visión de América' (1948).[3] In English-speaking Guyana W. H. Hudson's
Green Mansions (1904) and Wilson Harris's *Palace of the Peacock* (1960)
draw in their different ways on Carib accounts of mystic ascent to
Roraima up east-flowing rivers possessed of their own will and life. The
Brazilian Mário de Andrade turned to the Taupilang-Arekuna epic of

[2] Italo Calvino, *If on a Winter's Night a Traveller*, p. 94, quoted by Gerald Martin, *Journeys through the Labyrinth* (London, 1989), p. 356.
[3] See *Ensayos*, vol. 13 of *Obras completas* (Mexico, D.F., 1990).

Makunaima when writing his novel of the same title (*Macunaíma,* 1928), which sends this hero on a journey south from Uaricoera to São Paulo and back again. In Venezuela, the third country to share Roraima as a landmark, Rómulo Gallegos anticipated Wilson Harris's story 'Kanaima' in diagnosing Canaima, the title of his story of the north-flowing Caroni river (1935), as the particular homicidal madness which *Watunna* tells us was induced among the Carib by the White invasion. Other versions of Canaima appear in Eduardo Galeano's American trilogy *Memoria del fuego* which, moreover, opens with a creation passage from *Watunna.* It is just this continual resonance of Pacaraima cosmogony which prompted Carpentier's notable intuitions on the subject and his cross-references to the *Popol vuh* in *Visión de América* and *Los pasos perdidos.*

Another study could record a similar story of impact on Western literature more widely, that includes such figures as D. H. Lawrence, André Breton, Antonin Artaud, Alfred Döblin and many others. The intertextual phenomenon as such is decidedly twentieth-century, and definitive. Recovering native classics and sensing their continuing vigour in native societies today has been a turning point for many modern Latin American writers.

7

MUSIC, *c.* 1920–*c.* 1980

INTRODUCTION

In general terms, the history of Latin American art-music composition in the twentieth century begins with a period of nationalist assertion, with neo-Romantic and neo-classical countercurrents, followed by a period of openly experimental tendencies. These trends occurred at times concurrently in the various Latin American republics, but musical nationalism appeared above all from the 1920s to the 1950s, neo-classicism and other neo-tonal aesthetic orientations at various times from the 1930s, while experimentalism and the avant-garde in music prevailed from the early 1960s. The output of Latin American composers was considerable, revealing a wide compositional diversity, according to historical period, geographical location and special socio-cultural conditions and circumstances. There was at the same time a significant development of music professionalism, supported by professional associations and by institutions of learning, including the national conservatories inherited from the nineteenth century and, from the 1930s, some state and private universities. A number of opera houses were erected or reconstructed from the beginning of the century, and national symphony orchestras emerged in the major countries of the continent in the 1920s and 1930s.

Historically the art music of twentieth-century Latin America had its antecedents in the colonial period and, above all, in the nineteenth century when numerous elements of the great European classical tradition were implanted in the continent. Following the wars of independence, several of the emerging nations established national music institutions. They were, however, dominated by foreign professionals and visiting virtuosi, especially in the latter part of the century. Italian opera and lighter musical theatre genres, art-songs and piano music (mostly of the salon type) dominated the cultivated musical life, although symphonic and chamber music made their appearance in some of the larger cities during the second half of the century.

The earliest attempts to write music in a definable national style were generally undertaken after the mid-century. Opera proved to be particularly conducive to dramatic and musical expression of national themes and values. In Mexico, for example, the opera *Guatimotzin* by Aniceto Ortega (1823–75), premiered in 1871, relies on a libretto based on a romanticized Aztec theme and incorporates some native elements. In Peru, an Italian, Carlo Enrique Pasta, wrote the first opera on a Peruvian theme, *Atahualpa,* premiered in Lima in 1877 and José María Valle Riestra (1858–1925) attempted in *Ollanta* (1901) to create a national opera, but only the libretto had reference to national culture. The Argentine composer Francisco A. Hargreaves (1849–1900) drew on folk-music sources or simply folkloric associations in his operas, which include *La gatta bianca* (1875) and *El Vampiro* (1876). The operas *Pampa* (1897) and *Yupanki* (1899) by Arturo Berutti (1862–1938) borrow actual folk melodies from the *gaucho* and Andean Indian traditions. In Brazil, Antônio Carlos Gomes (1836–96) followed the Romantic Indianist movement in some of his operas, particularly *Il Guarany* (1870) whose libretto is based on a celebrated novel by José de Alencar and whose overture in its final version became virtually a second national anthem. Verdi who heard and saw *Il Guarany* in Ferrara in 1872 called it the work of a 'truly musical genius'. The native contents of Gomes's operatic style, however, are rather limited: his libretti treat Brazilian subjects (Indianism, abolition of slavery), but largely in a symbolic manner.

The late nineteenth century and early part of the twentieth century saw the emergence of musical nationalism, particularly in Mexico, Cuba, Colombia, Argentina and Brazil, under the influence of similar trends in Europe. Romantic nationalism at that time could be described essentially as the 'creolization' of European salon dances (polkas, mazurkas, waltzes, schottisches) together with a new attention to vernacular music genres, and the incorporation in a stylized fashion of certain characteristic elements of 'native' music into a prevailing European Romantic music vocabulary. It should be borne in mind that the aesthetic ideas of composers of such national music represented the typical middle class and upper class values of the time. That such values reflected the cultural-artistic dependence on Europe should surprise no one, since the art-music tradition in Latin America was part and an extension of Western civilization.

Among the numerous Mexican pianist-composers of the latter part of the nineteenth century who contributed substantially to the characterization of Mexican national music were Juventino Rosas (1864–94), an Otomí Indian whose set of waltzes *Sobre las olas* (1891) won him international fame, Tomás León (1826–93), Julio Ituarte (1845–1905), Ernesto Elorduy (1853–1912), and Felipe Villanueva (1862–93). Through a stylized arrangement of popular airs and dance rhythms, these salon-music, popular composers made vernacular music presentable to concert audiences. Elorduy and Villanueva, particularly, devoted themselves to the *danza mexicana,* influenced by the Cuban *contradanza,* the source of numerous Caribbean dance forms, such as the *habanera* and the *danzón,* all emphasizing typical syncopated rhythmic figures that became characteristic of numerous Caribbean and Latin American popular music genres.

In Cuba, Manuel Saumell (1817–70) and Ignacio Cervantes (1847–1905) cultivated the *contradanza* and through it took the first decisive steps toward musical nationalism. Saumell excelled in the small, intimate salon piano piece of a frankly popular style in which an extraordinary variety of rhythmic combinations prevails. Cervantes, a concert pianist, wrote twenty-one *Danzas cubanas,* for piano (1875–95), which incorporate elements of both Afro-Cuban and Guajiro folk music traditions into a Romantic piano style. Particularly conspicuous in these pieces is the use of one of the most typical rhythmic figures of Afro-Caribbean traditional music, the syncopated rhythm known as *cinquillo* in Cuba.

In Colombia, the first attempts to write music of a national character dated from the 1840s, when Henry Price (1819–63), born and educated in London, settled in Bogotá and wrote the piano piece *Vals al estilo del país* (1843), a stylized *pasillo,* one of Colombia's most popular dances. But it was at the end of the nineteenth century that nationalist composition within a Romantic style began to emerge more generally. José María Ponce de León (1846–82), composer of opera and sacred music, took an early interest in national music; works such as *La hermosa sabana* (1881) and *Sinfonía sobre temas colombianos* (1881) were partly based on typical folk dances like the *bambuco, pasillo* and *torbellino.*

The early phase of Argentine musical nationalism developed from the mid-nineteenth century, and centered on the cowboy (the *gaucho*) of the pampas who came to symbolize the national folk and to epitomize the country at large in the early part of the twentieth century. The various dances and songs of the pampas were the major sources to which the first nationalist composers turned. Francisco Hargreaves, for example, in his *Aires nacionales* (1880), for piano, stylized such typical folk songs and dances as the *gato, estilo, vidalita, décima* and *cielito*. The father of Argentine musical nationalism, however, is generally considered to be Alberto Williams (1862–1952) who first found his inspiration in gaucho folk music in the 1890s. The various albums of the *Aires de la Pampa* (begun in 1893), totalling over fifty pieces for the piano, include *vidalitas, gatos, zambas,* and a large number of *milongas,* one of the forerunners of the tango. In his *Primera Sonata Argentina,* Op. 74 (1917), Williams relied on the athletic gaucho dance known as *malambo* for the scherzo movement, thereby opening the way to similar treatment of the dance by later nationalist composers. A true understanding of the expressiveness of Argentine native music is found more readily in the works of Julián Aguirre (1868–1924) whose piano pieces (*Aires Nacionales Argentinos*) and songs (*Canciones Argentinas, Cueca, Vidalita*) reveal a strong empathy for native music and a sophisticated *criolla* inspiration.

In Brazil, the piano piece, *A Sertaneja,* written by the amateur composer Brasílio Itiberê da Cunha (1846–1913) and published in Rio de Janeiro in 1869, opened the path to Romantic music nationalism in its reliance on melodic and rhythmic traits of the urban popular music of the time, particularly the *modinha* (a sentimental song type), the Brazilian tango (especially as cultivated by Ernesto Nazareth, 1863–1934) and the *maxixe* (a popular dance deriving from the European polka). A closer adherence to national musical sources appeared in some of the works of Alexandre Levy (1864–92) whose *Suite brésilienne* (1890), for orchestra, ends with a *Samba* movement based on two traditional tunes and a multitude of rhythmic patterns closely related to contemporary urban popular music. Among the various works of nativistic persuasion written by Alberto Nepomuceno (1864–1920) were the piano piece *Galhofeira,* the String Quartet No. 3 (subtitled 'Brasileiro'), and the *Série brasileira,* for orchestra. *Galhofeira*'s syncopated accompaniment pattern is derived from similar rhythms found in urban popular forms, such as the *maxixe* and the *chôro*. The last movement, *Batuque,* of the *Série brasileira,* is based on the composer's early piano piece, *Dança de negros,* imitating symphonically Afro-Brazilian dance music, by stressing rhythmic elements and simulating through orchestral texture density the responsorial from Afro-Brazilian singing.

MUSIC NATIONALISM, 1920S TO 1950S

As an aspect of culture, music did not escape during the first half of the twentieth century the influence of the rapid development of nationalism in the socio-political life of the Latin American republics. Although musical nationalism lost its importance in Europe after about 1930, it remained a viable current in Latin America well into the 1950s. Latin American musical nationalism, however, cannot be defined in general terms; its expression, meaning and function varied with the individual composer and the specific socio-musical conditions in a particular region, country or even city.

Mexico

Although the composer Manuel M. Ponce (1882–1948), considered the pioneer of Romantic nationalism in Mexican music, advocated a native musical development during the years of the Mexican Revolution (1910–20), it was not until the late 1920s and the 1930s that the Indianist movement responded to the search for a national cultural identity and reached its full development in Mexican art-music. The central figure in this development was Carlos Chávez (1899–1978) who, in a 1928 lecture at the Universidad Nacional in Mexico City, praised the pre-Conquest virtues of Indian music as expressing 'what is deepest in the Mexican soul', and the musical life of pre-Columbian Indians as 'the most important stage in the history of Mexican music'.

Chávez exerted a profound influence in Mexican musical life from the 1920s to the 1950s, not only as a composer, conductor and a teacher but also as a writer on music and a government official. His own adherence to nationalist composition was followed by many of his students, although he was not an exclusively nationalist composer. His own direction toward Indianist, primitivistic style began with the ballet *El Fuego Nuevo* (1921) and culminated with the *Sinfonía India* (1935–6) and *Xochipilli-Macuilxochitl* (1940). Although the subjective evocation of Indian music (whether that of contemporary tribes or remote pre-Columbian high cultures) remained a fundamental concern, Chávez also paid attention to the mestizo folk tradition and to urban popular music. His music has been characterized as 'profoundly non-European' perhaps as the result of the obvious exoticism of his Indianist works but, more importantly, as the consequence of the unique, austere style of such works that combine modernistic and primitivistic elements. The indigenous musical features of his works identified by the composer himself are also found in several of his non-Indianist works and include modal melodies (both pentatonic and diatonic), frequent use of rhythmic ostinatos and consistent underlying rhythmic units, irregular metres, cross-rhythms and syncopation, and frequently changing tempos. In addition, the predominant linear (polyphonic) texture of many of Chávez's works can be related to his statements about polyphony in Indian music of Mexico and the primary value assigned to melody and rhythm rather than harmony in primitive music. The use of copies of ancient instruments, particularly the two-keyed slit drum, *teponaztli,* and the *huehuetl* (a cylindrical, one-headed Aztec drum), and of numerous other percussion instruments or the percussive treatment of other instruments, are also related to primitivistic Indianism. The harmonic vocabulary of Chávez is decidedly modern and akin to contemporary European practices. This vocabulary includes parallelisms, harsh dissonances, sevenths, ninths and octaves, and non-triadic three-note chords (quartal and quintal harmonies), that is, non-Romantic harmonies.

The *Sinfonía India,* one of the best-known Mexican orchestral works of the twentieth century, relies on authentic Indian melodies and native instruments, such as Indian drum (Yaqui drum), clay rattle, water gourd, *teponaztlis* and a large *huehuetl.* The melodic material of the various sections presents a Cora Indian melody used as the first theme of the first allegro, a Yaqui Indian melody used as the second theme, and a Sonora Indian melody as the main theme of the slow middle section. The grandiose finale of this work relies on a Seri Indian melody and epitomizes Chávez's Indianist style in its repetitious structure, brilliant orchestral and cross-rhythmic effects, and its exuberant, driving force.

During his twenty-one years as music director and conductor of the Orquesta Sinfónica de México (OSM, founded in 1928), Chávez favoured the contemporary repertory and championed the works of Mexican composers. His active participation in the International Composers' Guild and the Pan American Association of Composers also contributed to the development of Mexico City as an important musical centre of the hemisphere. As director of the National Conservatory (1928–34), he provided true academic leadership in music education by initiating basic reforms of the curriculum, organizing concerts of all kinds, and by establishing three research units for the study of folk and popular music, of music history and bibliography, and of new musical possibilities. His interest in electric sound reproduction while he was in the United States in 1932, resulted in his book *Toward a New Music: Music and Electricity* (New York, 1937).

Besides his incursion into Indian and mestizo folk music, Chávez also expressed on occasions his sympathies with the post-revolutionary ideology in such populist work as the 'proletarian symphony' *Llamadas,* the 'Mexican ballad' *El Sol,* and the *Obertura Republicana* (retitled later *Chapultepec*), involving an arrangement of the provincial military march, *Zacatecas,* the nineteenth-century salon waltz, *Club Verde* and the revolutionary 'canción mexicana', *La Adelita.*

Among Carlos Chávez's students who were directly influenced by their teacher in their early compositions were Blas Galindo (1910–93) and José Pablo Moncayo (1912–58). Together with Daniel Ayala (1906–75) and Salvador Contreras (1912–82) they formed the 'Grupo de los Cuatro' to promote their activities in nationalist music. Both Galindo's *Sones de Mariachi* and Moncayo's *Huapango,* presented at the Museum of Modern Art in New York in a series of concerts in conjunction with the exhibition Twenty Centuries of Mexican Art (1940), are overtly nationalist pieces with direct borrowing of mestizo folk tunes (particularly *sones*) and the imitation of specific folk dance rhythms and of regional folk music ensembles. In his later works, however, Galindo cultivated a neo-classic style and eventually adhered to the twelve-tone method of composition.

Next to Chávez, the nationalist composer who won the widest international reputation was Silvestre Revueltas (1899–1940). Most of his compositions date from the last ten years of his short life. His first orchestral piece, *Cuauhnahuac* (1930) ('Cuernavaca'), exhibits a highly chromatic, at times violently dissonant harmony, together with a colourful orchestration and a vigorous rhythmic drive. The latter is better expressed in another orchestral piece, *Sensemayá* (1938), considered Revueltas's best work. Inspired by the poem of the Afro-Cuban poet Nicolás Guillén, *Sensemayá* is a sort of onomatopoeic imitation of the sounds and rhythms of Afro-Cuban traditional religious music. The rhythmic ostinatos combined with highly dissonant harmonies and short, repetitive melodic motifs, remind one of Stravinsky's *The Rite of Spring.* Revueltas's good humour and spontaneity is clearly reflected in *8 x Radio* (*Ocho por Radio*) (1933), for an octet chamber group, and in the tone poem *Janitzio* (1933). (Janitzio is the resort island of Lake Pátzcuaro; Revueltas referred to this piece as his contribution to national tourism.) Indeed, such works derive their basic contents from characteristic mestizo folk music models. In other works, such as his *Homenaje a García Lorca* (1936), Revueltas combined his nationalistic tendency with neo-classicism.

Other Mexican nationalist composers of the same generation were Luis Sandi (b. 1905) and, to a lesser extent, Miguel Bernal Jiménez (1910–56). Sandi, particularly interested in choral music and conducting, followed the Indianist trend in such works as *Yaqui Music* (1940) and *Bonampak* (premiered 1951), while Bernal Jiménez, a native of Morelia, explored Michoacán's folk musical traits in his *Suite Michoacana* (1940) and *Noche en Morelia* (1941). His opera *Tata Vasco* (1941) written for the celebration of the fourth centenary of the arrival of the first bishop of Michoacán, Vasco de Quiroga, incorporates some national elements such as popular religious songs and traditional Indian instruments.

After about 1950, musical nationalism in Mexico declined rapidly when new aesthetics and their corresponding styles emerged. By this time Mexico had been able to establish a truly professional musical life, with the official backing of some government agencies, such as the Instituto Nacional de Bellas Artes (founded in 1946 by President Miguel Alemán), and even the possibility of music publishing with the appearance also in 1946 of the Ediciones Mexicanas de Música.

Cuba

Just as Mexican artists found in the Aztec Renaissance of the 1920s and 1930s one of the major sources for their artistic expression, Cuban artists of the same period rediscovered Afro-Cuban culture (known as *afrocubanismo*) as the essential source of national characterization. Despite the advocation of an Indianist approach to musical nationalism by Eduardo Sánchez de Fuentes (1874–1944) who, as an opera composer cultivated Italian *verismo* based on pseudo-Caribbean Indian music, all of the members of the 'Grupo Minorista' (established in Havana in 1923) explored the African elements of Cuban folk and popular culture. For the two most outstanding representatives of music nationalism in Cuba, Amadeo Roldán and Alejandro García Caturla, *afrocubanismo* remained the most appropriate source of national expression.

Amadeo Roldán (1900–39) wrote the first major symphonic work, *Obertura sobre temas cubanos* (1925), indicating the new trend. Besides the utilization of authentic Afro-Cuban musical instruments, this and other works by Roldán explore the prevailingly rhythmic character of Afro-

Cuban music. Roldán's most celebrated work, the ballet *La Rebambaramba* (1927–8), based on a story by the well-known poet, novelist and musicologist Alejo Carpentier, relies on numerous folk elements, such as Afro-Cuban mythology, Cuban *contradanzas* of the nineteenth century, and popular *comparsas* (processional groups of Afro-Cuban cultmen). His second ballet, *El milagro de Anaquillé* (1928–9), also based on a story by Carpentier, relies on both Guajiro (Cuban-Hispanic folk song and dance) and Afro-Cuban (Abakuá initiation ceremonial music) folk traditions. Roldán treated the folk music sources in a modern, dissonant style. In his six chamber music pieces, *Rítmicas* (1930), he tended to recreate subjectively the spirit of Afro-Cuban music, stressing at the same time the refinement of his harmonic and tone-colouring language. *Motivos de Son* (1934), eight songs for soprano and an ensemble of seven instruments, a set of Nicolás Guillén's poems, reveals the composer's skills as a lyrical melodist, a highly effective orchestrator, and an accomplished technician in his treatment of rhythmic intricacies associated with Afro-Cuban dances.

Alejandro García Caturla (1906–40), a student of Nadia Boulanger in Paris in the late 1920s, was exposed to the avant-garde music of the period and came under its direct influence, particularly in reference to poly-tonality and poly-rhythms. His profound empathy for Afro-Cuban culture and people is felt in all of his creative output. His approach to Cuban folk music (both Afro-Cuban and Guajiro) was unorthodox, in that he attempted to create his own unique style with some important elements derived from many folk music genres. His *Tres danzas cubanas* (1927), for orchestra, the Afro-Cuban suite *Bembé* (1928), and the symphonic movement *Yamba-O* (1928–31) on the poem *Liturgia* by Alejo Carpentier, all show a very advanced, exuberant style, with highly imaginative harmonies and instrumental and rhythmic effects. Pentatonic melodies related to Afro-Cuban folk music contribute frequently to the primitivistic nature of his music. The composer-musicologist Adolfo Salazar compared Caturla's style with that of the Cuban popular *son* itself. The main traits of that style consist of a 'generally pentatonic melody, presented by an instrument of a distinct timbre, in a tonally indefinable sonorous atmosphere, sustained by the multiplicity of simultaneous rhythms played by typical instruments'.[1] Both Roldán and García Caturla held a significant place in twentieth-century Cuban music not only be-

---

[1] Adolfo Salazar, 'La obra musical de Alejandro García Caturla', *Revista Cubana*, XI, 31 (January 1938).

cause of the high quality of their works, rooted on national sources but transcending these in unique, modern styles, but also because they contributed, each in his own way, to raising the level of music professionalism in their country.

In the 1940s and 1950s, the Spanish-born composer José Ardévol (1911–1981) dominated the Cuban music scene as an influential teacher and composer. He settled in Havana in 1930 and, although he shared at first the aesthetic ideals of the 'Grupo Minorista', he eventually adhered to neo-classicism which, in his view, carried a greater international meaning. He explored Cuban folk music elements on a few occasions, as in his *Suite Cubana No. 1* (1947) and *No. 2* (1949). Two of his students, Argeliers León (1918–91) and Hilario González (b. 1920), followed the nationalist trend up to the 1950s. Both as a composer and an ethnomusicologist, León maintained his interest in Afro-Cuban music, as revealed in his works *Escenas de ballet* (1944), *Danzón No. 2* (1945), *Yambú, Bolero y Guaguancó* (1956), and *Akorín* (1956), among others. González's most typical nationalist works include *Tres preludios en conga* (1938), *Danzas cubanas* (1938), and two cycles of *Canciones cubanas* (1940, 1945), in which the composer handles rhythmic patterns of folk and popular music in a very personal manner, within a strikingly dissonant style.

The Andean Republics

From around 1920 Vicente Emilio Sojo (1887–1974) and Juan Bautista Plaza (1898–1965) exerted strong leadership towards the renovation of music composition in Venezuela. Sojo helped found the Orquesta Sinfónica Venezuela (1930) and the choral association Orfeón Lamas. He taught at and directed (from 1936) the National School of Music of Caracas, and in those capacities, he influenced a large number of student-composers. In his compositions, he developed a rather overt national style combined with Impressionistic techniques. Plaza who occupied the post of chapelmaster at the Caracas Cathedral for twenty-five years wrote religious music and a series of works for various media in which he cultivated 'música criolla', that is, songs and dances of partially European origin, such as the *joropo*, Venezuela's national folk dance, related to the Spanish *fandango*. His *Siete canciones venezolanas* (1932) may have been inspired by the example of Manuel de Falla in his own *Siete canciones españolas*, each drawing on a different popular genre. Plaza set poems by

Luis Barrios Cruz, himself a nationalist and a 'poeta llanero' (of the plains or 'llanos' and hence of the popular tradition of that area). The settings borrow certain characteristics of popular songs and dances but there is no strict imitation. *Joropo* rhythmic patterns are cleverly combined in Plaza's *Fuga criolla* (1932), for string orchestra, with the essential polyphonic nature of the fugue.

Among the following generation of Venezuelan composers Evencio Castellanos (b. 1915), his brother Gonzalo Castellanos (b. 1926), Inocente Carreño (b. 1919) and Antonio Estévez (b. 1916), could be counted as nationalist composers, although not exclusively so.

The most influential Colombian composer of the first half of the twentieth century, Guillermo Uribe Holguín (1880–1971), combined a good technical command of the great tradition of European music with an excellent assimilation of national elements. The latter are particularly evident in the 300 piano pieces known as *Trozos en el sentimiento popular* (1927–39). The melodic, rhythmic and formal characteristics of such folk-popular dances as the *pasillo* and the *bambuco* provide the basis for some of these pieces. Other nationalist works, such as the *Second Symphony*, Op. 15 (1924), subtitled 'del terruño', and the *Suite típica* Op. 43 (1932), for orchestra, are programmatic and their musical descriptions or associations favour the vernacular elements.

Other Colombian composers representative of the nationalist trend were Daniel Zamudio (1885–1952), author of the study *El Folklore musical de Colombia* (1944), José Rozo Contreras (1894–1976) who relied in part on the Afro-Colombian folk music tradition of the Chocó area, and Antonio María Valencia (1902–52) who, as a student of d'Indy in Paris, received a solid training in composition. Valencia's *Chirimía y bambuco sotareño* (1930) originally for piano and orchestrated in 1942, and *Emociones caucanas* (1938) for violin, piano and cello, represent some of the best examples of his nationalist style, made up of evocations of national life and nature through the stylization of popular dance music. His early training in Europe is reflected in his frequent reliance on Impressionist techniques of composition.

Among those of the following generation of composers who maintained an interest in national music, albeit in an indirect and non-exclusive manner, were Luis Antonio Escobar (b. 1925) and Blas Emilio Atehortúa (b. 1933).

Musical nationalism in Ecuador found its first proponent in the Italian Domenico Brescia, director of the Quito Conservatory of Music from

1903 to 1911, and composer of such works as *Sinfonía ecuatoriana* and *Ocho variaciones* on an Indian song, both written in the 1920s. Indianist styles were developed subsequently in the works of Segundo Luis Moreno (1882–1972), a well-known folklorist and musicologist, Luis Humberto Salgado (1903–1977) and Pedro Pablo Traversari (1874–1956). These styles generally reveal an overt reliance on Indian music and dance, either through direct borrowing of themes and scales or through programmatic allusions to native legends and national history.

The search for national identity among Peruvian composers found a logical direction in the 'indigenismo' (Indianist) movement. A number of folklorist-composers active from the 1920s wrote piano pieces, art songs and fewer orchestral pieces, all reminiscent in varying degrees of highland Indian and mestizo traditional musical expressions. Traits related to such folk genres as the *huayno, triste* or *yaraví*, particularly descending pentatonic melodies and characteristic cadential and rhythmic practices, are found in the music of composers such as Daniel Alomía Robles (1871–1942), José Castro (1872–1945) and Manuel Aguirre (1863–1951). The most prolific and influential composer of nationalist persuasion was Teodoro Valcárcel (1902–42) whose 30 *Cantos de alma vernacular* and *Cuatro canciones incaicas* reveal an imaginative stylization and genuine understanding of traditional Indian music material.

Inadequate academic training in music in Peru was somewhat remedied with the settling in Lima in the 1920s and 1930s of several European-born musicians. Among these the most influential were Andrés Sas (1900–67) and Rodolfo Holzmann (1910–92). Sas not only taught a large number of Peruvian composers but stimulated through his own research a better penetration of pre-Columbian music. His own compositions exhibit a general folkloristic nationalist style, with clearly French Impressionist harmonic practices as can be seen especially in *Rapsodia peruana* (1928) and *Poema indio* (1941). As a professor of composition at the National Conservatory of Music, Holzmann exposed his students to the newest European trends, particularly atonality and serialism. Over the years, he collected and studied Peruvian folk and primitive music, but despite this interest he never did advocate for himself the Indianist style. Some of his works of the 1940s are related to a few aspects of Peruvian folk music, such as the *Suite sobre motivos peruanos* and the *Suite arequipeña,* but such incursions appear more circumstantial. His later works relied on other contemporary trends.

Bolivian nationalist composers during the first half of the twentieth century utilized a Romantic stylization of folk music elements rather than relying directly on traditional Indian music. Among others, these composers include Simeón Roncal (1870–1953), Eduardo Caba (1890–1953), Teófilo Vargas Candia (1886–1961), Humberto Viscarra Monje (1898–1971) and José María Velasco Maidana (1900–70). Roncal was particularly effective, as a composer, in the stylization of Bolivia's national dance, the *cueca*. His twenty *cuecas* for the piano are highly virtuosic pieces, written in the character and the spirit of nineteenth-century Romantic salon music. Velasco Maidana, considered by many the leading nationalist composer of his country, wrote ballets and tone poems describing or evoking Aymara–Quechua myths and music.

In Chile, Indianism and nationalism in general had few adherents; the cultivated tradition in Chilean music was strongly Europeanized. There were, however, a number of exceptions. Pedro Humberto Allende (1885–1959) was the first to cultivate a national style in a context of French Impressionist techniques. Musical Indianism was followed especially by Carlos Lavín (1883–1962) and Carlos Isamitt (1885–1974), both composers and folk music researchers. Lavín carried out field research among the Araucanian Indians and incorporated his knowledge and impressions in his own works, such as the *Mitos araucanos* (1926), for piano, and *Fiesta araucana* (1926), for orchestra. The same occurred with Isamitt whose works of most obvious Indianist persuasion include *Friso araucano* (1931), for voices and orchestra, and the piano *Sonata 'Evocación araucana'* (1932).

Argentina and Uruguay

A number of Argentine composers in the twentieth century kept alive the nationalist current initiated in the latter part of the nineteenth century in opera, ballet, symphonic and chamber music. In the 1930s, Juan José Castro (1895–1968) appeared as the leading figure of the movement, especially with his *Sinfonía argentina* (1934) in three movements ('Arrabal', 'Llanuras', 'Ritmos y Danzas'), and his *Sinfonía de los Campos* (1939), a 'pastoral' work evocative of the pampa folk traditions. His approach to musical nationalism, however, is not overt but rather based on a few references to folk or popular music genres (as in *Tangos*, for piano, 1941, or *Corales criollos nos. 1 and 2*, for piano, 1947), or a sublimation of these (as in the *Corales criollos No. 3*, for orchestra, 1953). His operas *La Zapatera prodigiosa* (1943) and *Bodas de sangre* (1953) on texts by García

Lorca, attest to his strong affinity with Spanish music. Castro's contemporary, Luis Gianneo (1897–1968), contributed to Argentine national music, over a period of thirty years, in a consistent and comprehensive manner. His nationalist style relied on Indian music elements of northern and northwestern Argentina, the *música criolla, gauchesca* tradition, and urban popular music represented by the *tango*. The latter is given prominence in his *Variaciones sobre tema de tango* (1953), for orchestra.

Alberto Ginastera (1916–83), recognized as one of the leading creative personalities in twentieth-century Latin American music, came of age during the high tide of Argentine musical nationalism. The first period of his activity as a composer reveals an objective, deliberate treatment of vernacular elements, but his reputation as the most notable national composer of his generation was established in the late 1930s and 1940s, with such works as the *Danzas argentinas,* for piano (1937), the ballets *Panambi* (1937) and *Estancia* (1941), *Obertura para el 'Fausto' Criollo* (1943), *Suite de danzas criollas* (1946) for piano, and several solo songs. This period that Ginastera himself has qualified as one of 'objective nationalism' (1937–47) is characterized by a strong reliance on the *gauchesco* tradition, both literary and musical, a clearly tonal musical idiom, including however, extremely dissonant passages. *Estancia* includes sung and recited excerpts from the epic poem *Martin Fierro* (1872) by José Hernández, which connects the work at once with the gaucho. Furthermore, the last section of *Estancia,* titled 'Malambo', establishes a direct link with the *malambo* dance, a vigorous, now extinct competitive dance of the gauchos. Here Ginastera makes the most of the intricate rhythmic organization of the dance. At the same time and as early as 1937 in the third of the *Danzas argentinas,* Ginastera tried his hand at polytonality, both melodically and harmonically, anticipating later stylistic developments.

From about 1947 to 1954, Ginastera moved into a phase of 'subjective nationalism', beginning with the first *Pampeana* (1947) and the First String Quartet (1948) and ending with the *Pampeana No. 3* (1954), for orchestra. Here the national musical elements are sublimated and stated in a subdued manner. Referring to his Piano Sonata (1952), for example, Ginastera maintained that 'the composer does not employ any folkloric material, but instead introduces in the thematic texture rhythmic and melodic motives whose expressive tension has a pronounced Argentine accent'. One particular trait reappearing until 1953–4 is the conspicuous use of the natural chord of the guitar, with the open strings (E-A-D-G-B-E) often presented in chromatically altered form. This 'symbolic' chord retained a close association with Argentine folk and popular music traditions. *Pampeana No. 3*, called a 'symphonic pastoral', still related indirectly to Argentine folk music, but the techniques of composition are based, for the most part, on non-national elements such as tone rows, although the feeling of tonality is still evident. Beginning with his String Quartet No. 2 (1958), Ginastera turned to neo-expressionist aesthetics and ceased to be associated with musical nationalism as such.

Uruguay's first nationalist compositions appeared in the 1910s and 1920s. The works of Alfonso Broqua (1876–1946), Eduardo Fabini (1882–1950), Luis Cluzeau Mortet (1889–1957) and Vicente Ascone (1897–79) are the most representative. Fabini, in particular, was the champion of nationalism in his country. His tone poem *Campo*, premiered in 1922, is generally considered the Uruguayan 'national' work par excellence. In this and other works, such as *La Isla de los Ceibos* (1924–6) and the series of *Tristes*, for various media (1925–30), he re-creates rather than imitates directly elements of Uruguayan folk music.

Brazil

The most prolific and creative composer of his generation in Brazil, indeed in Latin America, Heitor Villa-Lobos (1887–1959), approached the art of composition with spontaneity, sophistication and individuality. His non-conformity, in his life as well as in his music, often resulted in originality and success. He always felt a deep empathy and affinity with Brazilian popular culture and, although he was not an exclusively nationalist composer, his works of nationalist inspiration represent his most original contribution to Brazilian twentieth-century music.

Born and raised in Rio de Janeiro, Villa-Lobos's first musical experience as a guitar player originated among the *chorões*, or popular strolling, serenading musicians. This provided him with a first-hand, practical knowledge of urban popular music of the turn of the twentieth century. That music exerted a profound influence on him throughout his life. From about 1905 to 1913, he travelled extensively all over the country and discovered the richness of the various regional folk musical traditions, albeit his approach to such materials was not scientifically orientated.

In February 1922, Villa-Lobos participated in the 'Week of Modern Art' in São Paulo, that celebrated *modernismo* in modern Brazilian culture, a trend based on the principle of the adoption of avant-garde European techniques in the arts combined with a renewed promotion of national subject matters. (In fact, Villa-Lobos had already anticipated much of this, particularly in his ballets and tone poems, such as *Uirapurú, Saci-Pererê* and *Amazonas,* all composed in 1917.) Before leaving for Europe in 1923, he wrote the *Nonetto* (subtitled 'Impressão rápida de todo o Brasil'), one of his most typically nationalistic compositions. Besides the reliance of Brazilian popular percussion instruments (*chocalhos, cuíca, reco-reco,* among others), the work draws on the dance rhythmic character and colour blendings of popular music and stylizes somewhat the improvisatory nature of the music of the *chorões.*

During the 1920s, Villa-Lobos wrote some of his most celebrated piano pieces (*A Prole do Bebê No. 2,* 1921; *Cirandas,* 1926; *Rudepoema,* 1921–6), the series of *Choros,* and the songs of *Serestas.* The sixteen *Choros* were written from 1921 to 1929, a period of experimentation corresponding to his exposure to new European styles combined with his subjective re-creation of the musical manifestations of the various popular and primitive cultural traditions of Brazil. *Choros No. 5,* subtitled 'Alma brasileira' (Brazilian soul), for solo piano, characterizes the serenading music of the popular *chôro,* with its lyrical quality emanating from the *modinha,* a sentimental song genre of eighteenth- and nineteenth-century Luso-Brazilian tradition. The middle section of this piece, in contrast to the first, typifies the dance-like repertory of the *chorões,* with characteristic popular rhythmic patterns. *Choros No. 10* (1926), 'Rasga o coração' ('Rend my heart'), for large orchestra and mixed chorus, represents the composer's most successful attempt to integrate local musical elements with some of the European contemporary techniques of the time. The latter include above all a richly dissonant harmony with polytonal effects and multiple syncopations with polyrhythmic passages. The national elements are the subjective re-creation of primitivistic musical practices, particularly through the imitation of Indian melodic material and the use of onomatopoeic vocal effects, echoing the phonetic character of Indian languages.

The 1930s and 1940s were dominated by the composition of the nine *Bachianas Brasileiras.* The composer referred to this set as a 'genre of musical composition in homage to the great genius of Johann Sebastian Bach'. Conceived as suites, that is, a sequence of dance movements with preludes and arias, these works were intended essentially as a very free adaptation to Brazilian folk and popular music of certain Baroque procedures. Villa-Lobos felt, not without some justification, that there existed some clear affinity between certain of Bach's contrapuntal and rhythmic procedures and those of Brazilian folk and popular music. In effect, the *Bachianas* won international acclaim not only for the curiosity aroused by their evocation of Bach but also for their captivating melodic and harmonic contents and their exciting rhythmic qualities. With a few exceptions, each movement of the *Bachianas* bears a double denomination, one formalistic relating to the Baroque suite, the other clearly nationalistic. Their melodic contents tend to be quite lyrical and the harmonies Classical and strongly tonal. Examples of Romantic, lyrical melodies abound in the *Bachianas,* but none as expressive as the soprano line of the 'Aria-Cantilena' in *Bachianas Brasileiras* No. 5 (1938–45), the best-known work of Villa-Lobos. The improvisatory character of that long vocal phrase and the ingenious accompaniment (by a cello ensemble) suggesting an amplified version of a picked style of guitar playing add to its powerfully expressive qualities.

Brazilian musical nationalism also had strong adherents in Camargo Guarnieri (1907–93) and Francisco Mignone (1897–1986). Guarnieri's large production covers several decades of intense activity. His first works of clearly nationalistic character were the *Canção Sertaneja* (1928) and the *Dansa brasileira* (1928). Mário de Andrade, the influential Modernist writer and the spokesman for musical nationalism, acknowledged Guarnieri's *Sonatina,* for piano (1928), as the work of an extraordinarily imaginative composer. Among the chamber music works of the 1930s, Guarnieri began a series inspired by the popular *chôro* and his association with Andrade resulted in 1932 in a one-act opera, *Pedro Malazarte,* for which Andrade wrote the libretto. His numerous solo songs, from *Impossível Carinho* (1930) to *Vai, Azulão* (1939), are considered the composer's best contribution to this medium. His total song output reveals the effective use of Afro-Brazilian and Amerindian folksong characteristics. In the 1940s and 1950s he wrote his best orchestral pieces: three symphonies, an *Abertura Concertante* (1942) and several orchestral suites (*Brasiliana,* 1950; *Suite IV Centenário,* 1954; *Suite Vila Rica,* 1958). These works typify his unique style, based on the nationalist aesthetic, but with a substantial stylization of national elements, and a special attention to the technical craftsmanship of composition. Among the numerous piano pieces written by Guarnieri the fifty pieces in five albums entitled *Ponteios* (1931–59) are fine examples of this neo-classical linear writing and harmonies combined with rich lyricism.

Francisco Mignone was also prolific. His extensive production covers almost all musical genres of the Western tradition. He first cultivated a neo-Romantic style and, from around 1929 to about 1960, he combined a

strong native orientation with post-Romantic and neo-classic styles. Representatives of this orientation are the ballets *Maracatu de Chico Rei* (1933),
Batucajé (1936), *Babaloxá* (1936), and the four *Fantasias Brasileiras*, for piano and orchestra (1929–36). In them he uses Afro-Brazilian subjects and
actual themes or stylized folk and popular dances. Urban popular music
forms and contents influence overtly many piano pieces by Mignone, particularly the two sets of waltzes, *Valsas de Esquina* (1938–43) and *Valsas
Choros* (1946–55), which are reminiscent, in their Romantic inspiration, of
the piano music of the popular composer Ernesto Nazareth (1863–1934).
From the late 1950s, Mignone followed a more eclectic approach to composition. He was less directly concerned with nationalist expression and
gradually developed an interest in experimenting with new-music techniques, as in the *Variações em busca de um tema* ('Variations in search of a
theme') (1972).

Among the numerous Brazilian nationalist composers of subsequent
generations, José Siqueira (1907–85), Radamés Gnatalli (1906–88),
Luiz Cosme (1908–65), Cláudio Santoro (1919–89), César Guerra Peixe
(1914–93) and Oswaldo Lacerda (b. 1927) have been the most successful,
albeit not exclusively nationalist.

COUNTERCURRENTS, 1920S TO 1940S

Although musical nationalism prevailed in Latin America well into the
1950s, other currents, some opposed to nationalism and others indiffer-
ent to it, emerged from the beginning of the twentieth century. A
number of composers in the various republics attracted to the most advanced techniques and aesthetic of their period were frankly opposed to
nationalism; they felt that musical nationalism and particularly national
music styles demeaned Latin American music in general by resorting to
an easy exotic regionalist expression. They also sought to gain recognition
through the intrinsic quality of their works rather than through what
could be construed as external means. In general, however, the majority
of composers up to the 1960s followed an eclectic path, cultivating
varying styles which combined national and non-national stylistic elements. Specific countercurrents were not adhered to systematically, although the main trends were, besides post-Romantic and neo-Romantic,
Impressionist, neoclassical expressionist and, after mid-century as we
shall see, serialist and variously experimental.

As we have seen, the post-Revolutionary period in Mexico strongly favoured the development of musical nationalism. Yet one important figure who came to prominence in the 1910s and 1920s gave no attention to national music. Julián Carrillo (1875–1965) who studied in Germany and Belgium for almost five years came under the influence of late German Romantic music but also favoured in some of his early works a complex harmonic vocabulary, including at times extreme chromaticism and an intricate contrapuntal technique. He is, however, remembered essentially as one of the pioneers in the cultivation of microtonality. His theories of microtones, which he called *Sonido 13* ('Thirteenth Sound'), won him an international reputation. *Sonido 13* stood for him as the symbolic representation of the division of the octave beyond the twelve semitones, that is, microtones of various sizes down to sixteenths of a whole tone. In one of his first microtonal works, *Preludio a Colón* (1922) for soprano, flute, guitar, violin, octavina (a string instrument designed by the composer) and harp, Carrillo uses quarter, eighth and sixteenth tones. The microtonal effects enhanced by specific performance traits such as glissandi, harmonics, vocal portamentos and mutes, create a wailing, incantatory, eerie atmosphere which appeared quite futuristic for its time. For later works, he had instruments constructed to microtonal specifications, particularly microtonal pianos, which attracted the attention of the Czech Alois Hába and the Russian Ivan Vischnegradsky, both early proponents of microtonal music. In 1926, Carrillo's microtonal *Sonata Casi Fantasía* was performed in a concert of the League of Composers at New York's Town Hall, with resounding success. Leopold Stokowski himself took an immediate interest in Carrillo's theories and helped develop his reputation, by commissioning him to write a work for the Philadelphia Orchestra, resulting in the *Concertino* (1927) for violin, guitar, cello, octavina and harp (all in microtones) and orchestra (in traditional semitones). With this work, the composer applied for the first time his theories of 'musical metamorphosis', a forward-looking method of treatment of musical structures involving new possibilities of transformations and permutations of melodic, harmonic and rhythmic materials. Carrillo further explored microtonality in later works such as *Horizontes* (1951), various concertos, *Balbuceos* (1959) and the Mass for Pope John XXIII (1962). In retrospect, Carrillo appears as the precursor of ultrachromaticism and one of the most important pioneers in the field of sound experiments in the early part of the century.

While the ideas of Julián Carrillo were unique in Mexican music of the time, a number of Mexican composers were concerned with keeping up to date with European contemporary idioms, concurrently with their nationalist profession of faith. The case of Carlos Chávez himself is quite revealing. As a composer and the main conductor of the Orquesta Sinfónica de México, Chávez always strove to promote the 'new music' of a particular period. His *Seven Pieces for Piano* (1923–30), published in the United States in Henry Cowell's New Music Series in 1936, are written in the complex, international avant-garde style of the 1920s. In the period 1930–50, he wrote several non-nationalist works, relying wholly or partially on contemporary European techniques. Significant examples are the *Sinfonía de Antígona* (1933), the *Diez preludios para piano* (1937), the *Toccata* for percussion instruments (1942), and the Violin Concerto (1948–50). The *Sinfonía de Antígona,* one of Chávez's orchestral masterpieces, is certainly akin to the neo-classical style of Stravinsky, in its archaic modal flavour, sobriety, austere character, thematic polyphony and its wind-dominated orchestration. Likewise, the systematic diatonicism and linearity of the Ten Preludes, as well as their predominant two-voice polyphony and their diatonic, parallel static harmonies, identify them as excellent examples of the neo-classical movement of the 1930s. The Violin Concerto exemplifies the composer's mature compositional process. As a grand virtuoso work, this concerto reveals further the attachment of the composer to classical techniques, such as melodic inversions, variations, retrograde formal organization and highly demanding and effective virtuosic writing, all of them treated in a very personal, imaginative manner.

Silvestre Revueltas, the other major Mexican national composer of the time, also paid attention to neo-classical stylistic idioms. His *Homenaje a García Lorca* (1936), while maintaining a uniquely Mexican character, is one of the most successful examples of the assimilation by a Mexican composer of the neo-classical style. The second movement – 'Mourning for García Lorca' – particularly is neo-classical in its aesthetic, characterized by a static, contemplative character and a general economy of musical means.

The Spanish-born Rodolfo Halffter (1900–87) settled in Mexico in 1939 and exerted a profound influence on Mexican art-music developments in the subsequent decades, particularly as a professor of composition at the National Conservatory, as the editor of the journal *Nuestra*

Música (from 1946) and the manager of Ediciones Mexicanas de Música. As a composer, Halffter had a close affinity with Manuel de Falla's neo-classicism of the 1920s. He developed a personal language whose austere character and highly expressive restraint are conveyed through tonal and polytonal feelings, complex rhythmic patterns related to Spanish folk music, predominant linearity and contrapuntal elaboration, and refined diatonic and dissonant harmony. His most significant works written in Mexico in the 1940s are the Violin Concerto Op. 11 (1939–40), the ballet *La Madrugada del Panadero* (1940), *Homenaje a Antonio Machado* (1944), for piano, and the *Epitafios* (1947–53), for a cappella chorus.

Although Blas Galindo did not abandon altogether the nationalist expression of his early works, he cultivated in the 1940s and early 1950s a style reminiscent of neo-classicism. His harmonic practices especially became more cosmopolitan at that time, as seen in such works as the Violin Sonata (1945) and the *Siete Piezas para Piano* (1952).

Cuba

In Cuba, both Amadeo Roldán and Alejandro García Caturla had instilled their nationalist style with very modernistic practices, particularly harmonic and rhythmic complexities, that lend a contemporary expression. Beginning in the 1940s, however, José Ardévol became the leader of modern Cuban composition. In 1942, together with some of his students, he founded the Grupo de Renovación Musical whose aim was the creation of a Cuban school of composers 'which could reach the same degree of universality obtained by other countries'. The most important members of the group included Harold Gramatges, Edgardo Martín, Julián Orbón, Hilario González, Argeliers León, Serafín Pro and Gisela Hernández. Ardévol stood as the spokesman and leader of the group. While the credo of the group stressed the independence of its members from any pre-established trend, the neo-classical movement appeared at first as one of the most adequate currents for their purposes. Craftsmanship and competence in the knowledge and treatment of musical composition were emphasized. In the early 1930s, Ardévol himself wrote in an atonal style or followed the twelve-tone method. But gradually he adhered to neo-classicism in the late 1930s and the 1940s. His most revealing works of this period include six *Sonatas a tres* (1937–46), two Concerti Grossi (1937), the ballet *Forma* (1942), and the Concerto for

Piano, Winds, and Percussion (1944). The *Sonata a tres No. 1*, for oboe, clarinet and cello is conceived as a Baroque trio sonata as to instrumentation and form. Systematic imitations and contrapuntal elaboration occur throughout the work. In the ballet *Forma* for four-, five- and six-part choruses and orchestra, the voices are treated in the manner of ancient Greek drama, commenting upon the action in a non-participatory way. Once more, the harmonic staticity of the choral numbers is typical of neo-classical techniques of the period.

Almost all of Ardévol's students associated with the Grupo de Renovación Musical cultivated a neo-classical style, often combined with a neo-nationalism early in their career (the 1940s), but they followed quite different paths during the subsequent decades. The youngest and most independent member of the group, Julián Orbón (b. 1925), developed (together with Aurelio de la Vega) into the most outstanding Cuban composer of his generation. His earlier works, dating from the mid-1940s, exhibit a direct influence from the Spanish neo-classical style of Falla and Cristóbal Halffter. After 1950, he found a more personal style, harmonically more tense and less committed to tonality (as, for example, in his *Tres versiones sinfónicas*, 1953).

The Andean Republics

In Colombia Guillermo Uribe-Holguín came increasingly under the influence of French Impressionism, particularly in the harmonies and orchestration of his works of the 1920s. His compatriot Carlos Posada-Amador (1906–48) had the same experience in the 1930s, while Santiago Velasco Llanos (b. 1915) showed a preference for neo-classicism. And in Peru, Rodolfo Holzmann exposed his many students to various contemporary European styles and advocated openly an alternative to nationalism. He was himself influenced by Paul Hindemith's new tonal system and emphasis on craftsmanship in the composition training. In some of Holzmann's most characteristic works of the 1940s, including *Divertimento Concertante* (1941) for piano and ten woodwinds, the *Cantigas de la Edad de Oro* (1944), for small orchestra, the *Tres Madrigales* (1944) for voice and piano, and the *Concierto para la Ciudad Blanca* (1949) for piano and orchestra, his attachment to tradition can be seen in the formal designs, compositional processes and general reliance on the tonal system—treated, however, in a modern vein.

Among the Andean nations it was Chile, however, that took the lead position during the 1930s and 1940s in the production of significant non-nationalist compositions. Chilean musical life underwent a profound transformation in the 1920s, as the result of the activities of the Sociedad Bach under the leadership of Domingo Santa Cruz (1899–1987) and especially of the creation of the Facultad de Bellas Artes (1929) within the University of Chile. Santa Cruz exerted a considerable influence from the 1920s to the 1950s as teacher, administrator and composer. As Dean of the Faculty of Fine Arts at the National Conservatory, reorganized later as the Faculty of Musical Arts and Sciences, he helped establish a successful system of musical instruction in the country under the control of the university. As a composer, he wrote a number of important works. His first orientation went towards both Impressionist neo-classicism, and atonal stylistic elements. The *Five Pieces for String Orchestra,* Op. 14 (1937), for example, exhibit a rich, contrapuntal style with technical and formal elements akin to Baroque and Classic practices. At the same time the essentially horizontal writing generates at times a polytonal harmony. Later works, such as the *Sinfonía Concertante* Op. 22 (1945) and the *Preludios Dramáticos* Op. 23 (1946), illustrate further his attachment to the Western art-music heritage. He did not eschew, however, the 'Latinidad' of his own heritage: many of his themes reveal a strongly Hispanic character, particularly the type of melodic ornamentation associated with Andalusian folk singing or typical rhythmic motives associated with Spanish folk dances. Santa Cruz was also active and successful as a choral composer in the 1940s. His compositions include *Cinco Canciones* Op. 16, for mixed chorus or soloists, *Tres Madrigales,* Op. 17, for mixed chorus, *Cantata de los Ríos de Chile,* Op. 19, and *Egloga,* Op. 26. These represent a special expression of his aesthetics. The *Tres Madrigales,* for example, are highly dramatic settings (with texts by the composer), combining an expressively harmonic counterpoint with monodic, recitative-like designs.

Santa Cruz's contemporaries such as Enrique Soro (1884–1954), Alfonso Leng (1894–1974) and Jorge Urrutia Blondel (1903–1981) cultivated above all post-Romantic and Impressionist styles. Acario Cotapos (1889–1969), who lived in New York from 1917 to 1927, was associated with the avant-garde of the time and, like Edgard Varèse, refuted all academicism and established trends. His early works (for example, *Le Détachement vivant,* 1918, or the *Tres Piezas Sinfónicas,* 1923) reveal a vivid imagination and independence, which found further expression in his later works, such as *Balmaceda* (1958), considered revolutionary.

Of the next generation, Alfonso Letelier (b. 1912) and Juan A. Orrego-Salas (b. 1919) were quite active in the 1940s. Both belong to the generation of Chilean composers sometimes classified as 'formalists' because of their adherence to the stylistic aims of neo-classicism. Among Letelier's numerous works of this period, the *Sonetos de la Muerte* (1942–8), for soprano and orchestra (on sonnets by Gabriela Mistral), and the piano *Variaciones en Fa* (1948), exemplify his stylistic preference. In the *Sonetos* he succeeds in depicting the dramatic substance of the poems, by treating the vocal line as a free recitative, in the character of 'endless melody', by utilizing dissonant and dense harmonies and contrasting dynamics. Several of the variations in the piano *Variaciones* are stylized Baroque dance forms (gigue, allemande, minuet, gavotte), in which homophonic and polyphonic textures are combined.

Orrego-Salas enjoyed the widest international reputation among Chilean composers. He was influenced by the aesthetic orientation of Domingo Santa Cruz, his teacher of composition at the Santiago National Conservatory. Thus his early works of the 1940s follow an imaginative and effective neo-classic style. The *Canciones Castellanas* Op. 20 (1948), for soprano and a chamber ensemble are settings of early Luso-Spanish Renaissance poetry, in which modal and linear writing prevails. A rhythmic intensity and a skilful treatment of timbres quite characteristic of the composer's musical language pervade these songs. Occasional Spanish traits also appear in this work, such as arabesque-like figurations and rhythmic patterns. Orrego-Salas turned to the orchestra more readily in later works, but his First Symphony (1949) and his *Obertura Festiva* Op. 21 (1948) denote already a very colourful, virtuoso orchestral writing.

Argentina and Uruguay

In the 1920s a few Argentine composers began to move away from folkloric nationalism. Such figures as Juan José Castro, his brother José María Castro (1892–1964), Floro M. Ugarte (1884–1975), and Jacobo Ficher (1896–1978) attempted in varying degrees to assimilate European contemporary techniques. Juan José Castro's quest for a more international style is evident in his *Allegro-Lento e Vivace* (1930), for orchestra, in which Impressionist and Stravinskian influences abound. Although Ugarte's primary interest lay in music nationalism, some of his works of the 1920s are conceived within a post-Romantic style and aesthetic. Of

Russian origin, Ficher remained attached in the 1920s to the post-Romantic Russian composers, particularly Scriabin, but his subsequent works (symphonies, piano and violin sonatas) have greater affinity with neo-classicism.

Dodecaphony, considered in the 1930s the most radical trend in musical composition, had its first Latin American champion in the Argentine composer Juan Carlos Paz (1901–72). With the Castro brothers, Ficher, and others, Paz founded the Grupo Renovación in 1929, with the aims of advocating a deeper involvement of Argentine composers with European modern trends, leading to the renovation and updating of art music in their country. Paz, however, withdrew from the Group because of irreconcilable differences as to the methods to achieve such goals, and founded the Conciertos de Nueva Música (1937), eventually creating his own group, the Agrupación Nueva Música (1944). This latter organization went further in the promotion of the avant-garde, particularly the music of the serial composers Schoenberg and Webern, and the experimentalists such as Varèse, Cowell, Cage and Messiaen. Largely self-taught, Paz's attitudes and enthusiasm for new musical ideas had a beneficial influence on a number of later composers.

Juan Carlos Paz was the only composer of the period who sustained a consistent campaign against musical nationalism. Up to about 1934, he cultivated an essentially neo-classical style, characterized by a linear writing, polytonal and at times atonal harmony (*Three Pieces for Orchestra*, 1930, *Octet for Wind Instruments*, 1930). With the *Primera Composición en los 12 Tonos* (1934), Paz turned to dodecaphony, but always used the twelve-tone methods in a free, personal way, radically different from Schoenberg's manipulations. A good illustration of Paz's treatment can be seen in the *Tercera Composición en los 12 Tonos* (1937), for clarinet and piano. All four sections of the work – 'Toccata', 'Tema con variaciones', 'Canción', and 'Tempo de giga' – utilize the same row, in its prime and retrograde forms without inversions or transpositions of it. As opposed to Schoenberg, Paz does not avoid chordal or tonal implications in the arrangement of the basic row material. Here he utilizes octaves and chords such as triads, sevenths, and ninths quite deliberately, and he repeats several notes of the row or presents them out of order. Another aspect of Paz's musical style was revealed with the work *Rítmica Ostinata* Op. 41 (1942), for orchestra. This composition abounds in virtuoso contrapuntal and rhythmic writing. The title itself indicates the repetitive nature of the work, which has the character of a large toccata, due to the prevailingly fast tempo, constant quaver and semi-quaver figurations, numerous ostinatos, and to the brilliant orchestration. The harmonic idiom is wholly chromatic and dissonant.

Among other Argentine composers representative of the 'international' trend, Roberto García Morillo (b. 1911), the Spanish-born Julián Bautista (1901–61), and the Austrian-born Guillermo Graetzer (1914–92) stand out. García Morillo began writing in the 1930s in a modernistic style and appeared until the 1950s as an eclectic composer, thereafter showing a clearer orientation towards neo-classicism. In works such as *Las pinturas negras de Goya* (1939), *Tres pinturas de Paul Klee* (1944), and the cantata *Marín* (1948–50), he developed an increasingly complex language which includes an intensified, dissonant and often atonal harmony and an original treatment of rhythm. Bautista belongs to the Spanish neo-classic school of the 1920s to the 1940s. His style is primarily contrapuntal, harmonically advanced and formally traditional. Graetzer's training in Austria and Germany orientated him towards the new tonal style developed by Hindemith. As a teacher he became influential in the field of music education.

Among the few Uruguayan non-nationalist composers active in the early part of the twentieth century were César Cortinas (1890–1918) and Carmen Barradas (1888–1963). Cortinas wrote in a style combining Romantic elements of the late nineteenth century (especially in his piano works) with a Puccini-like lyric intensity (in his songs and his opera, *La última gavota*, 1915), while Barradas who wrote primarily for the piano was exceptional for her interest in experimenting with revolutionary notation. Beginning in the 1940s, Uruguayan music matured enough to be able to achieve an international reputation. The composers most in evidence during the 1940s were Carlos Estrada (1909–70), Héctor Tosar E. (b. 1923), and, to a lesser extent, Guido Santórsola (b. 1904). Estrada, who studied at the Paris Conservatoire, cultivated a sober neo-classical style. His incidental music for Paul Claudel's *L'Annonce faite à Marie* (1943) and Paul Verlaine's *Les uns et les autres* (1950) as well as his numerous settings of French poems reveal his strong empathy for French culture. Tosar's most important works were written after 1950, but his talent as a composer is already evident in the 1940s. In his *Sinfonía No. 2* (1950), for strings, for example, he reveals a decisively modernistic style of enormous rhythmic vitality, rich harmonic resources and original timbral and dynamic effects. The Italian-born Santórsola was particularly influential as a conductor and string player, having founded the orchestra of the Uruguayan Cultural Association. In his works he drew at first on Uruguayan folk music, but later turned to serial techniques.

A particularly important figure active in Montevideo from the 1930s was the musicologist Francisco Curt Lange (b. 1903), who had emigrated to Uruguay from Germany in the late 1920s. Besides his invaluable services as a researcher of Latin American music, he systematically promoted the music and musicians of Latin America the world over. He founded both the Inter-American Institute of Musicology and the unique Editorial Cooperativa Interamericana de Compositores which published numerous piano, choral and chamber music works by composers of the Western Hemisphere. In 1985, he received, together with the U.S. musicologist Robert Stevenson, the 'Gabriela Mistral' Prize awarded by the Organization of American States' Department of Cultural Affairs.

Brazil

During the first quarter of the twentieth century Brazil had a Europeanized school of composition represented mainly by composers such as Francisco Braga (1868–1945), a post-Romantic, Glauco Velasquez (1884–1914), an Impressionist, and Henrique Oswald (1852–1931), a post-Romantic eclectic. Alberto Nepomuceno himself wrote many works in a non-nationalist vein, such as *Sinfonía* in G minor (1894), *Valsas humorísticas* (1903), for piano and orchestra, numerous choral works, all of post-Romantic inspiration and technique. There is no doubt, however, that Villa-Lobos's works of the period 1915–30 represent the boldest achievement in Brazil in the assimilation of contemporary techniques of composition. Despite its nationalistic intention and substance, Villa-Lobos's music relied on such techniques as polytonality, polyrhythm, dissonant polyphonic textures and experimental tone colouring.

The major innovating movement in Brazilian composition came from the Música Viva group, founded in 1937 under the leadership of the German composer Hans-Joachim Koellreutter (b. 1915). The group's manifesto of 1946 declared its frank opposition to folkloristic nationalism and was viewed by many as an anti-national campaign. The current that became associated with this campaign was dodecaphony because Koellreutter himself favoured it in his own works of the 1940s. At first his treatment of atonality and twelve-tone techniques was rather dogmatic, as in *Música* (1941) and *Noturnos* (1945), but he used them more freely and personally in subsequent works. His influence as a teacher of composition was felt especially in Rio de Janeiro, São Paulo, and Salvador (Bahia), the three major centres in the country for the future development of new music. Among his many students were Cláudio Santoro and César Guerra Peixe (see above).

Santoro orientated himself between 1939 and about 1947 towards atonality and a pragmatic twelve-tone technique. His early works are abstract, with the exception of the semi-programmatic *Impressões de uma fundição de aço* ('Impressions of a steel foundry') for orchestra (1942). The Sonata for solo violin (1940) is written in an atonal style but retains the structure of the Baroque sonata. Moreover, this atonal style does not rely on the twelve-tone technique. In the First Sonata for Violin and Piano (1940), however, Santoro follows serial techniques in a free manner. In a few of his vocal works of the period he also follows Schoenberg's vocal technique known as *Sprechstimme*, as in *Asa Ferida* (1944) which includes a passage with the indication that the recitation of the text should be interpreted as 'spoken song'. Other works of the 1940s (Second and Third Symphonies, First String Quartet, *Música para cordas*) reveal Santoro's eclecticism with definite preference for classic structure, Baroque polyphony, atonal and polytonal harmonies and rhythmic drive. Guerra Peixe appeared in the 1940s as a decided apologist of atonality and twelve-tone music in Brazil. He wrote several works based on serial techniques, such as *Sonatina 1944*, for flute and clarinet. Soon, however, he turned to what he called a 'curious sort of music' that could combine two apparently irreconcilable trends – twelve-tone and nationalist music. The necessary compromise, which required some alteration of both serial technique and typically national musical elements, proved untenable. But Guerra Peixe produced original, well-conceived works (such as the *Trio*, for flute, clarinet and bassoon, in 1948) which need no theoretical affiliation.

Another composer associated with the Música Viva group was Luiz Cosme (1908–65), who turned to non-national sources in his later works. From 1946 to about 1950, he increasingly avoided the tonal system and made free use of the twelve-tone method. His last work, *Novena à Senhora da Graça* (1950), for string quartet, piano, narrator and female dancer, relies to a certain extent on some dodecaphonic techniques and is free of national implications.

From the 1930s to the end of his life, Villa-Lobos tended to write in a more abstract manner, that is, without the obvious programmatic intention of his earlier works. Although he remained close to Brazilian national sources as in his *Bachianas,* he concurrently displayed an interest in neotonal and post-Romantic styles with little or no nationalist references. The *Missa de São Sebastião* (1937), for example, and many other choral works, are good indications of this tendency. Among his later works, the *String Quartet No. 17* (1957) shows a new aesthetic direction towards an austere simplicity, expressed through a rather terse and abstract style.

In general, the countercurrents witnessed in Latin American music from the 1920s to about 1950 indicate the definite awareness of a number of composers of a need to innovate and rejuvenate Latin American composition by liberating it from the subjection of musical nationalism. The consequent individualism and eclecticism developed in full during the next three decades.

CONTEMPORARY MUSIC, 1950S TO 1970S

Since the middle of the twentieth century the profound transformations that have affected art-music in Latin America have resulted in a variety of styles and in a diversity of aesthetics. Before the Second World War social and intellectual conditions in Latin America had reflected a strong dependence on Europe and, to a lesser extent, North America; consequently musical nationalism appeared to many as a logical orientation since it responded to the need for national identity and assertion. But, although political and economic subordination, particularly in relation to the United States, continued after 1950, cultural dependence diminished considerably. A new tendency, at least in the larger cities, towards a greater cosmopolitanism gradually emerged. Foreign elements still prevailed but were deliberately assimilated within a new frame of mind. Many progressive Latin American composers speculated that in the process of assimilating the 'new music' of Europe and North America a natural qualitative selection would occur, followed by an imitation, recreation and transformation of foreign models according to the local artistic environment and individual needs and preferences. The progressive and avant-garde composers of the period realized that they had a great deal to contribute as Latin Americans to these new cosmopolitan musical trends.

In the 1960s new, experimental musical currents emerged in most countries of the continent. Those adhering to such currents, however, soon discovered that official support for the performance of their music by national orchestras or for its publication and commercial recording was not readily forthcoming. Several prominent Latin American composers were forced to settle in Europe, the United States and Canada. Conditions for new music composers did gradually improve, however, in the 1960s and 1970s, especially in Argentina, Chile, Brazil, Venezuela and Mexico. In co-operation with the International Society for Contemporary Music (ISCM), several national organizations were formed; a few electronic music studios were developed; some professional schools or universities updated their music curricula; state broadcasting systems gave some attention to contemporary music; and several private and state institutions began to subsidize festivals of new music. Beginning in 1958, the Organization of American States organized and sponsored the Inter-American Music Festivals in Washington, D.C., always premiering new works of Latin American composers. From the early 1960s, the OAS also promoted the publication of a series of scores, including some works by young composers. In the 1970s contemporary music festivals, summer workshops and courses, such as the Latin American Course on Contemporary Music held in various countries, occurred more frequently and brought together not only prominent figures from Europe but also young composers from the entire continent. Thus, the isolation of the majority of composers and the lack of interaction among them in previous decades tended to disappear. With it, a sense of new identity within the contemporary music scene became stronger among Latin American composers.

Mexico

Although Mexican musical life no longer revolved around him after about 1955, Carlos Chávez remained active as composer, conductor and teacher. He delivered the Charles Eliot Norton lectures at Harvard University in 1958–9, out of which came his book *Musical Thought;* and he opened a workshop in composition in 1960 at the Mexico City Conservatory, which he directed until 1964 and in which several young Mexican composers got their training and experience. Chávez's compositions of the period include four symphonies, the opera *The Visitors* (1953–6), the cantata *Prometheus Bound* (1956), *Resonancias* (1964), for orchestra, *Clio* (1969), a symphonic ode, the ballet *Pirámide* (1968), *Initium* (1971), for orchestra, *Concerto for Trombone and Orchestra* (1976), and several piano and chamber music pieces. In contrast to earlier works, *Sinfonía No. 4* (1953), subtitled

Romántica, is lyrical and emotional in character and rather classical in formal designs. *Sinfonía No. 5* (1953), for string orchestra, clearly indicates Chávez's penchant for neo-classicism. Among his most significant works of this period are *Soli II, III* and *IV* (of 1961, 1965, 1966, respectively). *Soli II* is for wind quintet, *Soli III* for bassoon, trumpet, timpani, viola and orchestra, and *Soli IV* for French horn, trumpet and trombone. The appearance of each instrument (or group of solo instruments) as soloist in each movement justifies the titles. The directing principle in these pieces, according to the composer, is that of non-repetition, the avoidance of standard sequence, symmetry and recapitulation and of the 'repetitive procedures implicit in the Viennese serial technique'. Instead, Chávez resorts to the element of renewal of musical materials. This principle affects the melodic writing which is made up of wide-ranging, disjunct and chromatic motifs that establish an improvisatory character, as seen in *Soli II.* In addition, the composer's concern for clarity, terseness and novelty of instrumental blendings finds its best expression in these works.

Twelve-tone and other serial techniques gained the attention of several Mexican composers during the 1950s and 1960s, at first under the guidance of Rodolfo Halffter who himself turned to twelve-tone methods in the early 1950s (for example, *Tres Hojas de Album,* for piano, 1953, and *Tres Piezas* for string orchestra, 1954). In these and subsequent works, however, he applies the techniques very freely, and the Spanish rhythmic traits noted in his earlier works reappear occasionally. Among Halffter's students who followed serial techniques was Jorge González Avila (b. 1926), primarily a composer of piano music. Atonality and serialism, that is, the serialization of more than one parameter, found more acceptance among younger Mexican composers. Joaquin Gutiérrez-Heras (b. 1927), for example, cultivated a free atonal style, in works such as the *Woodwind Trio* (1965). In the case of Mario Kuri-Aldana (b. 1931), another student of Halffter, we find the development of a highly individual style based on traditional procedures but expressed in a contemporary language mixed with neo-classical and neo-nationalist elements. His research on Mexican folk and Indian music influenced his compositions somewhat, as in works such as *Peregrina agraciada* (1963) or *Concierto Tarahumara* (1981). A modern style rooted in national sources also appears in some of the works of Leonardo Velásquez (b. 1935).

Foremost among the Mexican followers of avant-garde techniques and aesthetics from the 1960s were Manuel Enríquez, Héctor Quintanar, Eduardo Mata, Manuel de Elías and Mario Lavista. Enríquez (1926–94) was a student of Peter Mennin at the Juilliard School in the mid-1950s and at that same time came under the influence of Stefan Wolpe who orientated him to serial techniques. He then kept up with all avant-garde music developments and, as the director of CENIDIM (Centro Nacional de Investigación, Documentación e Información Musical 'Carlos Chávez') and the founder of the Mexican Society for Contemporary Music, was influential in the promotion and dissemination of such developments in his country. In 1971 he worked at the Columbia-Princeton Center for Electronic Music, but the electronic medium did not figure prominently in his works. Rather Enríquez favoured neo-expressionist atonality, serialism and aleatory music. His first serial work was *Preámbulo* (1961), for orchestra. He himself qualified his *Tres Invenciones* (1964), for flute and viola, the culmination of his admiration for Webern. After that date, chance operations appeared more frequently in his works, such as the Sonata for violin and piano (1964), *Ambivalencia* (1967) and *A Lápiz* (1965). From around 1967, he adhered more fully to indeterminacy, a principle first espoused by John Cage in the 1950s, whereby chance operations or random procedures create compositions with a certain degree of unpredictability and a variability of the sequence of sections in a work, often referred to as 'open form'. One of the first works by Enríquez relying systematically on open form was his *Second String Quartet* (1967), in which he applied graphic notation, a type of non-specific notation in which different symbols, drawings of different sizes and shapes, give general directions to the performer who can combine at will any of the numerous possibilities. In later compositions, such as *Él y Ellos* (1975), he wrote in a highly virtuosic, free style.

Héctor Quintanar (b. 1936) worked with Chávez in the Composition Workshop in the early 1960s and took over its directorship from 1965 to 1972. In 1970 he became the founding director of the electronic music studio at the Mexico City Conservatory. As a composer, Quintanar developed from a style akin to Webernian serialism and Penderecki-like experiments with new sonorities (in such works as *Galaxias,* for orchestra, 1968) to electronic music, aleatory techniques and mixed media. He pioneered the study and composition of electronic music in Mexico. Eduardo Mata (1942–94) combined freely in his works from the mid-1960s aspects of serial and aleatory techniques. In the 1970s and 1980s he dedicated himself primarily to his orchestra conducting career. Manuel Jorge de Elías (b. 1939) studied first at the School of Music of the National University of Mexico and at the National Conservatory, and later in Europe with Stockhausen and Jean-Etienne Marie. In the 1960s he cultivated a serial style mixed with aleatory procedures and also paid attention to the electronic medium. His *Vitral No. 3* (1969), for orchestra, sets forth some of the typical performance practices of new music, such as rhythmic patterns produced by tapping the mouthpieces of brass instruments with the palm of the hand, and it combines counterpoints of discontinuous, unrelated lines with various series of clusters.

Mario Lavista (b. 1943) represented in the late 1960s and 1970s the extreme left wing of the Mexican avant-garde. While a student in Europe he became acquainted with the Hungarian composer György Ligeti who exerted some influence on his aesthetic development. In the early 1970s he studied electronic music in Tokyo. More than his colleagues, he appears as a bonafide experimentalist. Improvisation and chance operations were utilized in the most unconfined manner. He explored new sonorous possibilities, combined electro-acoustic and visual elements, and attempted to expand the concepts of musical time and space. In works such as *Pieza para un(a) pianista y un piano* ('Piece for a pianist and a piano') (1970) he applied John Cage's principles of indeterminacy and non-self-expression.

The Caribbean and Central America

In Cuba the leader of the Grupo de Renovación Musical, José Ardévol, began to pay attention to atonality and serialism from around 1957. During the early years of the Cuban Revolution, he played a major role as National Director of Music in the reorganization of the country's musical life. Thanks to him, Cuba has enjoyed since then a remarkable freedom of musical expression, conveyed not only through his own stylistic development but through that of other members of the Grupo, like Harold Gramatges, Edgardo Martín, and Argeliers León, and of a number younger composers discussed below. From around 1965, Ardévol combined a post-Webernian serialist style with a few aleatory techniques, as in the cantatas *La Victoria de Playa Girón* (1966) and *Che Comandante* (1968). The same orientation is found in Gramatges's works, especially *La muerte del guerrillero* (1968), on a text by Nicolás Guillén, and *Cantata para Abel* (1974), for narrator, mixed chorus and ten percussionists. Martín ceased to compose during the period 1953–9 when he joined Fidel Castro's movement against the Batista regime. Several of his works of the 1960s reflect his political conviction. *Cuatro Cantos de la Revolución* (1962), *Así*

Guevara (1967), the cantata *Canto de héroes* (1967) and *Cinco Cantos de Ho* (1969), on texts by Ho Chi Minh, all reveal an eclectic language, with some serialist techniques permeating his abstract works of the period.

The younger, progressive composers most in evidence in the 1950s and 1960s included Juan Blanco, Aurelio de la Vega, Carlos Fariñas and Leo Brouwer. Blanco (b. 1920) learned on his own the techniques of *musique concrète* and electronic music which he was among the first Cubans to explore beginning in the early 1960s (*Música para danza*, 1961, *Estudios I–II*, 1962–3). Chance operations first appeared in *Texturas* (1963–4), for orchestra and tape, and with *Contrapunto espacial I* ('Spatial Counterpoint I') (1965–6) began a series of five major works belonging to so-called spatial music, that is, music in which the actual location of the sound sources, live or recorded but generally transmitted through loudspeakers, becomes integral to the structure of the work. In the last two of the 'Spatial Counterpoint' pieces, Blanco combined the spatial concept with that of theatre music, calling for actors and acting musicians.

Together with Julián Orbón, Aurelio de la Vega (b. 1925) is the best known Cuban composer of his generation. In the early 1950s, he developed a highly chromatic language combined with a strong rhythmic drive, and a virtuoso style of writing for traditional instruments which remained one of his constant concerns. He also cultivated free atonality, in such works as *Elegy* (1954) and *Divertimento* (1956), and unorthodox twelve-tone techniques, as in the String Quartet 'In Memoriam Alban Berg' (1957). From 1953 to 1959, he directed the music department at the Universidad de Oriente in Santiago de Cuba. Around the mid-1960s, by which time he was professor of composition at the California State University in Northridge, he abandoned gradually serialism for electronic means, open forms and aleatory procedures, while continuing to explore new sonorities. The effective expression of his colour blendings and structural organization is best expressed in two works of 1973: *Tangents*, for violin and pre-recorded sounds, and *Para-Tangents*, for trumpet and same pre-recorded sounds. The timbres and the expressive aspects of the solo instruments are explored in a dialogue fashion with the electronic sounds. Indeterminacy appeared in later works such as *Olep ed Arudamot* (1974) (the retrograde form of 'Tomadura de pelo', or 'Pulling one's leg') for non-specific instrumentation, the *Infinite Square* (1974), and *Undici Colori* (1981), with graphic projections by the composer.

Carlos Fariña (b. 1934) turned to serialist aesthetics in the 1960s, after an early interest in national music sources, and Leo Brouwer (b. 1939) after a similar nationalist concern became one of the most talented and recognized composers of the Cuban avant-garde. After the Cuban Revolution, Brouwer's contacts with the contemporary Polish avant-garde (Penderecki, Lutoslawski) and with Luigi Nono prompted him to adopt more readily new-music techniques. From around 1962, he wrote in a post-serialist and aleatory manner. His *Sonograma I* (1963), for prepared piano (following the ideas of Cage) is generally considered the first piece of aleatory music in Cuba. In the late 1960s and 1970s, he cultivated mixed media, first with *Cantigas del tiempo nuevo* (1969), and wrote major works for the classical guitar.

In Puerto Rico, new music has had several followers. Héctor Campos-Parsi (b. 1922) who had cultivated a rather overt nationalistic style in his early works and neo-classicism in the 1950s turned to atonality and serialism in the 1960s. He was active and influential in the promotion of music education in his country and of music research at the Institute of Puerto Rican Culture founded in 1955. Rafael Aponte-Ledée (b. 1938), a student of Ginastera and Gandini at the Buenos Aires Torcuato Di Tella Institute, followed such trends as serialism, electronics and indeterminacy.

Although he considers himself a nationalist composer, and his early works rely on aspects of Panamanian folk song and dance, the most significant works (since the late 1940s) of the Panamanian composer, conductor and teacher Roque Cordero (b. 1917) have been written in an almost exclusively serialist idiom. His *Second Symphony* (1956) exemplifies his treatment of the dodecaphonic technique. The symphony is based on three related tone rows used freely, that is, with melodic and harmonic repetitions and octave doublings. One typical trait quite common in Cordero's music is the use of frequent *ostinatos* which create a rather complex rhythmic organization. An increased concern for timbral effects, virtuoso writing and rhythmic intricacies appeared in his works of the 1960s, such as the *Violin Concerto* (1962) and the *Third Symphony* (1965). The *Violin Concerto* is a truly virtuoso work, with a technically very demanding solo part, and a virtuosic treatment of the orchestra. The basic twelve-tone set involves various forms and transpositions that make up the thematic and developmental materials. Further works (Concertino for viola and string orchestra, 1968 and Variations and Theme for Five, 1975) evidence Cordero's strong individuality in handling serialism while maintaining a Latin flavour without being nationalist.

Central American composers who have paid attention to non-nationalist currents include the Guatemalans Ricardo Castillo (1894–1967), José

Castañeda (1898–1978), who was one of the first to experiment with polytonality, microtonality and serialism, Salvador Ley (b. 1907), Enrique Solares (b. 1910) and Joaquín Orellana (b. 1937); the Nicaraguan Luis A. Delgadillo (1887–1964); the Costa Rican Bernal Flores (b. 1937), professor of composition at the University of Costa Rica and director of the department of music of the Ministry of Culture, who wrote in an atonal and serial style; and Gilberto Orellana (b. 1942), from El Salvador, who also adhered to serial techniques.

The Andean Republics

In Venezuela the development of contemporary composition from the 1960s was encouraged by the establishment of the Instituto Nacional de Cultura y Bellas Artes (INCIBA), which promoted national prizes for composition, the Caracas Music Festivals, and the creation of laboratories of electronic music. The composers most in evidence during the late 1960s and 1970s were Antonio Estévez (b. 1916), who turned to electronic music after 1970, José Luis Muñoz (b. 1928), who used aleatory techniques, and Alexis Rago (b. 1920), who wrote in a neo-tonal style. Alfredo del Mónaco (b. 1938) worked at the Columbia-Princeton Electronic Music Center and studied at Columbia University. He wrote in the electronic medium (*Cromofonías I*, 1967, *Metagrama*, 1970), in a combination of traditional instruments and electronic sounds (*Alternancias*, 1976), and in computer music (*Synus-17/251271*, 1972). With the settling in Caracas of the Greek composer Yannis Ioannidis (b. 1930), younger Venezuelan composers who studied with him were readily exposed to contemporary music. Among his students were Alfredo Rugeles (b. 1949) who shows an impressive command of contemporary techniques whether he writes for traditional instruments (*Mutaciones*, 1974, for string orchestra, *El Ocaso del Héroe*, 1982, for narrator, mixed chorus and chamber orchestra) or realizes his compositions on tape (*Things-phonia*, 1978).

In Colombia, the most active representatives of contemporary music have been Fabio González-Zuleta (b. 1920), Luis Antonio Escobar (b. 1925), Blas Emilio Atehortúa (1933), and the Belgian born Jacqueline Nova (b. 1938). In his Violin Concerto (1958) and Third Symphony (1961), González-Zuleta pursued a polytonal and atonal style; later works explored serial techniques. Atehortúa became in the 1960s and 1970s one of Colombia's foremost contemporary composers. His music incorporates a rich rhythmic construction with effective colour blendings. Occasionally he used serialist techniques rather freely (e.g. *Cinco Piezas Breves,* 1969, *Partita 72,* 1972), but remained essentially attached to neo-classical compositional ideals (e.g. *Brachot para Golda Meir,* for orchestra, (1980), *Suite* for String Orchestra, 1982).

The only Ecuadorian composer since the 1950s to have espoused readily experimental aesthetics is Mesías Maiguashca (b. 1938) who, after an early training at the Quito National Conservatory, studied at the Eastman School of Music in the United States, and at the Torcuato Di Tella Institute in Buenos Aires. He worked in close contact with Stockhausen during 1968–72 as a collaborator at the Electronic Music Studio in Cologne and then remained in Germany as a freelance composer. His discovery of electro-acoustic techniques led to such major works as *Hör Zu* (1969) on tape, *A Mouth Piece* (1970) for amplified voices, and *Ayayayayay* (1971) on tape. After his *Übungen für Synthesizer* (1972) he turned to mixed media, as in *Oeldorf 8* (1973).

In Peru, while Rodolfo Holzmann continued to develop the neo-classical style of his earlier works—as in *Introitus et Contrapunctus* (1974) and *Sinfonía del Tercer Mundo* (1979), for example—beginning in the 1960s some of his students gave Peruvian music a truly contemporary character. Composers such as Enrique Iturriaga (b. 1918), Celso Garrido Lecca (b. 1926), Enrique Pinilla (1927–89), Francisco Pulgar Vidal (b. 1929), Leopoldo La Rosa (b. 1931), José Malsio (b. 1924), and especially César Bolaños (b. 1931) and Edgar Valcárcel (b. 1932) advocated a clear anti-nationalist attitude but were also conscious of the need to assert a Latin American personality in their new music. Admittedly subjective and vague, such an attitude has nevertheless motivated these composers to a cultivation of contemporary styles treated in a unique manner. Iturriaga, for example, attempted to integrate some native and European elements. Garrido Lecca developed a style in which contemporary European practices (atonality, quartal and quintal harmonies) are juxtaposed with locally derived musical traits (use of pentatonic scales), as in his Suite for Woodwind Quintet (1956). Enrique Pinilla put into practice his conviction that the modern composer should try his hand at all techniques available to him. He therefore cultivated a polytonal and atonal language and, in the 1960s, serialist and electronic music procedures. Pulgar Vidal and La Rosa have written primarily in a modernistic neo-nationalist vein but also have cultivated freely twelve-tone and aleatoric techniques, while Malsio, a student of Hindemith at Yale University and of Schoenberg in

Los Angeles, favoured polytonality in his works of the 1950s and atonality in the 1960s.

César Bolaños and Edgar Valcárcel represented in the 1960s and 1970s the progressive avant-garde of Peruvian music. From the very beginning of his career Bolaños orientated his activity as a composer towards experimental music in the electronic medium and towards indeterminacy. He studied at the New York RCA Institute of Electronic Technology and at the Di Tella Institute in Buenos Aires in the 1960s. From about 1970 he carried out experiments, at Honeywell Bull Argentina, in the application of computer science to music composition. Works created by this process have been referred to generically as ESEPCO (Estructuras Sonoro-Expresivas por Computación) and have included *Sialoecibi* (ESEPCO I), for piano and a narrator-mime actor, and *Canción sin Palabras* (ESEPCO II), subtitled 'Homage to non-pronounced words', for piano with two players and tape. As theatre music, the stage action becomes an integral part of the instrumental performance. His use of mixed media involved a range of activities from performance-theatrical actions to abstract audio-visual environmental movements. Valcárcel cultivated various contemporary techniques, from dodecaphony to electronic and aleatory procedures. As one of the most creative personalities of the Peruvian avant-garde, his development as a composer has been symptomatic of the Latin American composer of new music in general, in its assertion of the composer's intellectual freedom and its attempts to contribute unique features to new music expressions.

Most Bolivian composers who developed an interest in contemporary music studied abroad and often felt alienated upon returning to their country. Jaime Mendoza Nava (b. 1925) cultivated a neo-classical style in which appear some elements of native music of the Bolivian plateau (pentatonicism and characteristic rhythms). Gustavo Navarre (b. 1932), a student at the Paris Ecole Normale de Musique, created a neo-Romantic language combined, on occasions, with traits of Bolivian folk music. Atiliano Auza-León (b. 1928) wrote in a neo-classical vein at first and turned to twelve-tone technique in the 1960s. The most in evidence of the Bolivian composers in the 1960s and 1970s was Alberto Villalpando (b. 1940). He began using serialism in his First String Quartet (1964) and *Variaciones Tímbricas* (1966), for soprano and chamber ensemble, but turned to electronic and aleatory techniques in later works.

In Chile, where the University of Chile continued to be the main pillar supporting the country's extraordinarily dynamic musical life, the foundation of the Philharmonic Orchestra of Chile (later renamed the Municipal Philharmonic), the establishment of several chamber ensembles at the Catholic University, and the issuance of commercial recordings of Chilean music and a series of score publications by the Instituto de Extensión Musical (1959), all strongly stimulated musical composition. Domingo Santa Cruz remained attached to his neo-classical style, characterized by contrapuntal textures and linear chromaticism, though he was not as prolific as in previous decades. His Opus 28 (*Seis Canciones de Primavera*) dates from 1950, Opus 32 (*Endechas*) from 1960 and Opus 37 (*Oratio Jeremiae Prophetae*) from 1970. He wrote in an increasingly dissonant harmony and textural complexity and his dramatic and highly expressionist sense was reinforced during this period. In the case of Juan Orrego-Salas, from 1961 director of the Latin American Music Center at Indiana University, the neo-classical elements of his earlier works remained the underlying basis of his style, but with the adoption of twelve-tone procedures (restricted, however, to pitch selection) atonality prevailed in his works of the 1960s and 1970s. His *Sonata A Quattro*, Op. 55 (1964) reveals the concern for formal clarity and balance, irregular rhythmic aggregates, and an artful handling of timbres with original instrumental effects. The monumental *Missa* 'In Tempore Discordiae', Op. 64 (1968–9) and the oratorio *The Days of God*, Op. 73 (1975) illustrate the composer's skilful writing for voices, his dramatically refined character, and his remarkable talent for combining traditional and contemporary compositional techniques and ideas.

Among the Chilean composers of the 1920s generation Gustavo Becerra-Schmidt (b. 1925) has been one of the most successful. His works cover a considerable range of styles and genres. He began in the early 1950s as a neo-classicist (e.g. in the Violin Concerto, 1950 and the First String Quartet, 1950), then adopted the serialist method of composition around 1955, but maintained classical formal concepts. Webernian influences are felt in such works as the Third String Quartet (1955) and the First Symphony (1955–8) in which pointillistic procedures (associated with Webern) appear frequently. In the early 1960s he combined the serial method with what has been called a 'complementary polychordal system', involving also the twelve tones of the chromatic scale but divided into groups or 'polychords', of various pitches. Becerra felt that such a system was less restrictive than dodecaphony. During the 1960s, he introduced aleatory techniques in his works, as in the Concertos Nos.

1 and 2 for guitar (1964, 1968), the String Quartet No. 7 (1961), and the oratorio *Macchu Picchu* (1966), on a poem by Pablo Neruda. Becerra's aesthetic thought has been moulded by his socio-political views, as his choice of texts indicates. Influenced by Marxist philosophy he set to music poems or texts by Chilean poets or writers such as Neruda, Gabriela Mistral and Nicanor Parra, or simply texts on such subjects as Lenin's death, the Guatemalan revolutionary struggle, the Vietnam war and Allende's death (in the work *Chile 1973*, for voice and chamber orchestra).

Other Chilean composers representative of the musical avant-garde have been León Schidlowsky (b. 1931), Fernando García (b. 1930), and Miguel Aguilar-Ahumada (b. 1931). In 1955 Schidlowsky became a member of the Agrupación Tonus, a private musical association for new music, which he directed in 1957. He has been influential as a composer conscious of his social function and deeply devoted to questions of a socio-political and religious nature. He has shown a particular concern for the misfortune of the Jewish people throughout the world, which accounts for the pronounced mysticism of many of his works. His large output reveals a phase of expressionist and dodecaphonic style (1952–6) followed by one of adherence to total serialism (1959 to *c.* 1963), then since about 1964, one of utilization of aleatory procedures. García also reveals a deep preoccupation with the socio-political conditions of the Third World (*América Insurrecta*, 1962, *La Tierra Combatiente*, 1965, both on texts by Neruda). His serial works of the 1960s reflected special care in the treatment of tone colour. Aguilar-Ahumada has been a rather eclectic composer. He developed from an early influence of Hindemith, Bartók and Stravinsky and the early expressionism of Schoenberg and Berg to a post-Webernian serialist style and in the mid-1960s to aleatory procedures combined with electronic sounds (e.g., *Texturas*, 1965).

The first experiments in electronic music were initiated by Juan Amenábar (b. 1922) and José Vicente Asuar (b. 1933), who created in 1955 the Taller Experimental del Sonido (Experimental Sound Workshop) at the Catholic University in Santiago. Amenábar's *Los Peces* (1957) is generally considered the first tape composition in Latin America. Asuar, a trained acoustic engineer who was influential in the establishment of electronic music studios in several cities throughout Latin America, experimented with electronic music pieces (the first, *Variaciones Espectrales*, in 1959), and computer scores programmed for traditional instrumental ensembles (such as *Formas I–II*, 1970–72, for orchestra), and for complete electronic sound synthesis.

Argentina and Uruguay

After 1950, Argentina (and especially the capital Buenos Aires) developed the most flourishing musical life in Latin America. This was due to the renewed vitality of older institutions, the upsurge of new-music activities in national and private universities, and the generally improved level of music instruction in both public and private institutions. Among the latter, the Latin American Center for Advanced Musical Studies at the Di Tella Institute in Buenos Aires was unique. Established in 1962 and directed by Alberto Ginastera, the centre offered two-year fellowships biannually to twelve composers from Latin America, contracted with world-renowned composers to conduct composition seminars, established an electronic music studio (directed by Francisco Kröpfl), and sponsored concerts and festivals of the faculty members' and fellows' works. Several groups for the dissemination of new music were created in Buenos Aires, including the Asociación de Jóvenes Compositores de la Argentina (1957) with such members as Mario Davidovsky and Alcides Lanza, the Agrupación Euphonia (1959) (later renamed Agrupación Música Viva) established by Gerardo Gandini and Armando Krieger, and the professional Unión de Compositores de la Argentina (1964).

Among the composers born prior to 1920, Ginastera and, to a lesser extent, Juan Carlos Paz continued to be productive during the 1950s and 1960s. Ginastera's phase of neo-expressionism began with the Second String Quartet (1958) which relied extensively on twelve-tone techniques but retained the strong rhythmic drive of earlier works. In this and later works (e.g. *Cantata para América Mágica*, 1960, for soprano and a large percussion ensemble), twelve-tone techniques are often combined with other procedures, microtonal, polytonal, non-serialist, or atonal. In his orchestral and instrumental works of the 1960s and 1970s Ginastera explored very effectively new-music techniques and continued to search for new sonorities in the established vocal and instrumental media. Works such as the Violin Concerto (1963), the *Estudios Sinfónicos* (1967–8), the Piano Concerto No. 2 (1972), the *Serenata* (1973), for cello, baritone and chamber ensemble (on text by Neruda), or the Sonata for Cello and Piano (1979) combine the colourful exploration of clusters, microtonal and aleatory structures, are highly virtuosic and retain a clear affinity with Classical formal designs. Ginastera's aesthetic ideals during the last twenty years of his life have been equated with Romantic surrealism, because of a noted predilection for the supernatural, the fantastic and the ritualistic. This predilection finds no better expression than in his drama works of the 1960s, namely the operas *Don Rodrigo* (1963–4), *Bomarzo* (1966–7) and *Beatrix Cenci* (1971). In both aesthetic philosophy and musical technique, these are typically expressionistic works, involving tragic situations emerging from the neurotic states of morbid and pathological characters. The resounding success of these operas resulted not only from their timely libretti (making them relevant to contemporary western society) but also from the large spectrum of musical means put into action to express their intense dramas. During the 1960s Paz wrote two orchestral works and a few chamber and instrumental works that revealed a free atonal, intuitive style open to all sorts of rhythmic and timbral experiments. His language retained a post-Webernian quality, especially in the pointillistic treatment of timbre and the high concentration of thought, as can be seen in the five *Núcleos* (1962–4) for piano.

Among the numerous Argentine composers active from the 1950s, Roberto Caamaño (1923–93), Hilda Dianda (b. 1925), Francisco Kröpfl (b. 1928), Alcides Lanza (b. 1929), Mario Davidovsky (b. 1934), Gerardo Gandini (b. 1936), and Armando Krieger (b. 1940) deserve mention here. Together with García Morillo, Caamaño was the most significant neo-classical composer. He wrote some orchestral works, but his major contribution was in sacred and secular choral music. From around 1960, Dianda developed an earnest interest in new-music techniques. Her search for new sonorities was evident in such works as *Núcleos* (1963), *Ludus I* and *II* (1968, 1969), in which a virtuoso writing prevailed. The Hungarian-born Kröpfl was one of the most successful composers of electronic music in Argentina. His original treatment of the medium is evident in the series of works that addresses some specific electronic technical problems: *Exercise in textures, Exercise with impulses, Exercise in motions,* and *Exercise with coloured noise,* all from the early 1960s. From his association with the Columbia-Princeton Center (1965–71), Lanza also developed a major interest in electronic music, but electronic sounds tended to be incorporated with those of traditional instruments (e.g. *Plectros II, Interferencias I* and *II*), or were associated with mixed media. In the 1970s, when he made his career in Montreal, he relied increasingly on indeterminacy, those works calling for traditional instruments disclosed at times electronically conceived aleatory, as in *Eidesis III* (1971). From 1960 Davidovsky was resident in New York, also working at the Columbia-Princeton Electronic Music Center. His early works exhibited an atonal, abstract lyric style. His first work exclusively in the electronic medium was *Study No. 1* (1961). Since then he has given more attention to the combination of electronic materials and traditional instruments, as shown in the series of several pieces entitled *Synchronisms* (from 1963 on), for various instruments and tape. Gandini, a pianist-composer, developed a coherent style based on a free utilization of serial techniques and a keen treatment of timbres. His *Música Nocturna* (1964) is an outstanding example of the composer's expressive power which includes numerous instrumental effects, contrasts between static parts and fast, elusive and delicate figures, and an acute pointillistic treatment of the minute material at work. In the late 1960s and 1970s aleatory procedures became an integral part of his compositions. Krieger first wrote in a largely post-Webernian vein but soon turned to aleatory procedures in his search for new sonorities with classical instruments. He has written considerably for the piano, his own instrument as a performer. Particularly striking and novel in his piano works are his experiments with registers, dynamics and timbre, including harmonics and sonorities extracted from clusters.

In Uruguay, the composers who followed some of the most advanced styles were León Biriotti (b. 1929), Antonio Mastrogiovanni (b. 1936), José Serebrier (b. 1938) and Sergio Cervetti (b. 1941). The music of Biriotti developed from a language imbued with considerations of craftsmanship (e.g., *Sinfonía Ana Frank*, 1964) to a total serialist style and the use of electronics. He has been particularly concerned with questions of set theory, which he refers to as a system of structures through permutations ('Sistema de Estructuras por Permutaciones') of ordered sets. This combinatorial-like method was applied in his *Espectros* (1969) for three orchestras, *Permutaciones* (1970), for chamber orchestra, and *Laberintos* (1970), for five instruments. Mastrogiovanni created a free serial style and from the early 1970s produced a few electronic music pieces and orchestral and chamber music works with special attention to new treatment of textures and timbres. Serebrier, on the other hand, attempted to instill a characteristic Latin American flavour in some of his works, especially through an intricate and clever treatment of rhythm (as in *Partita*, 1956–8, for orchestra). A resident of the United States for many years, he was very active as a conductor and helped disseminate Latin American contemporary music. In his works of the 1970s (e.g. *Colores Mágicos,* 1971) he explored simultaneously mixed media techniques, serialism and the concept of spatial music. Cervetti, who also settled in the United States, represents the left wing of the Uruguayan avant-garde. After an early interest in serialism he became attracted to electronic music (*Studies in Silence*, 1968; *Raga III*, 1971), chance operations, and mixed media in the form of theatre music in such works as *Peripetia* (1970) and *Cocktail Party* (1970), resorting to visually intricate and provocative graphic notation.

Brazil

Only after 1960 do we witness radical changes in Brazilian twentieth-century music. Important musical activities developed after that date in several major Brazilian cities, such as Rio de Janeiro, São Paulo, Santos, Recife, Salvador, and, to a lesser extent, Belo Horizonte, Brasília and Curitiba. Several groups were established to promote new music ideologies, such as the Grupo Música Nova in Santos and São Paulo, the short-lived Grupo Musical Renovador in Rio de Janeiro, and the very active Grupo de Compositores da Bahia in Salvador. Several festivals of avant-garde music took place in Rio (1962, 1966, 1969, 1970), a total of eighteen festivals Música Nova de Santos (1964–82), and several events since the late 1970s entitled Bienal de Música Brasileira Contemporânea, organized by the Sala Cecília Meireles of Rio de Janeiro. The Brazilian Society of Contemporary Music was formed in 1971 and became affiliated with the ISCM. With few exceptions, institutions of higher learning, however, paid little attention to new music.

The music of Cláudio Santoro underwent profound stylistic transformations, with a return to serialism (Symphony No. 8, 1963), the reliance on micro-tuning combined with static sound-blocks, and random choice of scraping instruments (e.g. in *Interações Assintóticas*, 1969). Aleatory procedures also entered into his compositions in the late 1960s (*Cantata Elegíaca*, 1970) and a combination of electronic music with traditional instruments often involving chance operations appeared in the works of the 1970s (e.g. the six *Mutationen*, 1968–72, *Aus dem Brecht-Zyklus*, 1974, for soprano and synthesizer, *Cantata 'Aus den Sonetten an Orpheus'*, 1979).

Edino Krieger (b. 1928), a student of Hans J. Koellreutter in Salvador (Bahia), then Copland and Mennin in the United States, turned to twelve-tone methods during the late 1940s but a few years later developed a slightly nationalist neo-classic language (as in *Chôro*, 1952; *Abertura Sinfônica*, 1955; and especially *Brasiliana*, 1960). From about the mid-1960s, he utilized freely some serialist organization and other advanced techniques, as in *Fanfarras e Sequências* (1970). As the Director of the Music Institute of FUNARTE (Fundação Nacional de Arte) since 1980 he has been influential in promoting further contemporary music in Brazil but has been less productive as a composer.

The members of the São Paulo/Santos Música Nova Group most in evidence during the 1960s and 1970s were Gilberto Mendes (b. 1922), Rogério Duprat (b. 1932) and Willy Corrêa de Oliveira (b. 1938). Mendes came to composition rather late and has been essentially an experimentalist. His earliest and most original works are settings of concrete poems by Brazilian avant-garde poets such as Décio Pignatari, Haroldo de Campos and José Lino Grünewald. The choral piece *Beba Coca-Cola* (1966), subtitled 'Motet in D minor', on a poem by Pignatari, explores the sonic structure of individual syllables, with microtonal vocal effects mixed with talk, chanting, howling and shouting. The ending of the piece calls for a theatrical display of a strip bearing the word *Cloaca* which appears as an altered form of 'Coca-Cola', in an obviously critical, anti-advertising and anti-imperialist gesture. Mendes has also been interested in exploring the visual aspects of the music world. Many works since the mid-1960s (e.g. *Blirium c-9, Vai e Vem, Son et Lumière, Santos Futebol Club, Pausa e Menopausa*) exhibit a clear affinity for Cage's concept of indeterminacy and music theatre. Duprat was, together with Mendes and Corrêa de Oliveira, the major spokesman for the Música Nova group. Beginning as an atonalist and serial composer, he later cultivated electronic music and mixed media. He also explored the application of a computer to electronic music (*Experimental Music*, 1963). From about 1965 he worked mainly as an arranger of urban popular music. Mass communication and its implications for new-music creation was one of the major interests of Corrêa de Oliveira. In the early 1960s he turned to serial techniques (e.g., *Música para Marta*, 1961) and wrote numerous scores for plays utilizing the electronic medium. But from about 1965 he was stimulated by aleatory techniques applied to sound collage of borrowed materials from Western music and combined with controlled passages (*Divertimento*, 1967). A number of original works also resulted from his association with Brazilian concrete poets. *Cicatrizteza* (1973) for female voice is a true tour de force of imagination in the various vocal effects and its treatment of theatrical elements.

Among the numerous composition students of Camargo Guarnieri in the São Paulo area, José Antonio de Almeida Prado (b. 1943) and Raul do Valle (b. 1936) deserve special attention. Almeida Prado succeeded in freeing himself from Guarnieri's influence around the mid-1960s, when he began to develop a style in which a post-Webernian serialist character (rather than strict techniques) often prevailed, together with highly individualized harmonic and timbral effects and rigorous formal structures. Later works (*Pequenos Funerais Cantantes*, 1969, *Livro Sonoro*, 1973, for example) reveal the mystic temperament of the composer. The oratorio *Thérèse, L'Amour de Dieu* (1975) shows some technical affinity for his former teacher Olivier Messiaen's *La Transfiguration de Notre Seigneur Jésus Christ*. Raul de Valle also developed a highly original language based on atonality and exploration of new sonorities. His most successful works include the Mass *Da Nova e Eterna Aliança* (1974) and *Cambiantes* (1974), for percussion.

Among the composers active in Rio de Janeiro during the 1960s and 1970s, Marlos Nobre (b. 1939) came to occupy a prominent position within the Brazilian avant-garde. Stylistically he moved from an early nationalistic concern mixed with the dissonant style of Milhaud to twelve-tone techniques, free serialism and aleatory procedures with nativistic overtones. Many of his works have the natural exuberance found in that of Villa-Lobos, particularly in their dramatic intensity, projected through special timbral effects, rhythmic drive and highly contrasting dynamics (e.g. *Ukrinmakrinkrin*, 1964; *Rhythmetron*, 1968; *Concêrto Breve*, 1969; *Mosaico, In Memoriam*, 1970). Also in Rio (in alternation with New York City) Jocy de Oliveira (b. 1936) has been successful since the 1970s in multimedia works.

The composer most in evidence in the new capital of Brasilia after 1960 was Jorge Antunes (b. 1942). As a trained physicist, Antunes developed a special interest in electronic music which he studied at the Di Tella Institute, then at the University of Utrecht and with the Groupe de Recherches Musicales in Paris. He pioneered in electronic-music composition in Brazil (*Valsa Sideral*, 1962, *Auto-Retrato sobre Paisaje Porteño*, 1969, *Historia de un Pueblo*, 1970) and cultivated from about 1965 what he called 'integral art' or mixed media including not only sounds and colours but odours and flavours (e.g. *Ambiente I*, 1965). In his orchestral, chamber music and choral works (e.g. *Isomerism*, 1970, *Music for Eight Persons Playing Things*, 1970–71; *Catástrofe Ultra Violeta*, 1974; *Congadasein*, 1976; and *Proudhonia*, 1973), he relied a great deal on aleatory procedures.

The Salvador (Bahia) Seminários Livres de Música were founded in 1954, under the leadership and direction of Hans J. Koellreutter, and became during the 1960s and 1970s a dynamic centre for new music. The person largely responsible for this development was the Brazilian composer of

Swiss birth, Ernst Widmer (1927–90) who settled in Bahia in 1956, and was very influential as the teacher of a whole generation of local composers. Widmer's own output shows him to be an eclectic. He developed from a moderately modernist style in the early 1950s to an intermittent involvement in avant-garde music in the 1960s. His profound dislike of dogmatic attitudes in composition resulted in a wide variety of compositional resources, from tonal, modal, polytonal and serial idioms (as in *Sinopse*, 1970), to an alternation of aleatory procedures and totally controlled elements (as in *Pulsars*, 1969; *Quasars*, 1970; *Rumos*, 1972), to aleatory and spatial-music effects (as in *ENTROncamentos SONoros*, 1972).

The most creative younger members of the Bahian Group of Composers have been Rufo Herrera (b. 1935), Lindembergue Cardoso (1939–89) and Jamary Oliveira (b. 1944). The Argentine-born Herrera settled in Brazil in 1963 and lived in Salvador in the 1970s as a freelance composer. Besides exploring new timbres in works for traditional instruments and electronically generated sounds, he has also experimented with aleatory procedures and collages. He was one of the first in Bahia to organize mixed-media events. Cardoso created a typical avant-garde local style in the late 1960s, made up of a combination of aleatory processes with fixed elements (*Via Sacra*, 1968, *Pleorama*, 1971, *Toccata* for piano, 1972). Oliveira, who also experimented with aleatory processes and was prepared to try any technique, tonal or atonal, that he believed might help to express a given idea, cultivated in the late 1960s an unorthodox twelve-tone technique. Among his most significant works were *Conjunto II* (1968), *Interações* (1970), *Congruencias* (1972) and *Ludus* (1973). In the late 1970s, he became interested in the application of computer techniques to music composition.

The younger generation of Latin American composers, born in the 1950s and early 1960s, have thus a vital tradition of art-music to draw upon. Some composers in the period from the 1950s to the 1970s no doubt suffered from what is called the 'terrorism of the avant-garde.' But in following international models the Latin American composer has automatically transformed them in order to authenticate them. Gustavo Becerra has referred to the Brazilian *sotaque* (regional accent) in contemporary music. This can be extended to the music of all Latin American countries. While it is difficult to point out precisely where and how the *sotaque* manifests itself in the considerable music production since 1950, its existence can hardly be questioned.

A NOTE ON POPULAR MUSIC

The term 'música popular' in both Spanish and Portuguese has denoted traditionally the generic sense of music of the people, encompassing what folklorists and ethnomusicologists call folk and traditional music as well as urban popular music. Since the 1950s, however, 'música popular' has gradually assumed the contemporary sense of urban, commercial and mass-mediated music. It is to this sense of popular music that the note addresses itself. Urban popular music represents musical repertories, genres and behaviours specific to urban areas. It is generally disseminated through commercial outlets such as the publication of sheet music, radio and television broadcasts and, above all, the recording industry. It reflects the social stratification of a particular area, whether social strata are conceived in socio-economic, generational, or ethnic terms. In addition, certain Latin American popular music movements, genres and styles have frequently resulted from socio-political participation and criticism.

As an urban phenomenon Latin American popular music first developed in the early nineteenth century, primarily as an upper-class activity involving semi-popular theatrical genres and salon music and as a parallel to art-music traditions. It is impossible, however, to attempt to trace a homogeneous, unbroken tradition of urban music because of insufficient documentary sources. In many cities and towns the interpenetration of folk and urban cultures remained dynamic well into the twentieth century. Since the 1920s, and particularly after the Second World War, however, urban growth in most Latin American countries resulted in a massive development of urban cultures. In some of the largest cities, this growth and the consequent cultural diversity have been quite extraordinary. Urban popular music has expressly reflected that diversity, often in ethnic and socio-economic terms.

Fashionable European and other foreign species of popular music have always been present in the major cities. Thus, the main nineteenth-century ballroom dances such as the waltz, mazurka, polka, schottische, contredanse, and others were readily adopted in all cities and with time suffered the process of 'creolization' or 'mestisaje', that is the transformation into local, national genres. The waltz, for example, served as a forerunner to a large number of popular dances in the whole continent, with different names such as *pasillo* or *vals del pais* in Colombia, *vals criollo* in Peru, *vals melopeya* in Venezuela and *valsa-choro* in Brazil. The great European salon music tradition also left a strong imprint on Latin American urban music and provided an important source for numerous popular genres of the twentieth century. In addition, the prevailing romantic character of many popular song types originated in that tradition whose gentility came to be combined with the *criollo* tradition of Latin American cities. The influence of North American Tin Pan Alley and other popular genres had its obvious repercussions in the hybrid forms that developed in the 1920s and 1930s (for example, the *rumba-fox,* the *Inca-fox* and the *samba-fox*). The big jazz band era of the 1930s and 1940s also left its imprint on the performing media of many Latin American urban popular forms. In the 1950s, several attempts were made, particularly in Cuba, Puerto Rico and Brazil, to develop Latin expressions of jazz, and the 1960s and 1970s witnessed assimilations of rock 'n' roll and rock music sometimes fused with local folk-urban traditions, which gave rise to substantial innovations. Concurrently *música folklórica* in urban contexts became part of the *peña* fashion established in the 1960s and was the point of departure of a new style associated with political movements, a style that in a short period of time took on a pan-Hispanic American character.

Mexico and the Spanish Caribbean

Much Mexican popular music of the nineteenth century was influenced by European salon music. One of the best examples of that influence comes from the set of waltzes *Sobre las Olas* (1891) by Juventino Rosas (1868–94), one of the first Mexican popular composers to win international fame. The most national popular genres of nineteenth-century Mexico were the *jarabe* and the *danza mexicana*. Since then the *jarabe* has been practised by most popular musicians in popular bands or ensembles, including *mariachis.* Those *jarabes* in triple metre were often easily transformed into fast-tempo waltzes, as was the case of the famous 'Cielito lindo', believed to have been written by a Quirino F. Mendoza during the Mexican Revolution. The *danza mexicana* stemmed from the Cuban *contradanza,* itself transformed by the Andalusian tango and the Cuban *habanera,* which stressed the duple metre structure and the basic dotted rhythm and the feeling of disjunction between duple and triple divisions of the beat that came to epitomize many Latin American and Caribbean popular dances. In Mexico, the *danza* was cultivated by composers such as Ernesto Elorduy (1853–1912), Felipe Villanueva (1862–93) in the salon music tradition, and later by Miguel Lerdo de Tejada (1869–1941) who was the first major popular composer who transformed the *danza* into a vocal genre. Many popular pieces originally written as simple songs were performed as *danzas* or *habaneras,* such as 'La Paloma' and the well-known 'La Cucaracha', popularized during the Mexican Revolution.

Despite the variety of dance music genres since the beginning of the twentieth century, the *canción mexicana,* and especially the *canción romántica mexicana* came to epitomize the whole domain of Mexican popular music. The modern history of the romantic *canción* begins with the publication in 1901 of Lerdo de Tejada's 'Perjura'. It is a history of catchy melodies that have remained in the collective memory of the Mexican people. Besides its obvious kinship with Italian opera, the *canción* has been influenced by other popular song genres, especially the Cuban *bolero.* The special type of *canción* known as *ranchera* is more distinctively Mexican in that it originated from folk-song tradition and retained specific performance characteristics of that tradition. As an urban genre, it appeared in the 1920s, at first primarily to accompany sound films, and was popularized in the 1930s. *Canciones* and *boleros* have been written by the hundreds since the 1920s. By far the most popular composer of his generation was Agustín Lara (1897–1970), whose song 'Granada' was an international hit. Other famous composers of *canciones* and other genres were Tata Nacho (Ignacio Fernández Esperón, 1894–1968), author of some two hundred songs, and Guty Cárdenas (1905–32), immortalized among his countrymen by his songs 'Rayito de sol', 'Nunca', and 'Caminante del Mayab'. The 1930s also saw the further development of urban popular music with the establishment of the first regular recording companies, the Victor Talking Machine Company, which opened its Mexican factory in 1935, and several years later Columbia Records. The first radio station to pay attention to popular music was XEW Radio in Mexico City ('La Voz de la América Latina') which began broadcasting in 1930 and maintained its leadership role until about the mid-1950s, when television took over.

In the 1940s, urban composers began to pay attention to the *corrido,* the folk ballad of Mexico. In the process of urbanization, the *corrido* underwent a few changes, that is, predominantly duple metre, *copla* (quatrain) literary form, vocal duet and trio performance in harmonized fashion, and *mariachi* and *norteño* ensemble accompaniment. The best illustration of the phenomenal popularity of a modern *corrido* is 'Juan Charrasqueado', written in the 1950s by Victor Cordero (b. 1914). José Alfredo Jiménez (1926–73) was very successful with his *corridos* evoking historical events or the beauty of the Mexican provinces performed in a *ranchera* style.

Cuba has exerted enormous influence on the development of numerous Latin American popular musical forms throughout this continent. From the *habanera*, the *son cubano*, the *danza cubana*, and the *bolero* to the *mambo*, *rumba*, *conga*, and *chachachá*, Cuban music has either shaped the *criollo* music genres in other countries of the continent or been adopted in toto at various periods as fashionable dance music. Of the many popular forms, the *habanera* and the *son* first characterized Spanish Caribbean music. A typical example of a composed *habanera* was Eduardo Sánchez de Fuentes's piece entitled 'Tú,' published in 1894. The *son*, which became urbanized during the 1910s, has a strong syncopated rhythmic accompaniment, resulting in the folk version in a typically Afro-Cuban polyrhythmic texture, and is generally considered the basis of modern *salsa* music. As a dance the Cuban *bolero* stresses a duple metre and the same rhythmic pattern of the early *habanera*. Since the 1920s, the *bolero* has been essentially a vocal genre of highly romantic and sentimental character whose lyrics stress love themes of the most varied types. One of the most popular composers of *boleros* was Ernesto Lecuona (1896–1963), immortalized by songs like 'Malagueña', 'Maria la O', and 'Siboney', and many others.

The traditional *rumba* has three recognized sub-types, the *guaguancó*, the *columbia,* and the *yambú.* Musically and choreographically, the first of these was the forerunner of the urban *rumba* that developed around the 1920s. As a dance, the *rumba* deals with courtship and the male domination over the female and involves extensive hip and shoulder motions and a pelvic thrust known as *vacunao.* The urbanization of the dance retained the hip and shoulder movement, but the *vacunao* was made less obvious or disappeared altogether. This urbanization was also due to numerous dance bands that developed in the 1930s, the first to gain popularity being the Havana Casino Orchestra of Don Azpiazu. The most commercialized of all in the United States was that of Xavier Cugat.

The specific new Cuban song known as *nueva trova* reflects the ideals, the history and the struggles of the Cuban Revolution. This musical movement, which gave rise to protest music in several South American countries in the 1960s, was not one of protest as such but rather of expression and promotion of the revolution's ideology. The movement started and grew spontaneously among young people who wanted to express through song their experience and feeling within the revolution.

Among the numerous Caribbean dances, the *merengue* which originated in the Dominican Republic, has enjoyed popularity throughout the Caribbean and South America, particularly in the Central American countries, Puerto Rico, Venezuela and Colombia. The Haitian *méringue* developed its own *créole* character but is related to the Dominican counterpart.

Venezuelan popular music shares common musical characteristics with both the Caribbean and the Andean area. The most popular genres, however, the *joropo*, the *valse*, and the *merengue*, are typical native (*criollo*) expressions. As a music and literary genre, the *joropo* has been cultivated by popular composers since the latter part of the nineteenth century and has remained the most characteristic national dance of Venezuelan popular music. In the 1910s, it was associated with light theatrical pieces, the most successful of which was the *joropo* of the *zarzuela* or comic opera *Alma Llanera*, written in 1914 by Pedro Elias Gutiérrez.

The Andean Countries

Since the beginning of the twentieth century, Andean urban popular music of clear national derivation has frequently consisted of urbanized renditions and therefore transformations of folk songs and dances. In Colombia the most popular forms have been the *bambuco*, the *porro*, the *cumbia*, and the *pasillo*. The vocal part of the urban *bambuco* involves a duet of male voices singing in parallel thirds, although originally it was a serenading song for solo voice. No dance form has had the lasting popularity in Latin America of the *cumbia*, originally an Afro-Panamanian and Colombian (Atlantic coastal area) folk dance. In its urbanization the *cumbia* lost some of its choreographic figures, such as the typical hip movement and the zig-zag motion of the male dancer, but the musical characteristics are generally similar. The *pasillo*, another widespread popular dance-song, also known in the nineteenth century as the *vals del país*, is a moderately slow waltz-like dance whose rhythm does not stress the downbeat as in its European counterpart. Sung by either solo voice or duet in parallel motion, it is accompanied by either piano (in the salon context), the *tiple* (a treble guitar) and guitar supported by tambourines and 'spoons', or an *estudiantina* (a string ensemble).

Ecuadorian popular music includes the *sanjuanito*, the *pasillo*, and the *cachullapi*, among other genres. Much like the Peruvian *huayno*, the *sanjuanito* is a dance in duple metre, strictly instrumental with syncopated melodies frequently in the minor mode, with a regularly and strongly accented accompaniment. The *pasillo* from Ecuador enjoys popularity both in the highland mestizo communities and in the coastal area, particularly the city of Guayaquil.

Popular music in the various Peruvian cities and towns reflects to a large extent local musical traditions. Thus, cities like Cuzco, Ayacucho and Arequipa exhibit a popular musical style akin to the mestizo folk music tradition of the highland region. The popular *huayno,* similar to its folk counterpart but performed by urban ensembles with an instrumentation foreign to the folk tradition, has maintained its strong status among highland urban communities. Coastal cities such as Trujillo, Chiclayo, or Piura in the north and Pisco and Ica in the south have popular music expressions related to the *criollo* tradition, for example, the *marinera* and the *vals criollo.* The Lima population at large favours the *criollo* music genres, especially the *vals criollo.* Originated in Lima between 1900 and 1910, the *vals* became the main musical expression of the urban working class throughout the 1920s and 1930s. Cultivated by composers such as Felipe Pinglo Alva, Laureano Martinez, Carlos Saco, Filomeno Ormeño and Alicia Maguiña, the *vals* contains lyrics that reflect in general the psychology of the Peruvian people at different times, their cultural personality, and their conflicts, attitudes, and value systems resulting from their reaction to social conditions. A specific type of urban popular music, identified particularly with the youth of the 1970s and 1980s, is *chicha* music, combining Caribbean-like and Afro-Peruvian dance rhythms with melodies of a predominantly Andean related style.

Bolivian popular composers have cultivated the *huayño popular,* the *cueca,* the *yaravi,* and the *taquirari.* The stylized *cuecas* for piano written by Simeón Roncal (1870–1953) continue to enjoy popularity among Bolivian pianists. As in the other highland Andean areas, the Bolivian *yaravi* is a melancholy love song. The *taquirari,* a sung dance, originated in the eastern provinces of Beni and Santa Cruz; the singing almost invariably calls for parallel thirds or sixths. In the cities and towns of the Bolivian plateau, the *bailecito,* similar to the *cueca,* has been extensively cultivated. The *carnavalito,* spread throughout the country, is a characteristic popular dance in which the rhythmic hemiola (a simultaneous duple and triple beat, thereby creating a rhythmic ambiguity) prevails. Since the 1960s, festivals of 'música folklórica' in urban settings have given rise to the development of a new style and sound of popular music recreating and stylizing aspects of indigenous and mestizo music. As a strictly urban phenomenon this trend toward folk music revival and 'música criolla' rested primarily in the hands of members of the middle and upper classes. These musicians became highly proficient performers on indigenous musical instruments and adopted truly traditional and folk music genres, albeit in a more or less free style. In 1965, the La Paz 'Peña Naira' opened as an urban cultural centre. This is where the group 'Los Jairas' began, at first under the direction of the famous *charango* (small ten-string guitar) player, Ernesto Cavour. In the 1970s, the most popular and influential group was 'Savia Andina', made up of four highly professional musicians consisting of a guitar player/singer, a percussionist, a *charango* virtuoso, and a player of *quena* (Indian end-notched vertical flute), *zampoña* (panpipe), and occasionally *tarka* (another Indian whistle, vertical flute) or *mohoceño* (large flute). Subsequently, the group 'Los Kjarkas' enjoyed wide popularity throughout the Andean nations.

In addition to the adaptations of international forms of popular music, Chilean urban music consists of such popular forms as the *cueca* and urban versions of *tonadas*, *tristes*, *carnaval*, and *tiranas*. The Chilean *cueca*, a dance with song, alternates rhythmic figures in 6/8 and 3/4 metres. The singing is done by one or two voices, accompanied by guitar, *charango*, flute and *bombo* (double-headed drum). The 'Nueva Canción' movement, which spread to the whole of Latin America in the 1960s, originated in Chile. Following the example of the Cuban model, this movement was associated with social protest, labour movements and reform, and the strongly revolutionary sentiment of the period. The New Song movement centred around a group of talented musician-poets of whom the main figures were Violeta Parra (Sandoval); her children, Angel and Isabel Parra; Patricio Manns; and Victor Jara.

Argentina and Uruguay

Among the various popular music genres of Argentina and Uruguay since the beginning of the twentieth century none epitomizes as deeply the social and cultural history of those countries as the tango. For this reason alone, the tango has remained by far the most important popular form that originated in both countries. In the Rio de la Plata area, the tango came to symbolize the hopes, successes and failures of the millions of European immigrants who hoped to work in the farms but settled in the *arrabal* or ghettos of Buenos Aires and Montevideo. The *milonga*, a dance of Afro-Argentine and Uruguayan folk tradition in duple metre and syncopated rhythm, probably contributed to the development of the tango in the area. Choreographically, the tango is in part a local adaptation of the Andalusian tango, the Cuban *danzón* and *habanera,* and, to a lesser extent, of the European polka and schottische. Essentially three types of tango developed: the strongly rhythmic instrumental *tango-milonga* for popular orchestras, the instrumental or vocal *tango-romanza* with a more melodic and romantic character, and the accompanied *tango-canción,* which is strongly lyrical and sentimental. It is in the *tango-canción* that the major themes characteristically associated with the tango as popular culture appear. Carlos Gardel (1887–1935), a popular idol who continued to fascinate most Argentines well into the 1970s and 1980s, was particularly important in making the tango fashionable throughout the Western Hemisphere and in Europe. His major contribution was to transform it into a song genre of social and cultural significance. Perhaps the most successful tango ever composed was 'La Cumparsita' (1917), written by Gerardo Matos Rodriguez in Montevideo. Other representative popular pieces of the 1920s were Julio César Sanders's 'Adiós Muchachos', Enrique Santos Discépolo's 'Yira, yira', Angel Villoldo's 'El Choclo', Juan Carlos Cobián's 'Nostalgias', Francisco Canaro's 'Adiós, pampa mia' and Edgardo Donato's 'A media luz'. The tango revival of the 1960s and 1970s brought about stylistic innovations. The so-called new tango movement, whose leading exponent was Astor Piazzolla (1921–92), included the appearance of tango suites transformed into ballets.

Brazil

The popular music of Brazil began to acquire stylistic originality during the latter part of the nineteenth century. The sentimental love song, *modinha,* and the song-dance *lundu,* cultivated in the salons since the period of Independence, began to be popularized among urban musicians in the 1870s. Local adaptations of European urban dances, particularly the polka, gave rise to new genres such as the *maxixe,* the *tango brasileiro,* and the *choro,* whose most successful composers were Joaquim Antonio da Silva Callado (1848–80), Francisco Gonzaga (1847–1935), and Ernesto Nazareth (1863–1934). The *choro* of the 1920s to the 1940s stressed virtuoso improvisation of instrumental variations and the consequent counterpoint of remarkable imagination as in the pieces of the Velha Guarda band of Pixinguinha (Alfredo da Rocha Viana, 1899–1973).

Carnival, first organized on a regular basis in the late 1890s in Rio de Janeiro, stimulated the development of urban popular music. At first simple marches, polkas and waltzes were used, but the most typical carnival genre, the urban samba, emerged during the second decade of the twentieth century. The first recognized samba to be recorded was 'Pelo telefone' by Ernesto dos Santos, nicknamed Donga, in 1917. From that date, the samba became standardized as an urban genre. Several species of the form appeared from the 1920s, including the folk-like dance known as *partido-alto* and the *samba de morro* (sometimes referred to as *batucada,* i.e., with percussion emphasis) cultivated by people of the *favelas* (hillside slums) and the first samba 'schools' of Rio de Janeiro. Around 1928 two significant new developments affected the samba: the creation of the first samba schools and the advent of the genre *samba-canção.* Both epitomized the dichotomy that separated the music of the lower classes and that of the middle and upper classes. The *samba-canção* was meant for middle- and upper-class consumption. Melodically and textually it was strongly reminiscent of the older *modinhas,* while harmonically and rhythmically it was influenced in the 1940s and 1950s by the Cuban *bolero* and the 'fox-blues'. Together with other hybrid forms such as *samba-choro* and *samba-fox,* the *samba-canção* dealt with love and unhappiness often in superficial or melodramatic terms. One of Brazil's popular idols, Francisco Alves (1898–1952), was a singer of *samba-canções.* Among the most recognized composers of urban sambas were José Luiz de Morais (alias Caninha) (1883–1961); Ary Barroso (1907–64), who won international acclaim with his samba 'Aquarela do Brasil'; Noel Rosa (1910–37); and Carlos Ferreira Braga (alias João de Barro) (b. 1907).

In the 1950s, the urban samba in its ballroom context suffered the influence of the big band with stereotyped arrangements seeking to emulate the American big jazz band sound of about ten years earlier. The reaction to such arrangements led to the development in the mid-1950s of the samba jazz phenomenon (influenced by the cool sound and aesthetics of Miles Davis) and, in turn, to the *bossa nova* movement of the late 1950s, which provided Brazilian popular music with new currents and a dynamic vitalization that brought about in the 1960s and 1970s highly sophisticated musicians, notably Antônio Carlos (Tom) Jobim (1927–94). The group of musician-poet-performers known as 'Tropicália' emerged in the mid-1960s and included such different personalities as Caetano Veloso, Gilberto Gil, Gal Costa, José Carlos Capinam, Torquato Neto, Tom Zé, Nara Leão and the composer-arranger Rogério Duprat.

Socio-politically, this group meant to awaken the consciousness of the middle class to the Brazilian tragedy of poverty, exploitation and oppression and to point out the true nature of the modern Brazilian reality. Musically, the 'Tropicália' movement brought about substantial innovations by widening the Brazilian musical horizon through adherence to and adaptation of the most relevant musical trends of the 1960s and 1970s, for example, the rock-Beatles phenomenon and the experimental new musics of the electronic age.

The history of recorded music represents an essential aspect of the development of popular music throughout Latin America and the Caribbean but can hardly be sketched at present with any degree of completeness and accuracy, except for the recording careers of some of the famous musicians.

CONCLUSION

This chapter has provided ample evidence of the great musical achievements of Latin America during the period under consideration. Especially since the 1950s the music of Latin America has been recognized in the major centres of the western world and many of its eclectic voices have been heard worldwide. As the century unfolds, we witness an acute new awareness of cultural identity in Latin American art and popular music that reflects the diversity of the Latin American nations and the Latin American people. Popular music genres especially have become key identity markers and have contributed to the considerable growth of pluralistic artistic expression. Art-music composers frequently complain about the diminishing possibilities of expansion of their artistic activities. Thus, we find numerous examples of music composition, especially in Mexico, Cuba, Brazil and Argentina, that unconsciously or intentionally blur the established boundaries of the popular and art-music traditions, thereby questioning the old aesthetics as the value system of the elite artist-composers. We might speculate that more attempts at integrating urban musics will occur. Although the Latin American art-music tradition of the twentieth century has been considered essentially an extension of that of Western Europe, new aesthetic processes may well change that perception within the next generations.

8

ARCHITECTURE, *c.* 1920–*c.* 1980*

INTRODUCTION

By the 1870s the majority of the newly independent Latin American countries appeared – to greater or less degree – to be on the road to social and political stability. Relative economic prosperity resulting from Latin America's accelerated integration into world economy during the following decades and the arrival of hundreds of thousands of immigrants from all over the world, but above all from Europe (especially the Mediterranean basin), had at least two important consequences for Latin American architecture. First, it brought skilled labour that was quite different from the local work-force; secondly, a new acculturation on a global scale meant exposure to styles and sensibilities distinct from those which had prevailed until then. Between the 1870s and the 1920s governments and the new rising bourgeoisie used architecture as one of the most visible means of giving themselves an aura of respectability, and they did so by imitating European and North American models.

During this period neo-classicism – refined or popular, as it was handled by masons steeped in the millennarian formulas of the Old World – began to disappear, giving way to eclectic designs typical of the late nineteenth century: neo-romanesque or neo-gothic, Italian Renaissance, Beaux-Arts, or simply the picturesque styles of the European countryside: Andalusian, Basque, Norman, Swiss or English, appropriated for suburban residences or homes built in the mountains or at the beach.

In general, architecture at the end of the nineteenth century met a common fate in nearly all the Latin American republics: there was a reaction against everything Spanish or Portuguese that might even re-

*A preliminary draft of this chapter was translated from the Spanish by Elizabeth Ladd. The chapter was substantially revised by the Editor. Sadly, the author died during the final stages of the editing.

motely conjure up memories of colonial dependence. Instead, the ideal was anything that evoked the rest of more highly civilized Europe: France, Italy, England, Germany. Progressive governments turned to foreign architects and engineers or to those natives who had European (or North American) technical and artistic training.

This movement towards modernity was so important that in assessing the period 1870–1920 as a whole the structures built by engineers – railroad stations, markets, ports, hospitals, prisons, schools, factories, warehouses, the first department stores – often appear more interesting and important than the works of architects. In the first years of the twentieth century, however, new architectural and design formulas, different from everything that came before, were adopted by Latin American architects: French and Belgian *Art Nouveau*, Viennese *Sezession*, Italian *Liberty* or *Floreale* and Catalan *Modernismo*. Compared to the routine attempts to re-use the traditional styles of the past, these ventures into a new aesthetic – while not always very well balanced – at least offered original solutions to the problems posed by contemporary buildings. These architects did not hesitate to make use of a variety of techniques simultaneously or to mix materials. On the contrary, they did everything possible to use metal structures combined with stone, brick walls, large windows and skylights of clear or multicoloured glass. All in an attempt to 'integrate' – rightly or wrongly – the 'box of walls' that contained the building proper, with its decoration in paint or in mosaic, ceramic, marble, wood or bronze.

For the most important public buildings it was usual to hold international competitions, which produced a great flow of foreign professionals, dominated by the French and Italians. In Mexico, the Palacio de Bellas Artes (1904–34) and the Central Post Office (1904), both in Mexico City, were the work of the Italian architect Adamo Boari. In Colombia the outstanding buildings in Bogotá were those that formed the National Capitol (1846–1926), by the Englishman Thomas Reed and an infinity of successors, among whom was the Italian sculptor Pietro Cantini, although the architect who changed the tastes of the epoch was the Frenchman Gaston Lelarge. Architecture in Chile was dominated by two architects who came from France to teach and, at the same time, managed to get the best commissions: C. F. Brunet de Baines, who built the first Municipal Theatre which burned down and was rebuilt by his countryman Lucien A. Henault, who also designed the University of Chile and the National Congress, both in Santiago. In Argentina the great event of the end of the nineteenth century was the founding *ex nihilo* of the city of La Plata. The plans were drawn by an Argentine architect, Pedro Benoit Jr. and the different public buildings were awarded – through competition – to a constellation of architects that included Germans, Swedes and a Belgian, Julio Dormal, who later settled in the country. In Montevideo, the great builder of that epoch was the Italian civil engineer Luigi Andreoni, who was responsible for the Uruguay Club and the new Italian Hospital, and who also finished the Central Railroad Station.

In Brazil the great architects at the turn of the century were, in São Paulo, Francisco de Paula Ramos de Azevedo (1851–1928), who was responsible for the Caetano de Campos School and the Government Palace; and in Rio de Janeiro a Spaniard, Adolfo Morales de los Ríos, who designed the School of Fine Arts. Later in São Paulo the Swedish architect Carlos Eckmann distinguished himself as designer of the School of Commerce, but above all of the lovely Villa Penteado. In Rio the Frenchman Victor Dubugras – who worked primarily in Argentina – designed the most elegant residences in the city.

From the 1920s there developed throughout Latin America a consciousness of national identity. The fundamental differences that separate everything Latin American – at whatever latitude – from the tradition of the West, taken in this case as an all-encompassing general term, became more apparent. Of course, there would still continue to be a considerable number of architects and plastic artists who were content to remain more or less repeating the academic ways. A few younger, more talented and, above all, more audacious architects would embark on an exploratory vanguard, influenced in particular by Le Corbusier. Finally, a third category which thought of itself as original, although it did not admit cosmopolitan novelties, would try desperately to find its own formula. In painting and sculpture this would be called 'indigenism', 'return to earth', with the consequent justification and exaltation of the artists' own cultures, autocthonous and colonial. In architecture, an equivalent movement would also seek motifs of inspiration in earlier forms, some in the pre-Columbian, but especially in an intense revival of the colonial.

MEXICO

Several buildings were erected in Mexico City in the neo-colonial style during the early years of the twentieth-century: the enlargement of the

University by Samuel Chávez; the rebuilding of the City Hall by Manuel Gorozpe; the Cervantes Library; the Escuela Normal and the Benito Juárez School by Carlos Obregón Santacila. Some years later, Augusto Petricioli would, in turn, contribute a new plan for the National Palace (1927), uncovering the *tezontle* – a dark red volcanic stone – that was part of the original construction which had been plastered over in the nineteenth century. The Mexican neo-colonial phenomenon is interesting because it occurred at least twenty years before the style appeared in the rest of Latin America, a situation doubtless due to the prestige of the omnipresent colonial buildings that served as models and inspiration. It is easy, therefore, to understand why the style passed rapidly to the domain of private building, for the most part badly interpreted.

The aesthetically contrary posture is the one which the vanguard quickly assumed. Along the most serious line of the strictly functional we find José Villagrán García (b. 1901), whose design for the Granja Experimental at Popotla (1925) influenced many of his own students, including Juan O'Gorman (1905–83) – also a distinguished painter, Alberto Aburto and Juan Legarreta. The style these architects used was simple and, because of that, economical, and this fact contributed to the state's commissioning several public works from them. The Hospital de Huipilco was built by Villagrán; the Centro Escolar Revolución and the Coyocán School were entrusted to O'Gorman, who between 1927 and 1938 took the opportunity to design about thirty school buildings, in addition to a dozen private houses, among them the home-studio of Diego Rivera.

The most orthodox functional works of the period – other than those already mentioned – were created by Enrique del Moral, Enrique Yáñez, Mario Pani and Salvador Ortega. These men built in the public interest some of the gigantic multi-family housing complexes. There were also innovations in religious architecture, like the church of the Purísima (1946) in Monterrey, by Enrique del Moral, who, in collaboration with Fernando López Carmona, also produced the church of San Antonio de las Huertas. The Spanish architect Félix Candela, in collaboration with López Carmona, created the Santa Monica Church (1966) and, working alone, built a little masterpiece – the church of the Medalla Milagrosa, both located in the Federal District.

The culmination of the 'international' style (as it was also called) can be seen best, however, in the Ciudad Universitaria (1950–54) which, under the direction of the architect Carlos Lazo, includes buildings by Villagrán García, Enrique del Moral and Mario Pani, and O'Gorman with Martínez

Velasco y Saavedra. The University buildings are important because of their scale and their deliberate monumental effect. The relative failure of some of the pavilions consists, perhaps, in the unnecessary and forced integration of mosaics, polychrome reliefs and sculpture – a 'plastic support' that this powerful architecture did not need.

At more or less the same time, but in the private sphere, Luis Barragán (1902–89), one of the greatest of modern Mexican architects, created the development of Pedregal de San Angel in what had been a field of lava considered worthless by real estate developers. Among the luxurious modern homes first built there are houses by Barragán himself, Pedro Ramírez Vázquez (b. 1919), and many others. In 1957, Barragán – collaborating with the then young German-born sculptor Mathias Goeritz (b. 1915) – designed and built the so-called Satellite City Towers, genuine 'monumentos a la nada', since they consisted of simple shafts of concrete, painted in different colours. They are fanciful towers whose mission is to provide a true 'centre of gravity' around which a confused suburban landscape is organized – for better or worse. The rest of Barragán's scarce but exquisite work lies exclusively in gardens, convents and private homes.

It appears that around the 1960s, the buildings commissioned by the state had to be obligatorily meaningful and even symbolic of the tacit message they embodied. They excelled in the modern style which, at that point, was already considered 'official'. Rising above the merely nationalist, it sought to create – in its own eyes and those of foreigners passing through – an image of Mexico as a country in the vanguard, in which the naive 'local colour' lent by well or badly imitated historical styles was kept in check. In this sense, the surpassing Mexican work of the century is, without doubt, the Museum of Anthropology (1963–5), by Pedro Ramírez Vázquez, in collaboration with Rafael Mijares. In this building unfolds a true transposition of pre-Columbian and colonial elements in terms of an architecture that is contemporary, bold and perfectly functional. These same architects designed the Museum of Modern Art (1964) and the Aztec Stadium (1965). Also worthy of mention in Mexican official architecture are the Olympic Pools and Stadium (1968), designed by, among others, Félix Candela. A colossal work of almost 'symbolist' proportions is the Military College (1977) by the architect Augustín Hernández, which tries to recapture something of the pre-Columbian grandeur, at the risk of losing everyday practicality.

In the 1970s the team directed by the architect Orso Núñez deserves mention; it was responsible for the Nezahualcóyotl concert halls and the imposing National Library (1974–9) on the periphery of University City and at the edge of the so-called Espacio Escultórico (see Chapter 9). However, dominating public and private commissions during these years were the team of Abraham Zabludovsky and Teodoro González de León. Their work includes the ultramodern buildings of Infonavit, the Colegio de México (1977) and the new Museo Tamayo (1980). In collaboration with F. Serrano they also designed the austere Mexican Embassy in Brasília, which is a fine example of the best contemporary Mexican architecture.

GUATEMALA

At the end of the nineteenth century there were few notable buildings in Guatemala, whose capital was built and rebuilt after the various earthquakes that dot its troubled history. And few were built in the early decades of the twentieth century, with the exception of the National Palace (1919), designed by Rafael Pérez de León. Architectural modernity arrived only slowly in this country, and when it did it seems to have followed its more simplistic patterns in which 'modern' was the equivalent of cubical, stripped, smooth and white. Those responsible for it lacked a true understanding of the principles of the best functionalism, which relate above all to floor plans and sections, not merely to volumes and façades. This seems clear, for example, in the Municipal Palace (1954–8), designed by Roberto Aycinema, whose exterior boasts the great mosaic *Canto a la raza* by the Guatemalan painter Carlos Mérida (who lived in Mexico). Something similar might be said of another voluminous structure, the Guatemalan Institute of Social Security (1957–9), also designed by Aycinema, this time with Jorge Montes Córdova. These semi-functionalist plans are also reflected in the Civic Center of Guatemala, which consists of several public buildings including the Dirección General de Bellas Artes, the National Radio Station, the National Theater and the Museum of Modern Art. Interesting works of the 1960s and 1970s are the Rectory of the University City, and, also in the capital, the National Mortgage Credit Building, the Bank of Guatemala and the National Library and Archives.

CUBA AND PUERTO RICO

In Cuba and Puerto Rico until the end of the nineteenth century the architectural models still came from Spain, but after the Spanish-

American War the influence of North American architecture was dominant. During the first three decades of the twentieth century the great buildings of Havana were for the most part designed by U.S. architects and built by U.S. companies. This was the case, for example, with the Hotel Nacional (now the Habana Libre), by McKim, Mead and White. The styles which still dominate in these buildings are either French classicism (revised by the Academie des Beaux-Arts) or 'Californian' on a gigantic scale, correctly designed but with no serious attempt at architectonic innovation. In the Havana of the twenties, other enormous buildings were erected like La Metropolitana, designed by Purdy and Henderson. The Parliament building (1929) was built in neo-classical style, with the indispensable cupola, designed by Raul Otero in collaboration with J. M. Bens and others.

In Puerto Rico, after a Hispanizing trend which produced the Puerto Rico Casino (1918), the Capitol (1925) was built in official classical style. However, in Río Piedras, the University Tower (1936–7) by Rafael Carnoega Morales and Bill Shimmelpfenning boasts a deep-rooted Spanish affinity. The same occurs, around the same time, with the Puerto Rican Atheneum and the School of Medicine, both in San Juan. Also in the 'colonial' style was the 'skyscraper' of the Cuban Telephone Company in Havana (1927), the first of its kind in the city, designed by the architect Leonardo Morales.

Within the current opposed to historicism, two movements began to reach the Caribbean, movements which moved in parallel in nearly all of Latin America in the 1930s. These were functionalism and, to abbreviate, the style we will call art deco. The latter, for example, was brought to Havana by the architect E. Rodríguez Castells, designer of a famous building for the Bacardi Company (1929), the noted rum distiller. Also on the Cuban scene various Spanish immigrants made their appearance, including the architects Martín Domínguez and R. Fábregas, many of them members of a group called GATEPAC which was affiliated to the Congrés International d'Architecture Moderne in Barcelona. People like Domínguez and Fábregas transmitted the message of functionalism, which would soon produce interesting designs like those by two local architects, Alberto Camacho and the future colonial art historian Joaquín Weiss (1894–1968). In Puerto Rico several excellent foreign professionals appeared: one was the Czech, Antonin Nechodoma (who died prematurely in 1928), an imitator of Frank Lloyd Wright, whose Prairie Houses he made known with great sensitivity and talent; another was the German, Henry Klumb (b. 1905), a direct disciple of Wright, from whom the new buildings on the university campus were commissioned.

By the 1940s, Cuba was already more in step with the derogatorily labelled 'international style'. The architect Emilio de Soto built apartment buildings in Havana along these lines, and even the Maternidad Obrera clinic (1939) in Marianao. However, the real point of departure for the best modern tendencies took place through people like Max Borges and Mario Romañach, who specialized more than anything else in private homes. Large projects, meanwhile, were awarded to Emilio del Junco, Miguel Gastón and Martín Domínguez, who designed, for instance, the Radio Center (1947).

In the fifties there was a great stirring of architectural activity throughout the Caribbean. Thus, for example, in Havana Arquitectos Unidos enlarged the Edison Institute (1954), while Ernesto Gómez Sempere completed the great residential complex of Focsa (1956). In Puerto Rico, Klumb on some occasions reminds one of Frank Lloyd Wright, as in the Fullana house, and on others of Le Corbusier in Ronchamp, as in the case of the Church of Carmen in Cataño. In the Caribbean it has frequently been the luxury hotels that have served to introduce and diffuse modern architectural trends. First there were those of the Vedado neighbourhood in Havana, later the Caribe Hilton in San Juan, Puerto Rico, by Toro, Ferrer and Torregrosa, the Sheraton in Kingston, Jamaica, by Shearer and Morrison, and the Hotel Jaragua in Santo Domingo, by G. González.

In Cuba after the Revolution the buildings best representing the new architectural experimentation were the East Havana Neighborhood Unit (1959–3), and the famous National School of Plastic Arts and the National School of Dance in Cubanacán (1960–3), which were an attempt at an original synthesis of African and colonial elements, the substrata of Cuban culture. Perhaps the most transcendental was, however, the Ciudad Universitaria José Antonio Echeverría (1961–70), on the outskirts of Havana. All the required conditions are present in this excellent design: consideration of the climate, transparency of walls, the provision of abundant areas of shade.

In the seventies, 500 schools were built for no less than 300,000 children. Three important projects should be mentioned: the V. I. Lenin Vocational School (1972–4), by Andrés Garrudo; the Máximo Gómez school (1976), in Camagüey, by Reynaldo Togores; and the Ernesto Guevara Palace of the Pioneers (1979), by Néstor Garmendia. Finally, built along very pure aesthetic lines, we must mention the new Cuban

Embassy in Mexico City (1977) and the José Martí Monument (1978) in Cancún, both created by the talented architect Fernando Salinas.

During this same period in Puerto Rico several important buildings were erected: the conventional Ponce Museum, by the U.S. architect Edward Stone; the María Libertad Gómez Elementary School in Cataño, the work of Lorenzo Rodríguez de Arellano; and the Library of the Interamerican University of San Germán. Finally, in the building for the legislators, the annex to the Capitol in San Juan, the partnership of Toro and Ferrer achieved a tropical lightness of great purity.

COLOMBIA

In Colombia, with the general prosperity of the beginning of the century and the growing need for public works, a few privileged architects dominate the principal projects. The most important were the French architect Gastón Lelarge and two Colombians, Julián Lombana (who died in the 1920s) and Mariano Santamaría (1857–1915). During the first quarter of the century the interior of the country was provided with a number of important buildings, such as the Government House of Antioquia, built by the Belgian architect Al Goovaerts, the one at Manizales, by the North American J. Vawter, and the Edificio Nacional in Cali, built by another Belgian J. Maertens. During the same period the cathedral of Villanueva, originally designed by the French architect Charles Carré, was built (1875–1929) in Medellín. The cathedral in Manizales (built 1927–37) was designed by another French architect, Auguste Polty. In the latter case the structure was of concrete and since it was left unfinished (it was projected as a 'gothic' building) it gives the false impression of having been an advanced work for its time.

Two local architects, Guillermo and Alberto Herrera Carrizosa, produced a true revolution in taste when they created the La Merced neighbourhood in Bogotá between 1937 and 1942, with the houses in 'Tudor' style. At the end of the thirties, the campus of a new National University – very deteriorated now – was planned by another foreigner, Leopoldo Rother, who was inspired by Le Corbusier's first period. The outstanding elements of this campus were the Faculty of Architecture building, the Hydraulics Laboratory and the Faculty of Law building. However, the more mature contribution was made by another architect from abroad, the Italian Bruno Violi, who between 1939 and 1943 built the Faculty of Engineering with obvious Italo-German references. The great national commissions continued: for example the Radium Institute (1937–9) in Bogotá designed by A. Wills, and his plan for the National Library (1937–9) which reflects a complex of evocations that run the gamut from contemporary fascist architecture to North American influences.

The most transcendent architectural turning point occurred, however, between 1946 and 1958. It began with the 'messianic' visit of Le Corbusier to Bogotá, for which a development plan was rapidly sketched. Two works greatly inspired by Le Corbusier were also built at this time: the '11 de Noviembre' Baseball Stadium (1947–9) in Cartagena, and the David Restrepo Maternity Clinic, built in the fifties. Then the second Corbusian generation began to return – including some who had worked directly with the master in Paris. The first great impact among young Colombian architects was made by Germán Samper, who participated in the group that designed and built the Central Mortgage Bank where he showed evidence of extraordinary adaptation and imagination. Perhaps the most outstanding of these collaborations was, however, that formed by Rogelio Salmona and Hernán Vieco in their design for a group of multi-family dwellings in bare brick, called San Cristóbal (1964–5 and 1967–8), whose form set themselves apart from the 'cubical' canons of architecture and approached the free integration of Alvar Aalto.

The work that is undoubtedly the mark of the decade of the seventies is the Park Towers (1968–72) designed by Rogelio Salmona, three skyscrapers of exposed brick with elegant curved stories that ascend in steps forming terrace gardens. This nearly obsessive reevaluation and return to brick – first carried out by Gabriel Serrano – has been brilliantly continued, not only by Salmona but also by Fernando Martínez. It is perpetuated in single buildings, like Los Cerros (1982), by Salmona himself, and in small residential developments in the environs of Bogotá like El Bosque (1972), Santa Teresa (1977–8), Sorelia (1974–5), Brapolis (1976–7) and El Polo del Country (1979–80). The dissident is the architect Jorge Piñol, whose best known works are not in exposed but in plastered brick, through which he tries to revive the white architecture of the architectonic cubism of the twenties.

VENEZUELA

It was not until 1937 that we first see symptoms of architectural and urban innovation in the Venezuelan context when the government of the day appointed a group of French urban planners to take charge of the modernization of Caracas. This group included Maurice E. H. Rotival, who presided over the preparation of a Master Plan approved in 1939. At the same time, the Venezuelan Cipriano Domínguez was put in charge of designing the Centro Simón Bolívar (1950–60), in accordance with the 'modernized' norms of the Beaux-Arts style: a great central avenue with identical buildings and two symmetrical coloured towers that were designed by the great architect Carlos Raúl Villanueva (1900–78).

Villanueva, a key figure in the history of Venezuelan culture, had earned his architecture degree in Paris in 1928, and scarcely a year later opened his own office in Caracas, a city in whose transformation he would later play a major part. As early as 1935 the authorities commissioned him to design the Museum of Fine Arts in the Los Caobos neighbourhood. Villanueva dared to conceive an edifice of a single story with an attractive sculpture patio in the shape of a quarter-circle. In 1939 he created the Gran Colombia School and, during the 1940s, he also developed the El Silencio neighbourhood, where he tried to preserve something of the colonial ambiance, designing a plaza with fountains and statues surrounded with porticos in the vernacular tradition. Villanueva's *magnum opus,* however, was the monumental University City in Caracas, completed in several stages over twenty years, from the middle of the 1940s to the middle of the 1960s. Here we find ourselves at the opposite pole from the contemporary Ciudad Universitaria in Mexico City. Indeed, the fact that the Caracas project is an individual undertaking and the Mexican one eminently collective is what separates them from the outset. Villanueva continued to contribute other projects: the Olympic Stadium (1952), with a capacity of 30,000 spectators; the Baseball Stadium, somewhat later and capable of holding the same number of fans; and finally, the Olympic Pool, whose galleries support a daring concrete roof.

In the private sector in Caracas, beginning in the fifties, there appeared an urgent demand for really modern structures adapted to the climate and the local style of life. In 1950, the architects Guinand and Benacerraf erected the important Edificio Montserrat. Among the first tall buildings – of which there would be so many later – was the Edificio Polar (1952–4) in the Plaza Venezuela, the work of the architects Martín Vegas Pacheco and José Miguel Galia, an Uruguayan who had settled in Caracas.

The system of multi-family dwellings – in spite of having been severely criticized – continued to be practised as the only answer to the enormous uncontrolled growth of Caracas. Thus, the Caricuao complex, designed by the architects Alcides Cordero, Carlos Becerra and others, was extended. Meanwhile, Guido Bermúdez was building the Unidad Habitacional Carro Grande (1951–4) in the Valley of Caracas. The Cerro Piloto (1954) was also supervised by Bermúdez but involved other participants including, as consultant once again, the omnipresent Villanueva.

Among the urban projects on a grand scale Ciudad Guayana deserves mention above all – an artificial creation, the product of a governmental decision, situated at the confluence of the Orinoco and the Caroni Rivers, where building began around 1960. During the 1960s other official commissions were made: for example, the School of Medicine of the Vargas Hospital (1961), designed by the architect Nelson Donaihi; the Maturín Industrial School, by Ignacio M. Zubizarreta; and, lastly, also by the same architect, the Escuela Artesanal El Llanito (1962) in Petare. We must also point out several later works by José Miguel Galia: the Bank of Caracas, the Banco Metropolitano and the interesting exposed brick tower of Orinoco Insurance. An Argentine who works successfully in Venezuela is Julio César Volante; he offered his own style in the Andrés Bello University with its severe façade. Finally, worthy of note are the Venezuelan Tomás José Sanabria, to whom we owe the Ince building, and the powerful Hispano-Venezuelan firm of Siso, Shaw and associates, who were responsible for the Parque Central – begun in the seventies – which contains three colossal 'cliffs' thirty-five stories high with a 400 meter façade, finished off with two towers of mirrors which – for better or worse – have definitively changed the urban skyline.

ECUADOR

After a glorious colonial past, Ecuadorian architecture entered a lethargic phase that lasted for at least 150 years. Modernity appeared very late, and that it did so at all is, in part, thanks to the strong personality of the Austrian architect Oscar Edwanick and to the fact that the Quito authorities in 1946 asked two competent architects Guillermo Jones, an Uruguayan, and Gilberto Gatto Sobral, an Ecuadorian, to organize a Faculty of Architecture. One of the first interesting vanguardist works, without doubt, is the San Francisco de Sales School (1955) in Quito, created by the Swiss architect Max Erensperger. Also outstanding are several private homes designed by Jaime Dávalos together with Gatto Sobral. Dávalos had studied in the United States and brought the latest architectural ideas to Ecuador. A worthy building from the 1970s – before oil wealth produced a rash of new buildings in Quito – is the Municipal Palace (1975), built near the Cathedral and the Government Palace on one side of the central plaza. Moderate in scale and neutral in design, it is the work of the architects Diego and Fausto Banderas Vela, who received their training and degrees in Montevideo.

PERU

Peru, like all Latin American countries, including Brazil, seems to have gone through a real architectural identity crisis between 1920 and 1940. On the one hand, there was a return to the pre-Columbian (the equivalent of 'indigenismo' in painting), although hardly a trace remains of the indigenous influence in the National Museum of Anthropology and Archaeology in Pueblo Libre, a suburb of Lima, and there is only the vaguest of hints in the Peruvian pavilion at the Paris International Exhibition (1937). On the other hand, by contrast revival of appreciation for the colonial assumed considerable proportions in Peru, doubtless because it is the country – in this part of the continent – where the greatest number of colonial buildings of value are still standing. The architect Rafael Marquina seems to have started the trend with his Desamparados railway station in Lima. Marquina, together with Manuel Piqueras Cotolí, developed (beginning in 1925) the Plaza San Martín in 'neo-colonial' style, in spite of the fact that in the surrounding area vaguely French style buildings were appearing as, for example, the Hotel Bolívar (1938). Similarly neo-colonial was the Plaza de Armas (1945), designed by the great historian of colonial architecture, Emilio Harth-terré (1899–1983) and José Alvarez Calderón. It is hard to believe that these four architects, plus other specialists like Carlos Morales Macchiavello and Héctor Velarde, could have succumbed to the same error: they allowed excellent buildings to disappear – they even demolished them – in order to reconstruct a historic city like Lima in 'pseudo-colonial' style, invented from head to toe. Velarde himself, in one of his books, defends this 'revival' which, at bottom, represents nothing more than a naive affirmation of nationalism.

Nevertheless, the Master Plan of Lima (1946), which literally gutted the old city, at the same time accepted the advent of the contemporary style that had already had an opportunity to manifest itself in several works by Alfredo Dammert, Juvenal Monge and Santiago Agurto Calvo. In this new spirit the National Stadium (1952) was constructed in Lima, with a capacity for 60,000 spectators. During this period the neocolonialist Alvarez Calderón 'converted' to modernism, and collaborated with Walter Weberhofer on the Atlas Building (1956), which exhibits obvious Corbusierian influence. Finally, the Colonia Huampani project (1956), by the architects S. Agurto, L. Vásquez, C. Cárdenas and J. Ramos, was an important step towards vanguard planning.

During the 1950s and 1960s the Peruvian government commissioned several modern buildings in Lima, including the Ministry of Finance by G. Payet, and the Ministry of Education by E. Seoane, both of mediocre quality. At the same time there were some excellent intransigently functionalist projects like the Jorge Chávez Airport in Lima, the Cuzco Airport, and a residence designed for the Peruvian Air Force. Other notable buildings in Lima were the Faculty of Architecture, part of the National University of Engineers; several neighbourhood developments such as San Felipe, Santa Cruz and Palomino; and, later, the Civic Centre (1971). This impressive, and controversial, agglomeration of spaces, terraces and little plazas in the 'brutalist' style has literally changed the old face of the city, since it rises between the colonial neighbourhoods, now very run-down, and the new residential sections which as yet have little character.

Among other distinguished Peruvian architects Miguel Rodrigo in particular deserves mention. Rodrigo designed, among other things, the Central Mortgage Bank of Peru in El Callao, the port of Lima and, with others, the Ministry of Fisheries, a very high quality structure, within an aesthetic of sharply contrasted masses made, deliberately, of exposed concrete. Also important are Walter Weberhofer, whom we have already mentioned, and Daniel Arana, creators of the Petroperu building, which for some time was the tallest building in Lima. Finally, other talented architects who worked in partnership are Federico Cooper Llosa, Antonio Graña and Eugenio Nicolini. They built several new pavilions for Lima's Catholic University, the San Miguel Trade Center and a multitude of private buildings, always displaying designs of the highest quality.

BOLIVIA

In Bolivia, the link between European-inspired architecture, the neo-colonial and modernity was the architect Emilio Villanueva (1884–1970), who was born in La Paz and received his degree in Engineering and Architecture in Santiago de Chile. Villanueva is important for his dual role as urban planner and architect, and for thirty years he exerted a powerful influence over the shape of his native city. As a young man he designed the Military College (1914, now demolished) and the General Hospital (1916), but his really important work is the City Hall (1925), which recalls the one in Brussels. It is built in an unexpected Flemish Renaissance style not often seen in South America. A brief neo-colonial period did not contribute much to his career, until after passing two years with his family in Paris, he returned to build two more interesting buildings: the Hernando Siles Stadium (1930, demolished in 1975) and, more important, the thirteen-storey tower in one solid block of the Universidad Mayor de San Andrés (1941–8) in La Paz. This functional construction – symmetrical in floor plan and façade – has only a few decorative elements at the entrance, inspired by motifs from the ancient Tiahuanaco culture.

From the 1960s modern architecture made forward strides, little by little, in the principal Bolivian cities, although many of the buildings erected suffer from more or less conventional design. A notable exception is the University of Oruro (1971), by the architects Gustavo Medeiros (who studied in Córdoba, Argentina) and Franklin Anaya. It consists of a series of powerful blocks made of rough concrete. Another interesting figure on the contemporary scene is the architect Alcides Torres, principally the author of the German Club in La Paz (1965) and the building for Yacimientos Petrolíferos Bolivianos in Santa Cruz de la Sierra.

CHILE

After the inevitable eclecticism, historicism and a few excursions into *art nouveau,* such as that practised by the Catalan architect A. Forteza at the beginning of the century, Chile moved more and more in the direction of modern architecture. In this vein we find two important figures, both native architects: Sergio Larraín and Jorge Arteaga, who designed the precocious 'rationalist' Oberpaur Building (1928–9) in Santiago. Arteaga also designed the Bulnes Gate (1923–32) in the Plaza de Armas in Santiago. During this period José Smith Miller and Josué Smith Solar built the monumental Hotel Carrera, also in the capital. In the centre of Santiago the Barrio Cívico represents, in turn, the most substantial urban planning effort of this era in Chile: it includes a series of solid public buildings – severe and smooth – surrounding the elegant Palacio de la Moneda, the neo-classical masterpiece of Joaquín Toesca completed at the end of the eighteenth century. Sergio Larraín was not only the teacher of several generations of architects, but also – with other collaborators – the de-

signer of the impressive Naval School in Valparaíso, which remained
unfinished for many years. In association with Diego Balmaceda and
others, he later created the Presidente Frei barrio in Santiago (1965).

Another important figure in contemporary Chilean architecture is
Emilio Duhart. A disciple of Gropius, Duhart later worked in Le Corbusier's studio in Paris during the period when he was drawing up the plans
for the city of Chandigarh in Northern India. He is best known for the
magnificent headquarters of the United Nations Economic Commission
for Latin America (1960–6), which he built in Vitacura, a suburb of
Santiago. The building, a dominant horizontal, recalls Corbusierian solutions, both in its relationship to the mountainous terrain – with which it
does not want to merge – and the visual play of its masses and the bold
use of rough-finished concrete. Duhart later designed the dignified and
refined Chilean Embassy in the Barrio Parque of Buenos Aires.

The Corporación de la Vivienda (CORVI) directs and organizes the
construction of multi-family housing for the entire republic. One of the
most interesting is that built in 1966 in Santiago by the architects V.
Bruna Camus, V. Calvo Barros, J. Perelman and O. Sepúlveda Mellado.
In the provinces at least two very successful CORVI projects deserve
mention: one in Salar del Carmen in Antofagasta, in which the architects
M. Pérez de Arce and J. Besa performed the difficult feat of harmoniously
adapting ultramodern cubic forms to a desolate landscape; the other in
Población Astorga in Valparaíso, the product of a collaboration between
O. Zacarelli and J. Vender.

Finally, we must mention a building of some purity, beyond the
merely utilitarian: the Benedictine Chapel and Monastery in Las Condes
(1964), near Santiago, designed by two architects who are themselves
members of the Benedictine order: brothers Gabriel Guarda (also a noted
historian) and Martín. They achieved, with a minimum of means, one of
the most attractive and restrained works in South American vanguardist
architecture of the post-war years.

ARGENTINA

The first young Argentine architects to follow modern ideas – then revolutionary – were Alberto Prebisch and Ernesto Vautier, who conceived a
project (never realized) for Ciudad Azucarera in Tucumán (1924), inspired
by two great French architects, Garnier and Perret. When at the end of the
1920s Le Corbusier gave a series of lectures in Buenos Aires, his ideas were

well received, not only among students and young professionals, but also among intellectuals and some of the ruling class. Thus Antonio U. Vilar and his brother Carlos, two architects who had begun their careers building 'historicist' buildings, soon converted to functionalism, becoming widely known among the public at large for a series of white service stations built for the Argentine Automobile Club.

Around this same time we encounter the original creations of two free spirits, the Italian Mario Palanti and the Argentine Alejandro Virasoro. From Palanti we have the Pasaje Barolo (1922) in Buenos Aires, a strange tower that has been classified as 'expressionist', consisting of bulbous forms that distract from its main lines. At the opposite pole, Virasoro is known as the 'champion of the right-angle': his signature work is the Casa del Teatro (1928), another structure of about twenty stories also located on a major central avenue in Buenos Aires. Virasoro's style is derived from art deco, a mannered style that does not, however, lack character and elegance.

Those who accepted neither functional vanguardism nor art deco practised eclectic international styles, including the 'neo-colonial', which we have already discussed in the context of Mexico and Peru. The best theoreticians and specialists in colonial art were Martín S. Noel, Juan Kronfuss, Angel Guido and Mario J. Buschiazzo, who fell into the temptation of practising the controversial 'revival' style. Noel built the Argentine Pavilion at the Iberoamerican Exhibition in Seville (1929), the Argentine Embassy in Lima, and a two-family residence for himself and his brother, today converted into the Fernández Blanco Museum of Colonial Art.

As if to neutralize this backward-looking effect, the first skyscrapers had already begun to appear in Buenos Aires – office and apartment buildings – which would radically transform the urban profile. The purest of them are the Comega Building (1933), by Joselevitch and Douillet and, above all, the true masterpiece which is the Kavanagh Building (1934–6), by Sánchez, Lagos and de la Torre, thirty-five stories high and for many years the tallest building in the entire world made of reinforced concrete. Alberto Prebisch, mentioned above, was a very gifted professional architect who, nevertheless, built relatively few buildings. His two principal works, however, continue to be highly visible in the heart of the Argentine capital, as it was he who designed the controversial Obelisco (1939) and the Gran Rex cinema (1936–7), a model of functional reserve and elegance, on Avenida Corrientes.

Among the architects of the next generation, Jorge Ferrari Hardoy and Juan Kurchan, who worked with Le Corbusier in Paris, stand out; their eight-storey house on Calle Virrey del Pino (1943) in the Belgrano district of Buenos Aires remains a classic in Argentine architecture. Other significant creations of the decade of the forties, several of them in the provinces, include the well-known 'Casa-puente' (1945) by the architect Amancio Williams in Mar del Plata, the Atlantic beach resort, and in Tucumán the new University built on a wooded hillside and the Hospital Antiluético (1948), both to the credit of the architects Eduardo Sacriste and Jorge Vivanco.

In the 1950s two large architectural practices in Buenos Aires appear to have vied for the majority of public and private commissions. One of them was formed by Sánchez Elía, Peralta Ramos and Agostini (known by the acronym SEPRA), which in addition to innumerable 'towers' of rental apartments, designed the great ENTEL Building (1951) in Buenos Aires and the more conventional Córdoba City Hall (1953). The other still powerful firm was directed by the brilliant architect Mario Roberto Alvarez who worked alternately alone or with different associates. He built, for example, with Oscar Ruiz, the impeccable San Martín Municipal Theater (1954–60) in Buenos Aires, which has not become dated.

Another figure, a little younger and more revolutionary, is the architect-painter Clorindo Testa (b. 1923), who often collaborated with other professionals without ever forming a stable partnership. With SEPRA Testa designed the most controversial building in Argentina of the last thirty years: the Bank of London and South America (1960–64) in Buenos Aires. At the opposite pole we find two architects, Claudio Caveri Jr. and Eduardo Ellis, who produced very little but were the fortunate designers of one of the most popular and influential buildings in Argentina – the little Church of Our Lady of Fátima (1956–7), in Martínez near Buenos Aires. In fact, although its design is modern, this church in its proportions and the way its materials are treated, recalls solutions within local tradition; one might even say it is a valid variation on the neo-colonial, similar to what Luis Barragán achieved in Mexico.

In the 1970s three practices captured much of the important work: Solsona, Manteola, Sánchez Gómez, Santos, Petchersky and Viñoly, designers of an important television station and numerous apartment buildings; Baudizzone, Díaz, Erbin, Lestard and Varas, which became known when it won the competition for the Municipal Auditorium of Buenos Aires (1972, never built); and Kocourek, Katzenstein, Castillo and Laborda, who – among other works – built the Conurbán Tower (1973) in Buenos Aires. In the interior of the country the leading figure was Miguel Angel Roca in Córdoba, his native province, where he won important commissions such as the Paseo Azul Commercial Center, the Conjunto Habitacional Consorcio Sur (1972–7) and the Consorcio Habitat (1972–8). Some Buenos Aires architects also designed for the provinces. E. Kocourek, mentioned above, is the author of the International Hotel (1978) in Iguazú, facing the Cataracts.

URUGUAY

In Uruguay the *magnum opus* of the first third of the twentieth century was the large and complicated construction of the Legislative Palace in Montevideo. This monumental edifice was first entrusted to the Italian architect Victor Meano. On his premature death in 1904 the job was temporarily assigned to J. Vazquez Varela and A. Banchini, and in 1913 it was awarded to another Italian, Gaetano Moretti, who only finished it 20 years later. In another category, the Palacio Salvo skyscraper (1923–8), for many years the tallest in South America, is, like the Pasaje Barolo in Buenos Aires, the work of Mario Palanti, although in the latter case the Italian architect collaborated with the engineer L. A. Gori Selvv. In a style more sober than that of these concrete skyscrapers, other important works were built in this era, including the Edificio Central (1931), a true tribute to art deco, and several 'modern' private residences, like the Perotti house (1931).

From the same period several designs and executions by the influential architect and teacher Mauricio Cravotto are worthy of mention. He was responsible for the design of the Palacio Municipal (1929, which in its realization was lower than in Cravotto's original plans), the Master Plan of Montevideo (1930) and later the Rambla Hotel (1940). Around the same time the architect Carlos Surraco built the Hospital de Clínicas (1930), important for its size and the quality of its design. The most significant event in the history of Uruguayan architecture in the first half of the century was, however, the appearance of the exceptional figure Julio Vilamajó (1894–1948) whose designs, from his private house on the Boulevard Artigas (1930) to his masterpiece the Faculty of Engineering (1938), demonstrate a constant striving for excellence. M. Muccinelli and R. Fresnedo Siri designed the Faculty of Architecture, much more conventional than that of Engineering, although not without its own brand of elegance.

The Spaniard Antonio Bonet, who practised in Argentina, realized his most transcendental work in Punta Ballena, Uruguay: the Berlingieri house (1946) and the Solana del Mar (1947), which were to have a marked influence on both banks of the Río de la Plata. The Uruguayan engineer Eladio Dieste, by contrast, was an 'outsider' who made himself the champion of the most traditional 'poor' material in South America: bricks. In his hands, however, bricks, together with iron reinforcements, join the most modern techniques to achieve structures of true vanguardist boldness without any folkloric or romantic concessions. In the fifties, the other outstanding figure in Uruguay was the architect Mario Payssé Reyes, who was impressive for his refinement in the use of materials, his elegance and innate sense of beautiful proportion. Later he built the new Embassy of Uruguay in Buenos Aires, a work which is, however, not one of his best. Finally, among recent Uruguayan architects of note, we must mention Nelson Bayardo, author of the admirable Urnario (1961) in the North Cemetery in Montevideo, and Mariano Arana, who in addition to being an architect and professor much admired by his disciples has, as head of the well-known Urban Studies group, done much to save the old parts of Colonia and Montevideo.

BRAZIL

The only modern school of Latin American architecture that has merited a worldwide reputation in this century has been the Brazilian, although today it must be said that, unfortunately, its hour of glory is already past.

Modernism had its origins in São Paulo. It was a movement stimulated at first by a group of intellectuals and artists, both older people and enthusiastic young people, all of whom organized the famous week of Modern Art in 1922. In architecture the movement was launched by the writings of Mário de Andrade and the practice of a Russian architect, Gregori Warchavchik (1896–1972), who had studied in Odessa with Tatlin and Lissitsky, and with Piacentini in Rome. Warchavchik came to São Paulo in 1923 and, barely two months later, published a pair of manifestos in defence of 'rationalism'. He built his first revolutionary house in 1927, followed by the Casa Modernista (1930) in Pacaembú, which was decorated with paintings by the artists Tarsila do Amaral and Lasar Segall.

During the revolution of 1930, which brought Getúlio Vargas to power, two tendencies which had appeared to be antagonistic – neo-colonialism and modernism – became united under the leadership of a highly prestigious architect, Lúcio Costa (b. 1902). There emerged, little by little, the elements which were to constitute the strength of modern Brazilian architecture: a functionalism *sui generis,* with local traits – like the use of tiles – and, above all, the exaltation of the climate and tropical vegetation. The two visits made by Le Corbusier to Brazil, one in 1929 and another in 1936, proved fundamental for the diffusion and triumph of rationalist principles. There is no doubt that the *pilotis* and the *brise-soleil,* so indispensable there for climatic reasons, are his influence, but in the hands of Brazilian architects they surpassed their merely functional roles and came to constitute a proud symbol of tropical affirmation. In chronological order the principal realizations of the movement are: the Ministry of Education and Culture (1937–43) in Rio de Janeiro, by the team directed by Lúcio Costa with the participation of Le Corbusier himself; the district of Pampulha, Belo Horizonte (1943–44) built by Oscar Niemeyer (b. 1907) – who would become the best-known Latin American architect of the century – and two 'classics' of modern Brazilian architecture, the residential complex Pedregulho (1950–2) and the Museum of Modern Art (1954–8), both in Rio de Janeiro, constructed by another great architect, Affonso Eduardo Reidy (1909–64).

In São Paulo, simultaneously, a parallel movement was developing which, while modern, nevertheless tried to distinguish itself from the Rio de Janeiro current. The two principal local figures there were Rino Levi and João Vilanova Artigas. The latter not only founded the Faculty of Architecture and Urban Planning in São Paulo (1961–8), but also built its main buildings; they are different–less theatrical and spectacular–from those by Niemeyer for the new capital Brasília.

The main event of this period was indeed the 1956 competition for the design of Brasília for which Rino Levi presented a very daring but practically unrealizable plan. The prize was won by Lúcio Costa, with Oscar Niemeyer as architect of the principal public buildings. From the moment of its conception, Brasília consecrated urban planning ideas – based on Le Corbusier's *Ville Radieuse* – that were already at least thirty years old. Now, with the benefit of historical perspective, its design, as well as the individual buildings, has been harshly criticized. Among the buildings designed by Niemeyer – who displayed in them the true imagination of a sculptor – we find the Cathedral, the Theater and the Civic Center, composed of two tall rectangular prisms and two segments of a sphere, each of which houses one branch of the legislature.

In São Paulo – in opposition to the school that gave rise to Brasília – the first disciples of Vilanova Artigas began to appear in the sixties. They were principally Paulo Mendes da Rocha, Pedro Paulo de Mello Saraiva, Carlos Millan, Décio Tosi, João W. Toscano, Abrahão Sanovicz, Ubirajara Giglioli and Fábio Penteado. The architect Joaquim Guedes designed innumerable public and private buildings in São Paulo. Rui Ohtake continues to astonish us with imaginative solutions of strange volumetric forms.

Brazil after the early sixties, however, seemed to be living on its architectural reputation. Rio de Janeiro, São Paulo and even Brasília were transformed by the intervention of great engineering companies, whose only interest was commercial. See, for example, the enormous Avenida Central Tower, by Henrique E. Mindlin, in Rio de Janeiro, which has no character: it is just one more North American style skyscraper. Nevertheless, there were a few who resisted this trend, notably the great architect Sérgio Bernardes (b. 1919). His contributions include the Mercado das Flores in Rio de Janeiro, the Palácio do Governo (1966) in Fortaleza, and the Hotel Tambaú (1971) in João Pessoa, a low circular structure, closed on the exterior except for the side facing the sea.

CONCLUSION

The architecture of Latin America during the second half of the nineteenth century was not always of the highest quality. New governments emerging from the morass of civil wars are not the best qualified or most cultivated vehicles capable of commissioning works of supreme aesthetic significance. Everything was improvised. Young local architects, just out of school, found themselves entrusted with major structures for which they were indubitably not ready. As for the foreign architects who came from a Europe already contaminated by eclectic historicism across the whole repertory of styles, they offered Latin America the same warmed-over dishes with which they had earned their livings – poorly or well – in their native countries. Some of the best, such as, for example, the excellent French architect René Sergent – famous on the European level – did not even bother to cross the Atlantic in order to supervise the three or four palatial homes he built in Buenos Aires for as many Argentine millionaires.

Nevertheless, some of the designs from the turn of the century are perfectly respectable: for instance the one of the National Theatre in

Mexico (now the Palace of Fine Arts), by the Italian architect Adamo Boari, which was an original attempt to integrate, within a modern European scheme, certain autochtonous elements. These are most visible in the sculptural decoration of the façades. Likewise the National Congress of Buenos Aires, by another Italian, Victor Meano, seems a noble and successful work with an original cupola of elliptical profile whose slender proportions confer an individual stamp on the building. Even today some of these buildings, with their excellent design, quality materials and skillful execution, remain outstanding points of reference in the majority of Latin American cities.

From the 1920s a choice had to be made between two options: the conservative, typical of the 'Southern Cone', which was in love with French and Italian architecture; and the modernist as, for example, in the case of the Mexicans who came immediately after the Revolution, or, thirty years later, the still more famous 'Brazilian school', which flourished from the 1940s to the mid-1960s.

Some twentieth-century Latin American architects can be placed at the highest international level: for example, the best of the Mexicans, Luis Barragán and Pedro Ramírez Vázquez; the Cuban Fernando Salinas; the Colombians Rogelio Salmona and Germán Samper; the Venezuelan Carlos Raúl Villanueva; the Argentines Jorge Ferrari Hardoy, Juan Kurchan, Clorindo Testa; the Uruguayans Julio Vilamajó and Mario Payssé Reyes; to say nothing of the veritable legion of great Brazilian architects (and urban planners) of the 'golden age': Lúcio Costa, Oscar Niemeyer, Affonso Reidy, Sérgio Bernardes and João Vilanova Artigas. Many of the above are distinguished enough to confer on Latin America a good place in the history of modern world architecture. It is true that some others, the most famous being the Cuban Ricardo Porro, the Chilean Emilio Duhart, the Uruguayan Carlos Ott, the Argentines César Pelli and Emilio Ambasz, have lived and practiced abroad, which is a way of reminding us that chronic political and economic crises do not favour budding architectural talents and that they, like delicate plants, can only flower fully when they can benefit from the opportunities to be found in the highly developed countries.

9

ART, *c.* 1920–*c.* 1980*

INTRODUCTION

Beginning in the 1870s Latin American art was gradually transformed by a dual phenomenon. On the one hand, increasing numbers of European (especially French, Italian and Spanish) teachers of drawing, painting and sculpture – some recruited, others simply on a 'cultural adventure' – arrived in the New World. At the same time increasing numbers of young Latin American artists, with scholarships or prizes if they did not have private resources, departed for Europe to pursue their studies in Paris, Florence, Rome, Madrid or some other centre of Western European art. Most Latin Americans returned to their own countries, either to teach or, commissioned by the government, to depict images of national heroes in bronze or on canvas, immortalizing the principal events of independence in large-scale works of art. Simultaneously, however, monumental change – in part a struggle against the inertia of the academies – was taking place in the art world in a number of different European cities: principally in Paris, but also in Vienna, Amsterdam, Berlin and Moscow. It was not for the avant-garde artists of Europe at first simply a question of subject matter, but something more immediate: the treatment of sunlight, the use of colour, as well as the validity of everyday themes which were considered pedestrian by the academies. In other cases, the driving force behind the new painting was the reinterpretation of the artists' own landscape or the assimilation of non-Occidental forms of art. In a word, the flight from the classical canons, a flight to which photography partly contributed, opened a door to other ways of perceiving and interpreting reality. And what happened was not confined to the limits of a few cities within national or

*A preliminary draft of this chapter was translated from the Spanish by Elizabeth Ladd. The chapter was substantially revised by the Editor. Sadly, the author died during the final stages of the editing.

continental boundaries. The most 'advanced' European art movements crossed the Atlantic and reached first the United States and then Latin America, albeit after a delay produced by the physical and psychological distance separating the two continents. Thus, Latin American artists were gradually exposed to naturalism, impressionism, post-impressionism and symbolism. But if the first exhibition of Impressionism dates from 1874, the Argentine and Mexican Impressionists – to cite only two examples – do not begin to express themselves in this style until twenty-five or thirty years later. Eventually, the delays in Latin America's reception of, and response to, the vanguard in art became shorter. In the case of Cubism and Fauvism, for example, there was a lag of only ten or fifteen years. And after the Second World War, thanks to modern media of diffusion, art, including Latin American art, became universal.

We do not find any extraordinary figures among Latin American painters and sculptors of the late nineteenth century as we do in literature (for example, the Nicaraguan poet Rubén Darío), but a considerable number of artists of the period deserve to be remembered. Thus, for instance, in the heroic genre of historic evocation, the Venezuelans Martín Tovar y Tovar and Arturo Michelena and, above all, the Uruguayan Juan Manuel Blanes were outstanding, as were the Colombians Epifanio Garay and Ricardo Acevedo Bernal, the Argentine Eduardo Sívori and the Catalan artist who practised in Mexico, Pelegrín Clavé, in the field of portraiture. At this time Latin American art was practically unaware of the continent's indigenous people; only the Mexican painter Juan Cordero dared to represent a few of his classmates with their own characteristic racial features. Other compatriots of his, such as José Jara, took advantage of historical themes to present a realistic version of the Indians, while the Peruvian Francisco Laso and the Brazilian Rodolfo Amoêdo idealized indigenous types in a semi-academic compromise.

Among notable artists painting in the style which might be called native *costumbrismo*, Teófilo Castillo, who was inspired by Ricardo Palma's *Tradiciones peruanas*, and the Brazilian José Ferraz de Almeida Junior, who was more faithful to the social reality that surrounded him, which he did not attempt to improve, are worthy of attention. In landscape painting a variety of painters fom all latitudes distinguished themselves: the Argentine Prilidano Pueyrredón depicted like no one else the vast transparent dome of sky that dominates the *pampa;* the Romantic Ecuadorian Joaquín Pinto did lyrical interpretations of the mountains of his land; and, in an opposing style, we have the Mexican José María Velasco, the 'scientific' observer who transcribed the landscape of his country, with its climate and its unmistakable geology and flora.

The female nude was practically a prohibited genre in respectable houses at that time, but nevertheless several artists dared to treat it, including the Brazilian Eliseu Visconti and – in a still more realistic manner – the Chilean Alfredo Valenzuela Puelma. On the other hand, *intimistas* were well received by a bourgeois society that liked to see its own world and faces reflected in realistic paintings. Good practitioners of this style were Cristóbal Rojas, a very sensitive Venezuelan who died young; the Argentine Severo Rodríguez Etchart, little known even in his own country; and the talented Chilean Juan Francisco González, a refined colourist. In social painting, which the Argentines later seemed to ignore, we nevertheless find two notable Argentine examples: Pío Collivadino and the eclectic and less literal Ernesto de la Cárcova, the author of *Sin pan y sin trabajo* ('No bread and no work'), a genuine political painting. Another Argentine Martín Malharro was an impressionist, although a latecomer, who interpreted the local landscape in somewhat romantic terms. We should mention, too, a contradictory Puerto Rican painter, Francisco Oller, who was alternatively a naturalist with little imagination and the best impressionist ever born in Latin America. In Paris he made friends with Pissarro and Cézanne and, under their influence, returned to his island to evoke the crude but beautiful light in the tropics as no one else has done.

In Latin America – as in the rest of the world – it has always been more difficult to find good sculptors than good painters, especially if we mention only the names of those who reached a truly high level of artistry. At the end of the nineteenth century, within the tradition of the heroic nude – especially the male nude – we have the Mexican Manuel Vilar, and if we look for a more modern expression we find his compatriot Miguel Noreña, who created the classic *Cuauhtémoc* on the Paseo de la Reforma in Mexico City. The Chilean Virginio Arias astonishes us even today with the pathos of his group *El Descendimiento* ('The Descent'). More along the lines of Carpeaux, Rodolfo Bernardelli, a Brazilian born in Mexico of European parents, became in his country the representative of a 'pictorial' type of sculpture which was dynamic and sensitive. Finally, the Argentine Francisco Cafferata, who would have become the greatest naturalist sculptor in his native land if he had not died so young, deserves mention.

We now turn to Latin American art in the twentieth century and especially in the period from the crucial decade of the 1920s to the 1970s and
1980s. The subject will be treated chronologically, country by country.

MEXICO

At the beginning of the twentieth century, there was only a handful of
important painters in Mexico. One, Joaquín Clausell (1866–1935), who
was a lawyer by profession, decided to paint in the impressionist style
after a brief sojourn in Europe and became its best representative in
Mexico throughout his long career as a painter. Clausell was above all a
great landscape artist who travelled tirelessly throughout his country and
was appointed director of the Ixtacalco School of Outdoor Painting.

In contrast to this objective painter, a faithful interpreter of nature,
Julio Ruelas (1870–1907), who was a subjective artist, lived a short but
intense life and 'burned himself out' with his iconoclastic and mysogynist
violence. He studied first in Mexico and later in Karlsruhe, Germany
with the master painter Mayerbeer. Ruelas distinguished himself more as
an illustrator for the *Revista Moderna,* founded in 1898 by a group of
intellectuals who considered themselves to be in the vanguard, than as a
painter. He is remembered above all for a splendid print, *La Crítica,* done
using the technique of etching which he had learned in Paris a few years
before his premature death.

Saturnino Herrán (1887–1918), who was twenty years younger than
Clausell and lived an even shorter life than Ruelas, was perhaps exaggerat-
edly glorified by the critics of his time but must be considered an indispensable element within the Mexican national conscience. What Clausell
did with landscape, Herrán tried to do with ethnic types and their
respective regional costumes. His *Tehuana* (1914) is a classic of Latin
American painting and, in spirit corresponds to what some artists like
Zuloaga had achieved in Spain, although Herrán always realized his work
in a lighter and more optimistic vein. Born in the same year as Herrán,
Roberto Montenegro (1887–1968), by contrast, enjoyed a very long life.
He studied in Paris from 1906 to 1919, but when he returned to his
native country he kept in mind the 'naive' artists, especially those who
had painted ex-votos. In this sense a meeting took place within him
between a cultivated and a popular orientation that contributed to the
Mexican artistic maturity. He painted at the easel; he did frescoes; he was

a printmaker; and he even wrote an important book on the art of Mexico in the nineteenth century: *Pintura mexicana, 1800–1860* (1933).

One figure who cannot be linked to any other because he played the role of a true precursor of mural painting was Gerardo Murillo (1875–1964), who called himself Dr Atl, the name by which he is best known. Atl was a man of action; in his youth he went to Italy and France, becoming involved with the Anarchist and Marxist movements, at the same time associating with the artistic avant-garde in Paris. A restless innovative painter he invented several 'dry' colours (the 'atl-colours'). With these he painted his views of volcanoes – the principal theme of his art, which he developed throughout his life. This did not prevent him from being, at the same time, an excellent portrait painter. His extreme nationalist attitude counted more than anything else in facilitating the advent of the muralist movement. By 1910, supported by a group of young people – which included José Clemente Orozco – he organized a successful dissident and revolutionary exhibition.

While Dr Atl was one of the cultivated forerunners, we also find popular antecedents of muralism. It should be remembered, first of all, that in nineteenth-century Mexico there had always been a tradition of naive mural painting, on the walls of, for example, the *pulquerías* – usually executed by anonymous artists. Secondly, there was also a line of popular graphic artists, like Gabriel Gahona (1828–99) or, much more important, José Guadalupe Posada (1851–1913). The case of Posada is extraordinary because working for newspapers, without any formal training, he became the 'natural illustrator' of the reality of his era. Most of his prints – generally woodcuts but sometimes metal engravings – reveal a formidable intuitiveness. A picturesque character, he worked in view of the public in his tiny studio in the centre of Mexico City. For artists like Rivera and Orozco, for example, his style represented an example of how to reach the public without being vulgar or condescending.

The topic of Mexican muralism must be approached as what it unquestionably is: the Latin American art movement that had the greatest repercussions on the continent as a whole and on the rest of the world in the course of the twentieth century. It will be discussed below by examining the work of its most famous figures, the artists traditionally labelled the 'big three': José Clemente Orozco, Diego Rivera and David Alfaro Siqueiros.

Today it seems relatively easy to discern the various causes that would explain the success of this true 'school', so different in its means and objectives from all the other great modern art movements of this century. From the outset we must realize that in the historical process – in any place or time – if a group of artists appears and behaves as a true 'generation', the effect on public opinion is much greater than if each of those same artists had tried individually to follow his own path. Furthermore, if the idea that motivates this group is simple and easy to grasp, better still: one can then say that the 'message' will be transmitted, and through it the contact between artist, work of art, and at least a portion of the public will be established to some extent. Finally, one indispensable element must be added: the work of art must possess positive values without which the message would not be captured – and these must be not only artistic values but also social and even ideological.

Mural art, when it reached its full expression, exhibited all those characteristics we have just listed as necessary for success and recognition, although it must be admitted that this recognition was somewhat relative. It certainly existed at the international level, but not in Mexico itself. The mass of the Mexican people were unable to decipher these painted murals, although the utopian aim of their creators was to 'reach the people' in order to contribute to their civic education. Today, of course, the situation looks totally different: mural art is accepted as 'historic' with as noble a pedigree as pre-Columbian or colonial art.

Leaving aside questions of quality and quantity, it is interesting to compare the Mexican with the Cuban case. After their Revolution the Cubans literally 'papered over' the island with posters, both normal-sized and monumental. Perhaps they had learned a lesson of Mexico: when they saw that 'the public did not go to the images', they turned things inside out and decided that 'the images would come to the people'. Between the two revolutions, that is between 1930 and 1960, what Mexican mural art represented from the aesthetic, social and political point of view – and it was certainly much better than the social realism of the Soviet Union – was quickly grasped and often badly imitated by a number of Latin American painters who, confronted with similar problems of expression, wished to convey a message which, if not revolutionary, was at least rebellious.

In describing the unique phenomenon of Mexican mural art in detail, it must be made clear from the outset that we are talking about the idea of a single intellectual and not an initial impulse by one or more painters. This intellectual was José Vasconcelos, who, on being appointed Secretary of Education in 1921, invited a series of young artists to execute huge mural compositions for several public buildings. And the truth is that Vasconcelos himself did not have very clear ideas about how to reach the objectives he had outlined. We might add that two of the future 'greats' – Rivera and Orozco – erred in their first efforts when they were unable to liberate themselves from the nineteenth-century notion of 'allegory' that was linked to monumental-scale painting. It was, instead, painters who were later considered less important, like the Frenchman Jean Charlot (1898–1979) and the Mexican Ramón Alva de la Canal (1898–1981), who best understood the importance of the themes that should be addressed: popular themes, with concrete references to familiar events, portrayed without falling into the misty symbolism with which Rivera and Orozco began their work on the walls of the Escuela Preparatorio in Mexico City.

Good mural art would be, by definition, revolutionary and Marxist, nationalist and indigenous. In this art, in rather Manichean fashion, the forces of good (those just mentioned) confront the forces of evil, represented by Spain, Catholicism, the *conquistadores* and, in modern times, capitalism. This is the ideological line followed by Rivera and Siqueiros; we will see that Orozco seems to have been more relaxed, treating these themes in a more general manner and with a greater power of synthesis that augmented the impact of his work.

Diego Rivera (1886–1957) was born in Guanajuato into a middle-class family and went to Mexico City as a young boy to study at the Academy of San Carlos. The precocious career he had undertaken later took him to Spain – on a scholarship – in 1907, where he studied with the painter Chicharro, a *costumbrista* of colourful brilliance. Beginning in 1908–9 Rivera tried his luck in Paris, where he associated with vanguard artists like Picasso and Braque, who were in the full swing of Cubism, a style Rivera imitated successfully. When he returned to Mexico in 1921, he accepted Vasconcelos' offer and, after a few tentative first efforts, began to decorate the Ministry of Education building (1923–8). From this moment he discovered his own language, which he would develop, if unevenly, for the rest of his life. Among Rivera's most famous murals are the ones located at the National School of Agriculture in Chapingo (1923–7) and at the National Palace in Mexico City (1929–35 and 1944–51). He also painted, with various degrees of success, murals in Detroit, New York and San Francisco. At the same time, Rivera always led a double career as a muralist and an easel painter (specializing in portraits).

José Clemente Orozco (1883–1949) was born in the state of Jalisco, but went to the capital as a child. As a young man he began to study at the School of Agriculture, where he unfortunately suffered an accident that left him with a maimed left arm for the rest of his life. Then he studied at San Carlos with Dr Atl, following the vanguardist movements in his teacher's footsteps. When his father died, Orozco had to earn a living as an architectural delineator and as a caricaturist, so that when he came to paint his first murals at the Preparatory School he sometimes approached the work with a markedly ironic intent, although he would soon realize that this was not appropriate. From 1927 to 1934 he had to live in exile in the United States, where he left several murals: for example Pomona College in California; the New School for Social Research, New York; and especially Dartmouth College, New Hampshire. When he returned to Mexico he did some of his best work, such as the murals that decorate the stairway of the Government Palace (1937) and the vault and cupola of the Hospicio Cabañas (1939), both in Guadalajara.

David Alfaro Siqueiros (1896–1974) might have become a great artist had he led a different life, but spent a third of his agitated life in jail, travelled extensively, took part in the Spanish Civil War, and was militant all his life on behalf of the extreme leftist ideas he always held. Nevertheless, his style was daring, such as, for example, the use of very exaggerated perspective and foreshortening that add drama to the themes presented. He was also innovative in technique, spraying industrial colours and using a new paint (pyroxiline) spread directly onto stone panels. Perhaps Siqueiros's best work, apart from some spectacular easel paintings, are the murals painted with a spraygun – *La Libertad, Cuauhtémoc* – which today occupy a place of honour in the Palace of Fine Arts in Mexico City. He painted large compositions in the Social Security Hospital and the Historical Museum in Chapultepec. He taught in the United States where he left at least one disciple who would become famous: Jackson Pollock, the inventor of drip painting.

Of course the 'big three' had numerous followers, to the point where it might be said that mural art held back the normal progress of painting in Mexico for many years. Among the most illustrious of these was Rufino Tamayo, scarcely younger than Siqueiros, whose career we will view in detail below. Others who should be mentioned are Juan O'Gorman, Alfredo Zalce, Pablo O'Higgins, Leopoldo Méndez, Jorge González Camarena, José Chaves Morado and Federico Cantú. Of these, perhaps Juan O'Gorman (1905–83) is the most interesting: an architect-muralist-painter of note, in association with other artists he not only planned the building for the Library of the National University in Mexico City, but also covered its cubical mass with a gigantic mosaic of coloured stones representing images inspired by pre-Columbian art.

This long and complex period of mural art – which by the middle of the century had become a real obstacle to the development of Mexican art – had major repercussions in the rest of Latin America. Cubans like Victor Manuel, Colombians like Pedro Nel Gómez, Ecuadoreans like Camilo Egas, Peruvians like José Sabogal, tried to imitate the formula and some even travelled to Mexico to learn it. In Argentina – through Siqueiros – there was a mural art movement whose best representative was Lino E. Spilimbergo. However, the Argentine who painted with a content that most paralleled Mexican mural art was Antonio Berni (1905–81), first through his large rectangular oil paintings and later through collages on a colossal scale, in which he used the cast-offs of the undiscriminating consumer society. Finally, from the point of view of absolute transcendence, the Brazilian Cândido Portinari (see below) was the one artist who could be compared in greatness to his Mexican predecessors; his strong celebratory compositions neither belittled historic themes nor themes of daily life. Thus, although some of the names mentioned here will appear again below, it should be made clear that when mural art is discussed in Latin America – praised or criticized, as is always the case with important movements – the reference is not to one country only nor one specific historical moment, but in a much more general way to a school that would forever transform the notion of Latin American art. In other words, it became one of the principal vehicles for that obsessive concern with *identity* – a concept that seems to make Latin Americans so anxious.

Leaving the world of mural art, the two most important creators who were contemporary with the movement were without doubt the Guatemalan Carlos Mérida, to whom we will refer later, and Francisco Goitia (1882–1960). Originally from Zacatecas, Goitia studied in Europe for eight years, first in Spain and then in Italy. When he returned to his own country it was to occupy himself first and foremost with archaeological and ethnographic questions. Thus a great artist was lost, and an original one within the context in which he lived and worked. As a painter, Goitia represents a violent expressionism, more direct but less 'committed' politically and socially than that of the muralists. His *Tata Jesucristo* (1927), for example, is a small masterpiece.

Four other interesting names from this period of Mexican art history are Castellanos, Agustín Lazo, Meza and Michel. Julio Castellanos (1905–47) was always under the influence of post-muralism, even when he did easel painting. His figures seem deformed, whether in pain or violent joy, reacting in the style of the humble folk who inspired them. Agustín Lazo (b.1910) belongs to another breed of artists. A cultivated man whose friends were writers, Lazo translated Goldoni and Pirandello and even designed the sets for their plays when they were staged. Guillermo Meza (b.1917), on the other hand, was a master of the nude who continued, to some extent, the line of the muralists, but he was more of a naturalist and less grandiloquent than they. Finally, Alfonso Michel (1898–1957) was a very fine 'chamber painter' who lived in Europe from 1923 to 1930, and only dedicated himself exclusively to painting during the last ten or eleven years of his life.

The impression has been given – perhaps exaggerated – that between 1920 and 1950 everything that happened in Mexican art came under the rubric of muralism. But there also existed dissident or simply naive artists who continued to express themselves as they could and as they wished. One of them – who has been newly appreciated in recent years – was Antonio Ruiz 'El Corzo' (1897–1964), author of the unforgettable *Sueño de Malinche* (1939) in which he realizes an ingenious syncretism between woman and landscape, united with deliberate symbolic meaning. An equally important figure is Maria Izquierdo (1906–55), who is not simply one more 'naive painter', but someone who tried to practice an art that was not academic in any way, a kind of painting which, precisely because of its total freedom, seems surprisingly modern today.

Along similar lines, but expressed with much more violence, is the art of Frida Kahlo (1907–54), who in spite of having been Diego Rivera's wife for many years, did not adopt a single aspect of the master's style. A brilliant, intuitive painter, she shows herself under two very distinct and perhaps complementary aspects. In some small 'autobiographical' canvases about her unhappy life – which she spent either in bed or in a wheelchair because of an accident – she does not surpass the mediocre quality of the ex-votos; by contrast, her portraits are admirable, especially the self-portraits, like the so-called *Las Dos Fridas* (1939), clearly her masterpiece.

The next escape from the dictatorship of muralism was achieved by a series of immigrant foreign artists. As a result of the Second World War, several surrealists came to Mexico, a place they saw as – in their own words – a providential country. We will begin with the most important, the Austrian-born Wolfgang Paalen (1905–59), whose international career was already quite advanced before he came to Mexico in 1939. Years later he founded the magazine *Dyn* (1942–4), of which only six numbers were issued. Paalen's mind-set was like that of the early Dalí or, even better, Yves Tanguy. In his best pictures he demonstrates a great power of evocation inspired by nature. A Spaniard, Remedios Varo (1900–63), and an Englishwoman, Leonora Carrington (b.1917), are painters of literary 'obedience'. Varo departs from an invented story which she 'dresses' in a concrete manner: elongated characters disporting themselves in a world of transparent objects. Carrington lets her uncontrollable imagination soar, painting beings who perform hard-to-comprehend actions. Both have a good sense of mystery and display a delicate and intriguing colour scheme.

Although because of his age and importance Rufino Tamayo (1899–1991) might have appeared earlier in this history, this is the best place to discuss him. On the one hand, he was a contemporary of the muralists – whom he survived by many years – and on the other he was already a modern painter who possessed all the boldness of the best universal painting of his time, integrating it into a decidedly Mexican figurative and chromatic scheme, without ever falling into the merely folkloric. It is true that Tamayo, in the beginning, also practised murals and painted in the traditional manner, at a time when as a young artist he could not refuse to do so. These paintings are, however, excellent, and bear his already unmistakable personal stamp. Above all, Tamayo was, more than anything else, an easel painter, as he himself realized early in his career. When he agreed to execute enormous mural paintings, he knew that he would do them with the same technique he always used, that is, by painting on canvas which was later attached to the wall in question. Tamayo's strange world consists of a very personal distortion in which the synthesized figures move across backgrounds of very strong or very pale colours – depending on the situation. The 'skin' of his painting is never totally smooth; it was rather granular and opaque.

It seems appropriate here to turn to Pedro Coronel (1923–85) who, without imitating Tamayo, was unable to avoid belonging to his tradition. Coronel was one of the few 'lyrical' abstract painters in Mexico who preferred pure form to figurative painting, always producing forms with well-defined contours, using ample quantities of paint and generally very 'thick', intense colours. Another 'outsider' who deserves mention is Juan Soriano (b.1920) of Guadalajara, who, like Pedro Coronel, belongs to the strange family of improvisers. Unbelievably precocious, this intelligent and lucid man is simultaneously a supreme craftsman. If he paints in an unpredictable manner it is not to surprise, but because he has so many resources to draw on that he himself does not know what he is going to conjure up on every occasion. Soriano's dominant characteristic is, after all, a certain way of seeing the world in which elements of reality mix with a strong dose of popular Mexican art, including its macabre connotations. He has often approached – successfully – abstraction, only to return immediately to his beloved figurative art.

As an introduction to geometric abstract art, we have waited until now to present a precursor like Carlos Mérida (1891–1984), who was born in Guatemala but from the thirties lived and worked in Mexico during the full flowering of mural art, in a way setting himself against this trend. Mérida's style has two roots: on the one hand his work may be read in a surrealistic key, but his main enthusiasm has been to 'geometrize' a coloured reality: characters, costumes, dances of his Guatemalan homeland. He returned there several times to carry out commissions for large semi-figurative mosaics, although he considered himself basically an easel painter.

If present-day Mexican painting is divided by generations, that of Tamayo and Mérida is followed by that of Coronel, Soriano and Gerzso. We have already discussed the first two. Gunther Gerzso (b.1915), for a long time a set designer for stage and screen, also dedicated himself actively to painting after the surrealists came to Mexico. He himself seems to have begun with this style, although his later work would scarcely lead one to suspect it. Fortunately, he stopped being an orthodox surrealist – with all its literary connotations – to become a pioneer in a kind of geometric painting in which several other very talented painters, whom we will analyse later, were to follow. Gerzso's painting always shows the obvious presence of different planes that are superimposed on one another, creating real depth. Each of these 'walls' – as they might be called – displays its own colour and its own material, and this gives his paintings, which take a long time to complete, a nobility of style which is not common in this period.

One of the most original and well-rounded Mexican artists is Manuel Felguérez (b.1928). He was born in Zacatecas and, after studying in Mexico City, spent some time in Paris working under the sculptor Ossip Zadkine. Felguérez was – with Lilia Carrillo – one of the few Mexicans who successfully practised 'informalism', a style of abstract art that exalted the materials his works were made of, whether in painting or sculpture – that is, its texture. Later he developed towards more purely geometric bases, two-dimensional or three-dimensional, where colour and surface still retain their importance. In the 1980s his work became more rigid and systematic – even to the point of working with computers – although he then returned to the search for effects of colour and materials, avoiding the smooth, homogeneous, brilliant surfaces that fascinated him for a time.

Although there are other examples of abstract artists in Mexico, Vincente Rojo (b.1932), one of the painters who had the most influence on the favourable reception of this type of art, especially in the field of graphic design, merits special attention. Born in Spain, he came to Mexico at the age of sixteen, where he has worked for nearly his whole career. This secretive man seems to feel comfortable when he organizes his work as the development of a series dictated by intuition. Each of these series confronts an artistic problem to which he tries to find a compound solution. Thus we have seen *Señales, Negaciones, Recuerdos* and, finally, in the 1980s a series entitled *Mexico bajo la lluvia.*

Figurative art did not lose its validity in Mexico during the 1960s, but, as in the rest of Latin America, in order to survive it had to focus on what we have elsewhere called 'critical figuration.' That is, the figure is treated in a negative, cruel manner – a desecration. This manner of returning to the world of objects and, primarily, to the world of people with their bodies and their faces, might be expressed through satire or inoffensive irony. Among the satirists, we must first mention Alberto Gironella (b.1929), who seemed to be leaning towards the study of literature when, beginning in 1958–60 with his 'variations' on the Niño de Vallecas and Queen Mariana of Austria – glorified by Velázquez – he began to express himself through painting. He was successful with this, and on trips to Europe he was received enthusiastically by the surrealist group, one of whom, Edouard Jaguer, became his sponsor. Gironella – a great craftsman and painter – was not content with these forms of expression. He also made huge collages, which are really 'assemblages', collections of heterogeneous objects which he seasons with acid pictorial commentaries, a sort of derisive, mocking monument.

Along similar lines, though less aggressive, we find two foreign artists who nevertheless made their careers in Mexico: Roger Von Gunten (b.1933), a Swiss, and Brian Nissen (b. 1939), an Englishman. The first, more attached to visible reality, transforms it through what we might call a 'joyful expressionism' that uses a beautiful palette dominated by the blues and greens of the countryside in which he lives, far from the large cities. Nissen's trajectory, on the other hand, is obviously related to English pop art of the sixties. Nevertheless, once in contact with the complex Mexican world, he evolved toward a delicate art, halfway between pure painting and three-dimensional creation.

The best known native Mexican of this generation is undoubtedly Francisco Toledo (b.1940), born in Juchitán, Oaxaca, to which he always returns, after prolonged stays in New York or Paris. This polymorphic artist is a talented painter, printmaker, ceramist and weaver. His expression seems to consist in a "return to the source' and his works are based on recapturing prehistoric caves where ancestral signs combine – the supreme irony – with the day-to-day instruments of our machine-age culture. The drawing is tense and precise in the prints, but in the paintings the sandy material with which he works obviates any possible rigidity. The opaque colours are always orientated towards a dominant hue (blue, ochre, red) which confers unity on each work. Another figure who deserves special mention is José Luis Cuevas (b.1933). A great draughtsman and graphic artist, he must today be placed beside the best contemporary painters of his country; he is unique and indispensable to current Mexican art.

In the 1970s a curious phenomenon occurred in Mexican art – equivalent to what we might call a 'lost generation'. There seems to have been few original artists born between 1940 and 1950, who would have been expected to reach maturity twenty-five or thirty years later. This vacuum was filled – precariously – by a few outbreaks of what was then considered the 'vanguard'. However, compared with the enthusiasm with which these manifestations (which we will summarize under the generic name of 'conceptual art') were practised in Argentina, Brazil and later Colombia, Mexican developments were relatively poor. Perhaps more interesting were the manifestations of 'street art', which deliberately mixed musical and literary elements with the plastic arts. All these phenomena had a political-social protest character, developing in a climate similar to that of the old 'happenings' of the fifties.

On the other hand, with the advent of the eighties, Mexico witnessed extraordinary renewal in the field of the visual arts. Painters, sculptors, draughtsmen and printmakers proliferated. New, fairly independent artists appeared, some of whom had begun to work during the 'conceptual' era. One of the most brilliant is the painter-sculptor Gabriel Macotela, whose ideas are interesting because although they reflect earlier experiences of other artists (Tamayo, Toledo) they appear interpreted in an original way and in a context other than abstraction. Also worthy of attention are painters such as the four Castro Ieñero brothers – each one with his specific individuality – Santiago Rebolledo and a few others. It is no longer possible to divide them into abstract and figurative categories, as we might have done twenty years ago. They already belong to a world which is eclectic by definition: novelty resides in the formula which each one finds to express himself.

Since colonial times, sculpture has been traditionally less important in Mexico than painting. Nevertheless, at the end of the nineteenth century a few competent, if not great, artists appeared; for example, Miguel Noreña (1843–94), who was trained in Europe and who, on his return, received several important commissions: the Monument to Hidalgo in Dolores; the Monument to Father Llanos in Orizaba; and the work that made him famous, the noble figure of Cuauhtémoc which stands in a plaza on the Paseo de la Reforma in Mexico City. At the beginning of the twentieth century the architect Antonio Rivas Mercado, collaborating with the Italian sculptor Enrique Alciati, raised the column of the Monument to Independence (1902–16) on the same broad avenue that leads to the Chapultepec woods.

True modernity made its appearance with a sculptor such as Guillermo Ruiz (1896–1964), who in 1934 raised a colossal statue of Morelos on the island of Janitzio in the middle of Lake Pátzcuaro. The work, forty metres high, is basically made of reinforced concrete covered with stone blocks which were cut to size after they were put in place. The enormous stylized figure lifts its right arm to the sky while the left grasps the hilt of the sword of justice. Two contemporaries of Ruiz were Ignacio Asúnsolo (1890–1965) and Oliverio Martínez (1901–38). They helped to fill the need apparently felt by every new country to cover itself with congratulatory monuments. Asúnsolo created the Monument to the Fatherland (1924) and Martinez, who died young, designed the powerful figures that decorate the outside of the dome of the Monument to the Revolution (1933). Luis Ortiz Monasterio (b.1906) chose also the stylized tendency of large masses and scarce details in the Monument to Motherhood in the Federal District, which can be compared to the statue of the same theme by Asúnsolo erected in Monterrey. Seldom do we find busts or heads among so much more or less allegorical monumental production. But those of the composer Silvestre Revueltas by Carlos Bracho and of the painter Francisco Goitia by his friend Asúnsolo deserve mention.

The fact that between 1900 and 1930 not many quality sculptors were born in Mexico may explain in part the influence of foreign artists who were ready to fill the need for three-dimensional expression, whether figurative or abstract. Several of these became famous. Preeminent was Francisco Zúñiga (b.1914), who was born in Costa Rica but spent practically his whole life in Mexico. Zúñiga was, without a doubt, the most popular figurative sculptor in spite of the sameness of his theme: the Indian woman, fullbodied and either nude or clothed only in her *huipil,* a kind of sleeveless blouse. At the opposite pole from Zúñiga we find another foreigner: Mathias Goeritz (b.1915), a German refugee with a degree in philosophy who, after fleeing the Nazi regime, came to Mexico in 1949. Goeritz alone would change the face of sculpture in his adopted country, by trying to recapture – through his intransigent abstract sculptures – the greatness and solemnity of ancient pre-Columbian art. Needless to say the architects saw him as an indispensable collaborator. Luis Barragán planned with the then young Goeritz the Towers of Satellite City (1957), one of the fundamental features of modern Mexico City. In spite of the fact that he had been internationally known for many years, Goeritz still produced new work, above all in the collective enterprise called Espacio Escultórico ('Sculpture Space') in Mexico City.

Another influential non-Mexican sculptor was Rodrigo Arenas Betancur (b.1921); born in Colombia, he went to Mexico to study in 1944, and has remained there ever since. Although in his native country he had the opportunity to execute a gigantic equestrian statue of Bolívar – whom he represented nude – perhaps his most popular creation is his vertical image of Prometheus (1951) in Mexico's University City. Finally, the Frenchman Olivier Séguin worked with success for several years in Mexico before returning permanently to his own country. To him is owed several large abstract sculptures in public places, especially in Guadalajara, which have certainly contributed to the diffusion of this form of non-figurative art.

Again in the abstract tradition two Mexican women sculptors of comparable talent, although their formal characteristics are opposed, are outstanding: Angela Gurría and Helen Escobedo. Gurría's work always seems like a memory of things seen, that is, her works are of 'biomorphic' inspiration; Escobedo, on the other hand, is a stubborn practitioner of the hard geometric line, with which she often achieves great artistic purity. Of the same generation there is another notable painter-sculptor worthy of mention: Federico Silva (b.1923), who worked first in Siqueiros' team, and later became completely independent. Today he is one of the best abstract sculptors on the continent, whose works, although reaching sometimes considerable size, show a subtle and balanced 'skeleton', as for example with a piece suspended above the central hall of the National Library. Fernando González Gortázar (b.1942) is an architect-sculptor who was born in Mexico City, but at the age of four moved to Guadalajara, where he still resides. In his double role as architect and sculptor he follows the tradition set in motion by the great landscape architect Luis Barragán. Gortázar is also fond of pure geometric form, which he plays with on every scale and with different materials, combining them frequently with water in motion to create fountains of great originality.

Goeritz, Escobedo and Silva all took part in the design and execution of the abovementioned Sculpture Space in Mexico City. On the campus of the Autonomous National University of Mexico (UNAM), a vast field of black lava, untouched by human hands since the creation of the world, was set aside. The intent was to erect several sculptural works there. After serious reflection, the artists concerned decided to leave the land intact, barely accenting it with a circle 120 metres in diameter formed of natural elements. The sculptures themselves were installed outside the lava field and represent some of the best examples of abstract sculpture on the continent.

CUBA

In Cuba which declared itself an independent country only in 1902 art – like culture in general – had been strongly marked by Spanish colonial rule. Even after the change in Cuba's political status the academies continued to dispense the same antiquated, conventional teachings. The most distinguished artists of the beginning of the twentieth century were Armando Menocal (1861–1942) and Leopoldo Romañach (1862–1951). Menocal, who had been a classmate of the great Spanish painter Sorolla, decorated the Presidential Palace in Havana, although his *forte* lay in the field of portrait painting. He stands out for having used a more brilliant palette than that of his immediate Cuban predecessors. Romañach, on balance, much the better painter, was also trained in the Spanish and Italian painting tradition, although he had occasion to visit Paris. In spite of this, he did not have any contact with impressionist or post-impressionist innovations, but only with the academic art of his time.

When Romañach returned from Europe, he was appointed professor of 'colouring' at the Academy of San Alejandro and around 1920 his pupils included, among others, Victor Manuel, Eduardo Abela, Fidelio Ponce de León and Amelia Peláez, which is to say, those who would be the best representatives of vanguard Cuban painting in the next thirty years. Little by little, these students lost interest in the obsessive 'chiaroscuro' that seemed to be Romañach's principal preoccupation as a teacher. The magazines and the reproductions of the great painting of the end of the nineteenth and the beginning of the twentieth centuries were now coming freely into Cuba and naturally the younger painters wanted to follow these new paths.

In 1924 Victor Manuel (1897–1969) rebelled against official teaching and took as a model Mexican muralism. In the same year Amelia Peláez (1897–1968), who had studied at the Art Students' League, had an exhibit in New York, where she had gone for training after spending several years at the Grande Chaumière, a private academy in Paris which was very popular among Latin Americans. In 1926 the Hispano-Cuban Institute of Culture was created to organize the more advanced exhibitions. A year later the poet Jorge Mañach began to publish the *Revista de Avance.* In 1929 the Lyceum was organized and, almost simultaneously, the Plastic Arts Foundation. It should be mentioned that the Communist Party and the José Martí Popular University were also founded in Cuba during the 1920s. Artists who considered themselves avant-garde identified with these popular struggles and their artistic creed followed the same path. This situation was demonstrated when Eduardo Abela (?–1966) exhibited his painting *Guajiros* (1928), which revealed the direct influence of Diego Rivera. In its violent colour, its search for a certain naivete, the use of national themes and figures, it introduces the deliberate line that avant-garde Cuban art was to take in this period. Later, the Estudio Libre de Pintura y Escultura, directed by Abela himself, would employ two young teachers about whom we will say more later: René Portocarrero and Mariano Rodríguez (who signed his name simply Mariano).

The Cuban painter Wifredo Lam (1902–82) is customarily regarded – along with Rufino Tamayo, the Mexican, and Roberto Matta, the Chilean – as one of a triumvirate of great Latin Americans all born around the turn of the century. Lam, who was of mixed Chinese and African background, after the obligatory presence at San Alejandro, went to Madrid where he pursued more or less conventional studies, and by the time he was twenty-six he had already exhibited in the Spanish capital. His fate, however, was determined on a trip he made to Paris where he had the opportunity to meet Picasso, with whom he formed a friendship that would last the rest of his life.

It seems odd today that Picasso, in Paris, would be the one to introduce Lam to black African art, a revelation that would definitively change the young Cuban's art. It was also providential that he met André Breton and the French painter André Masson in 1940 when the three of them sailed on the same ship from Marseilles to the Caribbean. The great 'popes' of surrealism accepted him on this historic crossing and from the moment Lam disembarked in Cuba one can say that his painting followed a sure path. The proof of this is his admirable painting entitled *La Jungla* (1941), which is perhaps his masterpiece and today hangs in the Museum of Modern Art in New York. However, while Lam may have found his racial and spiritual roots in his African forbears, this did not exhaust the possibilities of Cuban artistic expression. His contemporary Amelia Peláez, inspired by the coloured glass in tropical doors and windows, filled her canvases with a profusion of flowers, fruit, fish and everyday objects. She offered an optimistic, objective art, while Lam always followed the subjective, anguished path.

Fidelio Ponce de León (1896–1957), mentioned earlier, was an independent personality who having abandoned his art studies reappeared in the thirties. He is a kind of 'intuitive expressionist' who barely pays attention to drawing in order to concentrate on strong colours and thick paint. When he died the National Museum in Havana organized an exhibition (1958) of 115 of his paintings. Felipe Orlando (b. 1911), who through his irregular career went from figurative art to abstraction with a surrealist connotation which is very particular to him, emigrated permanently to Mexico in 1949. Mariano Rodríguez (1910–90) also had connections, although sporadic, with Mexico, since it was there that he was a disciple of the painter Manuel Rodríguez Lozano, who introduced him to the secrets of his trade. But while the master used neutral, somber colours, the disciple – when he began to find his own way – would be a man of a bright palette. His series of cocks and cockfights, figurative at first, became gradually almost abstract. This was his best period. A few years after, he regressed to a diluted figurative style loaded with confused political content, without achieving the direct effect of good 'propaganda' as represented, for example, by the best Mexican mural art. Another important Cuban painter was René Portocarrero (1912–85), who studied at the Academia Villate and later at San Alejandro. By 1945 he had exhibited in New York, and fifteen years

later the National Library in Havana organized a retrospective of his drawings and water colours. In 1966 he had a special gallery at the Venice
biennial and there he introduced a kind of *horror vacui,* the result of which is
that his canvasses are literally filled with signs presented frontally, all
worked in thick paint: a heavy 'static baroque'.

Cundo Bermudez (b.1914), who later emigrated to Puerto Rico, has
always been an inventor of strange themes linked to a kind of 'naive
surrealism'. Another voluntary exile is Mario Carreño (b.1913), who
visited Mexico, France, and Italy, lived in Spain for a few years and then
in New York for a time before settling permanently in Chile. His art has
'travelled' with him: starting as a figurative form of folkloric fantasy, it
became rigorously abstract and then returned to a cold and measured
representation. Another wanderer is Luis Martínez Pedro (b.1910), who
in 1932 moved to New Orleans. He participated, however, in the Exhibition of Cuban Contemporary Painting organized by the Casa de las Americas in 1960.

We must finally mention a few artists who have made their reputations in revolutionary Cuba. Some are exclusively painters, such as
Fayad Jamis (b.1930), a strange case of a poet-painter who studied at
San Alejandro and has exhibited in Europe at the Salon Réalités Nou-
velles (1956), the Paris Biennial (1959) and, above all, the Exhibition of
Cuban Painting in London (1967). Originally an abstract painter who
tended to use blots of dark colours, his work later derived – for better
or for worse – from what some writers call 'magic realism'. Other talented artists only practised easel painting sporadically, launched as they
were on a fundamental public mission, forming the official popular
graphics teams, in, for example, the Organization of External Support,
the Committee for Revolutionary Action, the Casa de las Americas, the
Union of Writers and Artists, and the Cinematographic Institute. In
spite of the fact that the works – posters or what they called 'vallas'
(enormous signs that might cover a whole building) – had to be anonymous, a few names always leaked out. Among the most distinguished
artists we must mention Raul Martínez (b.1927), who practised 'nationalist neo-primitivism', and Alfredo Rostgaard (b.1943), who created
some unforgettable poetic images.

In the same period, several fine Cuban painters for reasons of political
dissidence lived in exile, where they continued to produce art. Some of
the most famous include Emilio Sánchez, who lives in New York but who
tirelessly paints architectonic canvasses in which brightly coloured tropi-

cal houses are represented. Another talented Cuban, Agustín Fernández, works between New York and Puerto Rico. A painter whose art has nothing to do with the superficial image of a tropical country like Cuba. Fernández is a hyper-realist whose canvases are accumulations of metallic objects with reflections, all represented in solemn greys and blacks. Of the painters who live in Paris, two can be mentioned: Joaquín Ferrer and Jorge Camacho. Ferrer is one of the finest and most mysterious Latin American painters of all those who work in Europe. With perfect techniqúe, he draws angles and curves with ruler and compass, delimiting monochromatic areas, creating non-figurative paintings which nevertheless are fascinating to even the most demanding viewer. Camacho, a much younger man, shows the influence of the Chilean Roberto Matta and the Mexican Francisco Toledo, although his work is entirely original. Over neutral backgrounds – usually ochres – move strange half-human, half-animal forms, painted in iridescent and phosphorescent colours that make them even more dynamic.

As in the rest of Latin America, sculpture in Cuba is of lesser importance than painting. Juan José Sicre (1898–1974) is the most famous Cuban sculptor of his time. He began his studies in 1916 at the Academia Villate, and continued two years later at San Alejandro. Beginning with a scholarship in 1920, Sicre went to Madrid, Paris and Florence, remaining in Europe until 1927, when he returned to Cuba and was appointed to a teaching position at San Alejandro. His best known works are a statue of Victor Hugo (1936) in the El Vedado neighbourhood of Havana, a colossal head of heroic proportions representing José Martí (1939), and a series of portraits and contributions of a religious nature. Norberto Estopiñán (b.1920), born in Havana, where he later became Sicre's disciple at the Academy of San Alejandro, is also worthy of mention. He works in wrought iron or bronze, in a non-figurative style, inspired by primitive cultures. The best Cuban sculpture of this century, however, can be found in the work of one great figure: Agustín Cárdenas (b.1927), who was born in the Cuban providence of Matanzas, but who has lived and worked in Paris since 1955, achieving international fame. Cárdenas works directly on the most noble of materials: wood, stone and marble. He is also the type of artist usually characterized as having a 'biomorphic' inspiration. In his work masses always are defined by large twisting curves, melting into one another due to the great care with which he polishes the surfaces to make them gleam in the light.

DOMINICAN REPUBLIC AND HAITI

In the Dominican Republic it can be said that modern painting begins with Abelardo Rodríguez Urdaneta (1870–1932), an academic painter who did historical paintings and scenes of local colour. A breath of fresh air arrived later with the Spanish painter José Vela Zanetti (b.1913), who subsequently emigrated to Puerto Rico. Among local talents we should mention Jaime Colson (b.1904) and Darío Suro (b.1918), who studied first in his own country and later with Diego Rivera and Agustín Lazo in Mexico. Suro is probably the best known artist from the Dominican Republic, although he usually lives in the United States.

In the city of Santo Domingo in 1965 – motivated by the U.S. intervention – the combative and bold Frente Cultural was created. It brought together artists from different generations and artistic approaches, as is evident in an Exhibition-Competition held in November 1965 in the Palace of Fine Arts. Artists as different from one another as Silvano Lora and Ada Balcácer joined together to pose the question of art and the social function of the artist. Both still create art today in accordance with their traditional media: for example, Lora insists on political testimony; Balcácer uses myth and dreams to convey her message. A younger artist, Danilo de los Santos (Danicel) creates an obsessive female figure, Marola, who must be interpreted for her symbolic meaning. Another outstanding contemporary figure is Orlando Menicucci (b.1949), a self-taught painter who is always halfway between abstraction and representation.

Haiti achieved international recognition in the field of art with the founding of the Art Center in Port-au-Prince in 1944. The person responsible for this institution was the North American painter DeWitt Peters, who fought harder than anyone else to establish a meeting place for Haitian artists that did not depend on any government subsidy and that would provide them with a place to exhibit and publicize their work. Of those who participated at the outset, only three could be categorized as 'popular' artists: Philomé Obin (1892–1984), Rigaud Benoit (1911–86) and the sculptor Valentin. DeWitt Peters, however, was convinced that the most interesting aspect of Haitian art was primitive or naive art, especially the work of the exceptional Hector Hyppolite (1894–1948), who in addition to being a painter and decorator was a Voodoo priest. (He had long been a practitioner of *vévé*, a ritual design made with flour on the ground before the beginning of a ceremony.) Unlike Obin or Benoit,

Hyppolite, because of his role as an 'intermediary', had to paint in a hurry. Many other artists – too many, obviously – have tried to continue this naive tradition (genuinely or otherwise), to the point where Haiti has been turned into a marketplace for this type of painting – a marketplace in which there are many false primitives who nevertheless represent one of the country's richest sources of income.

CENTRAL AMERICA

The Central American countries do not have a strong modern art tradition. It might be said that they passed directly from a mediocre colonial art – with the notable exception of Guatemalan imagery – to the contemporary period without any major transition. After the Second World War, however, many talents were revealed, some of whom, like Carlos Mérida (Guatemalan) or Francisco Zúñiga (Costa Rican), have already been mentioned in our discussion of Mexico. Many artists from the Mexican provinces and from neighbouring Central American countries have always been attracted to Mexico City.

Guatemala seems to have produced the most distinguished artists. Besides Mérida, González Goyri, Mishaán and Abularach deserve mention. Roberto González Goyri (b.1924), a sculptor who was born in the capital, although he studied in the United States, executed between 1964 and 1966 a number of important reliefs in his native city. Rodolfo Mishaán (b.1924), also from Guatemala City, fell under the influence of the famous Mérida, considered a national hero. Finally, Rodolfo Abularach (b.1933) has become known in Latin America for a theme which seems to have become an obsession with him: the representation of a great open eye. Mishaán and Abularach have lived for many years in the United States. However, all in all – if we make an exception of Francisco Zúñiga – of the present generation the most important Central American artist is Armando Morales (b.1927). Born in Granada, Nicaragua, he went to the capital, Managua, where he learned drawing and painting. In 1957 he travelled extensively in South America, and three years later – on a Guggenheim grant – he went to live in New York, where he stayed for twenty years and pursued his aptitude for graphic art. Morales, who was an admirable abstract painter, returned some years ago to representational art of the metaphysical type, which he achieves through very pure drawing and a strange iridescent palette.

At the beginning of the twentieth century Colombia had only one out-standing artist: Andres de Santamaría (1860–1945), who was born in Bogotá, but was taken to Europe as an infant. There, he studied in England and France, finally taking up permanent residence in Brussels, where he later died. However, the seven years that he spent intermittently in his native country were enough to classify him as an indispensable link in the Colombian artistic chain of awareness. It has to be said, however, that most of the painting that was produced in Colombia during the first thirty years of the century was somewhat unimaginative. Among the few who contributed to different and revolutionary movements in the 1940s and 1950s was Guillermo Wiedemann (b.1905), who was born in Munich, Germany, and studied art in his native city. Fleeing from the Nazi terror, he took refuge in Colombia in 1939, and was at first overwhelmed – like so many foreigners – by the 'tropicalism' that he tried to express on his canvases. In the 1950s, however, with the same seriousness he had put into his figurative art, he began to cultivate 'lyrical' abstraction and was the major precursor of this style in Colombia.

Besides Edgar Negret – strictly speaking a sculptor – whom we shall consider later, two artists are considered to be indisputable abstract masters in Colombia: Obregón and Ramírez Villamizar. Alejandro Obregón (1920–92), born in Barcelona, lived from childhood on the shores of the Caribbean, which has always been his great source of inspiration. In 1958, he began an active career that fascinated the Colombian critics of the time, since they found him to be semi-figurative, semi-abstract, and able to pose the problem of Latin American expression in his paintings. Eduardo Ramírez Villamizar (b.1923) was an inspired painter-sculptor. He presents the opposite case to that of Obregón: he is one of the few Colombians – the other is Omar Rayo – who was tempted by the purity of geometry. Omar Rayo himself (b.1928), born in Roldanillo, is an artist who engraves obsessive, labyrinthine reliefs of black lines on a white ground, when he is not pursuing – as well – the revelatory relief on paper of a real object. Skipping a generation, there are two Colombian women painters who are interested in this same avenue, although they approach it in a less insistent manner: Fanny Sanin, who lives in New York and paints symmetrical pictures in muted colours; and Ana Mercedes Hoyos, of Bogotá, who at first created ambiguous canvasses in a style that lay between the figurative and the abstract, and more recently has made incursions into conceptual art.

In figurative art, the most famous figure is Fernando Botero (b.1932), who was born in Medellín and by 1951 was exhibiting in the capital. Later he studied in Madrid, at the Academy of San Fernando, where he doubtless learned his excellent technique. Is Botero a modern or a reactionary in art? Fifty years ago his paintings would have been rejected as conformist. Botero is a creator of *sui generis* images whose principal characteristic is that he 'inflates' everything he paints – people, animals, objects. Going against the tide of automatic avant-gardism, thanks to the quality of his work and his humour, Botero has commanded higher prices than any other Latin American artist. What remains uncertain is whether his painting will endure or whether it will become simply another momentary curiosity.

If in Botero we discern an element of social criticism, through the mocking treatment of reality, in his compatriot Beatriz Gonzalez this criticism becomes satirical and merciless. She attacks religious and patriotic myths and even the themes of daily life, and instead of applying her paintings on canvas, she affixes them – like permanent lacquers – on furniture or vulgar objects: an original use of Pop Art, Colombian style. Figurative artists to the core are the brothers Santiago and Juan Cárdenas Arroyo, but they are very different from each other in spite of their attachment to the visible 'document'. Santiago is the best hyperrealist in his country, using amusing *trompe-l'oeil* effects in which we see a tacit irony. Juan, perhaps less imaginative in his provocations, concentrates on representing people in enclosed or open spaces. An able portrait artist, perhaps his work as a printmaker is more interesting than his paintings.

The 1970s saw the appearance of the new art of Colombia, especially as it concerns a handful of draughtsman-painters. One of the most brilliant is, without doubt, Luis Caballero (b.1943), who studied in Bogotá and Paris – the city where he lives and where he began as a great figurative artist of distortions. Older now, he has become an inspired interpreter of the young male body in attitudes of maximum tension. Another of these excellent draughtsmen-painters is Gregorio Cuartas, from Medellín. Influenced by the Italian *Quattrocento,* which he studied first-hand, Cuartas draws with a hard line which also, recently, is enriched with strange sombre colours on small canvases of intense magic.

In Colombian sculpture as in Colombian painting at the beginning of the twentieth century there is only one name of any real interest, that of Romulo Rozo (1899–1964). Born in Chiquinquirá, Rozo studied in Bogotá, Madrid and Paris. As soon as he returned, his government sent him on a diplomatic mission to Mexico, which was a crucial episode, since he established his career in that country, building monumental sculpture and teaching. Rozo and Rodrigo Arenas Betancur (see above) have several things in common: not only did both emigrate to Mexico, but they also both aspired to the stylization of form, simplifying masses through the use of large planes without detail.

Later came a radical revitalization. Two great sculptors of the same generation as Arenas Betancur – Negret and Ramírez Villamizar, whom we have already mentioned as painters – entered the scene with new ideas that were diametrically opposed to what preceded them. Edgar Negret (b.1920) was born in Popayán and studied in Cali, where he would later settle. In 1948 he travelled to the United States and stayed there for about ten years, with intermittent trips to Europe. He sculpts in welded metal which he cuts, folds, perforates and embosses, as if he were trying to create fantastic 'useless machines'. These solemn and elegant creations are invariably painted monochromatically: in black, white, red or, most recently, yellow. They always have a matt finish with not a hint of reflection. Eduardo Ramírez Villamizar was born in Pamplona – in the north of Colombia – but he studied architecture and fine arts in Bogotá. As a painter, he revitalized the genre with his strictly geometric constructivism and his smooth technique. In 1955 he began to work in sculpture, first in small reliefs or large mural compositions. He also lived for several years in New York, concentrating there on three-dimensional sculpture which he sometimes painted in bright colours. His conception of form is basically monumental and accordingly he creates huge works which, in spite of their severity, are integrated with the landscape of his native country.

At the opposite pole we have Feliza Bursztyn, a sculptress who died young. She was the first and most gifted of the 'junk sculptors' in Colombia. At first she created static pieces by accumulating heterogeneous metallic materials; later she launched 'crazy machines', which both intrigued and irritated the Colombian public during the 1960s. The breach, however, remained open. Also worthy of mention is Bernardo Salcedo (b.1942), an architect and sculptor born in Bogotá. His temperament shows in his fabrication of invented objects, in which he arbitrarily combines certain elements taken from reality: old dolls, photographs, knives and saws which he modifies and combines in strange and elegant assemblages. His work adds an ironic note to contemporary Colombian sculpture.

VENEZUELA

In spite of the fact that Venezuelan painting had some outstanding artists at the turn of the century, it must be recognized that except for Emilio Boggio – an impressionist who lived in Europe – the rest were content with a more or less academic approach.

Something more meaningful took place, however, with the arrival on the scene of Manuel Cabré (1890–1983). Although he had studied with Herrera y Toro – one of the important precursors – Cabré had a new vision of painting, or to put it better, of the light of the Caracas Valley. The attempt to represent it on canvas was a task that occupied his entire long life. For him art was not a matter of portraits or heroic themes of Independence or even of the intimate details of daily life. What Cabré wanted was nothing less than to pay supreme attention to the nature of his region, which he interpreted on a monumental scale.

The fact that this approach became generalized into what we call the Caracas School does not mean that more advanced Venezuelan painters did not also experiment – at the same time – in other, frequently totally divergent, directions. We refer to the style of the greatest twentieth-century painter to have been born in Venezuela – Armando Reverón (1889–1954). This genial *clochard*-to-be of tropical painting began a sensible career first studying in Caracas (1904), then going to Europe ten years later (1914–21), with long stays in Madrid, Barcelona and Paris. It was only when he returned from Europe that Reverón began to explore the light of the Caribbean coast, first painting 'blue' with fuzzy technique and Goyesque themes, and later turning to a 'white' period, renouncing the city and taking refuge in the wild beach at Macuto. He then entered his 'brown' period, in which the brushstrokes are almost lost in the neutral colour of the burlap he used to paint on.

The First World War brought home Rafael Monasterios (1889–1961) and Federico Brandt (1879–1932) from Europe, bringing with them a fresh view of the new conception of painting. Brandt is a painter of people and things in the home; his palette is refined and cheerful. In contrast, with Monasterios we return to nature captured in a pale palette, without the subtle visual transposition of Reverón. A similar case is that of Antonio E. Monsanto (1890–1948), a good *plein-air* painter who had learned the lessons of Impressionism. In the following period the most interesting artists are Francisco Narvaez, Marcos Castillo and Juan V. Fabbiani. We will discuss in particular Francisco Narvaez when we turn to the topic of Venezuelan sculpture. Castillo and Fabbiani were above all painters of the nude – a genre not practised in Venezuela until then: the first treats them in flat colours, and the second in large masses. Since both taught at the School of Plastic Arts in Caracas, they naturally had a great deal of influence over the young artists of the day.

Hector Poleo (b.1918) is the painter who provides the link with the generations to follow. He went through several periods: he was strongly influenced by Mexican painting – both in subject matter and technique – and he then pursued a kind of highly constructed surrealism. Later he turned to mistier, almost abstract evocations.

From then it might be said that the history of modern Venezuelan art was written both in Caracas and in Paris, that is with the creation of the group that baptized itself 'The Dissidents'. It included Guevara Moreno, Debourg, Regulo Pérez, Barrios, Vigas, Arroyo and Peran Erminy. At first all of them were in favour of a violent abstraction that later would take the form of kinetic art or neo-plastic geometricism. However, there still remain vestiges of figurative art in some of them, which were given concrete expression by Oswaldo Vigas, Omar Carreño, Humberto Jaime Sánchez, Jacobo Borges and Alirio Oramas.

During the late 1950s several groups were formed in Caracas – for example, Sardio, El Techo de la Ballena, La Tabla Redonda and those around the publication *Crítica contemporanea* – and in Maracaibo two main movements arose: Apocalipsis, and another around the magazine *40° a la sombra*. From 1960 figurative painting became diversified. Younger artists began to express themselves: Virgilio Trómpiz with the stylized human figure; Hugo Baptista, who painted doors in dazzling colours, but developed towards more diluted, non-representational canvases. Marisol Escobar devoted herself completely to sculpture and went to New York where she pursued her career in pop art.

Venezuelan kinetic art in Paris had a complex internal history of its own. We will begin with Alejandro Otero (b.1921), who was in Paris from 1945 to 1952. A talented figurative artist, he learned a great deal from Picasso and began to use that influence successfully. Nevertheless, on his return to Venezuela he broke with that facile approach and invented what he called 'colour-rhythms': white panels painted in impasto, striped with black and containing geometric areas of intense colour. Later we will follow Otero's development that led him to three-dimensional expressions. Jesús Rafael Soto (b.1923), who had studied in Caracas and rapidly rose to be director of an art school in Maracaibo, was in Paris in 1950. During his first five years in Europe he did scientific research on certain phenomena known in optics but generally not used until that time in art. He discovered that if a freely moving element passes in front of a background with vertical black and white stripes, the human eye imagines it perceives a vibration. After thirty years of recognition, Soto created other intriguing optic illusions like his 'fields of bars' or, even better, his 'penetrables' – virtual forests of nylon threads which viewers traversed in amusement or alarm.

Carlos Cruz-Díez (b.1923) reached Paris in 1959, after a brilliant career in his own country as a prominent industrial designer. If Otero and Soto were above all intuitive, Cruz-Díez showed, in contrast, a systematic sensibility and mentality. He gave the name *fisiocromías* to his most widely known experiments, which consist of systems of vertical bars set on end and painted different colours. As the spectator moves in front of it, the panel is transformed into a series of successive geometric compositions, each one different from the others. As in the case of Soto, there is a virtual movement in the background – not only a real one – that justifies the label of kinetic art which is applied to this trend initiated first of all by Alexander Calder.

Venezuelan art in the 1980s, after the perhaps exaggerated 'boom' of kineticism, protected by the state, the foundations and the rich collectors, was beginning to concede the preeminent position to other manifestations. Jacobo Borges (b.1931), for example, always an interesting artist, became in his mature years probably the best neo-figurative artist in Latin America. His broad recent canvases possess a purely pictorial dynamism, that is, they are never simply drawings coloured in *a posteriori*. As in the work of the great colourists of earlier times, the form is born from the colour that the brush – as sensitive as a seismograph – applies on the canvas. Other talents continue to flourish and it is practically impossible to take account of all of them. Particularly worthy of mention is Edgar Sánchez (b.1940), first for his drawings, and then also as a painter. His art is mainly expressed through the amplification of details – on a colossal scale – of nude or clothed bodies which he represents with minute, icy precision. In other cases, his works consist of isolated features, like several mouths that appear to have separate lives of their own, without a face to support them, emerging painfully from a fragment of spread out skin.

In sculpture, the only great name from the beginning of the century is that of the already mentioned Francisco Narvaez (b.1908), who belonged to the generation of artists who produced stylized figures, and who were the vanguard of the era of his youth. His Fountain of Las Toninas in the El Silencio neighbourhood of Caracas belongs to this period. However, after 1950 Narvaez became an abstract biomorphic artist, with a more architectonic tendency in his latest works. He is a man who has worked in all techniques and with all materials, listening to what each medium has to offer and taking it as his inspiration.

We discussed the kineticism of Soto and Cruz-Díez under painting, because many of their works were murals. We cannot do the same with the recent work of Alejandro Otero: his 'pyramids' or 'rotors' are three-dimensional, that is, true 'spatial sculptures'. Ingenious, monumental, constructed of stainless metals, reflective of light from all angles, they are proliferating throughout the world as 'signs' of the Venezuelan spirit, that is to say, of a country orientated towards the future. As far as spatial sculpture is concerned, we must also mention the name of Gego (Gertrudis Goldmichdt, b.1939), a German architect established in Venezuela who displays an aerial conception of sculpture, using spiderwebs made of wire or knotted cords, which paradoxically reveal to the viewer the indeterminacy of open space. And finally, another architect, Domingo Alvarez (b.1935), deserves attention. He won a competition for the Monument to Venezuelan Aviation, which was, unfortunately, never built. It consisted of a Solar Plaza with mirrors that reflected the whole sky on the earth. Alvarez also constructed labyrinths of mirrors which, in their way, play with the ambiguity of space.

ECUADOR

The first new principle in Ecuadorean art in this century was stamped by indigenism, discussed above. Its most illustrious promoter was Camilo Egas (1899–1962). After 1912, a group of young men including Egas and his friend José A. Moscoso (who died in the prime of life) benefited from the presence in Quito of two men who had been 'imported' from

Europe. One was the Frenchman Alfred Paul Bar, summoned to teach drawing and painting; the other was an Italian, Luigi Cassadio, who acted as instructor of sculpture. In Egas's case, Bar's presence was crucial, since he made him see the Ecuadorean landscape in Impressionist terms. Egas would go to Rome and the Academy of San Fernando in Madrid to continue his studies, travelling extensively in Europe until he decided to settle in the United States, where he achieved a certain recognition by exploiting the lode of pre-Columbian America with its typical characters, attire and customs.

Victor Mideros (b.1888) also studied in Quito with Bar. Mideros followed the indigenist current – with more realism than Egas – before becoming interested in a mystical painting rendered in classical terms. He is an indispensable figure because he represents the nexus with the next generation, as he was, for example, the teacher of Eduardo Kingman (b.1911), another indigenist painter who shared with Egas the honour of creating the pictorial decoration in Ecuador's pavilion at the New York World's Fair (1939). The artist who attracted most attention, however, was a controversial figure: Oswaldo Guayasamín (b.1919), who was born in Quito and studied at the National School of Fine Arts there. In his work the traces of Mexican muralism are obvious, as well as the influence of Portinari in Brazil (see below) and even Picasso of a certain period. With these elements and his own statements, which he certainly does not lack, he has been able to elaborate a declamatory image of suffering humanity.

In the middle of the fifties the first signs of abstract art appeared in Ecuador. Two very different personalities initiated it: Manuel Rendon (b.1894), who was born in Paris, although his family was Ecuadorean, and was twenty-six years old when he moved to Guayaquil, where he has remained ever since; and Araceli Gilbert (b.1914), a native of Guayaquil, which is where she began her studies with Hans Michaelson before moving to New York to continue her training with Amedée Ozenfant, the French purist. Ecuadorean painting evolved a style we must characterize as concrete, that is, a severe non-figurative expression based on geometry.

Among the direct or indirect disciples of these two artists we may count younger men like Enrique Tábara (b.1930), who is also from Guayaquil. He began his career painting landscapes and regional themes, and when later he approached informalism it was under the influence of Michaelson and Rendon, although it was the years he passed in Barcelona that brought him to monochrome painting with emphasis on the material. When he returned to his own country, he attempted a pre-Columbian symbolism, pasting natural elements on his canvases, a collage worked with constructivist methods.

Luis Molinari Flores (b. 1929), like those mentioned above, was born in Guayaquil, but his training was more international since he studied in Buenos Aires and spent many years in Paris and New York. His works exhibit a rigorous geometry, inspired by Vasarely. Oswaldo Viteri (b. 1931), his contemporary, was born in Ambato; in contrast to the intellectual Molinari Flores, he aspired to a popular art, using burlap in his work, with which he fashioned little dolls that were supposed to represent the South American expression.

Later there was a return to figurative art, represented above all by artists like Felix Arauz, who through the use of oil paint and sand tried to approach that *art brut* practised by Dubuffet. Finally, even conceptual art seems to have reached Ecuador, in the person of Maurice Bueno, who was trained in the United States. His materials are taken from nature, such as water, earth and fire; his techniques are, by contrast, ultramodern and include neon light and laser beams.

In sculpture, the only interesting figure is the sculptress Germania de Breilh, who studied at the Faculty of Fine Arts in Ecuador and also, later, in the United States. The cast iron pieces by this artist are reminiscent of the solutions of the Spanish artist Chillida, while when she works full forms in andesite, one can not help thinking of the great French sculptor Arp.

PERU

The glorious colonial past of Peru, rather than being an advantage for the development of modern art in the country, has represented a burden, a true millstone around the art community's neck.

By way of introduction, we will begin our discussion with Daniel Hernández (1856–1932), who in spite of being still a traditional artist, served as a transition, especially in his work as a teacher. Born in a rural area, Hernández moved to Lima at the age of four, and after studying there was sent to Europe in 1875 by the government to finish his education. He spent ten years in Rome, and in Paris he made friends with the Spanish painters Pradilla and Fortuny, from whom he must have learned the cursive manner of handling his brushes. He was a fast and accurate painter, although his great historical paintings often seem grandiloquent. He portrayed many female nudes, and several portraits of much better workmanship and penetration than the large official pictures. From 1918 he was the director for many years of the National School of Fine Arts from where he exercised undeniable influence. Another important artist was Carlos Baca-Flor (1867–1941), a strange case of internationalism, whose situation was similar to what happened with Santamaría in Colombia and Boggio in Venezuela. In fact, one must ask whether Baca-Flor's cosmopolitan career had any influence at all on the painting of his native country. He lived in Paris and was a mundane portraitist of real universal fame.

Hernández had problems with several rebellious students at the School of Fine Arts. The one who stood out immediately as the leader of the future indigenist movement was José Sabogal (1888–1956), who by 1909 had already made a trip to Europe. Five years later we find him studying in Buenos Aires, and between 1922 and 1925 he lived in Mexico, linking himself closely to Rivera and Orozco. The indigenists pursued a regional and racial ideal that had to represent the human figure in accordance with local archetypes, although they also extended their quest to the portrayal of landscape, customs and dress. Among those converted by Sabogal were: Julia Codesido, Jorge Vinatea Reinoso, Alejandro González, Enrique Camino Brent and Camilo Blas. Their respective works are diminished by the extreme simplification of the drawing, the careless composition, the aggressive colours, all of which seem more fitting to tourist posters than to serious art. Perhaps the only Peruvian painter who reflects the life of the people spontaneously – and not through an intellectual process – is Mario Urteaga (1875–1959), a sort of *naif* artist born in Cajamarca, who had the grace (in both senses of the word) to be able to paint simply what he felt. His humble little rural or urban scenes, in muted tones like those of the real earth, tell us more about an authentic reality than any pompous declamation.

A wave of internationalism swept across Peru with two other painters: Grau and Gutiérrez. Ricardo Grau (1907–70) was born in Burdeos and studied in Brussels. Returning to the country of his parents, his catalytic role seems today even more important than his artistic career proper. In fact, Grau would launch three decisive battles in Peru: for colour (as the principal organizing element of the picture and not simply the subject), for the freedom to experiment (with emphasis on the individual in the face of nationalism), and finally, for the search for *plastic* thinking, instead of the 'literary' impositions from which indigenism had not been able to escape. Quite different, but important in his own way, was Sérvulo Gutiérrez (1914–61), who began as a self-taught artist until he was able to study for eight years in Buenos Aires with the great Argentine painter Emilio Pettoruti. Gutiérrez' masterpiece is without a doubt his canvas *The Andes* (1943), in which a crude, strong female nude represents – better than in the case of Guayasamin – the unavoidable South American reality. Perhaps the most noticeable difference between Sabogal and Grau, as compared to Gutiérrez, was that the latter was never an intellectual, and perhaps because of this his pictures offer a direct, living testimony.

Abstraction would also reach Peru thanks to a foreigner: A. C. Winternitz (b.1906), who was born in Vienna but as a young man moved to Italy where he specialized in mosaic and stained glass work. In 1939, when he moved to Lima, he taught the techniques of mosaic and founded the School of Plastic Arts at the Catholic University where he had as his disciple – among others – Fernando de Szyszlo, the most important present-day Peruvian painter. Winternitz, with his knowledge and sensitivity, was, then, an indispensable link in the evolution of art in Peru.

Fernando de Szyszlo (b.1925) studied first at the Catholic University, and then spent several years in Europe, where he went to complete his studies. When he returned to his own country, he himself taught at the same school where he had been educated. Szyszlo's art demonstrates that there is no hard and fast line between the figurative and the abstract. In his paintings what appears at first to be totally invented, in the end seems to evoke – voluntarily or involuntarily – the memory of something already seen, and that comes from the rich repertory of pre-Columbian art, to the point where his painting could be classified as 'indigenist abstraction', or, better yet, 'abstract indigenism'.

We must not neglect three painters from the intermediate generation who, in addition to practising their art, were also teachers. Ugarte Elespuru (b.1911) shows the influence of Mexican muralism, at least in the vast panel he painted for the assembly hall of the old Saint Thomas School in Lima. Ugarte Elespuru wrote, furthermore, the most useful of the manuals on modern Peruvian painting. Alberto Dávila (b.1912), although faithful to the regionalist theme, knew better than the indigenists how to construct his pictures, organizing them around geometric schemes, perhaps invisible to the uninitiated. Sabino Springuett (b.1914) is someone in whom there is also a struggle – as in Dávila – concerning the old conflict between localism and universalism.

Within Szyszlo's generation we find other painters whose style ranges from informalism to the most minute cult of detail. Among those who painted 'tactile mists', we have, for instance, Milner Cajahuaringa, Venancio Shinki and Arturo Kubotta, who today lives in Brazil. In the opposite camp are those who use reality as a starting point – seen or imagined – and then devote themselves to transcribing it implacably. The most important figure of this group is probably Herman Braun (b.1933), who was born in Lima and began his career as an architectural designer. In recent years he has become one of the best Latin American hyper-realists, although in his canvases some deliberate incongruity always appears, which links him almost in an obligatory way with surrealism. Braun has lived in Paris for many years. The surrealist *par excellence* is Tilsa Tsuchiya (1932–84), of Japanese lineage, but born in Lima, who also lived in Paris for a long time. Tilsa – as she is often called – was a patient and imaginative miniaturist who created her works in small dimensions, populating them with imaginary beings and illuminating them in pure, brilliant colours.

The isolated figure who embodies 'intellectualism' in Peruvian art today is the poet-painter Eduardo Eielson (b. 1923), who has lived in Rome for years. He has been creating modern *quipus* (knotted woollens used by the Indians to register dates and facts), perhaps of little interest artistically, but they are precursors of conceptual art. In a younger generation we find Gerardo Chávez, who after graduating from an art school in Lima, travelled to Europe in 1960, living first in Rome for two years and since then in Paris, where he exhibits frequently. Chávez, at the beginning of his career, was influenced by both Matta and Lam, although at present he is totally confident in his own art. He reveals himself as a 'fantastic' figurative artist of great imagination.

Modern sculpture in Peru really begins with Joaquín Roca Rey (b.1923), who was born in Lima and trained at the National School of Fine Arts, but perhaps received his real education beside the great Spanish sculptor Victorio Macho, who worked in Lima and left many sculptures there. Roca Rey has tried everything in sculpture: sometimes figurative work with a declamatory emphasis (for example, his *Monument to Garcilaso*, in

Rome); sometimes experimenting with complicated abstractions in iron, as he did in the 1950s and 1960s. However, his role as a teacher is important, not least for having helped to train the most distinguished contemporary Peruvian sculptor today, Alberto Guzmán, and another outstanding artist, Armando Valera Neyra.

Alberto Guzmán (b.1927) was born in Talara and studied in Roca Rey's classes in Lima. Later, in 1960, he won a scholarship to go to France, where he has remained ever since. Guzmán is the first Peruvian who seems to have really embraced modern art, not treating it superficially. Another well-known sculptor from Peru is Fabián Sánchez (b.1935), who was born in Ayacucho, studied in Lima and went to live in Paris in 1965. Sánchez is a very curious artist, in the sense that he neither carves nor models. Using old sewing machines, he makes them look like large 'insects' that move by means of a perfect and silent technique, which makes them even more alarming. The surrealist reference is clear, and in part it has validated his current reputation.

CHILE

The twentieth century in Chile begins with the figure of Pablo Burchard (1875–1964). Born in Santiago, Burchard studied successively at the German School, the National Institute and the University of Chile, graduating with a degree in architecture. Later he enrolled in the School of Fine Arts to study with Pedro Lira, one of the best Chilean artists of the previous generation. Comparing Burchard's mature style with that of his antecedents – Valenzuela Llanos, the landscape artist, or J. F. González, the brilliant *plein air* painter – we can see that Burchard is less aerial than they, since he 'constructs his paintings through colour,' colour that is thereby transformed into the dominant element of his painting.

From 1912 the School of Fine Arts was directed by the Spanish painter F. Alvarez de Sotomayor, a decided partisan of *costumbrismo*. This teacher was responsible for training excellent technicians in the use of painting materials (he initiated them in the tricks of the trade), but at the same time he held back all attempts at lyricism and that exploration of unknown paths that seems to be the supreme goal of youth. Some of these disciples belonged to the Group of 1913, in which several good painters were active: Pedro Luna (1894–1956), intimate and refined, whose canvases are characterized by their blurry contours; and his opposite, Arturo Gordon (1883–1945), who was slightly vulgar but, representing popular scenes as in *The Cockfight* or *La Cueca* (a great dance), became a great favourite. Finally, we must mention Julio Ortiz de Zárate (1885–1946), a solid constructor of still lifes, who after belonging to the Group of 1913 reappears in the Montparnasse movement (see below).

As art instruction had been deteriorating in Chile, an enterprising Minister of Public Instruction, Pablo Ramírez, decided in 1929 to close the School of Fine Arts. He sent about thirty promising young artists to Paris. Among those Chilean artists who returned (some, like Manuel Ortiz de Zárate, stayed) were the sculptors José Perotti, Tótila Albert, Laura Rodig and Julio A. Vásquez, and the painters Vargas Rozas, Camilo Mori and Julio Ortiz de Zárate. They joined to form the Montparnasse circle, led by Pablo Burchard, who only visited Europe during the last years of his life. The most famous figure from this group was Camilo Mori (1896–1976), who was born in Valparaíso, studied at the School of Fine Arts in Santiago, and later travelled extensively in Spain, Italy and France, where he lived for many years. Mori was a painter of extreme facility and elegance, with such versatile talent that perhaps this very virtue has damaged the judgement that his work deserves today. Landscapes, still lifes, figures, all were topics for Mori's avid brush; he painted in so many different styles that at times it is difficult to recognize him from one picture to another.

Of the so-called 'revolutionaries' in the decades from 1940 to 1960, the best known is Roberto Matta (b.1911), who was born in Santiago and studied architecture, receiving his degree in 1931. Three years later he was in Paris working in the studio of the famous architect, Le Corbusier. In 1937 he joined the surrealist movement and, at the same time, began to exhibit his strange drawings and then incipient painting. Before he was thirty, Matta had all his expressive means at his disposal: his drawings show an 'automatic' freedom (as prescribed in surrealist theory); his colours flow strangely and inventively, forming vast expansions that serve as the background for a multitude of machines and 'humanoids', engaged in actions that we cannot decipher. Another architect-painter, Nemesio Antúnez (b.1918), began to paint in the United States, where he had gone to do post-graduate work. Is Antúnez a surrealist too? We would say that what he does is, at least, 'fantastic' painting in which he deliberately presents a confusion between reality and pure imagination, to the extent that all of his paintings, instead of trying to solve enigmas, on the contrary seem to propose them. Enrique Zañartu (b.1921) is a painter and sculptor of reliefs, although his name more often is associated with printmaking, a medium in which he is a notable practitioner. After his abstract, dark-toned graphic work, Zañartu later surprised us with an antithetical attitude: the creation of small white reliefs of extraordinary refinement. Rodolfo Opazo (b.1925) presents yet another version of the 'latent surrealism' of many of the best contemporary Chilean painters. Instead of working with that elemental magma to which Matta is accustomed, Opazo practised a kind of free association of scales and diverse objects; whether real or invented, they intrigue us through their quality of 'ectoplasm', fixed on the canvas with extraordinary lucidity. Ricardo Yrarrázaval (b.1931), born in Santiago, is a painter-ceramist who carries on both careers in parallel. At first it seemed as if ceramics would be the dominant voice, since his paintings consisted of horizontal stripes of earthy colours superimposed in strata, but later he changed completely to caricatured figures in lively, sharp colours. On a very individual track, always bordering the fantastic, we find Ernesto Barreda (b.1927), also an architect, a fact soon revealed to anyone who sees his obsessive paintings. In them, he represents exclusively doors, windows and walls, dislocated in relation to each other, alarming in their very frontal presentation. This whole world appears decrepit and in ruins. Barreda, conscientiously imitating the texture of stone, the grain of wood, tries to transmit his vision using only white, black, grey and ochre.

The political situation in Chile from the early 1970s resulted in some unfortunate exiles, like for example José Balmes (b.1917) and Gracia Barrios (b.1926), two abstract artists of high quality who later turned to figurative art with an expressionist accent, and Guillermo Núñez (1930), a painter and set designer, who worked along conceptual lines. Balmes, Gracia Barrios and Núñez have all been living in Paris for several years.

Another artist integrated in the contemporary Chilean artistic scene is the Cuban Mario Carreño (b.1913). The style with which Carreño made his name was geometric, although inspired by forms from nature, a little like the case of Carlos Mérida. Beginning in 1958, when he moved to Chile, the architects immediately solicited his collaboration, which they thought would harmonize with the severity of modern buildings. Later in his complex career – perhaps in compensation for his earlier position – Carreño returned to figurative art encompassed in a kind of classical revival. Roser Bru (b.1924) was born in Barcelona, Spain, but is totally at home in her adopted country. In good Mediterranean style, one senses in this painter a kind of aplomb, a sense of proportion; the forms she uses, with their harmonious colours, produce works of great serenity.

Finally, we turn to several Chileans who live outside their country.

They could not be more different from each other. Claudio Bravo
(b.1936), of Valparaíso, after studying in Chile went to Madrid in 1961,
before moving to Tangier, where he continues to paint successfully. Bravo
is a hyper-realist, as the style has been called in recent years, with a
disconcerting visual acuity equalled only by the dexterity of his hand.
However, the spectacular duplication he achieves in his painstaking oils
astonishes or disquiets without moving us. This has not prevented him
from enjoying fame and commanding high prices. There are at least three
significant expatriates living in New York: Mario Toral, Enrique Castrocid and Juan Downey. Toral (b.1934) is a figurative artist who lets
himself be carried along by his galloping imagination, conjuring up
strange indeterminate objects before our eyes which almost always refer to
the female nude. He is a skilled draughtsman, and perhaps drawing is the
medium which best lends itself to the representation of his personal
fantasies. Castrocid (b.1937) is by contrast deliberately iconoclastic, without knowing too well what target to aim at. In 1966 he exhibited
sculptures and a series of robots which clearly attempted to announce the
future. Later – by several years – he turned to some curious 'anamor-
phoses', distorted representations which only appear recognizable from a
single point of view. Downey (b.1940), a disciple of Nemesio Antúñez,
after winning several prizes with semi-figurative painting, moved on to
compose 'fake' maps and graphics, which at first sight seem scientific but
in reality arise from his playful and delirious imagination.

Modern sculpture in Chile begins with the already mentioned José Perotti
(1898–1956), who belonged to the Montparnasse movement. In 1920 he
went to Madrid at the Chilean government's expense and his teachers
there were Sorolla, Romero de Torres and the sculptor Miguel Blay. In
addition he later worked in Paris with Bourdelle, and this strange combination of influences explains his eclecticism, a tendency which was also
characteristic of his time. A more significant figure is Lorenzo Domínguez (1901–63). He was born in Santiago and studied medicine in
Madrid, but in 1926 he abandoned this career to devote himself to
sculpture under the tutelage of the Spanish sculptor Juan Cristóbal.
When he returned to South America in 1931 he exerted great influence,
not only through his own works, which were solid and well defined, but
also through his dedication to teaching. Domínguez, who worked directly in marble and even harder stones, expressed himself through compact forms and hieratic, monumental content.

Chilean sculpture has been dominated by women. Juana Muller (1911–52), of Santiago, studied in Paris with Zadkine, although she was above all a follower of the great Brancusi. Her premature and accidental death deprived the art world in her country of a key figure. Lily Garafulic (b.1914) was born in Antofagasta and studied in Santiago. She was a pupil of the figurative Lorenzo Domínguez, but her own art was abstract. Marta Colvin (b.1917) was born in Chillan but educated at the Academy of Fine Arts in Santiago. In 1948, on a scholarship, she also worked with Zadkine in Paris. In 1957 she made an educational trip that took her to the highlands of Peru and Bolivia where – according to her own report – her interest in pre-Columbian sources was awakened. She later tried to evoke this character in her abstract sculpture, carved in stone or wood, without literally copying any earlier monument, although always inspired by the pre-Columbian. She lives today in Paris.

We conclude with Raul Valdivieso (b.1931), who belongs to a generation that cannot be described in terms of the essentially false abstract-figurative dichotomy. He began by manipulating non-representational forms and today is increasingly reverting to the transposition, in sculptural terms, of an image he extracts from human, animal, or vegetable forms. His masses, compressed like seeds or shells, follow the traditional path of compact sculpture, caressed by the hand or the chisel. Valdivieso alternates the materials, textures, finishes and even the colours of the stones with which he works.

BOLIVIA

The study of art in twentieth-century Bolivia must begin with Cecilio Guzmán de Rojas (1900–50). From a young age he exhibited his work in his own country, but then, thanks to a scholarship, he was able to continue his studies at the Academy of San Fernando in Madrid, where his teacher was Julio Romero de Torres. When he returned to his country in 1930, he was appointed director of the School of Fine Arts, and he used this position to exert his influence. Guzmán de Rojas is an indigenist in his own style, but he lacks the social concern that was the most important aspect of this movement. He concentrates solely on picturesque themes, which he stylizes in a decorative manner. It must be recognized, however, that his painting is of higher quality than that of most Peruvian painters of this school, and his colours are deep and intense. One of his contemporaries was Jorge de la Reza (1900–58), who studied at Yale and possessed, like his countryman, a great aptitude for mural decoration, which he hardly ever used. His colour range seems deliberately restricted.

Everything in the Bolivian art world changed with the revelation of its finest artist: Maria Luisa Pacheco (1919–74), originally from La Paz, who studied first in her native city and later in Madrid (in 1951–2) with Daniel Vázquez Díaz, an excellent Spanish figurative artist. From 1956 until her death she lived in New York, where she created most of her work. Since she gave considerable importance to the material she worked with, it is not unreasonable to assume that she was tempted by informalism, which was so much in vogue among South American artists of the 1950s. She did, however, resist this facile solution, partly because she aspired to achieve the 'plastic equivalent' of the rugged landscape of her own country, which must have been engraved on her retina.

Alfredo La Placa (b.1929) is another outstanding Bolivian painter who avoided figurative art, although his pictures always evoke a kind of 'ghost' of concrete things. Today he is one of the best known artists in Bolivia. Alfredo da Silva (b.1936) twenty years ago seemed to be a typical abstract lyricist, with emphasis on materials, as if the viewer had to re-translate the forms and colours of the painter into the terms of authentic nature. Enrique Arnal (b.1932), like the rest of his generation, returned to figurative painting, although his style is neither distorted nor critical. His object was, until a few years ago, to conjure up an anonymous figure from the highlands, a silhouette without features profiled against a back-lit scene, which is set off in many of his paintings by the simple frame of a door that leads to nowhere.

Moving to geometric and kinetic art in Bolivia, we mention here Rodolfo Ayoroa (b.1927), who was born in Bolivia and studied in Buenos Aires. For many years he has lived and worked in the United States, but without dissociating himself from his native country. Ayoroa is a precision creator of silent optical machines that cast a genuine spell on the viewer; recently he has also been painting canvases on a small scale in which he displays great geometric imagination and an exultant gamut of colour.

The only relevant figure in modern Bolivian sculpture is Marina Núñez del Prado (b.1910), who was born in La Paz, where she began her studies and soon became well known. During her career she passed from a fairly literal naturalism to a comprehension of form that cannot be interpreted as merely abstract, since in her work everything departs from the seen object, which she reduces to forces and tensions in an always elegant resolution. She works in *quayacan* wood and in the hardest Andean stones. She has lived in Quito for many years.

The seeds of modern art were planted in Paraguay by Ofelia Echagüe Vera (b.1904), a painter who studied in Asunción until the government gave her a scholarship to work in Montevideo with the Uruguayan D. Bazzurro and later in Buenos Aires with A. Guido and E. Centurion. Apart from her work itself, Echagüe Vera is interesting because she also devoted herself to teaching. Her disciples include Pedro di Lascio, Aldo del Pino and especially Olga Blinder. These artists form the traditional nexus from which the vanguard would afterwards become established. Olga Blinder (b.1921), originally from Asunción, began her studies at the Paraguay Atheneum. Later she worked with Livio Abramo, a Brazilian artist who has lived in Paraguay since 1956, with whom she further developed the technique of woodcut prints, a medium in which she excelled. Important as a well-rounded artist (she is also a painter) Olga Blinder is thus one of the fundamental promoters of change who was active in Paraguayan art circles in the 1950s. Of course, she was not alone. Josefina Pla (b.1909), who was born in the Canary Islands, was active alongside her. Pla is the widow of an important Paraguayan ceramist and painter who signed his name Julian de la Herreria. Herself a ceramist and critic, she took part in the arduous struggle to connect Paraguay with the rest of Latin America and the world. At this time – 1950 – the Center for Plastic Artists was created to oppose the traditionalists. However, when one of the members of this group went to the second Biennial in São Paulo, Brazil in 1953, the dynamic Pla founded the New Art Group, which included Olga Blinder, Lili del Monico and the sculptor José Laterza Parodi.

The best contemporary Paraguayan artists include Carlos Colombino and Enrique Careaga. Colombino (b.1937) was born in Concepción and is a painter-architect of great merit. At the beginning of his career he invented what he called 'xylopaintings' (wood panels carved and painted). Later, he also experimented with some large screens in the form of hands or figures of cutout profiles. Thereafter, still pursuing his xylopaintings, his images were not abstract but figurative – 'faceless portraits', as he calls them. Careaga (b.1944) was born in Asunción and is, by contrast, a pure geometric artist. He studied in Paraguay and later went to live in

Paris for a few years, where he discovered the world of Vasarely: that is to say, a *trompe l'oeil* art of hard edges and bright colours.

Modern Paraguayan sculpture is represented by two figures: José Laterza Parodi and Hermann Guggiari. Laterza Parodi began his career as a ceramics disciple of Josefina Pla. His initial sculptures were figurative and 'Americanist', although later they were derived from a not entirely gratuitous abstraction, since they are always related to the character of the wood from which they are carved. When he expresses himself as a ceramist, however, he resorts to another repertory – such as the human body – of highly stylized forms. Guggiari, although he took some lessons from the sculptor Pollarolo, can be called a truly self-taught artist. In 1943 he received a scholarship to go to Buenos Aires, where he associated with good teachers and fellow students. Three years later, he returned to his own country as a trained sculptor with mastery of all his expressive techniques. Of these the most important aspect is his skill in working metal until he produces certain lacerations which, although figurative, clearly signify the explosion of a frank violence and are not merely a pretext for decorative formalism.

ARGENTINA

Argentine art – like that of Mexico and Brazil – is more complex than the art of the rest of the continent, and there was important activity there at the end of the nineteenth and the beginning of the twentieth centuries. Perhaps we should begin with Miguel Carlos Victorica (1884–1955). Born in Buenos Aires he was so precocious that his family hired a private teacher for him until he was old enough to enroll in the Estimulo Association for Fine Arts, a private school where he studied with some of the most brilliant painters of the preceding generation: De la Carcova, Sivori, Della Valle and Giudici. Victorica went to Europe in 1911 and stayed there for seven years, which were crucial to his career. In modern Argentine painting, Victorica embodies expression through colour, since the weak structure of his paintings is organized – and saved – in exclusively chromatic terms. The forms take shape against neutral backgrounds by means of large isolated spots of iridescent colour which together form an extremely aerial and tactile kind of 'archipelago'.

The opposite pole – in terms of personality and artistic attitude – is represented by another great Argentine painter: Emilio Pettoruti (1892–

1971). Born in what was then the new city of La Plata (located fifty kilometres from Buenos Aires), Pettoruti was awarded a scholarship by the provincial government in 1913 to study in Italy, the country where his parents were born. Just as the First World War was about to begin, he left for Europe, to stay in Florence for several years; he also travelled all over Italy in order to study the Renaissance masterworks from which he learned his own impressive craft. The content of his paintings, however, arises from various sources. As the youngest of the futurists, he adopted from them the *parti-pris* of simplification, although to their dynamism he preferred a well-tempered staticism like that of synthetic cubism. Finally, there is also in his pictures a kind of magic that brings them close to Italian metaphysical painting. Pettoruti returned to Argentina in 1924 and it was there that he would realize his best work. By the time he moved to Paris for the last twenty years of his life, his career was already essentially completed.

Argentine painting tended to be cosmopolitan, especially after 1920. That is, in contrast to what was happening in other cultural centres, the Argentines had difficulty in finding an easy identity to assume, as had been the case, for example, with indigenism in the Andean countries. The vanguard was restricted, thus, to pursuing the European currents which, after a certain lag, reached the Argentine schools. The most impatient artists finished their own education in the Old World, in one of the great Italian cities of art or, better still, in Paris, studying for the most part not in the official but in private schools.

Among the best of those who went to Paris were Hector Basaldúa (1895–1978) and Horacio Butler (1897–1983), who caught the delightful fever of the Paris school. Basaldúa expressed it in pictures and theatre set designs, and Butler painted in grey and olive-green tones using short brushstrokes in pursuit of Cezanne. Only Raquel Forner (1902–87) liberated herself from this elegant contagion. Unlike the others, once she had learned her trade well, as they all had, she produced a much more fantastic and dramatic kind of painting, especially in her portrayal of the Spanish Civil War on bold monumental canvases. Another Paris-educated Argentine who did not follow the tacit assignments of the 'school' was the provincial Ramón Gómez Cornet (1898–1964), who reduced the violence of Mexican indigenism – the Andean version was so artificial it hardly mattered – to a note of melancholy village life. His characters are Indians or Mestizos, but since the reassertion of their proud heritage is absent or merely implied, they seem to consider themselves simply second-class citizens.

Argentina differs from the rest of Latin America in the sense that it has a generation of modern artists who might be said to fall into the category of what the French call *petits-maîtres,* offering an irreplaceable kind of 'chamber-painting'. These include Eugenio Daneri (1881–1970), an earthy painter of humble scenes of Buenos Aires and its neighbourhoods and Miguel Diomede (1902–74), who painted still lifes 'in a whisper'.

More assertive were another pair of painters: Spilimbergo and Berni. Lino E. Spilimbergo (1896–1964) was a great draughtsman and painter in the Italian style – that is, a classical painter – who bathed his figures in intense, bright colours. His pictures showed, at first, exaggerated 'fugitive' views, which he gradually abandoned in favour of anonymous portraits in which one can see solemn, monumental figures with large, staring eyes. Antonio Berni (1905–81) began painting surrealistic pictures, which eventually made political and social statements. The colours Berni used at the time were intense and crude, and the drawing showed an expressive, hard line. (Much later, another 'reincarnation' awaited him, when he was able to take advantage of the 'pop' experience to create large collages of popular celebration that had their moment of glory.)

In Argentina, unlike Chile, there is no stable tradition of surrealism. Nevertheless, one strange, indefinable personage is intriguing: Alejandro Xul Solar (1888–1963), a sort of follower of Klee but with esoteric facets, who is the exception that proves the rule, and perhaps because of this his work has gained favour today in critical opinion. Official surrealism, however, did not appear in Argentina until the arrival of the Spanish artist Juan Batlle Planas (1911–65), creator of grey deserts across which prophets stride carrying shepherd's crooks, and veiled women are draped in soft colours of blue and lavender.

Between 1930 and the end of the Second World War Argentina saw a healthy reaffirmation of local values, exemplified by figures like the Uruguayan Figari and the Argentine Victorica, who showed in their work that one could be 'national' without painting in a folkloric style, and that 'intimate-ism' is more natural to the Argentine character than the effects of sentimental pathos. On the other hand, the youngest and most restless artists were inspired – almost without knowing it – by the constructivism of another Uruguayan, the great Torres-García (without feeling themselves obliged to follow his tiresome symbolism), and also by that formal exactness and perfection that was always an essential feature of Pettoruti's work. We refer here to 'concrete' art, a hard abstraction which was undoubtedly inspired by everything that was *not* French in European art. Tomás

Maldonado (b.1922), who would later have a brilliant career as a theoreti-
cian and designer in Europe, and Alfredo Hlito (b.1923), the most important painter of the movement, were the heroes of this new path which, in
1945, baptized itself 'Agrupación Arte Concreto-Invención.' However,
under the impulse of the founders – Carmelo Arden Quin (b.1913) and
Gyula Kósice (b.1924) – another revolutionary movement was to emerge:
Madí, which postulated total freedom and allowed every kind of creation,
without distinguishing between painting and sculpture. Colleagues in the
first group were: José Antonio Fernández Muro (b.1920), Sarah Grilo
(b.1920), Miguel Ocampo (b.1922) and, later on, Clorindo Testa
(b.1923), better known as an architect. All of them had brilliant careers,
and their work is in general less rigorous and more sensitive than what they
had proposed in their youth.

Other artists born a few years later went to Paris in 1958 in search,
above all, for the sponsorship of the Hungarian-Parisian Victor Vasarely.
The principal figure among these *émigrés* is Julio Le Parc (b.1928), who
won one of the grand prizes in the Venice Biennial of 1966. Also worthy
of mention are Francisco Sobrino (b.1932), Hugo Demarco (b.1932) and
Horacio García Rossi (b.1929). They were the great inventors and practitioners of kineticism, an art based on the effects of optics and movement,
whether the real movement of the object or the virtual movement of the
spectator. Independent, but still in the same framework, are three other
Argentines in Paris: Luis Tomasello (b.1915), creator of what he calls
'chromoplastic atmospheres', and those two inspired optical machine 'engineers', Marta Boto (b.1925) and Gregorio Vardánega (b.1923).

The sixties was the great period of the Instituto Di Tella, whose art
section was directed by the well known and controversial critic, Jorge
Romero Brest. It was the heyday of everything rash and the triumph of
extreme youth, from which some elements of value, especially in the field
of theatre, would emerge. In 1961 under the name Otra Figuración four
new painters began to exhibit their work: Rómulo Macció (b.1931),
Ernesto Deira (1928–86), Luis Felipe Noé (b.1933) and Jorge de la Vega
(1930–71). The painting of these outsiders consisted of a kind of figurative expressionism. They represented a genuinely 'angry generation' of
Argentine artists.

What happened to the other movements that were never entirely extinguished? Lyrical abstract art ended up as 'informalism', as exemplified by
several notable black and grey canvases by Clorindo Testa, although in

most cases it became mixed with a kind of non-figurative surrealism, if one can use such an expression. Strict surrealists had already appeared between 1930 and 1940 in the group called Orion, which included, among others, Orlando Pierri (b.1913), Leopoldo Presas (b.1915), and Ideal Sánchez (b.1916), although the last two later abandoned the style. The best-known Argentine orthodox surrealist is Roberto Aizenberg (b.1928), who exquisitely interprets his rich interior world of desolate landscapes and mysterious architecture.

In conclusion, we must not omit the other independents, who include several of the best artists, some of whom stayed home in Argentina, and some of whom sought their fortune elsewhere, but especially in Paris and New York. Among the former is Rogelio Polesello (b.1939), a painter of canvases and a 'constructor' in transparent acrylics, who applies to all his works such geometric rigour and sensitive colour treatment that they become all exceedingly appealing. Of those who left home, the most outstanding Argentine in New York would seem to be Marcelo Bonevardi (b.1929), also halfway between painting and abstract sculpture, as he creates panels of wood covered with painted canvas, panels that are true architectonic 'constructions' and have niches and objects incorporated into them. Antonio Segui (b.1934), born in Córdoba, is the best known Argentine living in Paris. He is a combination of painter-engraver-draughtsman who, through the use of black humour, pokes fun at the stereotypes of his native country, defects and transgressions that stand out more sharply because of the distance created by the fact that he has lived and worked in Paris for the last twenty years.

If Argentine sculpture was perhaps less conventional than its painting in the first thirty years of this century, this is due to the presence of an exceptional artist – Rogelio Yrurtia (1879–1950). This sculptor was sent to Europe at an early age on a scholarship awarded by his own government. His case was unusual at the time, because instead of going to Florence or Rome, he went directly to Paris, where he breathed in the inspiring genius of Rodin. Both in Paris and on his return to Buenos Aires, Yrurtia contributed to the creation of some of the most impressive monuments in the Argentine capital: *Dorrego* (1907, erected in 1926), the *Hymn to Work* (1922), and the *Mausoleum of Rivadavia* (1932), in which, although the oppressive architecture is of questionable merit, the splendid figures of Action and Justice certainly are not. Pedro Zonza Briano

(1886–1941), a man of very humble origins, began his studies in Buenos Aires, but in 1908 he won the Rome Prize, which allowed him to go to Italy for the first time, although later he would establish residence in Paris. The nature of Zonza Briano's sculpture is different from that of Yrurtia: the younger man is frankly more in Rodin's orbit, as is very noticeable in the melting of one mass into another producing pictorial chiaroscuro effects.

There are too many good Argentine sculptors to permit us to speak at length about all of them. The only alternative is to group them according to style, putting those who model by pure sensibility on one side and those we will call the architectonic sculptors on the other. Among the first we have Alberto Lagos (1893–1960) and, above all, Luis Falcini (1889–1970), an admirable romantic. Among the second, we must mention with praise Troiano Troiani (1885–1963), grandiose in the best way, a little in the Italian manner, and on the highest level, José Fioravanti (1896–1982), more solemn than Troiani and more successful with his public works, several important monuments in Buenos Aires. Alfredo Bigatti (1898–1960) is more declamatory, but his figures perhaps gain in dynamism what Fioravanti's lose because of their static nature. Bigatti, who worked in 1923 in Bourdelle's studio, learned from the French sculptor a care for the treatment of form that we also find – even more exaggerated – in Pablo Curatella Manes, another of Bourdelle's Argentine disciples. Curatella Manes (1891–1962) was the first Argentine sculptor to pursue a notable double career as both figurative and abstract artist, having been a member of the Cubist movement since 1920. Although he simplified his figures into large straight or curved planes, when he approached abstraction his exceptional talents as a plastic artist asserted themselves still more.

Two other notable Argentine sculptors were trained in Paris, where they lived until their deaths. Sesostris Vitullo (1899–1953), who had studied in Buenos Aires, appeared in Paris in 1925 to join Bourdelle's studio. As in the other cases we have noted, Vitullo failed to catch the 'heroic' style of the master. He did learn from him, however, how to schematize form using a semi-abstract, semi-figurative approach, which he translated by carving directly on stone and wood. Alicia Penalba (1913–82) is an interesting case because of the about-face she executed during her career. At the advanced School of Fine Arts in Buenos Aires she had studied drawing and painting, but as soon as she reached Paris in 1948 she signed up for a course in printmaking at the Academy. Only later did she discover her true vocation, which was sculpture. She spent three years in Zadkine's studio, becoming his most brilliant disciple of that period. Penalba always practised that form of abstraction which we have already characterized as 'biomorphic'. Her works contain a reminder of the vegetal world which she interpreted on different scales, in different metals and finishes, from the monumental to the tiny jewel.

Among the best known sculptors who remained predominately in Argentina is Líbero Badii (b.1916). After studying in Buenos Aires he travelled to Europe following the Second World War, where he consolidated his style, which is always figurative in the last analysis, although it also exhibits a stylization that is one of his characteristics. Enio Iommi (b.1926) is a self-taught artist who grew up in a family of Italian sculptors. Before he reached his twentieth birthday he was already a concrete artist, following the movement we alluded to earlier in our discussion of painting. In this period Iommi was only interested in working with hard materials – like stone and stainless steel – to build geometric forms that expressed a 'gesture' almost without occupying a place in space. Much later, after 1977, he became interested in other problems, whose resolution involved the association of the most heterogeneous materials in the construction of 'ironic monuments', a tradition that appears in Latin America mainly among Colombians and Argentines.

URUGUAY

Like the incomparable Juan Manuel Blanes (1830–1901) in the nineteenth century an Uruguayan painter Joaquín Torres-García (1874–1949) brought fame not only to his country but to the whole continent in the twentieth century. It is difficult to summarize such a full life. The son of a Catalan family, he moved with his parents to Catalonia at the age of seventeen. Educated from youth at the Barcelona Academy, the young Uruguayan seems to have appropriated, during his career, the whole history of art for his personal use. Thus, beginning with a 'classical' period within the Mediterranean tradition, he spent some time in Italy and then passed two difficult years in New York (1919–21), where perhaps his response to the skyscrapers, with their vertical and horizontal masses, provided the seeds of his future constructivism. He returned to Paris in 1922, where he joined other artists who shared his tendency. There he painted 1,500 pictures in which he put his theories into practice. Finally, returning to Montevideo in 1934, he founded the Torres-García Workshop where he had some brilliant disciples, among them his own sons Augusto and Horacio. What is the nature of a Torres-García painting? It depends on the period examined. First, he moves from normal figurative art to a synthesis of flat mass and colour, without any chiaroscuro or volume. Later, at the culmination of the style, the painting is reduced to the division of its surface, according to the 'golden section', and the presentation of virtual 'logos' that represent the sun, man, a clock, and so forth. All is painted in white, black and grey, with an extreme severity that is never unintentional.

Although Pedro Figari (1861–1938) was born before Torres-García, he did not become a full-time painter until 1920, when he was nearly sixty years old. Figari studied drawing and painting as a child, but later concentrated on his career as a lawyer, which he practised all his life alongside his distinguished role as a politician. In 1921 he left all his duties in these fields and moved, first to Buenos Aires and later, in 1925, to Paris, where he painted for nine years. He is the antithesis of Torres-García. For Figari, what matters is a fleeting impression of the whole that also implies movement, translated into brilliant spots of colour. His South American themes portray city and countryside as they might have appeared in the nineteenth century. This featuring of local themes was important because it inspired other South Americans to try to recapture their own history without succumbing to facile folkloricism.

Another excellent painter who, like Torres-García, lived for relatively short periods in his own country, was Rafael Barradas (1890–1929), who left Uruguay at the age of twenty-two and returned later only to die young. Barradas settled in Spain, where he pursued his entire career. Spain thus claims him as its own artist. His painting consists of an interpretation of everyday life in terms of simplified lines and masses which are presented in a deliberately greyish, neutral colour scheme. Other painters like José Cúneo (1887–1970), on the other hand, in spite of making numerous trips to Europe, felt closely linked to their own country. It is revealing that his series have titles like 'Ranches', 'Moons', or 'Uruguayan Watercolours', and are treated in the expressionist manner – dark, dense, thickly painted interpretations of the tellurian South America. Later on, when he had switched to informalism, he signed his canvases Perinetti, which was his mother's maiden name. Unlike Torres-García, this excellent painter apparently left no artistic heirs.

José P. Costigliolo (b.1902) boasted of being an outsider, as was Cúneo in his way, *vis-à-vis* the tacit dictatorship of the Torres-García Workshop. Costigliolo began to paint abstractly in 1929, although until 1946 he had to earn a living working in advertising. His figurative painting is reminiscent of the work of the Guatemalan Mérida – the solutions are not infinite – but, on the other hand, his pure abstractions are completely original and quite unique in the Río de la Plata region.

Julio Alpuy (b.1919) seems to us – with the exception of the sculptor Gonzalo Fonseca – the most original of Torres-García's disciples. Without abandoning the master's method, he never renounced figurative art, which he projected onto his canvases or his carved, polychrome wooden reliefs. We must also mention Washington Barcala (b.1920), who joined the Torres-García Workshop in 1942, where he learned an austere discipline, but one that never lacked grace and sensitivity. In his later work Barcala did geometric painting of counterposed solid-colour planes with smooth surfaces, to which he added relief elements that enrich the texture of the whole.

To end this list – from which, naturally, many names are missing – we should mention two contemporary artists who are very different from each other. Nelson Ramos (b.1932) studied two different painters, the Uruguayan Vicente Martin, a figurative painter, and the Brazilian Iberé Camargo, a semi-abstract one. His most characteristic works are panels on which he builds up in a neutral pigment, with an occasional isolated element of bright colour, as if he were working in relief. He is not only looking for the 'material nature' of the work, but also trying to find a relation between verticals and horizontals, between surface and depth. The lesson of Torres-García has still not been completely forgotten in Uruguay. José Gamarra (b.1934) studied in Montevideo and Rio de Janeiro, thanks to a scholarship. He has lived in Paris for more than twenty years, where he launched a brilliant career creating a sort of 'pictograph', like the symbols in cave paintings, in which he alludes to America before the 'Discovery'. Now, for several years he has adopted the apparent stance of a *naif* wise man, whereby he denounces the political situation in most of the countries of Latin America. This style of admirably painted 'comic strip' allows him to recreate a continent that seems more like something dreamed of than something real.

Modern Uruguayan sculpture begins with several very talented artists who cannot, however, be called avant-garde. For example, José I. Belloni (1882–1965), the son of Swiss parents, who studied in Lugano, Switzerland and spent many years after in Europe, is a 'popular' sculptor in the best sense of the word. His best known work, *La Carreta* (The

Wagon) (1929), conferred a degree of fame on him that is difficult to match in the Río de la Plata. José Luis Zorrilla de San Martín (1891–1965), the son of the celebrated national poet Juan Zorrilla de San Martín, studied in Montevideo and won scholarships in 1914 to Florence and in 1922 to Paris, where he stayed for many years. A naturalist like Belloni, Zorrilla's style exhibits other characteristics. He is almost always grandiosely declamatory, but he nevertheless masters all the resources of his own theatricality. He created several heroic monuments both for his own country and for Argentina. His most serene work is without doubt the marble tomb of Monsignor Mariano Soler in the Cathedral of Montevideo.

Turning to the contemporary scene, we should first mention Germán Cabrera (b.1903), who was born in Las Piedras and began his studies with the Argentine Luis Falcini in Montevideo. He spent many years in Venezuela and later, in 1946, abandoned his figurative style to devote himself to welding metals in accordance with the informalist canon of the 1950s. Later, he made large roughcut wooden boxes, which contain in their centre a kind of explosion of abstract forms made of metal. Leopoldo Novoa (b.1919) was born in Montevideo, but spent his adolescent years in Spain, returning to Uruguay in 1938. Self-taught, he was indirectly influenced by Torres-García. Since 1961 he has lived and worked in Paris where, after a period of gigantism exemplified by the mural of the Cerro Stadium in Montevideo, he has turned to more sensitive creations on a normal scale.

One of the best contemporary Latin American sculptors is Gonzalo Fonseca (1922), who was born in Montevideo and who at the age of twenty had become one of Torres-García's first disciples. Later Fonseca, who worked as an archaeologist in the Middle East, tended towards solid sculpture. His works, which are usually on a small scale, are carved directly in stone. Rather than merely abstract, they tend to be architectonic, since they are reminiscent of tombs excavated on the slopes of mountains, processional staircases, sacrificial terraces – that is, any kind of monumental form with a solemn, severe appearance. We conclude with Enrique Broglia (b.1942), who was born in Montevideo, and had the good fortune to be able to study with the great Spanish abstract sculptor, Pablo Serrano. Broglia spent his early years in Madrid, later set up a studio in Paris, and finally settled in Palma de Mallorca. In his solid sculpture, his creations often play with the surprising effects of torn metal. In his later work, Broglia contrasts exterior surfaces of dark, opaque bronze with interior ones that are polished, bright and capable of reflecting the world around them.

Three isolated events set the stage for the advent of modern art in Brazil. The first was an exhibition by the Lithuanian painter Lasar Segall (1891– 1957) in São Paulo in 1913; the second a show of works by Anita Malfatti in 1917; and finally, in 1920, the 'discovery' by a group of artists and intellectuals of the work of the sculptor Victor Brecheret. Then came the famous Semana de Arte Moderna, also in São Paulo, in February 1922. An avant-garde group of intellectuals, sponsored by wealthy and influential patrons of the arts, organized a festival at the Municipal Theatre that lasted for three nights, with poetry readings, music recitals, lectures and visual arts exhibitions. The group, made up of musicians, poets, writers, architects and plastic artists, was trying to achieve something whose goal was, in the words of Mário de Andrade, 'to fight for the permanent right to pursue the aesthetic quest, the actualization of Brazilian artistic intelligence, and the establishment of a national creative consciousness'.

Among those present who were to have important careers were two women, Anita Malfatti and Tarsila do Amaral. Anita Malfatti (1896– 1964), who studied in Germany with Lovis Corinth and at the Art Students' League in New York, brought back a strident violence from her travels, unknown in Brazil until then. Unlike the more contained and sadder violence of Lasar Segall, Malfatti's projected itself through a heightened sense of colour that the painter would later lose forever. Tarsila do Amaral (1890–1973) only began to practise art at the age of thirty. In 1922 she went to Paris to study in the studios of Leger, Lhote and Gleizes, and she continued to experiment when she returned to São Paulo for a few months in time to attend the Week of Modern Art festival. Tarsila's first paintings collided with the taste of the aesthetes. They contained microcephalic figures with enormous feet and hands. It was really the first stage of the future movement of Anthropophagia, which Oswald de Andrade – Tarsila's husband – would develop later in the form of a Brazilian cultural theory. However, this 'ideological' period – which pleased her critical compatriots – lasted, in fact, only a short time. The artist turned afterwards to a highly constructed geometrical figuration in pastel tones. Another version of this 'Brazilianism' – carried to extremes – can be found in the work of Emiliano Di Cavalcanti (1897–

1976). He was born in Rio de Janeiro but had his first exhibit in São Paulo in 1917. Di Cavalcanti is, above all, a painter of women, especially mulattas, and the night life of Rio de Janeiro, where he spent his whole life. In a way he seems to be a precursor of Cândido Portinari, who never had Di Cavalcanti's charm, although on the other hand, he surpassed him in depth of meaning.

Cândido Portinari (1903–62) was born in Brodosqui, in the state of São Paulo, and was the second of twelve children. His parents, Italian immigrants, were humble farm workers. As a child he was sent to Rio de Janeiro where he completed his elementary education and then enrolled in the Escola de Belas Artes. He soon won a scholarship, which enabled him to spend two years in Paris, from where he made frequent trips to Spain and Italy, to be inspired by the great fresco painters of the Renaissance. His work was rewarded when in 1935 he won a prize from the Carnegie Institute in Pittsburgh. Suddenly his own country now 'discovered' him and showered him with commissions, many of which he carried out in collaboration with the architect Oscar Niemeyer. An example of this partnership is the chapel of Saint Francis in Pampulha, on the outskirts of Belo Horizonte. Portinari's passion was the monumental form, to which he then applied subdued colours which were nothing like the loud hues that might have been expected from a tropical painter. In spite of having been a man of leftist political attachments, Portinari also painted many Christian religious themes, and not only with respect, but with love.

Here it is necessary to compare the relative weight of the cultural movements in Rio de Janeiro and in São Paulo, cities which are traditionally rivals. In the thirties, a group of artists from São Paulo founded the Familia Artistica Paulista, which held exhibitions in the country's two major cities. Around the same time the Salon Paulista de Belas Artes began, followed by the salon of the Artists' Union and the May salons (1937–9). These were really an anticipation of the São Paulo Bienal, which began in 1951. In Rio de Janeiro, exhibitions began to be held on a more and more regular schedule, partly thanks to the efforts of the Association of Brazilian Artists. These shows took place at the Palace Hotel and were held from 1929 to 1938. The decade of the 1940s – with the resistance to the dictatorship of Getúlio Vargas and the euphoria over the end of the Second World War – reflects a liberation that can be seen in a certain trend of expressionism. Other names began to appear in both the major centres, like Volpi and Bonadei in São Paulo; and Guignard,

Cícero Dias and Pancetti in Rio de Janeiro. At the same time in the state of Rio Grande do Sul Vasco Prado, Danubio and Scliar are worthy of note, and in the Northeast, Rego Monteiro and Brennand.

Alfredo Volpi (1896–1988) was a figurative painter who began by painting female nudes but soon turned to the theme that made him popular: houses, flags, banners, anything that could be subjected to a geometric plan in bright, straightforward colours. Aldo Bonadei (1906–74) studied in Florence and exhibited characteristics of the Italian school of the 1930s. Using nature as a starting point, he abstracted it in harmonious, pale colours, although his figures always had a Mediterranean solidity.

Alberto de Veiga Guignard (1896–1962) studied in Florence and Munich but, reacting against tradition when he returned to Rio de Janeiro in 1929, decided to 'become' a *naif,* and painted several beautiful works that are pleasing precisely because of their anti-cultural aspect. Cícero Dias (b.1907) was born in Recife and worked in Rio de Janeiro after 1925. In his pictures, or more precisely in his watercolours, he reveals himself as a naive surrealist, and perhaps this is why he is important in the anemic Brazilian art scene of the period. After returning from a stay in Paris, Dias became interested in abstract art and in 1948 he executed a non-figurative mural in Recife that may have been the first one in the country.

Guignard, the 'cultivated *naif*', and Dias, the 'spontaneous *naif*', bring us to José Pancetti (1902–58), whose attitude was naive although his painting was not. A sailor whose wandering life oscillated between Italy and Brazil, he painted like a self-taught artist, sometimes giving away his paintings to his shipmates, until in 1932 he began to study art, and soon became one of the best landscape painters in the country. Carlos Scliar (b.1920) recorded scenes of the riograndense countryside in his linoleum prints. At the same time he pursued a praiseworthy pictorial career which consists of a kind of post-Cubism in warm but muffled colours. Vicente do Rego Monteiro (1899–1970) was a painter who divided his life between Brazil and Paris. His formal characteristic was to reduce the human figure to geometric forms, endowing it with a strong impression of actual relief; he generally used ochres and browns.

Until the 1940s Brazilian artistic activity was restricted. There were hardly any galleries and artists often had to earn a living with a second job, in the best of cases by teaching. Furthermore, art criticism remained almost exclusively in the hands of journalists, literati and poets, although professionals now began to appear on the scene. These include Brazilians like Lourival Gomes Machado and Mario Pedrosa, and foreigners like Jorge Romero Brest, the Argentine specialist who was invited to give a series of lectures in São Paulo in 1948.

Although the essayist Mário de Andrade had been insisting for ten years on the need to create museums in Brazil, only in 1947 did the wealthy newspaper proprietor Assis Chateaubriand found the Museu de Arte de São Paulo (MASP). In 1948 the São Paulo industrialist Francisco Matarazzo Sobrinho created the Museum of Modern Art (today called the Museum of Contemporary Art). In 1951 Matarazzo also founded the São Paulo Bienal, the most important show of its kind in Latin America which has been held every two years ever since. 1948 also saw the foundation of the Museu de Arte Moderna (MAM) in Rio de Janeiro, although the present building by Affonso Reidy belongs to the 1950s.

Perhaps unjustly, we must omit from our discussion certain fine artists of this period, including some, Heitor dos Prazeres (1898–1966) and the well-known Djanira da Motta e Silva (1914–79), who are categorized by Brazilian critics as 'primitives', and who seem to us, in general, overvalued. Some local painters, like Antonio Bandeira and Cícero Dias, still went to live in Paris. In exchange, some foreigners decided to live in Brazil; for example, Samson Flexor, who did geometric abstract art, Almir Mavignier, Ivan Serpa and Abraham Palatnik. New Brazilian talents, who were able to establish a 'bridge' between figurative and abstract art included Milton Dacosta, Maria Leontina and Rubem Valentin.

In 1956 the São Paulo Museum of Contemporary Art organized its first exhibition of concrete art, bringing together, as in 1922, poets and plastic artists. After the second exhibition, two groups began to take shape. One, formed around Waldemar Cordeiro, Geraldo de Barros and Luis Sacilotto, aspired to 'pure form' with no symbolism at all. The other, with Lygia Clark (1920–88) and Hélio Oiticica (1937–80), sought a more organic vision. As their differences grew, the movement baptized 'neo-concrete' emerged in 1959 at an inaugural show in Rio de Janeiro, only to dissolve two years later. This was the moment when figurative art infiltrated, in the new form of North American-influenced pop art.

We now turn to the 'traditional' abstract or semi-abstract artists, such as the painter-draughtsman Iberé Camargo (1914–94). He draws his native countryside with affection, and in contrast also builds up dark paint on paintings which are – for him – figurative, but with extreme distortion. Another first class artist is Tomie Ohtake (b. 1913), of Japanese origin, who composes impeccable canvases which are divided into 'free' geometric zones that she covers with strange colours and that harmonize very well with each other. To continue with the Japanese Brazilians we may mention Manabû Mabe (b.1924), whose colour work is astonishing, although his paintings gradually became less and less structured. A step further towards informalism is represented by Flávio Shiró (b.1928), who lives in Paris and paints in greys or dull colours that take shape in thick, opaque applications of paint. Different from all these artists is Arcángelo Ianelli (b.1922), who belongs to the hard edge school of abstraction. His style consists of the superimposition of translucent planes in only two or three colours, which nevertheless suggest the impression of depth.

In the early sixties art became politicized. There were groups of students who arrived at aesthetic questions only by starting with social reality. This process was, however, interrupted by the overthrow of democracy by the military in 1964. Now, with political art prohibited as subversive, a return to figurative art occurred, including manifestations such as 'happenings'. This did not prevent the period from 1967–72 from being in terms of art one of the most active the country had seen. Here is a list of the major manifestations: the Opinião exhibition (1965 and 1966), at the Museum of Modern Art in Rio de Janeiro; Brazilian Vanguard (1966), in Belo Horizonte; the Brazilian New Objectivity Show (1967), also at the Museum of Modern Art, which included artists like Vergara, Gerchman, Magalhães, Leirner and Nitsche. It was a figurative exhibition, but it was not organized in the traditional manner but with a critical eye, analysing the trend towards technology and utilization. It included the *object,* the *environment,* and even the spectator as *creator* of the work on display. At the same time it stressed the step from the 'object' to the 'idea', which the critic Roberto Pontual calls 'the leap from the retina to the mind'. That is to say, we find ourselves face to face with what is called conceptual art.

This does not mean that painting – as painting – had disappeared from Brazil. Here are two examples that demonstrate the contrary. Antonio Henrique Amaral (b.1935) is a São Paulo native who began as a printmaker and became one of the best painters in the country. Using a hyper-realist approach in the North American style, he nevertheless managed to imbue his paintings with explosive political content. At the beginning, Amaral discovered the theme of bananas: pierced, sliced, in bunches, he represents them in enormous, detailed images. Of course these paintings demand to be read differently from what they seem to represent. Later this painter found other 'tropicalist' motifs which, however, he did not carry off as well. João Cámara Filho (b.1944), of Recife, became the figurative *engagé* favourite of Brazilian criticism. His painting, more than simply aggressive, is truculent, with long series of paintings on political or sexual themes. They aim to do more than break a taboo, which is surprising in such a liberated country. The explicit message is overstated. On the other hand, not everyone appreciates the intrinsic pictorial quality of these works, which come dangerously close to pamphlet art.

At the beginning of this section we mentioned the sculptor Victor Brecheret (1894–1955) as a precursor of modern art. A native of São Paulo, he studied first in his own city, then from 1913 to 1916 in Rome, and the next three years in Paris where he fell under the combined influence of Rodin, Bourdelle and Mestrovic. He even adopted certain art deco mannerisms, which he later transformed into monumental sculpture. In 1920 he exhibited the maquette of his *Monument to the Bandeirantes,* but he did not begin work on the colossal sculpture until 1936; it was finally unveiled in São Paulo in 1953. Brecheret was a sculptor of compact, stylized figures with unmistakable round, glossy volumes. He was one of those rare artists who was equally at home on a small scale as on the monumental, and who moved with natural ease from bronze to smooth or rough-textured stone.

One of the pioneers in the field of women's sculpture, which has recently become so important in all of Latin America, was María Martins (1903–73). After starting out as a painter, she turned to sculpture and studied in Paris and then, during the Second World War, with Lipchitz in New York where she moved from surrealism to the strictest abstraction. She has important works in Brasília, both in the Alvorada Palace and the Ministry of Foreign Relations. The hero of Brasília, however, is Bruno Giorgi (1908–92), who was born in the state of São Paulo but lived in Italy, his parents' homeland, for many years. He began his studies in Paris with Maillol, whose influence is evident in his solid forms with vague details in stone. At other times, however, he worked with a linear silhouette which is very legible from a distance, as in the case of *Os Guerreiros,* which has become a kind of logo for Brasília. Franz J. Weissmann (b.1914) was born in Vienna, Austria, but moved to Rio de Janeiro at the age of ten, where he later studied sculpture with the Polish artist Zamoyski. In 1946 he moved to Belo Horizonte, where, together with the painter Guignard, he founded the first modern art school in that city.

Weissmann is an intransigent purist in contemporary Brazilian sculpture. His work is abstract, geometric and metallic, and these qualities are expressed through solemn structures on a large scale.

With Lygia Clark we completely depart from the framework of traditional sculpture, and find ourselves on the edge of certain experiments which at first could be assimilated into a sculptural approach, but later became pure 'actions' in which the artist encouraged the participation of the spectator through movement. A diametrically opposite approach – not intellectual but almost ecological – is found in the work of Franz Krajcberg (b. 1921), who was born in Poland and came to Brazil in 1948. After going through an abstract phase, in the sixties he began to use elements taken directly from nature in his work, such as stones, leaves and roots. He presented these either without modification or painted overall in opaque colours. Yet another view is the one of Ione Saldanha (b. 1921), who began as a figurative painter and then was overtaken by abstraction. In her most recent work she creates spatial sets in which she presents forests of bamboo shoots coloured horizontally in bright, lively hues. An outsider in his manner is Mario Cravo Júnior (b. 1923), from the state of Bahia. He is a draughtsman, printmaker, sculptor and man of action. He was one of the founders of the first modern art show in Salvador in 1944. In his sculptural work he uses every kind of material, including very modern ones like polyester. He built a large geometric fountain in the port area of the city of Salvador.

Certain 'marginal' artists whose production can be assimilated – with good will – into the category of sculpture include Wesley Duke Lee (b. 1931), who in 1967 began to show large constructions which he calls 'spatial ambientations', and his friend Nelson Leirner (b. 1932), who is interested in activating the participation of the spectator. Leirner works with objects from real life, linked together in an arbitrary manner with the use of new techniques such as neon light. There are other artists who are just as avant-garde as these, except that they do not seek to provoke, nor are they committed to the latest fashions in art. Abraham Palatnik (b. 1928) was born in Rio Grande do Norte and emigrated with his family to Israel, where he was educated. When he returned in 1948 he became the pioneer of kinetic art in Brazil, and was one of the first artists in the country to perceive the importance of technology as applied to the aesthetic experience. Sérgio de Camargo (1930–90), on the other hand, was purely a sculptor. He was born in Rio de Janeiro but studied in Buenos Aires with Pettoruti and Lucio Fontana. He lived in Paris until 1974, and then returned permanently to Rio. Camargo is a sculptor of truncated solids, which he 'accumulates' or presents in the form of totem poles or 'vibrating walls' all in one colour. At first he worked with white-painted wood, but then he used marble from Carrara which is undoubtedly a higher quality material. Camargo is considered one of the most important artists of his kind on the continent. Finally, Yutaka Toyota (b.1931) deserves mention. He was born in Japan and went to school there. After travelling through Europe he returned to São Paulo (which he had previously visited only briefly) in 1962. He is an abstract sculptor who uses shiny metal, to which he adds the effects of colour. Many of his voluminous public works are endowed with movement, which makes them even more fascinating.

CONCLUSION

After a rather dull period from around the 1870s to the First World War, where we find some academic artists following the European eclecticism of the time, at the beginning of the 1920s a kind of artistic 'explosion' took place throughout Latin America. It was one of the most fertile, inventive and innovative moments in the development of its plastic arts. Latin American artists, like North American, and for that matter Australian or Japanese, were fascinated by the European vanguard of the early twentieth century. The fact of their having been inspired by or having imitated the advanced western models and norms, in their transition from a more or less dead academic art, not only does not constitute an original sin, but was a most spontaneous and healthy response. Without anyone planning it in advance, around this time things began to change and become revitalized, in Mexico thanks to muralism, in Brazil with the Semana de Arte Moderna, and in the Southern Cone with the widespread success of the so called 'School of Paris'. Twenty-five years later, immediately after the Second World War the foreign model was what for convenience – without naming its subspecies – we call the 'New York School'. The best Latin American art of this century, however, is independent and distinct from its presumed models: only the mediocre and second-rate artists have naively or intentionally imitated what came to them from outside.

Here are some concrete examples. The three best known Mexican mural painters alone revived the mural, an art form that had fallen into disuse; their contemporaries, – with exceptions like Puvis de Chavannes – had been praticising the genre in a routine and lifeless manner. Each of those Mexican artists approached the mural in his own way. Rivera 're-read' the Italian *Quattrocento* and infused it with modern political content. Orozco worked on a monumental scale and relied on gray, black and touches of yellow and red to evoke apocalyptic flames and banners. Siqueiros introduced new sorts of pigments, exaggerated foreshortening and perspective. This had never been done before, and Europe and the United States at the time paid more than benign attention to this Mexican painting. The works of these three painters are still preserved on the walls of several important North American institutions.

When Torres-García, who was educated in Barcelona, Paris and New York, returned to Montevideo to found his Workshop, he was not influenced by Mondrian, as has falsely been said. Colleagues in the *Cercle et Carré* movement (which the Uruguayan had begun with the Belgian Michel Seuphor), Torres-García and Mondrian are, strictly speaking, two painters who are independent from one another. It is easy to see that constructivism, in the case of the Dutch artist, was carried to its theoretical extremes: white striped with black and the frugal use of primary colours. Torres-García, on the other hand, of Mediterranean origins, practised his art through that inherent quivering hand – 'with feeling', as they say in the art studios – investing his works with a strange symbolism. Nothing like that had ever been seen in the world.

Was Matta, the Chilean who was discovered by the 'official' surrealists, merely one more surrealist? Hardly. His formula, invented by him alone – and not pursued intellectually – is a fantastic visceral image vision, a premonitory biological-cosmic science fiction. And it is certainly not the case that he imitated the Armenian-North-American Arshile Gorky; rather the reverse is true, and this can be corroborated by comparing their respective chronologies.

And what can be said of the Argentine kinetic artists: Le Parc, Demarco, García Rossi, Tomasello and their Venezuelan counterparts: Soto, Cruz-Diez and Otero? They all went to Paris in the fifties and declared themselves followers of the Hungarian Vasarely (who came from the Bauhaus) and the North American Calder. All those stubborn South Americans produced innovations which for years were not appreciated in the very city where they wanted to be recognized, until the Germans, Italians and English began to imitate them. Then there are the North Americans themselves, who, when they talk about 'op art', only mean a brief cultural fad in New York – until it was snuffed out by advertising and design – a visual expedient which in reality they had copied from the art produced for years by the Latin American kinetic group in Paris.

Besides the great figures of the 1920s and 1930s we can perhaps find ten to twenty careers in Latin American painting and sculpture in the second half of the twentieth century, sharing originality and substance and making a distinctive contribution to the art of the world. The time has come to discover them, just as the best Latin American literary figures were discovered twenty to thirty years ago by a surprised and delighted international public.

10

CINEMA

INTRODUCTION: THE SILENT ERA

With the advent of the centenary of cinema, each country has a story to tell about the arrival of moving pictures in the last decade of the nineteenth century. On 6 August 1896, in Mexico, C. F. Bon Bernard and Gabriel Veyre, agents of the Lumière brothers, showed the President of Mexico, General Porfirio Díaz and his family the new moving images. Three weeks later they gave public screenings. And they began to film the sights of Mexico, in particular those in power in the land: Díaz on his horse in Chapultepec Park, Díaz with his family, scenes from the Military College. At the end of the year Veyre left Mexico and arrived in Cuba on 15 January 1897. He set up in Havana, at 126 Prado Street, and a few days later the local press announced screenings in the Parque Central alongside the Tacón theatre. Particular favourites were the 'Arrival of the Train', 'The Puerta del Sol Square in Madrid' and 'The Arrival of the Czar in Paris'. Veyre went down to the fire-station in Havana to film the activities there. He took along with him María Tubau, a Spanish actress who was the star of the theatre season. It is said that she wanted to see the fireman at work. What is more likely is her early fascination with a medium, still in its infancy – the shots of the firemen last one minute – which would incorporate theatre and its forms into a new language. It would not be long before the public would prefer actresses like María Tubau on screen to endless shots of their ruling families in public or at leisure, or of worthy demonstrations of civic duties, for the cinema released dreams of modernity, opening up new horizons of desire.

In 1896 moving images had also arrived in Argentina and Brazil. The first establishment in Rio de Janeiro to project the new medium on a regular basis was the aptly named Salão de Novidades set up by two

Italian immigrants, the Segreto brothers, in 1897. They soon changed the name of their hall to Paris no Rio, in deference to the pioneering work of the Lumières and as an assertion that the cultural modernity of the European metropolitan centers had found a home in the South.

Cinema took root in the developing cities of Latin America during the next twenty years. 'Along the way', wrote Clayton Sedgwick Cooper in Rio de Janeiro in 1917, 'sandwiched in between business, art, press, politics, are the omnipresent and irrepressible moving picture theatres, which here in Rio de Janeiro, as in every South American city and town from the top of the Andes to Patagonian Punta Arenas, give evidence by their number and popularity of the picture age in which we live . . . The people of the country . . . are getting expert with the moving picture camera, and more and more purely national subjects, having to do with the plainsmen's life or description or romances set in the interior of the big Republic, are finding their popular following.'[1] Speed, motorized transport (trams and trains), artificial light, electricity cables, radio aerials were signs of the changing perceptions of modernity and the growth of a culture industry in which cinema would become central. But it was also a 'peripheral modernity', in Beatriz Sarlo's apt phrase, in societies of uneven development.[2] In the case of cinema, progress required advanced technologies which increasingly only the metropolitan centres could provide.[3]

Cinemas, rudimentary or sophisticated, mushroomed in the urban centres and from these centres, the itinerant film-maker/projectionists could follow the tracks of the railways which, in the interests of the export economies, linked the urban metropolis to the interior, projecting in cafés and village halls or setting up their own tents (*carpas*). As early as 1902, there were some 300 cinemas in Mexico. A heterogeneous public learned to dream modern dreams. 'In the cinema', Carlos Monsiváis has written, 'they learned some of the keys to modern life. The modernization presented in films was superficial but what was seen helped the audiences to understand the change that affected them: the destruction or abandonment of agricultural life, the decline of customs once considered eternal, the oppressions that come with industrialisation . . . Each melodrama was an encounter with identity, each comedy the proof that we do not live

[1] Clayton Sedgwick Cooper, *The Brazilians and their Country* (New York, 1917).
[2] Beatriz Sarlo, *Una modernidad periférica: Buenos Aires, 1920 y 1930* (Buenos Aires, 1988).
[3] On 'peripheral' modernity in Brazil, see Roberto Schwarz, 'The cart, the tram and the modernist poet', in *Misplaced Ideas: Essays on Brazilian Culture* (London, 1992), p. 112.

our lives in vain.'[4] It was an audience whose horizons of desire were already being expanded by mass circulation popular literature, the sentimental serial novels, and new magazines in the style of the Argentine *Caras y Caretas,* which began publishing at the end of the nineteenth century, together with the radio and the record industry which made great advances in the 1920s.[5]

The values and themes embedded in the early filmic melodramas, as in the serial novels, hark back to 'pre-modern' moments, to the values and stabilities of the neighborhood, the *barrio,* as opposed to the dangers of the new. Critics have argued that the Mexican sentimental naturalist novel *Santa,* published by Federico Gamboa in 1903, contains many of the keys of later Mexican melodramas: the eternal values of the provinces (the book opens in the idyllic village of Chimalistac) as opposed to the vice of the cities (the heroine ends up in a brothel in the centre of the city). The provinces are populated by hard-working, respectful, honourable families, organized by beatific mothers, in the setting of harmonious nature. The city is the site of immorality, sensuality, disease and death. A woman is pure and good as a virgin, but can become perverted when seduced.[6] The first of many versions of *Santa* was filmed by Luis G. Peredo in 1918. The lyrics of tango, in the 1910s and 1920s in Argentina, work with similar simple oppositions: a protagonist is often stranded in the world of modernity ('Anclado en Paris' – anchored in Paris), dreaming and singing nostalgically of his mother, friends, the lovers' nest (*bulín*), the *barrio.* In contrast, an *ingenu(e)*, is propelled into the world of modernity, prostitutes have hearts of gold, the *barrio* offers the site for homespun wisdom. The trauma of the new is both desire and threat. If Peter Brook is correct to argue that melodrama is 'a fictional system for making sense of experience as a semantic field of force [that] . . . comes into being in a world where the traditional imperatives of truth and ethics have been violently thrown into question',[7] then it can be seen as a way of structuring the values of a post-revolutionary Mexico, or of the inhabitants of São Paulo or Buenos Aires caught in the maelstrom of the new.

Melodrama was also the dominant mode of the French and particularly

[4] Carlos Monsiváis, 'Mexican cinema: of myths and demystification', in John King, Ana M. López and Manuel Alvarado (eds.), *Mediating Two Worlds: Cinematic Encounters in the Americas* (London, 1993), p. 143.

[5] Beatriz Sarlo, *Jorge Luis Borges: A Writer on the Edge* (London, 1993), ch. 1.

[6] Gustavo García, 'Le mélodrame: la mécanique de la passion', in P.A. Paranagua (ed.), *Le Cinéma Mexicain* (Paris, 1992), p. 177.

[7] Peter Brook, *The Melodramatic Imagination* (New Haven, Conn., 1976), pp. 14–15.

Italian films that dominated the world market up to the 1910s, and millions of first and second generation Italian immigrants throughout Latin America as well as *criollos,* could enjoy the stylized gestures of the great divas, Francesca Bertini, Pina Menichelli, Hesperia and Maria Jacobini. Yet it would be to the Hollywood star system that audiences in Latin America would be drawn once the U.S. film industry resolved the disputes of the Patents War and began to invade the world market from the mid-1910s, initially with the successful superproductions of D. W. Griffith. Lillian Gish and Mae Marsh worked with Griffith and soon they and a number of other emblematic idols could be found in photojournals throughout Latin America: Theda Bara, John Barrymore, Rudolph Valentino, Mary Pickford, Gloria Swanson and in particular Greta Garbo and Marlene Dietrich. All over Latin America, dozens of such journals appeared: *Cinearte* in Brazil, *Hogar y Cine, Cinema Chat* and *Héroes del Cine* in Argentina, *La Gaceta Teatral y Cinematográfica* in Cuba. All disseminated modern dreams, marketing the desire for the new. And the emblems of the new were the stars of Hollywood. From about 1915, the preeminence of Hollywood cinema was established. By December 1916 the trade newspaper the *Moving Picture World* could remark, 'The Yankee invasion of the Latin American film-market shows unmistakable signs of growing serious. It may before long develop into a rush as to a New Eldorado.'[8] North American films could achieve such dominance because in general they were amortized in the home market (which contained about half of the world's movie theatres) and could thus be rented cheaply abroad. U.S. distributors, taking advantage of the semi-paralysis of European production in the First World War, gained control of foreign markets almost without competition and successfully combated renewed opposition after the war.[9] The modern dreams of Hollywood were more complex and more entertaining than rudimentary national cinemas as Jorge Luis Borges noted. He talks of going to the cinema in Lavalle Street which, even today, contains the highest proportion of cinemas in Buenos Aires. 'To enter a cinema in Lavalle Street and find myself (not without surprise), in the Gulf of Bengal or Wabash Avenue seems preferable to entering the same cinema and finding myself (not without surprise) in Lavalle Street.' Why support the national product, thought Borges, if it was badly made: 'To idolise a ridiculous scarecrow because it is autoch-

[8] Quoted in Kristin Thompson, *Exporting Entertainment* (London, 1985), p. 79.
[9] Thomas H. Guback, 'Hollywood's international market' in T. Balio (ed.), *The American Film Industry,* revised ed. (Wisconsin and London, 1985), p. 465.

thonous, to fall asleep for the fatherland, to take pleasure in tedium because it is a national product – all seem absurd to me.'[10]

If Hollywood provided the images of modernity and the technological sophistication of the new medium, Latin America, in particular Mexico, could offer the United States a series of exotic images of bandits, 'greasers', noble savages and beautiful señoritas. It is not the purpose of this chapter to explore U.S. or European images of Latin America, to chart the shifting positions of Hollywood as cultural ethnographer, creating rather than reflecting images of 'otherness'. This analysis can be found elsewhere.[11] It is interesting to note, however, that Mexico, in both U.S. documentaries and in fictional films (especially the Western), appears as both desire and threat. It has been well remarked that 'Mexico is the Western's id. South of the border is to the body politic of the Western what below the belt is in popular physiology – a place where dark desires run riot, a land not just of wine, women and song, but of rape, treachery and death.'[12] U.S. newsreel cameramen followed closely the vicissitudes of the Mexican Revolution. For a time, before he had the audacity to lead a raid across the border, Pancho Villa was the 'star' of the Revolution, a presence which beguiled journalists and film-makers from John Reed to Raoul Walsh. Villa even signed a film contract with Mutual Film Corporation and, in return for $25,000, gave them exclusive rights to film 'his' war. Publicity material on billboards and hoardings throughout the United States boasted Mutual's new signing: 'Mexican War, Made by Exclusive Contract with General Villa of the REBEL Army. First reels just in and being rushed to our branch offices. These are the first moving pictures ever made at the front under special contract with the commanding general of the fighting forces.'[13] Carlos Fuentes, the Mexican novelist, imagines Pancho Villa's relationship with his cameraman, Raoul Walsh. 'He promised Walsh, the gringo with the camera "Don't worry Don Raúl. If you say the light at four in the morning is not right for your little machine, well, no problem. The executions will take place at six. But no later. Afterward we march and fight. Understand?" '[14]

The overwhelming majority of films made in Latin America in the silent

[10] Jorge Luis Borges, quoted in E. Cozarinsky (ed.), *Borges y el cine* (Buenos Aires, 1974), p. 54 (both quotations).

[11] See George Hadley-García, *Hispanic Hollywood: The Latins in Motion Pictures* (New York, 1990).

[12] Ed Buscombe, '*The Magnificent Seven*'; in John King et al. (eds.), *Mediating Two Worlds*, p. 16.

[13] Quoted in Margarita de Orellana, *La mirada circular: el cine norteamericano de la revolución mexicana* (Mexico, D.F., 1991), p. 74.

[14] Carlos Fuentes, *The Old Gringo* (New York, 1985), pp. 170–71

era were documentaries. As Jean-Claude Bernadet, the Brazil critic, has
argued from his exhaustive study of the press in São Paulo, documentary
film-makers could carve out a niche that international competitors were
not concerned with: regional topics, football competitions, civic ceremonies, military parades. These documentaries reflected society's self-image,
especially that of the aristocracy: its fashions, its power, its ease and comfort in modern cities and in a spectacular rural landscape. The scenes of
virgin landscape could be incorporated into the discourse of modernity, by
showing the raw strength of these young developing nations.[15]

Fictional films, from the few remaining examples that are still available for viewing – the film heritage of Latin America from this period has
been largely lost through neglect, indifference, lack of money and resources, or catastrophic fires or floods in archives – reveal a melange of
styles: an imitation of Hollywood, a strong influence of theatre melodrama and the presence of acts and artists from the vaudeville shows,
burlesque reviews and circuses which were the main components of popular culture in the 1910s and 1920s. One temporarily successful attempt
to harness the popularity of music to the silent screen in Brazil was the
'singing films', where duos or even whole companies sang behind the
cinema screen, attempting a rudimentary synchronization. In Argentina,
the film-maker José 'El Negro' Ferreyra drew explicitly on the world of
the *barrio* conjured up in the lyrics of tango. He could sometimes count
on Argentine band leaders such as Roberto Firpo to give his films live
backing. Remarkably, the first animated feature film in the world was
produced in Argentina – *El Apóstol* (The Apostle, 1917), animated by
Quirino Cristiani and produced by Federico Valle. Most films, however,
did not reveal such technical virtuosity.

Ferreyra, the most prolific director in Argentina, was an auto-didact,
as were most of the pioneers of the medium throughout the region. All
sought to work in the interstices of the dominant Hollywood model and
found a certain support in local audiences who were not yet so used to the
sophisticated language and techniques of Hollywood that they would
turn their back on more rudimentary national products. Different countries could point to at least one director who could consolidate a body of
work: Enrique Díaz Quesada and Ramón Peon in Cuba, Enrique Rosas,
Miguel Contreras Torres and Mimi Derba in Mexico, or Humberto Mauro

[15] Jean-Claude Bernadet, 'Le documentaire', in P.A. Paranagua (ed.), *Le Cinéma Bresilien* (Paris,
1987), pp. 165–7.

in Brazil. A brief focus on Mauro reveals the limits of the possible for film-makers in Latin America.

Born in Minas Gerais, Humberto Mauro (1897–1983) was brought up in the region of Cataguases. His early work shows the artisanal dynamism of a pioneer. He began by dabbling in the new technologies, working with electricity, building loudspeakers for radios, learning the techniques of photography from the Italian immigrant Pedro Comello.[16] Mauro and Comello together studied the techniques for making movies. In 1925, Mauro set up Phebo Films and made a film *Na primavera da vida* (In the Spring of Life) using family and friends as actors: his brother is the hero who rescues Eva Nil (Comello's daughter) from a band of bootleggers. This film brought Mauro to the attention of the Rio-based critic and cultural maecenas Adhemar Gonzaga who founded the film journal *Cinearte* in the mid-1920s and later his own production company Cinédia. Mauro's next feature, *Tesouro perdido* (Lost Treasure 1926), which starred himself together with his brother and his wife Lola Lys, won the *Cinearte* prize for the best film of the year. After this success, Rio producers tried to attract him to the city. Come here, they argued, 'cinema is the art of the tarmac.'[17]

Mauro stood wavering between these two influences – urban Brazil and the *sertão* (the backlands) – a tension that structures his following film *Braza dormida* (Burned Out Embers 1928). A landowner from Minas lives in Rio, but returns to his country estate with a new overseer. The overseer falls in love with the landowner's daughter and she is sent to Rio to avoid his amorous advances. The film comments on Cataguases and Rio as opposite poles of desire. Rio would eventually draw Mauro in, when he was invited by Adhemar Gonzaga to film the stylish *Lábios sem beijos* (Lips Without Kisses, 1930). His last feature in Cataguases was only financially viable thanks to the investment of the actress Carmen Santos, who also starred in the movie *Sangue mineiro* (Minas Blood, 1930) which once again places sophisticated characters in a love triangle set in the interior of Minas. By this time Mauro, accompanied in his last two films by the inventive cinematographer Edgar Brasil, was recognized as the most accomplished director of the day in Brazil, a reputation enhanced by his stylish *Ganga bruta* (1933).

There was little avant-garde exploration of the medium itself in the

---

[16] On the fascination of new technologies in the 1920s, see Beatriz Sarlo, *La imaginación técnica* (Buenos Aires, 1992).

[17] Bernadet, 'Le documentaire', p. 231.

1920s. If certain theorists of modernism, such as Walter Benjamin, talked of the inherently radical and experimental nature of cinema, these arguments found few echoes among the practitioners. Nor did the modernists in Latin America itself spend much time discussing cinema – the favoured forms were poetry, the novel and in particular the plastic arts. When the visionary Minister of Education in post-Revolutionary Mexico, José Vasconcelos, sought to define a cultural project for Mexico and looked for emblems of post-revolutionary optimism, he turned to the plastic artists and not to film-makers. Vasconcelos was bitterly opposed to cinema: he saw it as the work of the devil of the North, the United States, and, furthermore, there were no great cineastes, on a par with Orozco, Siqueiros or Rivera.[18] Genuinely radical, avant-garde, movies were a rarity. One notable example, *Limite* (The Boundary, 1929), was filmed in Brazil by the precocious Mario Peixoto who at, the age of eighteen, revealed a vision and a technical mastery uncommon in Latin America at the time. In 1988, almost sixty years after it was made, a panel of critics voted *Limite* the best Brazilian film of all time.

The state of Latin American cinema at the advent of the talkies was thus parlous. Directors worked within a medium and a marketplace dominated by Hollywood, though some had the raw energy to draw on strong national traditions of popular culture – melodrama, theatrical spectacle, or vaudeville and tent shows – to make movies which could attract a local audience. In Billy Wilder's classic analysis of an ageing silent movie star, *Sunset Boulevard* (1950), the 'heroine' Norma Desmond (Gloria Swanson) looks with delight at one of her famous silent roles and remarks to her 'captive' young scriptwriter: 'We had faces then!'[19] What would happen when these faces would be required to speak? No one in Latin America quite knew. A columnist in the Mexican paper *Ilustrado* remarked on 3 October 1929 that the installation of the vitaphone would raise entrance prices and would flood the market with English speaking films, comprehensible only to the minority: 'the vitapahone is the most modern calamity. Synchronized films are capable of harming the ears through their never-ending, dreadful sound-tracks . . . And it is not just a question of music, for these films will impose the English language on us. And frankly, the only people who have the right to impose a language

---

[18] See Gabriel Ramirez, *Crónica del cine mudo mexicano* (Mexico, D.F., 1989), pp. 203–4.

[19] I am grateful to Carlos Monsiváis for reminding me of this scene. See Monsiváis's beautifully illustrated *Rostros del cine mexicano* (Mexico, D.F., 1993).

on ourselves are Mexicans. Or not?'[20] In Brazil, on the other hand, Adhemar Gonzaga greeted the arrival of sound with optimism: these developments, he felt, would deal a death-blow to foreign films, drowned out by the songs and vernacular of contemporary Brazil. He ought surely to have been right; but he was wrong.

THE 1930S: THE COMING OF SOUND

The availability of synchronized sound in the late 1920s created a new, complex, situation in Latin America. Many shared the optimism of Adhemar Gonzaga: if the image could be understood everywhere, surely language and music were particular to specific cultures? Yet the expense and complexity of the new systems were too much for poorer countries; they would wait for many years to have access to these technologies. At the beginning, in Europe, only the Elstree Studios in Britain and U.F.A. in Berlin had the equipment in place, and Italian, French and Spanish producers and directors flocked to their doors. The universal language of cinema now gave way to the Tower of Babel and the confusion of tongues. How would this affect the dominance of Hollywood in the world?

The conversion to sound coincided with the 1929 Depression, which slowed down, albeit briefly, new technological options. Dubbing films, for example, was impossible in the first years since there was no means of mixing sound. Hollywood was thus in some confusion. The first, rather desperate attempts to preserve their market share abroad was to make foreign-language versions of Hollywood films. N. D. Golden, the head of the Film Division at the U.S. Department of Commerce stated the policy: 'Hollywood must make films spoken in five languages – English, Spanish, French, German and Italian – if it wants to keep for its films its great foreign markets.'[21] Hundreds of actors and aspirant script-writers from Spain and Latin America – Carlos Gardel, Xavier Cugat, Lupita Tovar, Mona Maris, Juan de Landa, Imperio Argentina, Tito Guizar were among the most distinguished – flocked to Hollywood and to other studios that opened in New York, London and Paris, to take part in 'Hollywood Spanish-Language Films'. In 1930, Paramount set up a huge studio at Joinville, on the outskirts of Paris, which could initially make films in five languages. By working a twenty-four hour schedule, it at one stage

[20] Quoted in Angel Miguel Rendón, *Los exaltados* (Guadalajara, 1992), p. 212.
[21] Quoted in Juan B. Heinink and Robert G. Dickson, *Cita en Hollywood* (Bilbao, 1990), p. 22.

reached a delirious twelve languages. This experiment lasted until the mid-1930s, with peak production in 1930 and 1931. Historians have made a recent inventory of these films and show that sixty-three films were made in 1930 and forty-eight in 1931.[22] After that numbers declined.

There are many reasons for the relative failure of this scheme. Films were expensive to make and did not return a profit. Local audiences wanted to see the Hollywood stars and were not happy to tolerate their Hispanic substitutes. Accent, dialect and even physiognomy varied wildly with each line-up of Latin American and Hispanic actors, something that producers could not detect – to them one Hispanic looked and sounded very much like another – but a detail that did not escape the 'Hispanic' public, who were irritated when an Argentine had a Mexican brother and a Catalan sister. By the early 1930s, dubbing and subtitling had improved and Hollywood, coming out of the Depression, regained or even increased its market share. The Motion Picture Producers and Distributors of America (MPPDA), was an effective pressure group for U.S. films, seeking to maintain an 'open door' policy in the face of possible tariff, quota or exchange restrictions.

If the substitution of actors in mainstream Hollywood productions did not work, Hollywood could boast of a few successes in the field of Hispanic language films. Paramount had the wit to sign up tango singer, Carlos Gardel who, by the late 1920s, was a superstar throughout Latin America thanks to the growth of the record industry and the spread of radio. The simple plots of his films were structured around his extraordinary voice – Gardel needed to sing at least five tangos per movie and the audience often interrupted screenings to make the projectionist rewind the film and play the songs again. The main successes were *Melodía de arrabal* (Arrabal Melody, 1932), *Cuesta abajo* (Downward Slope, 1934) and *El día que me quieras* (The Day you Love Me, 1935). One Buenos Aires cinema cabled Paramount with the enthusiastic news that: '*Cuesta abajo* huge success. Delirious public applause obliged interrupt showing three times to rerun scenes where Gardel sings. Such enthusiasm has only rarely been seen here'.[23] The songs in *Cuesta abajo* are indeed worth hearing again, especially 'Cuesta Abajo', 'Mi Buenos Aires querido' (My Beloved Buenos Aires) and 'Olvido' (Forgetting), composed and orchestrated by the Argentine band-leader and composer Alfredo Le Pera in collaboration

---

[22] For a complete filmography, see Heinink and Dickson, *Cita en Hollywood*.
[23] Simon Collier, 'Carlos Gardel and the Cinema', in J. King and N. Torrents (eds.), *The Garden of Forking Paths: Argentine Cinema* (London, 1987), p. 28.

with Gardel. Song, dance, melodrama: these were the ingredients of Gardel's success with Paramount and these were also the ingredients of early sound cinema in Latin America: Gardel was being groomed to become a crooner in English-language Hollywood films (a slow process since he did not have a great ear for languages, as his few words of spoken French in *Cuesta Abajo* reveal), but his career came to a tragically early end when he was killed in a plane crash in Colombia in 1935.

Local entrepreneurs in Latin America soon realized the possibilities opened by sound and, in countries with a large domestic market – that is to say, Argentina, Brazil and Mexico – investment was made in machinery and in installations. Some rudimentary studios such as the Chapultepec Studios had been built in Mexico in the silent era. This complex was bought and expanded in 1931 by Nacional Productora to make 'talkies', beginning with *Santa*. Mexico Films followed suit – eleven of the twenty-one films made in 1933 were filmed in their studios. CLASA studios were set up in 1934. In Argentina two major studios were opened – Lumitón in 1932 and Argentina Sono Films in 1937 – to exploit the commercial potential of tango-led national cinema. In Brazil, Adhemar Gonzaga established the Cinédia Studios in 1930 and the versatile Carmen Santos, a pioneer woman in a male dominant industry, founded Brasil Vita Filmes in 1933, both in Rio de Janeiro, which was to become the almost exclusive centre of Brazilian film production in the 1930s and the 1940s. Other small Latin American economies found it difficult to respond to the new conditions. It would take until 1937, for example, for Cuba to produce its first feature length sound film *La serpiente roja* (The Red Snake), directed by Ernesto Caparrós, drawn from a popular radio serial.

Most of the first actors, directors, cinematographers and technicians, especially in Mexico, had received some rudimentary training in Hollywood or in New York, in bit parts or in small jobs, and early films showed both vitality and technical proficiency. *Santa*, for example, shot in 1931, was directed by Antonio Moreno, a Spanish actor who had worked in Hollywood; the cinematographer was a Canadian Alex Phillips and the two principal actors Lupita Tovar and Donald Reed had played Hispanic parts in Hollywood. By 1933, Mexico was producing films of lasting quality: among the twenty or so movies that come out in that year we find Fernando de Fuentes's *El prisionero trece* (Prisoner Number 13) and *El compadre Mendoza* (Godfather Mendoza) and Arcady Boytler's *La mujer del puerto* (The Woman of the Port). Russian emigré Boytler stylishly directed this film which, after *Santa*, firmly established the prostitute melodrama in Mexico. The heroine is betrayed by her fiancé who causes the death of her father. Bereft, she drifts into prostitution and, in a genuinely tragic ending, unwittingly sleeps with her long-lost brother. Andrea Palma – Dietrich in Vera Cruz – is a splendid Mexican vamp with her deep voice, hanging cigarette and haughty disdain. She had worked as a wardrobe assistant to Dietrich and manages to create one of the first lasting images of enigma and sadness in a rudimentary film milieu.

The films of Fernando de Fuentes of the mid-1930s establish the genre of the melodrama of the Revolution, reflecting and perhaps making sense of the huge social and cultural upheavals of the post-revolutionary period. De Fuentes early vision, like that of the novelists of the Revolution, is sombre. In *El compadre Mendoza* an opportunistic landowner is faced with the dilemma of remaining loyal to a kinsman, a general in Zapata's army, and a character clearly modelled on Zapata, and thus court economic ruin, or to betray the kinsman and save his own skin. Mendoza, under the mute, accusing gaze of his housekeeper, chooses to preserve his hacienda, but will be haunted forever by the sight of his compadre, hanged by Carranza's forces at the entrance to the estate. In the later *Vámonos con Pancho Villa* (Let's Go with Pancho Villa, 1935), Fuentes portrayal of the revolutionary forces is equally bleak as a band of friends, the Lions of San Pablo, decide to join up with the forces of Pancho Villa, but find their noble sentiments caught in a world of anarchy, stagnation and corruption. The final speech of a revolutionary in this film: 'Is this an army of men or a troop of dogs?' reverberates with tragic power.

De Fuentes captures a period and a nation in transition. 'The nation' is reflected in the faces of the principal actors, but also in the extras, as Carlos Monsiváis explains. 'Underlying philosophy: if the revolution taught us to look at ourselves, it is now necessary to specify who we are, that's to say, how the mirror of cinema accepts, essentialises or distorts us.' Soon, through persistent repetition, the 'people' of the cinema screen become 'the people': 'It is no exaggeration to state that when a Mexican of those years wants to conjure up an image of "the people", he or she can only refer to film images.'[24] These popular images are the backdrop to the main scenes of the Revolution, but they are also the faces of the family, the neighbourhood, people 'like us'. Director Juan Orol used Sara García as everyone's mother in *Madre querida* (Beloved Mother, 1935), the story of a boy sent to a reform institution, an action which causes his mother to

---

[24] See Monsiváis, *Rostros del cine mexicana*, p. 10.

die of a broken heart on Mother's Day. García later starred in a string of maternal melodramas such as *No basta ser madre* (It's Not Enough to Be a Mother 1937) or *Mi madrecita* (My Little Mother, 1940) and most famously, *Cuando los hijos se van* (When the Children Leave, 1941), directed by Juan Bustillo Oro.[25]

If Fernando de Fuentes made his most complex films about the Revolution, his most successful film – and one of the most successful films of all time in Latin America – was *Allá en el Rancho Grande* (Out On the Big Ranch, 1936). The image of the singing charro, the emblem of Mexican virility, was at one level clearly a reworking of Roy Rogers and Gene Autry films, but it added a particular Mexican pastoral fantasy to the model and also drew on Mexican popular cultural forms – the *canción ranchera* from Guadalajara and the Bajío. Song from the countryside was to become an essential part of national cinema, the sentimental underpinning linking scenes together and giving greater weight to specific situations. Singing stars – in this film Tito Guízar and in later *comedias rancheras* Jorge Negrete – become popular all over the continent. So popular that the film industry changed direction and concentrated its energies on rural dramas, set in rural bars, or in the world of Mexican *fiesta*, with *charros*, beautiful señoritas in folk costumes, mariachis and folk trios.[26] These rural melodramas are structured by paternalist feudalism, with casts of honest landowners and noble workers, harking back to a time before the Revolution when God was in heaven and benevolent, firm fathers such as Porfirio Díaz were in control and everyone knew their place. Ironically these films appeared during the radical administration of Lázaro Cárdenas (1934–40) who put agrarian reform as one of his firm priorities. Cárdenas, however, did not seek to interfere with a form that was becoming an important export item throughout Latin America. The image of the singing charro was Jorge Negrete who was arrogant, *criollo* and severe, an aristocrat, conquering the world and all its women. From his earliest film *La madrina del diablo* (The Devil's Stepmother, 1937), his image changes little: it offered the rural Mexican way of being a man.[27]

The urban equivalent to singing cowboys were the night-club crooners, Agustín Lara and, later, Pedro Infante. The scene moves from the rural cantina to the night-club or brothel, the cabaret. Lara sings the

[25] Charles Ramirez Berg has an interesting analysis of this film as a 'classically transparent text' in his *Cinema of Solitude: A Critical Study of Mexican Film, 1967–1983* (Austin, Tex., 1992), pp. 16–28.
[26] See Monsiváis, in P.A. Paranagua (ed.), *Le Cinéma Mexicain* (Paris, 1992), pp. 143–53.
[27] See Monsiváis, *Rostros del cine mexicana*, p. 12.

songs that become the stuff of *caberetera* melodrama articulating for the first time the desires and threats of a new morality, or amorality, when tradition had been turned upside down by the Revolution and by a developing, urban-centred, modernity. In Lara's idealized night life, the forbidden seemed almost within reach, the brothel was the space of exalted passions and sensibilities (*Santa* again). Pedro Infante, as we will see later, moves from night-club crooner, to the voice of the urban dispossessed in a number of key melodramas of the late 1940s. If Mexican cinema by the end of the 1930s could be said to have a toe-hold in the domestic market – figures for the decade show that Mexican films account for 6.5 per cent of the home market (Hollywood accounting for 78.9 per cent) – it was largely as a result of musical features.

It took Mexican producers a number of years almost to stumble over a successful box-office formula. Argentine producers knew from the outset that tango would be at the heart of their endeavours. Paramount in the United States had seen the profitability of Gardel: if Argentine cinema could not now afford Gardel, it could at least use his friends, the singers, band leaders and musicians of the cabaret circuit in Buenos Aires and abroad (for tango had swept Europe and the United States in the 1910s and 1920s). As in Mexico, the six hundred or so movie houses in Argentina in the early thirties were showing almost exclusively North American films, but exhibitors would not turn down a tango film. Manuel Romero, who had worked with Gardel as a librettist, was to become one of the most successful directors of the 1930s with films such as *Mujeres que trabajan* (Working Women, 1938) and the extremely popular *Los muchachos de antes no usaban gomina* (Back Then, Boys Didn't Use Hair-Cream, 1937), which starred Mireya, the woman oblivious to the advances of rich men around town. He followed these with a series of musical melodramas which often took well-known tangos as their titles, such as *Tres Anclados en Paris* (Three People Anchored in Paris, 1938). 'El negro' Ferreyra, the pioneer of silent cinema, made a successful transition to 'talkies' with a series of evocative portrayals of the *arrabales* (outskirts) and *barrios* of Buenos Aires, such as *Calles de Buenos Aires* (Streets of Buenos Aires, 1934) and *Puente Alsina* (Alsina Bridge, 1935).

In 1936, Ferreyra teamed up with Libertad Lamarque and helped to make her a star the rival of Gardel. Lamarque's life story, like that later of Eva Perón, seemed to come out of the plot of a tango melodrama. Born of humble origins in the provinces, she moved to the city and worked her way up through cabaret and vaudeville, eking out a meagre existence in a world of duplicitous men and false glamour. She wrote the script of, and starred in, the 1936 film *Ayúdame a vivir* (Help Me Live) directed by Ferreyra. This film set a style for the musical in Argentina in which the song lyrics, as in operetta or its Spanish cousin, the *zarzuela,* are built into the scripts as moments of dramatic punctuation. Gardel films, by contrast, stop when the star sings a song. These plots – the naive in the world of modernity, the tart with a heart, the *barrio* as pre-modern site of stability – and the songs could be repeated with small variations. The new immigrants to the city flocked to these movies and could empathize with the heroine who was pure and moral, struggling against the odds.

In Brazil, the musical vehicle was the *chanchada,* drawn from the vaudeville sketches of Brazilian comic theatre, as well as music and dance forms revolving around carnival. One of the first, Wallace Downey's *Coisas nossas* (Our Things, 1931), a 'Brazilian Melody', broke all box-office records in São Paulo on its release. Such films would incorporate singers already popular on the radio and in popular theatre: Paraguaçu and Noel Rosa and the orchestras of Gaó and Napoleão Tavares and Alzirinha Camargo. The amalgamation of different aspects of the developing culture industry was quite clear. Wallace Downey, for example, was a high-ranking executive in Columbia records. Cinédia Studios led the way, with successes such as Gonzaga's *Alô, Alô Brasil* (1935) and *Alô, Alô Carnaval* (1936), featuring the talented Miranda sisters. Carmen Miranda, as a singer and as a hoofer, became a major star in Brazil, with more than 300 records, five films, and nine Latin American tours, before she erupted onto the New York stage in 1939 and was immediately bought up by Fox. There, 'her explicit Brazilianness (samba song-and-dance repertoire, Carnival-type costumes) was transformed into the epitome of *latinidad.*[28] Even the most stylish Brazilian director, Humberto Mauro, was drawn to *samba* in *Favela de meus amores,* (Favela of My Loves 1935), a film which broke taboos by seeing samba not in its folklorist, tourist variation, but as a product of the vibrant popular culture of the shanty towns of Rio.

An essential aspect of *chanchada* was the stand-up comedian and the resulting plethora of verbal and visual gags. Two stars that were to emerge in the 1940s out of this tradition were Grande Otelo and Oscarito. But the first, internationally successful, comic of Latin American

---

[28] Ana López, 'Are all Latins from Manhattan?', in Lester D. Friedman (ed.), *Unspeakable Images: Ethnicity and the American Cinema* (Urbana, Ill., 1991).

cinema was Mariano Moreno, Cantinflas. He began as a tumbler, a dancer and a comedian in the popular *carpas* (tents). With his greasy shirt, crumpled, sagging trousers and large, scuffed shoes, he epitomized the *pelado,* the scruffy, street-wise neighbourhood wide-boy (the *arrabal* occupied a similar real and symbolic space in Mexico to the one we have already mapped out in Argentina), who deflates the pomposity of legal and political rhetoric. *Cantinflismo,* acting like Cantinflas, becomes a mode of speech where, delivered at breakneck speed, words go in desperate search of meanings. In his third film *Ahí está el detalle* (That's the Crux of the Matter, 1940), in the final court scene, he so disrupts the proceedings that the judge and the officials end up using the same nonsense language. In this movie he teamed up with Joaquín Pardavé, another comedian, whose trickster persona had the distinction of a resonant voice, a top-hatted elegance and a well-turned moustache. Manuel Medel was another perfect comic foil to Cantinflas in *Aguila o sol* (Eagle or Sun, 1937) and in *El signo de la muerte* (The Sign of Death, 1939). But it is the face and the acrobatics of Cantinflas that are memorable: his extraordinary arching eyebrows, leers, and his elastic limbs which contort into impossible positions. Cantinflas's films later became repetitive and hollow, but in the late 1930s and early 1940s he was at the peak of his inventiveness. It was not merely empty political rhetoric that caused Diego Rivera to include Cantinflas in his magnificent mural in the Insurgentes Theatre as a defender of the poor. Not a defender to lead them out of misery, but a man who could alleviate that misery with a few good or terrible gags.

Argentina, Brazil and Mexico, therefore, could maintain some presence in the home market and Argentina and Mexico even became successful exporters to the rest of Latin America by the late 1930s. The initiatives were based on private capital. The state, in Mexico under Cárdenas and even under Vargas's Estado Novo in Brazil, did little to protect or to sponsor local production. But several local producers exploited the market quite successfully. Apart from a number of 'quality' films that can be found in the canon of each country, the main concern is the box office, 'where', Monsiváis has written, 'success is assured by issuing films like orders, weep, repent, enjoy the beautiful unity of the family, swear never to break the rules, depart this vale of tears with an indulgent smile, get drunk . . ., serenade the whole town, kiss the hand of the little old mother, go directly to the nearest happy ending'.[29]

---

[29] Monsiváis, 'Mexican cinema', in John King et al. (eds.), *Mediating Two Worlds*, p. 145.

THE 1940S: A 'GOLDEN AGE' OF CINEMA?

Mexico

In 1940, Mexico and Argentina vied for Spanish-language dominance of the Spanish American film market. By 1945, the argument was settled in favour of Mexico, with more than a little help from north of the border. The U.S. Good Neighbor Policy of the 1930s had worked to improve the negative stereotyping of Latin America and, at the outbreak of war, a government agency, the Office of the Co-ordinator of Inter American Affairs (CIAA), was set up under Nelson Rockefeller to orchestrate economic and cultural programmes in Latin America. Nelson Rockefeller, for example, sent Orson Welles as a goodwill ambassador to Brazil in the early 1940s and supported Walt Disney in his two cartoon films *Saludos Amigos* (1943) and *The Three Caballeros* (1945), where Donald Duck teams up with new friends, the parrot José Carioca, symbol of Brazil, and the pistol-clad *charro* rooster Panchito. One bird absent from the jaunts was Martin the gaucho, since Argentina incurred the wrath – and, in the case of Secretary of State Cordell Hull, the obsessive hatred – of the State department by refusing to enter the war. The United States, as part of a package of restrictions, denied Argentina access to raw film stock, while simultaneously building up the Mexican film industry. While Argentina went into a partial decline in production, Mexico entered a fleeting 'Golden Age'. The success of Mexican cinema in the 1940s was thus given a boost by U.S. policies, but it was also guaranteed by the emergence of directors and cinematographers and the consolidation of a star system. Financial support was offered, from 1942, by the Banco Cinematográfico which was based on private capital, but with guarantees from state bodies such as the Banco de México. The closed shop union structures which were later to strangle the industry were evolved in these years.

Of the genres established in the 1930s, the revolutionary melodramas of Fernando de Fuentes found a worthy successor in the work of Emilio 'el Indio' Fernández, together with his 'team', the cinematographer Gabriel Figueroa, script writer Mauricio Magdaleno and the stars Dolores del Río and Pedro Armendáriz. In films such as *Flor Silvestre* (Wild Flower, 1943) and *María Candelaria*, 1943, Figueroa's expressive cinematography captures, in allegorical fashion, the moment of Adam and Eve in the garden of Mexico, the expressive physiognomies of the main characters, which harmonize with the expressive nature of the landscape: its lowering clouds, the emblematic plants, the play of light and dark, the shadows cast by the heat of the sun. Of course there are traces of Eisenstein's influence in this imagery (Eisenstein had spent nine months in Mexico in 1931 working on a film project that eventually he could not edit), and of photographers such as Paul Strand, but it is wrong to see the work of 'El Indio' and Figueroa as merely copying, or pandering to, European and North American images of the 'noble savage'. Both were original talents. Mexico, in these films, is elemental, atavistic, the site of primal passions, a violence from which can be forged a new progressive nation.[30]

The founding family on which this nation could be forged was made up of screen idols, Dolores Del Río and Pedro Armendáriz. Del Río had been a star in Hollywood from 1925 to 1942. There she appeared in twenty-eight films as the instinctual savage who could be tamed by love and western culture, or as a more distant, exotic, beauty. Her star appeal was beginning to fade in Hollywood by the early forties and her relationship with Orson Welles was running out of steam. She was ready for a change and 'El Indio' Fernández persuaded her to play a humble peasant girl in *Flor Silvestre* who falls in love with Juan, a landowner's son, and marries him secretly against the wishes of his severe parents. When the Revolution begins, the son's father is killed and he takes vengeance on the bandits masquerading as revolutionaries. They in turn take his wife and child as hostages and Juan, to save them, delivers himself to a firing squad, where Dolores faints over his dead body. Such were the cataclysmic moments of heroism and struggle, Dolores explains many years later to her son – a conversation which frames the main narrative – out of which modern Mexico could develop and prosper. This bald plot outline suggests conventional melodrama, but 'El Indio' carries it off with great gusto, while his 'perfect' couple, Dolores del Río and Pedro Armendáriz, convey tragedy in their stoic faces in a dialogue of elegant glances. Del Río was required to radiate a quiet, hieratic beauty. Her partner, Armendáriz by contrast was a mixture of passion, tenderness, rage and joy. Del Río went on to work again with 'El Indio' in *Bugambilia* in 1944, with Roberto Gavaldón en *La otra* (The Other Woman, 1946) and with Alejandro Galindo in *Doña Perfecta* (1950). These directors allowed her to escape from 'El Mexican aesthetics of 'El Indio' into other, more nuanced roles.

---

[30] Monsiváis, 'Gabriel Figueroa', in *Artes de México*, 2 (Winter 1988), p. 63.

The other major star in Mexico in the 1940s was María Félix. Octavio Paz has recently paid homage to her own distinct, beauty and appeal. He begins by analysing the myths of womanhood in Mexico, from the Virgin of Guadalupe and La Malinche to the revolutionary Adelita and adds: 'The myth of María Félix is different. In the first place, it is modern; secondly, it is not entirely imaginary, like all the myths of the past, but rather the projection of a real woman . . . she was, and is, defiant of many traditional conventions and prejudices . . . María Félix is very much a woman who has been bold enough not to conform to the idea of womanhood held by the machos of Mexico. Her magnetism is concentrated in her eyes, at once serene and tempestuous – one moment ice, the next fire. Ice that the sun melts into rivers, fire that becomes clarity.'[31] She came to play in a number of films whose titles reveal the on-screen persona outlined by Paz: *Doña Bárbara, Maclovia, La mujer de todos* (Everyone's Woman), *La devoradora* (The Devourer), *La generala* (The General). She had an impressive debut in *El peñon de las ánimas* (The Crag of the Spirits, 1942), playing alongside the already famous Jorge Negrete. Her third film, *Doña Bárbara* based on the famous twenties regional novel by the Venezuelan Rómulo Gallegos, gave Felix the image that would be repeated, with variations, over the next decade: the haughty, self-contained woman, the devourer of men. In marked contrast to the family melodramas of the 1940s, with Sara García as the self-abnegating mother, which rigidly upheld a patriarchal code, María Félix seemed to offer a revolt within this system. This revolt was, in the main, contained in the filmic narratives, which remain male centered. If Doña Bárbara humiliated other people around her, having been brutally raped, the film (and the book) is mainly concerned how an enlightened man Santos Luzardo, can tame and defeat this woman, rather than exploring the woman's point of view.[32]

That self-declared most macho of film directors El Indio Fernández sought finally to depict the taming of the shrew in his *Enamorada* (In Love, 1946), which paired Félix with Pedro Armendáriz. The plot, based loosely on Shakespeare, is straightforward. During the Revolution, general Reyes (Armendáriz) takes Cholula and falls in love with the beautiful Beatriz (Félix), daughter of the rich Don Carlos. She is going to marry a North American, Roberts, and treats the revolutionary badly. However, after a number of twists, Beatriz leaves Roberts on the eve of her wedding and fol-

---

[31] Octavio Paz, introduction to *María Félix* (Mexico, D.F., 1992), p. 13.
[32] See Ana López, 'Tears and Desire', in *Iris*, 13 (Summer 1991).

lows Reyes as his *soldadera*.[33] This is the film where the style of the cinematographer Gabriel Figueroa can be seen to excellent effect. Figueroa himself singles it out as one of his favourite films: 'Among the scenes I remember most enjoying as a cameraman is the end of *Enamorada*. I mention this scene because it has everything, and particularly an extraordinary visual emotion, as in the scene where the long shadows of the soldiers are projected into the heroine's house, and she begins to run among the shadows. That's a very striking scene, in which it is not technique but imagination that counts.'[34] Figueroa and other distinguished cinematographers – Agustín Jiménez, Jack Draper, Alex Phillips, Rosalío Solano – helped to define the dominant images of Mexican cinema throughout the forties and early fifties.

Not all Mexican stars were involved in revolutionary melodramas or in bucolic rural idealizations of hacienda life such as Jorge Negrete's *Ay Jalisco, no te rajes* (Oh Jalisco Don't Give Up, 1941). The modern city increasingly became both the backcloth but also one of the major themes of cinema. Director Ismael Rodríguez who had made successful *ranchera* films such as *los tres García* (The Three Garcías, 1946) turned to films which examined the culture of poverty of *barrios* of Mexico City: *Nosotros los pobres* (We the Poor, 1948) *Vds los ricos* (You the Rich, 1948), *La oveja negra,* (The Black Sheep, 1949). And in Pedro Infante he found an actor to personify the best aspects of the common man: tender, honest, handsome, long suffering, one of the boys. His saintly *novia* was often played by Blanca Estela Pavón and together they had a number of memorable scenes and song duets. These films are impossible to summarize since they contain myriad characters – structured loosely around a main character, the carpenter Pepe el Toro played by Pedro Infante, and his financial, amorous and family problems – who appear in different sketches. Among these are the lumpen women comedians, 'La Guayaba' and 'La Tostada' (Amelia Wilhelmy and Delia Magaña). *Nosotros los pobres* moves at a very fast pace, full of songs, gags, jokes and aching sentiments, and became for many years the biggest box-office success in Mexico.

While earlier images of the city are more earnest and attempt a gritty realism the films of Rodríguez had made no pretence to be realist. *Distinto amanecer* (A Different Dawn, 1943), directed by Julio Bracho, set mainly in the nightworld of Mexico City, successfully incorporates the structures of *film noir* into a political thriller. Alejandro Galindo's *Campeón sin corona*

[33] For an analysis of the film, see Jean Franco, *Plotting Women: Gender and Representation in Mexico* (London, 1989), pp. 148–52.
[34] Gabriel Figueroa, 'Un pueblo despojado de color', *Artes de México*, 10 (Winter 1990), p. 47.

(Champion Without a Title, 1945), examines the world of the urban poor and the attempts of a working-class boy, played by David Silva, to escape his background through his boxing talents. Interestingly, the theme of the underprivileged fighter trying to achieve advancement through his fists, became a favoured form in Hollywood narratives about Mexican Americans such as *Right Cross* (1950), *The Ring* (1952) and *Requiem for a Heavyweight* (1962). In Mexico, however, it was not boxers but rather masked wrestlers who would seize the popular imagination from the 1950s.

Awareness of the problems of Mexican Americans north of the border, but also of the fascination with border crossings help to account for the success of the comedian Germán Valdés, Tin-Tan. He plays a Mexican-American *pachuco*, the zoot-suited, upwardly mobile con man who can talk and dance his way out of any situation in a mixture of Spanglish idioms and border-music rhythms. By the late 1940s, the origins of Tin-Tan – the border towns such as Ciudad Juárez, the mass migrations (legal and illegal) across the border, the Americanization of Mexican culture – were all to become an irreversible part of the modern, urban Mexican experience. And Tin-Tan energetically expounds a frenetic, hybrid modernity in some of his best films, *El rey del barrio* (The King of the Barrio, 1949), and *El revoltoso* (The Rebel, 1951).

One of Tin-Tan's most regular co-stars was the exotic dancer Yolanda Montes, 'Tongolele'. Different rhythms were invading the nightclubs of Mexico City, from the North, but more particularly from the Caribbean and the south. Boleros were increasingly used in films to intensify particular heightened moments of melodrama, but there was also a considerable growth in more exotic rhythms, in particular the rumba, danced by the memorable María Antonieta Pons, Rosa Carmina and Amalia Aguilar, Meche Barba and, in particular, the Cuban Ninón Sevilla. Ninón Sevilla raised the heart-beat of audiences and critics throughout the world. The young critic turned director Francois Truffaut wrote in admiration in *Cahiers du Cinema* in 1954 under the pseudonym Robert Lacheney: 'From now on we must take note of Ninón Sevilla, no matter how little we may be concerned with feminine gestures on the screen or elsewhere. From her inflamed look to her fiery mouth, everything is heightened in Ninón (her forehead, her lashes, her nose, her upper lip, her throat, her voice) . . . Like so many missed arrows [she is an] oblique challenge to bourgeois, Catholic and all other moralities.'[35]

[35] Quoted in Jorge Ayala Blanco, *La aventura del cine mexicana* (Mexico, D.F., 1968), pp. 144–5.

To a certain extent, the films of Ninón Sevilla, directed in the main by Alberto Gout, continued the successful formula of *caberetera* films of the 1930s and 1940s, but the conditions of the late 1940s are depicted with a vulgar dynamism which is quite new. The post-war cosmopolitanism and early developmentalism which marked the Presidency of Miguel Alemán (1946–52) find a complex reflection in these extravagantly sexual and deliberately provocative movies. *Aventurera* (Adventuress, 1949) is the most accomplished film of Gout and Sevilla. Agustín Lara, the famous balladeer and crooner of the genre, once again supplies the appropriate lyrics, sung by Pedro Vargas, which serve as a leitmotif throughout the film: 'Sell your love dearly adventuress / Put the price of grief on your past / and he who wants the honey from your mouth / must pay with diamonds for your sin / Since the infamy of your ruined destiny / Withered your admirable spring, / Make your road less harsh / Sell your love dearly, adventuress.' Sevilla indeed exacts a price: by the end of the film, many of the protagonists have met grisly ends and genteel Guadalajara society is in ruins.[36]

Despite the excesses of these movies, the woman is still the site of 'spectacular' pleasure, the object not the subject of the narrative. Men occupied positions of power in the industry. The only woman film-maker of this period was Matilde Landeta, just as the actress and director Mimi Derba in the 1920s and the actress, producer and director Adela, 'Perlita' Sequeyro in the 1930s had been exceptional women film-makers in Mexico in earlier decades. Landeta had served a long apprenticeship as a script girl on almost one hundred features (from 1933) and later as an assistant to the major directors of the period. She made three features: *Lola Casanova* (1948), *La Negra Angustias* ('Black' Angustias, 1949) and *Trotacalles* (Street Walker, 1951). These films are interesting not merely as the work of a woman previously 'hidden from history' but also because they test the possibilities of an articulate pro-feminism in a male industry and society. Landeta would have to wait until the late 1980s, however, to be joined by a significant number of Mexican women working behind the camera.

The above analyses have pointed to the main trends in Mexico's most dynamic decade of film-making. The volume of output was considerable. Whereas in 1941, Mexican cinema had only 6.2 per cent of the domestic market, by 1945 this had risen to 18.4 per cent and by 1949, to 24.2 per cent. Over the decade, the average was 15.1 per cent. In 1949, Mexico

---

[36] See Eduardo de la Vega Alfaro, *Alberto Gout (1907–1966)* (Mexico, D.F., 1988).

produced a remarkable 107 films.[37] Figures are not available for the
market share of Mexico in the rest of Latin America, but the impact was
considerable: the stars of Mexican cinema, Cantinflas, Jorge Negrete,
Tin-Tan, Pedro Infante, Dolores Del Río, María Félix, Pedro Armendáriz
and Ninón Sevilla became firm favourites throughout the continent.
Mexico acted as a mini-Hollywood, making the battle for survival of
national cinemas even more difficult.

Argentina

Argentine cinema showed some of the dynamism, and indeed the quality,
of Mexican cinema in the 1940s, but was forced to struggle in the early
period against U.S. embargoes. This decade has received little critical
attention and indeed the films of the period have only in a few cases been
well preserved, so any analysis is necessarily provisional. In broad terms,
however, the most successful genre of the 1930s, the musical comedy,
continued until the mid-1940s, with Libertad Lamarque an ever-popular
star. In 1946, however, Lamarque quarrelled with the Perons and left for
Mexico where she established another successful career in films that often
aped directly the well-proven Argentine formulae. In *Soledad* (Solitude)
directed by Tito Davison in 1948, for example, she plays a young Argentine orphaned maid who is tricked into marriage, seduced and abandoned
by a self-serving man. In Mexico, she is portrayed as both mother and
entertainer and she holds her own with the greats. In 1946 Luis Buñuel
paired Lamarque with Jorge Negrete in *Gran Casino* (1946), though
Buñuel is not prepared to give her, or the portly Jorge Negrete, any special
treatment. As Michael Wood has pointed out, 'There are . . . nice gags in
this film: a love scene played straight by the principals while the camera
lingers resolutely on a sickening-looking patch of oily mud; an insistence
on showing Lamarque in extravagant close-ups and soft focus, so that she
looks like a movie-star in a museum, a rehearsal for *Sunset Boulevard*.'[38]

As urbanization increased and Argentine cinema became more secure,
more complex urban dramas took the place of the *barrio* melodramas. The
most interesting of the pre-1950 period was Luis César Amadori's *Dios se lo
pague* (God Bless You, 1948), which was nominated for an Oscar. The

[37] María Luisa Amador and Jorge Ayala Blanco, *Cartelera cinematográfica, 1940–1949* (Mexico, D.F.,
1982), pp. 373–8.
[38] Michael Wood, 'Buñuel in Mexico', in *Mediating Two Worlds*, p. 42.

location is the central streets of Buenos Aires, where an extremely intelligent beggar plies his trade outside a church and outside an aristocratic club. As the narrative develops, the spectator gradually discovers that the tramp is a mysterious millionaire who takes time out on the streets to obtain a clear perspective of the hypocrisy of life. The melodrama uses its urban locations to great effect: the main streets of Buenos Aires, where dandies and tramps rub shoulders; the *arrabal*, the Colón opera house (and an operatic conceit which requires a working knowledge of *Lohengrin*, the knight of the Grail to be fully understood); the aristocratic salons, the sight of conspicuous consumption and of the snares and delights of the modern; the town-house where the female protagonist is stifled and the Church, which resolves the tensions and blesses the new union. Other sophisticated and assured works, which mark a clear 'coming of age' include the urban comedy of manners directed by Francisco Mujíca, *Los martes, orquídeas* (Orchids on Tuesday, 1941), in which a father invents a romance for his melancholic daughter Mirtha Legrand (who suffers, like Catherine Morland, from reading an excess of romantic literature), an invention that gradually becomes a reality.

For historical-national melodramas Argentina lacked the symbols (a strong pre-Columbian past, a recent 'revolution' and a discourse of revolutionary nationalism) available to Mexico. The gaucho was only infrequently used as a symbol of a frontier society and there was little attempt to create a 'Southern' to vie with the symbolic strength and resonance of Hollywood's Westerns. Attempts at creating a national epic were made in the early 1940s by a group of writers, directors and actors who formed the group Artistas Argentinos Asociados (Associated Argentine Artists) and made two melodramas on nineteenth-century topics, *La guerra gaucha* (Gaucho War, 1942) and *Pampa bárbara* (Barbarous Pampa, 1945). *La guerra gaucha* in particular, based on the famous account by writer Leopoldo Lugones, that traces the Independence struggles of Güemes and his gaucho bands in Alto Peru in the 1810s, is full of achingly noble, Manichean, nationalist, sentiments and makes a rather rudimentary attempt to capture the grandeur of the landscape. It was a success at the box-office but came at a time when the mirror of liberal nationalism was being cracked, offering up new, unexpected and sometimes murky reflections.

In the artistic/intellectual community, most viewed the period of the first Peronist regimes (1946–55) as one of cultural obscurantism. Cinema was under the control of a Subsecretariat for Information and the Press, which acted as a form of propaganda ministry, monitoring newspapers and radio broadcasts as well as the cinema. Perón deliberately cultivated his matinée idol looks and his clear resemblance to Carlos Gardel, while Evita had come up through radio soaps and had had minor roles in the film industry as Eva Duarte. Both were, therefore, extremely conscious of the power of the image. A number of directors and actors found the regime claustrophobic and limiting and went to live abroad or else imposed strict self-censorship: Luis Saslavsky, who had directed a number of films, including the stylish comedy thriller *La fuga* (The Flight, 1937), Hugo Cristensen and the ineffable Libertad Lamarque. In these conditions, the quality of Argentine cinema fell and there was a marked decline in box-office receipts.

Perón did, however, offer the first state support for Argentine cinema. Up until his regime, producers were mainly weak and divided and at the mercy of distributors and exhibitors who had a strong investment in promoting North American films. Perón sponsored various measures to protect the Argentine film industry which included the establishment of screen quotas and distribution on a percentage basis for Argentine films, state bank loans for financing film productions, a film production subsidy programme and restrictions on the withdrawal of earnings from Argentina by foreign-controlled companies.[39] These measures were to have little effect, however, since the United States would not accept restrictions on repatriating profits, exhibitors ignored screen quotas and production money tended to be made available to safe, non-innovative, directors who could turn out formulaic, profitable B-movies. Money therefore chased, and generated, mediocrity. There are, of course, a number of clear exceptions to this state of affairs with distinguished films by Leopoldo Torres Ríos, *Pelota de trapo* (Rag Ball, 1948), his son Torre Nilsson (see below), Hugo Fregonese, in *Apenas un delincuente* (Just a Delinquent, 1950), and Hugo del Carril's evocative *Las aguas bajan turbias* (Muddied Waters, 1952) which returns to the genre of gritty realism. In the main, however, protectionism and autarchic nationalism did not generate any film renaissance.

Brazil

Given the linguistic 'limitation' of Portuguese, Brazilian cinema could never hope to reach the markets available to Mexican cinema. The battle,

[39] See Ana López, 'Argentina 1955–1976', in King and Torrents (eds.), *The Garden of Forking Paths*, p. 50.

therefore, was over the home market. It had managed to consolidate a domestic public through music, dance, song and comedy and these successful ingredients continued into the 1940s. A new production company Atlântida, the brainchild of cineastes José Carlos Burle, Alinor Azevedo and Moacyr Fenelon, had initially intended to support political, realist cinema and made a first feature *Moleque Tião* (Boy Tião, 1943) based on the life of Sebastião Prato, 'Grande Otelo', who was already a well-known actor. They soon discovered, however, that socially committed films could not guarantee economic stability as the title of a later film ironically pointed out: *Tristezas não pagam dividas* (Sadness Doesn't Pay Off Debts, 1944). Their commercial breakthrough came when they teamed Oscarito, Brazil's most brilliant comic, with Grande Otelo. This duo made a number of successful comedies throughout the forties, which attracted the attention of Luiz Severiano Ribeiro, who ran the country's major distribution and exhibition circuits. He bought Atlântida in 1947 and for the first time in Latin America, a country could boast a vertically integrated industry – one which, like Hollywood, had control over production, distribution and exhibition – however small this might be. Money could be made in *chanchadas* which featured Oscarito, Grande Otelo and other popular performers such as Zé Trinidade, Wilson Grey and Zezé Macedo. Ribeiro's buy-out occurred in the year in which the Vargas regime decreed that each movie house should show at least three Brazilian films a year. These movies were unashamedly 'popular' appealing to a large working-class audience. As such, they would be despised by middle-class critics, who aspired to a more modern, technically proficient and internationally acceptable cinema. The wish to provide an alternative to 'low brow' *chanchadas* would be one of the reasons for the development of the Vera Cruz Company in November 1949.

Production rose from ten features in 1946 to twenty in 1950 (one-fifth of Mexico's film output), as Atlântida helped to regenerate the industry. Cinédia, which had ceased production started up again and had a major success with *O ebrio* (The Drunk, 1947), directed by the multi-talented Gilda de Abreu who was already a singer, actress, writer and theatre director before she embarked on a film career. The most sophisticated comedy of the time was by an independent producer and director Silveira Sampaio, *Uma aventura aos 40* (An Adventure in the 1940s, 1947). Another woman cineaste, Carmen Santos produced, directed and starred in *Inconfidência Mineira*, 1948, a project that she had developed for over a decade, and which she could partly film in her own small studios. This artisanal approach would be derided in the overwhelming ambitions of Vera Cruz.

The Vera Cruz film company emerged from the optimistic conditions of post-war São Paulo, following the break-up of the Estado Novo, a return to conservative democratic practices and a brief economic boom. São Paulo lived through a time of intense cultural activity. In the short space of six years, the city witnessed the birth of two art museums, a prestigious theatre company, several schools, a film library, a biennial exhibition of plastic arts and a large number of concerts, lectures and exhibitions. Many of these cultural initiatives were financed by a group led by the industrialist Francisco Matarazzo Sobrinho. Vera Cruz was linked to the complex of institutions based on his prestige and fortune, notably the Museum of Modern Art and the Brazilian Comedy Theatre.[40]

The reasoning of the group was based on economic principles. Hollywood's hegemony, it was argued, relied on its access to the technologies which allowed it to 'universalize' its comparative advantages. The way forward, therefore, was to invest massively in the industry. The company built large, costly studios, imported all the most up-to-date equipment and brought over skilled European technicians. Approaches were also made to have Brazil's most internationally famous cinematographer, Alberto Cavalcânti, who lived in Europe, as head of the organization. He eventually took on the job but stayed for only one year. The project was posited on penetrating international markets, which proved impossible, and it was too expensive to be maintained by the domestic market alone: its productions cost about ten times the average Atlântida film. Up until 1954, it made eighteen films, the best-known being Lima Barreto's *O cangaceiro*, 1953, which was to have a great impact on the directors of the subsequent generation. In the end, however, the whole project was too overblown for the home market conditions of Brazil. Was there, then, an alternative to the *chanchadas?*

By the early 1950's it appeared that the creative energies of the forties were beginning to wane and that the market would increasingly dictate the type of movie available. In Mexico, it was found that quick formulaic films, *churros* (known after the doughy pastry) — singing cowboys, maternal melodramas, Cantinflas and Tin-Tan making up to six films a year,

[40] See Maria Rita Galvão, 'Vera Cruz: a Brazilian Hollywood', in R. Johnson and R. Stam (eds.), *Brazilian Cinema* (London, 1982), p. 273.

sex comedies – could provide acceptable profits. The structure of film financing, through the Banco Cinematográfico, favoured monopolization of a few producers, exhibitors and directors such as Emilio Azcárraga and William Jenkins. The major powers could set up an 'insider' financial operation, while the two main unions, the Sindicato de Trabajadores de la Industria Cinematográfica (STIC) and the elite breakaway union, the Sindicato de Trabajadores de la Producción Cinematográfica (STPC) ran a closed-shop policy which effectively closed the door on young film-makers for some twenty years.[41] A similar move to monopoly control by a few 'safe' producers has been observed in Perón's Argentina, where state credits chased mediocrity, which bred in these conditions of plenty. In Brazil, with the collapse of the Vera Cruz experiment, cinema was in a state of flux, though the popularity of *chanchada* showed no signs of diminishing as the spectacular parody *Nem Sansão, nem Dalila* (Neither Samson nor Delilah, 1954) reveals.

No other country in Latin America was experiencing a crisis since only a handful of films were made anywhere else and these tended to be timid imitations of Argentine and Mexican genres.[42] Film historians can find isolated titles in each of the Latin American republics, but no developed industry. In Chile an attempt was made in the 1940s to stimulate cinema through state investment. The state agency, CORFO, set up to deepen Chile's import-substitution industrialization and economic moderniza-tion, saw cinema as an important growth industry and in 1942 gave 50 per cent finance to set up Chile Films. Costly studios were erected but, as in the case of Vera Cruz in Brazil, the project was over-ambitious and Argentine film-makers ended up by using most of the facilities. Manuel Alonso's *Siete muertes a plazo fijo* (Seven Deaths at an Appointed Time, 1950) and *Casta de roble* (Caste of Oak, 1954) point to a certain vigour in film-making in Cuba before the Revolution. Isolated directors such as Rafael Rivero in Venezuela (*Juan de la Calle*, 1941) or the Colombian Máximo Calvo (*Flores del Valle*, 1941) and small production companies like Amauta films in Peru, which in the late 1930s and early 1940s produced some fourteen musicals and melodramas, show that all over the continent attempts were made to develop the new art form. Yet these are

---

[41] On the emergence of a 'new' Mexican cinema from the 1940s, see Berg, *Cinema of Solitude: A Critical Study of Mexican Film,* introductory chapter.

[42] For the early days of cinema in other countries, see, for example, Hernando Salcedo Silva, *Crónica del cine colombiano, 1897–1950* (Bogotá, 1981); Ambretta Marrosu, *Exploraciones en la historiografía del cine en Venezuela* (Caracas, 1985); Alfonso Gumucio Dagrón, *Historia del cine boliviano* (Mexico, D.F., 1983).

traces of individual works, rather than developed 'national' cinemas, in home markets dominated by Hollywood and, to a lesser extent, movies from Mexico and Argentina.

THE 1950S: TOWARDS A NEW CINEMA

The early 1950s witnessed a slow but appreciable shift in the appreciation of cinema among intellectuals and middle-class sectors more generally. Cine Clubs and discussion groups were set up, which explored the theory and practice of film aesthetics. It was from this moment that the gap between what Pierre Bourdieu has called the 'autonomous' principle in art (appreciation by peers, legitimation on the basis of aesthetic values) and the 'heteronomous' principle (value as constructed by the marketplace), began to widen.[43] While students debated the value of cinema, and talked about the new vogue of neo-realism, popular audiences still flocked to (and even now regularly support) the formula films. The great attraction in Mexico in the 1950s and beyond was the 'cine de lucha-dores', the masked wrestlers, in particular the legendary 'El Santo' (Rodolfo Guzmán Huerta) who had 15,000 bouts in the ring and starred in twenty-one films. In Argentina, audiences were much more interested in the increasing revelations of Isabel Sarli's body (in the sex comedies with Armando Bo) rather than in neo-realism. It is necessary to make these remarks since critical histories, especially those of the recent period of 'new cinema', tend to ignore what does not fit neatly into a progressive or socially concerned canon.[44]

In Cuba, the journalist and critic José Manuel Valdés Rodriguez founded a Department of Cinematography in the University of Havana in 1949 together with a cinémathèque which preserved copies of old prints. The cultural society Nuestro Tiempo was made up of figures who would later attract world attention such as Néstor Almendros, Guillermo Cabrera Infante and Tomás Gutiérrez Alea. In Brazil film journals like *Fundamentos* openly questioned the excessive spending of Vera Cruz and suggested that low-cost cinema should become the norm in Brazil. Film congresses met in São Paulo and in Rio in the early fifties to debate the different options. Cinema Clubs and filmothèques were set up in the

---

[43] See Randal Johnson's edition of Pierre Bourdieu's essays in *The Field of Cultural Production: Essays on Art and Literature* (London, 1993).

[44] The only book-length study of 'popular' cinema in Latin America is Jorge Ayala Blanco, *La disolvencia del cine mexicano: entre lo popular y lo exquisito* (Mexico, D.F., 1991).

major cities and influential critics, such as Alex Viany and in particular
Paulo Emílio Salles Gomes, presented alternative critical strategies. In
Chile a film club was established at the Universidad de Chile, which
edited a journal, produced a radio programme and gave weekly screening
of foreign films, and in 1959 a Centre for Experimental Cinema was
formed under the direction of a young documentary film-maker Sergio
Bravo. In Argentina, especially after 1955, film clubs mushroomed and
universities opened film departments. By 1955 in Mexico, there was
already in existence a federation of Mexican Cine Clubs. The winds of
change were beginning to blow across the continent.

Cine clubs and journals created a climate of increasing awareness of
cinema as an art form. They also provided a forum for debates about the
future of Latin American cinema. In the early 1950s, the major influence,
the most possible and appropriate model, seemed to be neo-realism.
Robert Kolker explains why: 'The neo-realists wanted the image to deal
so closely with the social realities of postwar Italy that it would throw off
all the encumbrances of stylistic and contextual preconception and face
the world as if without mediation. An impossible desire, but in it lay the
potential for yet other assaults on cinema history . . . [with] location
shooting, poor working-class subjects played by non-professionals, use of
the environment to define those subjects, an attitude of unmediated
observation of events'.[45]

Alongside the fascination with neo-realism, young French critics
around the journal *Cahiers du Cinéma* could offer interesting ideas to
young Latin American theoreticians/film-makers. The 'politique des
auteurs' spoke against the domination of bland and anonymous commercial studio productions and rediscovered individual voices rebelling
within the system. *Cahiers* critics would discover the mavericks within
Hollywood, and reassess the Western, or Minnelli or Hitchcock. Latin
American critics in the main dismissed Hollywood altogether and all of
the 'old' Latin American cinema, seeking instead the 'new' in terms of
social and political relevance.

Practical as well as theoretical models were thus on offer and a number
of aspirant film-makers made the pilgrimage to Italy, to learn at the feet
of the neo-realist theorist Zavattini and others. Gabriel García Márquez
talked in the mid-1980s of the strong influence of Italian cinema in that
period: 'Between 1952 and 1955, four of us studied at the Centro

[45] Robert Kolker, *The Altering Eye: Contemporary International Cinema* (Oxford, 1983), p. 44.

Sperimentale in Rome: Julio García Espinosa, Vice Minister of Culture for Cinema in Cuba, Fernando Birri, the great pope of the New Latin American cinema, Tomás Gutiérrez Alea, one of its most notable craftsmen and I, who wanted nothing more in life than to become the filmmaker I never became.'[46]

With hindsight we can perceive the contours of a new movement, but as yet film practitioners in Latin America were working in isolation, unaware of each others interests. We are still at least a decade away from being able to talk of a Pan Latin American movement. Certain precursor figures are important. In Brazil, Nelson Pereira dos Santos has recognized his debt to neo-realism: 'The influence of neo-realism was not that of a school or ideology but rather as a production system. Neo-realism taught us, in sum, that it was possible to make films in the streets; that we do not need studios, that we could film using average people rather than known actors; that the technique could be imperfect, as long as the film was truly linked to its national culture and expressed that culture.'[47] In 1955 Pereira dos Santos filmed the documentary *Rio 40 Graus* (Rio 40°, 1955) which focused on the slum dwellers of Rio, following the movement of five peanut-sellers throughout the city. Two years later he made *Rio Zona Norte* (Rio, Northern Zone, 1957), on the life of the Samba composer Espirito da Luz Soares. The composer is played by Grande Otelo who is given a different narrative function to that of black comic in numerous *chanchadas:* here he represents a man exploited by class and race, but who still inspires a strong popular culture. The young critic Glauber Rocha, saw Pereira dos Santos as an exemplary *auteur,* one who could give dignity to Brazilian cinema, showing that cinema could be made 'with a camera and an idea', a phrase that would later become one of the foundational definitions of Cinema Novo in Brazil.

In Argentina, Leopoldo Torre Nilsson and Fernando Birri offered two very different models. Torre Nilsson was the poet of aristocratic decadence. His *La casa del ángel* (The House of the Angel, 1957) was greeted with praise by 'new-wave' critics and film-makers such as Eric Rohmer who hyperbolically called it 'the best film to have arrived from South America since the beginnings of cinema.'[48] Torre Nilsson was a 'modern' *auteur.* Informed by Bergman, French New Wave and its British contem-

[46] Gabriel García Márquez, quoted in *Anuario 88,* Escuela Internacional de Cine y TV (Havana, 1988), p. 1.

[47] Quoted in Johnson and Stam (eds.), *Brazilian Cinema,* p. 122.

[48] Quoted in Jorge Abel Martin, *Los filmes de Leopoldo Torre Nilsson* (Buenos Aires, 1980), p. 30.

poraries Karel Reisz and Lindsay Anderson and in close collaboration with his wife, the writer Beatriz Guido, he explored the contradictions and decline of Argentine upper-class and genteel bourgeois society in such films as *Graciela* (1955), *Angel* (1957) and *La caída* (The Fall, 1959). Torre Nilsson gave prestige to Argentine cinema and helped to encourage a younger generation of cineastes, formed in the cine clubs and in film-making societies, who would create a temporary 'new wave' in the early 1960s.

While Torre Nilsson in Buenos Aires was exploring urban decadence, in the city of Santa Fé in the north Fernando Birri, on his return from the Centro Sperimentale in 1956, sought to use neo-realist principles to explore the hidden realities of Argentina. He set up a film school at the Universidad Nacional de Litoral and made an important early documentary *Tire Dié* (Throw us a Dime, 1958) helped by a large group of his students. They observed and recorded young shanty-town children who daily risked their lives running along a main railway line begging for coins. Before the final cut, he showed the film to the inhabitants of the shanty towns and incorporated their suggestions. He also took the film on tour, with a projector loaded onto an old truck, stopping at different remote communities who were outside main exhibition circuits. Birri in this and later documentaries and in his fictional feature *Los inundados* (Flooded Out, 1963) anticipated, and in fact theorized in a number of important essays, filmic practices which were to become important in the 1960s when, with the advent of portable, flexible 16mm cameras, the dream of 'a camera in hand and an idea in the head' could become a reality. Birri talked of national popular cinema, of the need to adopt and transform neo-realism in the context of Latin America and to break with the distribution and exhibition circuits of commercial cinema, incorporating working-class and peasant audiences into more democratic cultural practices. This final aim was to become one of the elusive chimeras of political film-making in the 1960s.

The Spanish exile director Luis Buñuel made some twenty films in Mexico between 1946 and 1965 including the memorable *Los olvidados* (1950), El (1952) *Nazarín* (1958), *El angel exterminador* (1962) and *Simón del desierto* (1965). He disagreed with the orthodoxies of neo-realism, seeking not to present things as they are, but rather how the desires and the state of mind of the observer charge these things with new meanings and new ways of seeing. His unique blending of documentary, psychological, religious and surrealist motifs were not fully appreciated in a 1950s

Mexican context dominated by formulaic films, but he became an example and an inspiration for Mexican critics and cineastes in the 1960s.

THE 'NEW CINEMAS' OF THE 1960S

The 'new' cinemas in Latin America grew up in the optimistic conditions of the late 1950s and early 1960s in Latin America. Two fundamentally different political projects were modernizing and radicalizing the social and cultural climate: the Cuban Revolution and the myths and realities of developmentalism in, for example, Kubitschek's Brazil and Frondizi's Argentina. We should not, as revolutionary Cuba lies in tatters in the mid-1990s, underestimate the radical impact of that revolution in Latin America throughout the 1960s. It seemed to most an exemplary nationalist, anti-imperialist movement which demonstrated a clear need for commitment and political clarity and held out the utopian possibility of uniting artistic and political vanguards. Cuba as a model influenced Latin American film-makers long before Cuban cinema came of age in the mid to late 1960s. This revolutionary impulse combined with a clear sense of cultural modernization in a decade in which the intellectual community felt that it could be 'contemporary with all men' in Octavio Paz's evocatively optimistic phrase. This optimism was, at least in part, grounded in economic and political realities, but realities that could be subject to acute variations. As an historian of cultural modernity puts is: 'All the modernism and anti-modernisms of the 1960s, then, were seriously flawed. But their sheer plenitude, along with their intensity and liveliness of expression generated a common language, a vibrant ambience, a shared horizon of experience and desire . . . The initiatives all failed, but they sprang from a largeness of spirit and imagination and from an ardent desire to seize the day."[49]

In every country, new agendas were being set, new problems debated: how Cuba would develop a state, 'socialist', cinema; the relationship between film-makers and the state in a dependent capitalist context; the problems of production in conditions of scarcity (what Glauber Rocha called 'the aesthetics' of hunger) or outside the main commercial networks (evolving what the Argentines Getino and Solanas would call a 'Third Cinema'); the problem of how and where to distribute and exhibit work, in a context controlled by strong local capital, or, more usually, by monopoly capital; the question of the appropriate film language for par-

[49] Marshall Berman, *All That is Solid Melts into Air: The Experience of Modernity* (London, 1983), p. 33.

ticular situations (which would be very different in the altiplanos of Peru and Bolivia to that in the urban centres of Argentina or Uruguay); the whole vexed question of what constituted a 'national' reality in the context of an increasing globalization of culture; the uneasy relationship between film-makers (largely middle-class intellectuals) and the people they purported to represent; and the very nature of popular culture itself.

Brazil

Brazil led the way, in both theory and practice, in a movement that became known as Cinema Novo. 'Cinema Novo is not one film, but an evolving complex of films that will ultimately make the people aware of its own misery.'[50] Here Glauber Rocha articulates one of the paradoxes of the process: that of creating 'popular' cinema for a public not used to political cinema inside the industrial complex, a popular cinema, therefore, that was not for popular consumption. The young, largely Río de Janeiro based, film makers of the early sixties, Glauber Rocha, Nelson Pereira dos Santos, Ruy Guerra, Carlos Diegues, Joaquim Pedro de Andrade adopted a variety of styles but shared the view that they were expressing a radical national, and Latin American, identity in opposition to a neo-colonial cultural system. Here the influential think-tank, the Instituto Superior de Estudos Brasileiros, offered a model of developmental nationalism, and the idea that an intellectual elite should be the critical conscience of underdevelopment. The key films of the period up to the military coup of 1964 were set in the main in the countryside, and in particular the desolate Northeast of Brazil, the deserted backland, the *sertão*, with its poverty, its mythical social bandits, the *cangaceiros*, and messianic leaders. Three films in 1963, Pereira dos Santos's *Vidas secas* (Barren Lives), Ruy Guerra's *Os fuzis* (The Guns) and Glauber Rocha's *Deus e o diabo na terra do sol* (Black God, White Devil) were all filmed in the northeast and explored the nature of unequal development and different forms of oppression. Glauber adopted some of the forms and structures of northeastern popular culture: the ballads and the mythical stories of *cordel* (broadsheet) literature. In these and other important fictional films, such as Carlos Diegues's *Ganga Zumba*, 1963, a film based on the seventeenth-century maroon community of Palmares, and Paulo Cesar

---

[50] Glauber Rocha, 'An Aesthetic of Hunger', quoted in Johnson and Stam (eds.), *Brazilian Cinema*, p. 71.

Saraceni's *Porto das caixas* (1962) there was a similar attention to the plight of the urban and rural poor and a shared utopian belief that the film-maker could lead the process of social change.

The military coup of 1964 effectively put an end to these left-wing and populist dreams, but for a time, until a more radical coup in 1968, left-wing culture still continued to flourish[51] albeit within state-defined limits. The state also began to invest in culture and set up a National Film Institute in 1966 to offer subsidies and to impose the compulsory exhibition of national films. Radical film-makers were thus wooed by 'the philanthropic ogre', Octavio Paz's telling phrase for the state, a complex situation which Glauber Rocha allegorized in his next film *Terra em Transe* (Land in Anguish, 1967). For critic Ismail Xavier, *Terra* analyses, 'The contradictions of a socially engaged artist who, misinterpreting himself as a decisive agent in the struggle for power in society, is obliged to confront his own illusions concerning the "courtly life" in an underdeveloped milieu and discovers his peripheral condition within the small circle of the mighty. Defeated, the artist enacts the agony of his illusory status, the death of his anachronistic view.'[52] Other films focusing on the ambiguous response of intellectuals to power were Paulo Saraceni's *O desafio* (The Challenge, 1967) and *O bravo guerreiro* (The Brave Warrior, 1968) by Gustavo Dahl.

The coup within the coup of December 1968 further radicalized the situation, heralding what critics have called the third phase of Cinema Novo, 'cannibalist-tropicalist' phase, where the nature of power and oppression was explored by allegory. Certain film-makers such as Glauber Rocha and Ruy Guerra were forced into exile for short periods, while others resorted to indirect forms of criticism, often through more popular forms such as comedy. Joaquim Pedro de Andrade's adaption of the 1920s novel by Mario de Andrade, *Macunaíma,* has cannibalism as a central metaphor and follows the racial and social transformations of the trickster Macunaíma (played by Grande Otelo) as he travels from the Amazon to the modern city of São Paulo. Pereira dos Santos's *Como era gostoso o meu francês* (How Tasty Was My Little Frenchman, 1971) has the sixteenth-century Tupinambá Indians ingesting, and taking on the powers of, the French colonists. Cinema Novo directors, despite the severity of dictatorship, still had hegemonic power and state subsidies. Their dominance was ridiculed by a brief but vigorous underground (Udigrudi) movement of

[51] See Roberto Schwarz, *Misplaced Ideas,* pp. 126–59.
[52] Ismael Xavier, 'Allegories of underdevelopment': From the 'aesthetics of hunger' to the 'aesthetics of garbage', unpublished Ph.D. dissertation, New York University, 1982, p. 116.

the late 1960s which, in Xavier's phrase, proclaimed an 'aesthetic of garbage', an aesthetic of futility, in the place of Glauber's rebellious, active 'aesthetic of hunger'. Rogerio Sganzerla's *O bandido da luz vermelha* (Red Light Bandit, 1968) and Julio Bresanne's *Matou a familia e foi ao cinema* (Killed the Family and Went to the Cinema, 1969) expressed this new, caustic sarcasm, which hurled its disgust, like garbage, in the face of Cinema Novo and the state. The compromises reached in the 1970s, however, would give the state an increasingly upper hand.

Argentina

In Argentina, the young film-makers initially followed the example of Torre Nilsson, rather than the more radical-populist proposals of Birri. With some help from the newly founded Film Institute, INC, Argentine 'new wave' followed its Parisian counterparts in exploring middle-class anomie and alienation or the sexual rites of passage of the young, set in the cafés and streets of Buenos Aires. Or, like their Brazilian counterparts, they drew inspiration from literature, in particular the work of Jorge Luis Borges and Julio Cortázar. Films like Manuel Antin's *La cifra impar* (The Odd Number 1962), and David Kohon's *Tres veces Ana* (Three Times Ana, 1961) were enjoyed by a sophisticated urban elite. Lautaro Murúa showed the sordid side of the 'City of Dreams' Buenos Aires in his *Alias Gardelito* (1960), while Leonardo Favio took Truffaut's *Les quatre cent coups* several brutal stages further in his analysis of orphanage life: *Crónica de un niño solo* (Chronicle of a Boy Alone, 1964).

The brief period of non-Peronist political regimes between 1955 and 1966 saw an ever increasing radicalization of politics and, by extension, of culture. Perón was in exile, but he in many ways controlled the political agenda. When the military under Onganía decided to take control in 1966, many artists and intellectuals reacted to these conditions by fighting the government in all areas of intellectual activity. The discourse, by now, was nationalist, populist and, in many cases Third Worldist.[53] Concepts such as 'the people', 'the nation' and 'The Third World' were given a new positive value and the word *extranjerizante* (foreign loving) was used as a term of abuse to describe the 'false' cosmopolitanism of the liberal tradition. The most representative film of this populist radicalism, in the tradition of Fernando Birri (whom it quotes),

[53] For an analysis of the period, see Oscar Terán, *Nuestros años sesenta* (Buenos Aires, 1991).

was Fernando Solanas and Octavio Getino's *La hora de los hornos* (The Hour of the Furnaces, 1966–8).

La hora is a colossal four-hour work, in three parts, which explores neo-colonialism and violence as the legacy of Argentina's economic and cultural dependency on Europe and talks of the present and future in terms of radical Peronism. It is a formally complex and ideologically Manichean work, but it became a rallying-point of resistance to Onganía and was seen clandestinely on the shop floor, in village halls or in private houses. Solanas and Getino theorized the work of their group Cine Liberación in a seminal essay 'Towards a Third Cinema', a term that has passed into the critical canon as a way of describing cinema from three continents, Asia, Africa and Latin America. The roots of Third Cinema for the film-makers, however, lie in Peronism. Third Cinema, posed an alternative both to first cinema, Hollywood, and to second cinema, a-political *auteurism*. Cinema in these terms had to produce works that the system cannot assimilate and which explicitly fought the system. Viewing *la hora* with hindsight, its faith in Perón seems pathetically misplaced. This is not to deny, however, the radical impact of the film, and the film-makers declarations, at the time. By 1970, Argentine politics and culture had entered a radical phase. All sectors looked to Perón to save a situation that was spiralling violently out of control. His return in 1973, however, was to create more problems than it solved.

Mexico

The strength and stability of state power in Mexico had always managed to defuse radicalism by coercion or cooptation. Equally the film industry was the most solid in Latin America, with jealously guarded vested interests. Change in this context was, of necessity, less spectacular than in other parts. Buñuel, as we have seen, spent the fifties making films in Mexico, but like Simon of the Desert (*Simon del desierto*, Mexico, 1965), one of his film titles, he was very much a voice crying in the wilderness; he could not rewrite alone the dull chapter of 1950s cinema. He would be an example, however, to a group of critics and cineastes – José de la Colina, Rafael Corkidi, Salvador Elizondo, Jomi M. García Ascot, Carlos Monsiváis, Alberto Isaac, Paul Leduc and Fernando Macotela – who in the 1960s formed a group *Nuevo Cine* (New Cinema) and edited a journal (which ran an excellent double issue on Buñuel). In 1962, Elizondo – later to become one of Mexico's best vanguard writers – bluntly attacked the reigning orthodoxy of protectionism and a fading genre and star system. 'The system minimizes risks and establishes a certain security for investors. The system, in short, approves the following theorem: *A bout du souffle* would have been a much better film if instead of being directed by Godard with Belmondo and Jean Seyberg, it had been directed by Cecil B. De Mille and Vivien Leigh and Marcello Mastroianni.'[54] One film came from the group in the early 1960s, Jomi García Ascot's depiction of Spanish exile life *En el balcón vacío* (On the Empty Balcony, 1961), but they would all become leading film-makers, writers or critics in the decade of the 1960s.

An incentive to renovate cinema came from the film union STPC, which organized an experimental film competition in 1964/5. The prize was won by Rubén Gámez's *La fórmula secreta* (The Secret Formula) with Alberto Isaac's *En este pueblo no hay ladrones* (In this Town there are no Thieves), the first major film adaptation of a García Márquez short story, as runner up. These films were part of a sixties movement in which, as Carlos Monsiváis acutely observes, the Mexican public was also looking for different self-images: 'Socially and culturally what happens is that this (new) cinema is a clear product of the demands of the middle classes to find reflected their problems and their desire for access to universality, to cosmopolitanism in the face of the excesses of a cultural nationalism that had lost its force and dynamism and had become a series of grotesque formulae.'[55] Cultural nationalism was opposed by a movement known as 'la onda' a rag bag of different modernisms, in fashion, music and avant-garde literature. The 'hip' director of the 'onda' was the Chilean Alejandro Jodorowsky with *Fando y Lis* (1967) and *El topo* (The Mole, 1970).

Modernization and internationalization were accompanied in the late 1960s by a major political crisis when the Partido Revolucionario Institucional (PRI) found itself opposed by a strong student movement. This crisis was resolved in a horrifyingly brutal fashion on 2 October 1968, when troops opened fire on a demonstration of mainly students assembled in the Plaza of the Three Cultures in Tlatelolco, Mexico City. Many hundreds died in this massacre, which marked a watershed in the development of modern Mexico. In the widespread revulsion following the massacre, all intellectual groups condemned the government. The next president, Luis Echeverría, who took power in 1970, needed to restore the prestige of the

---

[54] Quoted in *Hojas de cine: Testimonios y documentos del Nuevo Cine Latinoamericano*, Vol. II (Mexico, D.F., 1988), p. 42.
[55] *Hablemos de Cine*, 69 (1977–8), p. 26.

presidency through conciliation. A major platform of his campaign would be to garner the support of artists and intellectuals.

Cuba

It would take until the late 1960s for Cuban cinema to have much impact outside its national frontiers. One reason for this was the fact that the new revolutionary government was forced to begin almost with nothing. Conscious of the importance of cinema and radio in a revolutionary context it set up in March 1959, three months after the triumph of the revolution, the Cuban Institute of Cinematographic Art and Industry (ICAIC), which gradually, with the nationalization measures of the early 1960s, took over not only production but also distribution and exhibition throughout the country. The aims were lofty: to create a new cinema for the spectator, but also to create a new spectator for cinema.

Cuba had a small nucleus of film-makers with slight experience. A short documentary *El mégano* (The Charcoal Workers) had been made in 1954 as part of the Cine Club movement and the production staff on this short would become Cuba's earliest film makers: Julio García Espinosa, Tomás Gutiérrez Alea, Alfredo Guevara, Jorge Haydú and Jorge Fraga. Alfredo Guevara was put in charge of ICAIC and, in conditions of scarcity, gave over most of the limited resources to newsreel production and to documentary film-making, under Santiago Alvarez. It would be Alvarez who set the standards – supported by visiting European documentary film-makers such as Chris Marker and the veteran Joris Ivens – for radical, innovative documentary film-making during the years 1959–66, which can be seen as a period of apprenticeship.

How could the regime seek to create a new spectator for cinema when its own new cinema was evolving so slowly? A number of measures were adopted. A Cinemathèque was set up which showed film cycles from existing archive material. Television also included courses on film criticism. A film journal *Cine Cubano* began publication. In the countryside, mobile cinema units – projection equipment loaded on to Soviet trucks – toured the countryside, giving some outlying communities their first experience of the movie image. A ten-minute short by Octavio Cortázar, *Por primera vez* (For the First Time, 1967) recorded one such event in Oriente province.

Such educational advances, like that of the literacy campaign, were quantifiably successful. More complex, however, was the definition of the role of culture itself in the Revolution. Critic and film-maker Julio García Espinosa talked in *Cine Cubano* in 1964 of the existing splits: 'On the one side chauvinism, on the other cosmopolitanism; on the one side tradition, on the other fashion; on the one side sectarianism, on the other pseudo-philosophical speculation; on the one side the intransigent revolutionary, on the other the utopic liberal-spiritual confusion creates its own myths.'[56] A major dispute grew up over the temporary banning of a short documentary *P.M.*, made by Saba Cabrera Infante and Orlando Jiménez in a free cinema style in 1961. It caused Castro to intervene in 1961 and give his famous verdict in 'Words to the Intellectuals' which talked of the need for fellow travellers to commit themselves in the long term to the current process: 'within the Revolution, everything, against the Revolution, nothing'. A number of film-workers left Cuba in the early years: Néstor Almendros, Fernando Villaverde, Fausto Canel, Alberto Roldán, Roberto Fadiño and Eduardo Manet as well as the well-known critic and writer Guillermo Cabrera Infante. In general it can be said that ICAIC was in the liberal camp, trying whenever possible to defend artistic plurality against the more intransigent parts of the cultural political elite and providing an umbrella organization for artists in other disciplines whose experimentation was frowned upon: Saul Yelin's poster art, Silvio Rodriguez and Pable Milanés in music who joined Leo Brouwer's Grupo Sonoro Experimental and the multi-talented writer Jesús Díaz. It was to take until the 1980s for a clear Cuban exile cinema to express itself in the United States.

By 1966, film-makers could point to concrete advances. Santiago Alvarez had established a new style of newsreel and began working in documentary, turning scarcity into a signifier, remodelling second-hand sources such as news photos and television clips and developing a poetic and politically effective film collage in such documentaties as *Now* (1965); *Hanoi Martes 13* (Hanoi, 13 Tuesday 1967) and *Hasta la victoria siempre* (Until Victory, Always, 1967). It was to such work that Coppola would refer in a much quoted statement on a visit to Cuba: 'We do not have the advantages of their disadvantages.' 1966–7 saw two major fictional films: Tomás Gutiérrez Alea's comedy on bureaucracies *La muerte de un burócrata* (Death of a Bureaucrat, 1966) and Julio García Espinosa's picaresque parody *Las aventuras de Juan Quin Quin* (The adventures of Juan Quin Quin, 1967). *Juan Quin Quin* is to date the largest grossing Cuban film,

---

[56] Julio García Espinosa, *Cine Cubano*, 23–5 (1964), p. 20.

with over three million spectators. At last ICAIC could begin to make popular fictional films which helped to fill the gap left by the North American blockades and the rather stolid Hollywood substitutes that could be found in Eastern Europe. 1968 and 1969 saw several important works, Octavio Gómez's *La primera carga al machete* (The First Machete Charge, 1969), Humberto Solás' three-part *Lucía* (1968) and Gutiérrez Alea's *Memorias del subdesarrollo* (Memories of Underdevelopment, 1968), based on a novel by Edmundo Desnoes.

Towards the end of *Memorias*, a documentary insert shows Castro issuing a defiant speech to the world during the Missile Crisis in October 1962. 'No one is going to come and inspect our country because we grant no one the right. We will never renounce the sovereign prerogative that within our frontiers we will make all the decisions and we are the only ones who will inspect anything.' There was no space for individual questioning in such a polarized world, in 1962, or more acutely between 1968 and 1971, where a siege economy, the failure of the ten-million-ton sugar harvest, counter-revolutionary violence and political isolation helped to form an embattled mentality which claimed its casualties. The most notorious of these was the poet Heberto Padilla who was briefly imprisoned and gave an abject public recantation in 1971, much to the dismay of leading North American, European and Latin American intellectuals who wrote two open letters to Castro, complaining of the regime's actions. The decade of hope, therefore closed in crisis, heralding a period of what the Cuban critic Ambrosio Fornet has called the 'grey years' of Cuban cultural life.

Chile

In the south of the continent the decade ended with the optimistic hope that the Chilean democratic road to socialism could become a reality. Throughout the 1960s, film-makers in Chile had been actively involved in the political process. Sergio Bravo's university based Centre for Experimental Cinema helped to form young cineastes such as Domingo Sierra and Pedro Chaskel. Bravo himself made a documentary film of Salvador Allende's 1963/4 election campaign *Banderas del pueblo* (Banners of the People, 1964) which was banned by government censors. The defeat of the left alliance under Allende in 1964 caused a widespread internal debate not just over electoral politics but also about the need to work in the cultural field to wrest 'common sense' values away from the control of the right or Christian Democracy. Under the Frei administration (1964–70) there was to be a flowering of activity in theatre, music and cinema, and the years 1968–9 saw the maturity of Chilean cinema. Five features came out: Raúl Ruiz's *Tres tristes tigres* (Three Sad Tigers); Helvio Soto's *Caliche sangriento* (Bloody Nitrate); Aldo Francia's *Valparaiso mi amor* (Valparaiso My Love); Miguel Littín's *El chacal de Nahueltoro* (The Jackal of Nahueltoro) and Carlos Elsesser's *Los testigos* (The Witnesses). These film-makers came from different ideological and aesthetic tendencies, from the inventive maverick Raúl Ruiz to the sombre neo-realism of Francia, but they can be seen as a group, working with very scarce resources: the films by Ruiz, Elsesser, Francia and Littín were made consecutively, with the same camera. Aldo Francia, a doctor by profession, also organized a famous 'Meeting of Latin American Film makers' at the Viña del Mar film festival in 1967. This would be one of the key events in the growing awareness of cineastes across the continent that they were working with similar ideas and methods. Raúl Ruiz makes the point: 'Suddenly we found ourselves with a cinema which in a very obvious and natural way, without any cultural inferiority complex, was being made with very few resources, with the resources that we could acquire and with a freedom that earlier Latin American and European cinema did not have. Suddenly we found ourselves with all the advantages.'[57] These film-makers would support the Popular Unity campaign in 1970.

Bolivia, Peru, Colombia and Venezuela

A film-maker who attracted attention at Viña del Mar was the Bolivian Jorge Sanjinés, who came from a country with scant tradition in film. In the aftermath of the National Revolution of 1952, the government established the Bolivian Film Institute, the ICB, which produced government newsreels, but lacked the resources or the trained personnel to exploit to the full symbolic and propaganda aspects of the revolution. One film-maker stood out in the 1950s: Jorge Ruiz who made two important ethnological films *Vuelve Sebastiana* (Sebastiana, Come Home, 1953) and *La vertiente* (The Watershed, 1958). Social cinema was extended by Sanjinés and the group he formed around him, the grupo Ukamau (named after their first major feature *Ukamau* (That's How it is, 1966)). Sanjinés had studied in Chile at Sergio Bravo's newly opened film school and on his

---

[57] Raúl Ruiz, interview in *Araucaria de Chile*, 11 (1980), pp. 101–18.

return to Bolivia formed a friendship and working partnership with Oscar Soria, Bolivia's foremost script-writer, who had collaborated with Ruiz in the 1950s. Sanjinés's work in the 1960s, and beyond, looked to highlight the problems of Bolivia's workers, peasants and indigenous peoples, but not in any patronizing way: instead the group tried to find a language appropriate to the rhythms and practices of popular culture. Their most successful film was *Yawar Mallku* (Blood of the Condor, 1968), which helped bring an end to the activities of the U.S. Peace Corps in Bolivia. But the film did not satisfy the group at the level of form: 'It was not that they [the Indian peoples] could not understand what was being said', Sanjinés wrote, 'it was rather a formal conflict at the level of the medium itself, which did not correspond to the internal rhythms of our people or their profound conception of reality. The substantial difference lay in the way in which the Quechua-Aymara people conceive of themselves collectively, in the non-individualistic form of their culture.'[58] Film-making in future would deal with the history of the collective, seeking to reactivate the popular memory denied by the hegemonic powers: the memory, for example, of the massacre of miners in June 1967, in the Siglo XX mines, which the group reconstructed in *El coraje del pueblo* (Courage of the People, 1971). The Banzer coup of 1971 ushered in a new hard-line regime in Bolivia and caused the group to rethink their working practices.

In Peru, theoretical debates about cinema in the 1960s were more sophisticated than filmic practices. The journal *Hablemos de Cine* founded in 1965, took up debates about 'new' cinema in Latin America. There had been a tradition of ethnographic film-making in Peru, especially based in Cuzco around the work of Manuel Chambi (the brother of the famous photographer Martin Chambi) and Luis Figueroa. This Cuzco school remained strong throughout the 1960s. Peru could perhaps boast of one *auteur*, Armondo Robles Godoy, but the main impetus towards film-making would come in the 1970s, as a result of state measures following the 1968 military coup of General Velazco.

The same opportunities could be found for film-makers in Colombia and in Venezuela in the 1970s, when state support was consolidated. Before then, in the 1960s, film-makers worked infrequently and, in the main, in isolation. In Colombia, the documentary film-makers, Carlos Alvarez and in particular, Marta Rodriguez and Jorge Silva – with *Chircales* (Brick-Makers 1968–72) – followed the 'new cinema's' interest

---

[58] Jorge Sanjinés, quoted in *Framework*, 10 (1979), p. 3.

in social documentary. In Venezuela Margot Benacerraf made a remarkable documentary *Araya* in 1958, while Román Chalbaud's fiction *Caín
adolescente* (Adolescent Cain, 1958) showed an early talent which would
develop in more favourable conditions a decade later.

The decade of the 1960s, therefore, saw the emergence, out of different
national contexts, of a group of radical film-makers and critics who would
define their work as 'new Latin American cinema'. They sought to join
their diverse projects into a broader ideological and cultural agenda capable of encompassing the continent.[59] The idea was, of course, utopian,
but in the late 1960s it seemed as if the dream might become a reality.
Film-makers met in different congresses in Viña del Mar (1967 and 1968)
and in Mérida, Venezuela (1968), and proclaimed the birth of a new
movement of Latin American cooperation and solidarity. It was a moment
when theoretical statements about 'cinema of hunger', 'imperfect cinema'
or 'third cinema' seemed linked to a dynamic practice. Perhaps this
indeed was the 'hour of the furnaces' which would light up and guide
liberation struggles throughout the continent.

THE 1970S: STATE REPRESSION, STATE-LED
DEVELOPMENT

The decade of the 1970s witnessed several interlocking trends that profoundly affected the development of cinema: the brief revolutionary optimism of the early seventies, in particular in Chile, Argentina and Uruguay;
the spread of dictatorship throughout the southern cone with military
coups in Uruguay (June 1973), Chile (September 1973), and Argentina
(March 1976) which dislocated the intellectual community and sent many
into exile; and the growth of state-led cinema in Brazil (under somewhat
less repressive military rule since April 1964), in Mexico and in hitherto
'minor' film cultures, Venezuela, Colombia and Peru.

The narrow victory of the Popular Unity parties in the election of 1970
showed that the Chilean road to socialism would be full of hazards. The
film-makers greeted the election victory with an enthusiastic manifesto
penned by Miguel Littín, and Littín himself was put in charge of the state
institution Chile Films. He lasted for only ten months, tiring of bureaucratic opposition (many officials had guaranteed jobs in Chile Films and

[59] Zuzana M. Pick, *The New Latin American Cinema: A Continental Project* (Austin, Tex., 1993).

could not be replaced) and inter-party feuding as the different members of Popular Unity demanded a share of very limited resources. Few films were made between 1970 and 1973 and the state bodies could do little to affect distribution and exhibition. The United States imposed pressure in a number of ways. The Motion Pictures Export Association ordered the suspension of exports of U.S. films from June 1971 and Chile Films was forced into bilateral exchanges with Bulgaria, Cuba, Hungary and Czechoslovakia to fill the vacuum.

Raúl Ruiz was the most productive film-maker of the period, with a number of films in different styles such as *La colonia penal* (The Penal Colony, 1971), *Nadie dijo nada* (No One Said Anything, 1971), *La expropriación,* 1973 and *El realismo socialista* (1973). Littín was working on an ambitious feature *La tierra prometida* (The Promised Land) when the 1973 coup occurred and post-production took place in Paris. The most exemplary film which traced the radicalization of Chile in 1972 and 1973 was Patricio Guzmán's *La batalla de Chile* (The Battle of Chile), a documentary in three parts which was edited in exile in Cuba. The first part, 'The Insurrection of the Bourgeoisie' deals with the middle-class revolt against the Allende government in the media and in the streets. 'The Coup d'état' continues this narrative, adding in the bitter quarrels among the left over strategy, while the third part 'Popular Power' looks at the work of mass organizations in 1973. In the first years of exile, this film became Chile's most evocative testimony abroad and received worldwide distribution in campaigns of solidarity. Paradoxically, Chilean cinema, which had little time to grow under Popular Unity, strengthened and became a coherent movement in exile.

The military coup in Uruguay in 1973, put an end to what had been for a time a lively film culture. The main protagonists of the 1960s had been the documentary film-makers Ugo Ulive and Mario Handler, and they were supported by a local independent producer and exhibitor Walter Achugar who pioneered the distribution of Latin American new cinema in Uruguay as a way of stimulating local production. In conjunction with the Argentine producer Edgardo Pallero, they were responsible for setting up the Cinemateca del Tercer Mundo in Montevideo in November 1969, which worked in production, distribution and exhibition. In the political radicalization of the early 1970s, the Cinemateca was a very visible target. In May 1972, two of its directors, Eduardo Terra and Walter Achugar were arrested, tortured and detained. As the long night descended in 1973, the artistic community spread into exile.

Both Chilean and Uruguayan artists initially found refuge in Argentina, for Perón had returned in June 1973, ushering in a brief period of civilian rule. The situation was tense and violent, as all sectors, from the far right and the military to the guerrilla groups and the left, thought that Perón would offer them support but there was a brief period of nationalist, populist, anti-imperialist euphoria in the film industry. Between 1973 and 1974, fifty-four films were made and cinema audiences rose by some 40 per cent. Cineastes focused on the heroes of Argentine history and adapted literary texts by José Hernández, Roberto Arlt and Manuel Puig. The most successful films were the anti-imperialist epics: Héctor Olivera's *La Patagonia rebelde,* Richardo Wullicher's *Quebracho,* and Leonardo Favio's *Juan Moreira.* Some more gentle, intimate, themes were portrayed such as Sergio Renán's *La tregua* (The Truce), but in the main artists and intellectuals were caught up in a political voluntarism.

Perón's death in 1974 and the assumption to power of his minor actress wife, Isabel, caused a spiralling violence. Factionalism grew within Peronism, the guerrilla groups continued a campaign of violence and right-wing death squads acted with impunity. Film-makers were just one of the sectors affected by the growing terror and repression. Many received death threats and escaped into exile even before the coup of March 1976.

From the mid-1970s and for the rest of that decade and beyond, the countries of the Southern Cone of Latin America lived through the bleakest period of their history. While repression was at its height, cultural expression was severely limited. In film, production dropped and a diet of inoffensive comedies or musicals became the norm. In the main it was foreign producers and distributions that benefitted: the North American Motion Picture Export Association recorded greatly increased profits in Argentina in the late 1970s. Yet no one could benefit from the blatant censorship which banned certain foreign films, or mutilated others, rendering them incomprehensible. Military men intervened in the state cultural institutions, military minds 'defended' the morality of the nation and of the family. A small 'catacomb' culture built up in the different countries in an attempt to keep intellectual debate alive, but high-visibility industries such as cinema had few opportunities to express difference.

The exiles suffered different problems, of displacement from community and isolation within their host communities. Most have described the process in positive terms, as Zuzana Pick reminds us: 'Forced to communicate with and engage in new cultural (and sometimes linguistic) contexts, these film-makers broadened the thematic concerns of their work and extended their practices beyond the affiliation with national communities',[60] into new expressive territories. The best example of a director adapting to new circumstances is the case of Raúl Ruiz. He went penniless to Paris, with his wife, the editor and film-maker Valeria Sarmento. His first film, which dealt with the exile community there, was entitled *Diálogo de exilados* (Dialogue of Exiles, 1974). It was greeted with hostility by the Chileans, who thought that his ironic, playful tone was inappropriate to the seriousness of the situation. Ruiz, now in almost a double exile, moved towards the world of French film-making. He was fortunate that the specialist institution, INA (Institut National de l'Audiovisuel) had been set up to commission experimental work. With the support of INA and other institutions, Ruiz gained the reputation of being one of the most innovative directors in Europe, the subject of a special issue of the film journal *Cahiers du Cinéma* in 1983. He has remarked that working in the stable conditions of Europe has given him 'an experience of production and a sense of craft that does not exist in Latin America, the idea of professional development and advancement, and the possibility of various technical skills converging into one.'[61] His films constantly navigate, like the sailors in *Les Trois couronnes du matelot* (Three Crowns of a Sailor, 1982), between Europe and America, in a hybrid style which is neither narrowly nationalist nor cosmopolitan. Eduardo Cozarinsky, the Argentine film-maker who went into voluntary exile in Paris with the return of Perón in 1973 has remarked that Ruiz and other film-makers (like Cozarinksy himself and the Argentines Eduardo de Gregorio and Hugo Santiago) 'can illuminate France, and consequently its cinema with a lateral light that emphasizes volume and texture, rather than the harsh front-lighting which flattens everything out.'[62]

Valeria Sarmiento, Ruiz's wife, is one of several Chilean women cineastes to have developed their careers successfully in exile. It is from about the mid-1970s, throughout the continent, that the work of women film-makers became increasingly prominent, in different contexts, putting forward gender issues which had been largely ignored by the first wave of new cinema in the 1960s.[63] Sarmento's best-known film, *Un hombre, cuando es un*

[60] Pick, *New Latin American Cinema*, p. 156.
[61] Interview with Raúl Ruiz, in Pick, *New Latin American Cinema*, p. 177.
[62] Eduardo Cozarinsky, 'Les réalisateurs étrangers en France: hier et aujourd'hui', *Positif*, 325 (March 1988), p. 42.
[63] On the development of women film-makers, see Pick, *New Latin American Cinema*, pp. 66–96, Luis Trelles Plazaola, *Cine y mujer en América Latina* (Río Piedras, P.R., 1991), and the special issue of the *Journal of Film and Video*, 44/3–4 (Fall 1992 and Winter 1993).

hombre (A Man When He is a Man) 1982, was shot in Costa Rica with a crew of Chilean exiles from Europe and was edited in Paris. It explores the world of machismo through *ranchera* music and *boleros.* This success was followed by *Notre Mariage* (Our Marriage, 1984) and the feature *Amelia López O'Neill* shot in Chile in 1990. Marilú Mallet made a number of important documentaries in Canada, while Angelina Vásquez found great support in Scandinavia, working and filming on Chile. Miguel Littín, Chile's best-known director from the Popular Unity period, was exiled in Mexico, receiving the support of president Echeverría. He became an explicit spokesman of Latin American cinema in exile, making a large budget Third World epic *Actas de Marusia* (Letter from Marusia, 1975) before funding dried up in Mexico in the late 1970s. These directors and others like Gaston Ancelovici in Paris and Pedro Chaskel in Cuba, showed the great energy and adaptability of Chilean film-making in the diaspora.

This was not the case for every director in exile. Fernando Solanas, for example, completed post-production work on his Peronist *Los hijos de Fierro* (The Sons of Fierro) in 1978 in Paris, but felt himself to be marginal, as an Argentine, but also as a Peronist. He never became a critical success like Raúl Ruiz and worked for a number of years to finance his film on exiles *Tangos: el exilio de Gardel* (Tangos: the Exile of Gardel) which he began filming in 1981, but could not complete until the mid-1980s, when Argentina had returned to democracy and co-funding became available.

In Bolivia, the Banzer coup of 1971 caused the Ukamau group to split. One part, under Antonio Eguino, opted to stay in Bolivia, and make films which were commercial but also socially responsible: *Pueblo Chico* (Small Town, 1974) and *Chuquiago,* 1977 (the Aymara name for La Paz). Sanjinés pursued a more radical option in exile and managed to make *El enemigo principal* (The Principal Enemy, 1973) in Peru and *Fuera de Aquí* (Get out of Here, 1976) in Ecuador until the fall of Banzer allowed him to return temporarily to Bolivia in 1979.

The experience of exile was thus ambivalent. It allowed some directors the freedom of distance, while it closed possibilities to others. It could be seen as an extension of the premises and aesthetics of the New Latin American cinema, but also as a moment of closure, or shifting of interests. In a period of transnational globalization the nation itself became a prime target. In terms of film, Hollywood by the mid-1970s had staged a remarkable comeback and, writes Thomas Elaesser, 'it was American movies, the package deal and big-business production methods which became more than ever the dominant model on both European and world markets. The new independent cinemas, whether national, politically internationalist or author-based, gradually found themselves forced into coexistence on the Americans' own terms or all but vanish altogether. In so far as spectators returned to the cinema, it was to watch Hollywood blockbusters'.[64] There was a danger, in these circumstances, that the only audience for radical, exile, Latin American cinema was on the international festival circuit, where they became part of European radical chic.

Some countries sought to minimize this risk of deterritorialization by offering major state funding, and other support, for national cinemas. In this period, Brazil and Mexico led the way. By the time directors such as Glauber Rocha and Ruy Guerra had returned to Brazil from brief periods of exile in the early seventies, Cinema Novo had largely disappeared as an integrated *movement* for social change. It was the Cinema Novo directors, however, who would dominate film-making in the next two decades, under the aegis of the state. Embrafilme, the state body, had been set up in 1969 as an international distribution agency, but its activities extended and in 1975, it began to work in production and exhibition as well as distribution, taking virtually a monopolistic control over cinema in the country. The screen quota for Brazilian films increased dramatically from forty-two days in 1959 to 140 days in 1981. Under the direction of Roberto Farias (1974–79) Embrafilme's budget rose from $US 600,000 to $US 8 million. Embrafilme distributed over 30 per cent of Brazilian films in the 1970s and controlled between 25 and 50 per cent of annual film production. The market share of Brazilian cinema increased from 15 per cent in 1974 to more than 30 per cent in 1980 and the number of spectators for Brazilian films doubled.[65]

Such figures of growth seem to offer an irrefutable case for working with the state. Yet the dilemma remained that Embrafilme was supported by a repressive military government. Most film-makers decided to make a pact with the state and produce socially responsible films from inside the system, across the range of themes. Literary works were adapted, from light sex comedies, Bruno Barreto's *Dona Flor e seus dois maridos* (Dona Flor and Her Two Husbands, 1976) based on Jorge Amado's novel which became the most successful film in Brazilian history, to the sombre realism of Graciliano Ramos's fictional world, evoked in Leon Hirszman's *São Bernardo* (1972). History was reexamined in Joaquim Pedro de Andrade's *Os*

[64] Thomas Elaesser, 'Hyper-Retro-or Counter Cinema', in *Mediating Two Worlds*, p. 121.
[65] Randal Johnson, *The Film Industry in Brazil: Culture and the State* (Pittsburgh, 1987), pp. 171–2.

inconfidentes (The Conspirators, 1972) and Carlos Diegues' *Xica da Silva* (1977), while Nelson Pereira dos Santos revised the early Cinema Novo's view that 'the people' were alienated masses that had to be educated out of false consciousness, by positing instead that they are repositories of popular wisdom, that intellectuals should tap in to. His *O amuleto de Ogum* (The Amulet of Ogum, 1974) and *Na estrada da vida* (Road of Life, 1980) deal, in this respectful way, with both popular religion and popular song. Ruy Guerra brought up to date his *Os fuzis* in *A queda* (The Fall, 1976), which finds the main military protagonist of the earlier film now as a construction worker in São Paulo. Women film-makers such as Ana Carolina and Tizuka Yamasaki also begin to emerge in this period, perhaps the most successful in Brazilian history. Ana Carolina made the first of a trilogy of surrealist, anarchist films, *Mar de Rosas* in 1977. Yamasaki made shorts in the 1970s, before releasing her first feature, a study of Japanese immigration into Brazil, *Gaijin: Caminhos da Liberdade* (Roads to Freedom) in 1980.

In Mexico the Echeverría administration (1970–76) sought to alleviate the loss of confidence caused by the massacre of students at Tlatelolco in 1968, by deliberately wooing intellectuals. Many prominent figures gave the new president their support. Leading novelist Carlos Fuentes accepted the Ambassadorship of Mexico in Paris and argued that 'above all, Echeverría lifted the veil of fear that Díaz Ordaz had flung over the body of Mexico. Many Mexicans felt free to criticize, to express themselves, to organize without fear of repression.'[66] Echeverría was particularly active in the area of cinema. He put his brother Rodolfo in charge of the Banco Cinematográfico, which was immediately reformed. He founded the Mexican Cinemathèque, established a film school, the CCC (Centro de Capacitación Cinematográfica) and gradually increased the role of the state in production and exhibition. In 1971, the state funded five films and private producers seventy-seven films; in 1976 private producers funded only fifteen features, while the state's share had gone up dramatically to thirty-five features. The major studios, Churubusco and América were turned over to state cinema, and the first-run cinemas were required to screen Mexican films.

This modernization of the film industry was accompanied by the development of a new generation of film-makers who had trained in the 1960s and now found that they had financial backing for their projects. Arturo Ripstein's *El castillo de la pureza* (The Castle of Purity, 1972), Jaime

<hr />

[66] Carlos Fuentes, *Tiempo mexicano* (Mexico, D.F., 1971), p. 166.

Hermosillo's *La pasión según Berenice* (The Passion According to Berenice, 1976) and *Matineé*, 1976, Felipe Cazal's *Canoa*, 1975, Paul Leduc's *Reed: México insurgente*, (Reed, Insurgent Mexico, 1970) and his documentary *Etnocidio: notas sobre el Mezquital* (Ethnocide: Notes on the Mezquital, 1976) and Marcela Fernández Violante's *De todos modos Juan te llamas* (Whatever You Do, It's No Good, 1975) were all successful feature films in Mexico and abroad. The set-back to this success was the lack of continuity in presidential policies from one *sexenio* to the next. President López Portillo (1976–82) put his sister Margarita in charge of the film industry and she effectively dismantled the Echeverría system. The state withdrew funding, or else supported unsuccessful and very costly international co-productions and the old producers returned offering a diet for the late seventies of sex comedies, mild pornography, strong language and violent gun-runners.

The Cuban state in the early seventies, in the aftermath of the Padilla affair, clamped down on intellectual and artistic diversity. It is sometimes argued that the film industry escaped these restrictions[67] but such an analysis fails to convince. This phase ended in 1975 when a Ministry of Culture was set up. The ICAIC became part of that Ministry, but although output increased the range of topics under discussion did not. Just as the Brazilian military had supported films on slavery and independence movements, so the black Cuban director Sergio Giral found official approval for a trilogy on slavery and slave rebellions: *El otro Francisco* (The Other Francisco, 1973), *Rancheador* (Slave Hunter, 1975) and *Maluala* (1979). At one level it can be argued that these films celebrate black insurrection, but they also demonstrate a sense of nationhood forged by black struggle, posit an unproblematic transculturation, and create a pantheon of heroic guerrillas, a useful iconography for a black population about to engage in a bloody war in Angola. Rather than talk about contemporary problems of race, ICAIC preferred to 'imagine' a community based on harmony. In general ICAIC worked predominantly in historical themes, leaving the present to be explored only fleetingly.

A film more sensitive to contemporary problems, *De cierta manera* (One Way or Another, 1974), was made by Cuba's only woman feature director to date, Sara Gómez who died of asthma before the final cut. The work was completed by Alea and García Espinosa. It deals quietly and sensitively with worker's responsibilities, with *machismo*, with the black popu-

[67] See in particular Michael Chanan's analysis in *The Cuban Image* (London, 1985).

lation and with the alienating effects of popular religion. The campaign for women's rights was taken up in Pastor Vega's *Retrato de Teresa* (Portrait of Teresa, 1970) which portrays the break-up of marriage as the wife is involved in the home, in factory work and in cultural activities which incur the wrath of her two-timing husband. Gender is more interestingly examined than race in the films of the 1970s and in this the films reflect the political and social imperatives of the time.

Experimentation in narrative was largely abandoned as there was a deliberate shift to capture a more 'popular' audience, using a more transparent style. Fornet has called this the 'nationalization of traditional genres, by giving them new progressive contents'.[68] Several Manichean, conventional films were made in this way: Manuel Pérez's *El hombre de Maisinicú* (The Man from Maisinicú, 1973) and *Río Negro* (1977), and Octavio Cortazar's, *El brigadista* (The Literacy Teacher, 1977). All these are macho adventure stories, where the good guys are revolutionary and the bad guys are counter-revolutionary. No other nuances are needed or offered. Gutiérrez Alea made a complex film, also about slavery, *La última cena* (The Last Supper 1976) and Humberto Solás and Octavio Goméz made experimental films in this period, but there was a great deal of mediocre, conventional, work and few signs of new blood in either directors or actors. The Revolution was growing older and more bureaucratic and tensions – both internal and external – were hampering creativity. Solás's *Cecilia,* made in 1981 and released a year later, seemed to bring together a number of different worries. An established director had spent an inordinate amount of ICAIC's yearly production budget on a hackneyed costume melodrama and an ageing superstar cast. The part of Cecilia Valdés demanded a betwitching actress in her teens or early twenties. Instead the part was given to Daisy Granados, a splendid actress, but a woman looking her forty-plus years. Changes were clearly in order.

In Colombia, Venezuela and Peru, the state led significant developments in film-making in the mid-1970s. In 1971 a 'ley de sobreprecios' or 'surcharge law' was passed to support Colombian film-making, it stipulated that a Colombian short film should accompany any new release in the country. These would be subsidized by offering producers a share of raised box office prices. Results in terms of quantity were spectacular. In 1974 two feature films were made through private investment, but ninety-four shorts appeared through the surcharge system. A number of

[68] See Fornet's essay in P.A. Paranagua (ed.), *Le Cinéma Cubain* (Paris, 1990), pp. 92–6.

these were of poor quality, but in general it can be said that the scheme created new independent film companies and gave directors and technicians valuable training. Some directors – Marta Rodríguez, Jorge Silva, Carlos Mayolo, Luis Ospina and Carlos Alvarez – had already made documentaries in the 1960s, but others such as Lisandro Duque, Jorge Ali Triana and Ciró Durán also benefited from these new conditions.

Government measures also looked to encourage feature films. Screen quotas were imposed for national films (twenty days in 1977 and thirty days in 1978). Colombia had the third largest cinema audience in Latin America after Brazil and Mexico (80 million spectators in 1984) and it was felt that a percentage of that market could help to make Colombian films economically viable. A film governing entity FOCINE (Compañía de Fomento Cinematográfico) was set up in 1978 to promote national cinema, financed by an 8.5 per cent levy on cinema tickets. At the outset it offered advance credits to film projects up to 70 per cent of total costs and also credits to buy film equipment and stock. But when loan payments were not made, FOCINE decided in 1983 to move into full-time production. The limitations and benefits of the system would be seen in the next decade.

During the sixties a lively film culture had grown up in Venezuela, with the work of Román Chalbaud and Clemente de la Cerda among others. In September 1968 the University of Mérida had sponsored a festival of Latin American documentary cinema which brought together work by Solanas, Sanjinés, Santiago Alvarez, Glauber Rocha and Tomás Gutiérrez Alea, and six months later, as a direct result of the festival, the Universidad de los Andes (ULA) had founded a documentary film centre, which became absorbed into a department of cinema. This department became an important training ground and also production centre throughout the 1970s, with established directors such as Carlos Rebolledo and Michael New. In 1975, perhaps prompted by the critical and commercial success of the Mexican Mauricio Wallerstein's *Cuando quiero llorar, no lloro* (When I Want to Cry, I Don't Cry, 1974) and Román Chalbaud's, *La quema de Judas* (Burning the Judas, 1974), the state began to support feature films and between 1975 and 1980, with oil revenues booming, the state financed twenty-nine features. It was also stipulated, through this period, that at least twelve Venezuelan films should be exhibited a year. For once exhibitors needed little encouragement since most filmmakers adopted the strategy of making deliberately commercial, popular, films which would also contain elements of social protest. Ramón

Chalbaud's *El pez que fuma* (The Smoking Fish, 1977), Carlos Rebolledo
and Thaelman Urgelles's *Alias: el rey del joropo* (The King of the Joropo
Dance, 1978) and Clemente de la Cerda's *Soy un delincuente* (I'm a Criminal, 1976) are exemplary in this respect. In 1981, the Fondo de Fomento
Cinematográfico (FOCINE) was established to consolidate this work.

In Peru the military government that came to power in 1968 decreed
that Peruvian films should receive 'obligatory exhibition' in the country
and since there were very few feature films, the documentary short became the favoured form. Over 150 production companies were set up to
make films for this new exhibition space. As in Colombia quality varied,
but a number of important film-makers all made significant documentaries in this period: Luis Figueroa, Federico García, Arturo Sinclair, Francisco Lombardi and Nora de Izcué. The investment in equipment and the
growth of film making experience also inevitably led to the production of
feature-length films. Indigenous themes were explored in Luis Figueroa's
adaptations of the novel *Los perros hambrientos* (The Hungry Dogs, 1976)
and *Yawar Fiesta* (Bloody Fiesta, 1980) and Federico García's *Kuntur
Wachana* (Where the Condors are Born, 1977). 1977 also saw the first
feature-length film by Francisco Lombardi, *Muerte al amanecer* (Death at
Dawn) which was a great box-office success. At the end of the decade,
therefore, Peruvian cinema was in a relatively healthy state.

1980S AND EARLY 1990S: FROM REDEMOCRATISATION
TO NEO-LIBERALISM

The decade of the eighties began with cinema showing optimistic signs
of growth. At the outset of the nineties there were fewer grounds for
optimism, as most countries, in the cold neo-liberal wind, found investment in film a dispensable luxury. Throughout the decade, the economic problems were immense. All over the world cinema had to
maintain a market share against the other attractions of the entertainment industry, in particular television and the new world of cable and
satellite. In order to survive, Hollywood companies diversified and became part of conglomerate networks. This diversification was a hedge
against losses which was a luxury that no Latin American film-maker
could entertain, unless the state, in a few cases, was willing to pick up
the tab. Cinema was maintained precariously, against a background
of declining audience and the attractions of the new electronic media.

Television would prove to be a rival, rather than ally of cinema. The big media conglomerates, Globo in Brazil and Televisa in Mexico have successfully exported *telenovelas* throughout the world, but there is no tradition of commissioning feature films for television. In Brazil in 1981, 1792 films were shown on television; of these 88 were Brazilian (4.91 per cent of the total); of the 88, very few were quality Cinema Novo titles: they were in the main, *pornochanchadas*. Television would also increasingly become a place of work for film-makers unable to finance features or documentaries.

The strongest industries in the 1970s had been state-driven: Brazil, Mexico, Peru, Venezuela, Colombia and, in a different context, Cuba. For a time production remained strong in Brazil despite the economic crises and the dramatic fall in cinema audiences as the TV giant Globo increased its market share with successful game shows and, in particular, soap operas. Several Cinema Novo directors had untimely deaths – Glauber Rocha, Joaquim Pedro de Andrade and Leon Hirszman – but others such as Nelson Pereira dos Santos (*Memórias do cárcere*, 1984) and Ruy Guerra (*Erendira*, 1982, *Opera do malandro*, 1986) produced important work. Several women, Ana Carolina, Suzana Amaral and the Japanese-Brazilian Tizuka Yamasaki directed major features which were successful in the home market. Ana Carolina completed her trilogy of films begun in the 1970s with *Das Tripas Coração* (1982) and *Sonho de Valsa* (1987). Yamasaki followed the success of *Gaijin* with *Parahyba, Mulher-Macho* (1983) and *Patriamada* (1985). Amaral successfully adapted Clarice Lispector's final novel *A Hora da Estrela* in 1985. Yet this model of state-funding was entering into crisis. Randal Johnson summed up the situation as follows: 'Embrafilme became the major source of production financing, creating a situation of dependence between the state and so-called 'independent' film-makers and in itself became a marketplace where film-makers competed against each other for the right to make films. This, in turn exacerbated tensions within the industry and created a situation in which the play of influences was often more important than the talent of the film-maker or the quality of the final product. As a consequence, public sector investments in the cinema lost social legitimacy. Brazilian President Fernando Collor de Mello's dismantling of Embrafilme in 1990, represented the *coup de grâce* to a poorly conceived and misguided policy of state support.'[69] However misguided the state

---

[69] Randal Johnson, 'In the belly of the ogre', in *Mediating Two Worlds*, pp. 211–12.

support, it had at least sustained film-makers for twenty years. Without this support, there was in the early 1990s a dramatic fall in production.

The same problems of clientelism and bureaucratic wranglings dogged the development of Colombia's film industry. Some directors of FOCINE were popular singers or boxing promoters. Even though FOCINE could boast in 1988, its tenth anniversary, of some 200 feature, medium length and short films including Mayolo's *La mansión de Araucaima* (The Mansion of Arucaima, 1986), Ospina's *Pura sangre* (Pure Blood, 1982), and Jorge Alí Triana's *Tiempo de morir* (A Time to Die, 1985), from 1986 it scarcely managed to offer any support in production or exhibition. Few directors were able to make more than one feature, especially after FOCINE withdrew from production in 1990. The state, it seemed, had no strategy for the 1990s. In its place, film-maker Sergio Cabrera proposed *La estrategia del caracol* ('The Strategy of the Snail', 1993), which, in January 1994, was on its way to becoming the biggest grossing box-office Colombian film of all time. In the first month of its release in Colombia it attracted an extraordinary 750,000 spectators, a figure that rivalled the year's audience for *Jurassic Park* in Colombia. The film tells of a group of tenants who share a large old house in the centre of Bogotá and are subject to imminent eviction. Their resistance, stage-managed by an old exiled Spanish anarchist, with the help of a lawyer outwits the yuppie tenement owner, his corrupt legal advisers and brutal henchmen. The narrative structure – the resourcefulness and unity of the people, the traditional *barrio,* in the face of rapacious modernity – has been a constant in Latin American cinema since the earliest times, but Cabrera offers a fresh and witty inflection which avoids the sentimentality of melodrama or of neo-realism or the triumphalism of sixties and seventies revolutionary optimism. Whether Cabrera offers an example that can be followed by other directors remains an open question.

The same financial setbacks can be seen in Peru, where only a handful of directors were able to make commercially viable films. The most successful was Francisco Lombardi, with *La ciudad y los perros* (The City and the Dogs, 1986) and *Boca de Lobo* (1988). Venezuela, on the other hand, maintained a relative stability despite the contraction of the economy after the mid-1980s. FOCINE offered credits and special incentives for 'quality' films. Exhibitors were also enticed by financial incentives. The support of the public meant that in the early 1980s, the large distribution chains Blancica and MDF had invested in production. The Universidad de los Andes also continued in co-production. In these conditions Diego Rísquez made a trilogy of films on the conquest and history of the New World, Fina Torres won the coveted Caméra d'Ort at Cannes with *Oriana* (1985) and veteran film-maker Román Chalbaud continued to make stylish thrillers up to *Cuchillos de fuego* (Flaming Knives, 1990). Solveig Hoogesteijn's *Macu, la mujer del policía* became a box office hit after its release in 1987. Perhaps the most interesting film on the theme of the *quinto centenario* was Luis Alberto Lamata's *Jericó* (1991), which explored the assimilation of a Dominican friar by an Indian group. Although in the early 1990s it lacked the resources of the early 1980s, Venezuelan cinema continued to have a modest yearly output.

Cuba reorganized the film sector in 1982. Julio García Espinosa became the minister responsible for cinema and he initiated policy changes: a marked increase in production, a reduced shooting budget and the introduction of new directors. As a result the veterans allowed space for new film-makers who were more interested in contemporary issues and not afraid of comedy (the 1970s had been a particularly solemn period in film production). Orlando Rojas in *Una novia para David* (A Girl Friend for David, 1985) and *Papeles secundarios* (Secondary Roles, 1989), Rolando Díaz in *Los pájaros tirándole a la escopeta* (Tables Turned, 1984) and in particular Juan Carlos Tabío in *Se permuta* (House Swap, 1984), *Plaff* (1988) and most recently *Fresa y chocolate* (Strawberry and Chocolate, 1993), co-directed with Tomás Gutiérrez Alea, have cast a fresh eye on contemporary issues. Inventive work took place in animation, under the guidance of Juan Padrón, with *Vampiros en la Habana* (Vampires in Havana, 1985) and the series 'Elpidio Valdés' and 'Quinoscopios'. In 1987 these younger directors began to work in decentralized 'creative' groups under the direction of Tomás Gutiérrez Alea, Solás and Manuel Pérez, the most established film-makers in Cuba, who continued to make features throughout the decade. One important result of these 'creative' workshops was the group feature *Mujer Transparente* (Transparent Woman, 1990) which extended the discussions on gender issues in Cuba.

This attempt at decentralization and revival ran up against overwhelming economic pressures as the momentous changes in Eastern Europe undermined the economic (and increasingly the ideological) stability of Cuba. In the 1990s there was little finance available for film-making. Even though it is too early to have the picture clearly in focus it would seem that the 1990s has seen major ideological swings. Directors Sergio Giral and Jesús Díaz – whose *Lejanía* (Parting of the Ways, 1985) had been one of the most thoughtful films of the decade – went into exile, while Daniel Díaz Torres, the maker of *Alicia en el Pueblo de las Maravillas* (Alice in Wonderland, 1991), a mild critique of government policies, was forced into a humiliating recantation. The incident caused the dismissal of García Espinosa and nearly led to the shotgun marriage of ICAIC with the Institute of Radio and Television, (IRT), under the direction of the armed forces. Two years later *Alicia* was shown in international festivals and the Latin American International Film Festival in December 1993, set in Havana, gave its major award to the first ever open treatment of homosexuality in Cuban revolutionary cinema *Fresa y chocolate*. An independent film movement, grouped around the Hermanos Saiz Association, questioned the dominant orthodoxies. But the future remained unpredictable in the extreme.

The exile experience of Cubans – and it is estimated that over 10 percent of Cuba's current population lives in exile – has received some attention in film. Several exiled film-makers have had successful careers in the United States. These include Orlando Jiménez Leal, one of the directors of the notorious *PM* of the early sixties, and in particular the late Nestor Almendros who became perhaps the world's most successful lighting cameraman. These cineastes and others became increasingly outspoken against the Revolution from the early eighties, especially in the aftermath of the *marielito* wave of exiles, and there appeared a trilogy of explicitly denunciatory documentaries *The Other Cuba* (1983) and *Improper Conduct* (1984), both directed by Jiménez Leal and Almendros and *Nobody Listens* (1988) directed by Almendros and Jorge Ulla, which dealt with the treatment of homosexuality and political prisoners by the regime. Jiménez Leal also directed a fictional comedy *El Super* (1980) on the Cuban American experience, made, as the credits reveal by 'the people who brought you the rhumba, the mambo, Ricky Ricardo, daiquiris, good cigars, Fidel Castro, cha-cha-cha, Cuban-Chinese restaurants plus the Watergate plumbers'. *El Super* follows the trials and tribulations of a Cuban tenement supervisor in Queens who dreams of returning to Cuba and, in the end, has to opt for Miami.

A younger generation of film-makers, born in Cuba but trained in the United States – León Ichaso, Ramón Menéndez, Miñuca Villaverde, Iván Acosta and Orestes Matacena – have tended to work on projects which are not specifically Cuban-American, but have a rather more *latino* focus, such as Menéndez's *Stand and Deliver* (1988). With an increased contact between the United States and Cuba possible in the 1990s, it remains to be seen if the younger generations across the diaspora can enter into dialogues that might shake the fixed certainties of their parents' and grandparents' generations.

Cuba had always supported internationalism, giving shelter to exiled Latin American directors, hosting an international film festival and setting up a film school in 1985, but with a bankrupt economy and with little belief left in Latin America that 'new' cinema could be linked to 'revolutionary' or socialist change, this role became increasingly redundant. For a time the republics of Central America, going against the grain of history, picked up the revolutionary mantle from Cuba. The victory of the Frente Sandinista de Liberación Nacional (FSLN) in Nicaragua was captured in moving images by film-makers attached to the FSLN. The Sandinistas in power set up the Nicaraguan Film Institute (INCINE), based on Somoza's film production company, Producine. With scarce resources and with donations from other countries, a rudimentary film production was established in newsreels, documentary film, video and eventually in feature films. Work in video and in super-8 was most widespread due to the cost and difficulty in obtaining 16 and 35 mm film stock and to the need for processing film stock abroad. The then exiled Bolivian film-maker Alfonso Gumucio Dagrón ran a workshop in the techniques of super-8, which could be used by union activists. Longer documentaries included Ramiro Lacayo's *Bananeras* (Banana Workers, 1982) and Iván Arguello's *Teotacacinte 83* (1983) who also made the short feature *Mujeres de la Frontera* (Frontier Women) in 1986. Attempts to produce anything more ambitious, such as full length, co-produced features, largely ended in failure, apart from the Chilean Littin's *Alsino y el condor* (Alsino and the Condor, 1982), and even before the Sandinistas were voted out of power in 1990, INCINE was virtually bankrupt and film-makers were in bitter dispute about the best ways to apportion limited resources.

In El Salvador, the revolutionary struggles were recorded by Radio Venceremos, the communications organization of the FMLN in a series of documentaries, *Carta de Morazán* (Letter from Morazán, 1982), *Tiempo de audacia* (Time of Daring, 1983) and *Tiempo de Victoria* (Time of Victory, 1988), while in Guatemala, a few documentaries followed the vicissitudes of the civil war. In Costa Rica democratic governments supported documentary film-making from the mid-1970s, and independent producers and directors, such as Oscar Castillo could make the occasional feature, such as Castillo's *La Xegua* (1984), a melodrama about the greed and rapaciousness of colonizers. Patricia Howell also produced significant documentaries. In Panama, a state-led company, the Grupo Experimental de Cine Universitario (GECU), made documentaries in the 1970s under Torrijos, but was forced to cut back under Noriega and after.

In the Caribbean islands, only Puerto Rico had what could be called a film movement. A critical, national documentary movement had been fostered by the Community Education Division of the government of Puerto Rico (DIVEDCO) from the 1950s, with over seventy documentaries, and by the 1980s several directors were working in feature films. The most successful of these was Marcos Zurinaga with *La gran fiesta* (The Gala Ball, 1986) and *Tango bar* (1988), both of which starred the late Raúl Julia, and Jacobo Morales's *Díos los cría* (God Makes Them, 1980) *Nicolás y lo demás* (Nicholas and the Others, 1983) and *Lo que le pasó a Santiago* (What Happened to Santiago, 1989), which portrayed the Puerto Rican middle class, its dilemmas and anxieties. In Haiti, exile film-makers such as Raoul Peck and Arnold Antonin could find occasional funding, whilst the Dominican Republic produced only one major fictional film in the 1980s: *Un pasaje de ida* (One Way Ticket, 1988) by Agliberto Meléndez.

In the wake of democratization in the 1980s, several countries that had suffered under dictatorship had a chance to express new cultural freedoms. Both Ukamau groups could make films in Bolivia in the 1980s. Eguino filmed *Amargo Mar* (Bitter Sea) in 1984 and Jorge Sanjinés followed the documentary *Banderas del amanecer* (Banner at Dawn, 1983) with the fictional *La nación clandestina* (The Secret Nation) in 1989. But funds remain limited and a director as well-known as Sanjinés took on average five years to put together co-production finance to make a feature length film. Other cineastes worked in video. Uruguayan film was slow to recover after the dictatorship, but boasted a very well-stocked and well run Cinemathèque. Chilean exiles continued to work in the 1980s – in particular the prolific Raúl Ruiz – but inside Chile some film-making also became possible in the 1980s, from clandestine documentaries by Littin and Gastón Ancelovici, to feature films by Silvio Caiozzi. After the victory of the democratic parties in November 1989 work slowly began to appear from exiled directors who had returned and from a younger generation brought up under the dictatorship. Whether their work is sustainable remains an open question.

The country to show the strongest revival in film culture after dictatorship was Argentina. The Radical government under Alfonsín (1983–9) abolished censorship and put two well-known film-makers Manuel Antín and Ricardo Wullicher in charge of the INC. Antín's granting of credits to young and established directors and his internationalist strategy had an immediate effect. For several years there was a great flowering of talent, a development that was halted temporarily in 1989 with an economy in ruins and with inflation running at an annual rate of 1,000 per cent. The swingeing neo-liberal reforms of the Menem government in the early nineties restored some confidence and the INC resumed the award of credits, with an income based on a percentage of ticket sales. However, very few films could recoup their costs in the home market and, after a fashionable few years in the mid-1980s – which culminated with the award of an Oscar to *La historia oficial*, directed by Luis Puenzo in 1986 – not many films found a place in international markets. The most visible and successful directors of the period were Luis Puenzo, Fernando Solanas and María Luisa Bemberg while a number of talented directors Sorín, Subiela, Mórtola, Felipelli, Beceyro, Pauls, Barney Finn, Doria, Fischerman, Kamin, Polaco, Pereira, Santiso, Tosso and Stantic made important films, but struggled to maintain a continuity in their work.

There has been a great heterogeneity of styles and themes in Argentine cinema that cannot adequately be surveyed in a brief history. Two general points, however, can be made. After so many years of persecution and censorship, the film-makers showed a great energy and inventiveness in exploring the medium. Secondly, many of the films produced focused directly or obliquely on the traumas of recent history. The conditions that gave rise to a militant cinema in the 1960s no longer existed: new movies were not a call to arms, but rather reflections on society's ills and conflicts. Solanas, for example, realized that films need not simply be didactic weapons, but should also be a source of pleasure, and his *Tangos, el exilio de Gardel* (Tangos, the Exile of Gardel, 1985) and *Sur* (South, 1989) treat political, Peronist, themes through an exciting blend of dance, music, choreography which contain hauntingly evocative images, an effect enhanced by the expert cinematography of Félix Monti, Argentina's most accomplished and innovative lighting cameraman. María Luisa Bemberg, in contrast, has provided Argentina's first sustained feminist viewpoint in a series of intelligent, and commercially viable features: *Señora de nadie* (No One's Woman, 1982), *Camila* (1984), *Miss Mary* (1986), *Yo la peor de todas* (I the Worst of All, 1990) and *De eso no se habla* (We Don't Talk about It, 1993). Her former producer, turned director, Lita Stantic made perhaps the most complex film about the dirty war, *Un muro de silencio* (A Wall of Silence, 1993), a success with the critics, but ignored by the Argentine public who preferred to view politics and repression through a gauze of melodrama and rock music as Marcelo Pineyro's *Tango feroz* (1993). What strategies film-makers should adopt to maintain the viability of their films in a shrinking domestic market is an acutely difficult question to answer.

The only country to reverse the trend towards the withdrawal of state support from the film industry and to resist the chill winds of the neo-liberal market economy has been Mexico. In 1988 Mexican cinema had suffered from over a decade of state neglect and rampant commercialism under the presidencies of José López Portillo (1976–82) and Miguel de la Madrid (1982–8). Some two hundred B-movies on drug trafficking were made in the 1980s, with extreme violence, light pornography or fomulaic comedy as the market leaders. By 1987, Mexican cinema had lost 45 per cent of its national audience and 50 per cent in the United States, which was a major source of income. Independent film-making survived, but the work of Leduc, Ripstein and Hermosillo was confined to university and art house circuits.

President Salinas de Gortari (1988–94) recognized the need to open state enterprises to privatization, as a precondition for entering NAFTA, but was also interested in cultivating the intellectual and artistic community which, for the film sector, implied state investment in cinema. The compromise, put into effect by the head of IMCINE Ignacio Durán, was to mix public and private sector funding. State bodies working in production (CONACINE), distribution (Azteca films) and exhibition (COTSA) were privatized and the closed-shop unions were forced to open up to competition from independent production companies. IMCINE embarked on a policy of co-financing films and the success and prestige of the ensuing films has attracted private Mexican capital and also investment from abroad.

The runaway success of the period was Alfonso Arau's *Como agua para chocolate* (Like Water for Chocolate, 1991) based on the best-selling novel by Arau's then wife, Laura Esquivel, who wrote the script. This became the largest grossing foreign-language film of all time in the United States and was shown throughout the world to similar acclaim.[70] While no other film could match this extraordinary exposure – unique in the history of Latin American cinema – the overall standard remained high and many new directors came to the fore. Six women directors made eight

---

[70] See 'An appetite for cinema con salsa', *Newsweek*, 24 January 1994, pp. 44–5.

films between 1989 and 1993: the veteran Matilde Landeta, who made a come-back after forty years, Maryse Sistach, Busi Cortés, Dana Rotberg, Guita Schyfter and María Novaro. María Novaro followed *Lola* (1989) with a film that also penetrated the world markets: *Danzón* (1991) which adhered to the 1930s and 1940s successful formulae of combining melodrama with music and dance. Danzón, a Caribbean dance rhythm, experienced, in the wake of the film, a major revival in Mexico City promoting the leading actress María Rojo to open a dance club, El Salón Mexico, named after a famous cabaret film of the 1940s. Other directors to capture a mood of popular nostalgia were José Buil in *La leyenda de una máscara* (The Legend of a Mask, 1989) a homage to the masked wrestlers of Mexico, the *lucha libre,* and Carlos García Agraz in *Mi querido Tom Mix* (My Beloved Tom Mix, 1991), where the local cinema, as in *Cinema Paradiso,* becomes the site for memories of a time and place when dreams could be shared by a community. Inside and outside the cinema, an old woman can evoke the cowboy legend of the silent screen, Tom Mix, to redress wrongdoings in the present.

Films have been made on a variety of themes, from historical, *quinto centenario* based works *Retorno a Aztlán* (Return to Aztlan, 1990), directed by Juan Mora Catlett and *Cabeza de Vaca* (1990) directed by Nicolás Echevarría, to post-modern yuppie comedies of manners. A young director, Alfonso Cuarón, for example, has made a modern bedroom farce about a young advertising executive, an energetic Lothario, who is led to believe, through a medical report faked by one of his many rejected conquests, that he has AIDS. *Sólo con tu pareja* (Love in the Time of Hysteria, 1991) manages successfully to make us laugh at our deepest fears. In the period from 1989–93, Mexican cinema was the most dynamic industry in Latin America. Mexico had not solved, however, the perennial problem of guaranteeing distribution and exhibition. The cinemas, in the hands of private capital, still block-booked Hollywood products and there arose the paradoxical situation that it was often easier to see Mexican films of this period in festivals and art cinemas abroad than in Mexico itself.

One hundred years on from the first visits of the Lumière agents to the region, cinema in Latin America retains the resilience that has been the hall-mark of film-makers throughout the region, who made and continue to make films against the odds. In a world of increased globalization, when the concept of national cinema itself is under threat, in a possible deregulated transnational world of signs and electronic impulses, in the current unstable political and cultural environment, there is still a generation of film-makers with an idea in their heads and a camera in their hands. Some still pursue the dream of a Latin American consciousness, others try to work within the nation, which remains the bed-rock for film-making, others still pursue co-productions with European or US companies and institutions as a way of financing an increasingly complex and, some argue, anachronistic endeavour. Gabriel García Márquez encapsulates the optimism for the future in his speech to Latin American film-makers and students in the mid-1980s: 'Between 1952 and 1955, four of us who are [here] studied at the Centro Sperimentale in Rome . . . The fact that this evening we are still talking like madmen about the same thing, after thirty years, and that there are with us so many Latin Americans from all parts and from different generations, also talking about the same thing, I take as one further proof of an indestructible idea.'[71]

[71] Quoted in *Anuario 88*, 1988, p. 1.

INDEX

theatre, late nineteenth century, 57–9
Tiempo, César, 112
Timerman, Jacobo, 217
Toesca, Joaquín, 12, 383
Togores, Reynaldo, 375
Toledo, Francisco, 406
Toledo, Mario Monteforte, 174
Tolsá, Manuel, 11
Tomasello, Luis, 438, 453
Toral, Mario, 431
Toro and Ferrer, architects, 377
Torre Nilsson, Leopoldo, 479, 485, 486, 490
Torres, Alcides, 383
Torres, Fina, 511
Torres Méndez, Ramón, 16
Torres Ríos, Leopoldo, 479
Torres-García, Augusto, 442
Torres-García, Horacio, 442
Torres-García, Joaquín, 89, 441, 444, 453
Torrijos, Omar, 514
Tosar E, Héctor, 336
Tovar, Lupita, 463
Tovar y Tovar, Martín, 16, 394
Toyota, Yutaka, 452
Traba, Marta, 216
Traversari, Pedro Pablo, 322
Trenzo, Norberto, 212
Tresguerras, Francisco Eduardo, 11
Treville, E. Charton de, 15
Triana, Jorge Ali, 507, 510
Trinidade, Zé, 480
Troiani, Troiano, 440
Trómpiz, Virgilio, 420
Trotsky, Leon, 183
Truffaut, Francois (Robert Lacheney), 475, 490
Tsuchiya, Tilsa, 427
Tubau, María, 455

Ugarte, Floro M., 97, 334
Ugarte, Manuel, 136
Ulive, Ugo, 499
Unamuno, Miguel de, 171
Unzueta, Mario, 307
Updike, John, 164
Urgelles, Thaelman, 508
Uribe-Holguín, Guillermo, 76, 321, 332
Urondo, Francisco 'Paco', 273
Urrutia Blondel, Jorge, 333
Urteaga, Mario, 425
Uruguay: architecture, 387–8; art, 441–5; cinema, 498, 499; music, 323–5, 334–7, 353, 364–5
Uslar Pietri, Arturo, 164, 175

Valcárcel, Edgar, 347, 348
Valcárcel, Luis E., 118

Valcárcel, Teodoro, 96, 322
Valdelomar, Abraham, 117, 231
Valdés, Germán (Tin-Tan), 475, 481
Valdés, Hernán, 217
Valdés Rodriguez, José Manuel, 483
Valdivieso, Raul, 432
Valencia, Antonio María, 321
Valencia, Guillermo, 68
Valentin, 414
Valentin, Rubem, 448
Valenzuela, Luisa, 207, 208, 216
Valenzuela Puelma, Alfredo, 395
Valle, Federico, 460
Valle, Raul do, 355, 356
Valle Riestra, José María, 312
Vallejo, César, 118, 250–3
Vallejo, José Joaquín, 32
Vardánega, Gregorio, 438
Varèse, Edgard, 333
Vargas Candia, Teófilo, 323
Vargas, Getúlio, 146, 388, 446, 470
Vargas Vila, José María, 57
Vargas Llosa, Mario, 163, 172, 174, 183, 185, 186, 187, 188, 201, 203, 215, 223, 287, 308
Vargas, Pedro, 476
Varnaghen, Francisco Adolfo de, 24
Varo, Remedios, 403
Varona, Enrique José, 116
Vasarely, Victor, 424, 438
Vasconcelos, José, 230, 239, 240, 398, 399, 462
Vásquez, Angelina, 502
Vásquez Díaz, Daniel, 433
Vásquez, I., 382
Vásquez, Julio A., 429
Vásquez Varela, J., 387
Vauthier, Louis Léger, 13
Vautier, Ernesto, 384
Vawter, J., 377
Vega, Ana Lydia, 208
Vega, Pastor, 506
Vegas Pacheco, Martin, 379
Vela, Arqueles, 115
Vela Zanetti, José, 414
Velarde, Héctor, 381
Velasco Alvarado, Juan, 497
Velasco, José María, 80, 96, 394
Velasco Llanos, Santiago, 332
Velasco Maidana, José Maria, 323
Velásquez, Leonardo, 341
Vellejo, César, 160, 227, 228, 230, 247, 250–253, 257, 261, 262, 271, 272, 277, 282, 288
Vender, J., 384
Venezuela: architecture, 378–80; art, 419–22; cinema, 497–508; music, 320–1, 346, 362

Printed in the United States
107623LV00003B/22-30/A